Minting, State, and Economy in the Visigothic Kingdom

Minting, State, and Economy in the Visigothic Kingdom

From Settlement in Aquitaine through the First Decade of the Muslim Conquest of Spain

Andrew Kurt

Routledge
Taylor & Francis Group
LONDON AND NEW YORK

First published in 2020 by Amsterdam University Press Ltd.

Published 2025 by Routledge
4 Park Square, Milton Park, Abingdon, Oxon OX14 4RN
605 Third Avenue, New York, NY 10158

Routledge is an imprint of the Taylor & Francis Group, an informa business

ISBN: 9789462981645 (hbk)
ISBN: 9781041182924 (pbk)
ISBN: 9781003699842 (ebk)
NUR 684

Cover illustration: Alan Caomin Xie. Coin: ANS 2015.48.11, obverse and reverse.

Cover design: Coördeisgn, Leiden

DOI: 10.5117/9789462981645

Table of Contents

Acknowledgments 9

Introduction 11

1. Pre-Regal Visigothic Coinage 25
   A The Fifth-Century Kingdom in Gaul 25
   B The Kingdom in Spain, 507-c. 573 46

2. The King's Coinage: The Beginning and Development of the Regal Coinage (c. 573-c. 720) 81
   A The Transition to a Regal Coinage 81
   B Regal Coin Types 105
   C A Trimetallic System? 108

3. The Activities of the Mints from c. 573- c. 720 123
   A The Operation of the Mints 123
   B The Record of Mint Output 135
   C The Organization of the Mints 144
   D Metrological and Metallurgical Standards of Visigothic Regal Tremisses 157

4. Why Were Gold Coins Struck in the Visigothic Kingdom? 173
   A The Late Roman Context 173
   B Other Reasons for Minting 191
   C The Addition of Bronze to the Corpus 220
   D Visigothic Minting in the Context of Contemporary Monetary Systems 221

5. The Royal Control of Visigothic Minting 231
   A Evidence of Royal Control 231
   B The Significance of Centralized Monetary Authority 237

6. Coinage in Spain in the Aftermath of the Islamic Conquest 247

7. Visigothic Currency in the Early Medieval Economy 257
A The Other Side of the Coin 257
B Use and Circulation of Currency in the Kingdom 261
C Bronze Currency in Spain and its Mediterranean Context 272

Conclusion 283

Appendix I 291

Appendix II 329

Bibliography 387

About the Author 411

Index 413

List of figures

Figure 1 Frequencies of weights of tremisses in the name of Anastasius 71
Figure 2 Frequencies of weights of tremisses in the name of Justin I 71
Figure 3 Frequencies of weights of tremisses in the name of Justinian 72
Figure 4 Frequencies of weights of tremisses in the name of Justin II 72
Figure 5 Frequencies of weights of pre-regal tremisses arranged by attributed mints or minting regions 74
Figure 6 Timeline of gold coin sets – estimated chronologies and metrological values 79
Figure 7 Proposed order of hoard contents related to Leovigild's regal-name minting 97
Figure 8 Tremissis standards from averages immediately prior to and during Leovigild's reign 100
Figure 9 Proposed chronology of the earliest Visigothic regal issues 100
Figure 10 Principal early facing-busts type forms 107
Figure 11 Diagram of the patrimony's divisions and the flow of proceeds into the *fiscus* 134

Figure 12	Difference in average regal tremissis weights between central and peripheral mints	166
Figure 13	Gold content of tremisses leading up to Leovigild's facing-busts phase	169
Figure 14	Coinage within the kingdom's political-economic system	235
Figure 15	Transitional dinar in Latin letters of 94H = 712-713	251
Figure 16	Bilingual dinar of 98H = 716-717	251
Figure 17	Thulth (1/3 dinar) in Arabic of 102H = 720-721	252

Appendix I:

Figure I.1	Weight and fineness measurements of Visigothic pre-regal tremisses at the ANS	291
Figure I.2	Comparison of intrinsic values between tremisses of Byzantine *Spania*, Constantinople and the Visigothic Kingdom	295
Figure I.3	Graph comparison of intrinsic values – tremisses of Byzantine *Spania*, Constantinople and the Visigothic Kingdom	296
Figure I.4	Map of gold mints in Visigothic Spain (c. 575 – c. 714)	297
Figure I.5	Schema of bust types of Visigothic regal tremisses	298
Figure I.6	Visigothic copper-alloy coins compared to tremisses	299
Figure I.7	Table of known regal mints	300
Figure I.8	Number of known mints from each reign	304
Figure I.9	Southern mints' percentage of total corpus	304
Figure I.10	Individual mints' percentage of total in southern-central Visigothic Spain	305
Figure I.11	Weight and fineness measurements by Lauris Olson of 377 Visigothic regal tremisses	306
Figure I.12	Averages of fineness and other measurements of gold coins at the ANS	317
Figure I.13	Frequencies of weights of Visigothic regal tremisses	318
Figure I.14	Average weights of tremisses at mints of diverse volumes of output	324
Figure I.15	Percentage of fineness in Visigothic tremisses of three major samples	325
Figure I.16	Average fineness of 238 tremisses tested using X-ray fluorescent spectrometry method	326
Figure I.17	Fineness of Visigothic pseudo-imperial tremisses, Visigothic regal tremisses, and early Muslim dinars in Spain	327

Appendix II:
Plate I 335
Plate II 337
Plate III 339
Plate IV 341
Plate V 343
Tables of regal Visigothic tremisses attributed to separate engravers 344
Concordance of new ANS accession numbers for ex-HSA regal Visigothic tremisses 368

Acknowledgments

The long gestation of this book project makes it an even happier task to thank the many people who helped me along the way. A first version of this work, written at the University of Toronto's Centre for Medieval Studies, owes much to my parents, Mark and Suzanne Kurt. Now deceased, they were a great source of inspiration and assistance in more ways than I can express here. I am indebted to my brother John for help provided at a key moment when the going was hard late in the first round of the project. Andrew Watson proved an encouraging and thought-provoking guide early on, and his comments and questions have ultimately made this a much better piece of work than it could otherwise have been. Rigorous commentary by Walter Goffart and Jonathan Edmondson at an early stage also proved greatly beneficial.

Many thanks go to Alan Stahl for his generous guidance, first when I was a participant in the Graduate Seminar at the American Numismatic Society, and on numerous occasions since then. Good questions and helpful advice as one transitions toward publishing a complex book are not easily forgotten by a scholar still finding his way in the process. More recently, despite pressing duties as Princeton University's Curator of Numismatics, Alan graciously read a few of my chapters and provided remarks. For several years, David Yoon, Associate Curator at the American Numismatic Society, has furnished insightful conversation as well as assistance in all things regarding Visigothic monetary matters. His extensive notes after reading this book and his many email responses to queries and theories I put to him, deserve a mountain of thanks. I am very grateful to Andrei Gandila of the University of Alabama in Huntsville, Erica Buchberger of the University of Texas – Rio Grande Valley, and Damián Fernández of Northern Illinois University, each of whom read parts of my manuscript and provided helpful commentary. The same is especially true of Peter Bartlett, a scholar and collector of Visigothic gold coinage, from whom I have benefitted enormously for quite a while. I sometimes struggled to do justice to his astute and lengthy remarks on many aspects of this currency, but they have always been of help. He has been a solid source of information and a most generous friend in this field. Handing him a copy of this book when I finally visit his cabins and bird sanctuary in Costa Rica within the year will be a fitting gesture of our friendship. Naturally the responsibility for all shortcomings in the present work are my own.

Clayton State University has provided some of the wind behind my sails in the writing of this book. The facilitation and encouragement of my department chair, Adam Tate, and the support of the Dean of the College of Arts & Sciences, Nasser Momayezi, deserve acknowledgement. The assistance provided in the form of College of Arts & Sciences Minigrants, FY 2014-15 and FY 2018-19, and additionally of a C.A.S.E. Award from the College for FY 2016-17, were indispensable. They allowed me to conduct research on the marvelous collection at the American Numismatic Society and to keep abreast of the growing literature relating to the theme of this work. I thank the CSU library staff for their help in securing books and articles from around the country and occasionally from foreign libraries. I am also extremely grateful to Kyle Marcano of the Center for Excellence in Learning and Teaching for his great help with maps and images.

It has been a pleasure working with Erin Dailey of Amsterdam University Press. His patience and assistance are very much appreciated. The press's Late Antique and Early Medieval Iberia series is clearly in good hands. I would finally like to express huge gratitude to my wife Bridget and an appreciation of all that she does to make my life complete. I hope the completion of this sometimes overwhelming task, as well as its quality, will be a token of my love and thankfulness for her many sacrifices. I do not think I could have finished the race without her help.

Introduction

The Visigothic regime in Gaul and Iberia flourished during the latter stages of a long era now commonly referred to as late antiquity, which spanned from the troubles of the Roman Empire in the third century to the Islamic invasions across the vast expanse from Central Asia to Spain. The ancient Mediterranean, along which the Visigoths found their eventual home, is open to various conceptualizations. Ambitious approaches that examine a large span of cultures on a grand scale compete in a sense with a more isolated approach, focused, for instance, on Western Civilization. The latter perspective, channeled along a path centered on the developments of Greece and Rome, can be a legitimate focal point but should not be cut off from interactivity between the Mediterranean rim and regions well beyond it, not only in Western Europe but in the Near East and North Africa including the Red Sea region, which, in turn, was spurred by interaction with eastern Africa and the Indian Ocean peoples. The Mediterranean can be seen as a massive zone of contact with multiple micro-zones, which, at the same time, had unifying elements in political culture, economic activity, social and intellectual traditions, and religion. It saw tremendous continuity in some respects even as it experienced important changes as well as a diverse range. In studying the Mediterranean in the ancient and early medieval eras, one can work one's way around the region and become immersed in the particular characteristics of various sub-regions such as Hispania, Gallia, Italia, Graecia, and so on, but what can be at least as striking are basic consistencies. As new residents entered the European landscape and necessarily propeled modifications in public and private life, the firm foundation left by the Roman Empire established a pattern that deeply affected the new kingdoms of early Europe. This influence was felt to a greater or lesser extent in such areas as administration, religion, literary culture, military habits, rural and urban life and economy and, not least, currency.

The field of late antiquity has burgeoned in recent decades, as a new sense of the interconnections and significance of a broad sector of Afro-Eurasia

Kurt, A., *Minting, State, and Economy in the Visigothic Kingdom: From Settlement in Aquitaine through the First Decade of the Muslim Conquest of Spain*.
Taylor & Francis Group, 2020
DOI 10.5117/9789462981645_INTRO

across some five centuries has been accompanied by an enormous amount of specialized research focused within this world. It was an era of subtle and not so subtle transitions, when developments in the Roman Empire led to more pronounced differentiations in the provinces, which became separate barbarian kingdoms by the fifth century. Connectivity is evident even as political unity can be seen to have been breaking down and culture transformed. The tail end of Classical civilization in the West slowly reworks into the first stages of Western Europe. This becomes evident in the territories of western Gaul and Hispania as the Visigoths first entered and eventually dominated zones populated by Romans. As Roman culture in its varied character continued to have a significant influence on the Mediterranean world in subsequent centuries, the Levant and the northern littoral of Africa experienced directly the transformative influx of Muslims in the seventh century. It is in Iberia after the Islamic conquest in 711 that a part of Europe saw a new dynamic with the intermingling of Hispano-Visigothic and Islamic culture. Thus, it is instructive and exceedingly interesting to see what resemblance there is between several monetary systems that emerged from the imperial base yet developed under very different circumstances, and what resulted from their direct contact.

How currency fits into the big picture of this transformative era can be tricky. In a small editing change in the section of the *Cambridge Economic History of Europe* on medieval coinage, noticeable only to someone comparing the same part in the 1963 and 1987 editions, the first sub-heading was altered from 'Roman-Barbarian Continuity' to 'Roman-Barbarian Discontinuity', even though the contents of this first segment remain practically the same. What is more obvious to the user of both editions is the movement of the section on coinage from an appendix to a full chapter (XII) in the later version.[1] Both changes are indicative of the challenges involved in approaching the monetary history of late antiquity and the early medieval world. Should continuity or discontinuity be stressed? How significant was currency in the period in which Europe was in its early stage of formation? Given the fact that the barbarian kingdoms did produce their own currencies and that these were of Roman inspiration, can we correctly speak of continuity in this area if, in fact, whole regions such as Hispania were without Roman minting facilities and these therefore had to be newly adopted?[2] It is reasonable to

1 Peter Spufford, "Coinage and Currency" (appendix), in *Cambridge Economic History of Europe*, vol. 3 (Cambridge: Cambridge University Press, 1963), 576-602, and idem, "Coinage and Currency" (Chapter XII) in ibid., vol. 2 (1987), 788-863.

2 Useful discussion of the term 'barbarian' can be found in the chapter "Who are the barbarians?" in Edward James, *Europe's Barbarians, AD 200-600* (London: Routledge, 2009), 1-20.

ask if, across regime changes, we get the same or similar answers to directly related questions: For what purpose were coins issued, by which authority, and in which way was minting organized? On what basis can the answers be established? Such challenges are part of the wider problem posed by the transition in the West from the Roman Empire to a configuration in many ways different yet bearing the marks of several centuries of Roman tradition.

This examination of the largely neglected Visigothic monetary system has been undertaken with the conviction that an up-to-date, full-length study is vital to a well-rounded understanding of the government and the society of the Visigothic kingdom in southern Gaul and Iberia from the early fifth through the first phase of the Islamic conquest launched in 711. Monetary history is the study of the making of money, usually, as in this case, coinage. Naturally, the production of currency is linked to political and economic history, the latter allied to money's use, and these themes are explored here in relation to the monetary system of the kingdom, including some of the evidential challenges. Early medieval Iberia's place in the larger western European and Mediterranean monetary history is also examined in the chapters that follow.

The intended audience of this book is not limited to the few numismatists and economic historians focused on the fifth to eighth centuries, rather it includes scholars and students interested in late antiquity generally or late antique-early medieval Iberia in particular. It aims not only to make available a comprehensive study of a subject often consigned to the margins in the mounting scholarship on post-Roman western Europe, but also to suggest ways in which the numismatic data is intertwined with questions that continue to concern historians. The value of bringing archeological and other forms of research on material history into greater dialog with mainstream historiography has become obvious in recent decades through the work of those willing to delve beyond the narrow confines of traditional thematic divisions.

Some of the expanding scholarship on Iberia from late Roman to Islamic rule can be brought to bear on the how and why of minting under the Visigoths, yet it is equally true to say that the dissemination of poorly known data on Visigothic numismatics, here and in several other recent works, can be of great worth to historians who become familiar with terms and issues frequently left solely to specialists. The author hopes to contribute to filling a lacuna in Visigothic studies and at the same time to form a bridge between this specialized field and general studies of the period or other sub-fields concerned with political history, archeology, the history of administrative structures, and economic history. Advancement in the subject explored here is much needed. Where not neglected entirely, even in well-recognized works on the period one occasionally comes across errors as basic as misidentification of coins or upside-down images apparently unnoticed by author or editor. Old suppositions call for correction or nuance.

Production and utilization of coinage is a rich field of investigation. Technicalities of monetary research, such as details of the complex minting network, metallic alterations, or questions surrounding volume of coinage, all shed light on the workings of the state. Added to the higher political strength as demonstrated in longevity in Spain relative to other post-Roman western provinces, as well as singular legal and ecclesiastical mechanisms,[3] such facets of the kingdom's creation of currency demonstrate sophistication and ingenuity. Study of how the coinage in Visigothic lands was made and in later centuries discovered opens our eyes to a whole range of activity and movement otherwise considered only in vague terms if at all. The configuration of finds is an open road to several lines of inquiry about economic life and the relationship between various populations or with subjects and the crown.

Unfortunately, there remains a large gap between the study of the coined money – termed numismatics – and the historiography of the Gothic kingdom of the far western reaches. Indicative of a limited trend toward incorporation of monetary matters in the post-Roman period, the *New Cambridge Medieval History* has chapters treating this topic in both volumes on the early medieval period.[4] The Visigothic kingdom receives brief attention there, yet even the best modern histories of the Visigoths in English neglect the subject almost entirely.[5] Spanish historians have tended to be

3 On very early medieval Spain's potency, often repudiated but, in fact, not receding but increasing, see Chris Wickham, *Framing the Early Middle Ages: Europe and the Mediterranean, 400-800* (Oxford: Oxford University Press, 2005), 93-100.

4 Mark Blackburn, "Money and Coinage," in *The New Cambridge Medieval History*, v.1: c. 500-c. 700, ed. Paul Fouracre (Cambridge: Cambridge University Press, 2005), 660-74; idem, "Money and Coinage," in *New Cambridge Medieval History*, v. 2: c. 700-c. 900, ed. Rosamond McKitterick (Cambridge: Cambridge University Press, 1995), 538-60. Both chapters are excellent in their range and offer many useful points, but are limited and now outdated on Visigothic currency.

5 For example, Roger Collins, *Early Medieval Spain: Unity in Diversity, 400-1000*, 2nd ed. (London: Macmillan, 1995) and idem, *Visigothic Spain, 409-711* (Malden, MA: Blackwell, 2004); E. A. Thompson, *The Goths in Spain* (Oxford: Oxford University Press, 1969), with useful remarks on some coin inscriptions and specific issues of currency, but almost nothing on the minting system as such; Herwig Wolfram, *The History of the Goths*, trans. Thomas J. Dunlop (Berkeley, CA: University of California Press, 1988). The works of Luis A. García Moreno and José Orlandis mentioned in this Introduction and elsewhere in this book are exceptions. A number of shorter studies by other Spanish scholars cited later in the present work, such as those of Iñaki Martín Viso, Félix Retamero, Santiago Castellanos, and Miquel Crusafont have begun to transform

much better in this area in their studies on Visigothic Spain: José Orlandis, Luis A. García Moreno, and the contributors to R. Menéndez Pidal's *Historia de España* have not only discussed Visigothic mint organization and the gold currency competently, but have made a number of useful observations. Their treatments are necessarily general, and they cannot be expected to be perfectly up to date on numismatic research. Medieval economic surveys covering this period are of no help.[6] Even as germane a work as Peter Spufford's *Money and Its Use in Medieval Europe* (Cambridge, 1988), laudable in many respects, is woefully inadequate on Visigothic and, indeed, later medieval Spain. And it did nothing to correct Spufford's erroneous view from previous years on the disappearance of bronze (or copper-alloy) coinage in the West by the middle of the sixth century,[7] which had been refuted in various writings on Visigothic currency including in English by the late 1980s and early 1990s.[8]

There is nevertheless a considerable amount of specialized work now published on the topic of Visigothic gold coinage, which was modeled on the two main denominations of the late Roman Empire, the solidus – 1/72 to the pound – and its third, the tremissis or triens. The most significant work for over half a century was without doubt George C. Miles's 1952 catalogue of Visigothic tremisses, which have acquired the title of 'regal' because they are inscribed with the name of the reigning king at the time of issue.

the historiographical landscape with respect to monetary realities. Jairus Banaji, *Exploring the Economy of Late Antiquity: Selected Essays* (Cambridge: Cambridge University Press, 2016) presents a critique of the economic minimalism commonly applied to late antiquity, and specifically the neglect of coinage in Wickham, *Framing*, a work whose general project he largely extols.

6 Robert-Henri Bautier, *The Economic Development of Medieval Europe* (London: Harcourt, Brace, Jovanovich, 1971), completely skips over the Visigothic kingdom in his short discussion of early medieval coinage and economy; *The Cambridge Economic History of Europe* is too basic to be of use; there is nothing useful on the entire early medieval period (!) in N. J. G. Pounds, *An Economic History of Medieval Europe*, 2nd ed. (London: Longman, 1994). Matthew Innes, "Economies and Societies in Early Medieval Western Europe," in *A Companion to the Medieval World*, ed. Carol Lansing and Edward D. English (Malden, MA: Wiley-Blackwell, 2013), 9-35 omits currency and in its extensive bibliography and various categories for 'Further reading' does cite not a single title specifically treating coinage.

7 In fact, it reiterated this error (p. 14).

8 Miquel Crusafont i Sabater, "Un numerario visigodo de cobre?" *Gaceta Numismática*, nos. 74-75 (1984), 131-41; idem, "The Copper Coinage of the Visigoths of Spain," in *Problems of Medieval Coinage in the Iberian Area*, v. III, ed. Mário Gomes Marques and M. Crusafont i Sabater (Santarém, 1988), 35-70. Another otherwise excellent work, Alejandro García Sanjuan, *La conquista islámica de la península ibérica y la tergiversación del pasado. Del catastrofismo al negacionismo* (Madrid: Marcial Pons Historia, 2013), continues the claim that Visigothic copper minting was inexistent (154); in this he is persuaded by the formidable scholar Eduardo Manzano Moreno, *Conquistadores, emires, y califas. Los omeyas y la formación de al-Andalus* (Barcelona: Crítica, 2006).

Miles's book provided a classified inventory of the tremisses issued from the 570s to c. 713, updating the information in previous works concerning the identification of mints, the monarchs, and usurpers who issued coins, and the precise contents of modern collections. It also gave a short analysis of the various coin types and styles, and provided the weights and photos of many hundreds of coins.[9] A few years later, a monograph on so-called pre-regal coinage appeared, although it was actually more narrowly focused on the dominant occidental form of the tremissis, which, in the sixth century, became the main Visigothic gold denomination; since pre-regal coinage is without mint names or kings' names, it could not offer a definitive classification.[10]

A few works published since that time in various western European languages provide excellent treatment of specific aspects of Visigothic coinage. In 1976, Xavier Barral i Altet covered coin hoards and circulation, assessing the movement of gold currency around the kingdom and beyond its borders from an economic standpoint.[11] A more recent book by Miquel Crusafont i Sabater includes a short survey of the Visigothic monetary system, but its real contribution lies in its presentation of the 'copper' coinage.[12] A book of essays by Mário Gomes Marques and two other Portuguese scholars, published in 1995, provides stimulating considerations on pre-regal and regal minting, presenting data on weights and fineness from a large sample of coins.[13]

9 George C. Miles, *The Coinage of the Visigoths of Spain: Leovigild to Achila II* (New York: American Numismatic Society, 1952). The catalog incorporated information from an enormous array of literature, among which the following have special importance: Aloïs Heiss, *Description générale des monnaies antiques de l'Espagne* (Paris: Imprimerie Nationale, 1870); Wilhelm Reinhart, "Nuevas aportaciones a la numismatica visigoda," *Archivo español de arqueología* 18 (1945), 212-35; Felipe Mateu y Llopis, *Catálogo de las monedas previsigodas y visigodas del Gabinete Numismático del Museo Arqueológico Nacional* (Madrid: Imp. Gongora, 1936), and several major articles by the same author. At the heart of Miles's catalog was the outstanding collection of the American Numismatic Society, for which he served as the Islamic Curator. To Miles's work should be added a museum collection of Barcelona which was published in the same year and is therefore almost absent from the book: J. Amorós and A. Mata Berruezo, *Catálogo de las monedas visigodas del Gabinete Numismático de Cataluña* (Barcelona: Ayuntamiento, 1952).

10 Wallace J. Tomasini, *The Barbaric Tremissis in Spain and Southern France: Anastasius to Leovigild* (New York: American Numismatic Society, 1964).

11 Barral i Altet, *La circulation des monnaies suèves et visigotiques. Contribution á l'histoire économique du royaume visigot* (Munich: Artemis Verlag, 1976). Economic history examines one main aspect of monetary history, the use of coinage, while numismatics examines how currency is made and attempts to identify and classify coins.

12 Miquel Crusafont i Sabater, *El sistema monetario visigodo: cobre y oro* (Barcelona: Asociación Numismática Española, 1994).

13 Mário Gomes Marques et al., *Ensaios sobre história monetária da monarquia visigoda* (Lisbon: Sociedade Portuguesa de Numismática, 1995).

While extremely useful, the essays are based almost entirely on Portuguese collections, and the book lacks any detailed historical investigation, study of dies, stylistic analysis, treatment of minting techniques or personnel, or a full discussion of the possible motives of minting. Publication of *Corpus Nummorum Visigothorum: ca. 575-714, Leovigildus-Achila* offered a type catalog of the tremissis series in the king's name and much information, but it is unfortunately dogged by errors in some areas.[14] It was only with the publication in 2009 of Ruth Pliego's full catalog and accompanying study of the Visigothic regal series, which emerged under Leovigild's authority around the last quarter of the sixth century, that the most celebrated portion of minting in the kingdom had a full modern study. In this splendidly illustrated and elaborated set, a wealth of scholarship was brought to bear on the minting system and the current state of knowledge of the tremisses of nearly the last century and a half of the Visigothic regime.[15]

The present investigation, notwithstanding the author's admiration for these works, aims to be more comprehensive than any work to date on the problems of minting and the functionalities of coinage during the entire Visigothic period, providing an extensive overview of the entire evolution of the currency from beginning to end while examining many specific related themes. Several factors make such an undertaking desirable. The corpus of extant Visigothic coins has grown enormously since Miles and Tomasini published their books. Two massive hoard finds in recent decades have more than doubled the four thousand royal-name tremisses estimated by Miles.[16] Largely as a result of these hoards, a number of previously unknown issues – i.e. mint-ruler combinations – have been established. Moreover, several new mints have been discovered since Miles's 1952 catalog. Even since Pliego's study, hoards have continued to bring tremisses to light, and her work was not focused on currency before the 570s. With the pre-regal coinage it is rather difficult to estimate the number of known specimens, because identification is much less systematic compared with that for the

14 Jesús Vico Monteoliva, María Cruz Cores Gomendio, and Gonzalo Cores Uría, *Corpus Nummorum Visigothorum: ca. 575-714, Leovigildus-Achila* (Madrid: the authors, 2006). It is not, in fact, a corpus and must be treated with caution, but it does provide a Spanish-English guide with much of value.

15 Ruth Pliego Vázquez, *La moneda visigoda*, 2 vols (Seville: Universidad de Sevilla, 2009). Volume I: *Historia monetaria del reino visigodo de Toledo* (*c. 569-711*); Volume II: *Corpus*. This work is invaluable not only for providing a proper corpus to that point, but also in its judicious discussion of a number of areas as well as detailed treatment of hoards.

16 Miles himself included 3461 tremisses, but estimated a total of approximately 4000: Miles, *The Coinage of the Visigoths*, ix. See below, Chapter Three, section B, on the new finds.

regal series, and there has been comparatively less interest in it on the coin market. Nonetheless, discoveries of new coins have been made over the years. The current quantity of extant Visigothic coinage is also hard to pinpoint with the very active market and 'discreet' dealers of the past few decades, but great strides have been made from the confirmed evidence. This book brings together the whole of Visigothic currency matters in Gaul and Spain, not only tremisses but also solidi and other denominations of recent discovery. It looks carefully into not merely the minting of coins but likewise what is of equal importance yet frequently dealt with in separated fashion, the utilization of coined money.

As the chief primary sources in question, the gold coins must be considered closely. This means gaining a complete understanding of the vast variety of these physical objects, from the physical characteristics of the specimens themselves to the variegated manufacture to which they point, so that a proper picture can be drawn of the minting system overall. This can only be developed by analyzing the multiple characteristics of the entire body of known currency: weight and fineness measurements (allowing large-scale considerations of quality and possible reasons for its variation); differentiations of style (permitting more specific chronologies and giving clues as to the arrangement of artisan labor behind the crafting of dies and perhaps the emission of coins); the reigning monarch announced on each coin in the case of the regal series starting in the 570s (providing at least a basic chronology); and mint names in this series (allowing the geography of minting to be established). Physical data extended to deductions about the systematic whole can then be brought into relation with broader contexts of politics, law, and commercial, urban, and agricultural life in the Visigothic kingdom and of currency systems of the same period viewed in comparison.

Yet, for all the focus on gold when it comes to the Visigothic monetary system, two other components must be considered. It is now simply inaccurate to refer to the kingdom's monometallism, though this is still the habit in too much of the literature. Silver was probably only a minimal part of Visigothic minting and did not see a constant output across the early fifth to early eighth centuries, but even to conceive of silver coinage production in the two geographical stages of the kingdom is a novelty for many scholars of the early Middle Ages.[17] Whether the fifth-century kingdom in Gaul was responsible for scattered silver issues is a matter

17 Miquel de Crusafont et al., "Silver Visigothic Coinage," *Numismatic Chronicle* 176 (2016), 241-60 and pll. 28f.

of some doubt, though modern specialists have made the case for its start not long after settlement in Aquitania probably in 419, just as the argument is made regarding gold coinage. It is fair to say that attribution of gold to the Visigoths in that period is problematic enough, and there is little room for a definitive declaration about silver minting either way. Some possibly Visigothic silver pieces of the next century, found in Spain, open the possibility of a small output before the time of Leovigild, perhaps around the mid-point of that century. Its significance cannot have been great, given that the number of specimens cited remains very low. One can no longer minimize the very small-level currency sometimes referred to as copper but more properly termed bronze. Firstly, enough examples have come to light in recent years from overwhelmingly local zones as to make the initial scholarly skepticism of Spanish origin look unreasonable at this stage. Bronze currency of the lowest denomination, the tiny *nummus* and its multiples, has appropriately been deemed a critical component of the late ancient economy without which real understanding would be impossible.[18] Chapters Two and Seven of this book discuss the ways in which it is or is not fitting to speak of "Visigothic bronze coinage" or a "trimetallic system", and the specific role that Visigothic bronze currency played in a wider sphere in which bronze coins were a common feature.

The author has taken advantage of several studies on particular aspects of early medieval minting. There are now expanded data on weights and studies of fineness, a significant feature not treated in depth by Miles and only partly by Pliego; until now, the results of this research have not been consolidated and discussed as a whole. For numismatics to be truly useful it must be brought into relation with larger historical problems. There is further potential in placing Visigothic minting in wider contexts than strictly numismatic ones, for example: examining continuities and breaches from Roman administration and how coinage correlated with other concerns of government such as taxation; the degree to which minting was centrally controlled; the relationship of mints to one another; and the very motives for creating currency. Two works especially began to open the study of coinage

18 Ruth Pliego, "The Circulation of Copper Coins in the Iberian Peninsula During the Visigothic Period: New Approaches," *Journal of Archaeological Numismatics* 5-6 (2015-2016), 125-60, at 147, citing S. Moorhead, "Ever Decreasing Circles. The Nummus Economy at Butrint (Albania) and Beyond," in *Numismatic History and Economy in Epirus During Antiquity. Proceedings of the 1st International Conference (University of Ioannina, October 3rd-7th 2007)*, ed. K. Liampi et al. (Athens: Society of Numismatics and Economic History, 2013), 601-16.

in Visigothic Spain to such broader questions.[19] In the present volume, the greater wealth of data is used to take the answers to these inquiries to new lengths. Finally, a whole area of research has hardly been touched: the coin styles of the individual mints and die links, i.e. use of the same die at more than one place or time or with more than one opposite die (only the latter holds true of tremisses in early medieval Hispania). As I demonstrate, an increased knowledge of minting practices can lead to more informed inquiry about the economy, provincial structures, and how war is organized.

This book follows the traditional division of Visigothic coinage into two main chronological categories. The 'pseudo-imperial' or 'imitation' series was minted from some point after the Visigothic settlement in southwestern Gaul in 418 or at least until the time when Leovigild (568-586) had all coins marked with his own name instead of the emperor's.[20] This was followed by the 'regal' series, starting, as I will argue, in c. 573 and lasting until the end of Visigothic minting in c. 713, during which period tremisses alone were struck in gold. The addition of the king's name as well as the mint name on regal tremisses not only marked a significant change in the West, as we shall see, but it also has the fortuitous consequence of making the coins easier to study. By contrast, the earlier series, often referred to as 'pre-regal', is full of challenges as basic as whether or not it can be reliably attributed to the Visigoths. As we meet these difficulties in the first chapter, we shall see that large groups of coins can be confidently assigned as Visigothic.

Chapter One addresses the pre-regal series, describing two stages conveniently divided by the loss of most Visigothic territory in Gaul in 507 at the battle of Vouillé. Before this time, the gold pieces widely attributed to the Visigothic kingdom closely resembled coinage of the Roman Empire. Much of the similarity is due to the political interdependence between Goths and Romans in the Visigothic region of Gaul until the last quarter of the fifth century, as well as to the concentration of minting there at one or two sites. After 507, however, strict imitation of Roman coinage is no longer attempted. Under the authority of Theodoric, the Ostrogoth, the tremisses acquired their quintessential pre-regal reverse type, a unique depiction of the Roman Victory goddess. The solidus kept the obverse and reverse types of its imperial model, but within a few years it also departed from imitation

19 Marques et al., *Ensaios*; Michael F. Hendy, "From Public to Private: The Western Barbarian Coinages as a Mirror of the Disintegration of Late Roman State Structures," *Viator* 19 (1988), 29-78.

20 Crusafont et al., "Silver Visigothic Coinage," 243 discusses certain inadequacies of the terms used for the series and rejects the label 'pseudo-imperial'. I concur to a large extent but rest on the usefulness of the convention and the problems with other terms employed.

of the styles current in Constantinople. Visigothic currency, moreover, did not imitate exactly the very high Roman standards of weight and purity of gold. The latter finding has been previously suggested from small test samples, but is now corroborated by a larger set of tested coins. Fluctuating weight measurements and gold analyses of a large number of the barbarian coins are indicative of the gradual spatial expansion of the Visigothic mint system, as opposed to the concentration of Roman and Byzantine minting at a handful of sites within the vast Empire.

The historical and monetary circumstances of Leovigild's adoption of a regal currency are treated in Chapter Two. We establish a chronology of his various issues, demonstrating that a sporadic process of change towards an expressly Visigothic currency began very early in the king's reign and must be associated with his subjection of numerous parts of Spain through war. The first regal issues can be narrowed down to the early 570s, several years before the dates traditionally supplied by a few notable scholars. A detailed look at the altered standards of the coinage gives further indication of Leovigild's interest in monetary affairs and of his clear authority in these matters. This chapter also discusses the evolution of regal types, which was marked by Leovigild's influence for many decades, and the recent discovery of both Visigothic copper-based coinage, which possibly began in Leovigild's reign, and silver produced in the mid-sixth century. The antiquated portrayal of a monometallic currency system can be definitively put to rest.

Chapter Three examines the material aspects of minting and explains how the minting of gold, especially the regal tremisses, was organized. The Visigothic manufacture of coins already differed in some ways from that of late Roman times, but especially the Visigothic minting network assumed characteristics very different from that of the Empire. Known Visigothic mints tally today at ninety-eight. They can now be estimated to have numbered at least one hundred, based on the fruits of scattered research on mint sites and new discoveries of coins, including extensive hoards, since Miles published his corpus. A close look at styles suggests that the engravers of the dies used in minting were not usually attached to a single workshop, but instead traveled around a large territory in carrying out their work. Thus, the organization of mints may be linked to the itinerancy of engravers and possibly other laborers. It is the author's hope that the presentation of this material leads others to undertake their own research in this area, which could tell us more about monetary administration in the face of a complete dearth of literary sources. The chapter ends with a section on the metallic quality of the coins. Such an investigation is required in order to address the large and difficult question of why the Visigoths produced coinage during the entire course of the kingdom in Gaul and in Hispania, which is the subject of the following chapter.

Why did the Visigothic state strike coins? Not a single surviving document from early medieval Spain offers a direct answer to this important question. Chapter Four attempts to answer it by first framing the same question around the making of currency in the Roman Empire, since that is the context in which Visigothic coinage emerged. The conclusion made by those on one side of the scholarly debate, that the Roman gold currency of late antiquity was chiefly intended to facilitate taxation and expenditure, syncs with the situation in the Visigothic kingdom. There the state itself probably minted only gold coinage, but bronze eventually was made available by certain cities for the needs of their urban populations. Abundant evidence of taxation in the kingdom implies the use of gold coinage in tax collection until at least the later seventh century. The extended argument draws on the normally higher weight and fineness measurements of coins of the capital mint in each province to suggest that fiscal coinage revolved around these and a few other major mints. The great majority of the mints in Iberia, however, served an exceptional fiscal purpose: they became active only when armies operated in those specific areas. Sudden, large issues on these occasions resulted in debased coins of reduced weight.[21] The idea that many mints existed for the support of the army is not new, but it has not received full elaboration until now. Here, a detailed discussion of the literary evidence of warfare is combined with treatment of the identification of mints, data on recently discovered issues, and a wide array of test results on both weights and gold fineness. A clearer idea of the purpose of minting puts into better focus the answer as to why the minting network took the shape it did. Its considerable and somewhat beguiling variation makes more sense as the question of the purposes of minting is developed.

Chapter Five examines the level of the kings' control over minting. While royal authority over most minting throughout the regal series is often taken as axiomatic or sufficiently proven in earlier scholarship, some have doubted the court's control of the peripheral mints which consistently struck inferior coinage. The matter can be adequately probed only with the aid of the combined data of the previous chapters. Since all mints can be best explained by either fiscal/administrative or military contexts,

21 Debasement is the reduction in the amount of the principal precious metal of a coinage, usually achieved by replacing a certain quantity of this metal with a base metal such as copper, or replacing some of the gold with silver. It can also be achieved by lowering the standard weight of a given denomination (often while attempting to keep the coin at the same value).

the great number of workshops should not diminish but rather increase our estimation of how firmly the monarchy presided over the making of money. Mints were strictly the creation of kings, as far as the evidence indicates. Some kings were more in control of minting, some less so, and some were capable enough to command significant changes in the system; all were affected by the supply of gold. In these ways, the situation in the Visigothic kingdom was not so different from that of late Rome and early Byzantium. What radically differed by the latter half of the sixth century was the extremely wide dispersal of Visigothic mints. It is one of the major aspects of administrative transformation in the early medieval West.

Chapter Six provides a brief excursus on minting and currency in the first decade after the conquest of the Iberian peninsula beginning in 711. Once again, we see a major transformation in power and with it a series of changes in administration. One important part in the story of the changes that occurred under Muslim authority was the coinage system. In the immediate transitional stage, it is of great interest to compare the Visigothic and the Islamic systems, at the same time examining the effect of the one upon the other. We will see that while major modifications would soon take place, initially some elements of the currency were deliberately patterned after those of the defeated kingdom or maintained a strong influence of the Byzantine regime.

Finally, Chapter Seven addresses Visigothic currency from the perspective of its uses. Here, the state-oriented function of gold coinage carries over to the possession and utilization of coined money by the kingdom's inhabitants, considered to some extent by socio-economic groups. The segment explores gold as well as bronze, these two main currencies understood to have separate origins and discrete usage. The geographical distribution of finds sheds light on the possibilities of the role of coins, including the economic framework in which coinage played an essential part. The chapter demonstrates that the western Mediterranean zone of exchange is key to understanding the copper-alloy currency in Visigothic Spain, some of it made within cities of the kingdom, but much of it coming from outside the borders. As with the tremisses, the southern and southeastern regions were most responsible for production of small denominations as well as their use, it would seem. When literary references to currency are considered, the combined record implies regular and widespread use of coinage in early medieval Spain, if not outright monetization as strictly defined. As reiterated in the conclusion, the comparatively high level of coin utilization as well as direct government involvement at least in minting of gold, in spite of the challenges this presented, should leave no doubt of a sophisticated monetary system not dissimilar to its Roman model.

1. Pre-Regal Visigothic Coinage

Abstract
Chapter One examines the minting of gold under the Visigoths in Gaul up to the battle of Vouillé (507), then in Spain and southwestern Gaul in the first three quarters of the sixth century. The first stage within this so-called pre-regal period was characterized largely by imitation of Roman coinage, while the second stage saw a departure from strict imitation, especially of the reverse tremissis type of the Roman Victory goddess. The chapter reviews Visigothic attribution of gold coins over the entire period; the weight and gold purity of these solidi and tremisses are shown to be well below Roman standards. Fluctuating weights and gold analyses of a large number of specimens tested indicate expansion of the mint system.

Keywords: Kingdom of Toulouse; solidus; tremissis; attribution; weights; imitation

A The Fifth-Century Kingdom in Gaul

The Emergence and Growth of the Visigothic Kingdom

A study of the monetary culture of the Visigothic kingdom over its long course begins concretely with the Goths' settlement first in the western Gallic provinces in the early fifth century and later in Hispania, in tandem with consideration of their relations with the Roman Empire. There is, however, a Gothic history prior to these pivotal episodes that has some bearing on the subject under discussion. Much of this revolves around the migration into the Empire in 376 of Goths, or primarily a portion of a people sometimes identified as their ancestors (the Tervingi), and the subsequent troubled relationship with imperial authorities who had permitted their crossing south of the Danube. This is highlighted first by the battle of Adrianople in 378 in which Gothic victory entailed emperor Valens's death and second

Kurt, A., *Minting, State, and Economy in the Visigothic Kingdom: From Settlement in Aquitaine through the First Decade of the Muslim Conquest of Spain*.
Taylor & Francis Group, 2020
DOI 10.5117/9789462981645_CH01

by the assault on Rome under Alaric in 410. Today, basic questions persist as to whether 'Goths' actually existed before the Danube crossing and who they were in the years that followed, what their real association was with other groups north of the river both culturally and in terms of the mass movements of this era, and what role all the barbarian migrants played in the demise of the western Empire.[22]

While these are matters beyond the immediate scope of this work, germane here are a few points that form a backdrop to the moment in 418, or perhaps 419,[23] when the Visigoths were installed on Roman soil after four

22 The make-up and scale of *Gothi* before and after entering Roman territory below the Danube in 376, and whether the Visigoths in the fifth century were in greater or lesser continuity with the people in movement in the late fourth century, are contested themes. It is not the place here to elaborate on these major questions that continue to generate stimulating debate. Distinguished from a view of group continuity less complete than once supposed, but based on a core Gothic governing elite (e.g. Reinhard Wenskus, Herwig Wolfram, Walter Pohl), or of general continuity based on a wider leading populace with sundry accretion (Peter Heather), an expression of the present orthodoxy is the interpretation of the Visigoths as "a new people with a new cultural and political identity," forging their way as "a Gothic confederation and simultaneously as a Roman army" (Patrick Geary, *The Myth of Nations* [Princeton, NJ: Princeton University Press, 2002], 100-01). For brief overviews of the competing views and further references concerning Goths, see Collins, *Visigothic Spain*, 15-26, with a resolution similar to J.H.W.G. Liebeschuetz, "Alaric's Goths: Nation or Army?," in *Fifth-century Gaul: A Crisis of Identity?*, ed. John Drinkwater and Hugh Elton (Cambridge: Cambridge University Press, 1992), 75-83, viewing Alaric's Visigoths as a mercenary assemblage without ethnic cohesion; and J.N. Hillgarth, *The Visigoths in History and Legend* (Toronto: Pontifical Institute of Mediaeval Studies, 2009), 1-3, siding with Heather's assessment. Further introduction to migration, identity, and 'ethnogenesis' studies can be found in Guy Halsall, *Barbarian Migrations and the Roman West, 376-568* (Cambridge: Cambridge University Press, 2007), esp. 13-68 and 417-98 and A. Gillett, ed., *On Barbarian Identity: Critical Approaches to Ethnicity in the Early Middle Ages* (Turnhout: Brepols, 2002). Heather continues to argue for large-group migration into the Roman Empire, a key piece of his framework of continuity with a relegated claim to biological or ethnic association: "These large groups were not 'peoples', but new coalitions. It is usually impossible to say anything much about ethnicity (which is not the same as saying there were no cultural commonalities; in reality, the evidence is again usually just ambiguous), but some of the groups possessed a pretty robust collective *political* identity, which many members were committed to, even in the face of considerable personal cost and danger." Peter Heather, "Migration," *Networks and Neighbours* 3.1 (2015), 1-21, at 19; cf. idem, *Empires and Barbarians: The Fall of Rome and the Birth of Empire* (New York: Oxford University Press, 2010).

23 Although the chronicle of Hydatius completed in the late 460s gives us the traditional date of 418, it has been more recently acknowledged that closer in time to the event and probably to be preferred on the timing is Prosper's chronicle, in which the date of settlement is 419. Quite possibly, the plan began in motion in 418 and was not completed until the following year. See Halsall, *Barbarian Migrations*, 228, with appropriate references. The case made for or against an actual treaty behind the arrangement cannot dispel the absence of explicit evidence of its existence.

decades on the move and without a long-term agreement with the Empire.[24] In the years immediately following the sack of Rome and preceding the famous arrangement under Wallia (r. 415-419), Goths cooperated, at times vitally, with Roman leaders. After they took Narbonne, an embargo by the formidable Master of the Soldiers Constantius forced their retreat into Barcelona. Dire food shortage brought about their presence in Iberia for the first time, and soon Constantius turned this circumstance into Gothic collaboration, as he enjoined them to fight Alans and Vandals in Lusitania and Baetica for the (albeit temporary) recovery of all of Roman Spain apart from Suevic-controled Gallaecia. Their involvement in the peninsula would soon be repeated and eventually endure.[25] The long progression in Gaul and Hispania from assistance to occupation to sovereignty is congruent with the gradual passage from adoption of Roman currency to minting of pseudo-imperial coinage to – after a considerable interval – establishment of a royal monetary system. In this vein, the early stages of direct Gothic-Roman relationship in the late fourth and early fifth centuries have a corollary impinging closely on the monetary system the Visigothic state would later institute: familiarity with Rome had long occasioned knowledge and use of imperial money. The use and production of currency were parts of a long integrational process for the populations who migrated into the Roman empire from *barbaricum*. Insofar as minting under directives of the Gothic monarchy in authority in Gaul and Hispania was to perform a Roman practice with only confined pre-migration barbarian precedents, it was one of the fundamental changes in political personality of the new rulers emerging in the late antique period.[26] Generating, managing, and utilizing currency on a state level quite literally came with the territory.

24 The group names Visigoths and Ostrogoths were not in use by contemporaries, though it has been conventional to use them as a convenient way to distinguish the western and eastern 'Goths', as early medieval sources referred to them. On rare occasions we see Goths in Gaul referred to as *Vesi*.

25 Michael Kulikowski, *Late Roman Spain and Its Cities* (Baltimore, MD: Johns Hopkins University Press, 2004), 168-70.

26 The recent claims of limited 'Gothic' imitation minting of gold coins in the mid-third century in the Ukrainian and Polish regions where Cherniakhiv and Wielbark cultures flourished is intriguing, though they should not be considered proven. Apart from the assumption, based on confused ancient sources, that these are indeed Goths as they later became known, the archeological contexts or even authenticity are largely beyond certainty. What is established is that these 'Goths' did rapaciously enter territory in northwestern Turkey where Rome had a very active bronze mint, and that irregularly heavy Roman-like but not official imperial gold issues of this era have been recovered for over a century in the lands north of the Black Sea. However, the coins struck were not part of a monetary economy, having been pierced and used as prestige items and not adherent to metrological standards. For the assertion that these

In 418/419, Constantius granted the Visigoths a settlement in Aquitania Secunda in southwestern Gaul.[27] This arrangement with the Visigoths, best seen as an ethnic fusion surrounding an adapting warrior band that had been moving westward without a solution to the challenges of sustenance and advancement, formed the basis of what would become a Visigothic kingdom. At this stage, the Visigoths had not only a recognized and permanent king at their head and an emerging group identity, but also a defined territory and semi-autonomous rule.[28] Yet, they still existed within imperial lands and structures and were federates that the leaders of the western Empire hoped to use to maintain security inside Roman borders.[29]

gold pieces were produced by Scythians/Goths using Roman bronze dies they had seized see Aleksander Bursche and Kirill Myzgin, "Gold coins, Alexandria Troas and Goths," in *Studies in Ancient Coinage in Honour of Andrew Burnett*, ed. R. Bland & D. Calomino (London: Spink, 2015), 232-58, and Aleksander Bursche, "Gold barbarian imitations of Roman coins: The Ulów type," in *Honoratissimum assensus genus est armis laudare*. Studia dedykowane Profesorowi Piotrowi Kaczanowskiemu z okazji siedemdziesiątej rocznicy urodzin, ed. R. Madyda-Legutko and J. Rodzińska-Nowak (Kraków: Towarzysto Wydawnicze – Historia Lagiellonica, 2014), 317-327. On imitative silver denarii of a slightly earlier stage and further north in barbarian lands see for example Andrzej Romanowski, "An Extraordinary Barbarian Imitation of the 2nd-Century Roman Denarius from Central Poland (Osiny, Baranów Commune, Grodzisk Mazowiecki District)," *Notae Numismaticae/Zapiski Numizmatyczne* 10 (2015), 115-30.

27 Walter Goffart, *Barbarians and Romans, A.D. 418-584: The Techniques of Accommodation* (Princeton, NJ: Princeton University Press, 1980), provocatively challenged the notion of land partitions by Roman citizens to situate the Visigoths and other groups in this migration period. His 'fiscal' scheme of barbarian allotments, granting tax revenues to the Goths (one third to the king and two thirds to the troops), further developed by Jean Durliat, has been much discussed but far from broadly accepted. Seeing a Roman intention of making the Visigothic and other fifth-century barbarian settlements permanent contributes to one scholar's rejection of the fiscal argument: Wolf Liebeschütz, "Cities, Taxes and the Accommodation of the Barbarians: The Theories of Durliat and Goffart," in *Kingdoms of the Empire: The Integration of Barbarians in Late Antiquity*, ed. Walter Pohl (Leiden: Brill, 1997), 135-51.

28 The precise nature of Visigothic rule is not clear, particularly because in 418 a letter from the emperor Honorius established a Council of the Seven Provinces (of southern Gaul), which was to meet annually and included municipal leaders and provincial governors of these same provinces: *Ep. Arel.* 8 (MGH Ep. 3:13-14). A settlement date of 419 makes even more credible the supposition that the Council had an immediate role in the decision to settle the Goths: see Halsall, *Barbarian Migrations*, 231-2.

29 On the settlement see Wolfram, *History of the Goths*, 161-73; Peter Heather, *Goths and Romans, 332-489* (Oxford: Oxford University Press, 1991), 194-224; Ralph W. Mathisen and Hagith S. Sivan, "Forging a New Identity: The Kingdom of Toulouse and the Frontiers of Visigothic Aquitania (418-507)," in *The Visigoths*, ed. Alberto Ferreiro (Leiden: Brill, 1999), 1-62; C.E.V. Nixon, "Relations Between Visigoths and Romans in Fifth-century Gaul," in *Fifth-century Gaul*, ed. Drinkwater and Elton, 64-74. Convincing on the rationale for the settlement and its location, as a bulwark against potential resurgence of Gallo-Roman usurpation, is Michael Kulikowski, "The Visigothic Settlement in Aquitania: The Imperial Perspective," in *Society and Culture in Late Antique Gaul:*

With or without an actual treaty, the grant of 418/419 was the seedbed of what eventually became the 'kingdom of Toulouse', as it is known from its capital. It allowed the Goths to settle in western Gaul from near the Loire down to Bordeaux or a little further, and southeast somewhat beyond Toulouse. For several years, the Visigoths' territory did not change, but over time a combination of Gothic military campaigns and political involvements brought enormous growth to their area of domination. By the late fifth century, Visigothic monarchs ruled in their own right over the largest barbarian kingdom in the West, stretching from the Loire and the Rhone to southern Spain. This vast dominion endured until 507, when the Frankish army of Clovis and his Burgundian allies defeated Alaric II and his troops near Vouillé, greatly reducing the confines of the Visigoths in Gaul.

The rule of Theodorid (or Theoderic I), from 419 to 451, was a period of intermittent cooperation with the Empire and of growth of the king's authority within the Visigothic abode. By and large, the king honored the terms of a *foedus* established either in 418/419 or a few years later, but not without hostilities, which were not atypical of barbarian allies of Rome at the time.[30] In the 420s and in 430, the Visigoths marched several times on Arles, headquarters of the Praetorian Prefect of the Gauls, although they never captured the city. In 436, they laid siege to Narbonne, which was saved at the last moment by the imperial general Litorius. The Goths countered and ended up capturing and executing the same general in 439 when he went to attack them at Toulouse itself. The result was a new treaty that was very favorable to the Goths and that some scholars have considered as a convenient marker for the beginning of a recognizable kingdom.[31] Seven

Revisiting the Sources, ed. Ralph W. Mathisen and Danuta Shanzer (Aldershot, UK: Ashgate, 2001), 26-38; see also idem, *Late Roman* Spain, 170-2. Kulikowski's assessment is sustained together with possible secondary benefits by Halsall, *Barbarian Migrations*, 228-34. As Wolfram notes, whether the settlement of the Goths in Aquitania II was envisioned by the *magister utriusque militiae* Constantius or the Goths themselves as a permanent situation, they did remain and within a short time established an enduring kingdom with a developing institutional structure.

30 E.A. Thompson, *Romans and Barbarians* (Madison, WI: University of Wisconsin Press, 1982), 193 overstated the case by calling Theodoric's attitude one of "indulgent neutrality." Gothic clashes with Roman forces in these years have been seen as a kind of understood ritual by which the federates ensured their worth and good bargaining position (Wolfram, *History of the Goths*, 175), but they may also have wanted to test the possibility of gaining access to the Mediterranean. See Kulikowski, *Late Roman Spain*, 179 on Theodoric's imperial relationship specifically in the last twelve years of his reign.

31 Gothic attacks and the accord: Kulikowski, *Late Roman Spain*, 179 and 372-3 nn. 15-16. Importance of the treaty: Mathisen and Sivan, "Forging a New Identity," 17 and 26. Similarly, Halsall, *Barbarian Migrations*, 246: in bringing the Goths forward on equally sovereign terms as Romans and in recognizing their monarchy and hegemony within their boundaries perhaps

years later, Gothic auxiliaries joined a Roman force attempting to combat the aggressions of Sueves in Spain, but the campaign failed miserably. The Visigoths won greater leverage to act in their own interest by their participation with Aetius's collection of forces in the defeat of the Huns in Gaul in 451. A new course of expansion of the kingdom and increasingly independent action can be charted from this time.[32]

Visigothic movements of lasting impact into Iberia occurred in the second half of the century. The brief reign of Thorismund (451-453), whom at least one chronicler of the day viewed as antagonistic to the Empire, ended with his murder by his brother Theoderic II (r. 453-466).[33] During the latter's reign, the Goths intervened in Spain several times 'on Roman authority', as contemporary sources make clear, but significantly the army was now not under command of a Roman general but rather a Visigothic one, and reliance on these allies underpinned imperial policy regarding Hispania.[34] A Visigothic force led by another of the king's brothers moved brutally against bagaudae in the key province of Tarraconensis in 453 or 454.[35] Shortly after a Suevic army invaded Tarraconensis in 456, Visigoths under Theoderic's own command, with the assistance of some Burgundian federates, almost totally destroyed the Suevic kingdom.[36] A few months later, the remnant of

for the first time, 439 was decisive. Wolfram, acknowledging that "it is difficult [...] to grasp chronologically the stages in the territorialization of the Gothic royal power," suggests that the Visigoths may have set about to advance the development of the kingdom after 423, when the death of Honorius brought into question the status of a treaty possibly made in 418: *The History of the Goths*, 204.

32 See Peter Heather, "The Emergence of the Visigothic Kingdom," in *Fifth-century Gaul*, ed. Drinkwater and Elton, 84-94. In the wake of the 439 treaty, independent Visigothic foreign policy moves are in evidence, and in the mid-450s the sending of Gothic legates separate from the Roman emissary to the Suevic King Rechiar displays a growing sense of discrete authority: see Halsall, *Barbarian Migrations*, 247, 259, noting in between the general context of Rome's much compromised situation in these years.

33 Hydatius, *Chronicle*, 156.

34 E.g. Hydatius, *Chronicle*, 150. See Wolfram, *History of the Goths*, 178 n. 62; Peter Heather, *The Goths* (Oxford: Blackwell, 1996), 188; Kulikowski, *Late Roman Spain*, 182-6.

35 Hydatius, *Chronicle*, 148, 150. José Orlandis, *Historia de España: La España visigótica* (Madrid, 1977), 37. Bagaudae, variously considered as comprised of peasants or slaves or other disenfranchised poor, were in any case organized bands of marauders whose uprisings in late Roman Gaul and Spain were a cause of great concern to imperial authorities. See Kulikowski, *Late Roman Spain*, 182f.

36 Halsall, *Barbarian Migrations*, 260. Rechiar was apprehended and executed, as were many Sueves who had surrendered. The Gothic capture of Emerita (= Mérida) at that time was probably final, for twelve years later Visigothic troops came from the city to reverse the Suevic seizure of Lisbon, and in 483 a Visigothic count named Salla appears from an inscription to be the stable authority in that region. See Thompson, *Romans and Barbarians*, 190.

those Visigothic troops who had not immediately returned with Theoderic II from Gallaecia made their way back to Gaul, pillaging and killing. By now, the Visigoths were immersed in the imperial campaigns in Spain, which gave them de facto military control over much of the south – including the diocesan capital at Mérida – and brought them into repeated warfare with Suevic groups. A more self-serving Gothic relationship with the Empire is evident in the years 458 to 463, when Visigoths intermittently battled against Roman troops in a series of tangled alliances contesting the imperial throne. A sign of the breakdown of the Gothic-Roman alliance was that Theoderic now sent troops to Baetica in his own name, and that his army remained there.[37] In 462, the imperial government under Severus ceded Narbonne to the Goths, likely as a reward for assistance against the 'rebel' general Aegidius in northern Gaul, transferring effective control of military passage into Spain.[38]

Under Euric (r. 466/467-484), who murdered his brother Theoderic to gain the throne and who lacked the refined qualities a prominent noble Roman could admire in Theodoric, the *foedus* was suspended.[39] Euric sought to aggrandize the Visigothic kingdom and, either from the start of his reign or more likely as favorable circumstances opened up, to gain the full independence of Gothic territory. After Euric's men had waged a series of inconclusive battles for control of the Auvergne, in 475 the region was ceded by Julius Nepos, with whom the Visigoths made what turned out to be a short-lived treaty. Nepos was soon deposed and within the year Euric took Arles and Marseilles and indeed the surrounding cities, having seen "the feebleness of the Roman Empire," as Jordanes relates.[40] Despite challenges that arose

37 Thompson, *Romans and Barbarians*, 189. Kulikowski, *Late Roman Spain*, 190f depicts Hispania (essentially Tarraconensis) ultimately handed over to emperor Majorian's authority in 459; the same author makes the case that "Spain ceased to be part of the Roman empire" after Majorian's failed plan to attack Vandal Africa from the Spanish coast with Gothic assistance (151-3, 192) since neither Roman troops, nor administration existed there any longer; Gothic military expeditions in the 460s fell well short of a full occupation force, as Spain became a ground of contesting Roman and Suevic warlords (197-202). Gothic aggression is not emphasized by Wolfram, *History of the Goths*, 180.

38 Hydatius, *Chronicle*, 212; Halsall, *Barbarian Migrations*, 268.

39 Admiration of Theodoric II, based on Sidonius Apollinaris, is noted in Hillgarth, *The Visigoths*, 6, 8.

40 Jordanes, *Getica*, 244, ed. T. Mommsen (*MGH.AA* 5: 121): "Euricus rex Visigothorum Romani regni vacillationem cernens Arelatum et Massiliam propriae subdidit dicioni." Jordanes also affirms Euric's acquisition of 'totae Spaniae Galliaque' after Odovacer subsequently waged unsuccessful campaigns to contest Visigothic gains in Gaul. The *Gallic Chronicle of 511* refers to Euric assuming all of Provence in this chaotic period: "*Arelate capta est ab Euricho cum Massilia et ceteris castellis*" (*Chron. Gall. a. 511*, 81; XX [R. W. Burgess, "The Gallic Chronicle of 511: A New

after two decades elapsed, the incursions of Euric's forces in the early 470s into Tarraconensis, which had been the last imperial territory in Spain, may have opened the door to permanent settlement in the peninsula.[41] In the 490s, two movements of Goths, observed in the so-called *Chronicle of Caesaraugusta*, brought a new and substantial advance in Visigothic control of northern Spain, since until that time the only Gothic presence was in scattered military outposts.[42] Nonetheless, it was not won without Hispano-Roman defiance, and after the Frankish triumph in Gaul in 507 killed King Alaric and forced the Goths to retreat into Hispania, rebuilding of the kingdom would have to start in this contested land.[43]

Just as the military alliance with the western Empire often seems elastic or unsettled from our vantage point, so the political status of Visigothic

Critical Edition with a Brief Introduction," in *Society and Culture*, ed. Mathisen and Shanzer, 99]). Andrew Gillett, 'The Accession of Euric,' *Francia* 26.1 (1999), 1-40 refutes the notion that Euric's policy early on was anything other than continued cooperation with imperial designs, a scheme that changed by 471 due to Roman assaults.

41 Tarraconensis was the northeastern part of late Roman Spain, named after Tarracona, a Mediterranean city some 60 miles down the coast from Barcinona (=Barcelona). The expansion of the kingdom of Toulouse is well described against deteriorating imperial authority in this century in Roger Collins, *Early Medieval Europe, 300-1000* (London: Macmillan, 1991), 75-99. For the long-held view of Gothic settlement of this region in roughly the last quarter of the century see Orlandis, *Historia de España*, 17; idem, *Historia del reino visigodo español* (Madrid, 1988), 12. Kulikowski, *Late Roman Spain*, 203-6 correctly challenges the assumption that Gothic gains in the 470s – clear from *Chron. Gall. a. 511*, 78-79; XVI [Burgess, "The Gallic Chronicle," 99] – were sustained, since the next testimony we have demonstrates that in the 490s it was necessary to regain some of these very locales. While this is probably the best conclusion, several points are worth mentioning: the limited record indicates that Mérida continued under Visigothic authority, as noted earlier; the uprisings that had to be dealt with do not disprove some continued Visigothic occupation of Tarraconensis, or parts of it, before then; it is at least possible that the chronicle notation discussed below about Goths taking up residence in Spain in 497 does not signify merely military garrisons (Kulikowski, *Late Roman Spain*, 208) but some actual if partial migration, in which case the settlement wave presents the possibility that parts of the region were now secure.

42 Lately given the title *Consularia Caesaraugustana*, more appropriate for what are in reality marginal notes on the chronicles of Victor of Tunnuna and John of Biclar, with dating by consuls. *Cons. Caes.*, s.a. 494; 497 (ed. C. Cardelle de Hartmann, CCSL 173A, 71a & 75a, pp. 22f): "Gothi in Hispanias ingressi sunt"; "Gothi intra Hispanias sedes acceperunt [...]". For a brief discussion of the possible reason for Visigothic migrations and for notes on the source see Collins, *Visigothic Spain*, 32-37 and idem, *Early Medieval Spain*, 34-35; also the important treatment in Kulikowski, *Late Roman Spain*, 206-9.

43 As indicated in the *Consularia Caesaraugustana*, rebellions in 496 and 506 were severely dealt with. *Cons. Caes.*, s.a. 496; 506 (ed. De Hartmann, CCSL 173A, 74a & 75a, p. 23; 87a, p. 27). The Franks pursued the Goths from Vouillé all the way to Barcelona, though with the aid of Theodoric's Ostrogoths the province of Septimania, extending just beyond the Pyrenees along the French coast, was restored to Visigothic rule.

Gaul defies easy interpretation. The original settlement did not make a wholesale grant of a Roman region to the Goths.[44] As C.E.V. Nixon writes, "certainly Rome did not give up its theoretical claims upon federate-occupied land until the days of Euric"; only in 476, when Euric asserted Visigothic independence, did the king gain authority 'in and over' a larger but still relatively small part of the Roman Empire.[45] The exact degree of Visigothic authority before Euric is ambiguous. The Roman provinces in which Visigoths were settled in 418/419 still had Roman governors whose participation in the 'Council of the Seven Provinces' of Gaul, resurrected that year after a period of Gallic usurpations, was foreseen in imperial legislation (though it did not necessarily happen).[46] Roman magistrates were still appointed to Roman cities and provinces organized along traditional lines and run under imperial laws.[47] The evidence regarding state revenues in western Gaul at this time implies that taxes paid by Romans were sent to the Visigothic court at Toulouse. For several decades, campaigns of the Goths as federates were led by Roman generals appointed by the emperor. Not until Euric's reign did the king himself act with a completely free hand, but perhaps already Theodoric II made appointments of Roman commanders over Gothic troops acting for the empire in Spain.[48] The cultural situation of the

44 Mathisen and Sivan, "Forging a New Identity," 8; Kulikowski, "Visigothic Settlement," 32, 36.

45 Nixon, "Relations," 72.

46 Mathisen and Sivan, "Forging a New Identity," 11. The 436 attack on Arles and Narbonne looks to have been already a Visigothic attempt at winning a greater place in the empire: Halsall, *Barbarian Migrations*, 244.

47 Mathisen and Sivan, "Forging a New Identity," 11; Heather, "The Emergence," 86ff. At the same time, Iberia was technically still part of the empire until the dwindled Roman government apparatus unceremoniously expired in Majorian's reign (n. 37 above), but imperial involvement was sporadic and not wholly effectual.

48 Taxes: Nixon, "Relations," 72-73; A.H.M. Jones, *The Later Roman Empire, 284-602: A Social, Economic, and Administrative Survey* (Oxford: Blackwell, 1964), I:257-60 & III:50f (nn. 47-52); one source is *Vita Viviani*, 4 (MGH.SRM 3:96). Euric not only sent several commanders including Vincentius, *dux Hispaniarum*, into Tarraconensis in 473, he soon sent Vincentius *quasi magister militum* on a military expedition to Italy: *Chron. Gall. a. 511*, 78-80; XVI (Burgess, "The Gallic Chronicle," 99). It is probably wise to understand this figure as one of a number of one-time Roman commanders who moved from imperial to barbarian service in these decades but retained at least a modicum of Roman title: see Collins, *Early Medieval Spain*, 24; R. W. Burgess, "From Gallia Romana to Gallia Gothica: the View from Spain," in *Fifth-century Gaul*, ed. Drinkwater and Elton, 19-27 at 25; Andreas Schwarcz, "The Visigothic Settlement in Aquitania: Chronology and Archaeology," in *Society and Culture*, ed. Mathisen and Shanzer, 15-25 at 22; and Heather, "The Emergence," 91f. Kulikowski, *Late Roman Spain*, 191 & 377 n. 72 surmises one general (Nepotianus) who commanded a Gothic army jointly with a Goth in the early 460s was before that a general of Majorian until the emperor's murder in 461. The underlying point here is that military authority was sliding into the orbit of the Visigothic monarch.

Visigoths is even more difficult to define. The attraction of Roman culture led Theoderic I to see to his son's education in Roman literature and law, and the dynamics of Roman aristocrats' shifting associations alongside an atmosphere of continued discourse of classical and Christian culture is evident.[49] Yet, Gothic nobles and even kings were sometimes unlearned in Latin. Euric supposedly knew little Latin and could employ powerful symbolism by the use of the Gothic tongue;[50] he habitually dressed in animal skins. Most importantly, any legitimate king had to play the role of a successful war-leader at the same time as he had to please the factions among the Visigothic nobility.

The First Visigothic Coinage

One of the key elements in the fifth-century transition in Gaul, as in other provinces of the western Empire, was the making of currency. When the multi-ethnic peoples along the Rhine and the Danube first became established on imperial soil with varying relationships with Rome, the need for currency in the provinces was still satisfied by Roman mints that had long been in existence and were still run by Roman minting bureaus.[51] In the western Empire in the fifth century, gold coinage in particular was supplied by mints in Italy. By the end of the century, all the major barbarian kingdoms that emerged in the continental West – Visigothic, Frankish, Burgundian, Suevic, Vandal, and Ostrogothic – produced coinage.[52] Minting by the new kingdoms should be seen in the context of the increasing hegemony of barbarian groups in regions of the empire with urban traditions, extensive patterns of trade, massive movements of state revenues and expenses, and long histories of currency itself.[53]

49 Nixon, "Relations," 74. See the observations in Hillgarth, *The Visigoths*, 4-20.

50 As when he insisted on a running translation into the Gothic language of the Latin spoken during negotiations with one Roman general. Ennodius, *Vita Epiphanii*, 89-90 (ed. F. Vogel, MGH.AA 7, 95).

51 See below, n. 63.

52 See the convenient summary of fifth-century coinage in Philip Grierson, *Coins of Medieval Europe* (London: Seaby, 1991), 3-6; for extensive treatment of barbarian coinages, see the chapters on the respective kingdoms in Ph. Grierson and Mark Blackburn, *Medieval European Coinage*, I: *5th-10th Centuries* (Cambridge: Cambridge University Press, 1986). For wider coverage of the coinage of first medieval kingdoms see Mark Blackburn, "Money and Coinage" (v. 1); more recently Rory Naismith, "Gold Coinage and Its Use in the Post-Roman West," *Speculum* 89 (2014), 273-306.

53 Some other important topics related to the rise of Roman-based currency systems by barbarian kingdoms, including the receiving of imperial tribute and gifts of sometimes huge proportions, are discussed in Hugh Elton, "Roman Gold and Barbarian Kings," in *Medieval*

Initially, the western kingdoms closely imitated Roman issues by adopting imperial numismatic types, denominations, legends, and mint marks. Thus, the coinage is most often referred to as 'pseudo-imperial' or 'imitation' coinage.[54] By far the main currency produced in Gaul in the fifth century was of gold. The two principal late Roman denominations minted were the solidus, a coin that Constantine established at c. 4.548 grams, and its third, the tremissis or triens. The Visigoths do not appear to have minted any of the Roman denominations of bronze, and the few sporadic issues of silver attributed to them must be considered tentative.[55] Our focus in the first section of this study of Visigothic monetary history, therefore, will necessarily be on gold coinage produced in southern Gaul.

Perhaps the main reason why most barbarian gold currency until late in the sixth century is called pseudo-imperial is that it was struck with the names, not of kings, but of Roman emperors, though inscriptions were not always up to date with the current emperor.[56] After the deposition in 475 of Julius Nepos, the last legitimate emperor in the West, coins were issued in the name of the Eastern emperor. Thus, as Peter Spufford noted, "for periods of up to a century, the various barbarian rulers appeared to keep alive the fiction that western Europe was still a part of the Roman Empire, before proclaiming on their gold coinages that they had created new independent kingdoms."[57] Even when Euric thwarted imperial control, he sought to make the Visigothic kingdom in the image of the Empire, and each coin quite literally provided an imperial image within his realm. Production of coinage on the Roman model should also be attributed to the fact that the

Europe, 1992 (Conference on Medieval Archaeology in Europe, 21-24 September 1992, University of York), v. 5: *Exchange and Trade* (York: University of York, 1992), 25-30. On late imperial economy and government one may profitably consult Jones, *The Later Roman Empire*; G. Depeyrot, *Le Bas-empire romain: économie et numismatique* (Paris: Errance, 1987); Chris Wickham, *Framing the Early Middle Ages: Europe and the Mediterranean, 400-800* (Oxford: Oxford University Press 2005).

54 Type refers to the dominant design on either face of a coin; denominations are the variety of metals and values in a currency system; legends are inscriptions around the type; mint marks are abbreviations or signs which indicate where a coin has been minted. The general terms applied to barbarian coinage before the regal series can vary slightly depending on definitions and emphases. I employ both 'pseudo-imperial' and 'imitation' for the Visigothic pre-regal coinage as a whole, much as Grierson and others have, but Pliego, *La moneda visigoda*, v. 1, 72-79 makes a distinction between 'imitation' (c. 417-c. 484) and 'pseudo-imperial' (c. 484-507), followed by the VPW form taken up in the West.

55 See below, n. 73.

56 By contrast, there were regular royal series in silver and bronze by the mid-fifth century (Suevi, Vandals) and in the sixth century (Ostrogoths, Merovingians): see Grierson and Blackburn, *Medieval European Coinage*, 4-5 and the respective sections on each kingdom.

57 Spufford, "Coinage and Currency," in *Cambridge Economic History of Europe*, v. II, 791.

imperial guise offered the only assurance that the coins would be widely accepted, since emperors had always enjoyed the sole authority to mint in the Empire, and the peoples from beyond the borders had no coinage of their own and only in a few instances imitation issues. From the period before they crossed the Danube in 376 until they reached southern Gaul, the people who coalesced as Goths had used Roman currency.[58] Eventually, all the barbarian states developed 'national' coinages of their own – though still based on late imperial currency – which gave expression to their independent identities. The first king to place his own name on coins was the Sueve Rechiar, who was proclaimed on silver issues around 450.[59] Visigothic kings would not do so until about 573, as shown in Chapter Two. The difference in the fifth century was that the Sueves were not allies of the Empire and never had the sort of mutual reliance that formed between the Visigothic court and Gallo-Romans.[60] No 'regal' gold currency was minted in the fifth century, and only exceptionally in the next century until between 570 and 580, at which time several western kingdoms struck tremisses with royal names. Meanwhile, the solidus was "the coin that seemed *par excellence* to embody the pretensions of the Roman Empire," and minting it in a name other than the emperor's was considered a violation.[61]

Most of the fifth-century gold coinage found in modern France imitates styles and mint-marks used at imperial mints in Italy. Scholars have long had difficulty determining whether to attribute these simplified or bungled issues to the Empire, the Visigothic kingdom, the Frankish kingdom, the Burgundian kingdom, or powerful Gallo-Romans acting unofficially. Even after more than a century of progress in this field the origin of various

58 See Peter Heather and John Matthews, *The Goths in the Fourth Century* (Liverpool: Liverpool University Press, 1991), 91; also above at n. 26.

59 Grierson and Blackburn, *Medieval European Coinage*, 79; Grierson, *Coins of Medieval Europe*, 5. If we bear in mind that Suevic gold currency continued with imperial name and figure, it is overstatement that by circulating a coin with his own monogram Rechiar "was in effect declaring his withdrawal from the *imperium Romanum*" (Kulikowski, *Late Roman Spain*, 184f).

60 See Halsall, *Barbarian Migrations*, 250, 254f (brief treaty abandoned), 259f; Heather, "The Emergence"; Nixon, "Relations"; Mathisen and Sivan, "Forging a New Identity." The Sueves were perhaps the first to strike a stylistically recognizable pseudo-imperial coinage: Grierson, *Coins of Medieval Europe*, 4-5.

61 Grierson, *Coins of Medieval Europe*, 5; on acceptability of minting gold solely with the imperial image, see Filippo Carlà, "The End of Roman Gold Coinage and the Disintegration of a Monetary Area," *Annali dell'Istituto Italiano di Numismatica* 56 (2010), 53-55, 61-64. See below, p. 102, n. 282 on the famous example of the Frankish king Theodebert I (534-48), who drew the anger of the Byzantines by having his own inscription put on his solidi (Procopius, *Bell. Goth.* III.33.5-6). In the same note I discuss Theodoric the Ostrogoth's (r. 493-526) pseudo-imperial gold coinage, with its faint references to himself, and his full regal legends on silver and bronze.

coin groups which have been formed still can seldom be attributed with certitude. Fortunately, the name of a barbarian king sometimes appears on issues of imperial type from the sixth century, allowing these and contemporary pseudo-imperial coins of matching style to be attributed to the same kingdom.[62] Sometimes, a particular style can be traced back to the fifth century, because individual mints or minting regions often developed enduring techniques. Consistent habits or marks are known from late Roman coins with identical mint-marks, and it is widely understood that under the new regimes Roman die cutters and moneyers still ran the workshops in the new kingdoms.[63] Attributions of certain coins to the Visigothic kingdom in Gaul have been made by following the progression of their styles to sixth-century coins, which are undoubtedly Visigothic, given the Iberian preponderance of their find-spots and their marked resemblance to the first royal-name issues of the Visigothic monarchy.[64] These styles from the fifth century can be differentiated from those associated with Franks, Burgundians, and Sueves. The locations of the finds of tremisses and solidi of Gothic style provide added confirmation of their attribution, since the pieces have turned up chiefly in the regions of southern France under Visigothic control.[65]

The difficulties of attribution have led to a divergence of opinion as to when the striking of coins under Visigothic authority first took place. Around three quarters of a century ago, Wilhelm Reinhart made great strides in the identification of currency in Gaul and, for the sixth century, Spain.[66]

62 Style refers to the specific appearance of the type and epigraphy of a coin, or to express the same reality in other terms, to the particular execution of the type and epigraphy on a given die and thus on coins which are made from its use.

63 While mint records as such are entirely lacking for the barbarian kingdoms and the western part of the Empire in the fifth-century, the conclusion is based on continuity of artistic execution, the cohesiveness of late Roman *collegia* in general and minting *collegia* in particular (*familiae monetariae*), and the fact that the barbarians had not previously minted on their own. Tomasini, *The Barbaric Tremissis*, 80, refers to "barbaric imitators or perhaps more accurately, later provincial craftsmen working under barbarian governments." See below, Chapter Three, section A on imperial and early medieval minters.

64 See below, Chapter Two, section A. Because sites of finds are usually unrecorded, there has been an assumption that the locations of twentieth-century collections accurately represent the general region of at least the great majority of coin finds. Grierson and Blackburn, *Medieval European Coinage*, 44; Grierson, *Coins of Medieval Europe*, 14.

65 See the rather neat territorial divisions of Gallic coins from this period in C. E. King, "Roman, local, and barbarian," 184-95, here 188, fig. 16.1, and in Georges Depeyrot, "Les émissions wisigothiques de Toulouse (Ve siècle)," *Acta numismática* 16 (1986), 79-104, here 98-100, figs. 4-6.

66 Reinhart, "Die Münzen des tolosanischen Reiches der Westgoten," *Deutsches Jahrbuch für Numismatik* 1 (1938), 107-35; idem, "Die Münzen des westgotischen Reiches von Toledo," *Deutsches*

He accepted the possibility that solidi in the name of Honorius (395-423) were minted under Visigothic authority.[67] Barral i Altet mistrusted any of Reinhart's attributions before Anastasius (491-518);[68] yet, the article of Le Gentilhomme on which Barral i Altet relied argued that imitation issues began rapidly after the Visigothic settlement in Gaul in 418, thus with Honorius's name.[69] Since that time, several numismatists, most notably Philip Grierson and J. P. C. Kent, followed Reinhart's assertions on the earliest issues of gold currency.[70] Reputedly, Visigothic solidi with legends of Honorius and the initials RV on either side of the emperor on reverse, copying the Ravenna mint-mark, can be clearly distinguished from official coins of the Empire. On the former, the obverse portrait has an elongated, more line-drawn nose, the letters in the legend are smaller, tongues from the letter G (in the abbreviation AAVGGG on reverse) are much shorter, and the figure of the emperor on the reverse is taller than on official Roman solidi.[71] These scholars who corroborated Reinhart's work have convincingly shown the link between these features and stylistic modifications of Gothic issues

Jahrbuch für Numismatik 3-4 (19441), 69-101; and idem, "Nuevas aportaciones a la numismática visigoda," *Archivo español de arqueología* 18 (1945), 212-35. The last article represents his revised thoughts on the entire Visigothic pre-regal coinage (see p. 214 of that article). Reinhart pointed out that the styles and mint-marks of many fifth-century pieces from southern France were not in harmony with the vast majority which have an Italian origin.

67 Reinhart, "Nuevas aportaciones," 215.

68 Barral i Altet, *La circulation*, 46 and 54. It is perhaps not a coincidence that Barral was a student of Jean Lafaurie, who argued that several groups of coins attributed to the Visigoths were instead minted under the authority of Aëtius; for references and counterarguments by various authors see C. E. King, "Roman, Local, and Barbarian," 189.

69 As Barral i Altet himself relates in *La circulation*, 54; Pierre Le Gentilhomme, "Le monnayage et la circulation monétaire dans les royaumes barbares en Occident (Ve-VIIIe siècle)," *Revue numismatique* 7 (1943), 46-112, here 68, and *Revue numismatique* 8 (1944), 13-59.

70 Grierson: Grierson and Blackburn, *Medieval European Coinage*, esp. 44, 46 and pl. 10, no. 166; Kent: J. P. C. Kent, "Un monnayage irrégulier du début du Ve siècle de notre ère," *Bulletin du Cercle d'etudes numismatiques* (1974), 23-32, and the final volume (v. 10) of idem, *The Roman Imperial Coinage* (London: Spink, 1994), 220-29 and 450-62 with corresponding plates. Kent assigns to the Goths some issues in the name of Theodosius II (r. 408-450), presumed to be from the period after Honorius's death. C. E. King, "Roman, local, and barbarian," and Depeyrot, "Les émissions wisigothiques," do not refute the Visigothic attribution of coins in Honorius's name, but rather concentrate on solidi with the mint-mark RA on reverse and tremisses with the figure of Victory facing left, i.e. coins starting during the rule of Valentian III (r. 425-455).

71 The general pattern of the Honorius solidus of Ravenna and Rome: obv. – diademed and cuirassed emperor's bust facing right; rev. – emperor standing or sitting with labarum in right hand and crowning Victory on globe in left hand, standing on a captive, with COMOB in exergue (bottom). The Ravenna solidi of Valentinianus III and a few years later of Libius Severus were similar but after 450 the reverse Victory is commonly holding a cross in the right hand and has one foot on a human-headed serpent.

in subsequent decades under Honorius's successors. The assignment of this coin group is also based on its probable zone of circulation in southwestern Gaul.[72]

Kent broadened the range of Visigothic attributions in the fifth century to a fuller extent than other scholars, assigning to the kingdom of Toulouse several early silver issues and later gold coins all the way through the reigns of Julius Nepos and Zeno (r. 474-475; 476-491), with whose reign the final volume of *Roman Imperial Coinage* concludes.[73] If he is correct in this, coins were probably struck under almost all the Visigothic kings in Gaul from the death of Alaric I: Athaulf (r. 410-415), Theoderic I (r. 418-451), Thorismund (r. 451-453), Theoderic II (r. 453-466), Euric (r. 466-484), and Alaric II (r. 484-507). About the same time that Kent's volume appeared, however, a Portuguese study called into question the attributions to the Goths before the 450s.[74] That work offers an excellent demonstration, with good photographs

72 C. E. King, "Roman, Local, and Barbarian," calls attention to the lack of a firm provenance for most of the coinage in question. The locations of museums and coin-dealing companies where specimens show up is not altogether reliable evidence of the place of loss or of minting. Some nineteenth-century scholars remarked on find-spots in certain areas of Gaul: see Grierson and Blackburn, *Medieval European Coinage*, 44.

73 *Roman Imperial Coinage*, v. 10, 220-29, 450-62, and plates 76-79: silver siliquae in the name of Attalus (r. 414-415; nos. 3701-02); silver and various gold denominations in the name of Honorius (r. 395-423, nos. 3703-09); gold solidi in the name of Theodosius II (r. 408-450, no. 3710); gold denominations, including some rare solidi with the reverse type on those in Honorius's name, and silver naming Valentinian III in three separate phases, including a posthumous phase of the years c. 470-475 (nos. 3711-33); gold denominations in the name of Avitus (r. 455-456; nos. 3734-36), Majorian (r. 457-461; nos. 3737-50), Severus (r. 461-465; nos. 3751-64), Anthemius (r. 467-472; no. 3765), Nepos (nos. 3766-68), and Zeno (nos. 3769-75).
A lengthy critique of these attributions is beyond the scope of the present work. I offer a few observations, all of which strengthen Kent's conclusions: a) the solidus of 'Theodosius II' is extremely similar to a pair of solidi purporting to be of Valentian III but attributed by Kent to the Visigoths (nos. 3711-12); b) the imitative solidi the author places in a second series of Valentinian III (c. 439-455; nos. 3717-19) resemble in detail several solidi of the same attribution in *Medieval European Coinage* (pl. 10), and the same is true for his 'second series' tremisses (extremely close to *MEC*, pl. 10, nos. 171-72); c) the posthumous issues of Valentinian III are thought to be confirmed as such on the basis of the low fineness of one of the coins, which accords perfectly with the standards of Libius Severus's reign (widely considered as 461-465). Kent notes the coincidence of the supposed Visigothic issues and the reigns of emperors with whom the Goths enjoyed peace, and a conspicuous absence of the names of emperors with whom there was confrontation (p. 221). Given Kent's careful analysis of the coins, we may doubt the opinion that the majority of Visigothic-Valentinian III issues were from late in this reign (as argued in Marques et al., *Ensaios*, 14).

74 Marques et al., *Ensaios*, 14, where the authors fault the lack of rigorous study of coin provenance and the insignificant typological distinctions that have been made in connection with coins of the first half of the century. It must be observed that they have not themselves

set side-by-side, of how the Visigothic coins of the mid-fifth century are distinguishable from contemporary imperial issues.[75] Clarity of presentation is no small matter in being able to assess attributions, since some stylistic groups of fifth-century coinage are similar in appearance. Few historians have access to the scattered collections of coins, and even a numismatist must rely on good photographs. In short, 'Visigothic' coinage under Attalus, Honorius, and Theodosius II is possible but by no means certain, although most specialists have agreed on that of Honorius.[76]

Greater certitude lies in the attribution to the Visigothic regime of coins in the name of Valentinian III (r. 425-455), emperor in the West during much of Theodosius II's reign in Constantinople. From his reign onwards certain differences between gold coinage of the Roman Empire and the Visigothic series become more evident. The reverse type on the empire's Ravenna solidi was changed at this time (the emperor stands facing forward, his

performed the very daunting task of actually cataloging or assigning a wide array of individual pre-regal coins. The authors should have cited Reinhart's article of 1945 in addition to the one of 1938. Kent's discussion in *Roman Imperial Coinage*, v. 10, 223 of possibly Visigothic coinage bearing inscriptions of Valentinian III affords a glimpse of the ongoing debate on pre-regal coinage; there Kent rejects the views of Jean Lafaurie and Grierson.

75 See e.g. Marques et al., *Ensaios*, 13, fig. I: in contrast to a solidus from Ravenna, the letters of a solidus assigned to the Visigoths are uneven in size and employ exaggerated serifs, while the types are rather schematic and more heavily line-drawn than molded. The schematization is most noticeable in the bust of the obverse, but on close investigation can also be detected in the eyes, head, and hands of the reverse figure. The legend of a Gothic tremissis on the same page is blundered to the point that it is hardly legible; the cross held by Victory depicted on the reverse has a 'hollowed out' stem (double lines instead of one) typical of this imitation series. Similarly, though it is also found on genuine imperial gold issues from early in the century, volume one of *Medieval European Coinage*, dedicated to the early Middle Ages, lays out photos of Visigothic specimens in such a way that the subtle development of unique styles can scarcely be doubted. This owes much to the high quality of the plates and accompanying information, but especially to the uncommon skill with which Philip Grierson formed his collection on which the book is based.

Kent, *Roman Imperial Coinage*, v. 10, because of the sheer volume of material and the necessarily more complex catalogue entries (separated from the plates), makes comparison much less convenient; however, his commentary (pp. 220-29) adds greatly to the discussion. For greater detail on the supposed Visigothic style, but without illustrations of official Roman coins, see Depeyrot, "Les émissions wisigothiques" and idem, "Les *solidi* gaulois de Valentinien III," *Revue suisse de numismatique* 65 (1986), 111-32, partly summarized in C. E. King, "Roman, Local, and Barbarian."

76 Reinhart, "Die Münzen des tolosanischen," pl. 2, nos. 3-4, assigned one group of tremisses in the name of Honorius (with a Victory advancing right on reverse) as Visigothic on the grounds that their bust style and epigraphy resemble the solidi. Grierson, in Grierson and Blackburn, *Medieval European Coinage*, 46, implicitly concurs on this attribution, as does Kent (see nn. 70 and 73 above).

right foot crushing a human-headed serpent; in his right hand he holds a long, jeweled cross while his left hand holds a globe on which stands a Victory figure holding out a crown). One set of the imitative coins copies the new type and the RV mint-mark, but includes a tiny crown over the obverse portrait. A very similar set without the crown has the letters RA instead of RV.[77] In both, obverse and reverse types are less refined in their execution, particularly the Victory figure in the emperor's hand, which is now reduced to a sort of stick figure set over a circle. The imitations in the name of Severus (r. 461-465), which no longer include the tiny crown, begin to have unaligned letters and have solely the RA mint-mark.[78] The names of towns in the Visigothic kingdom that may correspond to such an abbreviation have been proposed, but none seem likely as mint-cities. It is probably best to see RA as a means of differentiating these solidi and the ones struck at the Ravenna mint.[79] The two Visigothic series with different mint-marks were produced either concurrently, perhaps at different mints in the kingdom, or successively as a change in the abbreviation was made some time in Valentinian III's reign.

After occupation of the imperial throne in the West ceased in 476, Visigothic solidi kept pace with changes in imperial types in the East. In Zeno's reign (c. 474-491), the reverses imitated the Victory figure holding a Christogram staff. On obverses in the name of Anastasius (r. 491-518) a facing emperor wearing a crown was introduced.[80] But by the later fifth century the solidus gave way to the tremissis as the principal coin in the West, including the Visigothic kingdom. The obverse type on Visigothic

77 Depeyrot, "Les *solidi* gaulois," argues that the first set has an earlier, distinct origin in northern Gaul but clearly influences the second set, which he considers Visigothic. On the basis of style alone, I favor the approach of Grierson, in Grierson and Blackburn, *Medieval European Coinage*, 44-45 and pl. 10, who assigns the whole lot to the Goths. (C. E. King, "Roman, Local, and Barbarian," 190, is correct to suggest that 'RV' imitations of Majorian's solidi should be included in attributions to the Visigoths, but had she referred to *Medieval European Coinage* she would also have known to include Valentinian III coins of that style and with the RV mark.)

78 RA-marked solidi come from the last few years of Valentinian III as well as Majorian's and Severus's reigns. Grierson and Blackburn, *Medieval European Coinage*, 45-49 and 75-77, repeating the suggested reading 'Rex Alaricus', in which case these were posthumous imitative issues. Kent, *Roman Imperial Coinage*, v. 10, 225 more convincingly concludes RA was probably "a barbarized amalgam of RV and AR" (the Arles mint-sign which after all marks the first two letters of the city, setting a possible pattern), though his observation that it was first found on late Visigothic solidi of Majorian represents a slightly delayed chronology. The provenance of specimens is the western half of France and southern Britain.

79 C. E. King, 192, and Depeyrot, "Les émissions wisigothiques," 85.

80 Grierson and Blackburn, *Medieval European Coinage*, 46 and pl. 10; Reinhart, "Die Münzen des tolosanischen," pl. 6.

pseudo-imperial tremisses from Valentinian III until about the 520s was the same right-facing bust as on fifth-century solidi. From the reign of Justinian until c. 584 this bust design assumed a characteristic trapezoidal cuirass and, with increasing frequency, a cross on the emperor's chest, a symbol started under Anastasius and predominant by the time of Justin I. Reverse tremissis types in the mid-fifth century incorporated either the Victory goddess (facing left and holding a 'hollowed out' cross) or the cross within a wreath.[81] Shortly after the turn of the sixth century a new reverse type originated, with Victory striding to the right and holding out a wreath. It will be taken up at length later in this chapter.

While there are differences of opinion concerning the identification of late antique coins, literary evidence may confirm Visigothic minting long before the shift of the focal point of the kingdom to Narbonensis and Spain in the early sixth century. A law of Majorian in 458 (*Novel* 7.14) singled out *solidi gallici* as being of low quality: "Henceforward no tax collector, on the basis of false disapproval, shall refuse a solidus of full weight, except in the case of a Gallic solidus, the gold of which is valued at a lesser worth."[82] The label has traditionally been thought to refer to imitation solidi from Gaul, since it is unlikely that the emperor should have called for the rejection of his own coins struck at Arles – the only imperial mint then in Gaul – by either the comitatensian mint traveling with him there, or the Ravenna mint-workers transferred there a few years before.[83] The law does not seem to allude to forgeries but rather to official coinage of some kind; yet, no specific mint or moneyers are mentioned, as one would expect if the coins and their mint-marks were of Arles. Possibly, the Visigothic kingdom received the right to mint coins from the Empire, as was argued long ago in the case of the Sueves.[84] Further indication that Majorian's law targeted imitation

81 For more on these types and their relationship to the solidi see Grierson and Blackburn, *Medieval European Coinage*, 44-46, and Reinhart, "Nuevas aportaciones," 215, both with accompanying plates.

82 "Praeterea nullus solidum integri ponderis, calumniosae improbationis obtentu, recuset exactor, excepto eo Gallico cujus aurum minore aestimatione taxatur.": *Theodosiani libri 16 cum Constitutionibus Sirmodianis et Leges novellae ad Theodosianum pertinentes*, ed. Theodor Mommsen et al., v. II (Berlin: Weidmann, 1962), 171. Jean Lafaurie translates the phrase 'calumniosae improbationis obtentu' into French as 'sous le prétexte qu'il est de bas aloi': "Les monnaies frappées à Lyon au VIe siècle," in *Mélanges de Travaux offerts à maître Jean Tricou* (Lyon, 1972), 139-205, here 194. On the importance of coin weight, see below, n. 87.

83 On the Arles mint, see Kent, *Roman Imperial Coinage*, v. 10, 28. Nevertheless, Majorian's law is "ironic in view of the poor quality of his own gold": ibid., 224.

84 See Marques et al., *Ensaios*, 12-15. Just as the Empire occasionally delegated the right of striking coin to Roman generals, as Lafaurie asserts, so the same authority was possibly granted

pieces is provided by analyses that have revealed that coins considered to be of Visigothic origin had lower weights and fineness than contemporary currency.[85] Imitation gold pieces from Gaul in Majorian's name issued after the promulgation of his law have much improved fineness.[86] The Visigoths may have regularly issued pseudo-imperial coins of low standards except when imperial or other strictures prevented their acceptance.

A Burgundian law of 501 attests to Visigothic minting very early in the sixth century. The law lists certain solidi that people in the kingdom did not have to accept, among them "those of the Goths, which in the time of King Alaric were debased."[87] In a letter written in 509 Avitus, the bishop of Vienne,

to the Visigoths as a result of the *foedus* possibly initiated in 418 or 419. The Visigoths were the only authority in Gaul in the mid-fifth century likely to have minted the solidi mentioned here. The weakness of Lafaurie's argument that Aëtius and Aegidius are responsible for what others have considered Visigothic issues has been demonstrated by C. E. King and G. Depeyrot (see C. E. King, "Roman, Local, and Barbarian," 189-95 for a review of the arguments and for references) and by Grierson (Grierson and Blackburn, *Medieval European Coinage*, 45).

85 Cl. Brenot et al., *L'or monnayé*, v. I: *purifications et altérations de Rome à Byzance* (Cahiers Ernest-Babelon 2) (Paris: Centre National de la Recherche Scientifique, 1985), 202-04, report the results from tests of a few solidi from each of the three main groups circulating at that time. Whereas the six official Roman coins analyzed have between 1.1% and 2.6% silver in the alloy, and the two with a crown have between 1.1% and 4.7%, the silver content of the three 'RA' coins is in the range of 23-27%. On the low weights, see also Depeyrot, "Les émissions wisigothiques," 82-83. At least some coins from the few years before and after Majorian held the throne possess a fineness of only 83-90% gold: see Grierson and Blackburn, *Medieval European Coinage*, 436-37 (= pl. 10).

86 Kent, *Roman Imperial Coinage*, v. 10, 5 and 224.

87 The text, with important variants in brackets, is the following (emphasis mine): "De monetis solidurum [iubemus] custodire, ut omne aurum, quodcumque pe[n]saverit, accipiatur praeter quattuor tantum monetas, hoc est: Valenti[ni]ani, Genavensis [prioris] et *Gothici, qui a tempore Alarici regis adaerati sunt*, et A[r]daricianos [*vel* ad Eurici annos: *infra*]. Quod si quicumque praeter istas quattuor monetas aurum pensantem non acceperit, id, quod vendere volebat, non accepto pretio perdat." *Leges Burgundionum*, ed. L. R. de Salis, *MGH.LL* sectio I.2, v.II.i (Hannover: Hahn, 1892), no. 7, 120-21. Here, it is clear that, with the exception of these four kinds with recognized lower fineness, acceptance of solidi was obligatory if they weighed an acceptable amount – an indication that, as in the Roman era, precious-metal coins were placed on a scale to ensure that full value was received since coins of different weights (but stable fineness) would have different values, and there would be a tendency to underpay using coins of lowest weights (Gresham's Law). A merchant who did not accept coins of proper weight besides these four would lose what he had offered to sell. On the practice of weighing in late antiquity, see Carlà, "The End of Roman Gold Coinage," 103-72, at 49, 52, 64, 77, 78 (esp. n. 150, where *pensans* is necessarily understood as 'of right weight': ref. S. Suchodolski, "Est-ce que les Burgondes ont été forcés d'accepter l'or au poids?," *Numismatica e antichità classica* 20 (1991), 247-51). Also Michael F. Hendy, *Studies in the Byzantine Monetary Economy, c. 300-1450* (Cambridge: Cambridge University Press, 1985), 329-33 on the great attention paid to proper weighing in this period; Kent, *Roman Imperial Coinage*, v. 10, 8-11 on late Roman *exagia*, weight standards. Pliego, *La moneda visigoda*, v. 1, 76-78, believes

attributed the ruin of the late king to the debasement of his coinage, which, in the later part of his reign, was the result of the special circumstances of preparing for war against Clovis's Franks.[88] The Burgundian law reveals that this was not the first of Alaric's poor issues. While no solidi of reduced gold from this period have been discovered, there are examples of debased tremisses, which occasionally were called 'solidi'; that is, when the term was used to refer generically to gold pieces. There is also an intriguing solidus of this period with a low weight and apparently a combination of the letters 'AL' at the end of the reverse inscription, quite possibly a reference to Alaric.[89] A famous description of Narbonne in a poem by Sidonius Apollinaris has led some to believe that a mint operated there in the fifth century. The verse has been taken by one scholar as an allusion to the minting there in 414-415, while for another it is a "very clear reference to a mint at Narbonne in the early 460s, probably operated by the Visigoths."[90]

the law sought to prevent weighing of coins, apart from the four specified, in order to prevent their rejection.
The meaning of the law is not that the first three coinages named were debased during Alaric's reign, but rather that all those mentioned were debased, including the Gothic coins specifically from the period of this particular king. Lafaurie's interpretation of 'Valentiani / Valentiniani' is coinage of Valentinian III; his interpretation of 'Genavensis prioris' is the coinage of Geneva, the former capital of the Burgundian kingdom. 'Adaricianos' possibly refers to Gallo-Romans living under the authority of Franks, Visigoths, Tungri, and Burgundians; they are mentioned several times by a similar name in Greek in Procopius's writings, Αρβορυχοι (Lafaurie, "Monnaies frappées à Lyon," 195-96). Naismith, "Gold Coinage," 280, interprets the first two mints as Valence and Geneva. Depeyrot adopts the ms. reading "Valentiniani", rejecting the "Valenciam" of the Besançon ms., and interprets as "ad Eurici annos" the variants "ardaricianus", "adaricianos", "adaricianus", "ardaricae annos" (Depeyrot, "Les émissions wisigothiques," 97). The rendering of Lafaurie and Depeyrot for this latter term have interesting implications in the context of this law, however I am not able to resolve this question at present.

88 Avitus of Vienne, *Epistulae* LXXXVII (ed. R. Pieper, *MGH.AA* 6.2, 96-97): '[...] cui corruptam potius quam confectam auri nondum fornace decocti crederes inesse mixturam; vel illam certe, quam nuperrime rex Getarum secuturae praesagam ruinae monetis publicis adulterium firmantem mandaverat."

89 Reinhart, "Nuevas aportaciones," 217-18 and fig. 1, no. 15; from the photo it is difficult to make out the letters referred to by Reinhart, who owned the coin.

90 Sidonius Apollinaris, *Carmen* 23, ll. 37-42ff (ed. Christian Luetjohann, *MGH.AA* VIII [Berlin: Weidmann, 1887], 250-51): "Salve Narbo potens salubritate, / [...] / portis, porticibus, foro, theatro, / delubris, capitoliis, monetis, / thermis [...]". In *Roman Imperial Coinage*, v. 10, 29, Kent associates these lines with the silver and possibly gold issues of Priscus Attalus, puppet-emperor of the Goths in 414-415 (see also 135, 141-42 on the coinage). The opinion concerning the later period quoted above is from Ralph Mathisen's review of Kent's volume in *American Journal of Numismatics*, second ser., 7-8 (1995-96), 299-305, here 302. The Visigoths acquired the city of Narbonne in 461/2 from Ricimer in exchange for lending military support in n. Gaul (hence Grierson overlooked an important fact in dismissing the poet's reference to an actual mint there in the 460s on the

It was observed earlier in this chapter that ascertaining which coins belong to which polities requires a somewhat indirect approach, since the mint sites are not mentioned on the coins until about 580/582 and one must often rely on nineteenth-century scholars for very general information on the location of finds.[91] In the same way, identification of pre-regal mints involves guesswork. For the several decades when the Visigothic kingdom had its capital at Toulouse the main mint was probably located there. Reinhart claimed to have come across a solidus with the combined letters T and L on the reverse field, which he took to refer to Toulouse. Unfortunately, he did not provide a photograph or other information about this coin. He did observe that certain coins include the single letters N and A at the end of the reverse legend, which may refer to mints at Narbonne and either Arles or Agde.[92] These, however, are not entirely firm grounds for mint attribution, a matter that cannot be resolved until more evidence is discovered. If it could be confirmed that these letters are mint-marks, their placement in the legend instead of the field would be a feature peculiar to Visigothic currency in that era. Yet, one coin whose inscription ends in A also has an N in the field.[93] There is too little numismatic or documentary evidence to tell whether the letters at the end of legends may refer not to mints but to moneyers, even if the suggested attributions to Toulouse and Narbonne mentioned here seem particularly appropriate.

If the Goths established these or possibly other minting sites apart from Arles, as must have been the case before their occupation of the imperial praetorian headquarters in 461/2, their policy on the making of currency already took a different direction from that of the Roman Empire. Imperial minting, especially of gold, was centered in very few mints (at times only one in the case of gold), none of which were located west of Arles. Minting in Gaul under the Visigoths, of which we can be most confident starting from the 450s, took place in towns which had never produced coinage before. The proliferation of sites continued in the following centuries of Visigothic control of Hispania.

grounds that "the city was then in imperial hands and no imperial coins are known": *Medieval European Coinage*, 44). Cf. Barral i Altet, *La circulation*, 54 n. 244 for different interpretations of Sidonius's verse.

91 See above, pp. 36-38.

92 T-L: Reinhart, "Nuevas aportaciones," 216. N and A: ibid. and fig. 1, nos. 13-14, with legends transcribed on p. 233; the suggestions of actual sites are my own. Detached letters at the end of legends on imperial solidi of 5th c. indicate mints: Kent, *Roman Imperial Coinage*, v. 10, 25. There are similar letters on the reverses of Visigothic solidi: Reinhart, "Nuevas aportaciones," (one is a tremissis: fig. 1, no. 14); in Grierson and Blackburn, *Medieval European Coinage*, it is hard to say what is a detached letter at the end of a reverse legend.

93 Reinhart, "Nuevas aportaciones," fig. 1, no. 17, and 233; see also no. 19, ending in A but showing A and T in the field.

B The Kingdom in Spain, 507-c. 573

The Re-Building of the Kingdom

When the Visigoths began to take at least temporary control of parts of the Iberian peninsula starting in the mid-fifth century, there was as yet no major Gothic settlement of these lands. The placement of military administrators and their troops in key cities seems to have sufficed to bring about a patchwork of Visigothic hegemony.[94] As outlined in the early part of this chapter, the diminishing presence of an imperial army in Spain, defeated in 422 at the hands of the Hasding Vandals, thoroughly dependent on the Goths in following decades, and non-existent after Majorian's failed attempt to launch an invasion of Vandal Africa from there in 460, gradually allowed the Goths in the second half of the century to assume greater control, however tenuous. Sueves were the only rival to the Visigoths on a large scale. Raids by the armies of both peoples at times strengthened and at times altered local power bases that grew up as the traditional authority disappeared.[95] Large movements of the Visigoths into Spain first occurred in the 490s, in two episodes specifically recorded in the *Consularia Caesaraugustana*. The same chronicle also reveals the occasional rejection of Visigothic authority on the local level, but these rebellions were severely crushed.[96] The first stage of the sustained conquest of Spain was completed by the end of Alaric II's lengthy rule (484-507).[97] That said, for the first few years after 507 the focus appears to have been southern Gaul.[98]

Alaric II's defeat and death in the great battle against Clovis near Vouillé began what can be considered a second stage in the Visigothic rule of Iberia, a period of generally feeble monarchical power that lasted until the time of Leovigild (r. 568-586). In 507/508, the Visigothic nobility elected Gesalic, the illegitimate son of Alaric II, as king. Immediately afterwards began what has been traditionally labeled the 'Ostrogothic

94 See Collins, *Early Medieval Spain*, 25, and Orlandis, *Historia de España*, 17 and 47.

95 Several examples from Hydatius and other chroniclers are discussed in the two works cited in the previous note; see also Kulikowski, *Late Roman Spain* and Heather, *The Goths*.

96 See above, nn. 42 and 43.

97 See Collins, *Early Medieval Spain*, 31 on the planned ecclesiastical councils for all Catholic bishops of the kingdom, including those in the Spanish territories, immediately following the Council of Agde in 506 (nonetheless notable at that moment for its complete absence of Spanish bishops: Kulikowski, *Late Roman Spain*, 257).

98 Kulikowski, *Late Roman Spain*, 258-62 and Halsall, *Barbarian Migrations*, 298f.

Interval', referred to simply as the Ostrogothic supremacy.[99] With the pretext of Gesalic's passivity in the face of Frankish and Burgundian attacks on Arles, Carcasonne, and Gesalic's own capital Narbonne, Theodoric the Ostrogoth sent an army to intervene on behalf of the Visigoths. He brought the region around Arles into the Ostrogothic kingdom, while a Visigothic protectorate would retain possession of Septimania in southwest Gaul and, for almost twenty years, an area of southern Novempopulana, which possibly included Toulouse. In 510 or 511, a general of Theodoric forced Gesalic's retreat from Barcelona and eventually killed him in a battle nearby a couple of years later as he tried to stage a return through southwestern Gaul. Theodoric's grandson, Amalaric, was the legitimate heir but a small child at the time. Through handpicked confidants, Theodoric ruled the Visigothic kingdom until his death in 526,[100] at which time Amalaric (526-531) was old enough to reign. The latter's "brief and inglorious" rule, as Collins puts it, ended with the invasion of Childebert I, his brother-in-law, who seems to have been provoked by Amalaric's mistreatment of his sister.[101] Amalaric was killed in 531, possibly by members of his own army after this second Visigothic defeat by the Franks.[102] The Visigoths who had remained in or around Toulouse were now overcome, "and went to Theudis in Spain, who was already acting the tyrant openly."[103]

Amalaric was succeeded by Theudis (r. 531-548), an Ostrogothic general in Spain who had already begun to set his own course under Theodoric's

99 As in Luis A. García Moreno, *Historia de España visigoda* (Madrid: Cátedra, 1989), 87-93. Ostrogothic administrative and military control was established and Spain sent annual tribute to Italy.

100 Despite the description in Procopius, *Bell. Goth.* V.12 and Jordanes, *Getica* 302 of these years as a regency, Theodoric's clear direction led contemporary observers to see him as the ruler of Spain; dating of the acts of ecclesiastical councils in 516 and 517 seem to confirm this (cf. Collins, *Visigothic Spain*, 41). He seems to have controlled the Visigothic kingdom through governors Ampelius and Liuviritus, the one apparently Roman and the other a Goth. The command of the army was entrusted to the Ostrogoth Theudis. Surviving letters in the *Variae* of Cassiodorus show that the governors dealt directly with the king in Ravenna. See Orlandis, *Historia de España*, 69.

101 Collins, *Early Medieval Spain*, 34.

102 He was killed by his own men according to Gregory of Tours, but see the two rather different versions of his death in Kulikowski, *Late Roman Spain*, 261 and 399 n. 36. Since Jordanes says that Amalaric's successor, Theudis, "invaded" the kingdom, it may be that this Ostrogoth was involved in the assassination: Orlandis, *Historia de España*, 69.

103 Procopius, *Bell. Goth.* V.13.13; *Cons. Caes.*, s.a. 531. See Wolfram, *History of the Goths*, 244-45. In Gregory of Tours' account Visigoths at this time were as far east and north as Beziers, Rodez, and environs, where Frankish forces successfully forced their retreat: *HF* III.21-22.

nominal sovereignty.[104] His reign saw the Visigothic defeat of a Frankish army that invaded northern Spain in 541; it also saw an ill-timed invasion of Byzantine Africa that ended in disaster. Like Amalaric, both Theudis and his successor Theudisclus (r. 548-549) were assassinated. In the next twenty years, bloody conflict among the nobility led to such a weakened monarchy that several areas were loosened from Visigothic control, and in 551/552 the rebel Athanagild called upon Justinian to intervene on his side in the Visigothic civil war. The Byzantines used this excuse to take a large strip of the southern coast and, as Athanagild soon discovered, they refused to relinquish it after he won the throne. This entire troubled period since 507 was therefore one of transition for the former kingdom of Toulouse, which cannot yet be called the 'kingdom of Toledo' for the simple reason that Toledo did not become the fixed capital until the reign of Leovigild. After Alaric II, the principal royal residence was initially in Narbonne and then began to move around Spain: it was in Barcelona in the first few years of Theudis's reign, then occasionally it was in Toledo[105] and perhaps in Seville, where it remained under Theudisclus; in Mérida under Agila (r. 549-554); and probably in Seville and finally in Toledo under Athanagild (r. 554-567). The next king, Liuva (r. 568-571/573), was elected in Narbonne and stayed there after he left the rule of all but Septimania to his brother Leovigild, who established himself in Toledo.

It took until the reign of Leovigild, whose capabilities were unmatched among the Visigothic kings, for the kingdom to be consolidated. His military campaigns subjugated most of the northern mountainous regions (570-578 and 581), recovered territories in the south that were part of the Byzantine enclave (570-572) and of the short-lived 'kingdom' of his rebel son Hermenegild

104 On this period, see Kulikowski, *Late Roman Spain*, 265f, 271-76; Orlandis, *Historia de España*, 59-98, Collins, *Early Medieval Spain*, 32-38, and García Moreno, *Historia de España visigoda*, 85-122. It should be noted that while Theudis was Ostrogothic, he was not part of the Balt dynasty that ended with Amalaric, and if Procopius is to be trusted Ostrogothic supremacy ended with Theodoric's death with a peaceful separation of realms and the return of the Visigothic royal treasure Theodoric had seized (cf. Kulikowski, *Late Roman Spain*, 260).

105 Josep M. Gurt Esparraguera and Cristina Godoy Fernández, "*Barcino*, de sede imperial a *urbs regia* en época visigoda," in *Sedes regiae (ann. 400-800)*, ed. Gisela Ripoll López and Josep M. Gurt (Barcelona: Reial Acadèmia de Bone Lletres, 2000), 425-66 establish that the old supposition that Barcelona was the long-standing capital following Vouillé and the city from which Byzantine imitation tremisses were circulated does not bear scrutiny, and the sources point to Toledo's growing importance in mid-century and Theudis's residence there at minimum in his final years. See in the same volume Isabel Velazquez and Gisela Ripoll, "*Toletum*, la construcción de una *urbs regia*," 521-78 and Gisela Ripoll, "*Sedes regiae* en la Hispania de la antigüedad tardía," 371-401.

(579-584), and conquered the Suevic kingdom in the northwest (585). In the process, he secured a good measure of stability to the throne. It is no coincidence that his reign saw a major turning point in the coinage. By replacing the names of emperors on the coins with his own, he created a coinage fully identifiable as Visigothic in its own day and, from a modern numismatic perspective, considerably easier to study. The adoption of regal coinage forms the focus of the next chapter. For much of the period before this transformation was set in motion, early in his reign, Visigothic coinage remained dogged by basic uncertainties.

The Gold Denominations and Their Respective Designs

During the seventy-year period from the defeat by the Franks until a national coinage was initiated in the early 570s, the design of Visigothic coins became more defined. Thus, the general classification of the coins as pre-regal Gallic, pre-regal Spanish, and regal, if slow to develop at first, has become a matter of consensus in the wake of Reinhart's seminal studies.[106] Reinhart established in the 1930s and '40s that the Visigothic kingdom after 507 continued to produce gold coins in two denominations. Visigothic currency was still strongly imperial in terms of appearance and circulation. What Tomasini wrote of the tremissis applies equally to the solidus: "Without an Emperor in the West, and because of commercial expediency for maintaining an acceptable international coinage, the [tremisses] were issued in the names of Anastasius, Justin I, Justinian and Justin II." However, it was not subservience toward the Eastern emperors that led the kingdom's minters to preserve the imperial inscription, but rather the long-standing Roman monopoly of the emperor's name and image on gold.[107] Visigothic currency

106 Reinhart, "Nuevas aportaciones," 212ff explained the process by which he discovered pre-regal coins of the two main stages, i.e. before and after c. 507. This classification, following the initial work of Aloïss Heiss in the nineteenth century (*Description générale*), showed concretely the minting that was suggested only vaguely by literary evidence. Given the confusing nature of a currency with imperial inscriptions but only a quasi-imperial appearance, most of the attention of numismatists until Reinhart remained with the regal, mint-named series commencing with Leovigild. Mateu y Llopis, *Catálogo*, notwithstanding the inclusion of pre-regal coinage in the title, was limited in its treatment.

107 Tomasini, *The Barbaric Tremissis*, 37. Carlà rightly describes the notion of early barbarian gold minting in the imperial name "as though the Roman Empire was still in existence" as simplistic (B. Ward-Perkins, cited in Carlà, "The End of Roman Gold Coinage," 63 n. 73). Nor were barbarian kings identifying themselves as 'vassals' of the eastern emperor by issuing coins in his name, or thereby demonstrating "the essential political coherence of the former Roman Empire" (citations in ibid., 67 n. 94). Rather, monetary necessity borne of political and economic

still operated within an integrated economic setting established by the Roman Empire. How long that would remain the case and what effect this had on barbarian money systems are broad and important questions discussed in later chapters.

Very few identifiable Visigothic solidi from the period of 507 to around 576 are extant: there were fewer than fifty several years ago but now there are more. Though essentially designed after the model of Byzantine solidi from Constantinople, these solidi can be fairly easily distinguished as Visigothic by their fabric and style.[108] Their origin is also determined by their having been found only in the Iberian peninsula.[109] Obverses have a facing bust of an emperor, with a round crown on his head, a spear over his shoulder, and an elaborate cuirass and a shield, these latter two elements being gradually confused into one by the die cutters of the Visigoths. Reverses kept the image of standing Victory looking left and holding either a long 'hollowed out' cross composed of broken lines or a long cross-*Rho* (turned left) of broken lines – frequently with a forked base, starting around 520 – even after Constantinopolitan solidi changed reverse type in 522 by substituting the Victory with a facing angel.[110]

Two tremissis reverse types were used throughout the Mediterranean world in the period dealt with here. The kingdom in Spain adopted only one of these, the 'VPW' (Victory-Palm-Wreath) type depicting the Roman goddess Victory with a palm in one hand and a wreath in the other, the figure normally standing or striding to the right.[111] This reverse motif

power and prestige maintained the habit regarding gold; but exceptional issues, monograms or letters, and royal minting in lesser metals all hint at the adoption of 'national' currency systems later in the sixth century.

108 Fabric is a numismatic term referring to the appearance of a coin resulting from how it is formed (size, thickness, etc.). Style refers to the general appearance of the types; it is treated at some length below in Chapter Three, section C.

109 Grierson and Blackburn, *Medieval European Coinage*, 47f.

110 Ibid., where the types are well described and illustrated in corresponding plates. It may be significant that, despite the change in the Byzantine type, the Ostrogoths maintained the profile angel through the end of their solidus minting in 536. My thanks to Alan Stahl for sharing this observation with me.

111 The ancient significance of the victory goddess is discussed at length in Tomasini, *The Barbaric Tremissis*. Three tremisses from the Zorita de los Canes hoard buried in c. 577/8 (see below, pp. 65-68) employ the other reverse type, the popular Western form since the late fourth century, what Tomasini called the 'VGC' type: Victory holding a Globe with a Cross on top, the *globus cruciger* (and holding in the other hand a wreath-crown). Tomasini was absolutely correct to point out that one of these tremisses very closely resembles the products of the Byzantine mint thought to have been established at Cartagena sometime in the early 540s. (While he does not explicitly assign the coin to the Cartagena mint, I am of the opinion that it should be so

is the quintessential pre-regal Visigothic type. The obverse type is a right-facing emperor wearing a pearl diadem and a tall trapezoidal cuirass usually with a pectoral cross. Tomasini explained the way in which, throughout the lands surrounding the Mediterranean and northern Europe in the sixth century, bust design on tremisses in particular underwent a simplification in which classical modeling gave way to the line-drawing of figures. In this respect, the appearance of tremisses and solidi in Spain follows a similar stylistic evolution as that occurring in the Eastern Empire. But engravers under the Visigoths developed consciously abstract, as opposed to realistic, forms. As a result, their products are, on the whole, easily distinguishable from those of the other western barbarian kingdoms.[112] The peculiar 'kangaroo' or 'standing insect' forms of Victory on the coins is noted everywhere in the literature.[113] The reverse type of the tremisses has an entirely different development from the more imitative design of the solidi. It is useful to trace its beginnings under Theodoric the Ostrogoth. Attribution of VPW tremisses to the Visigothic kingdom among others is a complex affair on which much work remains to be done. For now, an outline of the problem as it currently stands must suffice.

The VPW Tremissis Type and Its Development

The VPW was not an original creation of Theodoric's coin designers but a resurgence of a type with a long history in the Roman Empire. On gold coinage in the late Roman period the VPW reverse type was rare but almost solely of western usage.[114] It continued to be rare in the fifth century until the reign of Anastasius (491-518). At some point during his rule it was adopted by some of the old imperial mints in southern Gaul and northern Italy (we do not know precisely which ones among Arles, Lyon, Milan, Aquileia, Ravenna,

assigned.) His suggestion that the other two are "unofficial Visigothic imitations" is reasonable but cannot be proved. Ibid., 142 and pl. D (n.b. the numbers on the plate do not match the Zorita hoard numbers).

112 Ibid., 79ff. There is unanimous agreement on the distinguishability of Visigothic coinage from the sixth century, even if some individual coins have eluded total consensus.

113 One may best refer to the photographs and explanatory text of Marques et al., *Ensaios*, 17, fig. 2.

114 Tomasini, *The Barbaric Tremissis*, 1-11; for 3 exceptions, all 1 ½ gold scripulum pieces (1.70g) minted in the East in the fourth century, see ibid., chart II on p. 264. Along with the much rarer type of the cross-in-wreath, the VPW represented a numismatic tradition separate and distinct from the East, concurrent with much more common issues in imitation of the predominant eastern type, the VGC, which, in the West, was advancing right rather than facing.

and Rome).[115] By the long and powerful association of the 'VPW' form of the goddess *Victoria* with the city of Rome, and by the absence of the VPW on gold issues in the eastern part of the Empire in the fifth and sixth centuries, this resurrected type emphasized "the independent and separate nature of the West"[116] around the beginning of the sixth century. Two questions have thus been taken up by several scholars in the past century: Who re-instituted this model for the tremissis, copied by the other workshops in the region? To which kingdoms can the many surviving tremisses be attributed?

Tomasini addressed both of these questions in great depth. With respect to the first, he presented a very solid argument why only Theodoric, and not the Visigothic king Alaric II or any other ruler in Gaul, could have provided the prototype for the revival of the VPW on western tremisses in the early sixth century.[117] The Victory with palm and wreath type in Anastasius's name, first employed on only rare occasions at Italian mints but common in southern Gaul at a later stage of his reign, suited well Theodoric's role as 'proxy-Augustus' in forcefully repelling the Frankish and Burgundian invaders of Provence and Narbonne in 508.[118] The inauguration of a distinct type was also highly appropriate for the special

115 The mint at Trier closed in the 420s. Lyon's mint operated under the Burgundians. None of the other mints were under Roman administration by this time, those in Italy under Odovacer and Theodoric and the one in Arles under Alaric II and Theodoric. It is of note that there are some discrepancies in the attributions in Kent, *Roman Imperial Coinage* and Philip Grierson and Melinda Mays, *Catalogue of Late Roman Coins in the Dumbarton Oaks Collection and in the Whittemore Collection: From Arcadius and Honorius to the Accession of Anastasius* (Washington, DC: Dumbarton Oaks, 1992).

116 Tomasini, *The Barbaric Tremissis*, 3ff and 12ff.

117 Ibid., 43: the originator of the VPW in s. France had to be someone announcing his independence from Anastasius at that moment, had to be somehow closely associated with Rome by reason of the VPW, was influenced by non-religious or at least non-orthodox values in choosing such a type, had enough prestige to be imitated by others, and had to be firmly connected with s. Gaul, the Visigoths, and the Burgundians. "Certainly, none other than Theodoric and Rome could fit the picture." Tomasini (ibid., 52) believed Alaric II had no VPW tremisses, although Reinhart, Mateu y Llopis, and Le Gentilhomme thought he did; recently Pliego, *La moneda visigoda*, v. 1, 76-78 raises the possibility that Alaric II introduced the VPW, though I still incline toward Theodoric.

118 Ibid., 42 with the date 510, but that this occurred earlier is clear enough from the treatment in Kulikowski, *Late Roman Spain*, 258f and corresponding notes on 397. Grierson and Blackburn, *Medieval European Coinage*, 48, places Theodoric's first use of VPW in Gaul in 509.
The style of the obverse bust of the VPW tremisses derives from the mints at Milan and possibly Arles during the reign of Anastasius's predecessor Zeno (474-491); Milan is considered to have been the chief western mint in the late fifth century: cf. Tomasini, *The Barbaric Tremissis*, 82-86. Kent, however, does not allow that any proof has yet been found for minting activity at Arles in Zeno's reign: Kent, *Roman Imperial Coinage*, v. 10, 28 and 216, with appropriate references.

fiscal and economic situation Theodoric faced because of the war and the requirements of maintaining the peace in subsequent years.[119] Visigothic striking of the VPW type began concurrently, since Theodoric assumed the rule of the Visigoths from 510 or 511 until his death in 526, during the minority of his grandson Amalaric.

The related question is whether one should attribute the VPW tremisses only to the Visigothic kingdom and the territories of southern Gaul under Theodoric's control. Differences in style and findings of the Anastasius tremisses throughout southern France imply that the Frankish and Burgundian kingdoms also minted tremisses of this type, which followed different lines of development in each realm. Tomasini, following on from the research of Reinhart, asserted that although the VPW type appears on some Merovingian coinage – a small minority of the tremisses – it did not originate with the Franks, but rather was imitated by their minters not long after its first appearance.[120] In fact, he concluded that the Merovingian VPW issues were almost completely confined to former imperial mints that the Franks took over from the Visigoths or Burgundians, mints that had maintained a strong association with Italian imperial currency types in the last decades of the fifth century.[121] It is not always possible to distinguish between Visigothic and Merovingian VPW pieces, as is apparent from the numismatic literature in this field.

119 Tomasini, *The Barbaric Tremissis*, 56-58, reviews the very clear effort of Theodoric to rehabilitate the areas damaged by the war, re-establish normal commercial activities, and relieve the inhabitants of the burdens of taxation for a year (September 510 to August 511) while at the same making sure to re-open this normal channel of state revenue in order to pay the costs of war, then garrison troops, and in addition new administrative expenses in the acquired territories.
The resurrected VPW type agrees with Theodoric's tone in a proclamation to his new subjects in southern Gaul. There the King, triumphantly acclaiming the reestablishment of the Gallic Prefecture, spoke of victory in Roman terms: the people could now enjoy "the triumph of Public Right." He urged them, "Obey the Roman customs. You are now by God's blessing restored to your ancient freedom; put off the barbarian; clothe yourselves with the morals of the toga [...]" (Cassiodorus, *Variae* III.17, as cited in Tomasini, *The Barbaric Tremissis*, 57).

120 Tomasini, *The Barbaric Tremissis*, 28ff: "The major French collections based largely on French hoard finds contain the largest number of the VPW tremisses for the Anastasius period, and their collections diminish in the number of these coins for each successive emperor [...]. Spanish collections on the other hand tend to develop in the opposite direction, with the Anastasius pieces being the smallest in number" (cf. his Charts VII and IX).

121 Lyon and Arles were perhaps the only imperial mints involved. From royal monograms it is known that Burgundian coinage was indeed struck in imitation of the Ostrogothic/Visigothic VPW issues until the Frankish conquest of 534. As explained above, Toulouse may have acted as a kind of semi-imperial mint in the fifth century, run under Visigothic authority but in cooperation with the Empire.

Although Tomasini's book has received some criticism, it has not been superseded and deserves greater recognition than it has been given. It was scathingly reviewed by Jean Lafaurie, a noted scholar of early medieval French coinage.[122] Lafaurie correctly pointed out certain shortcomings of Tomasini's work, for example his apparent unawareness of significant Merovingian hoards, and the lack of comparison with contemporary issues from Frankish mints. The chapter on style was harshly criticized. Yet, Tomasini's considerations on style were extremely careful and well-illustrated for the pieces he attributed to the Visigoths, and remains the only developed treatment of the tremisses. Besides the information on provenance provided by Tomasini, the best information on pre-regal Visigothic coins of both denominations is the hoard of Zorita de los Canes (buried c. 579), which includes a mix of pre-regal and regal coins, the latter identifying the hoard positively as Visigothic. Tomasini, giving the Zorita hoard due prominence, showed the strong evidence for stylistic continuity of the coins from Anastasius's time to Leovigild's. His book offers a good assessment of the problems of attribution of the VPW-type coins and builds the most credible case regarding the sequence of events: to the Ostrogothic administration in Gaul is owed the initiation of the VPW, to the Visigoths its most common use, and to the Burgundians and Franks scattered imitations.

Much confusion surrounds the application of the term 'imitation' to Visigothic coinage. Tomasini did not include Visigothic VPW tremisses within the category of imitation coinage.[123] The term refers to obvious but often simplistic efforts to copy Byzantine issues, for example those of the VGC-type tremisses found in the West, or Visigothic solidi. VPW tremisses of Visigothic origin, on the other hand, form "distinct issues whose consistent reverse type implies a conscious policy to separate them from the actual Byzantine tremissis."[124] Even the obverse bust took on distinctive features. In this respect, the VPW tremisses were the Visigoths' 'own' coinage, a kind of inchoate 'national' coinage. The monetary administration of Spain had, as Tomasini remarked, a "total commitment to the striking of the VPW type until Leovigild's numismatic reforms," whereas Merovingian issues of the VPW and other types were haphazard and unsystematic. Moreover, there is an obvious discipline in the Visigothic coinage in comparison with the

122 J. Lafaurie, review of *The Barbaric Tremissis in Spain and Southern France, Anastasius to Leovigild*, by Wallace J. Tomasini, in *Revue numismatique*, ser. 6, 8 (1966), 336-38.

123 Here, we are concerned only with imitations of Byzantine coinage, not of other barbarian coinages.

124 Tomasini, *The Barbaric Tremissis*, 1; see also p. 30.

Merovingian.[125] Tomasini considered the basic uniformity of the Visigothic Victory image to be the result of a directed stylistic system that implies government control of minting, whereas with Merovingian coinage centralized control appears to be lacking.[126] Hand in hand with the growth of an independent Visigothic style came a gradual lessening of imperial aesthetic standards, as occurred in all the barbarian kingdoms.[127]

The Mint Locations and Minting Authority

There were no official imperial mints at all in late Roman Spain. The only minting was of the silver and bronze pieces in Maximus's brief usurpation (410-11)[128] and the Suevic coinage in Gallaecia starting in the early fifth century.[129] The absence of mint-marks from Hispania correlates to the absence in written records of the imperial appointment there of a *comes metallorum* or a *comes thesaurorum*, who oversaw the running of mines and the storing of precious metals and other goods, respectively.[130] Both functions were important corollaries for the operation of mints. It is clear that the Visigoths introduced the minting system on the peninsula, probably only after 507.

One may ask how appropriate it is to speak of a 'minting system' in the Visigothic pre-regal period since, without mint names on the coins, the existence of numerous workshops cannot be known with certainty. If there was a multitude of mints, were they centrally controlled and to what extent? These are areas where the study of engraving style and other numismatic

125 Ibid., 34. "Legends never usurp their boundaries, do not invade the field, do not mix with the types."

126 Ibid., 30.

127 Ibid., 47. Concerning legends, it is evident from the plates in Grierson and Blackburn, *Medieval European Coinage* how the D and C at the beginning and end of the obverse legends become symmetrical circular attachments at the bottom of both sides of the cuirass, while retaining their function as letters in the inscription: cf. pl. 11, especially nos. 192, 198, 199, 201, 205, 206. Note the *theta*-like B of CONOB and the similarly geometrized and simplified R on a Visigothic coin (no. 205) from Justin II's reign (565-578). Could the *theta* form derive from imperial monetary influences, perhaps via Carthage? That is probably the case, although it could also have been inspired by looking at coins of Theodoric, since Ostrogothic mint-workers used the *theta* to represent his name (Tomasini, *The Barbaric Tremissis*, 35-36).

128 Kent, *Roman Imperial Coinage*, v. 10, 29.

129 On the Suevic coinage, see Grierson and Blackburn, *Medieval European Coinage*, 77-80 and Grierson, *Coins of Medieval Europe*, 5f.

130 Javier Arce, "La transformación de Hispania en época tardorromana: paisaje urbano, paisaje rural," in *De la antigüedad al medievo: ss. IV-VIII* (León: Fundación Sanchez-Albornoz, 1993), 227-49 and discussion 267-75, here 239.

features can be of service. Variations in standards, in legends, and in styles within the same obverse and reverse types show that the sixth-century Visigothic tremissis "moves in the direction of greater complexity and confusion," as Tomasini firmly established.[131] Such a condition could occur if there were initially a few mints, then gradually several more, a supposition borne out not only by the coins, but also by the southward movements of the royal residence. The number of mint sites grew after 507 from one or two at Narbonne and possibly still at Toulouse (until 531).[132]

The increasing range of styles suggests that several mints operated in the peninsula in the first three quarters of the sixth century. Tomasini's assessment is probably correct: different stylistic progressions imply several different mints. As he put it, "designs and legends are often too consistently distinguishable to be products of the same mint."[133] He specifically cites the omission of a pectoral cross among whole groups of like coins over several decades, at the same time that other groups included the cross. Nevertheless, Tomasini admitted that not every subgroup necessarily came from a separate

131 See especially the chapter on 'Style Groups and Processions,' Tomasini, *The Barbaric Tremissis*, 135-72; the citation is from 136 (this observation could also be applied to the solidus, albeit on a lesser scale). This is a perfectly valid and significant contribution, which Lafaurie skipped over in his negative assessment of the book.

132 Proliferation of mints probably emerged more by circumstance than by deliberate design, since the opening of new mints appears to have gone hand in hand with the movement of the royal residence. Evidence of these locations mark a royal foothold for an era in which the degree of monarchical power is left largely uncertain. A more localized structure of minting came into formation as former capital mints presumably stayed open and some secondary mints were created. The growth of the minting system in the regal period offers some clue to the number of mints in operation around the end of the pre-regal period. If we could know that a gradual trend and not a sudden increase is reflected in the fourteen earliest known mints and sixteen later mints of Leovigild, it would be appropriate to think in terms of approximately ten to fifteen workshops issuing gold currency by the 570s (regal mints are discussed below in Chapter Three; totals are provided in Appendix I, Figure I.8). In a recent article, however, it is estimated that between twenty to fifty mints were active in the pre-regal era: D. M. Metcalf et al., "Sixth-Century Visigothic Metrology, Some Evidence from Portugal," *American Journal of Numismatics*, second ser., 3-4 (1991-92), 65-90 and pl. 7. While fifty is far too many in consideration of output, the extent of Leovigild's minting, and the still limited Visigothic authority in the peninsula, the temporary military minting which we propose at the end of this chapter lends some support to the lower end of the estimate.

133 Tomasini, *The Barbaric Tremissis*, 138. Reinhart ("Nuevas aportaciones," 220) made essentially the same point, which Grierson has reiterated (*Coins of Medieval Europe*, 15). Metcalf et al., "Sixth-Century Visigothic Metrology," 66, poignantly observe that there is little reason to "doubt that the coins were struck at a variety of mints, even though they give no formal indication of their place of origin. The social context of the coinage did not change overnight: the same cities existed in 570 as in 590. The difference is that the coins are uncommunicative before Leovigild's reform."

mint.[134] Even if the many groups in his system have seemed excessive to some numismatists, he is probably close to the reality, that is, that a large number of die engravers rather than many different mints account for most of the variations. If die engravers moved around, their movements could account for the connections between several groups in Tomasini's diagram of the progression of groups. Indeed, in the regal period, die cutters worked in various locations, as did the engravers of fifth- to seventh- century Francia and elsewhere.[135]

Late in his reign, Theodoric felt compelled to correct a number of abuses in Spain that had been called to his attention, among them one involving minters. He wrote to his governors in *Hispania*, Ampelius and Liuviritus, between 523 and 526: "We have learned that moneyers, who have been specially placed in the public service, as is well known, have turned to the profit of individuals. With this presumption removed, may they be devoted to public duties according to the nature of their resources."[136] The profit referred to might have come from circumventing the crown fee for striking coin, called seigniorage. But a more likely possibility is that the moneyers were pocketing the profits instead of handing them over to the crown. This was a potential problem in late medieval and early modern mints, where seigniorage was expected to pay the costs of mint operations, but also yield a profit to the ruler (usually addressed by farming out the mint contract).[137] Either way, the language of the law seems to refer to several moneyers within a whole system of mints. If there were just a handful of mints with small staffs, it might well have been possible to point out the guilty parties by name or with reference to their cities.

Unofficial mints may have emerged in the climate of political instability in the middle decades of the century, or mints may have lacked detailed

134 Tomasini, *The Barbaric Tremissis*, 88; elsewhere he left question marks concerning the attributed mint site.

135 See Chapter Three, section C. Metcalf et al., "Sixth-Century Visigothic Metrology," 67 suggest that stylistic variants could result from the activity of many engravers at a few key mints. See Alan M. Stahl, *The Merovingian Coinage of the Region of Metz* (Louvain-la-Neuve: Institut Superieur d'Archeologie et d'Histoire de l'Art, 1982) for seventh-century Francia, where clearly several die engravers worked at a single mint in numerous cases, while at the same time some die engravers worked at more than one mint.

136 Cassiodorus, *Variae* V.39.8 (ed. Theodor Mommsen, *MGH.AA* XII [Berlin, 1894], 165): "Monetarios autem, quos specialiter in usum publicum constat inventos, in privatorum didicimus transisse compendium. Qua praesumptione sublata pro virium qualitate functionibus publicis applicentur."

137 Lafaurie, "Monnaies frappées à Lyon," 196, believes it may refer to charging less than the full fee. My thanks to David Yoon for his observations about this matter.

or at least uniform instructions on style, allowing the small distinctions in the coins to arise. A published discussion of the many tremisses with unintelligible legends is pertinent here. These coins, often with a meaningless arrangement of characters along the lines of VIVIVIVIVI/////, possibly constituted the majority of tremisses minted in the reigns of Justinian and Justin II.[138] Marques and his co-authors have labeled them 'unofficial parallel products' issued by rebel groups or areas at the same time that the state issued official coinage elsewhere. There is good reason to think they did not come from forgers working for their own profit: their rather high fineness would leave little if any margin for the forger.[139]

The dating of coins with unintelligible legends poses a particular challenge. These numerous pieces are very generally dated by their resemblance in typology to imperial coins, namely from Justin I to Justin II, i.e. 518 to 578. This span of years may be divided into three sub-periods. During the period when Theodoric the Ostrogoth and his immediate successors reigned, the striking of non-official coinage by rebels is improbable, and even ordinary forgers must have faced a high risk – we have seen that Theodoric was vigilant against the abuses of official mint-workers in Spain. Unofficial production also does not seem likely to have come from the years immediately prior to the regal series begun by Leovigild in the 570s; even his pre-regal coinage exhibits the firm control that contemporary literary works attributed to him in other areas. But between 548 and about 573 the production of coins with unreadable inscriptions by rebel zones does seem possible.[140]

Insurrections in this span of years, the locations of hoards from the same period, and Tomasini's classifications all associate the illegible coins with the south. While jumbled inscriptions appear everywhere in the kingdom, unintelligible inscriptions appear primarily on coins that Tomasini attributed to Mérida and parts of modern Andalucía. It must be remembered that during most of the sixth century the kings did not possess firm control over the whole peninsula. Currency was issued in the south probably only from the 540s onward,[141] shortly after the time when Visigothic domination of Baetica and southern Carthaginensis was first established, as some scholars believe.[142] The illegible issues are viewed by some as a response to

138 See the tallies in Marques et al., *Ensaios*, 37, Quadro II.

139 Ibid., 19; see below, pp. 75f.

140 Ibid., 19-21.

141 Tomasini, *The Barbaric Tremissis*, 170-72.

142 See García Moreno, *Historia de España*, 96-102, and J. N. Hillgarth, "Historiography in Visigothic Spain," in *La storiografia altomedievale*, Settimane di studio del centro italiano di studi sull'alto medioevo, v. 17 (Spoleto: Presso la sede del centro, 1970), 261-313, here 266; Thompson,

the need for currency in areas rejecting Visigothic authority. According to this theory, the legends were unintelligible, not because rebel die cutters were incapable, but because issuing currency in an emperor's name without authorization was deemed too bold.[143] In our discussion of standards at the end of this chapter, we will see that the king's need for currency for the military engagements provides a better explanation of these tremisses.[144]

Tomasini demonstrated that, despite the variations of style, Visigothic coinage before Leovigild exhibited overall "consistencies in aesthetic attitude," giving it a unity which set it apart from other western coinages. He wondered whether the consistencies were the result of "centralized official policy, common sources of origin, or mutual regional influences."[145] In regard to the first possibility, it may be noted that Leovigild's facing-busts type, whose rapid and universal adoption in the years 584-586 could only have been the result of centralization, still allowed for obvious regional differentiation. Similarly, the single obverse and single reverse bust of the pre-regal coinage may indicate a centralized minting policy at the same time that they exhibit regional variation. Not enough work has been done on the pre-regal series to answer categorically any of the three possibilities presented by Tomasini. All three seem to have had a part in giving unity to the coinage.

The Groupings of Tomasini and Others

In the absence of obvious letter mint-marks, and given the general similarity of artistic forms and die-cutting techniques, the attribution of extant pre-regal coins to specific mints is a daunting task. Groups

Romans and Barbarians, 194, suggested that Baetica came under Visigothic authority shortly after 500, but he believed it was the province of the Spanish kingdom least populated by Goths. On the difficulties of establishing and maintaining authority in southern Iberia see Chapter Two.

143 Marques et al., *Ensaios*, 19-21; the Byzantine presence in Spain would supposedly be a motive for rebels to avoid striking in the name of the emperor. Tomasini, *The Barbaric Tremissis*, 145, explained that illiteracy was not the reason for unreadable legends, for the name of Leovigild was easily managed everywhere in the 570s. After the period of meaningless legends "the pattern is immediately replaced once Leovigild feels strong enough to assert his independence and dynastic right." Marques et al. allude to an interesting area of possible future research: "rebel zones" have not yet been tested carefully to see if find spots coincide.

144 Tomasini, *The Barbaric Tremissis*, 144-45, ascribes the blurring of legends to "either technical or political reasons or both," but correctly emphasizes the growing inability to create good letter forms. His observations on the re-working of dies and the increased use of punches in confused legends give me greater confidence in the mostly southern attributions of such coins, since I have seen ample cases of the same phenomena on regal tremisses of the south but nowhere else.

145 Ibid., 136.

of coins that seem to have a common mint of origin have been formed. With few solidi at his disposal – apparently, only the fifteen for which he included photographs – Reinhart demonstrated that their attribution to the Visigoths was reliable, and he grouped them by the name of the emperor under whom they were issued. He could do more with the thirty-five tremisses in his possession that he identified as Visigothic. Reinhart made his attributions mostly on the basis of provenance, but he was also mindful of artistic similarities.[146] (The fact that he formed his tremissis groups without regard to imperial reigns poses problems to which we will return below.) On the assumption that the location of modern collections corresponded to the location of finds, he suggested four regional attributions. To Narbonne and possibly Barcelona were assigned coins found primarily in southeastern France and northeastern Spain; to Seville and Cordoba the coins predominantly from southern Spain; to Mérida the specimens known in Portugal and western Spain; to Toledo coins from all over Spain bearing obvious resemblance to later mint-marked coins from the royal city. Reinhart only claimed to be sure of the Toledo grouping, the evolution of which is the easiest to follow.[147]

Reinhart developed what has been called a 'capital theory' of pre-regal minting sites, the notion that coinage must have been produced in the city where the king resided, on the grounds that this practice corresponded both to the practice in Toulouse and to that of the Roman mints 'with the emperor' (comitatensian).[148] But while it is reasonable to assume that the largest stylistic groups of extant specimens emanate from the main mints, it cannot be assumed that the main mint at all times was located in the capital of the kingdom.[149] The capital might have been the site of the principal mint, but was not necessarily so for several reasons: a) more than one group of extant coins from some imperial reigns stand out,[150] an indication that no single center of production predominated; b) the mint associated most closely

146 Reinhart, "Nuevas aportaciones," fig. 2 (following 218) and fig. 4 (following 224), with explanations in the text.

147 Ibid., 229-31.

148 As described in Tomasini, *The Barbaric Tremissis*, 154. On the comitatensian mint see Kent, *Roman Imperial Coinage*, v. 10, 23ff; Jones, *Later Roman Empire*, v. I, 437.

149 This mistake made by Reinhart was followed by Tomasini, *The Barbaric Tremissis*, 154.

150 In the reign of Justin II, several mints have roughly equal numbers of surviving coins, according to the mint attributions in Tomasini, *The Barbaric Tremissis*, 168ff (Chart VIIIa, comparing his and Reinhart's assignments) and 185ff (the corpus): Córdoba, 37; Seville, 35; Mérida, 23; the number of 'CVRRV' coins attributed to Toledo is 52, but these are thought to have been minted only in the latter half of Justin II's reign (p. 165f).

with the king may have traveled with the king along with the treasure,[151] so that another mint site became temporarily more productive; c) factors other than political importance, such as economics or war, might result in the main mint being in a non-capital city[152] (the extant corpus of regal coins suggests Toledo's mint was second to Mérida's in output from c. 582 to c. 711). The political factors might even draw a king to move his capital to that city, meaning it would not be the chief mint site by reason of its being the capital from the start but instead would become the capital for reasons which had already heightened its role in minting.[153] To know if the main Visigothic mint was in the 'capital' at any given time, it is necessary to know if by far the largest attributed group from specific years matches the period when that city was the capital. Unfortunately, such chronological precision is not possible because imperial and Visigothic reigns do not correspond exactly. It is only possible to say that the largest number of extant coins seems to come in Anastasius's and Justin I's reigns from Narbonne, in Justinian's reign from Barcelona, and in Justin II's reign from Toledo,[154] a pattern that fits with the 'capital theory' although it cannot prove it.

Tomasini used a slightly different approach from Reinhart, first dividing coins with the same eastern emperor's name into several groups according to criteria of style and provenance (the latter often presumed). Then he established chronological links between like groups, working backwards from the early mint-name series whose appearance associates them with late pre-regal groups. From the somewhat broken lines of progression that resulted, he made assignments to the appropriate mints.[155] Tomasini also

151 A custom of Visigothic kings was to take the royal treasure with them on military expeditions – whether the whole or only a portion is not known. Striking gold coins from the treasure was probably the motivation in transporting it with the king. See Pablo C. Díaz and M. R. Valverde, "The Theoretical Strength and Practical Weakness of the Visigothic Monarchy of Toledo," in *Rituals of Power From Late Antiquity to the Early Middle Ages*, ed. Frans Theuws and Janet L. Nelson (Leiden: Brill, 2000), 59-93 and below, Chapter Four.

152 This consideration looks forward to the question of the motives for minting, on which see below, Chapter Three, section A. The available data will be found in Pliego, *La moneda visigoda*, v. 2, 46-48 (Emerita: 1537 tremisses; Ispali: 1240; Toleto: 1031). Alan Stahl has pointed out to me the weak, or negative, correlation between political centers and minting activity in Merovingian Gaul at least in the seventh century – such mints as Banassac dominate the coinage but are not known to have had any political importance and only conjectural economic importance. Similar cases obtained in subsequent centuries in France.

153 These were deciding elements in the movement of Theudis's capital to Barcelona, then apparently Seville, of Agila's capital to Mérida, and of Athanagild's to Toledo. See Orlandis, *Historia de España*, 75 and 91-93; Collins, *Early Medieval Spain*, 34, 38, and 40.

154 See Tomasini, *The Barbaric Tremissis*, 168-72, and the corpus, 185-264.

155 Ibid., 288 (Chart VIII: Style group progressions).

assigned mints to the capitals, but not always by means of the same groups as Reinhart (though some subgroups usually corresponded), and he conjectured that there were more mints than Reinhart had supposed.[156]

Are there, as Tomasini believed, stylistic continuities between late pre-regal tremisses and Leovigild's mint-name issues that make it easier to determine the origin of the pieces without mint name from the first three quarters of the sixth century? Tomasini wrote that, owing to the uniformity and standardization of the regal coinage started by Leovigild and continued by his successor Reccared, it was hard to see a carry-over of traits from the pre-regal period.[157] Yet, despite the general uniformity initiated by Leovigild, distinctive styles and even types within regions and individual mints were manifest in his coinage.[158] Tomasini would have been more accurate to say it was the drastic change in type to two facing busts which made it hard to see enduring traits from the anonymous coins, for at that point styles can no longer be compared.[159] The transitional pieces, those bearing inscriptions with 'CVRRV' and the named coinage of Leovigild before the change of type on both sides, hold the key to elucidating what direct links there might be between anonymous and mint-name issues. They will be dealt with in the next chapter.

Some lingering problems are perhaps unavoidable with coins without mint names. Subjectivity enters into the assignment of individual coins to a group,[160] and only a partial consensus has been reached by the few scholars who have attempted classification.[161] Reinhart himself changed his opinions on the matter after publishing a major article. A great deal of time might be spent minutely assessing the stylistic groupings made by various scholars, but still fail to produce absolute confidence in one's own or someone else's attributions. Tomasini often admits that certain coins in his corpus may not be Visigothic. Concerning the association of groups to each other and to mints, matters are complicated by the mixing of stylistic influences. For example, the obverses of a Justin II group are very like a

156 He suggested nine possible mints sites in all from c. 507 until the pre-regal coinage ended in Leovigild's rule: Toledo, Mérida, Évora, Seville, Narbonne, Córdoba, Barcelona, Tarragona and Saragossa. (Ibid., 155)

157 Ibid., 141.

158 Miles, *The Coinage of the Visigoths*, 43-50, had already commented on this point.

159 On the facing busts type see Chapter Two.

160 This Tomasini fully acknowledged (*The Barbaric Tremissis*, 135).

161 Chart VIIIa in ibid., 168-70, compares the attributions of Reinhart, Tomasini, and (for late Justin II) Miles. Grierson adhered to Reinhart's groupings: *Medieval European Coinage*, 45-49. All now agree that the coins marked 'AMR' in the field are not Visigothic issues of Amalaric, but rather Burgundian issues of Gundomar II.

Justinian group, while the reverses are probably associated with another Justinian group assigned to a different mint.[162] Die cutters might move from place to place or copy another style.[163] Such possibilities do not inspire confidence in the assignment of parentage of groups, the essential step for determining mint sites.[164]

Grierson faulted Tomasini for his lack of numismatic expertise;[165] he was no doubt persuaded by Lafaurie's review. Elsewhere Grierson wrote of "the weakness of reliance on style alone," asserting that the study of style should be accompanied by study of die linkage.[166] The main criticism he directed at Tomasini's work is best quoted in full, for it goes to the heart of the challenge posed by pre-regal Visigothic coinage:

> The pseudo-imperial tremisses struck by the Visigoths in the sixth century can be broken down into a number of well-marked stylistic groups, which on a meager basis of find records, lavishly reinforced by conjecture, have been attributed to different regions and even mints in Spain (Tomasini 1964). But if one applied the same reasoning to a number of Merovingian coins of the seventh century bearing a royal bust of a very distinctive type and style, all or most of these would be assigned to a single mint, when in fact we know from the inscriptions on the coins that they were struck by different moneyers at nearly twenty localities in northeastern Gaul [...].[167]

Grierson raised a real problem. Stylistic reasoning has its limitations, and Tomasini failed to address die linkage. Two points should be kept in mind, however. First, the pre-regal and regal series of both coinages show that Visigothic die engraving did not operate by the same norms as Merovingian

162 See Tomasini, *The Barbaric Tremissis*, 122 ('J II 4') and 288.

163 As is implied throughout in ibid. and was pointed out in Lafaurie, review of *The Barbaric Tremissis*, by Tomasini, 336.

164 The peculiar form of the letter R in the inscription of numerous coins does justify group J II 5 but does not help in connecting the group with the supposed parent, J I 3, which has a different form of R entirely: cf. Tomasini, *The Barbaric Tremissis*, 124; pll. XXVII-XXVIII and pl. X.

165 Grierson and Blackburn, *Medieval European Coinage*, 39. Tomasini's main field was Italian Renaissance art history.

166 If coins with slightly different styles of an obverse bust, for example, have reverses from the same die (a 'die link'), it is highly probable that the coins were issued from the same mint.

167 Ph. Grierson, "Numismatics," in *Medieval Studies: An Introduction*, 2nd ed., ed. James M. Powell (Syracuse, NY: Syracuse University Press, 1992) 114-61, here 131. This critique must be taken with great caution in its own right since Grierson here conflates the 'monetarius' whose name appears on the coin with the die engraver, a notion refuted for at least one major Frankish region by Stahl, *Merovingian Coinage* (see at nn. 689f).

die-engraving. Mint-named coinage proves that die cutting in Spain was much more regular, that is, it adhered largely to recognizable provincial patterns, and the work of individual engravers or their schools can often be traced throughout several reigns.[168] Second, the foundation for Reinhart's work was supposed provenance, yet the place of modern discovery is no guarantee that a coin was issued there. The later period makes absolutely clear that many coins traveled very far from the mint site.[169]

Tomasini's thinking on each of the groups and on style in general was explained in far greater detail than Reinhart's and seems more careful. Its basis was 660 tremisses, several times more than Reinhart's total. Tomasini was able to show beyond doubt the evolution of bust forms and epigraphical features, which have been similarly tracked in regal coinage at various stages. Perhaps a fuller, up-to-date study of pre-regal tremisses will be completed.[170] But until Tomasini's arguments can be proved erroneous his work will remain a useful approach to the problem of ascertaining the location of the mints of Spain from c. 507 to c. 582. Our treatment of styles and differentiation in regal coinage (in Chapter Three), anchored by the knowledge of the origin of each specimen, serves to demonstrate that Tomasini's method makes sense.

Pre-Regal Hoards from the Sixth Century

The study of Visigothic coin hoards, while frequently hindered by the disappearance of the evidence, has been of enormous benefit to those concerned with early medieval Spanish numismatics and economic history. In his book *La circulation des monnaies suèves et visigotiques*, Barral i Altet showed that the value of hoards goes far beyond the immediate addition

168 The best reference with which to compare styles is Grierson and Blackburn, *Medieval European Coinage*. There, Grierson is more careful to make the crucial distinction between Merovingian die engravers (possibly the same men striking the coins) and 'moneyers' whose names appear on the coins. I discuss mint-laborers and style in Chapter Three below.

169 This fact is amply proved throughout Barral i Altet, *La circulation*; see also the graph in D. M. Metcalf, "Some Geographical Aspects of Early Medieval Monetary Circulation in the Iberian Peninsula," in *Problems of Medieval Coinage in the Iberian Area*, v. I, ed. Mário Gomes Marques and M. Crusafont i Sabater (Ávila: Sociedad Numismatic Avilesina, 1986), 307-24, at 314, which demonstrates that roughly a quarter of the single finds from c. 575 to c. 713 were found between 500-1000 km from their place of production.

170 We look forward to the corpus and study of pre-regal currency being undertaken by Ruth Pliego. On the key sixth-century hoards from Spain see Peter Bartlett, David Yoon and Ruth Pliego, "Weight, Fineness, and Debasement in Visigothic Tremisses from Theudis to Leovigild: New Evidence from the Hoards of Seville and Reccopolis," *American Journal of Numismatics* 29 (2017), 149-211. The authors illuminate the benefits and drawbacks of Tomasini's categorization. I am grateful to the authors for the opportunity to see an early draft of this work.

of numerous coins to the corpus of a series.[171] Hoards composed of more than a few pieces normally also give a rough idea of the year of burial (or the cessation of additions to the hoard),[172] a sample of the coined money circulating at a given time, and a better overall picture than single finds can offer of the distances which coins traversed.[173]

Most of the twenty-nine or so Iberian hoards of Visigothic coins that have been uncovered contain specimens from the regal period alone. Only two hoards from Spain with significant pre-regal contents have been published, though a few hoards from France have offered significant Visigothic content.[174] Fortunately, both of the former are rather large and offer a wealth of

171 In spite of the usually prompt publication of the finding and contents of hoards, very few have received careful scholarly attention. Theft of one sort or another has diminished the contents of many hoards, and this rapid dispersion has impeded thorough analysis of even some major finds. Barral i Altet discusses 23 hoards (pp. 78-142), but full series of photographs of only a few have ever appeared in print and only the hoard of Zorita de los Canes is fully published. See Ruth Pliego Vázquez, *La moneda visigoda*, 2 vols. (Seville: Universidad de Sevilla, 2009), v. 1, 83-86 and 231-59. Although Visigothic coinage holds an advantage over Merovingian coinage in having a true corpus of the regal series (Pliego 2009 supersedes Miles, *The Coinage of the Visigoths*, 1952) and a partial corpus for the principal type of the pre-regal series (Tomasini, *The Barbaric Tremissis*, 1964), up until Pliego's major study and supplementary articles the state of knowledge of Visigothic coin hoards has been far behind that of Merovingian hoards. Lauris Olson, "Visigothic Coin Hoard Structure," Paper presented at the 24th International Congress on Medieval Studies, Kalamazoo, Michigan, 4-7 May 1989, 1 reviews the situation at that time and establishes the *desiderata* which is only now being remedied.

172 Much greater precision in dating hoards can be achieved with regal as compared to pre-regal coinage. Several factors make this the case. More detailed historical information is available from the late sixth and early seventh centuries. Justinian's long reign, together with confusion between coins of Justin I and Justin II are obstacles to close dating of pre-regal hoards. Finally, one can make use of the inscription of the place of minting on regal coins to help determine earlier and later issues. An example may be seen below in Chapter Two in the case of the three phases of Leovigild's coinage.

173 See the maps of mint distribution of Visigothic hoards in Barral i Altet, *La circulation*, 78-142. Rory Naismith, "Introduction," in *Money and Coinage in the Middle Ages*, ed. Rory Naismith (Leiden: Brill, 2018), 11f makes astute observations about hoards and their limitations, and reminds us of the clearer picture of circulation that a large number of individual finds can offer.

174 In addition to the two Spanish hoards discussed here consisting largely of VPW tremisses, there are also French hoards containing VPW tremisses which have received Visigothic attribution. One is from Roujan, near Béziers (then in Visigothic Septimania), deposited c. 520s; now mostly in the archaeological museum at Lattes, its publication is M. Dhénin and C. Landes, "Le tresor 'de Roujan' (VIe siecle)," *Etudes Héraultaises* 26-27 (1995-96), 11-14, available on the web at http://www.etudesheraultaises.fr/wp-content/uploads/1995-1996-02-le-tresor-de-roujan-vie-siecle.pdf. A few of the pieces have sold separately; see the following (lots 165, 207, 210): http://www.ogn-numismatique.com/upload/PDF/14062010_collection_Bernard_Chwartz_2eme_partie.pdf, accessed 19 September 2018. Other French hoards are from Alise-Sainte-Reine (c. 550), Viviers and Var (both c. 570-580): See Sebastian Heath and David Yoon, "A Sixth-century Tremissis from

information. One is called 'Seville I', after the city in which it was discovered in 1972, or 'Calle Cuna', after the street in that city where it was found in a wall. Jean Lafaurie is not alone in considering this hoard, along with the other called 'Zorita de los Canes,' as "the most important document for the study and identification of coins struck by the Visigoths in the sixth century."[175] Because Seville I contained both tremisses and solidi, it definitively proved Reinhart's earlier attribution of solidi to the Visigoths, an assignment that he had only been able to make with isolated pieces found in Spain.

The Seville hoard, deposited approximately in 548-554, was composed of thirteen Visigothic imitation solidi in the names of Anastasius (1), Justin I (1), and Justinian (11), twenty-three Visigothic 'VPW' tremisses with legends of Anastasius (1), Justin (7), and Justinian (15), plus thirty-nine imperial solidi of Honorius (r. 393-423) and two of Arcadius (r. 383-408) struck at Milan.[176] Among the imitation solidi are a pair of die-duplicates, a die link outside of the hoard, and one specimen with an obverse sub-type previously known from only one coin.[177] Each of the tremisses can be matched on stylistic grounds with one of the five groups that Tomasini assigned to areas in the southwest: Andalucía, Mérida, Seville (2 groups), Évora/Andalucía.[178] The

Psalmodi (Gard, France)," *American Journal of Numismatics*, Second series 13 (2001), 63-80. A hoard of Gourdon contained some Justin I VPW tremisses of Visigothic attribution. Spanish hoards of Alcàsser (in Valencia, called La Senda de L'Horteta, 570s?), Santander (La Hermida, c. 580/581), and Huelva (Real de la Jara, c 574/576), containing coins of the transition period into regal currency, were dispersed without recording but a few coins from them have been published. These are discussed in Pliego, *La moneda visigoda*, v. 1, 83-87, with references to Barral. On hoards of regal coins unearthed since the publication of Barral's book, see below, Chapters Two and Three. On the hoard of '*curru*' tremisses from the transitional period, found in the late 1990s near Ecija, see p. 96 below.

175 Barral i Altet, *La circulation*, 7. On Seville I/Calle Cuna see Ruth Pliego, "A hoard of Late Roman and Visigothic Gold," *Numismatic Chronicle* 176 (2016), 377-91. For Zorita de los Canes see Pliego, *La moneda visigoda*, v. 1, 85-87 and Manuel Castro Priego, "Los hallazgos numismáticos de Recópolis: aspectos singulares de su integración en la secuencia histórica del yacimiento," *Zona arqueológica*, Nº. 9, 2008 (Dedicated issue title: *Recópolis y la ciudad en la época visigoda*), 131-141. Bartlett et al., "Weight, Fineness, and Debasement" investigates the metrological data as discussed later in this chapter.

176 Pliego, "A hoard," 377f, updating Barral i Altet, *La circulation*, 79ff. One additional coin reported from the original discovery was not recovered by authorities. Anastasius: this coin probably shares an obverse die with Tomasini 82 (A 3) but is also a die duplicate of Tomasini 171 and 172 (J I 1c), so whether it is Anastasius or Justin I (or even Justinian, considering Tomasini's ruminations on J I 1) is unclear.

177 A die link occurs when one side of a coin has been struck from the same die as that of another coin; duplicates are the products of the same two dies for both sides of two or more coins.

178 Cf. Tomasini, *The Barbaric Tremissis*, 152-72; Lauris Olson, "Visigothic Coin Hoard Structure," Unpublished paper presented at the 24th International Congress on Medieval Studies, Kalamazoo, Michigan, 4-7 May 1989, 3.

hoard's burial in Seville and its basic stylistic uniformity support Tomasini's assignment of groups to southwestern Spain, since it can be demonstrated from the regal period that hoards tend to be comprised primarily of locally or regionally issued coins.[179]

The inclusion in Seville I of solidi of Honorius and Arcadius, with a gap of about seventy to one hundred years until the next earliest coinage, may seem surprising. It is somewhat less remarkable if one realizes that coins of Honorius form the single majority – twenty-four percent – of all Roman coin finds in Spain,[180] and that a plethora of hoards of solidi in Honorius's name has been recovered in the Iberian southwest.[181] The long gap in the hoard's issues can possibly be accounted for by a combination of two hoards formed in different periods, though in general hoards of the late Roman and early medieval period with tremisses and solidi over a century old at the moment of burial were quite common.[182] The economic implications of the hoard's divided timetable, one of similar indications of the curtailed supply of gold currency in Iberia for around a century, will be explored in the final chapter.

The chronologically separate parts of Seville I offer an enlightening perspective on the difference between the late Roman and early medieval minting systems.[183] The late Empire in both East and West made use of very few mints for the striking of gold, each of which served vast areas.[184] We have

179 A regional 'bias' obtains even though hoards often have a geographically broad distribution of mints. See Barral i Altet, *La circulation*, 96-142; also below, Chapter Four, pp. 195-98. No. 198 (pl. 11) of Grierson and Blackburn, *Medieval European Coinage* was placed in group JAN 3, which Tomasini had assigned with a question mark to Andalucía; in Grierson's words this is "an attribution supported by the presence of several specimens in the 1972 Seville hoard" (p. 438).
180 Olson, "Visigothic Coin Hoard Structure," 2; Jean-Pierre Bost et al., "Hallazgos de aurei y solidi en la Península Ibérica: introducción a su circulación en época imperial," *Numisma* 33 (1983), 137-76, here 174, c. 1; see also Kent, *Roman Imperial Coinage*, v. 10, lxxxii.
181 According to Kent, some Honorius solidi found in southern Spain are possibly Suevic (Kent, *Roman Imperial Coinage*, v. 10, 230), but it must be noted that since Suevic coins used an immobilized Honorius type they are not relevant to the specific context of imperial gold pieces of Honorius as in Seville I.
182 See Carlà, "The End of Roman Gold Coinage," 53 including references in n. 34, though many examples across northern Europe and the Mediterranean regions could be brought to bear.
183 What is said here of the Visigothic system could also be applied to minting in the Frankish and Suevic kingdoms and, to a lesser extent, the Anglo-Saxon kingdom.
184 Each diocese, made up of many provinces, had a mint, though by the fourth century the minting of gold was normally concentrated at the two comitatensian mints alone. See Jones, *The Later Roman Empire*, v. 1, 435-37; J. P. C. Kent, "Gold Coinage in the Later Roman Empire," in *Essays in Roman Coinage Presented to Harold Mattingly*, ed. R. A. G. Carson and C. H. V. Sutherland (London: Oxford University Press, 1956), 190-204, here 200-01; Kent, *Roman Imperial Coinage*, v. 10, esp. 23-24; also below, Chapter Five (p. 243).

seen that no permanent mints were established in Roman Spain. The early fifth-century solidi in Seville I, all struck in Milan, provide an example of the very distant movements of coinage required by the condensed Roman minting network. Conversely, the Visigothic coins in the hoard are thought to have come from various workshops in the southwest, just one of the regions of Spain with active mints at the time. Although the Visigothic kingdom in the mid-sixth century was much smaller than the western half of the Empire a century earlier, its minting system was much more dispersed.

The hoard found near Zorita de los Canes (Guadalajara province) in 1945 was buried in the basilica of the Visigothic city of Reccopolis, founded (or re-founded) by Leovigild in 578. While Juan Cabré Aguiló, the excavator, originally dated the hoard to c. 580-583, he soon adjusted this to *ante* 580, and Barral i Altet fixed a date of c. 577, though a date two or three years later is equally possible.[185] 'Zorita de los Canes' consists of ninety tremisses, seventy-nine of them Visigothic VPW issues, and is the only Iberian find to also include non-Visigothic and non-Suevic coinage.[186] The bulk of the Visigothic coins in the hoard is pre-regal, but five of the tremisses have Leovigild's '*curru*' legend and nine are '*Rex Inclitus*' pieces, the first to include the name of the king.[187] As mentioned above, its greatest significance is that it provides a direct link between Leovigild's named coinage and many earlier pseudo-imperial pieces. It confirms the attributions of pseudo-imperials in the name of Anastasius, Justin (I and II), and Justinian to the Goths.

Standards of Weight and Fineness

While the lack of information included on pre-regal coins limits our knowledge of the minting organization in the fifth and sixth centuries, the physical

185 Juan Cabré Aguiló, *El tesorillo visigodo de trientes de las excavaciones del plan nacional de 1944-45 en Zorita de los Canes (Guadalajara)* (Madrid: Ministerio de Educación Nacional, 1946), revised in idem, "Un hallazgo de monedas de oro en la ciudad de Recópolis. El problema de la fundación de dicha ciudad," *Crónica del II Congreso Arqueológico del Sudeste Español* (Albacete, 1947), 349-56.; Barral i Altet, *La circulation*, 79-81 and 91; see also Miles, *The Coinage of the Visigoths*, 96-99 and 172; Tomasini, *The Barbaric Tremissis*, 142-43; Olson, "Visigothic Coin Hoard Structure," 4-5. To these must now be added the works referenced in n. 175 above. In particular, Castro, "Los hallazgos numismáticos" touches on the stratigraphic reanalysis of the excavation by Lauro Olmo Enciso and others. An approximate date is suggested largely due to the absence at Zorita of the cross-on-steps tremis reverse introduced by Tiberius II in late 578 and known to have been soon adopted by Visigothic mints. The importance of this hoard for analyzing the chronology of Leovigild's early 'regal' coinage is discussed below, n. 263.

186 See Tomasini, *The Barbaric Tremissis*, 142 and 171.

187 Both transitional series are taken up in Chapter Two.

characteristics of weight and fineness offer helpful evidence concerning the monetary system. During the past century, the scientific methods have improved and the number of Visigothic coins tested has increased. Here, the data from several significant test sets are combined for the first time. We will see that the standardization of weights and gold concentration at various times suggests that the state closely controlled most of the minting operations in the kingdom.

Reinhart indicated that Visigothic coins were generally struck at rather high-weight standards from the fifth century until the mid-sixth century. With relatively few coins at his disposal, however, he did not aim at a systematic study; we saw above that fifth-century coinage was often sub-standard compared to Roman coinage.[188] Tomasini, with the large number of weight measurements in his catalog of the sixth-century tremisses, could be more comprehensive in his treatment of this important information. His work forms a good foundation from which to establish the modal range of weights during each imperial reign starting with Anastasius.[189]

When the modal range has a substantially higher number of coins than the other weight classes of a set, it represents the limits within which the observed weight standard lies, i.e. the weight that laborers in the mints actually sought to achieve in practice.[190] As is normal for minting in the pre-modern era, a large percentage of the Visigothic coinage always veered from the standard, owing no doubt to the lack of absolute precision or care or honesty on the part of the workers. At a tightly controlled mint, the deviation from the standard would be very limited in extent, depicted by a graph in which the curve descends more or less gradually from the peak across

188 See above, n. 85. Reinhart, "Nuevas aportaciones," 232; the weight standards that he approximated are 4.45 g for the solidus and 1.45 g for the tremissis. Most of the weights of solidi listed in ibid., 232-35 are well below the supposed standard.

189 Philip Grierson, "Visigothic Metrology," *Numismatic Chronicle*, 6th ser., 13 (1953), 74-87, showed the advantage of placing weight measurements in a frequency table, i.e. a graph displaying the number of specimens in a set which fall into each weight class of a small division such as .04 or .05 grams. From such a graph a mode, or 'most frequent' range of weights, emerges. I elaborate on the frequency table on pp. 158f below, where I discuss the more complex assemblage of evidence from the regal series.

The pre-regal data set in Figures 1-5 is drawn from two sources: Tomasini, *The Barbaric Tremissis*, Chart XI (296-97), subtracting coins regarded as non-Visigothic (cf. 168-69); and the measurements of W. Oddy, which appear in Grierson and Blackburn, *Medieval European Coinage*, 435-441 (incl. pll. 10 & 11), subtracting the few coins which already appeared in Tomasini's catalog. My weight classes are scaled to .05 g, as in Tomasini, *The Barbaric Tremissis*.

190 An observed (or real) standard is distinguished from a theoretical or legal standard, that known from a decree or inferred on the basis of other evidence such as the supposed relationship to other coins.

several lower-weight classes while sinking sharply and ending abruptly in the direction of the higher weight classes.[191] This was the pattern of weight dispersion that pertained in the minting of tremisses throughout the pre-regal period in Visigothic Spain and Septimania, aside from a double weight standard that came into effect some time before the reign of Justin II.[192]

Figures 1-4 below neatly demonstrate these points. The graphs here, drawn from Tomasini's and Oddy's measurements, show a clear modal class for tremisses in the names of Anastasius, Justin I, and Justinian. The observed standard during the rule of Anastasius was within the range 1.46-1.50 grams (Fig. 1), close to the theoretical Roman standard of 1.516 grams. In Justin I's reign, the Visigothic standard decreased slightly to between 1.41 and 1.45 grams (Fig. 2), where it would remain in the years 527-565, when Justinian ruled the Empire in the East (Fig. 3). The weight standard in the period of Justin II seems to have returned to the former higher weight somewhere between 1.46 and 1.50 grams, although an almost equal number of coins in the weight class just below this obscures the mode (Fig. 4). What is certain is that at least one additional, lower-weight standard probably between 1.16 to 1.25 grams was used at that time for a lesser portion of the tremisses. The existence of a second standard is already suggested in previous reigns by a small peak at a low weight in the corresponding graphs.

These findings are largely corroborated by the results of weight measurements from two sets of data somewhat different from those discussed above. In one case, a careful selection of coins from Tomasini's catalog was made and thirty-two unpublished specimens were added; in addition, the data is arranged slightly differently.[193] The coins in this set are divided into categories according to the legibility of their inscriptions – correctly spelled, confused but readable, and illegible. If data from the graphs for the separate categories are combined, the main Visigothic weight standards in the reigns of Justin I, Justinian, and

191 See Grierson, "Visigothic Metrology"; this is discussed at greater length in Chapter Three.
192 Dispersion is the term commonly used in the literature to designate how widely measurements varied.
193 Marques et al., *Ensaios*, 34, where a list of the 352 specimens from published sources is not provided but the great majority of weights are said to be taken from Tomasini, *The Barbaric Tremissis*. The selection from the latter is restricted to coins accompanied by a good photograph and about which Tomasini did not express doubt in his attribution to the Visigoths. To these are added thirty-two unpublished tremisses in Portuguese collections. (Since the total of the data set can be confirmed at 382 tremisses, if the thirty-two unpublished coins on pp. 66-70 are all included the sum of published coins in the set must be 350 rather than 352.)
The weight classes in the graphs (Marques, 50-53) are scaled to .04 g instead of .05g. Unfortunately, the scale for the number of coins differs among the various graphs. I have tried to correct this in my own graphs by adding grids, which, no matter what their size on the page, are always scaled to ten.

Figure 1: Frequencies of Weights of Tremisses in the Name of Anastasius

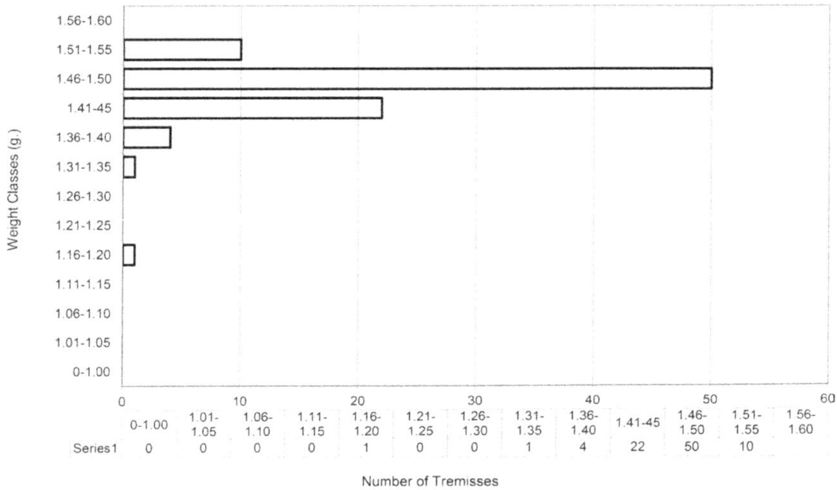

Figure 2: Frequencies of Weights of Tremisses in the Name of Justin I

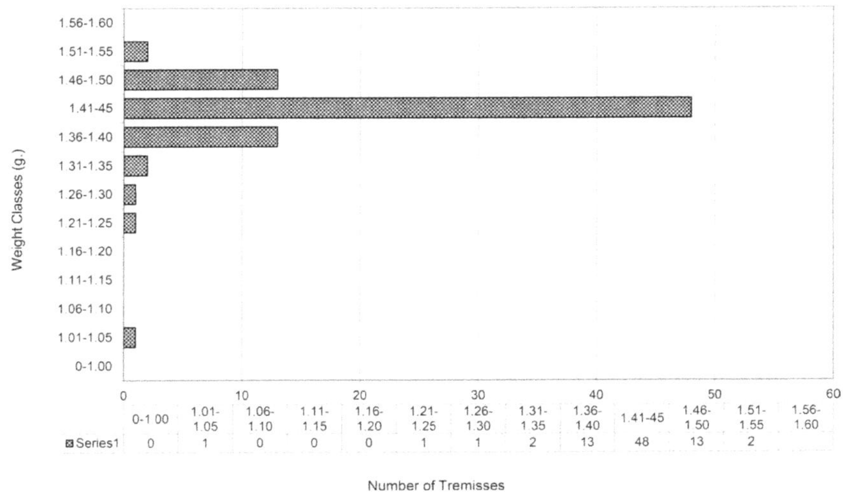

Justin II approximate those found in Figures 2-4 (coins naming Justin II lack an unambiguous weight standard in both sets).[194] The same is true in Figure 1 for

194 The mode from the time of Justin I and Justinian in Marques et al., *Ensaios*, 50-51, is definitely 1.42-1.45 g. For coins of Justin II my graph (Fig. 4) includes twenty-three coins in the range 1.46-1.50 g and twenty-two coins in the range 1.41-1.45 g; in ibid., 52, 13 coins are in the range 1.46-1.49 g and seventeen coins are in the range 1.42-1.45 g. (The addition of the weights

Figure 3: Frequencies of Weights of Tremisses in the Name of Justinian

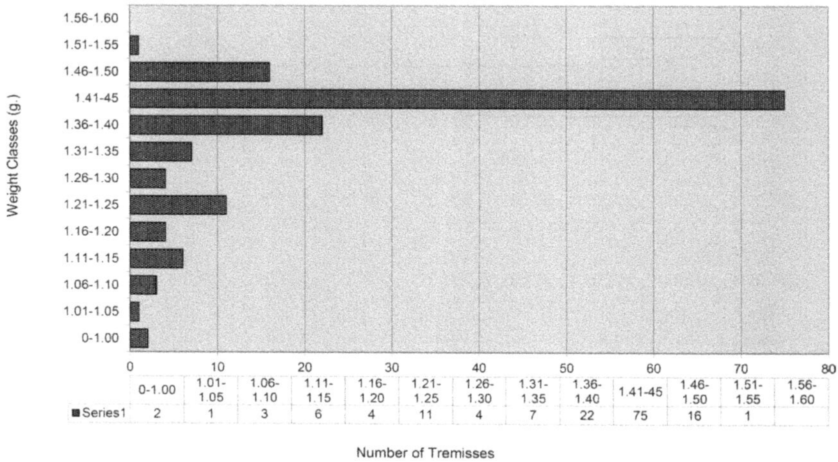

Figure 4: Frequencies of Weights of Tremisses in the Name of Justin II

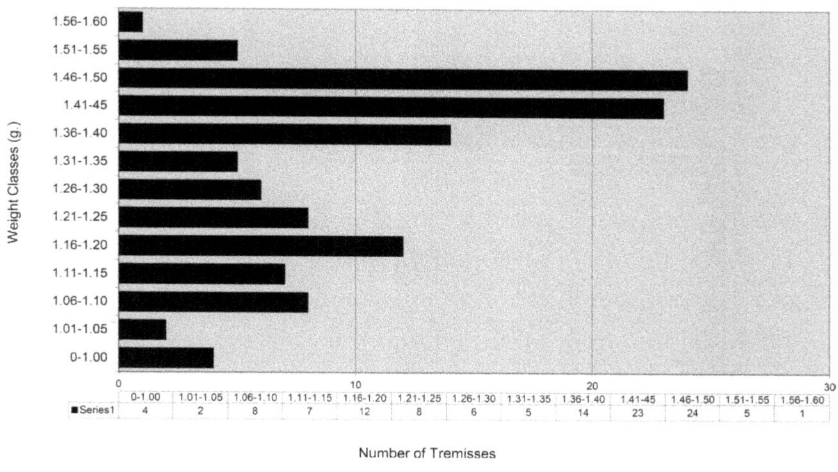

the reign of Anastasius, when a higher observed standard had been in place for most of the period from c. 508 to 518. The suggestion that a drop in the weight standard occurred in c. 515, supposedly concurrent with the first issues with jumbled legends, is unconvincing since it is based on too few coins.[195] In the

of the six unpublished Justin II coins in ibid., 69 does not change Fig. 4 in essentials, but it does bring the 1.41-1.45 g weight class even with the 1.46-1.50 g weight class – twenty-four tremisses in both.)

195 Marques et al., *Ensaios*, 44. In neither graph of Anastasius coins (ibid., 50) – those with correct legends and those with jumbled legends – does a single modal range of weights predominate. In the second category, only four coins are between 1.46 and 1.49 g, and seven are between 1.42

second testing sample, many of the coins in Tomasini's catalog were re-weighed. In most instances, there was no difference in the weight class of the coins. The several measurements that do move coins into a neighboring weight class actually confirm the modal classes of the three relevant figures here.[196]

A graph of the frequency of tremissis weights categorized by attributed mints or minting regions helps to explore the question of whether the main standard was the same everywhere (Fig. 5). The modal class for all but two minting areas during the whole period from c. 508 to c. 576 was 1.41-1.45 grams. Tomasini's Narbonne and Córdoba groups stand out for having a higher overall standard, somewhere between 1.46 and 1.50 grams, but when the supposed minting at these cities is broken down chronologically, it can be shown that they also fell in line with the slightly decreasing real standard. Tremisses attributed to Narbonne are at the higher standard (1.46-1.50 grams) in Anastasius's period and at the lower standard (1.41-1.45 grams) after that. During the period when minting is first specifically attributed to Córdoba, in the reign of Justin II, it was in line with what seems to have been the principal standard at that time, 1.46-1.50 grams.[197]

No doubt there was some monetary chaos during Athanagild's reign, yet the conclusion to be drawn from the uniformity of the main weight standard in all places – including when the standard changed – is that pre-regal minting was centrally controlled, even if that control was not always tight. Although the standard was reduced sometime in the middle decades of the sixth century, the state still ensured that the majority of tremisses remained fairly close to the Roman standard. Solidi were almost invariably struck with weights three times that of the majority of tremisses.[198] State supervision of minting is probably also the reason why dispersion of weights remained low except, according to Tomasini's attributions, in the southwest, which

and 1.45 g. The supposed date of c. 515 for the new standard is based on the comparatively few coins with jumbled legends. A late date in Anastasius's reign for the change in standard may or may not be correct, yet there is no reason to assume minting would then be confined to lower-standard tremisses with incorrectly spelled inscriptions.

196 See Appendix I, Figure I.1 for the results of tests performed by Lauris Olson in 1985 at the American Numismatic Society (New York, NY). Appendix I, Figure I.11 explains Olson's testing method.

197 To judge from extant coins, the mints held to be of the region around Seville had the greatest dispersion of weights and produced the most coins at the lower-weight standard. Figure 5 implies – albeit on the basis of few coins – that two lower- weight standards were employed alongside the higher weight in those years: 1.16-1.25 g, and 1.06-1.10 g. The former included all the minting regions, while the latter is limited to mints of the SW and the mint of Narbonne.

198 1.41-1.50 g multiplied by 3 is 4.23-4.50 g. Almost all the solidi in Reinhart, "Nuevas aportaciones," 233-34, plus the three relevant solidi in *Medieval European Coinage*, pll. 10 and 11, 436-39, fall in this range.

Figure 5: Frequencies of Weights of Pre-regal Tremisses Arranged by Attributed Mints or Minting Regions

(from Tomasini, *The Barbaric Tremissis*, 296-97, Chart XI, with additions from the Gabinete Numismática de Cataluña in ibid., 150-51)

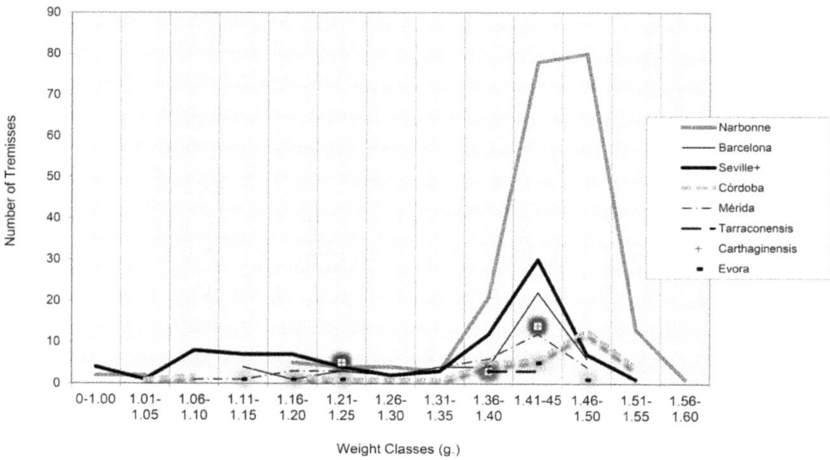

does not seem to have started heavy minting until the 540s or the 550s. The pattern of observed weights thus suggests that central, presumably therefore in some sense royal, control of minting was generally effective during the reigns of Theodoric the Ostrogoth, his grandson Amalaric, and his former general Theudis. During the years of civil war and the Byzantine incursion, the minting authority failed to avert a reduction in the quality of minting. A small resurgence in the weights of coins marked with the name of Justin II was finally achieved by Leovigild, a singular figure in the history of Visigothic coinage, although this fact must be weighed in conjunction with what was happening to the coins' fineness.

We cannot know whether the double weight standard that prevailed mainly in Andalucía, following the Tomasini attributions, was approved by state officials in charge of minting. As we saw earlier in this chapter, the independence of some areas of Andalucía in the mid-sixth century provides grounds for suspecting it may have been the result of unofficial minting. However, an explanation more in keeping with evidence from the regal period, when mints sites are displayed on tremisses, is that the state issued lighter coins in certain places where military engagements took place.[199] During wars, a greater number of coins were needed and had

199 See below, Chapter Three, section D (esp. pp. 203-06) and Chapter Four, section B.

to be produced rapidly. Providing a new swell of coins obliged minters to diminish the weights at such places and caused a drop in artistic quality, as was the case later with military coinage with regal inscriptions.[200] The military hypothesis, fully developed in later chapters with respect to the regal series, can only be inferred in the case of pre-regal tremisses because we have no specific information on where fighting or minting took place.

If extraordinary minting accompanied campaigns against the Byzantines or rebels before the advent of explicitly regal coinage, as evidence suggests,[201] a new interpretation of the many unintelligible legends can be offered. To this point, the most reasonable interpretation has been that coins with completely muddled legends came mainly from peripheral mints, sufficiently minor and perhaps far enough away from the principal mints that they lacked qualified personnel and close supervision from state officials.[202] According to this theory, similarities in design styles between specimens with incorrect inscriptions and those with correct ones is not the result of the two categories of coins having been produced at the same mints; rather, engravers at outlying mints imitated the work of engravers at the chief mints.[203] It is quite reasonable to suspect that peripheral mints were responsible for the inferior inscriptions and lower weights, largely because

200 See below, Chapter Four, section B.

201 See below, Chapter Two, section A and Chapter Four, sections A (esp. pp. 183-84) and B. Most of the high-output mints producing JII coins seem to have maintained higher fineness, whereas the eighteen from the Zorita hoard were low in both fineness and weight (ave. 77% and 1.15 g, and these and other JII specimens represent a new drop in real standards: Bartlett et al., "Weight, Fineness, and Debasement," 164f). Since JII 3 was a minor mint, it could be taken to have been a 'frontier' mint; either way, given the number of die links in the Zorita hoard it seems to be the source mint with which the owner of the hoard had most contact. (My thanks to David Yoon, who alerted me to this insight.)

202 Marques et al., *Ensaios*, 32f. As the authors explain, a growing technical incapacity of die engravers in general is not a credible explanation because correct legends are found throughout the period from c. 507 to c. 576. Nor does it seem likely that some die cutters were capable of producing coins with correct legends while others at the same mints were not. Since most of the letters in the garbled legends were properly formed, presumably the less literate engravers – or apprentices – would be corrected in their errors. The coins in question might naturally be suspected of being contemporary forgeries. Yet, the fact that they were struck at the same generally high fineness and the same weight standard as coins with perfectly readable legends eliminates the one obvious motive of a typical forger, i.e. to profit by producing coins with less gold which could pass as good coin in the market. That the vast majority of specimens during Justinian's and Justin II's reigns have incorrect inscriptions also casts doubt on the possibility that most were forgeries.

203 Ibid., 33. The opening of one or more peripheral mints before 518 may be the reason why the lower weights of some tremisses naming Anastasius coincide with designs and legends of lesser quality than those of higher-weight coins: ibid., 44.

that is exactly what the record shows for the later mint-named series. Such a situation, however, is not incompatible with royal command of the secondary mints. It may have been simply that the mints were strained by an enlarged demand for coins, a limited supply of gold, and unskilled die cutters taking on the task.[204] In light of the king's clear role in military minting a few decades later, as well as the inferior quality of workmanship of campaign mints in the south at that time, the flawed pre-regal issues are best explained as official coinage struck in special circumstances, which adversely affected their quality.

Tests of the concentration of gold of pre-regal tremisses tell much the same story as do the weight measurements.[205] Centralized control is indicated by the fact that the gold fineness of the great majority of the coins from this period taken as a whole was high, between ninety-three per cent and ninety-nine per cent. When measurements are separated into groups by reign, one can see that the chronological trend fits the development of the minting system described in this chapter. Among coins naming Anastasius and Justin I the concentration is highest (nearly all between 96-99 per cent) and dispersion is very low. The level of purity is still generally high during Justinian's reign (most between 93-98 per cent), but a trend toward dispersion begins. Lower readings (between 65-91 per cent) of several of these coins, presumed by the imperial name to date to 527-565 or perhaps slightly later, can be ascribed to an increase in the number of mints and perhaps a heavier reliance on them. Since the coins known to Tomasini with low concentrations fit within his style groups, and because there was normally only one such coin per group (though there are now more), they do not seem to be products of forgery but rather of poor work. Measurements

204 Erratic metrological and metallurgical values in the many JII groups and their significant stylistic variation "may point to the existence of significant amounts of coining on an unofficial basis" (Bartlett et al., "Weight, Fineness, and Debasement," 181), or these may derive simply from the rush of a minting blitz undertaken at state mints without very organized standards of production.

205 See Appendix I, Figure I.1. One may also consult Marques et al., *Ensaios*, 61, Fig. 2, to which one can compare the measurements of gold percentage in my Figure I.1. Note that Olson tested the specific gravity of Anastasius coins in water, and Justin II, '*curru,*' and '*Rex Inclitus*' coins in Freon 113 (see Appendix I, Figure I.11). The different methods of analysis of metallic content are treated in Marques at al., 55-58 and Peter Bartlett et al., "The Byzantine Gold Coinage of *Spania* (Justinian I to Heraclius)," *Revue Numismatique* 167 (2011), 351-401, at 352-57. The results of the specific gravity method are regularly below those of other current methods, as much as ten per cent; for fine gold coins, surface methods such as X-Ray Fluorescence has greater accuracy, but for gold coins of fineness below around eighty per cent, the SG method of bulk analysis is preferable. This has to do with the problem of surface enrichment whereby baser metals are drawn out by soil or in acid-based cleaning, affecting surface measurements.

of fineness are quite similar, though marginally lower, for coins naming Justin II and for the *'curru'* series from an early stage in Leovigild's reign.[206]

From the obscurity that a hard look at the real facts of the sixth-century pseudo-imperial currency reveals, given the absence of mint name and questions about accurate and precise dating, a more refined view of this minting is lately emerging from a culmination of metrological–metallurgical examinations and hoard study.[207] Some new chronologies among Tomasini's groupings are now being suggested on the basis of careful examination of stylistic features as well as the contents of the two major sixth-century Spanish hoards – which coin groups appear or do not appear in burials whose date is known with rough precision. One significant aspect of this research is that some altered group chronologies, which Tomasini tied to capitals during given reigns, extend alternative possibilities of minting location. Another is that trends in metallic measurements appear to accord with the narrowed interpretation of style progressions, thus conclusions on a more precise timing of changes can now be proposed.[208] One of the most intriguing lines of inquiry is the calculation of intrinsic value, the mass of pure gold in a coin (leaving aside whatever silver content it has). After all, whatever the exact values of weight and fineness and minor or major variations in either aspect of a coin, ultimately it is the two factors together that determine the actual amount of gold in a piece of money. None of these aspects is fully detectable to the naked eye, but weight and, to some extent,

206 Instructive here is the table in Bartlett et al., "Byzantine Gold Coinage of *Spania*," 358, which sets gold pieces believed to have come from Byzantine Spania within a comparative analysis alongside Constantinopolitan and Visigothic issues; it works from various sets of previous metrological/metallurgical data in addition to new test results. The table is reproduced with minor modifications in Figure I.2 in the Appendix. On the 'curru' series, see the first section of Chapter Two. Note that Olson's JII4 (= Justin II, subgroup 4) and C4 (= Curru subgroup 4) groups reveal especially low measurements, but one cannot make conclusions based on very few coins.

207 In particular Bartlett et al., "Weight, Fineness, and Debasement" and Bartlett et al., "Byzantine Gold Coinage of *Spania*."

208 E.g. there is good reason for dating the JAN 2 subgroup between the 540s-560s, later than Tomasini supposed. This large subset probably emanated from the largest Justinian-era mint in Visigothic Spain, perhaps located in the south of the kingdom rather than in Barcelona, though it incorporates finds from northern Spain and southern France. JAN 2 specimens of Zorita can be divided between those with decreased standards and two (Zorita 20 and 21) of simpler technique with exceptionally low fineness (ave. 65.5 per cent), weight and intrinsic value; comparison with Seville I and non-hoard specimens of the same subgroup therefore suggest it includes some non-standard coins that may be products of different mints. JAN 5 is shown to be from late in Justinian's reign and possibly from Tarraconensis rather than Seville as Tomasini thought. These and other stimulating suggestions can be found in Bartlett et al., "Weight, Fineness, and Debasement," esp. 161f.

fineness could be determined by simple testing methods employed in late antiquity: the balance and the touchstone.[209]

On the grounds of stylistic and metallic characteristics the kingdom's tremisses struck during the lengthy term of Justinian can be distinguished in a chronological divide established by the burial date of the Calle Cuna (or Seville I) hoard, i.e. c. 548-554. Metallurgical and metrological results come into play with this therefore dateable hoard set of coins before around mid-century, shown to be relatively high in fineness and weight (tremissis ave. 95.3 per cent and 1.446 g). Low standard deviation implies that minting was well controled. If the majority of another ensemble of tested coins of this period was issued *after* 554,[210] at the time of the Byzantine incursion in Spain, the data (ave. 93.4 per cent and 1.376 g) indicates that a decline, above all in the weight standard, took place at some time around the beginning of the second half of the sixth century. If so, a lower intrinsic value (an ave. of 1.38 g of gold dropped to 1.29 g of gold) likely began in the milieux of royal assassination and civil war followed immediately by a prolonged struggle to repel Byzantine occupation. Below, we can visualize the suggested dates of the sets' contents (represented by the length of the highlighted bars) in tandem with average values of the gold coins.

An essential point from advancing research on metrology is that Visigothic gold currency was already subjected to attenuation before the so-called national, or regal, tremissis issues of Leovigild,[211] which saw further reduced levels that became the norm in the kingdom. These operating standards even affected imperial coinage in the region. Clear data demonstrates

209 See n. 87 above. Ancient sources and modern testing convey a probable accuracy of gold assay by touchstone within a little over four per cent: see Bartlett et al., "Byzantine Gold Coinage of *Spania*," 360f, where it is also proposed that while some merchants and mint workers may have been capable of this kind of fairly precise estimation, most people cannot be assumed to have had this capacity. Intrinsic value is explained in Bartlett et al., "Weight, Fineness, and Debasement," 152.

210 Suggested by the fact that standards and certain style clusters match joint-named JII-Leovigild tremisses and initial issues in Leovigild's name alone, all produced at the earliest in the late 560s or early 570s. See Bartlett et al., "Weight, Fineness, and Debasement," 158 including measurement results. Arguing for the date of 554 for the imperial invasion of southern Spain is J. Fossella, " 'Waiting Only For a Pretext': A New Chronology for the Sixth-century Byzantine Invasion of Spain," *Estudio Bizantinos* 1 (2013), 30-38.

211 Cf. the discussion of specific data in Bartlett et al., "Byzantine Gold Coinage of *Spania*," 360 in relation to my suggestion earlier in this chapter of a dual weight standard among the JII pseudo-imperials. Reduced tremisses values may be set against the greater gold purity of solidi, including the extremely high fineness of some Visigothic solidi from a few years prior presumed to be from southern Spain and among the last produced, as emissions ended with Justinian's reign: ibid., 360.

Figure 6: Timeline of gold coin sets - estimated chronologies and metrological values

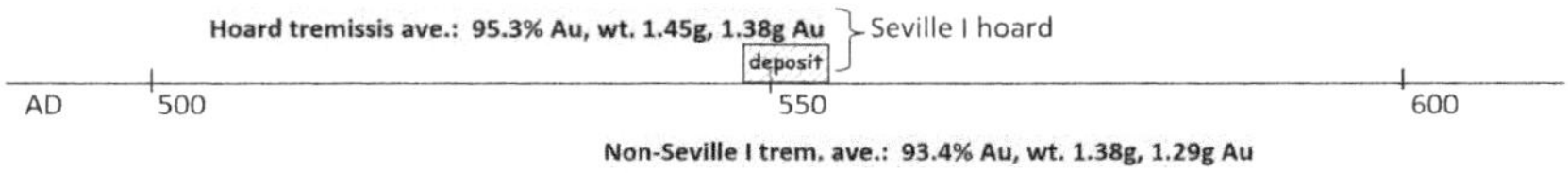

that standards of the Byzantine tremisses of Spania province, notably the sole gold denomination there, declined in rough correspondence with the kingdom's, since they remained well below the levels in Constantinople but generally higher than Visigothic currency though following its downward trend in subsequent decades (see Figures I.2 and I.3 in the Appendix). Fineness measurements suggesting a basic harmony with official imperial gold currency up to approximately 570 are possibly related to circulation of Visigothic pseudo-imperial coins in the post-Roman Mediterranean.[212] Approximation to Roman currency standard as well as imperial image allowed a limited wide circulation to occur. This, of course, has economic implications and will be revisited in the final chapter, which considers Visigothic coinage within the late antique economy more generally.

Finally, one may detect in the pseudo-imperial tremisses a correspondence between coinage and the relative strength of monarchs that will manifest itself more clearly in the later regal series. In the period of Theodoric's regency, when obverse coin legends named Anastasius and Justin I, the effort to maintain Roman models of government resulted in well-controlled minting. While standards do not decline very much as rivalries and war ensue by the mid-sixth century and as more mints appear to be operating, the same care in production is no longer in evidence. Visigothic coinage, almost on a par with imperial coinage in the first quarter of the century, becomes gradually more distinct. The following chapters demonstrate that even when monetary reforms were effective in the regal period, they only brought the tremissis back to standards inferior to those used in imperial coinage. The slow decline in standards was the consequence of a policy of diffusion of minting begun in Spain in the sixth century.

212 See Carlà, "The End of Roman Gold Coinage," 63f and 70-73, a suggestion advanced long before by Metcalf et al., "Sixth-century Visigothic Metrology," 82 specifically in relation to solidi, given their elevated gold quality. Lack of finds of barbarian gold coins in eastern Roman territories is possibly the result of re-minting. Visigothic debasement affecting Byzantine Spanish gold is treated in Bartlett et al., "Byzantine Gold Coinage of *Spania*," 359f and is repeated in Bartlett et al., "Weight, Fineness, and Debasement," 151.

2. The King's Coinage: The Beginning and Development of the Regal Coinage (c. 573-c. 720)

Abstract
Chapter Two analyses the transition from a pseudo-imperial coinage to an overtly Visigothic regal coinage under Leovigild. The chapter proposes a chronology of the various steps of that significant evolution, taking into account key stages in Leovigild's reign including the rebellion of his son, Hermenegild. As the tremissis became the sole gold currency, intensified manipulation of standards and values developed alongside growing appreciation of the propagandizing use of minting, which frequently had a strong association with military operations. The chapter examines an apparently experimental period of silver coinage and a much more abundant bronze currency in certain areas, possibly emitted under the authority of municipalities or the Church. Copper-based currency brought parts of Spain in step with other Mediterranean regions.

Keywords: Kingdom of Toledo; VPW type; regal coinage; tremissis; Leovigild; copper

A The Transition to a Regal Coinage

The currency of Visigothic Spain, like other currencies, reflects the political circumstances of the period. We have seen in the first chapter that for much of the sixth century Visigothic coinage was modeled on imperial coinage in its type and inscription, although in some ways it significantly diverged from its model. Both solidi and tremisses were struck according to Byzantine practice. Centers of coin production were probably few, although

Kurt, A., *Minting, State, and Economy in the Visigothic Kingdom: From Settlement in Aquitaine through the First Decade of the Muslim Conquest of Spain.*
Taylor & Francis Group, 2020
DOI 10.5117/9789462981645_CH02

their number was increasing. Numerous finds of foreign coins in Iberia and abundant evidence of the circulation of Visigothic gold pieces throughout France show the integration of the currency with that of other kingdoms in a large area of monetary exchange.[213] All of these facts show that the pseudo-imperial coinage did not have a 'national' character, one that was markedly Visigothic in its design and its usage. The reason is that the Goths did not yet have true dominion in Iberia in the first three quarters of the century.[214] Only parts of Spain were firmly in the Goths' control and, with the exception of Theudis, the kings of this period had a tenuous hold on power. Theses decades saw rivalries among Visigothic noblemen, assassinations of kings, a Byzantine invasion in the middle of the century, and rebellions in northern and southern Iberia. Northwestern Spain was in the hands of the Sueves, rivals whom the Goths could not completely overcome and who were under the influence of Francia and possibly Byzantium. But a change in the fortune of the Visigothic monarchy in the last third of the sixth century would have a considerable impact on Visigothic coinage.

Leovigild

The kingdom in Spain attained a measure of unity and stability during the reign of its greatest king, Leovigild (r. 568-586). Just a year after King Liuva I, his older brother, had ascended to the throne in late 567 or in 568, he entrusted Leovigild with the rule of the entire kingdom except Septimania, which he himself governed until his death in 573, according to John of Biclar. Perhaps Liuva felt the burden of rule was too great, but he must also have

213 See Barral i Altet, *La circulation*, esp. 147, fig. 20, a map of finds of Visigothic coins issued before c. 575, though more recently the French hoards and finds mentioned in the previous chapter would alter the count. The coins circulated throughout France, and several reached Kent in SE England. Idem, 64-66, discusses the presence of foreign currency in Spain during the same period. See below, n. 226 for a related note. A major database project underway at Princeton University, Framing the Late Antique and early Medieval Economy (FLAME), promises to make available the enormous amount of data concerning minting and coin finds for all Western Afro-Eurasia from 325-725, providing visualizations of quantities and geographical interconnections.

214 Best articulated in Kulikowski, *Late Roman Spain*, 261-86, which stresses the lack of Visigothic predominance throughout most of the peninsula at this time and views Leovigild effectively as the creator of a new kingdom; in that vein, the restorationist angle of John of Biclar and Isidore is appropriately tempered. Hillgarth, *The Visigoths in History and Legend*, 50 writes, "It was only with Leovigild [...] that Visigothic rule effectively began." A more traditional approach that traces the rise of the Goths, but still emphasizes the disunity in sixth-century Spain, is presented by Collins, *Early Medieval Spain*, 41-50; idem, *Visigothic Spain*, 38-63 inclines toward interpreting Leovigild's achievements as a reconstruction of the kingdom after long deterioration.

sensed the great potential for leadership in his younger brother.[215] Leovigild seems to have had a plan from the first years of his reign to bring the entire peninsula under his hegemony. He devoted much of his energies to crushing rebellious peoples.[216] Already in 570, he began attacking the eastern imperial forces which occupied parts of the southern tip of Spain and perhaps by this time Cartagena. He was distracted from that war by the revolt of his son Hermenegild (579-584) and then by a Frankish invasion of Narbonensis in 585. After holding back from completely devastating the Sueves, he finally annexed the Suevic kingdom a year before his death in 586. The so-called Kingdom of Toledo, which united most of the territories of Spain and which endured into the eighth century, really began with Leovigild.

With good reason, the two contemporary chroniclers in Spain, John of Biclaro and Isidore of Seville, portrayed Leovigild as the strongest of Visigothic kings, though his Arianism prevented them from making him an unqualified hero. This status was accorded to the son who inherited his achievements, King Reccared (r. 586-601), because of his conversion to Catholicism in 587. The chroniclers indicate that Leovigild was a visionary of the royal power, who was, nonetheless, not above using harsh or illegitimate means to establish his supremacy. Bent on creating a Visigothic state that could rival even the Byzantine Empire,[217] he attempted to forge a religious unity between Romans and Visigoths by converting Catholics, most of whom were Romans, to Arianism. His efforts were ultimately unsuccessful, although he provoked the conversion of some nobles, including bishops. He then resorted to persecution of Catholics, according to Isidore, removing the revenues and privileges of their churches and exiling many bishops.[218] Aware of the influence of Catholic religious fervor and of the crucial episcopal role,

215 John of Biclar, *Chronicon*, s.a. 569, 5 (divided rule), s.a. 573, 2 (Liuva's death); Isidore, *Historia Gothorum* (*HG*), 48 (Isidore's blurred and less reliable dating would position Liuva's ascension in 567/8 and his death in 570/1). The preferred date for Liuva's ascension is 568 in Collins, *Early Medieval Spain*, 40 and Kulikowski, *Late Roman Spain*, 283f and 411 n. 134; Collins leans toward John's dating of his death in 573.

216 John of Biclar, *Chronicon*, s.a. 569, 5: "[...] he wonderfully restored to its former boundaries the province of the Goths, which by that time had been diminished by the rebellions of various men" (trans. Kenneth Baxter Wolf, *Conquerors and Chroniclers of Early Medieval Spain* [Liverpool: Liverpool University Press, 1990], 64).

217 The histories took on this perspective, but with Reccared: see Hillgarth, "Historiography"; also Wolf, *Conquerors and Chroniclers*, 1-27. Hillgarth, *The Visigoths in History and Legend*, 15-18 discusses immediate precedents through post-Leovigildan efforts to forge a distinct direction for the Iberian kingdom of the Goths, set within Byzantine models and evident rivalry but far from employing wholesale imitation.

218 Isidore, *HG*, 50.

the king tried to gain control of the cult of the most celebrated saint in Spain at the time, Eulalia.[219] Isidore summarized his accomplishments in this way: "He extended his power over the greater part of Spain, for previously the people of the Goths had been confined to a small area. But the error of impiety tarnished in him the glory of such success."[220] In his quest for firm control, Leovigild went so far as to have nobles who posed any threat to him killed or banished.[221]

Many of his initiatives, however, had no nefarious quality. He made Toleto the permanent capital, likely because of its central location and its position on the Tajo River, a major waterway that flowed to the Atlantic. He founded and adorned cities, as Roman emperors did,[222] adopted regal paraphernalia similar to those of the eastern Empire,[223] and revised the laws of the Visigoths. In a less positive light, he was also the first king in Spain to expand state property holdings and enlarge the treasury by numerous confiscations.[224] The extant coins from this period reveal a new awareness of the important role the production of money could play in building up royal authority.

A major change in Visigothic coinage took place during Leovigild's reign. Leovigild is widely credited with creating the Visigothic regal series, that is, a coinage inscribed with his own name where the emperor's name had always been. At the same time, it was a currency that, after a period of transition, no longer copied the bust types of the Empire but instead displayed a consciously and visibly distinct image of the king. Toward the close of his reign, he appeared on both sides of the tremisses with long hair and frequently wearing a *paludamentum*, a customary Roman military cloak

219 *Vitas Patrum Emeritensium*, V.8, 1-4; see Roger Collins, "Mérida and Toledo, 550-585" in *Visigothic Spain: New Approaches*, ed. Edward James (Oxford: Oxford University Press, 1980), 189-219, and idem, *Early Medieval Spain*, 51-52. Also Andrew Kurt, "Lay Piety in Visigothic Iberia: Liturgical and Paraliturgical Forms," *Journal of Medieval Iberian Studies* 8.1 (2016), 1-37 at 26-29.

220 Isidore, *HG*, 49 (trans. Wolf, *Conquerors and Chroniclers*, 102).

221 Ibid., 51.

222 John of Biclar, *Chronicon*, s.a. 578, 5 (Reccopolis) and s.a. 581, 3 (Victoriacum).

223 The famous passage on Leovigild's royal vestments and throne appears only in mss. with the short version of *HG*, and can be found in Isidore, *Historia Gothorum, Wandalorum, Sueborum* (51), ed. C. Rodríguez Alonso, *Fuentes y estudios de historia leonesa*, 13 (León: Centro de Estudios e Investigación San Isidoro – Caja de Ahorros y Monte de Piedad de León, 1975), 258.5-10. See some important clarifications on the passage in Michael McCormick, *Eternal Victory: Triumphal Rulership in Late Antiquity, Byzantium and the Early Medieval West* (Cambridge: Cambridge University Press, 1986), 298-300. As Hillgarth, *The Visigoths in History and Legend*, 14f observes, the ceremonial helped Leovigild put himself at a remove from a sometimes-threatening nobility while providing a sense of continuity to the populace.

224 Isidore, *HG*, 51; see Luis A. García Moreno, "Estudios sobre la organización administrativa del reino visigodo de Toledo," *Anuario de Historia del Derecho Español* 44 (1974), 5-155, here 21-40.

fastened over one shoulder. This can be seen as a long progression after early phases when the obverse legends designating the emperor became increasingly muddled. In addition, Leovigild's name was added on the reverse and before long simply replaced the emperor entirely; a series labeled '*curru*', after variations of the word CVRRV in the legend, fits somewhere amidst this original transformation. Subsequently, the inscription on the reverse of each coin also included, for the first time in Visigothic history, the name of the mint city. Perhaps because of the turning away from imperial legends and images, Visigothic minting of the solidus ceased sometime around 570 in favor of the tremissis.[225] The physical changes in the currency went hand in hand with the sole use of the royal coinage within the boundaries of the kingdom, possibly the result of a prohibition of the circulation of foreign coinages.[226] Thus, Leovigild is said to have produced what is loosely termed a national coinage, "an effective symbol of the monarchy and of national unity."[227]

Who Struck First, Leovigild or Hermenegild?

In recent decades, the assumption that Leovigild was the originator of the regal series, held since at least the time of Henrique Florez in the eighteenth century,[228] gave way to debate over the possibility that Hermenegild initiated

225 Barral i Altet, *La circulation*, 79-81. Naismith, "Gold Coinage and Its Use," 281f discusses the trajectory of solidi and tremisses in Gaul and Spain, where both appear in contemporary documents as active currency and units of account. A close study of the Leovigildan monetary cycle will be found in Pliego, *La moneda visigoda*, v. 1, 79-95, with references to catalog listings in ibid., v. 2.
226 With the exception of at least some Byzantine gold currency (Bartlett et al., "Byzantine Gold Coinage of *Spania*," 376-78; Jaime Vizcaíno Sánchez, *La presencia bizantina en Hispania, siglos VI-VII: La documentación arqueológica* [Murcia: Universidad de Murcia, 2009], 706, 723), foreign gold coins were presumably melted down, given the almost total absence of such finds in Iberia from the period covering the late sixth century until the end of the kingdom, in contrast to the period from c. 500 to c. 575. See Barral i Altet, *La circulation*, 64-66; Metcalf, "Some Geographical Aspects," 310. Similarly, the Merovingian mints, particularly of Provence, re-minted Byzantine and Visigothic money, much of which then flowed northwards: Barral i Altet, *La circulation*, 151. While over thirty Byzantine tremisses of Spania province are recognized by numismatic specialists, find locations are almost never known, although the fact that they have surfaced in different parts of Spain (and only Spain) is likely indicative of circulation beyond the Byzantine zone.
227 Metcalf, "Some Geographical Aspects," 310-11. The earliest use of the term 'national coinage' is perhaps Felipe Mateu y Llopis, *Catálogo de las monedas previsigodas y visigodas del Gabinete numismático del Museo arqueológico nacional* (Madrid, 1936), 161; see also Miles, *The Coinage of the Visigoths*, 48. National unity here should not be taken to signify complete ethnic fusion, as Goths remained ascendant although their separateness wanes over time: see Hillgarth, *The Visigoths in History and Legend*, 35-41.
228 Henrique Florez, *Medallas de las colonias, municipios y pueblos antiguos de España hasta hoy no publicadas, con las de los reyes Godas*, v. III (Madrid: D. Antonio de Sancha, 1773), 175-80.

the change during his rebellion. The question is whether the very few extant coins that display the name of Hermenegild represent the first instances of the transformation, an innovation that Leovigild then imitated and later developed into what would become the primary Visigothic coin type of the revived kingdom. There are several versions in the numismatic literature of the chronology around which the debate revolves. Those who suggest Hermenegild was the first to have currency struck with his name must place the *terminus a quo* of all regal coinage at 579 or later, since it was in that year that Hermenegild received a part of the kingdom in southern Spain and began to rebel against his father.[229] Other scholars, to the contrary, have assigned a very early date to the start of regal issues under the authority of Leovigild, between five and ten years before Hermenegild began to rule.[230] Although the various issues of both rulers cannot be dated with exactitude, the matter can be given plausible resolution. On close examination of the first named coinages the argument that Hermenegild took the first step in the process, while intriguing, is unconvincing compared to the more traditional account. This section lays out the lines of reasoning at some length. The reward for careful consideration of the entire question is detailed knowledge of one facet of a kingdom whose workings are often frustratingly opaque. Readers who wish to skip ahead to the author's final conclusions toward a proposed chronology of minting may now turn to the table in Figure 9 on pp. 100-02.

The range of possible dates of issues in the name of Leovigild is from c. 571/573 – since he shared the throne up to that time with Liuva, who left no coins with his name[231] – until 586, the year in which he died. Within this period, three phases can be distinguished, although firm dates can be assigned only to the last one. The earliest phase comprises issues in which

229 The hypothesis was first proposed in an unpublished manuscript by Philip Grierson, who shared his ideas with Hillgarth. Hillgarth developed the idea in two articles: "La conversión de los Visigodos: notas críticas," *Analecta Sacra Tarraconensia* 34 (1961), 21-64, and "Coins and Chronicles: Propaganda in Sixth-Century Spain and the Byzantine Background," *Historia* 15 (1966), 483-508. Tomasini, *The Barbaric Tremissis*, 67-75 commented at length on the argument from Grierson's ms. and Hillgarth's first article on the matter. Pliego, *La moneda visigoda*, v. 1, 81-95 makes her own synthesis of the literature and emerges as the major current proponent of the argument.

230 The earliest suggested date I have come across is 570 or so (Barral i Altet, *La circulation*), but this is too early.

231 See n. 215 above. Some scholars following L. J. Velazquez, *Congeturas sobre las medallas de los reyes godos y suevos de España* (Málaga, 1759), 27-29, have read one or more confused inscriptions as LIVVA, but Tomasini explains why this reading is mistaken: Tomasini, *The Barbaric Tremissis*, 66.

the legend on one or both sides bears Leovigild's name and the weight standard has been reduced to 1.326 g from the 1.516 g or c. 1.45 g standard of most pre-regal tremisses. During this time, the tremisses still employed the Victory with Palm and Wreath (VPW) reverse type and the obverse profile bust type of pseudo-imperial tremisses naming Justin II and his predecessors. A few surviving coins from one of the earliest stages of the transition display the names of Justin (II) and Leovigild on opposite sides.[232] One special series within the first phase has been variously dated. It may be referred to as the '*Rex Inclitus*' series, so named from the reverse legend, an epithet for '*Livvigildvs*' on the obverse. The predominant group within the series is formed by extant specimens of an extremely regularized style from a single engraver, whose work was probably copied by one or two other engravers.[233]

A second phase is defined by a change in reverse type, Leovigild now imitating the cross-on-steps (COS) image introduced by the emperor Tiberius II Constantinus (r. 578-582). The cross-on-steps was first used by Leovigild sometime after the type first appeared in the East late in 578, though probably not for a few years after this date.[234] Approximate years may be assigned to several Visigothic coins of this type because they have inscriptions associating them with key moments in the war against Hermenegild. It is plausible that the earliest striking of the COS was at Emerita (=Mérida) to announce Leovigild's initial triumph over the rebel forces there in 582.[235] Along with the new reverse motif, the remainder of these coins now also included the name of the city in the surrounding legend.

232 See Miles, *The Coinage of the Visigoths*, 175-76. It has been speculated that Leovigild had an illegible transitional series minted after his imperial issues but before his own named tremisses, in order to test whether pieces falling short of Roman standards would meet acceptance. This may be the case, but either way the value changes were made obvious by physical appearance.
233 On the two or three design styles of the series see Pliego, *La moneda visigoda*, v. 2, 58-61; important albeit now dated treatment in Mateu y Llopis, *Catálogo*, 169-71 and Miles, *The Coinage of the Visigoths*, 178-81. I prefer to use the title '*Rex Inclitus*' rather than the '*Inclitus Rex*' (IR) used in much of the literature, since the former is the proper reading of the legend (i.e. in its full form, which instead is often spelled *Inclitv, Inclv*, or the like).
234 Tiberius II introduced the cross-on-steps between September and November, 578: see Miles, *The Coinage of the Visigoths*, 44 and Ph. Grierson, *Byzantine Coins* (Berkeley, CA: University of California Press, 1982), 44.
235 Greg. Tours, *HF* VI.18, a passage included within a broader narrative seemingly attached to 582, though Gregory does not specifically pinpoint this date for the event. A single instance of a '*Rex Inclitus*'/COS triens recently come to light in a hoard with 19 other COS trientes, all with mint names and presumably later in date, can be confidently stated to infer this particular sequence: IR/VPW > IR/COS > EMERITA VICTORIA/COS. Cf. the interpretation of Ruth Pliego in Pedro Mateos Cruz et al., "Un tesoro de tremises visigodos hallado en el llamado 'Foro Provincial' de

The imperial motto '*Victoria Augustorum*' that remained in abbreviated form on all previous gold currency is changed to reflect the king's own achievement: DN LIVVIGILDVS REX – EMERITA VICTORIA.[236] Late in the next year until early 584, Leovigild laid siege to Seville, the capital of Hermenegild's rebel kingdom.[237] By this time, Leovigild had already gained control of the "the ancient city of Italica," situated eight kilometers to the northwest, and restored its walls, "which proved a great disadvantage for the people of Seville."[238] The words CVM DE[O] O[PTINVIT] ETALICA on tremisses with the COS type imply that Leovigild occupied the city after his victory over the rebel's army, although this is left unstated by John of Biclar. These coins should be dated shortly before coins emanating from the same die engraver with the inscription CVM D[E]O OPTINVIT SPALI, which declared Leovigild's capture of Seville very early in 584.[239] That the king's gold pieces proclaimed a religious message for the first time can be explained by Hermenegild's conversion to Catholicism probably in 582 and possibly by the latter's use of religious propaganda at this time on his own coins, as we shall see below.[240] Leovigild also had tremisses of COS reverses with the words '*cum Deo*' struck at Roda, no longer thought to be Rodas (or Rosas) in northeastern Spain but an otherwise unknown city in Andalucía, possibly the Roman town that is now Ronda la Vieja (approx. 50 km north of Gibraltar): CVM D[EO] I[NTRAVIT] RODA. Roda was no doubt one of the "cities and fortresses that his son had seized" but which Leovigild quickly recaptured after the fall of Seville.[241] A lingering question is when other

Augusta Emerita," *Archivo Español de Arqueología* 78 (2005), 251-70, at 261-64; see also Pliego, *La moneda visigoda*, v. 1, 85-87, 231f.

236 Miles, *The Coinage of the Visigoths*, 194-95 and corresponding plates; Pliego, *La moneda visigoda*, v. 1, 85, 94f. As explained in this section I argue for a somewhat different chronology. DN is an abbreviation for '*Dominus Noster*', long a part of Roman inscriptions.

237 John of Biclar, *Chronicon*, 55 and in the same context 66, 67, 69. Gregory of Tours refers in the *Historiae Francorum*, V.38, to a battle taking place at Hermenegild's capital, although he does not mention the name of the city. From the geographical context of the events described it is undoubtedly Seville, where John notes the rebellion began.

238 John of Biclar, *Chronicon*, 67 (trans. Wolf, *Conquerors and Chroniclers*, p. 73).

239 Miles, *The Coinage of the Visigoths*, 191-92 and pl. II.15, 16 and pl. III.1. Cf. the different version in Pliego, *La moneda visigoda*, v. 1, 90-95, where the dates of these issues nonetheless coincide.

240 On the likely date of conversion in 582 and on the religious strife following the Arian council held in Toleto in 580 see Collins, *Early Medieval Spain*, 47-51 and idem, "Mérida and Toledo," 215-18; idem, *Visigothic Spain*, 58 refers more broadly to "some time after the beginning of the revolt in 579, possibly even as late as 582," but the detailed analysis is missing.

241 Anna Balaguer, "El problema de la localización de la Roda visigoda," *Acta Numismática* 13 (1983), 109-18; Pliego, *La moneda visigoda*, v. 1, 82, 90. Alternate reading: CVM D[E]I RODA. A second coin from Roda which has since come to light confirms Balaguer's assertion: Swiss Bank

COS issues were made. Mints at *Cesaragusta* (= Zaragoza) and, apparently, *Toleto* put out tremisses of Leovigild with VPW reverse type.[242] Tremisses of Leovigild with COS reverse were emitted at these same mints as well as others known from inclusion of the name of the minting city in the reverse legend: *Elvora, Reccopolis, Tirasona*, and *Barcinona* (= Barcelona). In addition, the lone '*Rex Inclitus*' coin with COS reverse type points to scattered and, to some extent, simultaneous minting; but as all other known IR coins are of VPW design, this one COS minting was later. VPW issues of '*Rex Inclitus*', Toleto, and Cesaragusta inscriptions look to have run side by side, then the new type succeeded with these legends. Whether this represents a strict order and whether, as fits best with the southern proximity to the imperial model, these other COS emissions followed or were simultaneous with the CVM DEO course must be left to educated guess. Because the named mints were far from the scene of fighting, it appears that at least the new cross-on-steps reverse design was enjoined upon almost all the major mints for a short time in order to spread the news that Leovigild won victories by the power of God and ruled as an equal of the eastern Roman emperor.[243]

It is possible that the first cross-on-steps coins were produced not at Emerita but at Toleto, for the changes in the coinage must generally have been directed by the court.[244] What is certain is the close association of

Corporation, *Auction 42, Basel: January 23, 1997*, no. 2551. See now Pliego, *La moneda visigoda*, v. 2, 71 (50a and 50b, respectively). This new coin, especially, appears to have emanated from the same die engraver responsible for a coin of Ispali (cf. Miles, *The Coinage of the Visigoths*, 191, no. 31(b) and pl. II.16). It is easy to see why the coin in Miles's catalog (ibid., 185, no. 18 and pl. II.6) was assumed to have been a coin of Rodas. J. N. Hillgarth was quite reasonable to have placed it in 585 as a witness to the battle with the Franks ("Coins and Chronicles," 503-506), but on grounds of style, spelling, and context his argument can no longer be accepted. See Appendix II, where coins of Roda and Ispali are compared.

242 A single tremissis of profile and VPW types and inscriptions LIVVIGILDVSI – TOLETO REX CONO was drawn in the eighteenth century but is now lost. Florez, *Medallas*, 175; Tomasini, *The Barbaric Tremissis*, pl. B.2; Hillgarth, "Coins and Chronicles," 506; see Pliego, *La moneda visigoda*, v. 2, 67 (no. 41) and ibid., v. 1, 93 for questions about this specimen.

243 It is curious that Narbona is not among the mints that issued cross-on-steps coins, but this could well be due to the brevity of this phase and the greater time required for minting instructions to reach such a distance. The interpretation of Fernando López Sánchez, "Moneda civil y moneda militar en Hispania (350-711)," in *Militares y civiles en la antigua Roma*, ed. Juan José Palao Vicente (Salamanca: Universidad de Salamanca), 227-52 at 245f of COS being employed by the southern cities as a mark of their independence makes little sense.

244 Pliego, *La moneda visigoda*, v. 1, 93f outlines the way Toledo and Cesaragusta appear to have led in the inauguration of regal coinage. It could be added that, besides the preeminence of Leovigild's capital in other respects, it "would have been the major mint for Leovigild, as indicated by the predominance of coins in his name from Toledo after the mint was added." Bartlett et al., "Byzantine Gold Coinage of *Spania*," 365f.

the mints of the capital and of Reccopolis and Elvora, whose tremisses all seem to have emanated from the same die engraver.[245] In the case of Reccopolis this is not surprising, given its royal foundation in 578 and its location some 65 km up the Tajo River from Toledo; the possibility has even been raised that Leovigild wished to transfer the capital there.[246] The coins struck with the mint name 'Elvora,' on the other hand, were once commonly thought to have come from the rather distant mint of what is now Évora in southeastern Portugal, then an episcopal see in the province of Lusitania. More recently, the suggestion that Elvora should instead be identified with Talavera la Reina, west on the Tajo some 80 km by road from Toledo, eliminates the problems posed by the great distance between this supposedly southern Lusitanian mint and the kingdom's capital and by the very different styles of coins from Emerita and Elvora.[247] The style of tremisses from Elvora unmistakably matches the work of the Toleto engraver, while in no obvious way resembling the distinctive Lusitanian style. The same is true during the later reigns from which coins of Elvora survive. Chapter Four will address the evidence and implications of the same die engraver appearing not only among several mints but even in multiple provinces.

Leovigild's coinage of the second main phase (COS) was almost certainly discontinued in early 584, when a new coin type with the king's facing bust on both sides was struck at Cordoba, with a legend alluding to the capture of Hermenegild there. The issues proclaim 'LEOVIGILDVS REX – CORDOBA BIS OPTINVIT,' in which *bis* ('twice') refers to the capture of the city at this time and in 572 when Leovigild crushed the city's rebellion, a feat Agila was unable to accomplish. Apparently, a new type was considered appropriate for the victorious end of the war. The facing-bust type embodies the final

245 See the map of known mints in Appendix I, Figure I.4 and the comparison of the coins in Appendix II. M. Castro, "Los hallazgos," 135 links the first regal minting with COS reverse (c. 579) with the Tajo River valley, noting it represents the zone of greatest royal control.

246 Collins, *Early Medieval Spain*, 45.

247 D. M. Metcalf, "For What Purposes Were Suevic and Visigothic Tremisses Used?" in *Problems of Medieval Coinage in the Iberian Area*, v. 3, ed. M. Gomes Marques and M. Crusafont i Sabater (Santarém: Instituto Politécnico de Santarém, 1988), 15-34, revives the identification Heiss made in 1872 of Elvora and Talavera de la Reina, although he gives reasons why he prefers nearby Talavera la Vieja as the true location. Metcalf's argumentation is based on medieval place names, the comparative distances of the proposed mints from Toleto, the topography of coin finds (favoring one of the Talaveras as the true site of the mint), and stylistic analysis. I take the stylistic evidence further in Appendix II. For further support for the proper location of the mint in the farthest eastern limit of central Lusitania see also Pliego, *La moneda visigoda*, v. 1, 124f.

phase of Leovigild's coinage. Its dates can be confined to the years 584 to 586 on several grounds: the nearly uniform spelling of Leovigild's name at all mints as LEOVIGILDVS – a form that did not appear on the cross-on-steps or Victory types; the uniform use, apart from the triumphal issues, of new epithets to describe the king (IVSTVS and PIVS); the naming of the mint-city on all reverse legends; and a change in standards of weight and fineness of gold.[248] The now unmistakably Visigothic tremisses, easily differentiated from the imperial coinage followed for so long, were brought back to the imperial standard of 1.516 g, although their gold was reduced to eighteen carats (seventy-five per cent Au).

The range within which Hermenegild's coinage must be placed is the five years of his self-proclaimed reign in the south, 579 to 584. According to the theory of Grierson and Hillgarth, followed today by Pliego, Hermenegild initiated the regal coinage of the Visigoths not long after his coronation, which is dated by the authors to 580 at the latest.[249] Of the two different legends on Hermenegild's tremisses, the one held to have been on the first issue is ERMENEGILDI – REGI A DEO VITA, which might best be translated 'Long life to King Hermenegild from God.'[250] The authors observe that the specific inspiration for such an inscription may well have come from African coins of Justin II (565-78) with the word VITA and the names of Justin and Sophia in the dative case. Grierson suggested that Hermenegild's inscription might also have been inspired by the coronation *laudes* (*N. ... regi vita*) used in the late Roman era and in medieval rituals, and presumably during the Visigothic period. The words '*a Deo*' are added by Hermenegild to emphasize the righteousness of his religious struggle in the face of persecution. At some later point, Hermenegild issued coins that proclaimed him as 'the renowned king' (ERMENEGILDI – INCLITI REGI).[251] According to this version of events, Leovigild responded to the rebel's initial propagandistic gesture with his own legends, initially ones that were hastily ordered and therefore irregularly executed (c. 580/81); then 'LIVVIGILDVS – REX INCLITVS' a short time later, also on coins of what is called here the phase one type (VPW); then the mint names of Toledo and Zaragoza with that type as well as 'LIVVIGILDVS – REX INCLITVS' surrounding a cross-on-steps (581-583); followed by 'CVM DEO' and 'EMERITA VICTORIA' and the rest

248 See below, Chapter Three, section D.

249 Hillgarth, "Coins and Chronicles," 505. Pliego, *La moneda visigoda*, v. 1, 89-95 views religion as central to the reason for Hermenegild's revolt and his minting as almost immediate.

250 This legend has been much discussed. See Hillgarth, "Coins and Chronicles," 504; Tomasini, *The Barbaric Tremissis*, 70-71; and Pliego, *La moneda visigoda*, v. 1, 89-93.

251 Cf. Tomasini, *The Barbaric Tremissis*, 70-71; Pliego, *La moneda visigoda*, v. 1, 90 and 92-94.

of the mint-city legends with COS, when the facing-bust type takes over the field of both sides of the tremisses in 584.[252]

One necessary consequence of this hypothesis is that all Leovigild's named coinage before the facing-bust type has to be placed within the same five-year period of Hermenegild's rule. At the same time, the stages that strongly suggest themselves as transitions toward a fully regal coinage – garbled emperor's name, J II-Leovigild, and *curru* – must be rejected as such. According to this view, after an uncertain J II-Leovigild period commencing in the early 580s, with the IR legend surrounding VPW rapidly copied by Hermenegild's coinage, the minting jumps immediately to a combination of the earliest labeling of mint-city and the IR legend around COS, then quickly to the COS with various mint-name legends. The transition to placing Leovigild alone on the currency was not by organized plan, nor was it the evolution Miles neatly laid out; rather, it must have been produced simultaneously in different places. One virtue of the argument of Hermenegild's instigation of the change is in its understanding of overlaps that must have occurred, so that a particular series does not necessarily indicate the end of a previous one. A problem, however, is that it requires too many simultaneous issues especially in the collapsed time frame. If coinage with the cross-on-steps was indeed issued between 582 and 584 and offers no reason to be considered concurrent with regal coinage of the Victory reverse type – at least at those mints that issued the cross-on-steps – then a great variety of Leovigild's tremisses within the first 'regal' phase must have been issued from c. 580 to 582. The difficulty here is whether it seems probable that the many varieties of 'mintless' issues (including '*Rex Inclitus*') were all produced in that short time, either simultaneously at the different mints or in stages. The scenario in which Leovigild's regal series is limited to very few years is plausible only in the case of simultaneous, diverse emissions. Is it true, as Grierson asserted, that what George Miles "believed to be a variety of early phases are really a single phase"?[253]

252 The slightly expanded and updated version will be found in a table provided by Pliego, *La moneda visigoda*, v. 1, 95, with Grierson's and Hillgarth's essential order and dates conveniently displayed in ibid., 84. Grierson changed his earlier opinion concerning the order, placing *Incliti Regi* before *Regi a Deo vita*: Grierson and Blackburn, *Medieval European Coinage*, v. 1, 50. The order in Hillgarth, "Coins and Chronicles" is somewhat unclear, since his primary concern in that article was coins with religious legends.

253 Grierson and Blackburn, *Medieval European Coinage*, v. 1, 49. A later section of this chapter elaborates the phases of coin types in Visigothic Spain, the first three of which were executed under Leovigild. These three are (by obv./rev. types): I – profile bust / VPW; II – profile bust / cross-on-steps; III – facing bust / facing bust.

To answer this question, we need to see if there is evidence of a succession of legends in the first phase of Leovigild's currency, a fact that would suggest a succession of issues rather than a variety of inscriptions and type styles used more or less simultaneously at different mints. Such a succession of issues would make it doubtful that all tremisses of the first phase were produced in just two to three years. In fact, there is internal evidence that the currency of Leovigild's first phase appeared in successive stages.[254] In the first place, Leovigild's 'regal' tremisses with the name of the emperor Justin II on one side must come before coins on which the emperor's name is removed, given the radical break this implied and the way in which the transition can ultimately be seen to have moved. We may suppose that a clear command of the king would be required to overturn the well-established minting practice.[255] Furthermore, issues with forms of the names *Justinus* and *Leovigildus* on either side usually employ the genitive case, as had imperial and pseudo-imperial currency bearing Justin II's name; when Leovigild's name is joined with the epithet REX, his side of the coins reads LIVVIGILDI REGIS.[256] The genitive form is not used, however, with either the cross-on-steps or facing-busts types. Most legends are already changed to the nominative forms, beginning with coins with the name LIVVIGILDVS on both sides. The epithet PIVS, as mentioned above, comes to be used only on coins from the second phase onward. While this fact indicates a succession of issues – a change in type concurrent with a change in inscriptions – what has not been observed in the literature is that the letters PS on a tremissis

254 However, the data does not indicate the same exclusivity of stages that characterized the second and third phases. Two observations reinforce the notion that minting of tremisses of the last phase, facing busts (FB), was not concurrent with the minting of tremisses of the first two phases. In the period of regal coinage still employing the Victory reverse, the letters DN (for *Dominus Noster*) at the start of inscriptions naming the emperor also appear on issues including or solely bearing Leovigild's name, as is also the case on some cross-on-steps issues. By the facing-bust phase the DN abbreviation disappears almost entirely (it is still part of the inscription on some coins minted in Narbona [cf. Miles, *The Coinage of the Visigoths*, 183f] and Barcelona [ibid., 195f].) Something similar occurs with the abbreviation CONO(B) or ONO (for *Constantinopolis Obryzum*, "pure gold at the Constantinople mint"), a remnant from Eastern gold pieces found on pseudo-imperial coinage. This exergue, or lower segment of the coin design, remains on much regal coinage of the first and second phases, but on none of the third phase.

255 It is possible, however, that both kinds of issues came as a result of a general order to the mints to include the name of Leovigild on all tremisses, without further instructions being given. This could result in a great variety of inscriptions.

256 There are a few examples in which genitive and nominative cases are combined: Tomasini, *The Barbaric Tremissis*, 237, no. 474 (LIVVIGIΔIREXPS – LIVVIGILΔIREXN) and ibid., 243, no. 528 (LIVVIGILDVS – LIVVIGILDIREGIS).

with Leovigild's name and a Victory reverse type (phase I) is probably an early abbreviation for later use of the full word PIVS.[257]

The theory that Visigothic regal coinage originated with Hermenegild encounters greater difficulty in the matter of the order of both rulers' issues. The supposed link between the REGI A DEO VITA legend and Leovigild's imitation of it with his CVM DEO legends is greatly weakened if the former originated in c. 580, since the latter did not appear until 583/584. The similar style of Leovigild's main *'Rex Inclitus'* issues and Hermenegild's *'Regi a Deo Vita'* coins also presents a problem. If one confines the comparison to these coins alone, it is clear that one engraver was copying the other's work, and we are left with the question of which was first. According to Grierson, the style of Hermenegild's engraver was imitated on Leovigild's *'Rex Inclitus'* coins after the period (of perhaps one or two years) of confused legends. But he overlooked the fact that Leovigild's *'Rex Inclitus'* series has an obvious stylistic forerunner in his so-called *curru* coins.[258] The obverse profile bust and reverse Victory of these tremisses are surrounded by mysterious legends with various forms of the word 'CVRRV' running forwards and backwards on right and left, respectively, and by some form of ONO in the exergue of the reverse.[259] Because none of the specimens bears the name of Leovigild, and because the spelling is extremely erratic, this series belongs to a period before the first named coinage. In theory, it is possible that the die sinker working for Hermenegild copied the style of *'curru'* coinage (Tomasini's subgroup C3), while for the legend he put his master's name. Yet, in this case, as in other scenarios, every consideration of style suggests that Hermenegild's engraver copied from Leovigild's, not vice versa.[260] As Tomasini persuasively argues, "It would be improbable for Leovigild to adopt the coin design of the mint of Seville and of his son Hermenegild and continue to use the obverse face in his later cross-on-steps. It would not be improbable for Hermenegild to adopt a coin that his father has established as the official national coin

257 As listed in Miles, *The Coinage of the Visigoths*, 178, 7(i) = Tomasini, *The Barbaric Tremissis*, 237, no. 474 = Cabré Aguiló, *El tesorillo visigodo*, no. 83 (see previous note). Pliego, *La moneda visigoda*, v. 2, 10(b) supplies PP for these letters; the various photos do not lend a definitive reading.

258 See Tomasini, *The Barbaric Tremissis*, pll. XXIX-XXXIV and Miles, *The Coinage of the Visigoths*, pl. I.

259 See Appendix II.

260 Most notable is the distinctive dot under the legs of Victory on the *'curru'* coins, which was already present in pseudo-imperial coinage dating back to Justinian: cf. the photos of the 'JAN 8' group in Tomasini, *The Barbaric Tremissis*, pll. XVIII-XIX. One should observe that the wedge-shaped serifs of Hermenegild's *'Regi a Deo vita'* coins, which appear as exaggerated additions to otherwise line-drawn letters, seem to imitate the serifs more intrinsic to the letters of Leovigild's *'Rex Inclitus'* specimens.

and place his own name on it."[261] This argument is all the more convincing if we concur that Leovigild's '*Rex Inclitus*' series was produced mainly in the capital of the kingdom, a most unlikely place to copy a rebel's coinage. Neither Grierson, nor Hillgarth gave sufficient consideration to the '*Rex Inclitus*' coins, and none to the '*curru*' coins, yet they are key pieces in the puzzle of the beginnings of the royal coinage, especially since the volume of C3 and IR minting was considerable.[262]

The '*curru*' series make clear that, by the time Hermenegild first minted, a long process of monetary change had already begun under Leovigild. It probably denotes the first step in Leovigild's currency reform.[263] In a number of respects – type, style, badly garbled legends, and varied weights (most around 1.3 g) – the '*curru*' series fits perfectly alongside the coinage in the name of Justin II with jumbled legends, which Miles dated from prior to 568 until c. 574.[264] Since the same engraving style, and probably the same die sinker, can be traced back to Visigothic pseudo-imperials in the name of Justinian without there being any Justin II groups of this style, we may conclude that the '*curru*' series emerged in the very early part of Leovigild's reign, concurrently with 'JII' coins.[265] What is one to make of these legends,

261 Tomasini, *The Barbaric Tremissis*, 72.

262 The same could be said of Pliego, *La moneda visigoda*, v. 1 as referenced above. On the high volume of C3 and IR, based on numerous specimens but few die links: Bartlett et al., "Byzantine Gold Coinage of *Spania*," 364.

263 Tomasini, *The Barbaric Tremissis*, 67f., where the author suggests that '*curru*' tremisses represent the first step in the creation of a uniform national coinage; he dates the first such coins to the years Leovigild still ruled jointly with Liuva. Hillgarth does not seem to have known of Tomasini's work and does not discuss the '*curru*' series. Grierson (in Grierson and Blackburn, *Medieval European Coinage*, v. 1, 49) treats it briefly, but does not attempt to explain its connection with the transition. Knowing when the Zorita de los Canes hoard was buried would help to determine if Hermenegild's issues could have preceded the regal coinage of his father. The date several scholars have given to the hoard on the basis of its different series – somewhat cyclical reasoning without external evidence to help – is 579 or 580. Such an early date for '*Rex Inclitus*' coins does not allow Grierson's synopsis because the series must be preceded by the '*Regi a Deo*' series (starting in c. 580) and a number of early regal series of Leovigild. The same difficulty exists even if the hoard is placed in 582, the latest probable date given the absence of pieces with the cross-on-steps. '*Rex Inclitus*' is normally dated much before (Barral i Altet, *La circulation*, 90: 576-579, Zorita in 579; Tomasini, *The Barbaric Tremissis*, 64-75: 578-580, Zorita in 580 [following Pio Beltrán Villagrasa, "Monedas de Leovigild en el tesorillo de Zorita de los Canes (año 1945)," in *Numario Hispánico*, II, 3 (1953), pp. 19-52]; Miles, *The Coinage of the Visigoths*, 45 and 97: c. 576-578, Zorita in c. 580; Pliego, *La moneda visigoda*, v. 1, 95 and 84: 581-583 and Zorita in c. 580).

264 A few of these same observations can be found in Tomasini, *The Barbaric Tremissis*, 127-30, although I arrived at them independently of his work.

265 Ibid., 288, Chart VIII (Style Group Progressions). Following Tomasini's usage, JII = Justin II.

which have long baffled scholars? They possibly refer to military triumph achieved by Leovigild. 'Triumph' is one meaning of the word *currus*, used here in the ablative case (meaning perhaps 'in triumph').[266] In view of the many military successes Leovigild is reported to have gained from the very first years of his rule, it is reasonable to consider this series as the king's first initiative to propagandize his military strength by means of his currency. It is noteworthy that the only abundant finds of '*curru*' tremisses are from hoards discovered in recent decades in central-southern Spain, where Leovigild won several victories in the years 570-577.[267]

The contents of hoards buried in Leovigild's reign strongly imply several stages in the various Leovigildan issues, though these finds cannot offer an absolute chronology. The hoard at Zorita de los Canes (the location of Reccopolis) presents a good sample of Leovigild's coins (a minimum of eleven of the ninety-two or more originally in the hoard, but at least sixteen if counting '*curru*' specimens). It includes tremisses identifying Leovigild as king and with the VPW reverse, but there are no mint names yet. It is therefore earlier than the Mérida hoard, consisting solely of the COS reverse type and with nineteen of the twenty coins displaying the city where minted. Neither hoard contains a Hermenegild issue, which would offer something close to a hard date, however the Mérida hoard's unique IR tremissis with COS and no mint name suggests relative dates as it fits logically just after the IR/VPW mintless coins but before the COS type is surrounded by mint names. This

266 The inscription LIVVIGILDI REGIS is most often preceded by C or VC (cf. Miles, *The Coinage of the Visigoths*, 175f and Pliego, *La moneda visigoda*, v. 2, 55f, set nos. 1, 2, 8). We find the explanation for the genitive case if we read these as abbreviations for the words CVRRV and VICTORIA (the former having appeared previously for some years, the latter found on pre-regal coinage and used again in 582 at Emerita in the reverse legend EMERITA VICTORIA).

267 One unpublished hoard found a couple of decades ago, reportedly in or near Andujar, approximately 60 km northeast of Cordoba on the Guadalquivir, is thought to have amounted to hundreds of tremisses, many from Leovigild's day. A trustworthy source with whom I have communicated has seen pictures of this hoard being held by a private dealer in Spain; I have viewed rather complete descriptions of the coins. The Mérida hoard of twenty coins was comprised of '*curru*' tremisses of the C3 category. I infer a link principally between the CVRRV inscription in the south and Leovigild's initial victories at Baza (Basti) and Málaga in 570 and Asidona in 571 (see John of Biclar, *Chronicon*, s.a. 570, 2 and 571, 3), and perhaps additionally his crushing of resistance in Cordoba in 572 and in Orospeda to the east in 577 (ibid., s.a. 572, 2 and 577, 2). Luis A. García Moreno, *Leovigildo. Unidad y diversidad de un reinado* (Madrid: Real Academia de la Historia, 2008), 40-52 correctly affirms the successful seizure of both Baza and Málaga while also constructing an interesting case for Leovigild's primary concern to recapture the royal treasure Cordoban rebels had seized in 550. A few years later, Seville and Cordoba were the points of transition between the cross-on-steps and facing-busts type. If the Victory-type 'Toleto' coin is authentic, '*Rex Inclitus*' and C3 coins are probably from Toleto – and that style was copied by other engravers of '*curru*' coinage, perhaps working in southern cities.

Figure 7: Proposed order of hoard contents related to Leovigild's regal-name minting

	Number of tremisses	*Legend*	*Reverse type*	*Most likely date*
Zorita hoard	5	CVRRV	VPW	pre-575
	1	J II – Leovigild	VPW	573-577
	7	Leovigild – Leovigild	VPW	pre-579
	3	Leovigild – REX INCLITVS	VPW	575-579
Mérida hoard	1	Leovigild – REX INCLITVS	COS	580-582
	19	Leovigild – mint name (incl. EMERITA VICTORIA)	COS	582-584

lone IR/COS piece likely reveals a brief stage in which the cross-on-steps was introduced at Mérida around the time of the battle against Hermenegild in c. 582.[268] (See the table in Figure 7 above, which supposes some time for the first few series listed to develop.) The hoards imply sequentialism even if it may not be definite but rather may entail some simultaneous issues.

Despite the variety of chronological interpretations, the four mints of the Mérida hoard are commonly deemed to have been the first with mint names, albeit initially with VPW reverse. Zorita, when related to a few other hoards buried shortly before and after, suggests the basic order of Leovigild's issues:[269]

(1) confused pre-regal (JII groups 2 and 3, and 4 and 5 without Leovigild's name): mid-560s to early 570s
(2) '*curru*', concurrent with later emissions of the former and possibly early issues of the next: late 560s to c. 575
(3) Leovigild's name on one side, then both sides (JII 4 and 5), and '*Rex Inclitus*'-VPW: mid- to later 570s
(4) COS, including continuation of limited '*Rex Inclitus*' issues: early 580s

268 Mateos Cruz et al., "Un tesoro de tremisses," no. 1. The specimen is possibly from before 582, but the association in this gathering with Mérida coins of a subsequent stage (six EMERITA VICTORIA, the single majority from the hoard) and by hoard location with the city itself, plus the otherwise close time of the hoard's emissions, make the date of c. 582 a strong conclusion. Other small hoards help fill in the picture: see the convenient chart of Leovigild-era hoards in Pliego, *La moneda visigoda*, v. 1, 87.

269 Mint names in the Mérida hoard: Pliego in Mateos Cruz et al., "Un tesoro de tremisses," 267-69; cf. Pliego, *La moneda visigoda*, v. 1, 93f. I express my gratitude to David Yoon for specific suggestions on the chronology; Peter Bartlett advocated the introduction of Leovigild's name as marking a specific phase.

There are other reasons to doubt that Hermenegild 'struck first.' It has been argued that ordering his engravers to replace the traditional inscription of the emperor with his name would be an affront to the Byzantines, with whom he was seeking an alliance.[270] No such problem existed for Leovigild, who was at war with the Byzantines. The different standards of the tremisses issued under Leovigild and Hermenegild also pose a problem. Hermenegild's few surviving tremisses indicate that they were struck at a higher-weight standard, between 1.34 and 1.37 g, compared with Leovigild's standard between 1.3 and 1.33 g – which suggests more precisely a seven-*siliquae* standard of 1.3265 g.[271] Testing of Hermenegild's tremisses for fineness of gold appears to demonstrate a moderately higher purity compared with many '*curru*' and especially '*Rex Inclitus*' coins.[272] If Leovigild issued his first named coinage only after Hermenegild's own coins appeared, one may wonder if he would be likely to have done so with tremisses of lower standards of weight and fineness. Such a move would risk popular rejection of the king's currency in favor of that of his rebel son, the last thing Leovigild would have wanted. In the principal group of '*curru*' coins (C3), which have been attributed to Toleto, Leovigild was already introducing new standards of weight and fineness;[273] subsequently, the

270 Mário Gomes Marques et al., *Ensaios sobre história monetária da monarquia visigoda* (Porto: Sociedade Portuguesa de Numismática, 1995), 23.

271 Grierson made an ingenious argument for Leovigild's alignment of late pseudo-imperial and early regal currency with a supposed Germanic standard of 1.3 g (20 grains, instead of 8 *siliquae*, or 1.516 g, on the Roman model). This idea has been cast in doubt by recent testing results, which are discussed below in Chapter Three. A completely different standard was used for Justin II coinage (between 1.42-1.45 g), and most coins from two of the '*curru*' groups and regal phases I and II fall in the weight class above 1.3 g, corresponding instead to the 1.326-g standard. Cf. Marques et al., *Ensaios*, 52-53 and 108.

272 See Figure 8 below, an interpreted synopsis of Bartlett et al., "Byzantine Gold Coinage of *Spania*," 388-93, which draws in part from specimens of the latter groups tested at the American Numismatic Society – see Appendix I, Figure I.11, Miles No. 7(e)1, 8(h)1, 8(i)1 and Appendix I, Figure I.12. Recent collection of measurement data on the Zorita hoard should make it possible to lend greater precision to specific categories of coins. Preliminary suggestions appear to indicate a continued reduction in weight and fineness through much of the Leovigildan era, and a wide variance in observed standards indicating less control of minting in at least in some locations.

273 This is illustrated by the research of Lauris Olson on '*curru*' coins, in a graph he placed on the web but which appears to be no longer available: http://pobox.upenn.edu/~olson/visicoins/currugraph, accessed in digital archive 3 January 2018. My point is corroborated by a remark of Metcalf, et al., "Sixth-century Visigothic Metrology," 73: "Any other of Tomasini's [JII] subgroups which deviate significantly from the 1.41-1.45 norm, such as JII2 or JII5, fall under suspicion of being late issues from mints that did not produce C3, IR, and H [=Hermenegild]." Such issues could be late or early, but were not yet affected by the modified and regularized standard emerging at the capital mint where, following Tomasini, C3 and IR were probably made. Bartlett et al., "Weight, Fineness and Debasement," 364f.

first phase of regal issues and *'Rex Inclitus'* fully established the lower values that had already begun a small decline since at least the reign of Justin II. C3 tremisses were struck at a lowered weight standard of approximately 1.3 g but at a relatively high concentration of gold at around ninety-two per cent, then a clearly separate step was taken as IR minting reduced both weight and fineness (1.3 g, seventy-five per cent Au). Minting of the COS coins, datable by inscription to 582-584 (except for the solitary IR/COS example that precedes the rest), adhered to the same depressed levels.[274] A good deal of experimentation with weights and gold purity was underway, and while an attempted coin reform may be supposed with the various series bearing Justin II's name,[275] the first use of the king's name coincides with an intentional skimping on the standard weight and fineness level. Ultimately, the manufacture of facing-busts type stabilized a higher intrinsic value by virtue of joining the same low fineness with a raised weight that averaged close to 1.5 g. The table below traces the significant changes and provides intrinsic value figures from recent scholarship, with boxes highlighting noteworthy alterations.[276]

These monetary innovations are yet another indication that Leovigild was setting Visigothic currency on a course of significant change, which – in the context of his efforts to increase the power of the monarchy – fittingly culminated in the regal series. Thus, it is highly probable that Hermenegild issued regal currency only after that of his father was in circulation, and apparently tried to win acceptance with better coins. His striking of coinage in his own name is a sign of the importance of money as a vehicle by which he could promote his claim as the legitimate king.

The following table summarizes the earliest regal issues as I have discussed them above, proposing their launch very soon after Leovigild became the sole ruler, in 573 according to John of Biclar. Here, I propose a more specific chronology of the beginning of the regal coinage than has been suggested thus

274 Tomasini asserts that the monetary reforms undertaken by Leovigild in the last years of pre-regal coinage entailed a greater degree of standardization of weight, fineness, and style. However, his graphs of weights do not bear this out, except in the case of C3 and RI which I have pointed out. One is hard-pressed to see a standardization of style among the JII coins. See Tomasini, *The Barbaric Tremissis*, 148-49, and 298-99, Charts XIa and b. Bartlett et al., "Weight, Fineness, and Debasement" treat the complex results garnered over the course of several years.
275 Bartlett et al., "Weight, Fineness, and Debasement," 179.
276 From Bartlett et al., "Byzantine Gold Coinage of *Spania*," 366, with graphic emphases added. The approximate dates, while not identical to mine at the end of this section, are consistent with my own. In ibid., n. 60 it is explained: "Fineness is estimated based on the assumption that a system of units of 1/24 like the present carat system was in use and the values could be 23/24 (96%) for the first stage and 22/24 (92%) for the second stage." The test samples, methods, and breakdown of groups is slightly different in the table of measurements below in Figure 13 on 169.

Figure 8: Tremissis standards from averages immediately prior to and during Leovigild's reign

Stage	Type	Weight	Au %	Intrinsic V. (wt. x Au%)	Start date	End date
1	VPW – (JAN 8 to C-1&2)	1.4-1.5	96	1.305	c. 565	c. 573
2	C-3	1.3	92	1.183	c. 573	?
3	IR	1.3	75	0.975	?	c. 580
4	COS	1.3	75	0.975	after 578	584
5	Facing Busts	1.5	75	1.125	584	586

far.[277] A breakdown of the basic issues is required by the variety of Leovigild's early gold currency. There is little question that some of the first categories below were simultaneous. In view of the uncertainties, their proposed dates are given with appropriate caution. The sequence of the later issues can be worked out with reasonable certainty, as we have shown. The suggested locations of the minting of certain VPW issues are based on those of Tomasini.

Note: { } signifies letters that occur only in some instances of the same legend.
[ ] signifies supplied letters that can be discerned from other issues of this period.
( ) signifies one of several variations in word order or one of several locations.

Figure 9: Proposed chronology of the earliest Visigothic regal issues

Issue designation	Inscription form	Type	Years	Reference to photos
	[garbled JII:] IVIVIVIVIVIVIVIVI – [garbled:] IVIVIVIVIVIVIVI CVVII	Profile / VPW	pre-569 –c. 571	Tomasini, pl. XXV; cf. Pliego, v. 1, 79 fig. 15
	[garbled JII:] DN IVSTINVS PPAVC – [garbled:] VICTORIA AVC {I}	Profile / VPW	pre-569 –c. 571	Tomasini, pll. XX-XIX
'curru'	[garbled:] CVRRVTII CVRRVΛII - [garbled:] VVRRVI VRRVRRII	Profile / VPW	c. 568 –c. 575	Tomasini, pll. XXIX-XXXIII; cf. Pliego, v. 1, 81, fig. 17
	Regal coinage			
JII – Leovigild	ƆNTSNV IVNSTC – ILIVVI ƆICVSI CO	Profile / VPW	c. 573	Tomasini, pl. XXIV; Pliego, v. 2, 56 no. 3.1

277 The proposed chronology of issues from 579 to 584 is based on some progression of types and legends as well as the associated events known from the historical record. The start of regal issues according to the most notable scholars is as follows. Pliego, *La moneda visigoda*, v. 1, 95: 580-582; Barral i Altet, *La circulation*, 56: c. 570; Miles, *The Coinage of the Visigoths*, 45: c. 575-576; Marques et al., *Ensaios*, 22-26: c. 576; Tomasini, *The Barbaric Tremissis*, 66: 577/78; Grierson and Blackburn, *Medieval European Coinage*, v. 1, 49-51: c. 580.

Issue designation	Inscription form	Type	Years	Reference to photos
"	[garbled:] IVSTINI AVC – {V}{C} LIVVIGILDI REGIS[278]	Profile / VPW	c. 573 –c. 575	Miles, pl. I.1; cf. Pliego, v. 1, 91, fig. 19; ibid., v. 2, 55-56
"	Emerita? [garbled:] DN LIVVICILDV{S}- [garbled:] IVSTINVS	Profile / VPW	c. 573 –c. 575	Miles, pl. I.2
Leovigild – VICTORIA AVC	DN LEVVCILDI R[EGIS] – [garbled:] VICTORIA AVC	Profile / VPW	c. 573 -c. 575	Miles, pl. I.3; Pliego, v. 2, 56 no. 4.2
Leovigild – Leovigild	Andalucía? VC LIVVICCILDI REGI{S}- VC LIVV•GILDI REGIS	Profile / VPW	c. 575 –c. 579	Miles, pl. I.4; Pliego, v. 2, 56 no. 8a.3
"	LVICOVS REX – LVVVV•VS REX	Profile / VPW	c. 575 –c. 579	Miles, pl. I.6; Pliego, v. 2, 58 no. 10c.1
DN Leovigild – DN Leovigild	DN LIVVIGILDVS REX - DN LIVVIGILDVS REX	Profile / VPW	c. 575 – c. 579	Tomasini, pl. XVI; cf. Pliego, v. 1, 92, fig. 20; ; ibid., v. 2, 57
Leovigild – IR / VPW reverse	Toleto LIVVIGILDVS – REX INCLITV{S}	Profile / VPW	c. 577 –c. 580	Miles, pl. I.8; Tomasini, pll. XXXIII-XXXIV; cf. Pliego, v. 1, 92, fig. 21; ibid., v. 2, 55-61
Hermenegild – IR	**Hermenegild >** ERMENEGILDI – INCLITI REGIS[279]	Profile / VPW	**579/ 580 – c. 582**	Miles, pl. III.13; Tomasini, pl. XXXIV; cf. Pliego, v. 1, 92, fig. 22; ibid., v. 2, 77f
Leovigild – Leovigild	Emerita? LIVVIGILDI REX P[IV]S – LIVVIGILDI REX N IDNO	Profile / VPW	c. 578 –c. 579	Miles, pl. I.7; Pliego, v. 2, 58 no. 10b.1
Leovigild – mint name	Toleto, Cesaragusta LIVVIGILDVSRE – CESARAGVSTA ONO	Profile / VPW	c. 579 – c. 582	Pliego, v. 1, 93, fig. 23; Pliego, v. 2, 63f
DN Leovigild – mint name & COS reverse	Toleto, Elvora, Reccopolis, Cesaragusta, Tirasona, Barcinona DN LIVVICILDVS – (TOLETO REX) CONOB	Profile / COS	c. 579 –c. 584	Miles, pll. II.9,11 & III.2-4; Pliego, v. 2, 67 etc.
Leovigild – IR & COS reverse	Emerita?[280] SVDLIIVVIL – REXINCXV ONO	Profile / COS	580-582	Pliego, v. 2, 61, 18.1

278 Here, the name of Leovigild is beginning to be spelled with a good degree of regularity, while the emperor's name is not. 'VC,' then later just 'V,' must be an abbreviation of *Victoria*, which had been on the reverse of JII coinage. 'C' alone must be a vestige from the '*curru*' legend, which had essentially the same meaning. The legend seems to be a direct precursor to those on coins which Tomasini tentatively attributed to Andalucía, the region of Leovigild's victories at that time.
279 Apparently, a blend of both Leovigild's '*L... Regis*' legend and his '*Rex Inclitus*' legend, the latter put in the genitive form. If this is, in fact, Hermenegild's first series, it is noteworthy that he did not start his regal minting with a religious inscription.
280 Mateos Cruz et al., "Un tesoro de tremisses," hold this issue as Emeritan, preceding the EMERITA VICTORIA legend.

Issue designation	Inscription form	Type	Years	Reference to photos
Hermenegild – REGI A DEO VITA	**Hermenegild >** ERMENEGILDI – REGI A DEO VITA	Profile / VPW	**c. 580/ 582**[281] **– c. 583**	Miles, pl. III.14; cf. Pliego, v. 1, 91, fig. 18; Pliego, v. 2, 77
DN Leovigild – EMERITA VICTORIA & COS reverse	Emerita DN LIVVICILDVS REX – EMERITA VICTORIA	Profile / COS	582-584	Miles, pl. III.8-9; Pliego, v. 1, 94, fig. 25; Pliego, v. 2, 73-75
Leovigild – CVM DEO OPTINVIT… & COS reverse	Ispali, Italica, Roda (REX LIVVICILDVS) – (CVM DE OPTINIT SPI)	Profile / COS	583-584	Miles, pll. II.6, 15-17 & III.1; Pliego, v. 1, 94, fig. 26; Pliego, v. 2, 69-71 etc.
Leovigild – CORDOBA BIS OPTINVIT of dual FB type	Cordoba LEOVIGILDVS REX – CORDOBA BIS OBTINVIT	Facing busts	584	Marques et al., pl. I.3; Pliego, v. 2, 69 no. 45a.1

The Reasons for the Change

If Leovigild did not issue royal coinage in response to earlier autonomous minting by Hermenegild, why did he decide to do so? We should remember that the idea was not new, since regal issues of various denominations were issued by other barbarian kings in the first half of the sixth century.[282]

281 The inscription is to be linked with either Hermenegild's coronation in c. 580 (Hillgarth, "Coins and Chronicles," 505) or his conversion in c. 582 (Collins, *Early Medieval Spain*, 47-51; idem, "Mérida and Toledo," 215-18).

282 As far as we know, only one barbarian king preceding Leovigild, Theodebert I of Metz (534-548), had full regal legends on gold coinage (see Grierson and Blackburn, *Medieval European Coinage*, v. 1, 116). The legends on his solidi and tremisses usually included DN THEODEBERTVS REX (or VICTOR), and may be the direct inspiration for Leovigild's inscriptions. Theodoric the Ostrogoth (490-526) had the words VICTOR GENTIVM placed on some of his tremisses, and his silver coins had on the reverse DN THEODORICVS REX or a monogram of his name. He and his successors included their own names in legends on the reverse of silver and bronze money (ibid., 28-38). Ostrogothic coinage ceased by 554 or shortly before. The Vandals minted regal silver and copper, but apparently never minted gold coins at all. The coinage ended in 533 with Belisarius's conquest and its legends are the least likely to have affected early Visigothic regal coinage. There is no merit to the suggestion that the placing of the king's name on the coinage coincides "with the disappearance of the kingdom of the Ostrogoths, which was the protector of the Visigoths for a long time," since the Ostrogoths as such had ceased control with the death of Theodoric in 526. (Jean Lafaurie, "Les trouvailles de monnaies des Visigots en Gaule," in *Actes du 94e congrès national des societés savantes, Pau 1969 (section d'archéologie)* [Paris: Bibliothèque Nationale, 1971], 111-28, here 120.)

Furthermore, we must place the change in Visigothic Spain within a similar transformation of tremisses, which came about in the Merovingian and Suevic kingdoms in approximately the same years.[283] It is possible that the first Merovingian regal inscriptions on gold on a regular basis began shortly before Leovigild's autonomous coinage. This seems unlikely, however, and was certainly not the case with Suevic gold currency, which merely imitated that of its neighbor.[284] Rather, Leovigild took up an old practice, which, in turn, was soon followed by other kingdoms. Was his primary aim to standardize the weight and fineness of the coins, which would now have the official guarantee of the king? The evidence gives some support for this hypothesis: the collective drop in the standards of the largest '*curru*' group may have fixed the lower norms used shortly thereafter in the inaugural stages of regal currency.[285] Similarly, the facing-busts type was introduced as another change in the weight standard was brought about in Leovigild's final phase, one which consciously raised the total (intrinsic) value of the triens.[286]

We have also seen above that Leovigild's creation of the Visigothic regal coinage must be placed in the whole context of his efforts to establish strong control over Spain. The beginning of an openly recognizable Visigothic coinage came in the wake of Leovigild's military victories, strengthened political and fiscal organization of the kingdom,[287] and imitation of imperial trappings of authority. Was it a show of resolve to the invaders and, as Hillgarth argued,

283 There may have been economic reasons why solidi ceased to be struck in Spain and in France, with the exception of Provence, by mid-560s and the early 570s, respectively. (See Grierson, *Coins of Medieval Europe*, 9 and 19.) A similar underlying economic shift may explain why Byzantine Spania did not mint solidi.

284 The starting date of Merovingian regal gold minting after Theodebert I is very confused, but is "probably 587," though possibly some years earlier: Grierson and Blackburn, *Medieval European Coinage*, v. 1, 90-93. Not by mere coincidence did regal tremisses of Chlotar II (584-629), who unified all the Frankish kingdoms, make pronouncements of his victories. He copied Leovigild's late issues.

285 In addition to what is discussed above in relation to the chronology question, see group 'C3' in Marques et al., *Ensaios*, 53 (weights) and 60-61 (fineness).

286 Leovigild's standards are taken up in detail in Chapter Three, section D.

287 See García Moreno, "Estudios"; E. A. Thompson, *The Goths in Spain* (Oxford, 1969), 58-64; D. Claude, *Adel, Kirche Und Königtum Im Westgotenreich* (Sigmaringen: Jan Thorbecke Verlag, 1971), 55-77. On construction and embellishment of cities as facets of *aemulatio imperii*: Manuel Castro Priego, "*Reccopolis* y los contextos numismáticos de época visigoda en el Centro de la Península Ibérica," *Revue Numismatique* 6 (No. 171, 2014), 463-95 at 463-67, and Javier Martínez Jiménez, "Crisis or crises? The End of Roman Towns in Iberia, Between the late Roman and the Early Umayyad Periods," in *Tough Times: The Archaeology of Crisis and Recovery. Proceedings of the GAO annual conferences 2010 and 2011*, BAR IS 2478, ed. E. Van der Wilt and J. Martínez Jiménez, (Oxford: Archaeopress, 2013), 77-90, esp. 81-84.

a means of propaganda?[288] It was, but such a view is in no way incompatible with the idea that Leovigild endeavored to regularize Visigothic gold currency.[289] This dual purpose is made clear by the fairly rapid transition from very garbled legends on pseudo-imperial coins to ones that were standardized or of a triumphant nature, no doubt ordered by the king or his court. The essential question remains as to why Leovigild would place a literal stamp of his own monarchy on coins of reduced value. It has been explained above that reduction was a process already slowly taking place and then made part of his own minting operations by the dawn of the '*curru*' series. He could perhaps get away with it in a mostly closed peninsular currency zone, though the adjustment in his final stage may show the prudent limits of coin adulteration. Most cogently, he must have concluded he could only mint in great quantities this way. The urgency of his minting needs is apparent, primarily to conduct frequent warfare, since it is precisely in the midst of his campaigns against the Romans that he made this decisive order for a radical monetary change. The tête-à-tête with Hermenegild reflected in his currency was a heightened stage of minting adaptation. The incisive adoption of an outwardly sovereign currency by which Leovigild forced his way into the palms of his subjects also makes sense if understood as part of an attempted resolution of contested cohabitation between ruling Goths and the vast majority Hispano-Romans.[290] Each tremis was a token of the new order he was effecting that could project his singular domination and powerful regal persona.

288 Hillgarth, "Coins and Chronicles." Stanislaw Suchodolski, "Les débuts du monnayage dans les royaumes barbares," in *Mélanges de numismatique, d'archéologie et d'histoire offerts à Jean Lafaurie* (Paris: Société Française de Numismatique, 1980), 249-56, maintains that the beginning of national gold coinages of the 'Germanic states' – particularly Visigothic Spain – was triggered by the desire for propaganda and the celebration of victories. The concurrence of the Byzantine occupation with the decision to commence the regal coinage is not sufficiently emphasized in the literature (Barral i Altet, *La circulation* is a notable exception). The chronology provided above disproves the claim of Michael McCormick, *Eternal Victory*, 318, that "the first issues of Visigothic coinage proclaiming the king's victory were forged in the crucible of internal strife," in other words, during the rebellion of Hermenegild. The issues that he deals with are certainly not the first of the regal series.

289 According to Tomasini, *The Barbaric Tremissis*, 67, "Considering Leovigild's strong dynastic instincts and his policies toward national unity, it is not incongruous that his currency should become more uniform and systematic."

290 Michael Kulikowski, "Ethnicity, Rulership, and Early Medieval Frontiers," in *Borders, Barriers, and Ethnogenesis: Frontiers in Late Antiquity and the Middle Ages*, ed. Florin Curta (Turnhout: Brepols, 2005), 247-54, at 250f discusses, in the context of ethnic difference, Leovigild's attempt in 580 to forge an acceptable religious union between the (Gothic) Arian and (Hispano-Roman) Catholic populations. Within the creative tension of forced interaction, I believe the coins of just this time demonstrate a self-conscious emphasis of the Gothic identity through a multi-layered projection of Leovigild and his feats.

A Reorganized System

Reform of the minting system was a major undertaking. Tomasini suggested that regal coinage first appeared sporadically and without decisive central control,[291] but in the progressive standardization we can see before long the growth of what may have been the first full exercise of royal power in this area. Leovigild's keen interest in his gold currency is also manifested in the shifting of standards and in the adoption of new styles of epigraphy and bust design that perhaps also point to new minting personnel. Whatever the structure of the minting system before, it was now basically centralized. While Leovigild's mint-named coinage comes from at least twenty-seven mints, most of it was struck in the big cities of the time: the capitals of the six provinces and a few others such as Cesaragusta and Cordoba.[292] Several other mints, which are generally known from only one or two surviving coins, may have been connected to military campaigns, as at Italica, Roda, and Ispali. Finally, the inclusion in the legends of the place of minting undoubtedly served a purpose in Leovigild's reorganization. In addition to a kind of declaration of monarchical authority over each town where minting was carried out, mint names and separate provincial types (if only loosely followed) would likewise facilitate the identification of coins. So too would other distinguishing features such as stars or multiple abbreviation marks or the like, which appear only occasionally on Leovigild's gold currency but increase starting in Reccared's reign. Easy counting of the tremisses, which does not seem to have been a feature of pseudo-imperials, would help in keeping track of mints and production and perhaps collection of coins.

B Regal Coin Types

Perhaps out of reverence for the figure of Leovigild, or simply because his coin design perfectly suited the revived monarchy, the facing-busts type was the only one used until the joint reign of Chindasvinth and Reccesvinth (649-53). Its most characteristic feature is the king's long hair flowing down into what seem to be braids or curls at the shoulder. In the new Visigothic bust, Miles saw "a true reflection of the 'national' quality" of the coinage, which presents evidence "not only of a divorcement from imperial ties but of the conscious creation of a proud and peculiarly Gothic independence

291 Tomasini, *The Barbaric Tremissis*, 66.
292 See Appendix I, Figures I.7 and I.8, both discussed in Chapter Three.

of style."[293] He found no immediate prototype for the facing busts, but held it to have been essentially inspired by the Byzantine facing bust design.[294]

For a detailed explanation of how the basic types and their many categories unfolded, Miles's essay on the subject is indispensable; an article by Octavio Gil Farrés is also seminal. Pliego builds on this analysis to form her own careful study of this complex matter, including identification of the assorted vestimenta adorning the figure of the king.[295] As she explains, her facing-busts types two through six were the main designs of Leovigild's tremisses and the most frequently used for over half a century afterward, although there is a great variety of specific forms sometimes associated with a particular city or set of mints. The schematic here depicts some early generalized types.

Immediately noticeable in the evolution of types is the iconographic shift during the reign of Reccesvinth (653-72), a change that began in his joint reign with his father Chindasvinth. Like their predecessor Leovigild, these kings were reformers who ruled with an iron fist; it was no doubt their desire to recapture past greatness after a period of decline that led to the creation of new types and a return to Leovigild's coin design of a right-facing bust and a cross-on-steps. Some possible motives for the changes will be explored in a section on standards in Chapter Three. The facing-busts type ceased at some point under Reccesvinth, and was not adopted again by his successors. The profile bust of Wamba (r. 672-80) introduces a scepter-with-cross in the king's hand. Two other major obverse types emerged after this time. One was an obverse facing bust, of which several forms vaguely resemble the contemporary Byzantine figure of Christ, accompanying a cross-on-steps reverse. The other was the "confronting busts" type of the joint reign of Egica-Wittiza (698/700-702).[296]

Miles speculated that, in several instances, Byzantine tremisses provided the model for a Visigothic type or for certain categories of a particular type. Comparison of the relevant specimens in his work and in Pliego's leaves no

293 Miles, *The Coinage of the Visigoths*, 48.

294 Ibid., 46; see p. 47 on the contemporary Merovingian facing-bust type. Pliego, *La moneda visigoda*, v. 1, 158 and fig. 94 demonstrates the obvious similarity to contemporary Roman facing busts.

295 Pliego, *La moneda visigoda*, v. 1, 29-42 (index of types), 155-73. Miles, *The Coinage of the Visigoths*, "The Evolution and Distribution of Types," 43-66; see also ibid., 67f on the inscriptions, in which the most common epithets were PIVS and IVSTVS. Octavio Gil Farrés, "Algunos aspectos de la numismática visigoda: consideraciones acerca del 'tipo tercero' de Leovigildo," *Numisma* 5 (no. 17, 1955), 25-61.

296 Revived profile bust – COS: Pliego, *La moneda visigoda*, v. 1, 166-71. Scepter-with-cross: ibid., 168. Figure of Christ: ibid., 167, 171f and idem, "El origen de la representación de Cristo en la moneda del rey visigodo Ervigio," *Numismatica e antichità classiche: quaderni ticinesi* 42 (2013), 251-62. Confronting busts: ibid., 172f.

Figure 10: Principal early facing-busts type forms[297]

(following type categories 2-6 in Pliego, *La moneda visigoda*, v. 1, 157)

Toleto Cordoba Emerita Tarraconensis far NE

doubt that those suggestions are correct.[298] Numismatic iconography was just one of many areas of Byzantine influence on the Visigothic kingdom, and provides clear evidence that autonomous coinage and even a successful war against the imperial army did not erase the prestige of the Empire felt all the way across the Mediterranean.[299]

The variety of types used on Visigothic tremisses is related to other aspects of their making, as we shall see in later parts of this book. Provincial types and regionalization of styles within the main types merit separate treatment.[300] For now, it is interesting to note that on perhaps a majority of the coins the specific bust design is more consistent in its execution than the legends are. The rather inconsistent spelling of the kings' names is demonstrated by Miles's and Pliego's catalogs and is discussed succinctly in the volume of *Medieval European Coinage*, which deals with the early Middle Ages.[301] What should be added here is that inconsistencies in spelling

297 Images adapted from selections in Mantis, the digital database for the ANS collection (numismatics.org.search, accessed August 22, 2019): 1/ 2016.29.9 (Leovigild-Toleto) 2/ 2015.48.41 (Reccared-Cordoba) 3/ 2015.48.20 (Leovigild-Emerita) 4/ 2013.40.1 (Sisebut – Tarragona) 5/ 2016.29.4 (Leovigild-Rodas).

298 Miles, *The Coinage of the Visigoths*, 51 referred to two sub-types with close resemblance to busts on coins of Constantine IV, r. 668-685 (2 a and d in ibid., 55). An earlier likeness can be found, namely their resemblance to tremisses of Constans II (641-668). Compare, for example, the Reccesvinth-Bracara coin in Miles, pl. XXVIII.9 with the one of Constans II in Grierson, *Byzantine Coins*, 510-12 and pl. 28. Similarly, Pliego, *La Moneda visigoda*, v. 1, 167 (fig. 95) and 171f (fig. 97).

299 Some of the Byzantine influences apparent in Visigothic Spain are dealt with in Hillgarth, "Coins and Chronicles"; see Barral i Altet, *La circulation*, 62 specifically on Byzantine artistic and numismatic influence. The copying of the depiction of the head of Christ in the late seventh century is treated in Grierson, *Coins of Medieval Europe*, 23 and Grierson and Blackburn, *Medieval European Coinage*, v. 1, 51.

300 See Chapter Three, section C below.

301 Grierson and Blackburn, *Medieval European Coinage* (v. I), 52. For expanded remarks on spelling see Pliego, *La Moneda visigoda*, v. 1, 175-79.

can be seen on coins produced contemporaneously at the same mints and sometimes by the same engraver.

C A Trimetallic System?

According to all of the standard works on Visigothic coinage until recently, only gold was minted in the Spanish period.[302] It was natural to think so, since gold coins are relatively abundant and easy enough to identify, whereas no silver or bronze pieces were known to have been made in post-Roman Spain.[303] The moderately numerous bronze coins found in the peninsula, when attributed at all, were usually attributed to the Empire and to the Vandals. But to some scholars, it seemed implausible that the Visigothic monetary system should have made only coins of high value. As one historian asserted, though without much archeological evidence from hoards to substantiate the notion, "coins of lower denomination must also have

302 The standard literature on regal Visigothic coinage is composed of the following works, in order of publication:
L. J. Velazquez, *Congeturas sobre las medallas de los reyes godos, y suevos de España* (Málaga: Oficina de Francisco Martinez de Aguilar, 1759), 2f, who mistakenly believed five of the authentic coins then known were silver, but added "hasta oy no se conoce alguna acuñada en otro metal: prueba de que en España los Godos dexaron correr la Moneda Romana de cobre" ("To this day we know of no minting in another metal: proof that in Spain the Goths allowed the flow of Roman copper money"); A. Heiss, *Description générale des monnaies des rois wisigoths d'Espagne* (Paris: Imprimerie Nationale, 1872); Felipe Mateu y Llopis, *Catálogo de las monedas previsigodas y visigodas del Gabinete numismático del Museo arqueológico nacional* (Madrid: Imp. Gongora, 1936); Wilhelm Reinhart, "Die Münzen des westgotischen Reiches von Toledo," *Deutsches Jahrbuch für Numismatik* 3-4 (1940-41), 69-101, and "Nuevas aportaciones a la numismática visigoda," *Archivo Español de Arqueología* 18 (1945), 212-35; George C. Miles, *The Coinage of the Visigoths*; L. G. de Valdeavellano, "La moneda y la economía de cambio en la península ibérica desde el siglo VI hasta mediados del siglo XI," in *Moneta e scambi nell' alto medioevo* (Spoleto: Presso la sede del Centro, 1961), 203-30; O. Gil Farrés, "La moneda sueva y visigoda," in *Historia de España*, v. 3, ed. R. Menéndez Pidal (3rd ed.; Madrid: Espasa Calpe, 1963), 177-91; X. Barral i Altet, *La circulation des monnaies suèves et visigotiques* (Munich: Artemis Verlag, 1976). Grierson and Blackburn, *Medieval European Coinage* (Cambridge: Cambridge University Press, 1986) carries the old view of monometallism, as does Blackburn, "Money and Coinage," v. 2, 531, but brief treatment of Crusafont's evolving work is given in Ph. Grierson, *Coins of Medieval Europe* (London: Seaby, 1991). Miles wrote (p. 154): "Nor is there any genuine Visigothic copper or bronze coinage, and again the plentiful Celtiberian and Roman bronze must have served for small change."

303 Mateu y Llopis, *Catálogo*, 295, 327, 395f, was of the opinion that a few of the known silver coins were contemporary with the Visigothic series, but were perhaps not products of official mints. Miles dismissed these as forgeries.

circulated."[304] These scholars argued that Roman silver or bronze coins were still used in the Visigothic period.[305] To others, the monometallic currency system was another sign of the decline of commerce in the early Middle Ages.

In recent decades, a Spanish numismatist has demonstrated that minting under the Goths was not monometallic. Starting in 1984, Miquel Crusafont i Sabater began to publish his discoveries of 'copper' pieces, better referred to as bronze, which gave indication of a Visigothic origin.[306] Rough likenesses to gold typology on both sides of many of the base metal pieces directed much of Crusafont's analysis. His later monograph provided an early systematic treatment of the coins and their Visigothic attribution, which, over time, has generally won acceptance.[307] The evidence lay both in new hoards and in a re-examination of a few old hoards in which bronze coins had been mistakenly attributed to other peoples or left uncategorized. Crusafont's initial discoveries eventually led to the amassing of a 'working corpus' of 229 specimens of what were deemed various denominations of *nummi* (one nummus through pentanumion), simple in their design and their execution, but for the most part easily distinguishable from other like pieces of late antiquity; now, several

304 P.D. King, *Law and Society in the Visigothic Kingdom* (Cambridge: Cambridge University Press, 1972), 193.

305 Cf. Mateu y Llopis, *Catálogo*, 184f (also quoting Pío Beltrán, who follows the opinion of others before him) and Miles, *The Coinage of the Visigoths*, 154 (see n. 32).

306 The terms copper and bronze are used here, as by Crusafont, without technical precision since the metallic content has only recently been tested, and only on a sample from the Seville region. Some uncertainties regarding composition and nomenclature is generally true for late Roman and early Byzantine copper-based alloys, which sometimes varied: see Kent, *The Roman Imperial Coinage*, v. 10, 17. But the purportedly Visigothic base metal specimens appear safely in the category of bronze, a mix of copper with some amount of tin; technically, they are high-leaded bronze. Lead may improve the casting properties of bronze slightly, but lead is poorly miscible in copper. As a result, the cast flans would have uneven composition, causing variation in malleability, resistance to corrosion, etc. Clearly the emphasis was on making cheap flans easily, rather than on a high-quality product or on the intrinsic value of the coins. (My thanks to David Yoon for clarification on this matter.) For test results showing a nearly equal mix of copper and lead, plus 5-10 per cent tin, see Álvaro Fernández-Flores, et al., "Nuevos hallazgos de bronces visigodos en la provincia de Sevilla: Una aproximación metrológica y de composición metálica," *Journal of Archaeological Numismatics* 3 (2013), 275-304 at 293f; see Miquel de Crusafont et al., "Silver Visigothic Coinage," *Numismatic Chronicle* 176 (2016), 241-60 and pll. 28f, at 259f for the various metallic levels in Visigothic gold and silver coinage.

307 Miquel Crusafont i Sabater, *El sistema monetario visigodo: Cobre y oro* (Barcelona, 1994), preceded by: "¿Un numerario visigodo de cobre?," *Gaceta Numismática* 74-75 (1984), 131-41; "The Copper Coinage of the Visigoths of Spain," in *Problems of Medieval Coinage in the Iberian Area*, v. 3, ed. M. Gomes Marques and D. M. Metcalf (Santarém: Instituto Politécnico de Santarém, 1988), 35-88; "The Copper Coinage of the Visigoths of Spain: New Evidence," *Spinks Numismatic Circular* 98 (no. 9, Nov. 1990), 303-04.

hundred more are known, though many await proper study and publication and the majority are without specific archeological information.[308]

Crusafont had to answer the question why no one had ever known before of the Visigothic bronze coinage, if, in fact, it was always there. One reason is that the images on the coins are normally hard to make out; bronze coins were made with less precision than gold coins and are corroded and more worn. They also do not have full inscriptions that make them as readily identifiable as some other bronze coinages. Compared to the tremisses they are small, rarely measuring more than thirteen millimeters in width and often between five and ten millimeters. At a supposed value of 1/2333 of a gold tremissis, there was little reason to include them in hoards of gold money. Furthermore, most have little market value today by reason of their minimal intrinsic worth and their comparatively dull appearance. For these reasons, therefore, no one was looking for them. When they have survived, they have been deemed negligible.[309]

Minting of bronze in Visigothic Spain is understood by the locations of a progressive number of finds that have occurred in several far southern cities as well as in cities of the southern half of the eastern coast.[310] While most of the unearthed coins are from Seville and its surrounding area, many have also been found across the center-south of Spain and especially in Málaga.[311] Crusafont's basic find pattern has thereby been confirmed, though, of course, the continuing search for bronze may enlarge the find zones. Discovery sites, including within Byzantine Spania, but also occasional finds as far as Arles and even the Peloponnese, portray a distribution wider

308 Fernández-Flores et al., "Nuevos hallazgos de bronces," 276 n. 5 notes over a thousand recovered from two locations within Seville.

309 Later Roman lower denomination equivalencies to gold is notoriously difficult, and the proposed value should be seen merely as a suggestion and, in any case, not applicable at all times. We should note that Crusafont's own search was greatly aided by one large and rich find of coppers washed up by heavy rains in a rural town fifteen km from Seville, called Salteras. If he were not notified of this chance discovery, his case would have progressed much more slowly. Cf. Crusafont, *El sistema*, 17f. On the difficulties in finding the small currency and how sifting and metal detectors are together the keys to effective recoveries, see Fernández-Flores et al., "Nuevos hallazgos de bronces," 296f.

310 A lack of finds in central-western Spain dampens Crusafont's attributions to urban locations there.

311 See Pliego, "The Circulation of Copper Coins," 137, Fig. 6, a map of finds before and after 1994. Fernández-Flores et al., "Nuevos hallazgos de bronces" covers new finds of the Seville área until a few years ago. Crusafont et al., "Silver Visigothic Coinage," 244f, citing many coins found in Málaga, Cadiz and other sites in the far south, though the reference to Málaga should be qualified by the explanation in Pliego, "The Circulation of Copper Coins," 140f of a confusion of a distinct type from Crusafont's original Cordoba group found in Málaga.

than originally known.[312] With recent finds, the classification Crusafont established has expanded from his twelve groups to Pliego's sixteen, but continuing discoveries will extend this further since there are already new types among the unpublished large, private collections.[313]

Mint attribution presents a major challenge. Crusafont's attribution to Seville has found common agreement because the majority of finds he published are from the area, many of which have the initials SP or SPL on reverse, abbreviations for ISPALI used on gold coins and in epigraphy as well.[314] His attributions to Toleto and Emerita are not obvious. For these, the interpretations of the design as monograms of the respective cities must be considered a stretch in the most favorable light, but Toleto should be considered less sure. Given the few specimens with other designs, Crusafont offered with appropriate caution three more possible sites of bronze minting: Cordoba, Bracara (= Braga), and Egitania (= Idanha a Velha in modern central Portugal).[315] These might eventually prove convincing but, as in the case of his first 'SP' coins, await a greater number of substantiated and photographed finds in order to be verified. Some confusion rooted in subtle, overlooked type distinction has led to new mint ascriptions, but these remain just as tentative.[316] A larger problem is the lack of finds in the cities of Crusafont's assignments apart from Seville, and the pattern of new finds has impeded any corroboration on these supposed points of origin. However, because the obverse busts of the bronzes in question

312 T. Marot, "La península ibérica en los siglos V-VI: consideraciones sobre provisión, circulación y usos monetarios," *Pyrenae* nos. 31-32 (2000-2001), 133-60, at 145.

313 Pliego, "The Circulation of Copper Coins," 127-29, including a list with descriptions and cross-references, plus photos on 128; also ibid., 131, Fig. 4, a convenient chart of all Crusafont groups with additional information on values, locations of finds, and suggested reign when each group started. A few notable collections from Seville and the surrounding area are De la Oliva (close to 300), Cores, Tonegawa.

314 Pliego, "The Circulation of Copper Coins," 142f demonstrates why the last remains of doubt in this particular case should be abandoned.

315 Crusafont, *El sistema*, 62f. With just six specimens, he only tentatively attributed to Córdoba the minting of coppers whose busts resemble unique Cordoban gold coin types. The other possible attributions, to Braga and Egitania, rest on the similarity of the busts to tremissis designs employed mainly at these mints, and in the case of Braga, on the letters BR. One is left to wonder what happened to the author's proposed bronze mint at Acci, suggested on the basis of a bronze coin with the letter A on the reverse: idem, "Copper Coinage...: New Evidence," 304. Somewhat arbitrarily, Mora "Old and New Coins" has moved Crusafont's attributions surrounding Córdoba to Málaga.

316 See Pliego, "The Circulation of Copper Coins," 140f.

closely resemble those on tremisses from these cities, the matter remains inconclusive.[317]

At this time, the few mints issuing bronze currency seem to have been located mainly in the central-south region of the kingdom, possibly with a few also active along a western strip.[318] The exciting aspect of all this is that our knowledge is growing with the fast pace of discovery. A guide for now is the apparent local movement of the majority of the bronzes, which suggests their very purpose was attached to the same locale in which they were made. In Chapter Seven, this clue will add to the discussion of money and the economy in early medieval Spain as part of the Mediterranean domain. The picture of regional differentiation in whether, how, and when to strike bronze should not be surprising. Regional differentiation and even disunity are a common feature in the literature. Variation is evident in a number of ways, such as topography, commercial engagement, minting styles and metrology of gold currency, religious patterns, as well as in manifestations of independence demonstrated in southern cities of the latter half of the sixth century, for instance.

Who was behind the many issues in bronze? Naturally, the types and of course inscriptions of any sort might offer a hint, especially when compared as a whole with the gold currency which clearly had centralized, royal direction. Initials and monograms had long been employed on Roman and Byzantine currency, and the practice was copied at times by barbarian mints in the West. Cruciform monograms introduced on Byzantine bronzes in the sixth century can be confidently said to have inspired similar forms on the bronzes struck in Spain and Merovingian France in this era, and later found vigorous expression on the kingdom's gold currency, starting under Chindasvinth and Reccesvinth.[319] The multiple factors suggesting Ispali as

317 See Appendix I, Figure I.6 (= Crusafont i Sabater, *El sistema monetario*, 35, plate I) for the remarkable similarity of designs on copper and gold coins. Most Visigothic bronzes do not have inscriptions, with the exception of clear monograms and those Crusafont assigned to Emerita bearing partial inscriptions, discussed below. Crusafont's attributions to Emerita and Toleto rest primarily on the basis of claimed monograms on the reverse emerging from a stylized M or T in combination with the other letters in the city names.

318 Cf. Crusafont, *El sistema*, 29, Map I (finds of bronze coinage of the Visigoths, Vandals, and Byzantines) and 41, Map II (gold mints at which tremissis types could have provided the model for bronze coin designs). For a more up-to-date geography of finds, see Marot, "La península ibérica"; Pliego, "The Circulation of Copper Coins"; and Crusafont et al., "Silver Visigothic Coinage."

319 Beginnings under Justinian: Grierson, *Byzantine Coins*, 33; Grierson and Mays, *Late Roman Coins*, 80. On the inspiration and development of Visigothic monograms, see Crusafont, *El sistema*, 50-59; Ildar Garipzanov, "Monograms as Graphic Signs of Authority on Early Medieval Coins (from the Mid-Fifth to Seventh Centuries)," in *Graphic Signs of Identity, Faith, and Power*

the predominant center of bronze emissions, in addition to the prodigious ecclesiastical stature of the city, inspired an attractive explanation. When Crusafont first reported the finds, he conjectured that the Visigothic bronze currency, so much of which displays a cross on the reverse, was episcopal. He noted that the cities to which bronze minting is attributed were invariably bishoprics. The hypothesis is plausible because the government of towns in Spain, as elsewhere in the Mediterranean world in the early Middle Ages, was in the hands of royal officials and bishops.[320] From this perspective, the episcopal attribution of bronzes made sense. In Spain, the authority of the Catholic bishops among their people had been strengthened in some respect under the Arian regime because of the defensive posture they were forced to take up against the minority rulers. Cities in the later sixth and seventh centuries were no longer the same thriving centers of trade and civic pride that they had been in the first centuries of the Roman Empire. Rather, they were generally small, fortified enclaves concentrated near churches and episcopal palaces.[321]

While Crusafont had not abandoned the notion of an episcopal origin of this minting by the time he wrote his fuller study, he emphasized instead the growing evidence of its urban context. The inscription CIVITA was then pieced together from remaining letters on coins attributed to Emerita.[322]

in Late Antiquity and the Early Middle Ages, ed. I. Garipzanov et al. (Turnhout: Brepols, 2017), 325-50, esp. 344.

320 There is an excellent example of this in the surviving inscription of the repair of the bridge at Emerita in 483, carried out by both the count of the city, Salla, and the bishop of Emerita, Zeno: J. Vives, ed., *Inscripciones cristianas de la España romana y visigoda*, 2nd ed. (Barcelona: Consejo Superior de Investigaciones Científicas, 1969), 126f, no. 363.

321 See Kulikowski, *Late Roman Spain*, esp. 287-309, on the shifting urban topography. The essay in Collins, *Visigothic Spain*, 213-22, offers useful points even if the archeological citations are somewhat dated (see the review by M. Kulikowski, *English Historical Review* 123 (2008), 160-61. Cf. Roger Collins, *Spain: An Oxford Archaeological Guide* (Oxford: Oxford University Press, 1998), 18 and passim (i.e. what can be inferred from the differences between Roman and early medieval urban excavations); also the numerous articles in *Complutum y las ciudades hispanas en la antigüedad tardía*, ed. Luis García Moreno and Sebastián Rascón Marqués (Actas del encuentro hispania en la antigüedad tardía, Alcalá de Henares, 16 de octubre de 1996) (Alcalá, 1997). While suggestive on many points, older works such as these latter must be treated with caution since archeological advances recommend altered views. On the transformation of towns in this period in the Mediterranean in general see the discussion and bibliographical notes in Averil Cameron, *The Mediterranean World in Late Antiquity, AD 395-600* (London: Routledge, 1993), 152-75 and 227-32.

322 A form of this word was inscribed on the dies for certain Merovingian tremisses. "*Civitas* (CIVI, CIVE, etc.) was reserved for places that had once been Roman administrative centres and in the Frankish period were all episcopal sees": Grierson and Blackburn, *Medieval European Coinage*, v. 1, 120.

Finds of increasing number all came from in or around major cities in a relatively confined area. At the same time, it had become clearer that royal busts on tremisses were a model for the obverses of the bronzes, some of which he now attributed to the mint of Toleto. He related the cross designs to the crosses on the reverse of gold coins issued under Leovigild (from c. 579 to 584) and his successors of a few decades later (from c. 653 to c. 713). The question is whether the production of this currency was under the close control of the Visigothic kings as was the case with the gold tremisses. Crusafont presumed that the minting of bronze was not without royal sanction,[323] yet none of the coins unequivocally bear regal names and there are none of the titles that appear on the gold coinage. He concluded that it was a secondary production running parallel to the precious metal mintings in selective cities, carried out mainly at central mints that were located in either provincial capitals or important administrative centers.[324] As in other early medieval kingdoms, most if not all of the bronze currency in Visigothic Spain was indeed probably municipal in character, the initiative of local inhabitants, albeit not necessarily a practice only of major centers.[325] Precisely in the southern part of Spain, cities of Crusafont's attribution such as Seville, Cordoba and Málaga, rebellions and autonomy were prevalent. That these cities would instigate their own base metal coinage is therefore not out of character.[326] The purpose of the coinage was to supply a need for currency smaller than gold coins in cities with significant commercial

323 Crusafont, *El sistema*, 60. Castro, "Los hallazgos numismáticos," 135: Bronzes of various origins from the sixth century still circulated in the seventh century. The regal authorities were not going to try to eliminate a residual circulation of low-value coinage that was quite separate from the king's monetary emission.

324 Crusafont demonstrates that the four bronze mints to which the most specimens were identified correspond to the four main gold mints: ibid., 45. Córdoba was not a provincial capital, but was a city of great importance and had a major mint. Egitania was the principal town of a large area in the westerly zone where bronze money was struck. Cf. Miles, *The Coinage of the Visigoths*, 115f.

325 Pliego "The Circulation of Copper Coins," 142f agrees with the bulk of the scholarship on this point, but wisely cautions that we should not assume with Crusafont that only significant cities struck base metal coins. On bronze of the Merovingian, Burgundian, Ostrogothic, and Vandal kingdoms – the latter two believed to have had municipally-issued bronze initially, before it came under apparent regal authority – see Grierson and Blackburn, *Medieval European Coinage*, v. 1, 21-23; Crusafont, *El sistema*, 65; and Michael F. Hendy, "From Public to Private: The Western Barbarian Coinages as a Mirror of the Disintegration of Late Roman State Structures," *Viator* 19 (1988), 29-78, here p. 44.

326 Autonomous local governments primarily in the southern-central Spain, is a phenomenon discussed earlier in this chapter. See also Marot, "La península ibérica," 146.

activity.[327] Ecclesiastical authorities could have been involved in some of this minting.[328] Such a connection makes sense, especially if we consider that the Church was regularly in possession of a large proportion of movable and immovable wealth and would thereby already be entangled monetarily. It remains a fact that where archeological contexts of the bronzes are known, in several cities finds can be associated with episcopal church complexes, though exactly how these were related is not known.

We may never know exactly the entire chronology of Visigothic minting of bronze coins. They appear to have circulated alongside Justinianic currency, a strong if not altogether precise indication of the chronology of the initial bulk of the currency. A handful of Hermenegild bronzes, as discerned from the letters ERM on reverse, solidifies the original attribution by Crusafont to the famous rebel prince some time very near his rebellion in 579.[329] A very recent attribution of a bronze piece with monogram now links Leovigild with issue as well. Royal names appeared on bronze currency in all the barbarian kingdoms of continental western Europe at least briefly, so the appearance of the Visigothic kings' names is not surprising.[330] Type similarity between a whole set of bronzes and Leovigild tremisses designs, the profile bust and cross-on-steps then the facing bust, occurred precisely in that same limited time frame and in the same southern cities linked to bronze series. Together with an attribution to Reccared based on a monogram that corresponds most plausibly with that name in the current state of knowledge, a chronology for some of the coins from approximately 580 to

327 Crusafont, *El sistema*, 64f.

328 Ibid.; Marot, "La península ibérica," 145; Pliego, "The Circulation of Copper Coins," 142f, 149f. Since the distinct specimens (simple cross and *delta* on either side) that appear to have been produced at Cartagena lack imperial imagery or epigraphy, the leading specialist on the matter posits an initiative of traders in the city who may have had ecclesiastical support. M. Lechuga Galindo, "Una aproximación a la circulación monetaria de época tardía en Cartagena: Los hallazgos del teatro romano," in *V Reunió d'Arqueologia Cristiana Hispànica: Cartagena, 16-19 d'abril de 1998* (Monografíes de la secció histórico-arqueologica 7), ed. J. M. Gurt and N. Tena (Barcelona: Institut d'Estudis Catalans, 2000), 342; see also Pliego, "The Circulation of Copper Coins," 152-55.

329 Pliego, "The Circulation of Copper Coins," 148 and 154 concurs, keeping to her regal chronology in supposing Hermenegild took the lead, establishing the pattern for other Seville emissions with letter abbreviations; but of course the order could be the other way around as I have propounded in my regal chronology above in Figure 9, with Hermenegild following a practice already in place (see ibid., 151 for the possibility of much earlier minting).

330 Leovigild: Pliego, "Kings' Names on Visigothic Bronze Coins: A New Minimus from Ispali in the Name of Leovigild," *American Journal of Numismatics* 30 (2018), 245-58. Other barbarian bronze currency: idem, "The Circulation of Copper Coins," 144f.

600 can be stated confidently.[331] This might be the starting point of bronzes in Visigothic Spain, though the total evidence of all bronzes in circulation in the kingdom makes a start several decades earlier in some cities appear more likely.[332] As for how long they lasted, as Pliego asserts, despite scholars regarding the Visigothic bronzes as strictly sixth-century productions, type evidence makes seventh-century emissions a near certainty and nothing prevents the conclusion of their being used throughout the duration of the kingdom.[333] In fact, very late ancient bronze currency in general makes this highly probable. At the time of Chindasvinth and Reccesvinth (r. 649-653) at the earliest, the bronze coinage underwent a change of weights and types, some of the latter beginning to resemble those of the gold currency.[334] Production also seems to have increased then, to judge from the number of known coins of these types. Minting of bronze in Toleto is thought to have begun during Wamba's reign (672-680).[335]

With some clarity on timing, attribution, and authorization, we take up the overall problem of whether it is appropriate to call these coins in question 'Visigothic bronzes'. Pliego's answer in the affirmative makes good sense. Even if the authorization seldom or perhaps never came from the king or the royal minting establishment, since we call all denominations by other early medieval kingdoms by the barbarian group name, the appellation 'Visigothic bronzes' is fitting.[336] Still, it requires caution. So too does speaking in terms

331 Pliego, "The Circulation of Copper Coins," 138-40 carefully picks apart the circular reasoning that has prevailed, *contra* Crusafont, largely founded on site chronology, which, in turn, is sometimes based on coinage of uncertain date; on the limits of archeological contexts for dating see ibid., 135. Pliego notes that "the chronological implications of typology have been overlooked, perhaps because of the rigidity of Crusafont's scheme," and offers five main conclusions that can be safely established on the time ranges of several types, though it must be said they themselves require certain assumptions. On Leovigild-era types and for the reconsideration of the coin with monogram R-C-D-(R?), earlier posited by Pliego as a Córdoba emission, as instead bearing Reccared's name: ibid., 148f.

332 Crusafont et al., "Silver Visigothic Coinage," 255-58 propose two narrow ranges for the beginning of bronze emissions: Leovigild's reign and Achila's reign, so roughly 570 or 550. One useful observation either way is that "the wide range of varieties and metrologies suggests that they were minted for a long time" (p. 258). Worth noting is that these varieties would match the oscillations in Leovigild's gold emissions. See below on silver for the argument that the emergence of bronze minting was related to the termination of the silver minting of the mid-sixth century.

333 Pliego, "The Circulation of Copper Coins," 139f. Vandal and Ostrogothic *nummi* still circulating into the seventh century lends perfect credibility to an extended use – not to mention manufacture – of Visigothic low-value coinage.

334 See Appendix I, Figure I.6, which reproduces photographs from Crusafont, *El sistema*.

335 Crusafont, *El sistema*, 32, 50f, 63f.

336 Pliego, "The Circulation of Copper Coins," 153f. B. Mora Serrano, "Old and New Coins in Southern Hispania in the 6th Century AD," in *Produktion und Recyceln von Münzen in der*

of a 'Visigothic system'. If one thinks of the system as the gamut of monetary realities, then the bronzes were part of a system, or the money made, used, and circulated. There is no evidence that the monarchy disapproved of the minor currency operating in numerous localities. But, as there is little sign of parallels between the bronze currency and gold currency with respect to volume or far-flung distribution or regal character, aside perhaps from a limited sample from the late 500s, the term 'system' should not be taken to indicate royally driven minting as in the case of gold currency. Although the bronze appears to have been overwhelmingly, if not exclusively, unofficial, the gold-bronze dual currency during most of the Kingdom of Toledo period put Spain in sync with the fifth-century Roman system made up of the same metals,[337] as well as with that of other barbarian states, though these were far from uniform in coin varieties. To take one example, the world's preeminent scholar of early medieval Italian coinage maintains the same sort of autonomous local response to monetary necessity in Italy under the Lombards.[338]

In 2014, the discovery of a hoard of silver coins added an unsuspecting monetary dimension to the Kingdom of Toledo. Six silver coins were found on a coastal site in Les Tres Cales (mod. L'Ametlla de Mar, Tarragona), 150 km southwest of Barcelona and some thirty km northeast of Tortosa, near a vessel that seems to have contained these as well as a few Visigothic pre-regal tremisses in the name of Justinian. With an average diameter of eight mm and average weight of 0.068 g, the coins' extremely small size presents an anomaly; even the quarter *siliquae* of the Ostrogoths (usually between 0.6-0.8 g) weighed many times more. The only similar silver issues by post-Roman kingdoms in the West were by the Lombards, which had an anonymous series of 12-13 mm and between 0.13 and 0.26 g.[339] The type imagery resembles

Spätantike. RGZM – TAGUNGEN 29, ed. J. Chameroy and P.-M. Guihard (Mainz: Schnell & Steiner, 2016), 139–53 at 149, however, differs: "Therefore, we do not agree with its designation as 'Visigothic bronze/copper coinage,' as the use and production of these *nummi* is extraneous to the monetary policy of *Regnum Visigothorum*."

337 Pliego, "The Circulation of Copper Coins," 142: The imperial minting of that time "only consisted of high value gold coins – *solidus, semissis, tremissis* – and low value base metal *nummi*." Citing S. Moorhead, "Ever Decreasing Circles," 603.

338 Pliego, "The Circulation of Copper Coins," 146, citing E. Arslan, "Ancora sulla questione della cosiddetta 'moneta in rame nell'italia longobarda'. Una replica e problem di metodo," *Rivista Italiana di Numismatica* 108 (2007), 11-28, at 11.

339 See Crusafont et al., "Silver Visigothic Coinage," 241 and 252-55 for physical characteristics and comparison. Variance with other early medieval silver affords greater assurance of their origin in Visigothic Spain. Another unrelated silver in the name of Anastasius is described in ibid., 253. Crusafont's suggestion that it is possibly a one-eighth silique is confused, since he states

very crude versions of the pre-regal gold coinage of the period and helps to distinguish them from imitation fractional silver coinage in the name of Justinian. There is a resemblance in the letter forms (I and V or Λ) of their indecipherable inscriptions to the jumbled pseudo-imperial tremisses or the '*curru*' series in or near the early years of Leovigild's sole reign.

Because the most recent unearthing of silver pieces was near Barcelona and that city served as the Visigothic capital in mid-century, Crusafont and his co-authors suppose they were minted there. The three other known silver specimens thought to be Visigothic were probably minted in Narbonne prior to that. Accepting an order of issues indicated by a change in type, the authors see a lowering of weight to the point that a new denomination, well below a siliqua, was created, in parallel with the paring down of gold currency to the tremissis alone befitting a reduced degree of exchange.[340] The rare Visigothic silver emissions probably ceased at some point during or before Leovigild's monarchy. Leovigild's reign, as we have seen, was a moment of experimentation and change in the currency of Visigothic Spain. It makes sense to see the rapid cessation of silver minting and the dawn of bronze emissions based on the question of practicality; the miniscule size of the precious-metal coinage cannot have been very convenient.[341] The query has been raised whether the frequent reference to *siliquae* – late Roman silver coins – in the laws and in the much-discussed document *De Fisco Barcinonensi* (592) about tax collection is merely to a unit of account, as has almost invariably been claimed. It is proposed that the literary evidence may signify actual coins from not only the fifth century but the sixth as well.[342] This is doubtful. If the references are taken to be to hard money, however, the very few discoveries of silver and the greater number of contemporary written references to solidi should not lead to exaggerated estimation of silver currency.

(255) "siliquae usually ranged from 1 to 1.4 grams," and eighths should range from 0.12 to 0.175 g. One other Justinian-era silver specimen found in Barcelona was published: T. Marot, "La ciudad de Barcino durante los siglos V y VI: Nuevas aportaciones sobre el circulante," *Anejos de Archivo Español de Arqueología* 20 (1999), 415-22, at 420; see also idem, "La península ibérica," 147.

340 Crusafont et al., "Silver Visigothic Coinage," 255f. Whether the coins actually followed the Byzantine model of the silique and its fractions as asserted is left doubtful by the invariably tiny size and weight of the known pieces.

341 Ibid., 256-58. The article places the start of the bronze and concomitant end of silver minting in approximately 550, but observes the possibility the tiny silvers commenced under Leovigild while bronze mintings were already occurring according to similarities of type with gold coins. For now, the sequentialism, assuming cause and effect between the two denominations, must be recognized as hypothetical.

342 Marot, "La península ibérica," 147.

The discovery of bronze and silver coinage enables us to see that the Visigothic monetary system was very similar to that of other barbarian kingdoms of Western Europe. Coppers or bronzes were produced under the Merovingian, Burgundian, Ostrogothic, Lombard and Vandal kings. However, none of these coinages was being issued when Visigothic bronzes first appeared if, in fact, this occurred just about 580.[343] Visigothic minting from around Leovigild's reign on gives the impression of having directly imitated the bimetallic system of Byzantium, and therefore no longer included silver currency,[344] unlike the Merovingian and Lombardic systems in the late sixth century and the Ostrogothic up until the mid-550s. The weights of Byzantine base metal coins cannot be exactly defined because they vary even within the same denomination. Although Visigothic bronzes also varied in weight, Crusafont attempted to establish at least an approximate equivalency to copper or bronze units used by Byzantine mints.[345] This is perhaps the murkiest part of his study. His conclusion regarding the general relationship of Visigothic and foreign bronze is more useful. Small Byzantine, Ostrogothic, and Vandalic base metal coins have increasingly been found in recent years in Spain, not least of all in the south and on the eastern littoral. Crusafont supposed they were brought by the Byzantines during their occupation of this territory starting in the 550s, after the Empire had regained control of Italy and North Africa, and lasting until c. 625.[346] It can be affirmed that many, though not all, were injected into the Iberian economy at that time.

As we shall see in the next chapter, southern Spain is where several large cities were located and where the majority of Visigothic gold coins were produced across numerous mints, as indicated by the evidence. Based on evidence that the foreign bronze began drying up in the same period in which the Visigothic bronze coins emerged, Crusafont suggested that some cities within the kingdom started to satisfy the need for small change by themselves when it was no longer being provided by the Byzantine presence. There is some basis for this conclusion, though archeological

343 See the chart in Pliego, "The Circulation of Copper Coins," 145 and the chapters on the various kingdoms in Grierson and Blackburn, *Medieval European Coinage*, v. 1, and the chapters on western coinages of the fifth, sixth, and seventh centuries in Grierson, *Coins of Medieval Europe*.

344 Crusafont, *El sistema*, 83. Cf. Crusafont et al., "Silver Visigothic Coinage," 256-58.

345 Crusafont, *El sistema*, 47. I.e. he does not consider the *nummus* as a coin but as a unit of .3 g, on which the different Visigothic, Byzantine, and Vandal denominations are based.

346 Crusafont, *El sistema*, has 552, but the date of 554 for the invasion is now to be preferred, as discussed in Jason Fossella, "'Waiting Only for a Pretext'."

research of the past few decades allows us to elaborate on many aspects of the fifth- and sixth-century influx of bronze currency into the Visigothic kingdom and explore its larger implications.[347] Crusafont and co-authors more recently propounded a shortage of gold and bronze, the first based on the fact that foreign gold currencies of the Sueves and Merovingian Franks were not re-minted, the latter on joint circulation of Visigothic with Byzantine bronze coinage.[348] In Spain, the circulation of three metals from all over the Mediterranean clearly occurred for most of the sixth century. In the seventh century, whether or not the acceptance of foreign coinage changed, monetary circulation appears to have been reduced primarily to the kingdom's own gold – with occasional exceptions and a continuation of some Byzantine Spanish gold until the takeover of Spania in c. 625 – and bronze from various foreign origins until almost this time and a resurgence of Visigothic bronze minting not long after the Byzantine presence ended.

We eagerly await more revelations about the bronze coinage of early medieval Spain as new specimens are discovered. Even if our knowledge about this currency is still developing, already some inferences can be drawn from it, as we have seen. Certain conclusions based on the complete absence of bronze can be shown to be wrong. Grierson held this absence to signify that the fully agrarian structures of Visigothic society had no need for small currency.[349] The difference between the economic situation in the 'barbarian' kingdoms and in the Byzantine Empire was, in his view, very great. Crusafont's discovery may serve to moderate this common idea. Pierre Le Gentilhomme argued that both the late western emperors and the Visigothic kings had an 'anti-social' monetary policy that concentrated on the production of gold[350] – a quite limited volume of gold, as it appeared to him in the 1940s. From what we have seen above and from the growing corpus of Visigothic gold coins discussed in the next part of this study, Le Gentilhomme's premises can be dismissed. Whether the primary purpose of the coinage of any successor states of the western Empire was public convenience – trade and storage of wealth – as opposed to enabling the state

347 Crusafont, *El sistema*, 98-107; Crusafont et al., "Silver Visigothic Coinage," 245-47. Chapter Seven below addresses Visigothic currency within the Mediterranean economic zone.
348 Crusafont et al., "Silver Visigothic Coinage," 245. The notion of 'permeability' of the kingdom's monetary system refers to its openness to foreign coins: ibid., 245 and 258. Naismith, "Gold Coinage and Its Use," 299f affirms a gold shortage in the western kingdoms with the effect of adulteration of gold currency, or in Frankish Gaul the shift to silver. A complete picture can only be achieved by also bearing in mind what transpired with low-value coinage.
349 Cf. Crusafont, *El sistema*, 95.
350 Ibid.

to collect revenues and make payments, should be considered doubtful. Barbarian gold was fiscal in nature just as Roman gold was.[351] One should not conclude, however, that commerce among ordinary people was absent or relied totally on barter. Crusafont's discovery shows that government authorities of some level were making bronze coins of a lower denomination available in parts of Visigothic Spain; these must have been intended largely to provide the medium of exchange for small commercial transactions.

351 I develop the administrative needs basis for Visigothic gold coinage, within the context of other late ancient-early medieval systems, in Chapters Four and Seven below. On the role of barbarian gold currency in general, see e.g. Hendy, "From Public to Private" and Naismith, "Gold Coinage and Its Use." Specifically on Visigothic currency, see Marques et al., *Ensaios*, 265-74; and Luis A. García Moreno, "Cecas visigodas y sistema económico," in *II^a reunió d'arqueologia paleocristiana hispànica* (Montserrat, 2 al 5 de noviembre de 1978) (Barcelona: Institut d'Arqueologia i Prehistòria, 1982), 333-45. Pliego, *La moneda visigoda*, 97-153, 187-98 and other works by the same author support the fiscal role. Naismith, "Gold Coinage and Its Use," 301-06 sees the initially primarily fiscal purpose of the gold diminishing by the seventh century, as in Merovingia.

3. The Activities of the Mints from c. 573- c. 720

Abstract
Chapter Three surveys the material aspects of coin production and explains how the minting of gold in the regal period was organized. Close to one hundred Visigothic mints are now known, although the actual site is not identified in all cases. Knowledge of the mints' organization cannot rely directly on contemporary documentation, but rather on coin types and painstaking study of styles. The chapter argues that die engravers (and their teams) were often not attached to a single mint but instead traveled across large territories for coin production at several sites. Although minting frequently followed a loose provincial or regional organization, engravers crossed into neighboring provinces. An analysis of the coins' metallic quality and its vicissitudes rounds out the chapter.

Keywords: mints; gold; types; style; weight; fineness

A The Operation of the Mints

For information on the techniques of coin production and the personnel involved at all levels in late Roman and early Byzantine minting, one can draw on written, epigraphical, and pictorial sources. By contrast, only a small amount of written material is left to inform us of those responsible for minting in the Visigothic kingdom, and nothing remains about their methods of work. For the latter, one is forced to rely on the coins manufactured at Visigothic mints, as well as on other contemporary currency that they resemble.

Kurt, A., *Minting, State, and Economy in the Visigothic Kingdom: From Settlement in Aquitaine through the First Decade of the Muslim Conquest of Spain.*
Taylor & Francis Group, 2020
DOI 10.5117/9789462981645_CH03

Material Aspects

As the successor states of the Roman West developed their own coinages in the fifth and sixth centuries, the currency kept most of the physical features of imperial coinage on which it was based. Some of the barbarian kingdoms minted coins in three metals, as Byzantium continued to do. As we have already seen, in Gothic Spain from the late sixth century onward the tremissis was the main coin and was the only gold denomination. In weight standard (1.516 grams), it conformed to the original model of the Byzantine tremissis, though the diameter of imperial issues had undergone changes by the time of Leovigild and the size of Visigothic tremisses had become much larger (usually 18-20 mm).[352] The similar appearance of Visigothic and Byzantine tremisses, aside from their use of the same types for many years, is due to similar techniques of production.

Although there are no extant dies from the Visigothic period that one can compare with dies surviving from the late Roman world, the coins themselves indicate that the technical process involved had not changed much.[353] Visigothic tremisses were made from disks of gold struck between two engraved dies. The disks were formed either by being cut out from flattened sheets of gold or – less likely – by molten gold poured into separate ingot molds.[354] No great effort was spent on making the disks perfectly round. The person who literally hammered coins into being (the *signator* or *malleator* of Roman sources)[355] held a metal punch in his hand or in a

352 Most official coins of Anastasius and Anastasius VPWs are approx. 13-14 mm in diameter, but by the time of Leovigild the Visigothic minters were using sheet-metal flans approx. 18-20 mm, while the Byzantine tremisses of Justin II are only about 14-16 mm. "The production of coins required the prior establishment of legal standard for weight and value whose acceptance was obligatory. Only a continuous relationship between the pieces and the legally instituted units of weight and account could avoid the dissipation of coins into mere metallic objects." *Seigniorage* added further to the currency value. Félix Retamero, "Coinage, Minting of," in *Medieval Science, Technology, and Medicine: An Encyclopedia*, ed. Thomas F. Glick et al. (New York: Routledge, 2005), 130f.

353 For the description of moneying in antiquity and the Middle Ages I have relied heavily on Philip Grierson, "Note on Stamping of Coins and Other Objects," in *A History of Technology*, II, ed. C. Singer et al. (London: Oxford University Press, 1956), 485-92.

354 Based on the thin width of tremisses, less thick than a US dime, it is safe to suppose they were formed from hammered sheets of metal. Cf. Pliego, *La moneda visigoda*, v. 1, 193. Other terms for the blank disks are flans, pellets, ingots, or simply blanks.

355 The exact roles of these workers, known from a set of inscriptions from 115 A.D., have been discussed at length. See Jean Lafaurie, "Familia monetaria," *Bulletin de la Société française de numismatique* (July 1972), 267-71 and Grierson and Mays, *Late Roman Coins*, 51. Late Roman terms for laborers in a mint in general, or perhaps sometimes the hammermen in particular,

clamp,[356] at the end of which was the upper die, or trussel; by the definition applied to Greek coinage this is the reverse die. One or more blows were made over the disk, which rested on a die placed in an anvil. Obverse dies generally have a longer life than reverse dies. While it is standard in the literature to equate the obverse of Visigothic tremisses with the side bearing the royal bust ('heads' in English), die breakage appears on the bust side of coins more frequently, a fact that suggests that busts might actually have been on the reverse, or upper dies. Visigothic tremisses are usually cleanly struck, without much double-striking and more or less on center. A certain degree of technical precision is also evident from the very high percentage of coins with a die-axis[357] of six o'clock or close to it, which would have been facilitated by a small mark or device on the punch.[358]

When we read the inscriptions on a medieval coin or compare one image with another, we are looking at the work of a die engraver. An artist or smith of some kind had to produce all features desired on the coins in 'intaglio,' that is, carved into the surface of both dies. When hammered into a gold blank, the dies made an impression in low relief on the coin. The engraving of dies must have been a demanding task. It is not certain whether engravers at imperial and early medieval mints cast their iron and bronze dies after heating them. Among the many Visigothic tremisses I have examined under microscope, some exhibit small deposits of rust around parts in relief, which suggests that minting under the Visigoths was done with steel or iron dies. If this were the case, carving would have been easier on an annealed surface, that is, after the metal has been heated and then slowly cooled in order to make it softer. Only a small part of die-cutting

were *aurifices solidorum* or *monetarii*: see Hendy, *Studies*, 389, 391, 393; Jones, *The Later Roman Empire*, v. I, 435ff. In Merovingian Gaul, the term *monetarius* referred to a maker of coins (but not the engraver), whose name on the coins provided a guarantee of authenticity: Grierson and Blackburn, *Medieval European Coinage*, v. 1, 97-102 and Grierson, *Coins of Medieval Europe*, 24-25.

356 The greater relief of Roman coins of the classical period required hammermen to hold their large mallets with two hands while other workers (*suppostores*) placed flans on the lower die (J. Lafaurie, "Familia monetaria," 270). In the early Middle Ages, lower relief allowed striking to be done with one hand on the hammer. See F. Panvini Rosati, "La tecnica monetaria altomedievale," *Settimane di studio del Centro Italiano de studi sull'alto medioevo* XVIII (1971), v. 2, 713-44.

357 Die axis is the relation of the reverse side to the obverse side (i.e. 'heads').

358 Miles, *The Coinage of the Visigoths*, 149ff. Variations in die axis and in the centering of the hammer blow prove that dies were not hinged together, for example on a tong. For detached dies in Merovingian depictions of minting see Jean Lafaurie, "Triens mérovingiens avec représentations d'un monétaire," *Bulletin de la Societé française de numismatique* 19 (1964), 342-43 and idem, "Flan de monnaie mérovingienne trouvé a Bordeaux," *Bulletin de la Societé française de numismatique* (May 1970), 528-30.

was actually engraving, however. Miles pointed out that much of the work on legends and devices was done by using punches with small shapes, mostly triangles, circles, and semi-circles.[359] The decorative outer rim on every tremissis was formed by a great number of hammer blows around the die on a small wedge-shaped punch. On copper coins, the rims are often sloppy and left largely off the surface, and it is obvious that less attention was paid to this currency. The simpler designs of copper pieces did not call for as much use of punches.

Mint Personnel

Though we are without contemporary sources to inform us directly about the personnel at the mints, we can at least surmise that staffs at the numerous Visigothic mints were much smaller than those at the few and very large mints of the Roman system. While steps of production similar to those used at imperial mints would still have been followed, the specialized crews of Roman and Byzantine mints were probably replaced by a few men performing several duties: die cutting, smelting, refining, hammering out sheets of gold and cutting them into disks, weighing blanks, and striking the coins.[360] The closest we come to a reference to coin makers in the Visigothic kingdom comes from a section of the law code pertaining to those who debase precious metals – *'De falsariis metallorum'*.[361] The two laws there pertaining to counterfeiters imply that the extensive team of specialized workers that existed in mints of the late Roman Empire was not necessary in order to produce passable tremisses on a much smaller scale.[362] One person might have sufficed.

359 Miles, *The Coinage of the Visigoths*, 151. An illustrated discussion of some of the specific techniques of minting craftsmanship of Visigothic and other coinages of late antiquity can be found in David Yoon, "Art, Craft, Innovation, and Efficiency: Early Medieval Minting Technology," *ANS Magazine* 14.2 (2015), 18-27.

360 On the extensive teams of workers at imperial mints see Grierson and Mays, *Late Roman Coins*, 51 and Lafaurie, "Familia monetaria". For the minting of solidi alone there were ten *officinae*, or mint divisions, at Constantinople, but this was under a structure in which palatine mints were virtually the only mints: see Grierson, *Byzantine Coins*, 51 and Hendy, *Studies*, 398-404.

361 See the discussion in Ruth Pliego, "La falsificación y manipulación de la moneda visigoda," en *Falsificació i manipulació de la moneda, XVI Curs d'Història monetaria d'Hispania* (Barcelona: Museu Nacional d'Art de Catalunya, 2010), 81-102.

362 Later Roman sources show a particular concern with the many *monetarii* engaged in counterfeiting. See Hendy, *Studies*, 321, 326f. Contemporary Visigothic forgeries did circulate with authentic coins, as observed in hoard evidence by Barral i Altet, *La circulation*, 77 n. 400 and 91; Pliego, "La falsificación," 82-84 maintains that these were probably few in number.

LV VII.6.i **Concerning the torture of slaves in place of their masters for corrupting money, and the reward of those who inform of having seen such corruption**

We do not forbid the torture of slaves in place of the lord or lady for false money, in order that the truth may be learned more easily by such torture; so that if a slave of another brings this accusation forward and what he reveals is found to be true, let him be freed if his master wishes, and his value should be given to his master by the royal treasury; but if his master does not wish to free him, three ounces of gold should be given to the slave by the treasury. But if he be a free man, he deserves six ounces of gold for revealing the truth.

LV VII.6.ii **Concerning those who have debased solidi or other money**

Whoever has debased, clipped, or shaved coins should be arrested as soon as the judge learns of it. And if he be a slave, his right hand should be cut off. But if afterwards he should be found doing the same deeds, he should be brought into the presence of the king, that sentence be carried out in whatever way the king decides concerning him [...]. But if the one who has done this be a free man, the treasury should acquire half his goods. A lower-class person will lose his freedom [...]. Whoever engraves or makes counterfeit money, whoever he may be, will fall under a similar sentence.[363]

In addition to the laws, stylistic evidence that a die cutter would often travel to several non-permanent mint sites raises the possibility that one person, or least very few people, carried out the minting duties at all but a

363 The *Leges Visigothorum* is published in Karl Zeumer, ed., *Monumenta Germaniae Historica. Leges*, Sectio I, Tome I (Hanover: Hahn, 1902), pp. 309-10. *LV* VII.6.i [Reccesvinth, Ervig]: "De torquendis servis in dominorum capite pro corruptione monete et eorum mercede, qui hoc visi extiterint revelasse. Servos torqueri pro falsa moneta in capite domini domineve non vetamus, ut ex eorum tormentis veritas possit facilius inveniri; ita ut, si servus alienus hoc prodiderit, et quod prodidit verum extiterit, si dominus eius voluerit, manumittatur, et domino eius a fisco pretium detur; si autem noluerit, eidem servo a fisco tres auri uncie dentur; si vero ingenuus fuerit, sex uncias auri pro revelata veritate merebitur." *LV* VII.6.ii [Reccesvinth, Ervig]: "De his, qui solidos et monetam adulteraverint. Qui solidos adulteraverit, circumciderit sive raserit, ubi primum hoc iudex agnoverit, statim eum conprehendat, et si servus fuerit, eidem dextera manu abscidat. Quod si postea in talibus causis fuerit inventus, regis presentie destinetur, ut eius arbitrio super eum sententia depromatur [...]. Quod si ingenuus sit qui hoc faciat, bona eius ex medietate fiscus adquirat; humilior vero statum libertatis sue perdat, cui rex iusserit servitio deputandus. Qui autem falsam monetam sculpserit sive formaverit, quecumque persona sit, simili pene sententie subiacebit."

few mints.[364] The laws raise the possibility that moneyers were goldsmiths, since the same section of the code passes from a prohibition of making false money or debasing coins to laws forbidding artists entrusted with precious metals to debase them or filch a part.[365]

There are several signs that minting was carried out locally at the site named on the coins rather than at one or more central workshops. The locations of coin finds, for the most part close to the cities whose names appear on the reverse, point to local production. This is confirmed by the absence of die links between mints. Moreover, even closely related mints exhibit differentiations in style[366] and module (diameter), in the legend (different use of letter punches, varied spellings and forms of ONO until the later sixth century), and in inscriptions related to the place of minting. The assertion that minting was local is also corroborated by the rough uniformity of metallic standards in certain places, although this is not a strict criterion to which all the coins adhere and it depends on prior categorization of coins by mint name.[367] An observation by Philip Grierson points to the same reality: "[...] one suspects that despite the general 'regal' appearance of the coinage [at peripheral mints] much really depends on local initiative."[368]

Production of coins at many non-permanent, even obscure, sites can be accounted for by the movement of die engravers from place to place, as we demonstrate in a later section of this chapter. When the Roman or Byzantine imperial court wished on occasion to open a new mint, it sent part of the

364 See section C of this chapter. Merovingian die cutters often worked for numerous moneyers in many different locations: Grierson, *Coins of Medieval Europe*, 24 and Grierson and Blackburn, *Medieval European Coinage*, v. 1, 97-102.

365 Pliego, *La moneda visigoda*, v. 1, 191 offers useful comments on the likelihood of goldsmiths' direct involvement in minting and offers ideas about the general placement of mints within the urban environment. Also on goldsmiths' probable part in minting: Ruth Pliego, "La acuñación monetaria en el Reino Visigodo de Toledo: El funcionamiento de las cecas," *Els tallers monetaris: organització y producció, XII Curs d'Historia monetaria d'Hispania* (Barcelona: Museu Nacional d'Art de Catalunya, 2008), 117-41 at 125f and idem, "La falsificación," 84f. The letters and monograms of some Visigothic signet rings, made of gold and other metals, bear some resemblance to those of the coinage. W. Reinhart, "Los anillos hispano-visigodos," *Archivo español de arqueología* 20 (no. 68, 1947), 167-78 discusses the rings and provides photos. On Merovingian goldsmiths as moneyers see Grierson and Blackburn, *Medieval European Coinage*, v. 1, 98-100.

366 Somewhat confusingly referred to by Miles as 'types,' but which I refer to as 'specific types' or 'sub-types,' by which is meant a particular design within a general type. See below in this chapter, section C.

367 See below in this chapter, section D.

368 Grierson and Blackburn, *Medieval European Coinage*, v. 1, 53. The inconsistency of the spelling of the king's name (ibid., 52) may well result from local variations.

staff from one of the existing mints.[369] In view of a certain expertise involved in minting, something similar must have occurred in the Iberian peninsula in the sixth and seventh centuries. An engraver and perhaps a small crew could have been sent out from the provincial capital, since the evidence gathered so far usually shows an engraver working at multiple sites to have worked in the capital city. The fact that Visigothic mints greatly expanded in number and were not limited essentially to the primary mints until the mid-seventh century was possibly the main reason why fineness and weights became erratic and engraving was often careless.[370] The impression one gets is that irregular minting and supervision led to irregular products.

One control device on minting is in evidence. Perhaps a third or more of Visigothic regal tremisses include control marks, as many Romano-Byzantine coins did.[371] They appear most often on tremisses from mints in the northeast. A complete study of the marks has yet to be carried out, but such an endeavor could be expected to provide clues about the organization of the mints. The evidence reviewed to this point suggests that the marks do not signal multiple engravers or multiple mints in one place, although neither possibility should be ruled out in the case of the principal cities. Nor do they regularly seem to provide an indication of separate issues, since identical marks appear on some coins of the same style but from distinct dies, with nothing else to easily distinguish them.[372] As separate control

369 Grierson and Mays, *Late Roman Coins*, 51.

370 Hendy, *Studies*, 396, extends the same observation to Merovingian coinage. See below in this chapter, sections C and D and Chapter Four, section B on reasons for the decreasing standards and artistic quality of the tremisses. Miles, *The Coinage of the Visigoths*, 151-52, reviews the poor engraving in the first half of the seventh century.

371 Control marks are any kind of symbols which allow minters or other officials to immediately identify coins according to a predetermined classification (e.g. coins minted by a certain person or within a certain year). A promising start to this field of investigation for early medieval Spain, though without definitive solutions at this stage, may be found in Peter Bartlett, Gonzalo Cores Uría and María Cruz Cores Gomendio, "The Use of Dots as Control Marks in the Coin Legends at the Visigothic Mint of Ispali During the Reign of Sisebut (612-21)," *XIII Congreso Internacional de Numismática* (Madrid: Ministerio de Cultura, 2003), 1127-33. Although Visigothic coins have an almost entirely different set of marks, one suspects a Byzantine inspiration for a few of them. For a brief treatment of contemporary Byzantine control marks see Grierson, *Byzantine Coins*, 41 and Hendy, *Studies*, 423. On late Roman control marks see Grierson and Mays, *Late Roman Coins*, 56.

372 For examples, see Miles, *The Coinage of the Visigoths*, pl. XIV, nos. 145-48; see also ibid., pl. IV, nos. 3-5, different Reccared-Barcinona issues all from the same die engraver and employing the same mint mark. In no. 6 the same engraver uses a different control mark. Also ibid., pl. XXII.1-19 (=273.a-g, excepting f): Without doubt the distinct control marks are from dies of the same die cutter. We may be certain the dies were cut at separate times because, among coins from several different dies at individual cities, there are groups which have in common

marks were used for each separate issue, it can be said that marks were not indiscriminately copied by engravers as one more feature of numismatic art. Their purpose may have been to separate the production of coinage of a certain period for the sake of counting, e.g. to count the coins of a fiscal year. Each symbol has small variations, but it is unclear whether slightly different forms should all be regarded as constituting one set of marks or not.[373]

We can only suppose that there was local supervision of minting. There must have been vigilant officials at the mints in the major cities of the kingdom, since the coins there were normally struck close to the standard weight of 1.516 grams.[374] Mint overseers in Roman times were called *procuratores monetarum*, but neither this term, nor any other has come down to us from Visigothic Spain, although the post is known to have survived in Ostrogothic Italy.[375] Merovingian kings did not make use of such officials as far as we know, but rather entrusted minting at each site to the moneyers named on the coins.[376] Over 1600 of these moneyers are known.[377] Only rarely did their products bear the king's name. By contrast, Visigothic mints from at least the reign of Leovigild onward, when tremisses were strictly royal in character,

a divergent spelling or some small distinguishing feature; there are die links between coins of the same control marks, but not between those with different marks.

373 Grierson and Blackburn, *Medieval European Coinage*, v. 1, pl. 12, nos. 221, 222 are Reccared-Ispali coins from the same engraver, with the same superscript dot at the end of the legend, but one is on the obverse side, one on the reverse side. Nos. 211 and 217 are from the same die engraver at Elvora, one dating to Leovigild's reign, the other to Reccared's; both have dots on the forehead, but the number of dots is not equal. Pl. 13, nos. 238 and 239 are tremisses of Suinthila-Emerita from the same engraver, who made a dot at the end of the reverse legend of 239 but not in that of 238. Another good example can be seen from two tremisses of Reccared from Elvora illustrated in ibid., pl. 12, nos. 217 & 218. The coins have small differences in their inscriptions (IVSTOS, PIVS), spellings (ELVORA, ERBORA), epigraphic style, and style of busts, yet are similar enough to suggest close copying (the engraver of 218 probably copied 217 or a like specimen, since the die sinker who produced 217 is known from Leovigild's reign while the engraver of 218 is not known to have existed previously). Copying did not prevent the second engraver from employing different control marks – a pair of double dots (:) in the reverse legend, instead of dots on the forehead of the king's bust.

374 See section D of this chapter.

375 On the Ostrogothic *procurator monetae* see Cassiodorus, *Variae*, VII.32 and related discussion of Ostrogothic resemblance of late Roman minting administration in Hendy, "From Public to Private," 41-45 and idem, *Studies*, 395f.

376 Grierson and Blackburn, *Medieval European Coinage*, v. 1, 101: even royal coinage was 'private,' in the sense that minting was farmed out to moneyers, whose names often appeared along with the king's.

377 Ibid.; Grierson, *Coins of Medieval Europe*, 24. According to Naismith, "Gold Coinage and Its Use," 291 there were around 2000 *monetarii* in the Merovingian period.

were clearly state-run.[378] The issuing authority was ultimately the king, not the moneyer. The developments in Leovigild's coinage reviewed above imply state control of minting. Behind the seemingly complex organization of mints elaborated in the next sections was a basic uniformity of type and inscription. Whether the moneyers in Spain still minted for private individuals, as they did during Theodoric's rule, is impossible to determine. Theodoric may or may not have been successful in eradicating this cause for complaint that he raised in a letter to the viceroys of 'the province of Hispania.'[379] Either way, it was not uncommon in the ancient world for people to bring their gold to the mints – in the form of bullion or old coins – and some scholars believe this was the normal way in which coins were made. Roman *procuratores* of the mints could not stop the practice, and Visigothic officials would have to have been extremely effective to do so.[380]

We do not know with certainty which of the king's officials was in charge of all the mints throughout the Visigothic kingdom. Laws and acts of ecclesiastical councils have left a haphazard record of the titles of several high-ranking offices. No mention is ever made of the *comes sacrarum largitionum*, the Roman and early Byzantine period official whose responsibilities included supervision of minting. The one Visigothic administrator whose title seems to correspond to such a duty is the *comes thesaurorum*, a post only known from late in the Visigothic period.[381] Overseeing the treasure(s) would presumably include overseeing not only the stocks of gold – bullion or coins – but the entire process of making coins. In the late Roman and contemporary Byzantine monetary system, which the Visigothic system resembled in many respects, *thesauri* and mints always coincided.[382]

378 García Moreno, "Cecas visigodas," 337, writes in terms of "el firme establecimiento de la regalía sobre la moneda" under Leovigild.

379 Cassiodorus, *Variae*, V.39.

380 A Roman law in 369 banned private minting, but perhaps the continued practice brought about a law of 374 that allowed it, simply requiring a fee of 1/6 of the metal for the state: Roland Delmaire, *Largesses sacrées et* res privata: *L'*aerarium *impérial et son administration du IVe au VIe siècle* (Rome, 1989), 501.

381 Only a single mention of the *comes thesaurorum* remains, in XIII Toledo of 683, though it is possible the title belonged to the chief of mint operations earlier than this. Hendy, "From Public to Private," 51 n. 69 comments, "It is tempting to regard the *com. thes.* as having been responsible for mints and *fisci* – someone of his rank must have been so responsible, and it is just possibly no coincidence that his title is identical with the Greek *komés tón (theión) thésaurón*, equivalent to the Latin *comes sacrarum largitionum*, who was certainly so responsible" (see Hendy *Studies*, 381-85, 405).

382 Hendy, *Studies*, 383-84, 389-91. Jones, *The Later Roman Empire*, v. 1, 428-30 explains the *sacrae largitiones* and its diocesan and provincial divisions: "The *sacrae largitiones* had a number of depots (*thesauri*) in the provinces, in which gold, silver, and other goods (presumably clothing)

The great number of mints in Gothic Spain seems to have necessitated a provincial or even regional division of *thesauri*, which can be equated with the term *fisci* when this refers to movable goods and not to land.[383] Who was at the head of these divisions is uncertain.[384]

It is in this regard that we must attempt to make sense of the institutional problem. There are several competing interpretations of the terms *fiscus*, *patrimonium*, and *thesaurus*, and indeed Visigothic usage of these terms can be confounding. Contemporary references are piecemeal and from different sorts of documents, at varied times, and within a variety of phrases and contexts which makes perfect certainty on the matter unattainable. The Visigothic regime looks to have conflated Roman financial departments over a long period of time,[385] while at the same time contraction is universally acknowledged. The best that might be

were collected and stored and from which they were either issued locally or transmitted to the *comitatus*." (428)

383 Evidence of the regional division is found in a document attached to the acts of a church council in 592, called '*De fisco Barcinonensi*' (José Vives, ed., *Concilios visigóticos e hispano-romanos* [Barcelona-Madrid: Consejo Superior de Investigaciones Científicas, 1963], 54). It is a letter to the Barcelona *numerarii* appointed by the *comes Patrimonii*, from the four bishops of the territories paying taxes to the fisc in Barcelona ('omnes episcopi ad civitatem Barcinonense fiscum inferentes'). The letter confirms the bishops' approval of what seems to be the rate of *adaeratio*, but whether the commutation rate or the taxation rate itself is in question, the units of payment are monetary units ('siliquae,' eighths of a triens, used as a money of account). See the discussion in Hendy, "From Public to Private," 53-56.

384 Canon 1 of II Seville (619) refers to a person who served as the *rector rerum fiscalium*. It has been supposed that this official, who is heard of only in this single instance, may have been in charge of all financial concerns within the province of Baetica: see José Orlandis, *Hispania y Zaragoza en la antigüedad tardía* (Zaragoza: Caja de Ahorros – Monte de Piedad de Zaragoza, Aragón y Rioja, 1984), 81-82; see also idem, *Historia del reino visigodo español* (Madrid: Rialp, 1988), 160 and Thompson, *Goths*, 216. How long this post was continued and whether the other provinces had it is unattested in the scant sources for Visigothic government. In his biographical sketch of Bishop Eladius, we find Ildephonsus of Toledo referring to his subject's late-sixth century service as *rector rerum publicarum*, specified as a member of the *aula regia* or highest rank of court officials: *De viris illustribus* VI, 2, ed. C. Codoñer, *El 'De viris illustribus de Ildefonso de Toledo* (Salamanca: Universidad de Salamanca, 1972). It cannot be determined definitively how these two posts relate to one another or whether they correspond in some way to the *comes Patrimonii*. A correspondence of Eladius's role with the *comes thesaurorum* has been suggested; see Amancio Isla Frez, "El *Officium Palatinum* visigodo. Entorno regio y poder aristocrático," *Hispania* LXII/3, no. 212 (2002), 823-47 at 837.

385 García Moreno, "Estudios," 23; John Haldon, *Byzantium in the Seventh Century* (Cambridge: Cambridge University Press, 1990), 190f n. 69 notes the malleability of the imperial fiscal administration as it developed. Even going back to Augustus there had been crossover between personal property (*patrimonium*), the imperial treasury (*fiscus*), and the public treasury (*aerarium*): Sitta von Reden, *Money in Classical Antiquity* (Cambridge: Cambridge University Press, 2010), 12-15.

said is that *fiscus* has different but related meanings that apparently all have to do with the totality of state, or crown, property; that is to say, not the king's personal holdings but the possessions acquired by the head of the realm and forwarded to successive rulers as such. This was the patrimony of the crown, placed under the *comes patrimonii*, which included the extractions from both royal lands as well as privately held, taxable lands – be they in kind or in specie.[386] Just as the Roman *actor rei privatae* with the charge over imperial lands had no power over the provincial population, which was taxed under the jurisdiction of the Praetorian Prefect, so in the western Gothic kingdom a separation of fiscal powers was maintained whereby the crown lands and their *actores* and *agentes* who extracted from lands worked by *servi fiscales* were separate from lands worked by *privati*, though all lands paid into the *fiscus* under direction of the *comes patrimonii*.[387] In this light, all tributary proceeds

386 Luis A. García Moreno, "Algunos aspectos fiscales de la Península Ibérica durante el siglo VI," *Hispania Antiqua* 1 (1971), 233-56 at 244-46 considers the office of *comes patrimonii* as the successor of the imperial Praetorian Prefect; similarly María del Rosario Valverde Castro, "Monarquía y tributación en la Hispania visigoda: el marco teórico," *Historia Antigua* 31 (2007), 235-51 at 246. Theodoric the Ostrogoth's *comes patrimonii* corresponded to the imperial *domus divina* who oversaw the emperor's household and personal lands, but it swelled by way of gifts, confiscations, and taxes of Sicily, Dalmatia and later Spain, and satisfied expenses of the outlying areas including army provisions: Jones, *Later Roman Empire*, I, 255f and III, 48f n. 44. For a different view, wherein taxation is thought to have been totally separate from fiscal activity – collections from the *fiscus*/royal patrimony served by *servi fiscales* – see S. Castellanos, "The Political Nature of Taxation in Visigothic Spain," *Early Medieval Europe* 12 (2003), 201–28 ("the *fiscus* was no more than the treasury of the royal patrimony": 210) and idem, "Tributa and *Historiae*: Scale and Power at a Turning Point in Post-Roman Spain," in *Scale and Scale Change in the Early Middle Ages: Exploring Landscape, Local Society, and the World Beyond*, ed. Julio Escalona and Andrew Reynolds (Turnhout: Brepols, 2016), 187-214.

387 Hence it is correct to view the *actor fiscalium patrimoniorum* (sometimes *actor fisci* [*nostri*]) of III Toledo as the superintendent in charge of royal lands, but this revenue source should be recognized as part of the entire patrimony. See García Moreno, "Estudios," 24, where it is also shown that III Toledo c. 18 makes separate mention of the royal lands, held under officials referred to as *iudices locorum*, and those held by *privati*. (The council went on to establish the election by the bishops and the people of *numerarii*, or regional taxation supervisors.) Likewise, the language of the letter known as *De fisco Barcinonensi*, from the several bishops of the cities "paying into the fisc" of that region around Barcinona, does not give any indication only royal lands were in question and instead implies that the taxes of the region's general populace were the basis of the notice. A secular law from the very same period, the reign of Reccared, differentiates the "count of the patrimony" and "administrators of our properties" (LV XII.1.2). It sought to inhibit fraudulent collections by government officials of various ranks and sectors that were apparently occurring, and begins by proclaiming that "A count, his deputy, or a royal estate overseer shall not dare to oppress the people with taxes, tributes, or labor, or compulsory requisitions for their own benefit

Figure 11: Diagram of the patrimony's divisions and the flow of proceeds into the *fiscus*

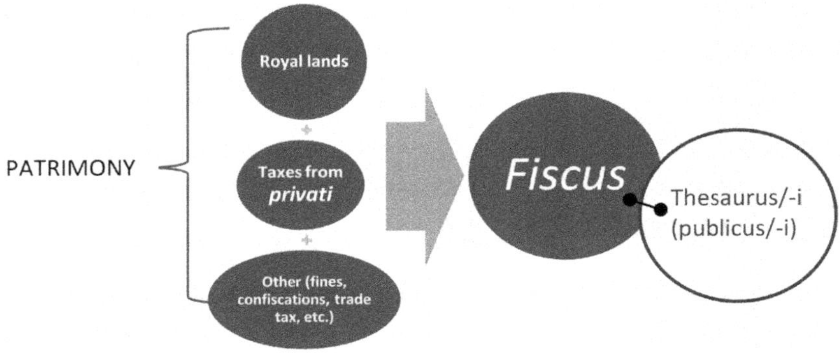

formed the patrimony and flowed into the fisc, which was the public treasury from which currency emanated through the hands of minters. This may be modeled as follows:

Based on sources of the sixth and seventh centuries the use of the term *fiscus* referencing crown lands (often by the adjective *fiscalis*) must be distinguished from the use of the same term for the general repository of all tributary collections (in this sense equivalent to *thesaurus/-i publicus/-i* and possibly *aerarium*). The precise meaning must therefore be sought in the context. *Thesaurus* applies in the Visigothic documentation to the monarchy's collection of mobile goods, a source of some royal payments, while *thesaurus publicus* signifies the collective fiscal assemblage in revenue terms.[388] In real terms, the diagram above would be multiplied to incorporate the various provincial divisions.

[...]." The law leaves the door open to confusion for us in the later line: "By the same command, we order the governor of the province, the count of the royal patrimony, and the administrators of our properties that they have no power over free people and they shall not harass them." This might be taken to mean the *privati* of the realm, as opposed to the *servi fiscales* of the royal estates, were not subject to *comes patrimonii*, although the general context and the reference to *populi* seems rather to indicate that none of the officials overseeing the extraction process had the power to abuse any subjects by demanding more than what was rightly owed. See García Moreno, "Algunos aspectos fiscales," 248 n. 82 and Damián Fernández, "Statehood, Taxation, and State Infrastructural Power in Visigothic Iberia," in *Ancient States and Infrastructural Power Europe, Asia, and America*, ed. Clifford Ando and Seth Richardson (Philadelphia, PA: University of Pennsylvania Press, 2017), 243-71 at 250f.

388 Valverde Castro, "Monarquía y tributación," 247-49, including the suggestion that the royal treasure was used more for public displays of power and wealth, whereas the public treasure was dedicated to the regular state expenses.

B The Record of Mint Output

New Finds

George C. Miles's remarkable book on the gold currency, *The Coinage of the Visigoths of Spain: Leovigild to Achila II* (New York, 1952), was an invaluable guide to several aspects of minting in the 'regal' period. It was first and foremost a corpus of unearthed Visigothic tremisses that he had built up from extensive research in North America and Europe. A table he made to summarize the number of coins from each mint during the reign of each king served for decades as a handy reference of the record of mint output.[389] Since the time of his research many new finds have been made. Miles's corpus and treatment of the royal-naming tremissis series has been updated and superseded by Ruth Pliego's two-volume *La moneda visigoda*, a well-illustrated corpus with extensive discussion of numerous aspects of the coinage.[390] Figure I.7 in the first appendix of the present work provides a table based on tremisses known to her in 2009, with her addition of a supplement three years later as well as one coin of very recent appearance (Arofre).[391] It is remarkably comprehensive but necessarily not definitive, since new coins are now emerging on the market every year and, as Miles had pointed out in regard to his own extensive investigations, some public and private collections end up being missed if only for lack of time and information. Significant additions are primarily of newly discovered issues or of issues known previously only from one or two specimens. Several of the new coins in Pliego's corpus are housed in public collections in Europe.[392] Though the provenance of newly published coins is rarely noted, a few of the coins added to the

389 Miles, *The Coinage of the Visigoths*, 70-74.

390 Ruth Pliego Vázquez, *La moneda visigoda*, 2 vols. (Seville: Universidad de Sevilla, 2009). Volume I: *Historia monetaria del reino visigodo de Toledo* (*c. 569-711*); Volume II: *Corpus*.

391 Pliego, *La moneda visigoda*, v. 2, 47-50; idem, "La moneda visigoda: Anexo I," *SPAL* 21 (2012), 209-33. Regnal dates are provided with various figures in my appendix.

392 In Pliego, *La moneda visigoda* many previously unpublished collections are recorded, e.g. Museo Arqueológico Nacional (MAN), Bode Museum in Berlin, many Portuguese collections, etc. Among the many coins that Miles was unaware of in 1952 are some in the collection of the Gabinete Numismático de Cataluña (see his later article on the same, "Notes on the Visigothic Coins in the Gabinete Numismático de Cataluña," *Numisma* 5, no. 16 [1955], 57-62). He was apparently unaware of the Visigothic tremisses in the Cabinet des Médailles of the Bibliothèque Royale Albert Ier in Brussels (7 of the regal period). Several new coins included in Marques et al., *Ensaios* are housed in public collections in Portugal.

corpus must come from individual finds, while the majority derive from several hoards recovered after 1952.[393]

One extraordinarily large hoard found in 1984 accounts for many new tremisses that have been regularly appearing on the market ever since. Only a portion of the hoard is found in auction catalogs.[394] Reliable sources indicate that the hoard was comprised of as many as several thousand coins, which alone would more than double the corpus published sixty-five years ago.[395] It was discovered at Fuentes de Andalucía, between Seville and Ecija.[396] Because most of the coins bear the name of Sisebut and Suinthila (r. 612-21 and 621-31), and based on the number of coins and their styles, the date of burial is estimated at c. 625 at the latest.[397] Another Visigothic treasure was found in Andalucía around 1996, at the same site where 'La Capilla' was unearthed in 1891. 'La Capilla II,' as it has been called, is thought at minimum to match the roughly one thousand coins of the old hoard.[398] There are rumors that a substantial, if not quite massive, treasure was uncovered in the 1980s in Galicia, although this may be confusion with the hoard found in that decade near Ecija. Dealers keep quiet about the exact contents of the recent hoards, and it is difficult to know which new coins

393 For individual finds up until 1976 see Barral i Altet, *La circulation*. For the known hoards, see Pliego, *La moneda visigoda*, v. 1, 231-59.

394 400 pieces that passed to Bank Leu (later Leu Numismatik) in Switzerland are included in Pliego's study. Larger portions of the hoard are known to be in the hands of Spanish coin dealers.

395 The total number of tremisses Miles recorded was 3461. He estimated that the actual number of genuine unearthed coins at the time was close to four thousand: Miles, *The Coinage of the Visigoths*, ix. Pliego's study includes almost 7500 tremisses, of which only 44 are traced to this hoard. See also remarks on the hoard and its size (c. 4300), in Bartlett et al., "Byzantine Gold Coinage of *Spania*," 369 and 376 (see n. 76). At this time, the number of unearthed Visigothic tremisses must stand somewhere around 10,000.

396 C. 225 km east of Sevilla.

397 Alan Walker, "The Identification of the Coinage of Reccared II: New Evidence from the Visigothic Mints of Emerita and Eliberri," in *Numismatics – Witness to History* (IAPN Publications no. 8; Wetteren: Moneta, 1986), 73-86, pl. 16-18; Marques et al., *Ensaios*, 172; and personal communications in 1999/2000 from a scholar in Spain researching the matter. The title "Reccared II" has been used in discussions of the hoard, since several specimens contained in it demonstrate that tremisses were struck during that king's very brief reign. See, in addition to the above, Gonzalo Cores and Anton Casariego, "Nota sobre las monedas de Recaredo II," *Numisma* 35-36 (nos. 192-203, 1985-86), 39-46; Bank Leu A.G., *Auktion 41* (*Mittelalter/Neuzeit*), Zürich: 14 October, 1986, 9f.; and most recently, Gonzalo Cores, J. M. Peixoto Cabral, Luis C. Alves, and Peter Bartlett, "Visigothic Mint Practice, March 621: What Can the Coins of Reccared II Tell Us?," in *Homenagem a Mário Gomes Marques*, ed. M. Castro Hipólito (Sintra: Instituto de Sintra, 2000), 195-223.

398 Bartlett et al., "Byzantine Gold Coinage of *Spania*," 369 and 376 (see n. 76 where it is the third hoard discussed).

come from such finds. Thus, there is a danger of counterfeits especially of previously unknown issues, which draw the most interest among collectors and scholars and which are not surprising to find in such enormous hoards. Some fakes have been easily detected, but questions over a few coins remain unresolved.[399] Nevertheless, stylistic analysis helps to confirm most of the present additions to the corpus.

It is primarily thanks to the large hoards that many unknown mints and issues have come to light, and the possibility that more sites and issues will be revealed over time is now wide open. Although Miles's table covered what must be the majority of the mints, and all the kings except one (Reccared II), it must now be considered inadequate. In 1952, Miles knew of seventy-nine mints of royal tremisses, but today about 100 are known.[400] Several still cannot be located with certainty, especially in the province of Gallaecia.[401] New workshops from each province of the kingdom except Narbonensis have become known. Five new workshops are in evidence from Tarraconensis (Amiasio [location unknown], Cestavi, Labeclosa, Lebea,[402] Volotania); five from Carthaginensis (Aorariola, Iliocrici/Eliocrica, Mave, Oliovasio [location unknown], Valentia[403]); two from Baetica (Carmona and the central southern town of Roda, to be distinguished from a mint already known to Miles called Rodas, in NE Spain); two from Lusitania (Adonis, Olisipona [= Lisboa; also called Elissa?]); and from Gallaecia nine (Asturica, Conteno, Decrinos [location unknown], Ewesis, Mertia, Palentiaca, Turico,

399 See now the section on false tremisses in Pliego, *La moneda visigoda*, v. 1, 261-78. Cf. "Counterfeit Visigothic Gold," *Bulletin on Counterfeits* 20 (no. 1, 1995), 8-10, and A. Domingo, "Sobre la autenticidad de los trientes visigodos," *Acta Numismática* 20 (1990), 79-82.

400 In addition to the ninety-eight workshops in Appendix I, Figure I.7 based primarily on Pliego, *La moneda visigoda*, v. 2, 47-50, there are possibly still a few whose unique issues are in the possession of a private collector in Spain and which are still to be published. Most of these are Gallaecian mints.

401 See the map of mints in Appendix I, Figure I.4 and the discussion of each of the mints in Pliego, *La moneda visigoda*, v. 1, 102-53, superseding the still valuable commentaries in Miles, *The Coinage of the Visigoths*, 76-146. A great amount of literature on mints, including their locations, can be found in the bibliography at the close of this book. On locations and new finds in NW Hispania, see now Ruth Pliego Vázquez, "*Gallaecia* en tiempos del reino visigodo de Toledo: sus emisiones monetarias," in *Introducción a la Historia Monetaria de Galicia*, ed. F. Cebreiro Ares (A Coruña: Labirinto de Paixóns, 2012), 65-104.

402 Listed among the unlocated mints in Gallaecia in Miles, *The Coinage of the Visigoths*, map following 68.

403 Oliovasio is listed among the unlocated mints in Gallaecia in Miles, *The Coinage of the Visigoths*, map following 68. Valentia was included in the 1952 catalog under Tarraconensis (Miles...., 70; see also 90f), but correctly listed as a Carthaginensian mint in Pliego, *La moneda visigoda*, v. 1, 149 (see explanation on 112f).

Vallesalsa).[404] Several mints cannot be assigned to a province with certainty (Adonis, Tulluco, Valle.../Valegia?).[405] It is not surprising that all of them were in obscure or relatively less important cities in the Visigothic era.

A few mints deserve particular attention. Iliocrici and Aorariola are of special interest because they are the only minting sites known to date in the vast area of Carthaginensis between Acci and Valentia. Until these mints were identified in recent years, it was assumed that the Visigoths did not strike coins at all in the southeast corner of the peninsula.[406] The case is similar with respect to the southwestern coast, where it was long thought that no mint was set up. The vacant area would be even larger when one takes into consideration an important change reflected in the map in Appendix I, Figure I.4, that of the new location of Elvora treated earlier in this book.[407] If Elvora is no longer to be identified as modern Évora in Portugal, where Miles and others believed it was located, a large part of Lusitania might seem to have lacked a mint. In fact, the previously vacant part of the map between Toleto and central Lusitania turns out to have had a workshop. The appearance of a coin of early medieval Lisbon ('*Olisipona*') fills what was believed to have been a gap in minting on the Atlantic coastline. Two mints in northern Tarraconensis which Miles rejected have been included in some historians' maps of mints. Egessa and Cestavi were put forward in Heiss's and Mateu y Llopis's volumes on the basis of coins in their name, specimens that Miles later held to be fakes.[408] Although these mints have not been confirmed by the appearance of any new coins, Miles's arguments against them must be considered unconvincing.[409]

404 Several mints Miles included (in Lusitania and Gallaecia) are discounted by Pliego. Some are assigned to a different province (e.g., Lebea shifted from Gallaecia to Tarraconensis), while different names are occasionally used for others (e.g. Miles's Arros and Celo of Gallaecia are identified as Susarres/Susarros and Inceio in Pliego).

405 See Pliego, *La moneda visigoda*, v. 1, 151.

406 Pliego, *La moneda visigoda*, v. 1, 115 provides some commentary; more extensively on Iliocrici/Eliocrica, see Andrew Kurt and Peter Bartlett, "Nueva ceca visigoda: Lorca (Iliocri[ca]) y sus nexos con las cecas del sur," *Numisma* 48 (no. 241, 1998), 27-39. On a Visigothic military zone here see below, n. 605.

407 Above, Chapter Two.

408 Orlandis, *Historia de España*, 200; García Moreno, *Historia de España visigoda*, 333; idem, "Cecas visigodas," following p. 338, adding 'Cestavi' only; Marques et al., *Ensaios*, 103. Unfortunately, none of the authors explains the reason for including the mints.

409 Egessa (LIVVICILDVS—REXEGESSA): A. Heiss, *Description générale des monnaies des rois wisigoths*, pl. I, no. 11; Mateu y Llopis, *Catálogo*, 281; Miles, *The Coinage of the Visigoths*, 453, no. 9 (as a forgery). Although Heiss saw only a silver copy of the coin, nothing in his drawing marks it out as non-authentic. Pío Beltrán's discounting of the mint because the town of Egessa was not the seat of an administrative division is not sound reasoning. The record of Visigothic

The new coins in the table make valuable contributions to our knowledge of mint activity. Several mint sites are now known to have been active for a longer period of time than was previously believed, or their use revived after a period of cessation. We may point by way of example to Aurense, Bergancia, and Georres in Gallaecia, mints whose use had seemed intermittent or experimental, in each case not very prolonged. Recent evidence shows otherwise. Aurense was formerly known to have a mint only at sometime within the years 642 to 653. In the last thirty years several new tremisses have expanded its chronology considerably, bringing its activity back at least to Sisebut. We may expect that more apparent gaps in the life of many mints will be closed as new revelations are made over time. Particularly helpful finds are those of Reccopolis coins from the reigns of Sisebut and Suinthila, since they demonstrate that this city, which Leovigild established for his son and successor, Reccared, was not destroyed shortly afterward, as asserted by the early excavators of the site.[410] We have noted the recent discovery of issues in the name of Reccared II, who ruled two decades later. It was always assumed that Reccared II's reign of a few days, according

administrative units is not so perfect, and not every mint site had such a standing. Whether Egessa was a mint or not is for me an unsettled question, though I incline toward Pliego, *La moneda visigoda*, v. 1, 263, whose consideration of the two coins with the name Egessa as fakes is unfortunately without specific explanation; see photos and description in ibid., v. 2, 496, nos. 840 and 841.

Cestavi (two coins whose legends are a version of '*Reccaredvs—Cestavi Ivstvs*'): 1/ C·ESTAVVIIVST: (Heiss, *des monnaies des rois wisigoths*, p l. III, no. 42, '*localité indeterminée*'; Mateu y Llopis, *Catálogo de las monedas previsigodas y visigodas*, 283; Miles, *The Coinage of the Visigoths*, 206, no. 59. 2/ *C·E:T:VI:V:TV: (Miles, no. 57(b)). Pliego, *La moneda visigoda*, v. 1, 107f affirms the mint. Miles regarded both coins as authentic but included them as aberrant versions of *Cesaragusta*. Several clear forgeries have thrown added confusion on this mint: see Miles, 458, 19(b).1-9. While I do not refute the forgeries, I cannot agree with Miles's argument that the two coins above should be read as products of Cesaragusta: "Quite apparently some of the contemporary die engravers became careless in the rendering of the abbreviated mint name (which takes so many forms) to such an extent perhaps that they ignored the significance of the letters" (206). The abbreviation symbols (:) in the mint name in all Miles's listings of '*Cesaracosta*' coins account for exactly one letter (e.g. CE:AR:C·O:TA, the single dot not an abbreviation but a standard control mark); the Cestavi piece no. 57(b) is no different, as is shown by the unabbreviated piece no. 59 which provides the full reading. There is nothing very confusing or careless about the legend – here are two different mints but one and the same engraver.

410 Miles, *The Coinage of the Visigoths*, 96-99. See Castro, "*Reccopolis*," and Pliego, *La moneda visidogoda*, v. 1, 111f and 148. Cf. also Peter Bartlett, "Reccopolis, ceca inédita de Suinthila (621-631)," *Gaceta Numismática* (no. 135, 1999), 19-20. Miles distrusted the arguments for the supposed early ruin of Reccopolis, but concluded that the single, damaged specimen of Wittiza was an insufficient basis for discussion. For more on original excavations of the site, see Roger Collins, *Spain: An Oxford Archaeological Guide* (Oxford: Oxford University Press, 1998), 223-25 and references on 318.

to Isidore, was too brief to have left any coins. Finally, the huge increase in the corpus in recent decades suggests that the output of Visigothic tremisses was much greater than has been commonly supposed. Not only are more mints and more issues becoming known, but also the die links among the new coins are less than fifty per cent; these facts indicate that the number of known dies is fast increasing, thus the production of coins must have been many times greater than the total of surviving specimens. This evidence makes it probable that Reccared II remained at least several months on the throne.

We can learn more about Gothic minting by making good use of the statistics created from the arrangement of extant tremisses. For example, certain mints have been designated as primary while others have been seen as secondary.[411] That is, a very few mints accounting for the majority of known specimens were primary in the minting organization; for instance, Emerita (=Mérida), Ispali (=Sevilla), Toleto (=Toledo), and Cordoba are the origin of about two thirds of the entire corpus. At the same time, most of the mints are minor or secondary mints, accounting for approximately a quarter of the corpus only. The majority of the minor mints were located in the mountainous province of Gallaecia.[412] Another criterion for deciding which mints were major and which were minor is duration, since most of the mints were active only for several years at a time. If we establish the criterion for a major mint as one that demonstrates evidence of issuing for at least five kings in a row (except for Reccared II and Roderic, whose reigns were brief), or otherwise was consistently active over the entire 'regal tremissis' period, the following can be placed in this category:

Narbonensis (1) -- Narbona
Tarraconensis (5) – Barcinona, Cesaragusta, Gerunda (after 680), Tarracona, Tirasona
Carthaginensis (3) – Acci, Mentesa, Toleto

411 James Spaulding, "The Mint-cities of Visigothic Spain: Leovigild to Achila II" (PhD, Duke University, 1970), ch. 1, concluded that there were fourteen central, or 'permanent,' mints; Miquel Barceló, "A Statistical Approach to Multiple Mint Issues of Royal Coinage: The Case of the Visigoths in Hispania (585-711)," *PACT* 5 (1981), 139ff: six mints; Grierson, *Coins of Medieval Europe*, 22: six mints (but see Grierson and Blackburn, *Medieval European Coinage*, v. 1, 53, where he refers to the 'big four' mints, i.e. Emerita, Toleto, Ispali, and Cordoba); Metcalf, "Some Geographical Aspects," 310: four mints; Gil Farrés, "Algunos aspectos," 188: fifteen mints. See the recent analysis in Pliego, *La moneda visidogoda*, v. 1, 111f and 146-53: seven mints, all episcopal sees and well-connected on the major roadways.
412 Many mints in this northwestern province taken from the Sueves in 585 are known only from between one and three specimens.

Baetica (5) – Barbi (from 612-653 only), Córdoba, Eliberri, Ispali, Tucci (from 612-653)
Lusitania (4) – Egitania, Elvora, Emerita, Eminio (through Chintila only)
Gallaecia (5?) – Bracara?, Georres, Luco?, Senabria, Tude[413]

Total: 23 mints

Underlined here are the principal mints within each of the six provinces, defined in terms of both quantity of known output and duration over the greatest number of reigns. One will notice that these are the capitals – both political and ecclesiastical – of the provinces. The hierarchy of the Visigothic minting network in the regal period can be best summarized thus: the primary mint city of each province was the capital; the kingdom as a whole had a little more than twenty major mints, five or six of which were most productive, and approximately seventy-five secondary mints.

This is not to say that secondary (i.e. temporary) mints never produced significant amounts of coinage. According to the record of surviving tremisses, the output of some of them equaled or exceeded that of the provincial capital for a time. Appendix I, Figure I.7 allows us to discover which mints and minting regions predominated at a given time. A dramatic change in patterns of output can be seen among mints in the southern part of the kingdom from 612 to 636. The sharp rise in their production at this time suggests that special circumstances were at play in the south. Even at other times, when it had only a few mints in operation, the combined region of Baetica and southwestern Carthaginensis provided over thirty per cent of the corpus during most reigns. Appendix I, Figure I.9 illustrates both points clearly.[414] It has been observed from the record of extant coins that the proportional number of specimens from the various provinces varies

413 The comparatively sparse minting in Gallaecia and the southerly location of the giant hoards leave a reduced record for this province. Only three mints (Braga, Luco, Tude) continued from early until late in the regal period. They could be considered major mints not with respect to the system as a whole but within Gallaecia.

414 The graph was made from the information in Miles's table, 70-74 and the additional thirty-one coins not known to Miles in Grierson and Blackburn, *Medieval European Coinage*, v. 1, 442-51, pls. 12-14. I have discussed this evidence in a previous article, where I also explain that 'hoard bias' in the south does not negate an especially high number of coins from that region: Andrew Kurt, "Visigothic Minting and the Expulsion of the Byzantines from Spain in the Early Seventh Century," *The Picus* (Toronto: 1996), 133-66, here 138f. Some elaboration of the observations made above will be found in Chapter Four. I have not added the many new coins which appeared since the 1980s since so many originate from the massive hoard in southern Spain known as Fuentes de Andalucía, which would add to regional distortions already present from the Capilla hoard.

from reign to reign.[415] Excluding the special circumstances just mentioned, nowhere is this more evident than in Gallaecia, where almost half of the mints were located for the first seventy years or so of the 'regal' period of minting. Only under Witteric (r. 603-610) and Chindasvinth (sole rule 642-649) did Gallaecian minting seem to reach close to twenty per cent of the total, rising above a level usually far below ten per cent. Beginning around the year 650, under Chindasvinth's and Reccesvinth's joint reign, Gallaecian minting was halted almost entirely. The reason for the fluctuations in the initial period have been generally attributed to the swings inherent either in tax collection or in recovery of gold deposits, although particularly since few extant coins are in question for that province the limitations of our knowledge is always a factor.[416] The nearly complete suspension of minting in the northwest is the best indication of a reorganization of the minting system.

When we use statistics of surviving currency, as with any archeological artifacts, a flag of caution should always be waved over the discussion. The tallies of surviving coins should by no means be taken as an absolute indication of comparative production, since the number of coins necessarily depends on unequal duration of reigns and for some kings is distorted by a hoard buried late in the reign or shortly after a king's death. But neither should the tallies be disregarded. We must avoid gross generalizations and try to pinpoint the distortions as well as possible. One indication from the table in Appendix I, Figure I.7 is that the two to four years of the joint rule of Egica-Wittiza (c. 698-702)[417] left a surprisingly large number of tremisses. Even if the record of extant pieces in this period is 'biased' by a fairly large hoard (110 trientes) buried between 702 and 710 in northern-central Iberia, the totals of the mints relative to one another right before and after the turn of the eighth century are not likely to misrepresent the reality significantly if we keep in mind the find location near Salamanca when considering each whole region.[418] It is therefore interesting to see what looks to be a

415 See Marques et al., *Ensaios*, 269, *Quadro I* (the percentage of coinage contributed from the six provinces for each reign, based on Miles's table).

416 Ibid., 265-74; Hendy, "From Public to Private," 57f; Metcalf, "Some Geographical Aspects," 307-24.

417 The exact year in which it began is unknown, and is generally proposed as either 698 or 700. Miles takes the high number of coins as suggesting the earlier date for the beginning of Egica's formal association with his son on the throne: *The Coinage of the Visigoths*, 36. Collins, *Visigothic Spain*, 108 cites the high number of coins specifically as a reason for following a charter rather than the *Chronicle of 754* and starting the joint reign in 694.

418 On this hoard ('Abusejo') and all the hoards of Visigothic gold coins before 1976 see Barral i Altet, *La circulation*, 78-142. Updated study of Abusejo is now available in Pliego, "El *tremis*

rise in production at Gerunda – and to a lesser extent Cesaragusta – and a corresponding even level and then reduction at Tarracona, and a huge increase at Elvora and Cordoba as well as Ispali and Emerita with a simultaneous drop at Toleto (still with significant output). Against the background of totals from these mints from other years, which seem normal if we figure in the presence of large hoards, these anomalies suggest a temporary shift based on changing needs of some sort.

A slightly safer body of evidence than the number of extant coins is the number of known mints active under each ruler, illustrated in Figure I.8 of Appendix I.[419] The period under consideration begins with Leovigild, whose opening of new mints is known from a wholesale change in type in the last two years of his reign. At least three new workshops were added to the monetary network after he conquered the Suevic kingdom in 585. The expansion in mints – and most probably in production, judging from the number of unearthed coins – continued under his son and successor, Reccared (r. 586-601). Liuva II's reign (601-03) was too brief to leave many coin finds from Gallaecia today, but we can see that Witteric still had numerous mints there. The longer reigns that follow show a possible increase in mint sites in the northwest (including upper Lusitania) until the marked contraction under Reccesvinth.[420] As the graph demonstrates, fewer mints were active throughout the kingdom during his reign. Once again, this points to monetary reorganization. The evidence suggests that reforms were already undertaken in the joint reign with his father.[421] Up until that time Visigothic Spain as a whole had probably an average of between thirty and fifty-five active mints at any given time, if we estimate by extrapolating data

de los últimos años del Reino Visigodo (702-714)," in *Monnaies du haut Moyen Âge: Histoire et archéologie* (*péninsule Ibérique – Maghreb, VIIe-XIe siècle*), ed. Philippe Sénac and Sébastien Gasc (Toulouse: Presses universitaires du Midi – Collection Méridiennes, 2015), 17-58 and idem, *La moneda visigoda*, v. 1, 250-52.

419 The table supersedes Pliego, *La moneda visigoda*, v. 1, 148-51 by adding to that impressive tally 155 coins, all but one (the recently appeared Arofre) gathered in idem, "La moneda visigoda: Anexo I."

420 The famous hoard of La Capilla, containing about 1000 tremisses, and the much larger and more recent hoard of Fuentes, have revealed a greater number of northwestern mints than would otherwise be known. On Gallaecian minting in particular, see D. M. Metcalf, "Many Mint-Places, Few Coins: Visigothic Coinage in Gallaecia and Northern Lusitania," *Homenagem a Mário Gomes Marques*, ed. M. Castro Hipólito et al. (Sintra: Instituto de Sintra, 2000), 175-94. Metcalf's ranking of northwestern mints is only slightly modified by the information contained in this book.

421 The very advanced age of Chindasvinth by this time, and the fact that Reccesvinth's name appears on the obverse of a Toleto coin from these years, leads me to believe that the latter was already taking control of the kingdom.

from reigns for which significant hoards are known to those without such finds. After the reduction a new growth in the number of mints seems to have occurred in the last two decades of the seventh century, although the Abusejo hoard distorts the evidence somewhat for these years as compared to the middle decades without such a large find.

The main concern of this section has been to present the advances in knowledge of Visigothic minting. The reasons for the existence of a large number of mint sites producing gold coins have been discussed by the present author and many others elsewhere, and are taken up in Chapter Four. In broad terms, the question comes down to the following: If Rome and Constantinople satisfied the enormous need for coinage in the Roman Empire with very few mints, why did the Visigothic rulers establish so many? No doubt the answer lies essentially in the difference of efficiency of the state and the apparatus required for a centralized system: roads, personnel, communication, and a mentality of massive structures built up over centuries. Various motives have been proposed for the particular locations of the many Visigothic mints, including the requirements of trade, taxation, or running an army, the desire for propaganda, and the proximity to gold deposits. Scholarship of recent decades tends to ascribe a variety of motives to the extensive minting network in this barbarian kingdom.[422] The picture will become sharper the more we become aware of exactly which sites composed that network.

C The Organization of the Mints

Gains and Limitations of Past Research

Extant coins are the only source of information on how the Visigothic kings organized the gold mints, yet they are a more valuable resource in this regard than, for example, the well-studied Merovingian coins. Specimens from the Merovingian kingdoms are much more numerous but have a notoriously ambiguous chronology and irregular geographical pattern, since the hundreds of sites named on the coins were often temporary and not necessarily the place of issue.[423] The organization of mints in most other barbarian kingdoms of this period was much simpler than in Francia, since the centers of coin production were very few. With nearly one hundred mints

422 For example, Metcalf, "Many Mint-Places"; Marques et al., *Ensaios*, esp. 265-73.
423 See Grierson and Blackburn, *Medieval European Coinage*, v. 1, 113-38.

in Spain, the Visigothic minting system stands somewhere between these two extremes. The crux of its geographical layout had been established even before Miles published his corpus, but in that volume the author carefully sifted the authenticity of questionable coins and the true location of many obscure mints.[424] In an effort to learn more about the manufacture of the coins and the organization of the minting system, he also brought the complex patterns of bust design into sharper focus, building on the work of Felipe Mateu y Llopis and Aloïss Heiss. According to all three authors, behind the great variety of coin designs was an essentially provincial organization of mints. Yet, a detailed study of numismatic style reveals that this notion must be considerably qualified.

Knowledge of where minting took place in the regal period, obtained from reverse inscriptions, does not answer questions as to how mints were related to one another or how they were managed. We have already touched on the important question of whether minting was carried out only at one or more central locations or in fact at the many sites stamped on the tremisses, arguing that mint names do indicate the place of striking. Did the mints operate separately or were they closely associated with other mints? Is there evidence that some mints or administrative cities had control over minting elsewhere? Such questions have to be answered by studying precise similarities in appearance, principally bust designs, in order to see which patterns of production emerge.

The first to adopt this approach was Aloïss Heiss, whose *Description générale des monnaies des Rois Wisigoths d'Espagne* appeared in 1872. Heiss categorized the busts of the regal tremisses on two levels. He began by enumerating the general types, which others have since elaborated and which are discussed in the second chapter above: type I, the profile bust with VPW reverse; type II, the profile bust with a cross-on-steps reverse; type III, the facing busts; and so on.[425] He then identified regional types from each of the six provinces, which existed only within type III up to Reccesvinth's reign. In the 1930s, Felipe Mateu y Llopis developed Heiss's regional divisions, using them as the basis for his catalog of the great public collection in Madrid.[426] There he showed that certain sub-types of type III were most closely or sometimes solely associated with a particular mint or a region of

424 Miles was able to give special attention to the Visigothic coins of the ANS since he was the Islamic Curator there.
425 See especially Gil Farrés, "Algunos aspectos."
426 Mateu y Llopis, *Catálogo*. The collection was stolen in the same year as the book's publication (1936) at the outbreak of the Spanish Civil War.

mints. The maps over which Mateu y Llopis placed illustrations of the main bust designs at key sites were those of the administrative boundaries of the six provinces of the Visigothic kingdom. He thereby showed the general correspondence of bust designs to provincial boundaries. But he noted that mints near provincial borders were influenced by the sub-types of the neighboring province and in some cases assumed the other provincial type completely. Therefore, provincial types were not static at all mints, since at times they changed and sometimes changed back again. From these observations it should be inferred that the network of mints was not organized strictly by administrative provinces.

In 1952, the comprehensive catalog of Miles made an enormous contribution in this area as in others. Miles systematically classified the immense variety of Visigothic busts into thirteen categories of regional types and distinctive design types, breaking each one down into specific sub-types (1a, b, c...; 2a, b, c..., etc.) and illustrating the characteristic form of each one.[427] Miles also listed the rulers and mints for which each sub-type was known. Most of the categories have five or more sub-types, and two of them have well over twenty. His aim was to classify all known busts. At the end of his commentary on the evolution and distribution of the facing-busts type, he argued that the organization of mints was less complex, but also less strictly provincial, than might appear. "As Reinhart has pointed out, there has been a tendency to classify Visigothic coins too rigidly along provincial lines and according to too many type categories. There are, in fact, only four main types: the Tarraconese (with Narbona), the Carthaginensian and Baetican (of which the Gallaecian is a crude variety), the Córdoban, and the Emeritan."[428]

It is necessary to ask whether Miles's division of sub-types makes good sense, since these specific types form the reference by which all historians and numismatists for over half a century have identified the designs of Visigothic coins, and because his division affects our picture of how mints were organized. Two questions should be posed: Are his sub-types accurate, in other words do the several issues[429] from the different cities he listed –

427 See Miles, *The Coinage of the Visigoths*, 54-66. His categories are: 1) Profile busts: early Visigothic type; 2) Profile busts: later types; 3) Facing busts: distinctive Leovigildan types; 4) Facing busts: Tarraconese type; 5) Facing busts: general types; 6) Facing busts: Barcinona type; 7) Facing busts: Lusitanian or Emeritan type [reverses]; 8) Facing busts: Lusitanian or Emeritan type [obverses]; 9) Facing busts: Cordoban type; 10) Facing heads: Cordoban type; 11) Facing busts: later types; 12) Facing busts and heads: anomalous types; 13) Confronting busts.

428 Ibid., 50. The reference to Reinhart is from "Die Münzen des westgotischen Reiches," 89-90.

429 Here referring to ruler-mint combinations, not the total emanation from the same pair of dies.

some of them from very distant parts of the kingdom – really belong together under the one bust depiction given? If the sub-types are accurate, do they support the implications about minting organization to be drawn from Miles's summary of the facing-busts types above? Miles was indeed on the right track. The categories of regional and distinctive types make perfect sense, as one can verify by poring over a sufficiently wide collection.[430] The depictions catch the essence of the sub-types, of which there are numerous minute variations. He was also correct in cautioning against a too rigid 'provincial' classification, given the exceptions. The category referred to as 'general types' or 'common types' is made up primarily of sub-types employed in both the south and the northwest, and a number of types in this category are employed by Baetica and Carthaginensis at the same time. There is also the case of Valentia on the Mediterranean coast. It was under the Metropolitan See of Toleto, belonged to the ecclesiastical province of Carthaginensis, and presumably lay within the same civil borders, as it had under Diocletian's territorial divisions. Yet, when the mint of Valentia was first opened it proved by its design to be a mint of Tarraconensis, matching the style of coins from Tarracona, Tirasona, and other mints in the northeast.[431]

While most of Miles's sub-types correspond accurately to the issues listed, some of the sub-types should be realigned or the assignment of issues to the depiction should be reconsidered. Examples are 5n, 5a, and 5d. The last is shown in three variations that we will label 5d(1), 5d(2), 5d(3).[432] A careful review suggests that, while it is appropriate to provide three variations of this specific type, it would be better to combine 5d(1), 5a, and 5n in one sub-type. Although there are slight differences in the style of the bust depictions, in reality features of the head and the cuirass interchange variously in all

430 Twice I have tested the classification by sorting a few dozen randomly chosen coins of the ANS collection solely on the basis of similarity of bust type, without looking at the names of the mints. In both cases, the various mints and bust types fell neatly into Miles's regional scheme, though the few Gallaecian coins seemed appropriate as a separate category.

431 Miles, *The Coinage of the Visigoths*, 49, 90, 277, 322-23. Valentia was part of Tarraconensis in the early Roman Empire, and it may be for this reason that when its mint opened during Suinthila's reign (621-631) it was associated with that province. On the other hand, this association may have something to do with its proximity to Sagunto, located just inside the southern border of Tarraconensis; the convenience of having the same minter strike in both places rather than adhering strictly to a provincial separation is precisely consonant with the argument I wish to forward. In an apparent reorganization, the two known tremisses of Valentia from Chintila's reign (636-639) fairly closely resemble coins from Toleto. The style at Valentia in the late seventh century, when minting resumed there, appears still to be that of Carthaginensis.

432 Ibid., 58 and 60.

three types, often on the obverse and the reverse of the same coin.[433] Yet, few such changes seem to be called for.

What should at least have provoked commentary from Miles is that he assigned a good number of his sub-types to mints in regions very distant from each other. How, for instance, did the Lusitanian type (category no. 7) come to appear not only at Emerita but at Bracara and Pannonias, or how did several of the 'general types' (5a-f, j-n) appear across the peninsula? Something more than the position of some mints on the frontier between provinces is involved. Only part of the answer lies in the copying of designs used in other cities.[434] The difficulty is to determine the extent to which Miles's regional types and sub-types actually reflect provincial administration of the mints. The three authors we have mentioned in this section at least implied that provincial types point to a provincial organization of the mints. In so far as this was the case (bearing in mind significant exceptions), one is led to infer that the monetary organization not only ran parallel to the provincial administrative structures but was a part of them. There is abundant evidence of the provincial units into which the government of the kingdom was divided, units whose responsibilities included the administration of financial matters.[435] Pliego's major study has provided an invaluable updating not only of the general provincial administration and, more importantly, mint locations, but also a reconsideration of the type and sub-type categories.[436] These categories are well described and referenced in

433 For 5n Miles listed "Liuva: Toleto; Witteric: Bracara, Nandolas, Vallearitia." In fact, the cuirass of the Liuva-Toleto coin in the corpus (pl. VII.2) resembles more a combination of 5a and 5d(1); so does the face on the obverse, whereas on the reverse the face alone is that of 5n. See Miles, *The Coinage of the Visigoths*, 189 n. 2, in which the author indicates his awareness of variations at Toleto.

434 Such a practice raises the possibility that particular mints were imitated, perhaps because of their authority or the eminence of the cities in which they were located. In Appendix II it is observed that some Emerita trientes give indication that their die sinkers copied the style employed by the 'Toleto hand': see pl. I, (d) and (e) and pl. V, 1324 and 1327. Some Gallaecian mints appear to copy Emeritan or Toledan style.

435 The Late Roman provinces of Spain stayed in place into the Visigothic period. For the fifth century transition, see Thompson, *Romans and Barbarians*, 176-77. One finds many references to the provinces in Isidore's *Historia Gothorum*, and the law code has similar references such as the one which is addressed by Reccared to all the provinces in the kingdom ('Flavius Reccaredus rex: universis provinciis [...]': *LV* IX.2.viii). The governor at the head of each province was called a *praeses* or *rector* (or *iudex*) provinciae, but by the latter half of the seventh century he was called a *dux*, a term that should be distinguished from the *dux* of Roman tradition who led an army in the field.

436 Pliego, *La moneda visigoda*, v. 1, 97-153 addresses the organization of mints at least in their provincial setting and the identity and brief history of the nearly 100 known mints, a few of which

correspondence with the mint network, laid out as in Miles's text by province, regional groups, and individual mints. However, the types and sub-types do not obey provincial lines, leaving open the question of how minting as a whole was arranged. In order to explain the wide geographical spread of many bust types we must go beyond the myriad types to the engravers of dies. A detailed study of bust as well as epigraphic style allows us to do just that. The geographical patterns of engravers' work justify a reconsideration of Visigothic mint organization.

Stylistic Evidence

All coins have their own style, the particular way in which the type or sub-type has been executed on the die, and similarly with respect to inscription. Within the Visigothic sub-types depicted by Miles and more recently by Pliego there is a great variety of subtle differences: eyebrows that touch or do not touch in the middle; a long or short nose; a nose or hair that ends with a dot, two dots, or a triangle; a trapezoidal cuirass as opposed to a triangular or rectangular one, etc. Certain patterns are observable. It is possible to argue, though never with complete certainty, that a very similar bust design at different places is the result, not of imitation, but of die engraving by the same hand. One is guided in the first place by varieties of dies made at the same location within the same period, whose similitude plainly shows them to be from the same engraver. Comparison can then be made to details of bust design, epigraphy, and other features of coins from other areas in order to see whether they fit within the same norms. he style-study undertaken here includes coins from the emergence of the facing busts late in Leovigild's reign up to Chindasvinth's reign. Though necessarily incomplete, it is the only study of its kind for Visigothic coins and brings instructive results.[437]

There is no evidence of the same obverse die being used in two different places, and naturally that is true of the reverse since mint names were

have not yet been pinned down geographically. Ibid., 155-73 is an exposition of the iconography and typological developments. Hers is a provincial and sometimes local basis for understanding of the iconography, colored by a strong sense of the Byzantine and in some measure later Roman iconographic models, which were followed all the way until late in the Visigothic period. Until that time, the essential forms were not original, but the stylization of figures and schematization of the types or sub-types were: ibid., 155. Pp. 105-08 above reviews the Visigothic tremissis types.

437 My criteria for deciding which coins are from dies cut by a particular engraver are explained in Appendix II, which includes photos and commentary. I have learned of a case for the same die engraver among different Suevic gold mints, though I have not been able to consult the article: Harold V. Livermore, "The Coinage of the Suevic Period," *Nummus*, 2nd ser., 12-13 (1989-90), 39-49.

inscribed on that side. There is copious evidence, however, that a few die engravers worked in many different cities – including across provincial boundaries – and during several reigns. The style-study that I have detailed in Appendix II suggests that several main engravers worked at multiple locations in the early half of the regal period to which I refer. It is perhaps best to begin with a group of engravers whose attributions are the clearest. The first four die cutters worked at the highly productive mints of the central-southern area of the Visigothic kingdom, what was then southeastern Baetica and southwestern Carthaginensis. The next engraver can be traced in the west, center, and south of the kingdom. The last four moved about in the northeast.

1) The work of the '*southern engraver*' (So.), as he may be called, is probably the easiest to identify as a single die cutter.[438] Starting at the latest in the reign of Suinthila, the engraver cut dies along a path stretching from Córdoba down to Tucci, Mentesa, Eliberri and Acci; then, in the next reign, he was also active at Castelona and east as far as Iliocrici. The mint of Iliocrici was not known before a damaged tremissis struck there entered the market in the late 1990s.[439] There may be a prelude in this region to the labors of this engraver. He may have begun in Sisebut's time to cut dies at Acci, Aorariola, and Iliocrici – the latter two issues rather recent revelations – and possibly other near mints. Whether it is a case of the handiwork of this same engraver over a few decades, the newer finds from Aorariola and Iliocrici attest to an extremely similar style sometime in the 610s or as late as 621.[440]

2) Another southern engraver, who may be called the '*Ispali engraver*' (Isp.), worked in Seville and at a few mints located mostly in the province of Baetica, but a number of coins in this style eventually from Acci and later Mentesa indicate that he traveled into the southwestern corner of Carthaginensis (see Appendix II, plates II, IV, V and Table).[441] He also sank dies in Cordoba and in Asidona, a mint that did not open until Suinthila's

438 An early treatment of this observation is in Kurt and Bartlett, "Nueva ceca visigoda". Refer to Appendix II for specific observations to support the engraving styles listed here, for example pl. IV, G and H for 'So'.

439 Ibid.

440 The last three coins pictured in Pliego, *La moneda visigoda*, v. 2, 167 (258.1=Acci, 259.1=Aorariola, 260.1=Iliocrici, all of Sisebut) share with this attribution the same left lean of the letters, a distinctive S (with a straight top, but at times S also sideways), a distinctive R especially in its angle and in the way the bottom right wedge meets the next letter, a distinctive B, and similar features of the cross if both sides are taken into account. These observations can be extended to other Acci coins on the page.

441 Pliego, *La moneda visigoda*, v. 1, 161f describes the parameters within the kingdom of the type group she calls 'Hispalense A'. Further work may demonstrate specific correspondences

reign (621-631). Ispali is surely the mint of origin, since the engraver appears to have begun his work there under Reccared (r.586-601) at the latest, well before he was present at other mints. Because this engraver and the immediately preceding and following engravers turn up at many of the same sites and have a few similar features, an explanation of what distinguishes the styles is provided in Appendix II.

3) *'Baetica/Carthaginensis'* (B/C) is so called because it appears so far only at mints near the border of the two provinces: Eliberri, Acci, Mentesa, and Barbi. The earliest coins of this kind which the present author has seen bear the name of Witteric and are from Eliberri and Mentesa. The style, while showing similar features to other hands at times, is certainly distinct from others in this region. It may be suspected that the work of this engraver was linked to war being waged there against the Byzantines.[442] Extant finds tell of this engraver's heavy activity in Barbi during Suinthila's reign. His travels do not seem to have extended any further than the border area described and, if the record of his issues is complete, he may have stopped altogether by 631; but as this study is not exhaustive differed conclusions may yet be reached on these points.

4) The *'Cordoba engraver'* (Cord.) is one of possibly four engravers active in the 620s and 630s in this important commercial city, which would later become the capital of Muslim Spain. Notes on this particular engraver are not included in Appendix II, but the separate style will be apparent on review of these coins in Miles's or Pliego's catalogs. His work is virtually unique to Cordoba, the apparent exception being some Chindasvinth-Eliberri issues. Miles devoted one category of three sub-types to these Cordoban facing busts, which originated under Leovigild. The 630s saw the emergence of Cordoban types of facing heads (no busts), which Miles placed as a separate category.[443] Two different engravers are involved in these two separate type groups, though I have not been able to examine whether the style of coins with heads alone is that of another die cutter listed here.

5) The style group that can be called the *'Toleto workshop'* (Tol.) is also in evidence for Baetica and Carthaginensis, but the work of this school was not primarily in the south. It was by far the most extensively traveled engraver team, as I suppose this source of dies, if the attributions offered are correct.

of the labors of individual engravers, or engraving groups, with major categories such as this one, her 'Cordobés A, B, C', and several others.

442 We know early in Sisebut's reign (612-620), around 614-615, there was heavy fighting near Barbi, for example. See Bank Leu AG Zürich, *Mittelalter Neuzeit: Auktion 41* (*Zürich, 14 Oktober, 1986*), 8, commentary on coin no. 24.

443 Miles, *The Coinage of the Visigoths*, 62-63.

During the last couple of years of Leovigild's rule, it seems to have followed a path from the center of the kingdom, minting at Reccopolis and Elvora and into Lusitania, then down to Ispali. It apparently went further south, to Eliberri and Mentesa, during Reccared's reign, but at some point, in the same period, traveled up to Gallaecia. Although that itinerary is difficult to imagine in the mostly provincial organization of minting proposed in the literature up to now, it should be observed in its favor that four of the northernmost mints in Gallaecia under Reccared have so-called victory legends, including one that reads 'IN TVDE,' likely pointing to the presence of the king there with his army. Such circumstances may explain why a die cutter would work in very distant parts of the kingdom.[444] Even apart from possible travels with the king's military campaigns, Toleto is to be preferred as the principal site of the engraver. The reason is not only because Toleto was the capital, but also because it was one of the few mint cities already with this style in Leovigild's reign, and because it was of much greater significance than the two other mint cities of that sort on the Tajo River.

Because of the great number of mints involved and the use of 'general types,' attributions to a single die cutter are less than certain. It is possible that imitation rather than a single engraver accounts for some of the styles. It is also possible that some early seventh-century coins from Emerita and surrounding mints should be considered products of a distinct engraver (see Appendix II, plates III and V). Sometimes, it is difficult to bridge the gap between the likenesses of Emerita coins and Toleto/Elvora coins on the one hand, and Emerita and Gallaecian coins on the other, since many Toleto/Elvora and Gallaecian tremisses have several different stylistic features. But, in the cases illustrated and commented on in Appendix II, there are enough similarities to suggest that possibly a single engraver or more probably a school of engravers was at work in perhaps more than a dozen locations. If the dies emanated from multiple engravers, these artists were few and there must have been at least indirect influences among them.

More than one single person may have been responsible for so many issues, or for some of them in separate cities, since this style group employed a slightly different engraving style at each place in Carthaginensis, Baetica, and Gallaecia where a general type was used.[445] The group assumed a

444 I deal with the subject of minting for the needs of war in the next chapter.

445 Among numerous examples in Appendix II, plate III is a tremisses of Reccared-Portocale (in Gallaecia; Marques et al., *Ensaios*, pl. II.32 = Pliego v. 2, 146 c.2) and one of Liuva II-Toleto (ibid., pl. II.33 = Pliego, v. 2, 160 b.1). Especially the faces on both coins, but also other stylistic features, make it clear that they both proceed from the same engraver. Yet, the cuirass of II.32, while quite similar, is not cut exactly in the conventional Toledan style.

different provincial bust type altogether in Lusitania and sometimes in Gallaecia. It also adapted the style of letters within different regions.[446] This particular work continued for several decades, ending perhaps in the reign of Sisenand or Chintila, although I am less certain of the later attributions.

6) The last four die cutters worked in northeastern Spain and do not show strong stylistic influences from other parts of the kingdom. My research on the Tarraconensian mints and that of Narbona is very limited, but a division of die cutters in the region is quite evident. Mateu y Llopis and Miles pointed out the distinct style which seems to have emanated from Barcinona (= Barcelona).[447] The engraver I call the '*Barcinona*' engraver (Barc.) was already cutting dies with the facing-busts design late in Leovigild's reign. My brief study of tremisses of this region has revealed his activity in two other places in Reccared's reign, Rodas and Tarracona. He probably produced the dies at Gerunda which generated quite similar tremisses during Witteric's rule, after which time the Barcelona mint surprisingly fell inactive for several decades.[448]

7) The '*Narbona*' engraver (N), although also active at Rodas in Leovigild's reign, must be presumed to have been based in Narbonensis, given the greater importance of its provincial capital. It is likely that there was only one die engraver in Narbona under Leovigild and his successor, which are the only reigns I have been able to investigate. I have reached this tentative conclusion because Leovigild-Narbona coins with different but related bust styles – Miles's 3a, 3b, 3c; Pliego's 3a, 4a, 7a, 8 – all have a very similar epigraphic style.[449] Die cutting was carried out by the same person in the time of Reccared and well beyond. Mateu y Llopis noted that the same basic style was kept up in Narbona until c. 621, when the tremisses of Suinthila assumed a Tarraconensian type; under Sisenand, the style was once again Narbonensian, only to revert back to a Tarraconensian model under Chintila and his immediate successors.[450] I have not yet determined whether these

446 In the last analysis, this may be evidence in favor of several die cutters rather than one, but the photos and commentary in Appendix II demonstrate that stylistic variants sometimes occurred at the same mint and even on the two sides of the same coin across the span of Visigothic regal issues. I take this to be an inevitable consequence of an engraver's frequent movements and stylistic variations.

447 Mateu y Llopis, *Catálogo*, 258; Miles, *The Coinage of the Visigoths*, 48, 61. This is reflected in the 'Barcinonense' grouping in Pliego, *La moneda visigoda*, v. 1, 159f (see also 106 on the Barcinona mint).

448 See the table in Appendix I, Figure I.7.

449 Miles, *The Coinage of the Visigoths*, pl. II.1-3; see ibid., 57 for the Leovigildan sub-types at Narbona. Pliego, *La moneda visigoda*, v. 1, 166 and the Index of Types in ibid., 29-42.

450 Mateu y Llopis, *Catálogo*, 236.

changes were the result of one engraver copying the designs of nearby mints or rather of a turning over of die cutters.

8) There are two principal sub-types of Tarraconensis from the period under consideration. One was in all likelihood based in Cesaragusta (= Zaragoza), a city and mint of importance. In Reccared's long reign, the '*Cesaragusta*' engraver (Ces.) also cut dies for the coins of Tirasona (= Tarazona) and Tarracona. By the reign of Witteric this minter toiled no longer in Tarracona but in Cesaragusta and a few smaller mints to the northwest.

9) The other main Tarraconensian sub-type is from the '*Tarracona*' engraver (Tarr.), as I suppose the capital city to be the most important site of his work. Beginning under Witteric, he appears to have an engraving style extremely close to that of the Cesaragusta die cutter. Perhaps the two engravers had worked together at first but now split responsibilities. The Tarracona die sinker continued his work in this city for many years, and appears to have engraved dies in the same style at Sagunto starting in Gundemar's reign, and at Valencia when this mint just beyond the provincial border opened in the 620s under Suinthila. His minting activity can be traced in coins of Gerunda struck in these years. If the attributions made here find acceptance, Tarracona was the city with the most die engravers in the province, at least three from Leovigild's reign through Sisenand's.

Several different styles, and therefore probably multiple engravers, were present in tiny mints cropping up in Gallaecia in the first few decades after its conquest by Leovigild. I have not undertaken extensive research for that very complicated zone of minting. An excellent introductory commentary on these styles can be found in the chapter on Gallaecia in Mateu y Llopis's book.[451]

The nine die cutters above are no longer in evidence when we come to the reign of Reccesvinth. By that time, and perhaps already in the reign of Chindasvinth, a different minting organization emerged. Reforms involving a drastic reduction in the number of mints were undertaken. Coins of the major mints, which were almost the only ones remaining under Reccesvinth, have a more uniform aspect, although styles still varied from mint to mint. The matter awaits more investigation, but it seems that a single die engraver worked at each of the dozen or so workshops, and that the engravers did not travel between mints.

Some further observations can be made from the stylistic study described in Appendix II and summarized above. The first is the habitual itinerancy

451 Mateu y Llopis, *Catálogo*; an updated type study of Gallaecian tremisses is in Pliego, *La moneda visigoda*, v. 1, 164-66.

of several engravers in the years c. 579 to c. 649. It has often been remarked that Visigothic Spain had a rather large number of mints in that period, but it has never been recognized that the kingdom had a much smaller number of engravers than mints. Nonetheless, certain mints had several engravers during the same reign, some of them probably active at the same time.[452] The death or removal of engravers, increased volume of output, or changing itineraries could all be reasons why more than one engraver would appear at one mint in a single reign. Second, what I have called sub-types derive in each case from an individual engraver; it appears that no two engravers ever produced the same sub-type. This is easy to understand if we consider that each sub-type has, within a range of tiny variations, its own fine points which are peculiar to the engraver working the die. How was it possible for Miles to attribute several sub-types to mints that have no apparent geographic link? The answer, which he had not yet discovered, is that some engravers traveled to various locations.

Conclusions

The facing-bust sub-types fall into a pattern that is primarily regional rather than provincial. Minting regions are simply those areas in which the traveling engravers worked. Regional organization of minting explains why most border mints do not obey what looks otherwise like a mainly provincial scheme. It explains why in Carthaginensis the same style appeared only in the central part and perhaps the sector to the south. Tarraconensis had two principal types used virtually only in that province – which Heiss, Mateu y Llopis, and Miles called the Tarraconensian provincial type – but they were not the only types used there, and more than once one of them crossed into Carthaginensis where it was used on coins of Valentia. The northernmost mint of the province, Rodas, did not use the quintessential Tarraconensian sub-types in the reign of Leovigild, but one by the engraver at Narbona. In the next reign, it used the special type of Barcinona, as did Tarracona down the coast, creating a new minting zone. In Lusitania, most of the gold coins adhered to a provincial type, but here again we have noted the presence of Carthaginensian designs at times. The fluidity of minting regions is merely the product of engravers' movements.

Yet, the Visigothic monetary organization operated on several levels at the same time. Coin production itself was carried out in regional arrangements

452 In Appendix II plates and tables I have occasionally pointed out where two different engravers possibly account for the inscription and the bust, respectively.

according to where each die cutter was told to go (or where he encountered demand for new coinage, if private persons could sometimes request the minting of their own gold, as seems unlikely). The 'Toleto engraver' gave local traits to his coins in the many places where he labored. Others included control marks on the tremisses as well as small variations at separate sites – not only dots, but exact execution of the face, cuirass (e.g. sometimes a dot on the neck, sometimes not), or hair (endings blending in with the cuirass or made of dots). Moreover, as we shall see in the next section, many secondary mints issued coins of standards lower than those of major mints. All of this implies some kind of monetary administration at a local level. With whom that local authority lay is not clearly known. If, as I believe, many secondary mints did not exist as permanent workshops but were instead dependent upon the temporary visit of an engraver or minting crew, then that person or group of workers could have determined local matters of money-making. It seems unlikely that such questions would have been decided by a local official such as the count of the city. The loosely provincial types established by a few engravers might represent a third level of administration, perhaps that of the provincial governor or a high-ranking financial officer. Provincial types can now be reduced to three: Lusitanian, Carthaginensian (central), and Tarraconensian.[453] Because their use turns out to be rather confined, we may suspect that provincial authority over at least the fine points of the making of money was limited.

The considerable regional, provincial, and local characteristics seen in a number of aspects of the coins should not make us overlook the evidence of centralized control over the workshops. Centralization is suggested by the general conformity of inscriptions after the very first years of regal gold coinage.[454] Centralized instructions from Leovigild's court must account for the use of the facing busts and an almost uniform version of the obverse legend[455] throughout the kingdom, particularly in Gallaecia starting in 585, when the Suevic kingdom had just been overthrown. While the degree to which mints were managed from Toleto is uncertain, "only government intervention can explain the changes in weight and fineness of Leovigild's reign and the two conspicuous changes in type and inscription under Chindaswinth, Recceswinth and Egica," as Grierson remarked.[456] It

453 Gallaecian sub-types are too varied to compose a provincial type.

454 Tomasini, *The Barbaric Tremissis in Spain*, 72 wrote of a gradual standardization by the late pre-regal and early Leovigildan period, but the opposite seems to be true, as can be seen in the great variety of spellings on JII coins and early in Leovigild's reign.

455 LEOVIGILDVS REX.

456 Grierson and Blackburn, *Medieval European Coinage*, v. 1, 53. And further, "Only the government can have laid down that the coins should bear the names of both king and mint, and not

is reasonable to postulate that these directives were sent out by the *comes thesaurorum* or whomever held command of minting. But effective central control of minting may have been achieved by only a few Visigothic kings, a point that will become more evident when we turn our attention in the next section to metallurgical analyses of the tremisses.

The style study described in this chapter goes well beyond the scope of Mateu y Llopis, Miles, and Pliego's investigations, and the conclusions that I draw from it suggest a different kind of organization for the first half of the life of the facing-busts type. Yet, the observations of these scholars about exceptions to the provincial scheme already pointed in this direction. I am well aware that the present style study raises as many questions about mint organization as it answers. In the case of the engraver whom I suppose to have been based in Toleto, his adaptation of styles points to both provincial and extra-provincial elements in the administration of mints. If indeed a single person or a small group under his influence is behind such wide-ranging issues, he has kept largely to a provincial division in terms of bust design and even epigraphic style, but established a connection between mints in vast stretches of the kingdom, a connection which appears to spring from the royal city. In the south, neither the geographical division of labor, nor the coin designs were based on provincial boundaries at all (the Cordoban style being more local than provincial).[457] Further research on dies and sub-types holds out the hope of clarifying certain engraving styles and the relationship between provincial types and particular engraving styles.

D Metrological and Metallurgical Standards of Visigothic Regal Tremisses

The coins of any era are produced at some kind of standards of weight and fineness, which give currency a more or less fixed value. The theoretical standards of Visigothic pseudo-imperial tremisses conformed to those of Roman tremisses: c. 1.516g and c. ninety-eight per cent fine. But the regal gold currency standards underwent changes, and the real weights and fineness of the coins were often different from the standards. Investigation

those of moneyers as in Gaul." Reccesvinth's sub-type 1h (Miles, *The Coinage of the Visigoths*, 51 and 54), used in many parts of the kingdom, reverted back to an early Leovigildan style and could not have occurred without a mandate from the center. The same is true of Egica-Wittiza coins, all with two busts facing each other on the obverse, but with an enormous stylistic variety at the many mint sites.

457 In the next chapter we will examine the special circumstances that account for this.

of when and where standards were adhered to and where fluctuations occurred helps to ascertain important characteristics of minting in Gothic Spain.

The best method of determining the weight standard(s) of a given set of coins, as well as the variability of real weights – how close the coins came to the standard – is the frequency table. When placed on a graph, this shows the number of coins that fall into each weight class of some small division, e.g. .04 or .05 grams, from which one or more classes will emerge as the modal class(es), if in practice minters have tried to keep coins close to the predetermined weight(s). While the frequency table often shows small clusters of coins that occur far off an observable standard, it reveals the standard more accurately than does a general average including coins of abnormal weights. It avoids another potential inaccuracy of the average, which fails to account for the normal asymmetric curve of a graph of real weights, with a gradual slope downward below the modal class but a sharp drop above those weight values. This occurs because minters of gold coin aiming for a given weight tended to err toward lower weights, which would pass as acceptable, rather than toward higher weights, which would entail a waste of gold. Wear and clipping would produce the same results. In order to have sufficient numbers of Visigothic tremisses for frequency tables, the products of all mints during one reign often have to be joined in a single set. When there are enough extant coins from a particular mint, the frequency table will usually give a clear indication of the modal weights in various reigns; a pattern may emerge which suggests the recommended weight at that workshop.[458]

An attempt can be made to determine the official weight standard (or legal weight) in the kingdom despite fluctuations, as well as the recommended weight (or actual standard) in the many cases where there are not enough coins for a proper sample from individual mints. For the legal weight one is fairly secure in relying on the modal weight from Toleto, which, apart from a late exception mentioned below, was always an exemplary mint in terms of weight and fineness even though it was not always the most productive mint, at least as far as one can determine by the volume of extant coins. If one then finds the modal weight class at what the corpus implies is the most productive mint – or the second most productive when Toleto takes this role – one can form a reasonable hypothesis that the recommended weight lay within the limits of this class, based on the supposition that a mint with enormous production would be under close supervision and therefore

458 I.e. the observed standard suggests the weight recommended to the workers.

would have to adhere to the officially recommended weight.[459] We shall see, however, that small mints often did not comply with the same standard.

Test Results

The weight measurements used in this section come from several sources. The majority are from statistics of 1,975 tremisses compiled by three Portuguese numismatists, among them Mário Gomes Marques. The preponderance of their data is from a careful selection of weights in Miles's catalog, to which are added measurements from 237 unpublished coins weighed by the authors.[460] Another sample comprises 377 tremisses, most of them tested by Lauris Olson in 1986 at the American Numismatic Society in New York City.[461] Olson re-weighed tremisses whose measurements already appeared in Miles, using more accurate instrumentation and obtaining slightly different results. To his own measurements, Olson attached published results from seventy-three coins at the Fitzwilliam Museum at Cambridge University and five at the Ashmolean Museum at Oxford University.[462]

From this broad pool of data, it is evident that the theoretical weight of regal Visigothic gold currency continued to derive from that of the Roman tremissis, which was based on the Constantinian solidus of twenty-four *siliquae*: 1/3 of a solidus of 24 *siliquae* = 8 *siliquae* = c. 1.516g.[463] The second chapter of the present study touched on the temporary reduction of the weight standard during Leovigild's rule. With the inauguration of the facing-busts design in 584, the coins struck at Toleto fall almost invariably into a modal class with a central value of 1.515g, or in the next modal class below, with a central value of 1.475g.[464] Marques and his colleagues have

459 Marques et al., *Ensaios*, 92. Pliego, *La moneda visigoda*, v. 1, 210, Table 18 displays metrological data from coins of Toledo, Ispali, and Emerita. The several tables furnished in ibid., 199-213 are from a much larger set of tremisses than my own and combine various testing groups. The metrological intervals used are .10g.
460 These are published in Marques et al., *Ensaios*, 92; see the authors' explanation on p. 83.
461 See Figure I.11 in Appendix I.
462 These are labeled as MEC (Grierson and Blackburn, *Medieval European Coinage*) and O (for Oxford, in D. M. Metcalf and F. Schweizer, "Milliprobe Analyses of Some Visigothic, Suevi, and Other Gold Coins of the Early Middle Ages," *Archaeometry* 12 [1970], 173-88). Olson did not include three repaired coins from MEC which could not be properly analyzed: nos. 259, 281, and 284.
463 *Siliquae* is the Latin term for weight units and should not be confused with late Roman silver coins by the same name. The Greek term for such units is *keratia*, 'karats' in English, but because of possible confusion I have used this term only when dealing with fineness.
464 Marques et al., *Ensaios*, graphs on 114-17; Pliego, *La moneda visigoda*, v. 1, 210, Table 18 demonstrates the same essential fact. In the cases where 1.475g is the main weight division

calculated the number of *siliquae* in tremisses and solidi with these modal values.[465] 1.515g is equivalent to 7.99 *siliquae*, or a solidus of 23.98g; a tremisses of 1.475g weighs 7.78 *siliquae*, corresponding to a solidus weight of 23.35 *siliquae*. Even the lower weight is proximate to the imperial standard and rules out a correspondence to the light-weight solidi of 20, 21, or 22 *siliquae* that circulated in the West. What may account for the weights several tenths below the Roman standard is a different 'tale,' that is to say, the number of coins cut from each large unit of gold. Imperial tremisses of eight *siliquae* were cut at a tremisses-per-pound ratio of 216.[466] The Portuguese scholars demonstrate that the most productive mint in each of the reigns for which they had enough specimens to test – usually Emerita, but occasionally Ispali – produced at the same or almost the same modal class as the Toleto mint.

There are, unfortunately, too few coins in each testing group to make a frequency table for every mint site in every reign. We must be content for now with comparing the results from all extant coins of each king and from coins struck at certain mints.[467] It must be borne in mind that the

average, the 1.50-1.53g weight class is always the second most frequent. Two exceptions to the high-weight mode at Toleto are from the coins of Egica and Egica-Wittiza, the modal class of which was well below 1.516g, but in both cases the second most frequent class is 1.54-1.57g and 1.50-1.53g, respectively. It is possible two different standards were employed at Toleto in these years.

465 Marques et al., *Ensaios*, 96, Quadro III.

466 To determine the weights of an issue moneyers might have been told how many coins were to be made from a pound (the 'tale' or 'cut'), from which would derive an average weight. Or, they may have been told, or simply decided themselves, a weight at which they would try to measure each disk. It is impossible to tell if Visigothic tremisses were struck *al pezzo* – by individual weights – or *al marco* – by a fixed number of coins per weight unit. Striking *al marco*, with the attendant changes in the tale that could take place, might explain better the wide dispersion of weight values. In the fifth century, Sozomon wrote of the minters of Cyzicus having to render a fixed number of coins to the fisc each year, which suggests that late Roman minting was done by tale: Delmaire, *Largesses sacrées*, 501; Jones, *The Late Roman Empire*, I, 439.
A law of Julian of 363 (*CTh* 12.7.2) stipulated that in every city in the Roman Empire an official weigher of solidi, called a *zygostatēs*, should be employed. The particular concern expressed in the law was that the high number of clipped coins in circulation was reducing the buying and selling of gold currency: see Kent, *Roman Imperial Coinage*, v. 10, 8. The work of these officials is recorded in succeeding centuries: see Jones, *Later Roman Empire*, v. I, 445 and III, 115 n. 84. We hear nothing of *zygostatēs* in the early Middle Ages, but must assume that weighing was carried out frequently. A law of Leovigild prohibited anyone from rejecting "a solidus of full weight" (*LV* VII.6.v), and anyone who clipped coins was to be arrested as soon as the judge learned of it (*LV* VII.6.ii). No doubt, the coins in question were placed on a balance to find out their true weight. The practice of weighing solidi especially in the late Roman and early medieval periods is well attested: see Carlà, "The End of Roman Gold Coinage," (see above n. 87) 49, 52, 64.

467 Pliego, *La moneda visigoda*, v. 1, 204-09 furnishes metrological data by province. The tables tell that the trend toward lower and more dispersed values in the 620s and 630s, discussed in

weights in the capital city and in the few most important cities were higher than average, and therefore bring up the weights of the set as a whole. The periods when the mode of the entire set is lower than Toleto's are times when recommended weights at some mints were less than the official standard;[468] this occurred in most reigns. Under a few kings, the general modal weight was in the same range as the legal weight. At other times, however, it is impossible to determine if only one standard was used since no single modal class predominates in the data pool. Such errancy in weights could result from the use of more than one standard or from irregularities of which people involved in minting or in the monetary administration may or may not have aware.[469] The following section summarizes the chronological pattern of weights considering all mints together.

Weights from Leovigild to Achila II

Some mid-sixth century Visigothic tremisses issued before Leovigild ascended to the throne seem to have had a standard of about 1.3g or somewhat less.[470] Most, however, had weights between 1.41-1.50 g, probably following the theoretical standard of the full-weight solidus but with decreasing precision. Already in the early years of this reformer king monetary changes were put in place. The first two phases of Leovigild's national coinage (reverses with Victory and a cross-on-steps) exhibit modal weights of which the central value is 1.32g, just below the weight in grams of a tremissis of seven *siliquae* (1.3265g). Such a weight standard would correspond to the 21- *siliquae* Byzantine solidus used in the western Mediterranean.[471] It is possible, however, that instead Leovigild established a tremisses-per-pound ratio of 246, which would correspond to a coin weight slightly higher than seven *siliquae* (1.33g).[472]

relation to warfare and supply of gold in the following chapter, was an effect felt broadly across Hispania including in Gallaecia (but not in Narbonensis). Ibid., 210, Table 18 informs that Toledo was only lightly affected at that time, and Emerita even less. Ispali's issues had lowered weights in Sisenand's reign but were still well controled comparatively speaking.

468 See Marques et al., *Ensaios*, 99, Quadro IV and 105, Quadro VII.

469 Ibid., 92.

470 In addition to the graphs discussed in the first chapter above (see pp. 72-74), see several examples in Grierson and Blackburn, *Medieval European Coinage*, v. 1, 438, pl 11; on pp. 14 and 50 Grierson raises his theory of a Germanic weight standard of 1.3g.

471 Marques et al., *Ensaios*, 80, 86, 94.

472 The fact that Hermenegild's coins are heavier than seven *siliquae* has been taken to support this interpretation, based on the assumption that he could utilize the propaganda of his better coins: ibid., 94. The few specimens from Hermenegild's reign in this sample weighed an average of 1.34g, with little variation in weight. His heavier coins also provide further support for the

Whichever is true, the weights of coins from c. 575 to 584 peak on a graph at 1.30-1.33g, with a classic curve in the table which indicates a well-defined standard for all or at least most mints.[473] We may conclude that Leovigild's innovative facing-busts type was issued to mark a change in the weight standard, a reversion to the old imperial weight standard of eight *siliquae*. Or, it could be, vice versa, that the return to the traditional Roman weight standard was seen as a necessity for issuing a Visigothic national design.

The improvement in weight was maintained by the monetary administration of King Reccared. However, from Liuva II through Chintila (601-39), the modal weight was no longer in the range of 1.50-1.53g (central value = 1.515g), but rather in the two frequency ranges with central values of 1.475g and 1.435g.[474] Still, in each of the eight reigns in this period a significant percentage of coins was struck within the 1.50-1.53g range, and the classic sharp drop in weights still occurred just above this range, which implies that the recommended weight of approximately 1.516g was not abandoned, or at least not everywhere. If certain mints were turning out coins with lower weights while some kept the old standard, one might suspect it was the minters at peripheral locales who took advantage of less close supervision. We will revisit this question below.

We can see the advantages of focusing on mode instead of average as we assess the weight measurements from coins made in the 620s and 630s and beyond. During Suinthila's reign (621-31), the average weight of tremisses fell to only 1.41g, whereas in Leovigild's third phase it had been about 1.47g or 1.46g. The modal weight is still fairly high, however. From 631 to 639, the average weight fell to about 1.36g; the reason for a lower average is an apparent second recommended weight somewhere near 1.21/1.22g, and possibly a third one near 1.32g.[475] The average fell during Tulga's reign (639-42) to

opinion that the rebel's issues were produced on the model of coins of Leovigild's second stage, rather than being the motive for the cross-on-steps design.

Marques et al. (ibid., 86) suppose that the standard weight in phases I and II was 1.3265g. Since the real average weight was close to 1.276g, the authors suggest that about .05g, or 4%, of the precious metal given over for striking may have been retained as brassage, the labor costs of minting. But one cannot make this conclusion from weight averages, since the modal value is still c. 1.32g in spite of the supposed withholding.

473 Figure I.13 in Appendix I.

474 Ibid. With only two coins from Reccared II, Marques et al. did not form a graph for that reign, but they have given the average of these pieces as 1.455 g: Marques et al., *Ensaios*, 85, Quadro I (table of average weights from Leovigild to Achila II). Although using larger frequency intervals, Pliego, *La moneda visigoda*, v. 1, 202, Table 10 showing averages and modes is still useful for comparison and leads to similar conclusions.

475 Figure I.13 in Appendix I.

its lowest point (1.3g) since Leovigild had established the 8-*siliquae* weight standard for the facing bust. The main recommended weight seems to have shifted to the lower-weight mark in use in previous years, while a second one remained high. From Sisenand to Tulga weights are so dispersed that it is impossible to resolve which weights were actually being targeted.[476]

Some interesting modifications were made to Visigothic money during the rule of Chindasvinth from 642 to 649, before he shared power with his son Reccesvinth. The average weight of the tremissis came up to about 1.45g, nearly the level around which it had hovered until 612 or so. The modal weight returned to a range whose central value is 1.515g. Dispersion was sharply reduced, and a significant percentage of coins was struck at weights higher than the theoretical standard. Nevertheless, the small levels of improvement in fineness at this time mean that the amount of gold in the coins bearing Chindasvinth's name was not returned to its previous level from 584 to 621, in spite of the fact that he had confiscated the property, and presumably much of the money, of hundreds of members of the nobility who were condemned to exile or execution for their alleged treason against him.[477] Monetary reforms continued during the joint reign of Chindasvinth and Reccesvinth (649-53), when the fineness of gold in the tremisses was increased along with their weight. A couple of tremisses from the very small set from this reign even reached around 1.6g. Reccesvinth was able to make further improvements in weight and fineness of tremisses during his long rule alone, presumably drawing upon his father's accumulation of wealth. The average weight of 1.49g obtained during the sole rule of Reccesvinth was very close to the standard of twenty-four *siliquae* to the solidus and was the highest during the entire period of regal Visigothic coinage. Concurrent with this improvement in standards was a vast reduction of mints in the kingdom, which we saw earlier in this chapter.

After Reccesvinth's reign came another gradual drop in coin weights. Under the joint rule of Egica and Wittiza, the average weight fell to 1.36g. It slipped further when Wittiza ruled alone (702-10), but an important clarification has recently been made. Careful review of the evidence demonstrates

476 Ibid.

477 Marques et al., *Ensaios*, 87. In the assessment of Pablo C. Díaz Martínez, "Confiscations in the Visigothic Reign of Toledo: A Political Instrument," in *Expropiations et confiscations dans les royaumes barbares. Une approche régionale*, ed. P. Porena and Y. Rivière (Rome: École Française de Rome, 2012), 93-112, Reccesvinth turned liabilities such as his father's personal acquisition of confiscations, rather than for the patrimony, into legitimization and strengthening of his position, but the necessity of placating magnates through gifts proved a vicious cycle for the monarchy.

that Wittiza's coinage should not be treated as a single group but instead can be divided in three groups: one with extremely low weights (an average of 1.20g) and two others with much higher averages (1.46g and 1.48g). This division probably corresponds to three phases, since the lower-weight coins bear the same typology as in the preceding reign and the coins with vastly improved weights have two distinct types.[478]

It has always been considered curious that the last period of the Visigothic regime (710-713), one in which the monarchy was contested, saw an increase in average coin weight in comparison to that of Wittiza's reign, since it is difficult to imagine the kings directing an improvement in coinage in this politically unstable period. But that comparison was made from an average of all of Wittiza's coins, whereas the division made by the Portuguese scholars strongly suggests that Roderic and Achila II (r. 710-11/12 and 711-14?) merely followed the recuperated standard set by Wittiza in the latter part of his reign, though in fact falling below it.[479]

Our discussion so far has implied that it is profitable to break down the combined data for each reign into sets from particular mints, as far as that is possible. Measurements from the largest sample of coins in the present discussion have been divided into those from large, medium, and small mints.[480] From this data, we can now get a more refined picture of the first period of severely deteriorating weights. It is not exactly correct to hold that tremisses between Reccared and Chindasvinth saw an almost constant drop in weight, as Miles's graph of the general average implied.[481] Rather, *some* of the coins sank in weight, while others remained near the full legal standard. It is important to note that monetary authorities could, or perhaps only wanted to, keep weights high at the central mints but not at the secondary mints. Sisenand's coins from small mints have a particularly low average (c. 1.29g).[482] Reccesvinth, on the other hand, was able to ensure high weights at all mints. A still moderately strong tremissis was sustained under Wamba, Ervig, and Egica throughout the kingdom, albeit with many fewer workshops since the mid-century reforms. Then, in Egica's and Wittiza's

478 Marques et al., *Ensaios*, 88. Pliego, *La moneda visigoda*, v. 1, 202, Table 10 reflects the same post-Reccesvinth trends and same phenomenon under Wittiza but by way of two phases.
479 Marques et al., *Ensaios*, 88.
480 Ibid., 114-17 (frequency tables for most reigns showing Toleto and the most productive mint when not Toleto) and 104, Quadro VI (= Appendix I, Figure I.14: table showing averages at the most productive mint, then at mints which account for greater than 10% of volume, 3-10% of volume, and less than 3% of volume).
481 Miles, *The Coinage of the Visigoths*, 155.
482 See Appendix I, Figure I.14.

joint reign, the downward trend in weights resumed, this time affecting large mints including Toleto. Frequency tables exclusively for Toleto coins make clear that two standards were then employed at the capital, one at 1.50-.53g and the other at 1.30-.33g.[483] Only a concerted effort to halt the trend sometime in Wittiza's reign brought the general average up again on a par with Reccesvinth's currency.

Miquel Barceló was the first to demonstrate a correlation between low-weight averages and the most extended range of weights.[484] The dispersion of weights compared to the average weight is calculated by means of what is called the coefficient of variation. Using this method, Barceló was able to show clearly the coincidence of low weights and wide variation of measurements precisely at small mints. The large drop in average weight that occurred from the reigns of Sisenand through Tulga (631-642) coincided with by far the greatest diversity of weights,[485] with the exception of a short phase during Wittiza's reign. It will be remembered that the number of mints had become greatest in the preceding decades. Barceló carries his results further when he writes that "a circuit of peripheral mints was in use to strike lower-weight coins" in this period.[486] It may be less a matter of policy of the crown, however, than simply poor control at the peripheral mints.[487] Primary mints generally had a tighter range of weights, although this is less true from 621 to 639 and under Egica (when dispersion was in the direction of very *high* weights, curiously).[488] The minimal variation of weights at all mints under Reccesvinth and his successor testify to the effectiveness of his condensing of the monetary network. Barceló's observations and the conclusions that he drew from them have some rich implications that we

483 Marques et al., 117; see also 83f. Similarly, Pliego, *La moneda visigoda*, v. 1, 210, Table 18. Idem, "El *tremis* de los últimos años," 29 explains that the mid-seventh century consolidation of minting and improvement in metrology dissipated under Wittiza, apart from Gallaecia, but a shoring up of weight later under this king's rule coinciding with new type imagery is in evidence, centered on Toledo.

484 Miquel Barceló, "A Statistical Approach to Multiple Mint Issues of Royal Coinage: The Case of the Visigoths in Hispania (585-711)," *PACT* 5 (1981), 138-54, esp. 141-51.

485 For fuller information on average weights, standard deviations, intervals of confidence, and coefficients of variation, see the corroborating figures in Marques et al., *Ensaios*, 85, Quadro I.

486 Barceló, "Statistical Approach," 149.

487 Some notably high and low weights from the sample of coins drawn up by Lauris Olson can be seen in Appendix I, Figure I.11. One of the surprising aspects there is the exaggeratedly high weight of several Gallaecian tremisses.

488 Compare our frequency tables for the coins of all mints with the tables for Toleto coins alone in Marques et al., *Ensaios*, 115-17. Pliego, *La moneda visigoda*, v. 1, 210, table 18, similarly relates the behavior of the main mints (Toleto, Ispali and Emerita).

will see in the following chapter when we discuss the motives for striking coinage.

Although it was shown in an earlier section in this chapter that minting did not adhere completely to provincial boundaries, there is some value in looking at weights by provinces. For three key reigns, Barceló calculated the difference in weight means between central and peripheral mints in the four provinces for which there was sufficient data.[489] The difference is expressed here in grams:

Figure 12: Difference in average regal tremissis weights between central and peripheral mints

Reign	Tarraconensis	Carthaginensis	Baetica	Lusitania
Suinthila	0.05 g	0.10 g	0.05 g	0.09 g
Sisenand	-0.16 g	0.27 g	0.10 g	0.11 g
Chintila	-0.12 g	0.26 g	0.20 g	0.20 g

The greatest disparity in average weights between central and non-central mints in the provinces was in Carthaginensis. That is because Carthaginensis incorporated the mint at the royal city of Toledo as well as numerous temporary mints far to the south during the long war against the Byzantines (see Chapter Four). In the three provinces encompassing the southern half of the kingdom the difference in average weights grew significantly in the period studied. When we look at statistics from the entire regal period, what happens when the average weight for each province in each reign is compared to the total average for each reign?[490] It can then be seen that Tarraconensis was below the general average in almost every period and Lusitania was almost always above it. Meanwhile, the other four provinces swung back and forth between higher- and lower-than-average weights. Erratic differences should not be surprising, given the number of secondary mints in the first half of the seventh century in Tarraconensis, Carthaginensis, and Baetica. Nor should it be surprising that the least conformity between weight means in the different provinces was during Tulga's reign, while the highest conformity was in the reign of Reccesvinth.

489 Barceló, "Statistical Approach," 149. Note that the statistics were compiled according to the old view of Elvora being located farther west in Lusitania, and without information on the new mint sites discussed further above.
490 See Marques et al., *Ensaios*, 101, Quadro V.

Fineness in the Regal Period

The weight of a coin is not, of course, the only criterion by which to know how 'good' or 'bad' it is. Equally important is the quality of a coin, in other words, the fineness of the metal. One should keep in mind that neither real weight, nor fineness alone determine the gold content of the tremisses. A coin could be very heavy but have comparatively less gold content than a light coin because a large amount of silver is mixed in with the gold. The gold content of Visigothic tremisses is highly variable, with as much fluctuation in fineness as in weight. In fact, whereas a theoretical standard weight was maintained from the late sixth century to the late seventh century, the theoretical standard of fineness was unstable.

A much greater amount of labor is required to test the fineness of the tremisses than their weights. Miles did not attempt to test finenesses in the vast collection at the American Numismatic Society. But after the pioneering work of Philip Grierson in this area, then of Metcalf and Schweizer followed by Oddy and Hughes,[491] great gains were made by Lauris Olson and the three scholars who tested coins in Portugal. Olson's sample is the same as that for which he gave weight measurements: 377 coins, including the seventy-eight from the Fitzwilliam and Ashmolean Museums. *Ensaios sobre história monetária da monarquia visigoda* discusses results from the authors' own tests on 237 coins and those from the earlier research cited here, excluding Olson's work since it was not published at the time.[492] In the chapter of that book on the concentration of gold in regal tremisses, the authors point out that different methods have been used, producing unequal results. X-ray fluorescence gives higher measurements than the specific gravity method, sometimes up to ten per cent higher; it is debated which method is more accurate. Yet, the tables and graphs presented in their study, some of which are reproduced in Appendix I, make appropriate distinctions between testing methods but also demonstrate the parallelism

491 The results of these samples and their own tests are discussed in Marques et al., *Ensaios*, 119-70. For the original articles see the following: P. Grierson, "Visigothic Metrology," *Numismatic Chronicle*, 6th ser., 13 (1953), 74-87; D. M. Metcalf and F. Schweizer, "Milliprobe Analyses"; W. A. Oddy and M. J. Hughes, "The Specific Gravity Method for the Analysis of Gold Coins," in *Methods of Chemical and Metallurgical Investigation of Ancient Coinage*, ed. E. T. Hall and D. M. Metcalf (London: Royal Numismatic Society, 1972), 75-87.

492 Marques et al., *Ensaios*, 128 and 151-70, have proved that silver was the only principal alloy, the copper content not exceeding 3.2 per cent and usually under two per cent. The chemical analysis helped the authors to determine the doubtful authenticity of many coins. Twenty-eight out of thirty coins that they had already suspected of being fakes turned out to have between four per cent and 10.9 per cent copper content on the surface.

of the results. They may differ by a few percentage points for most periods, but the fluctuations follow almost the same pattern.[493]

What is not harmonious is the discussion by the various scholars on the results obtained. Unfortunately, Grierson's account of trends in fineness are not in full accord with his data.[494] This has led to some confusions regarding the quality of Visigothic tremisses. The first and most serious one involves Leovigild's coinage. Grierson asserted that in its first two 'regal' phases the coins were about ninety per cent fine and weighed c. 1.3g,[495] but that the facing-busts issues were made at a weight of c. 1.5g – virtually the Roman legal standard – and with only seventy-five per cent fineness. He raised the possibility that the higher weight was meant to conceal the reduced quality. The difference in gold content would indeed have been significant: .045 grams less gold in the later series. The problem is that the fineness Grierson recorded of a single coin from each of Leovigild's first two phases is only eighty-six per cent from the first phase and seventy-one per cent from the second, and the first coin is really of the transition period before the emperor's name was removed. Also, the larger samples of Olson and of Marques and his colleagues indicate that at the beginning of Leovigild's named coinage fineness was already brought below ninety per cent.[496] When average gold content is calculated from these results, contrary to what Grierson's assertion would force us to conclude, the

493 See Appendix I, Figure I.15, which compares the results obtained by Olson, Oddy (in Grierson and Blackburn, *Medieval European Coinage*), and Marques et al., *Ensaios* (the last two copied from the graph in ibid., 133, Fig. 3). For the X-ray fluorescent method used by Marques and his colleagues see ibid., 129f. Olson's specific gravity measurements were done by extremely careful procedure, including three tests on each coin on the same day and re-testing if any result differed significantly. The account of his procedures is in Appendix I, Figure I.11. Oddy's procedure for the specific gravity measurements that appear in Grierson and Blackburn, *Medieval European Coinage*, v. 1, 442-51, are unfortunately not laid out in that work, but it is assumed to be the same method described in Oddy and Hughes, "Specific Gravity." Metcalf and Schweizer used a method of X-ray fluorescent spectrometry outlined in Metcalf and Schweizer, "Milliprobe Analyses."

494 Grierson and Blackburn, *Medieval European Coinage*, v. 1, 39-54, and the figures in 442-51 from Oddy which are said (53) to supersede the figures in Grierson, "Visigothic Metrology".

495 Grierson's hypothesis of a Germanic weight standard based on the grain and set at 1.3g may be found in Grierson and Blackburn, *Medieval European Coinage*, v. 1, 14 and 50. His division of Leovigild's regal coinage into three series is slightly different than the three phases found in Marques et al., *Ensaios*. The first series is made up of coins without mint name, the second of coins with profile bust and mint name (including both VPW and cross-on-steps), the third of facing busts. (Grierson, "Visigothic Metrology," 84.)

496 Olson repeated the error, in spite of his own measurements, which show the fineness of Leovigild's coins to have hardly departed from the range of 70-75%; see Olson, "Coin Hoard Structure," 6.

overall quality of the tremisses can be seen to have improved with the facing-busts series. A devaluation did occur, but it came as the regal series was inaugurated and not as a result of the adjustments within that series. The evolution of the metrological features at that time is sketched in the following table.

Figure 13: Gold content of tremisses leading up to Leovigild's facing-busts phase

Period of Tremisses	Modal Weight	Average Fineness	Gold Content (weight x fineness)
Late ps.-imperial (JII)	c. 1.48g (higher of 2 modes)	c. 95% [Marques et al.]	1.4g
CVRRV	c. 1.44g (one group at 1.32g)	c. 95% [Marques et al.]	1.3g
Leovigild – ph. I (VPW)	c. 1.32g	c. 85% [Marques et al.] *c. 73% [Olson / MEC]*	1.12g *0.96g*
Leovigild – ph. II (COS)	c. 1.32g	c. 84% [Marques et al.] *c. 73% [Olson / MEC]*	1.11g *0.96g*
Leovigild – ph. III (FB)	c. 1.515g	c. 85% [Marques et al.] *c. 74% [Olson / MEC]*	1.29g *1.12g*

The new standard established by Leovigild, which may have been set at eighteen karats fine (= seventy-five per cent), was maintained during the fifteen years in which his son Reccared held the throne. It is perhaps a sign of the strength of Reccared's control over the monetary system that the coefficient of variation in measurements of fineness of his coins is practically the same as that of his father's facing-busts coinage.[497] In the forty years that followed, the average fineness decreased at a fairly rapid rate until it reached as low as fifty per cent, although only from 639 to 642 was quality highly variable. In Chindasvinth's reign (642-49), a dramatic improvement can already be seen in the results from all the samples, which show average fineness of approximately sixty per cent. More improvement was made in the joint reign of Chindasvinth-Reccesvinth (to roughly sixty-five per cent by SG method, seventy-nine per cent by X-ray fluorescence) and in the initial part of Reccesvinth's sole rule. The bulk of Reccesvinth's tremisses average between sixty-seven per cent and seventy-five per cent. If the seventy-five per cent average obtained

497 See Appendix I, Figure I.12, which lists the averages from Olson's sample. Cf. Pliego, *La moneda visigoda*, v. 1, 211, Table 19 – concentration of gold in the tremisses throughout the regal series, assembled from assorted testing methods and samples.

by X-ray fluorescent spectrometry is more accurate, as would seem from scientific investigation of the method, Reccesvinth's minters probably fixed the standard at eighteen karats, as it appears to have been during Leovigild's reign. Simultaneous with improvements in weight and fineness under these kings was a reduction in the divergence from the standard of both components.[498]

The trend for the remainder of the Visigothic regime is similar to that of the weight means in the same period. The quality of the metal fell progressively until reaching its nadir of c. thirty per cent in Wittiza's reign. But the division of Wittiza's coinage into three stages by Marques and his team suggests that the slide continued only at the beginning of his rule, after which time a major upgrade was undertaken.[499] With only two tremisses tested from Wittiza's latest stage, one cannot confirm whether the average of seventy-five per cent marks a revival of the original standard, but it is tempting to think so.

The graphs that Olson and the Portuguese scholars have produced from the growing body of test results help to emphasize the fluctuations in fineness from the beginning to the end of the regal period. Grierson fell into an erroneous generalization in later works touching on this question by painting a picture of a steady, unbroken decline in quality after Reccared. In doing so, he contradicted his own data and an earlier article that accurately described the significant reversal of debasement in the reigns of Chindasvinth and Reccesvinth.[500] The reality is that in some periods there was a strong tendency toward decline, while some kings showed themselves capable of arresting a slide in fineness. Such information brings a more refined knowledge of monetary affairs, and also opens up questions as to why debasement occurred, how certain kings were capable of achieving sharp improvements, and what purpose this fluctuating currency was meant to serve. The following two chapters address these questions.

498 Olson has isolated two coins from Reccesvinth's sole rule as part of a separate, early phase ('A'). The fineness of one of them is just fifty-four per cent, which accounts for the surprisingly large standard deviation shortly after 650 in his graph.

499 Olson's average is about forty per cent (see Appendix I, Figures I.11 and I.15), but Marques et al. give quite different values from the three groups of coins (Appendix I, Figure I.16, a reproduction of Marques et al., *Ensaios*, 131, Quadro VI).

500 Grierson and Blackburn, *Medieval European Coinage*, v. 1, 54: "The coins remained at this figure [18 carats] under Reccared, after which further reductions took place. From the mid-century onwards the coins are only about 50% gold, though the fineness differs somewhat from mint to mint." A similar account is found in Grierson, *Coins of Medieval Europe*, 22. For the earlier version see "Visigothic Metrology," 84-87.

The scholars using X-ray fluorescent spectrometry have charted the results from the four most productive provinces and from Toleto, Emerita, and Ispali.[501] All the graphs follow the same high and low trends, but to a greater or lesser degree. For example, Tarraconensis and Baetica have much lower percentages of fineness than the general average; figures from Lusitania and Carthaginensis are equal to or just above the general average. Graphs of the three predominant mints are somewhat predictable. Emerita did not quite reach the lowest levels of debasement that occurred elsewhere, and during the years of greatest debasement in the 620s and 630s (average fifty-three per cent), Toleto coins remain closely between 63-69 per cent. Therefore, while the chief mints in the kingdom also produced coins of lower quality in those years and never reached more than seventy-eight per cent fineness after Reccared's reign, it was the secondary mints that brought the average down by several more percentage points. However, not even the primary mints avoided the extreme debasement reached during the reign of Egica and Wittiza and in the beginning of Wittiza's reign. In fact, the figures from Toleto are the lowest of all, dropping below thirty-five per cent. It can be concluded from the graphs of individual mints that nowhere was there a uniform standard of fineness as there was for the weights from the late sixth to the late seventh centuries.

Throughout most of the seventh century, a considerable number of tremisses were struck at very high weights, 1.5 g or even more, perhaps in order to hide or to some extent make up for inferior metallic quality. Grierson has pointed out that even at contemporary imperial mints such high weights were exceptional.[502] This habit of producing debased coinage at or above the legal weight standard was acquired and even exaggerated by Muslim minters in Spain shortly after the conquest, in sharp contrast to the Muslim practice further east of minting gold coins of regular weights and high fineness.[503] In a matter of years, the minters in al-Andalus brought dinars and thulths (one third dinars) back to nearly twenty-four-karat quality, as Olson's graph illustrates.[504]

If the Visigothic kingdom had not been overtaken in the early eighth century, would its gold currency have given way to a silver coinage instead? Grierson made this argument based on the conversion from gold to silver currency in Merovingian France around 670, which seemed to him to be

501 Marques et al., *Ensaios*, 136-42, Figs. 4-10.

502 Grierson and Blackburn, *Medieval European Coinage*, v. 1, 54.

503 Ibid. See also George C. Miles, *The Coinage of the Umayyads of Spain* (New York, 1950).

504 Appendix I, Figure I.17.

foreshadowed in Spain by marked decline in fineness and the decline and irregularity of weights in the final years of the kingdom.[505] He may well be correct. Not many years after the invasion of 711, Muslim Spain converted to a silver-based currency system.[506]

505 Grierson, *Coins of Medieval Europe*, 22. He drew an interesting conclusion with respect to the change in Merovingia: "The introduction of silver, with its lower purchasing power, must certainly imply a change in the economic pattern of life" (ibid., 20). The silver phase corresponded not to a gold drain but to a proliferation of local markets. Since Visigothic gold currency underwent marked improvements, albeit of short-term success, it does not seem that changing patterns in the economy in Spain were having – or were allowed to have – the same effect. But a general trend in the West toward debasement or a change to silver currency in the seventh century is undeniable. English silver was also introduced after a period of debasement. In the middle of the century Byzantine gold coins in the West became gradually less fine (W. A. Oddy, "The Debasement of the Provincial Byzantine Gold Coinage from the Seventh to Ninth Centuries," in *Studies in Early Byzantine Gold Coinage*, ed. W. Hahn and W. E. Metcalf [New York: American Numismatic Society, 1988], 135-42).
506 Issues of silver dirhams probably began in 721/722 (AH 103) and quickly accelerated, while the minting of gold slowed after 720 and ended in 745 (AH 128): see Chapter Six.

4. Why Were Gold Coins Struck in the Visigothic Kingdom?

Abstract
From descriptions of tremisses, mints, and their operations, Chapter Four aims to explain why the Visigothic state minted gold currency. A smaller category of primary mints played a key role in fiscal operations: the major cities were the destinations for tax revenues and took the lead in minting. Secondary mints, widely dispersed, were a much larger category. Military connections emerge as the single obvious factor in the placement of these temporary mints. These connections explain how a seemingly odd geographical distribution was deemed convenient and could result in exceptionally high output. Southern Iberian mints, late on in the war against Byzantine occupation, are only the most obvious case here. Under Leovigild, propagandistic legends were also incorporated into numerous emissions.

Keywords: purpose; primary mints; secondary mints; taxation; fiscal; military

A The Late Roman Context

The previous chapters have described the Visigothic minting system in Gaul and Spain as well as it can now be known and have offered evidence of the manner in which minting was carried out at the many sites. Equipped with extensive data on the minting network and operations – the 'what and how,' so to speak, of monetary production in the Visigothic kingdom – the much broader question of why the coins were made can be addressed. This second field of inquiry is every bit as important as the first. Without contemporary documents to inform us about the matter, the question of why minting was undertaken is unfortunately impossible to answer with the relative

Kurt, A., *Minting, State, and Economy in the Visigothic Kingdom: From Settlement in Aquitaine through the First Decade of the Muslim Conquest of Spain.*
Taylor & Francis Group, 2020
DOI 10.5117/9789462981645_CH04

precision which one can attain about the facts of coined money now above ground. The coins yield much information about what the workshops were doing, but tell nothing directly about the reason for their being struck.[507] The answer is in the realm of conjecture, yet with more numismatic data now in hand we are in a position to judge which hypotheses concerning the purpose of minting are most tenable.

Some of the earliest authors to take up the matter concluded from the legends of Visigothic solidi and tremisses, and from occasional holes in the coins or attached loops, that the gold pieces served primarily as political monuments and as decorative pendants.[508] Such a simplified view of the coins no longer holds merit in explaining the manufacture of coins on a large scale, if only for the much greater volume of coins and rather widespread circulation that we have become aware of in the past century and a half. The propaganda value of inscriptions on regal tremisses has been emphasized by some scholars, who have awakened others to the great importance and the rich variety of this element of Visigothic currency.[509] Propaganda, however, is now widely recognized as a secondary factor, a use to which kings put the coins and not an explanation of why money was struck in the first place. For the better part of the last century, when the reason for producing coinage was discussed in the literature on the currency of Visigothic Spain, it was assumed that the motivation of the state was to facilitate general economic activity, even though it was acknowledged that the use of currency was combined with or even overshadowed by barter systems of exchange. In recent decades, a different view has begun to prevail. Several scholars have argued that satisfying the state's fiscal needs and especially its military expenses was not only an important use made of coinage, but the predominant reason for minting coins.

Before we elaborate and assess the ideas mentioned above, we should bear in mind some of the main points brought forth in the previous chapters, which are phenomena that must be explained by any sound hypothesis about

507 Miles, *The Coinage of the Visigoths*, addressed the first point of inquiry but not the second.

508 E.g. A. Fernández Guerra, *Historia de España desde la invasión de los pueblos germánicos hasta la ruina de la monarquía visigoda* (Madrid: El Progreso Editorial, 1854); see Tomasini, *The Barbaric Tremissis*, 35. See also Miquel Crusafont i Sabater, "Monete suebe e visigote," in *I Goti*, ed. V. Bierbrauer et al. (Milan: Electa Lombardia, 1994), 348-51, here 350 n. 22, and idem, "The Copper Coinage," 55-56; also the comment in Orlandis, *Historia del reino*, 282. In 1759, Velázquez, *Congeturas sobre las medallas de los reyes godos, y suevos de España*, used the words 'medallas' and 'monedas' interchangeably.

509 Esp. Hillgarth, "Coins and Chronicles"; McCormick, *Eternal Victory*; F. Mateu y Llopis, "El arte monetario visigodo. Las monedas como monumentos (un ensayo de interpretación)," *Archivo Español de Arqueología* 18 (1945), 34-58; and Suchodolski, "Les débuts du monnayage."

why coins were struck in the Visigothic kingdom. We recall that the record of minting in the regal period shows some mints to have been regularly active (provincial capitals being foremost in each region), some less so, and as much as a third or more apparently open only temporarily. Some rather large areas had very few mints or – as far as finds reveal so far – none at all. Gallaecia was the probable site of forty-five of the ninety-eight workshops currently known, yet its extant coins form a very small percentage of the total. Mints in the south were not especially numerous, but together were apparently far more productive than the mints of any other region. Emerita, Ispali, and Toleto have yielded the greatest number of surviving tremisses. Certain coins, especially from the south and the northwest, bear victory inscriptions which fall into chronological patterns. Furthermore, these appear to correlate with the spheres of activity of individual engravers whose work was not confined to single provinces. We have also seen in detail how actual metallic standards fluctuate over time and that they are generally higher in major urban centers and lower at peripheral sites.

A fiscal coinage?

It may be fruitful to frame our examination of why coins were made in Visigothic Spain in the context of the scholarly debate that has heated up in the last few decades over the purpose of coinage in the Roman Empire. Two camps have arisen on the question of Roman currency, one that sees its almost sole purpose *from the point of view of the Roman government that produced it* as a fiscal instrument, and another that views its minting as largely intended to provide the means for the vast economic activity throughout the Empire. No one denies the underlying purpose of imperial gold coinage as a means for the state to collect taxes and make expenditures conveniently.[510] There is disagreement, however, as to the exclusivity of this aim and the extent to which coinage was used in the economy as a whole.

510 It is true that the principal taxes and modes of supply and payment were sometimes in the form of grain (*annona, capitus*). This was due largely to the unavailability of precious metals at times, which strengthens the point at hand about convenience. Yet, what is at issue is the entire incentive for making coinage, seen here from the perspective not only of its immediate use but its complete cycle of use before being lost entirely. The phases of taxation in kind and in coin from the fourth to the eighth centuries will be found in various sections of Jones, *Later Roman Empire*, and Hendy, *Studies in the Byzantine Economy*; see also the particular treatment of expenditure in kind or coin by the Byzantine Empire in John Haldon, "The Army and the Economy: The Allocation and Redistribution of Surplus Wealth in the Byzantine State," *Mediterranean Historical Review* 72 (1992), 133-53, and idem, "Military Service, Military Lands, and the Status of Soldiers: Current Problems and Interpretations," *Dumbarton Oaks Papers* 47 (1993), 1-67.

Michael Crawford positioned himself at one extreme when he wrote, "the use of coined money as a means of exchange was largely limited to the cities of the Empire," and "the Roman government had no policy concerning the supply of coinage and no monetary policy except in matters which directly affected its own interest or standing."[511] Contrariwise, it has been argued from literary, numismatic, and archeological evidence that coinage was used plentifully for all kinds of everyday transactions and payment of services, in addition to other uses such as gift-giving – in other words, Rome had "a fully monetized economy."[512] Elio Lo Cascio set out to demonstrate that, in the first three centuries after Christ, the Empire pursued a monetary policy through a number of measures to control supply, standards, and denominational values in currency, and others have shown similar concerns on the part of the late Roman administration regarding currency.[513]

511 M. Crawford, "Money and Exchange in the Roman World," *Journal of Roman Studies* 60 (1970), 40-48, here 45, 48. Similarly, Moses Finley, *The Ancient Economy* (Berkeley, CA: University of California Press, 1973).

512 As it is put by F. Millar, "The World of the Golden Ass," *Journal of Roman Studies* 71 (1981), 63-75. Elio Lo Cascio's model of the empire's 'intensely monetized economy' as the currently reigning interpretation is discussed in Banaji, *Exploring the Economy*, 13f, ref. E. Lo Cascio, "The Function of Gold Coinage in the Monetary Economy of the Roman Empire," in *The Monetary Systems of the Greeks and Romans*, ed. W. V. Harris (Oxford: Oxford University Press, 2008), 160-73. For a still relevant overview of evidence in favor of monetization in the Roman world, with an accompanying bibliographic essay, see Kevin Greene, *The Archaeology of the Roman Economy* (London: B. T. Batsford, 1986), 50-65.

513 E. Lo Cascio, "State and Coinage in the Late Republic and Early Empire," *Journal of Roman Studies* 71 (1981), 76-86. Lo Cascio regards the issue of early imperial bronze coinage as intending to serve economic activity. This same purpose loomed large in the making of fourth-century bronze currency, according to Michael Fulford, "Coin Circulation and Mint Activity in the Late Roman Empire: Some Economic Implications," *Archaeological Journal* 135 (1978), 67-114.
Christopher Howgego has also reacted against the view, orthodox until recently, "that coins were struck for no other purpose than to allow states to make payments, with little or no regard to how they would be used subsequently": C. Howgego, *Ancient History from Coins* (London: Routledge, 1995), 33. Elsewhere, he refers to scattered evidence from ancient societies to demonstrate that there were other motives to coin, including "[...] not only technical monetary factors, such as re-coinages connected with monetary reforms or closed currency systems [and] the need to renew worn coin [...] but also the substantial concerns of profit, pride, and politics." The denial "that coined money had in the ancient world an economic reason for existence seems to run counter to the evidence for measures taken in reaction to popular pressure to ensure the smooth functioning of the currency as a means of exchange, and fails to explain adequately steps taken to improve the supply of coinage at times of shortage. It is the clear testimony of ancient authors that coins could be struck to facilitate exchange between individuals, the payment of taxes and external trade" (C. Howgego, "Why Did Ancient States Strike Coins?" *Numismatic Chronicle* 150 [1990], 1-25, here 24-25). Although "government expenditure was the engine that drove the Roman economy," the location of late Roman mints before the extreme centralization of

The strictly 'fiscal' interpretation of Roman minting rests on the ample evidence of a massive system of taxation on the one hand, and of massive expenditures on the other. The greatest costs were the burgeoning administration and especially the army.[514] Coinage assumed a greater role in fiscal policy in the fifth and sixth centuries when currency became the standard form for tax payments and government output.[515] Michael Hendy argues for a "gigantic fiscal and redistributive cycle" of late Roman gold coinage through the repetition of tax collection and state expenditure.[516] The 'economic' interpretation has the great challenge of having to show the state's interest in public economic dealings when it minted – or when it made such decisions about minting as when, where, and in which metal to coin, and the amount to produce.[517] Aside from the bronze currency the

minting in the fifth century was arranged to suit the economic life of the provinces, according to K. Harl, *Coinage in the Roman Economy, 300 B.C. to A.D. 700* (Baltimore, MD: Johns Hopkins University Press, 1996), 230 and 211. Harl argues that even without an explicit monetary policy, Roman government reacted to fluctuations in money supply and exchange rates (207-09); still, "fiscal reasons dictated production of coinage" (250), and "the Roman state's budget generated the means whereby coins were put into circulation" (249).

514 For a discussion with comparative analysis and explicit sixth-century evidence: Hendy, *Studies*, 158; John Haldon, "Administrative Continuities and Structural Transformations in East Roman Military Organisation c. 580-640," in idem, *State, Army and Society in Byzantium* (Brookfield, VT: Variorum, 1995), V, 1-20, here 3; and idem, "Army and Economy," 139. See now, idem, "Late Rome, Byzantium, and Early Medieval Western Europe," in *Fiscal Regimes and the Political Economy of Premodern States*, ed. Andrew Monson and Walter Scheidel (Cambridge: Cambridge University Press, 2015), 345-389, esp. 351. The predominant place of the army in the early Empire can be seen in Richard Duncan-Jones, *Money and Government in the Roman Empire* (Cambridge: Cambridge University Press, 1994), 106 *et passim*. Description of fifth- and sixth-century gold expenditures especially on the army can be found in P. Spufford, *Money and Its Use in Medieval Europe* (Cambridge: Cambridge University Press, 1988), 7ff and 14f.

515 Hendy, *Studies*, esp. 294, where commutation of taxation in kind to taxation in coin is said to have become systematic probably under Anastasius. Also essential on late Roman fiscal policy is Jones, *Later Roman Empire*, esp. I, 411-469 and corresponding notes in III, 95-131; Haldon, *Byzantium*, 173-207.

516 Hendy, "From Public to Private," 36; see also idem, *Studies*, 157, 386; C. E. King, "The *Sacrae Largitiones*: Revenues, Expenditure and the Production of Coin," in *Imperial Revenue, Expenditure and Monetary Policy in the Fourth Century A.D.*, ed. C. E. King (Oxford: BAR International Series, 1980), 141-73. A similar characterization of monetary flow is implied by the description of imperial finance in Averil Cameron, *The Later Roman Empire, A.D. 284-430* (London: Fontana, 1993), esp. 116; idem, *The Mediterranean World in Late Antiquity, A.D. 395-600* (London, 1993), 95; Warren Treadgold, *Byzantium and Its Army, 284-1081* (Stanford, CA: Stanford University Press 1995), esp. 166-67; Jones, *Later Roman Empire*, esp. 441 (where he notes that the copper currency "ceased to matter essentially for public finance: it became merely a medium of exchange between subjects of the empire"); Haldon, *Byzantium*, esp. 173-76; idem, "Late Rome," 351.

517 These were decisions made at the highest level in the Roman Empire: see J.-P. Callu, "The Distribution and the Role of the Bronze Coinage from A.D. 348 to 392," 95-124, and idem, "Silver

evidence in favor of this motivation in striking coin is very thin. That the Roman world was in general highly monetized can scarcely be doubted.[518] What has not been proved is that precious-metal currency, no matter what its myriad uses and public benefits, was made in the early or later Empire for any primary purpose other than the fiscal one.

Some scholars have applied similar lines of interpretation to the Visigothic kingdom. Michael Hendy and Luis A. García Moreno were two early proponents of the position that the overwhelming motivation for minting the tremissis was to supply the fiscal structure.[519] More is known about taxation than about expenditures. There is substantial evidence of the collection of taxes in the Kingdom of Toulouse in various laws of Alaric's *Breviarium*.[520]

Hoards and Emissions from 324 to 392," 213-54, in C. E. King, ed., *Imperial Revenue*. For later centuries, see Haldon, *Byzantium*, 190f.

518 See Duncan-Jones, *Money and Government*, 109-12, where the number of precious-metal dies produced each year is estimated in the tens of thousands and precious-metal coins each year in the multi-millions; Greene, *Archaeology*, 56, 59, 65; Patrick Bruun, "The Charm of Quantitative Studies in Numismatic Research," in *Die Münze: Bild – Botschaft – Bedeutung; Festschrift für Maria R.-Alföldi* (Frankfurt am Main: Peter Lang, 1991, 65-83 (quoting estimates of yearly coin output in the first century in the hundreds of millions); William E. Metcalf, "The Joint Reign Gold of Justin I and Justinian I," in Hahn and Metcalf, eds., *Studies in Early Byzantine Gold Coinage*, 19-27 (for several weeks in 527 almost one solidus obverse die was used per day, no doubt for thousands of coins each); Harl, *Coinage in the Roman Economy*, esp. 230 (hundreds of millions of coins collected and spent each year) and 250-89 (extensive treatment of coinage in daily life).

519 Hendy, "From Public to Private"; García Moreno, "Cecas visigodas"; Crusafont, *El sistema*, 89 and idem, "Monete suebe e visigote," esp. 350; Naismith, "Gold Coinage and Its Use," 303-05 reinforces the enduring relationship between gold coin and taxation. See also I. Martín Viso, "Tremisses y potentes en el nordeste de Lusitania (siglos VI–VII)," *Mélanges de la Casa de Velázquez* 38 (2008), 175–200 and Castellanos, "The Political Nature of Taxation"; stressing the regional variation apropos the monarchical project of taxation kingdomwide is María del Rosario Valverde Castro, "La ideología fiscal en el reino visigodo de Toledo," in *Between Taxation and Rent: Fiscal Problems from Late Antiquity to Early Middle Ages = Entre el impuesto y la renta: problemas de la fiscalidad tardoantigua y altomedieval*, ed. Pablo C. Díaz and Iñaki Martín Viso (Bari: Edipuglia, 2011), 163-88. Wickham, *Framing*, 93-100 develops the taxation framework but with coinage only implied, and with land and goods explicitly the main factor of tribute and distribution later in Gothic rule.

520 See Dionisio Pérez Sánchez, *El ejército en la sociedad visigoda* (Salamanca: Universidad de Salamanca, 1989), 78, n. 113; E. A. Thompson, *The Goths in Spain* (Oxford: Oxford University Press, 1969), 126-31. Several laws sought to maintain the tax on land of which ownership was transferred. A few laws in Leovigild's code, but possibly of earlier origin, sought to protect land tax revenues in a similar way. On this and related protection of public funds see Pérez Sánchez, *El ejército*, 116-17. The best study of transitions in Visigothic taxation and the public officials responsible for it is García Moreno, "Estudios," which convincingly demonstrates that in its essentials the office of *comes patrimonii* derived from the late Roman Praetorian Prefect (esp. 37-41), while that of the *comes thesaurorum* derived from the *comes sacrarum largitionum* (54-65). On taxation in general useful if brief treatment will be found in Orlandis, *Historia de España*, 126f, 223-26

The extent of the continuity of taxation in Hispania in the sixth and seventh centuries is not altogether clear, but the imposition of some of the basic taxes of the later Roman Empire is not in doubt, nor is the fact that at least sometimes currency was employed.[521] Under Theodoric the Ostrogoth, the land tax and commercial taxes were collected along the lines of the late Roman system, although abuses had set in.[522] The involvement of bishops in the process of taxation as a means of preventing abuses is mentioned in the acts of two church councils toward the end of the sixth century.[523]

and, especially from seventh-century evidence, in P. D. King, *Law and Society*, 64-71, 78; more detailed examination will be found in references which fill out this section and the treatment of taxation in Chapter Seven below.

521 In Theodoric's Italy – and perhaps Spain during the interregnum – "the taxes were, as they had been under the last emperors, paid wholly in gold, and supplies required for the troops were obtained by compulsory purchase (*coemptio*)": Jones, *Later Roman Empire*, I, 254 and III, 47 n. 41. Cash is implied in Theodoric's objection to the fortunes of Hispano-Roman inhabitants becoming subject to the whims of arrears officers ('arbitrio compulsorum suggeruntur provincialium subiacere fortunae'): Cassiodorus, *Variae*, V.39.2 (ed. T. Mommsen, *MGH.AA* 12, 164). Another source of royal objection is that both kind and cash were demanded of the provincials to pay salaries of prebends granted by the king ("Praebendarum tenor adscriptus, quem nostra diversis largitur humanitas, provincialibus suggeritur intolerabilis cause esse damnorum, quando et in species exigitur et impudenter eius pretium postulatur"): *Variae*, V.39.12 (ibid., 165).

522 Cassiodorus, *Variae*, V.39. Theodoric complained to his two chief officials in Spain that *exactores* (tax-collectors) and *compulsores* (collectors of arrears) were extortionate, and demanded that he should receive all the revenues due to him, those from the time of Alaric and Euric ("quem Alarici atque Eurici temporibus constat illatas": 13). He charges that taxes were not being collected according to the tax registers, 'polyptichis publicis' (2). For references to customs dues and taxes on trade, from this document and from the *Breviarium* of Alaric II, see Thompson, *Goths in Spain*, 126-27 and García Moreno, "Algunos aspectos fiscales," 240-43. *Conductores domus regiae*, the lessees of crown lands, were salaried at this time, representing a government expense (*Var.* V.39.6, where I adopt the alternative reading *salaria* for *solaria*, which fits the passage better and agrees with *pensionis* in the same line; see *MGH.AA* 12, 164-66 at 165 l. 15).

523 Both are problematic as to their precise meaning. The first is III Toledo (589), c. 18: "[...] ne in angariis aut in operationibus superfluis sive privatum onerent sive fiscalem gravent" (Vives, ed., *Concilios*, 131). We see here and in the law codes a distinction between *privati*, free landowners, and *servi fiscales*, slaves working on or supervising the fiscal estates. In c. 20, the bishops are exhorted not to act like *exactores* by harassing the people with *indictionibus*. Also from the reign of Reccared is a secular law attempting to avert abuses by the tax officials themselves, who are already rewarded by the king: *LV* XII.1.2 (ed. K. Zeumer, *MGH.LL*, sectio I, 407), "[...] iubeamus, ut nullis indictionibus, exactionibus, operibus vel angariis comes, vicarius vel vilicus pro suis utilitatibus populos adgravare presumant nec de civitate vel de territorio annonam accipiant; quia nostra recordatur clementia, quod, dum iudices ordinamus, nostra largitate eis conpendia ministramus." For an excellent recent look at the bishops' accrued responsibility in providing just oversight of annual taxation payment, considered an adaptive method not indicating weakness but rather fortifying the monarchy (and magnates simultaneously), see Fernández, "Statehood, Taxation."

One of these is the so-called *De fisco Barcinonensi*, a document from 592. This is a letter from bishops of the territories paying taxes to the Barcelona fisc ('omnes episcopi ad civitatem Barcinonense fiscum inferentes') to the *numerarii*, or local tax officials there, appointed by the *comes patrimonii*. In accord with the episcopal involvement indicated in the acts of III Toledo, canon 18, the signing bishops approve what seems to be the rate of *adaeratio*, or conversion into gold of a 'modius canonicus,' a unit of taxation in kind. Payment is thus measured in monetary units of account (*siliquae*, eighths of a triens, found frequently in the *LV*).

> We decree that you [*numerarii*, or fiscal officials] or your assistants must require for one legal *modius* of barley [...] fourteen *siliquae*. [...] If anyone refuses, however, to adhere to our consensus or undertakes to pay you in kind less than what is established, it will be seen to that he bring forth his fiscal sum.
> *Decreuimus ut tam uos [numerarii] quant agentes, siue adiutores uestri pro uno modio canonico ad populum exigere debeatis* [...] *siliquas XIIII inibi hordeo.* [...] *Si quis sane secundum consensum nostrum adquiescere noluerit uel tibi inferre minime procurauerit in specie quod tibi conuenerit, fiscus suum inferre procuret.*[524]

Hendy was likely correct in his assertion that, together with numismatic data from the mint at Barcinona, one can find "no clearer demonstration of the direct connection between the extraction of state taxation, inevitably the land tax, and the minting of coin, in the entire monetary history of the barbarian successor states, and few better examples of the procedural continuity between those states and late Rome."[525]

524 Vives, ed., *Concilios*, 54. See the discussion of this document in Hendy, "From Public to Private," 53-56; Fernández, "Statehood, Taxation," 254f; Jones, *Later Roman Empire*, I, 258; M. Vigil and A. Barbero, "Algunos aspectos de la feudalización del reino visigodo en relación a su organización financiera y militar," *Monéda y Credito*, no. 112 (1970), 71-91 at 74; García Moreno, "Estudios," 35ff; Pliego, *La moneda visigoda*, v. 1, 223. P. D. King, *Law and Society*, 70 n. 1, against the opinion of others, sees 'modius canonicus' as a fiscal unit of land. All are agreed that the document ultimately deals with taxation. For the proper dating of '*De fisco*' to 592, see M. C. Díaz y Díaz, *Index Scriptorum Latinorum Medii Aevi Hispanorum* (Salamanca: Universidad de Salamanca, 1958), vol. 1, no. 41.

525 Hendy, "From Public to Private," 55, and the discussion of minting data as known at the time of publication, 54-55. The extant coins of Barcinona saw a large temporary increase in Reccared's reign, which Hendy links to the fact that the *fiscus* of a great area along the coast of Tarraconensis was located there in these years as indicated by *De Fisco*. The implication is that in other reigns the *fiscus*, or tax collection point perhaps falling under the term *thesaurus*, was located in Tarracona

Seventh-century laws of Gothic kings attest to a variety of exactions. According to a law of 612, freed slaves had to be included in the tax registers for the purpose of making a fiscal assessment on their property.[526] Chindasvinth and Reccesvinth enacted the only personal tax known from the Visigothic era in Spain, that on slaves.[527] Sometimes, kings remitted unpaid arrears of taxes in special circumstances, as did emperors of late antiquity. E. A. Thompson observed that the fiscal administrators listed in Ervig's declaration of remission, the Edict of 683, bore titles very different from the Roman ones in the *Breviarium*. The titles furthermore suggest that most of these officials were Gothic, and Thompson is probably correct in claiming that the financial administration as well as other areas of government came more into the domain of Visigoths after reforms were carried out by Chindasvinth and Reccesvinth in the middle of the seventh century.[528] Some

or another city in this tax zone. Such a rotation is indeed suggested by the language of III Toledo, c. 18 (Vives, ed., *Concilios*, 131): "Semel in anno in locum, quem Metropolitanus elegerit, episcopi congregentur: iudices vero locurum vel actores fiscalium patrimoniorum, ex decreto Gloriosissimi Domini nostri [...] die Kalendarum Novembrium in unum conveniant; ut discant, quam pie et iuste cum populis agere debeant [...]." Tarracona also has a large temporary increase in known tremisses in Reccared's reign; an unrecorded hoard from this period may be a factor in the unusually high number of coins from all provinces of the kingdom, or the region's *fiscus* may have been relocated there later in the reign. Pliego, "Dertosa, ceca visigoda bajo el reinado de Recaredo I (586-601)," *Acta Numismàtica* 45 (2015), 81-90, esp. 85-89 provides an updated treatment of minting in Tarraconensis during the reign of Reccared. Jean Durliat, *Les finances publiques de Diocletien aux Carolingiens (284-889)* (Sigmaringen: Thorbecke, 1990), 111 sees the taxation in '*De fisco*' as falling only on public, i.e. crown, lands out of the whole of taxable holdings. With Hendy (51 n. 70 and 57 n. 91), I favor the interpretation of Jones, *Later Roman Empire*, I, 254-56 and 258: the *comes patrimonii* was in charge of all state taxation since the rule of Theodoric the Ostrogoth, who regarded the whole Visigothic kingdom as a personal acquisition. This special arrangement certainly applied to Sicily and Dalmatia for several decades after the fall of the last western emperor, and the expenses of these territories were paid from the personal treasuries which made up the respective *patrimonii*. I believe a distinction is made in III Toledo, c. 18 between the collectors of ordinary taxation ('iudices locurum') and those responsible specifically for crown lands ('actores fiscalium patrimoniorum'); see also n. 523 above. As Hendy indicates, the interpretation here is compatible with the 'fiscal' scheme of barbarian allotments in Walter Goffart, *Barbarians and Romans, A.D. 418-584*, whereby only one third of tax revenues went to the king and two-thirds went to the Gothic troops.

526 *LV* XII.2.13: "[...] ad statum ingenuitatis [...] revertantur et prenotati in polipticis publicis adque secundum eorum peculium iustissima aderatione censiti vitam in propriis laboribus ingenuitate transigere valeant [...] et descripti sicut ceteri eorum libertati, census pro eo peculio illis inponatur" (ed. K. Zeumer, *MGH.LL*, sectio I, 419, ll. 4-7; 420, ll. 3-4).

527 *LV* X.2.4 (Recces.); see the related law X.2.5 (Egica). Chindasvinth was responsible for V.4.19, which attempted to maintain liability for fiscal payments on lands, houses, and slaves in the case of alienation.

528 Administrative reforms: see Thompson, *Goths in Spain*, 131, 210-17. Isidore, *Historia Gothorum*, 55 wrote that Reccared "was so merciful that he often reduced the tribute [*tributa*] of the people

Spanish scholars in particular have championed the idea of 'militarization' of government and the dawn of a protofeudal state by the latter half of the century, in which currency played a very diminished role.[529] In this regard, the totalizing (and perhaps teleological) cause, though not the effect, has been doubted.

Hendy upheld that the coincidence of major mints and administrative capitals is indicative of the fiscal nature of these mints.[530] The regular and large production at the provincial capitals accords with this theory. There is an important corollary: if all mints, or even just permanent mints, served the purpose of a fiscal coinage, can one infer that the Visigothic kingdom did not collect taxes centrally in Toleto but rather at numerous tax points, which may even have shifted at times as we have seen?[531] It seems so, since coinage inscribed with Toleto is far below Emerita and just below Ispali in the total number of finds, and the map of find locations by no means demonstrates heavy coin loss in central Spain.[532] Yet, such a conclusion cannot be reached on these grounds, since there is a southern bias of hoards from the 630s at work and because government payouts from Toleto of tremisses minted elsewhere and collected centrally could then go in all directions and did not have to stay at home. Rather, the nearly fifty per cent of individual coin finds within 200 km from their mints most clearly proves that most coins were not forwarded to the court.[533]

by a grant of indulgence" (trans. Wolf, *Conquerors and Chroniclers*, 105). Remissions of arrears of 'tributum' were granted by Ervig in 683 (XIII Toledo, *Tomus*; *LV* XII.1.3) and by Egica in 691 (III Zaragoza, *epil.*; XVI Toledo, c. 8). Taxes and large fines on Jews who remained as such are known from the time of these two kings, but possibly had been instituted previously: see R. Collins, *Early Medieval Spain*, 134-35.

529 See especially García Moreno, *Historia de la España visigoda* (Madrid: Cátedra, 1989), 170-90, 332-37 and idem, "Estudios," 125ff; Vigil and Barbero, "Algunos aspectos." Pliego, *La moneda visigoda*, v. 1, 222-24 assesses the fiscal operations as a mere shadow of the late Roman system rather than transformed by a militarizing process; but see also idem, "El *tremis* de los últimos años," 38 suggesting some use of coinage in relation to the army even as privatization of fighting forces was occurring.

530 A view based also on the mainly provincial organization of styles and generally the concentration of production at a few mints in each province: see Hendy, "From Public to Private," 53. A persuasive argument for the administrative nature of the principal mints can be found in Spaulding, "Mint-cities," 48ff, although trade is included as a factor (ibid., 82). Note that very few of the permanent mints were on the seacoast or very close to it, which one might expect if trade were the leading dynamic behind the minting of gold.

531 García Moreno, "Cecas visigodas," 341 envisions Toleto as the destination of taxation, but this does not find corresponding evidence in the extensive numismatic data from the Visigothic era.

532 Barral i Altet, *La circulation*, 153.

533 See D. M. Metcalf, "Some Geographical Aspects," 314, fig. 3, based on Barral i Altet, *La circulation*. Marques et al., *Ensaios*, 267 and 273 n. 2, propose the possibility that collectors sent

Collection and expenditure at the local or provincial level may be the reason why control marks were included even on very similar tremisses from the same workshop, since groups of coins at that site say, from two or three moneyers involved in re-minting, could then be counted without confusion, whereas if each city sent coins to Toleto the local mint name alone would be enough to distinguish them.[534] It may be significant that Toleto's coins begin to rather consistently outnumber those of Emerita and Ispali from Reccesvinth's reign until the Muslim invasion,[535] and one wonders whether Chindasvinth and Reccesvinth imitated the concentration of imperial minting and fiscal activities, which in the eastern Mediterranean were centered in Constantinople by 630.[536]

Very little is known specifically on the side of expenditures, although we get a vague idea from a few massive payments to other states, the activities of the military, patronage of buildings and cities, and court pageantry.[537] As in the Roman Empire, military costs are believed to have been the greatest outlay of the government, at least in times of war. We know that in the early sixth century Alaric II continued the late Roman practice of making

tax money not to Toleto but to the nearest royal treasury, from which it would then be disbursed. The reason why regional treasures go unrecorded is because they were much smaller than the central one and therefore did not draw the attention of contemporary writers. There is in fact nothing to prevent this reading of 'fiscus,' and it seems much more practical that payments of the oft-mentioned monetary fines and occasional awards from it should be made closer to home than from Toleto. Hints of this arrangement appear in '*De fisco Barcinonensi*' and perhaps in the plural object of the title 'comes thesaurorum' from at least the late seventh century (XIII Tol.).

534 The local use as well as collection of tax monies in the barbarian kingdoms is an important theme in Durliat, *Les finances publiques*. I hope to address some of his provocative arguments in a future publication.

535 See Appendix I, Figure I.7.

536 Hendy, *Studies*, 417-20.

537 Known examples of massive payouts are the 30,000 solidi Leovigild paid to the Byzantines in 583/4 (Greg. of Tours, *HF* V.38) and the 200,000 solidi Sisenand paid for Dagobert I's support in 631 (Fredegar, *Chronicle* IV.73). Although Sisenand was not yet king at the time but rather a usurper, he was a member of the *comitiva* and may already have had access to the immense gold *missorium* plate weighing 500 lbs; after the victory the Goths rejected giving this as payment, instead handing over the solidi. See John of Biclar, *Chronicon*, a. 587, 6 (Reccared as founder and patron of churches and monasteries); Isidore, *Historia Gothorum*, 50 (Leovigild enticing Catholics with gold and property to become Arians), 55 (Reccared distributing treasures among the poor), 61 (Sisebut using his treasure to redeem captives).
Several *palatii* in different towns throughout the kingdom have recently become known: for connection with coinage see Félix Retamero, "As Coins Go Home: Towns, Merchants, Bishops and Kings in Visigothic Hispania," in *The Visigoths from the Migration Period to the Seventh Century: An Ethnographic Perspective*, ed. Peter Heather (San Marino: Center for Interdisciplinary Research on Social Stress, 1999), 271-320, here 273. See below for more on court ceremony and military campaigns.

a *donativum*, or periodic cash reward to soldiers.[538] During Theodoric the Great's rule over the Visigoths, beginning shortly after the Visigothic defeat by the Franks at Vouillé in 507, a form of the *donativum* was still given to the troops.[539] Monetary and military evidence in connection with the reconquest of Byzantine areas of the kingdom, discussed below, strongly suggests a continuation of such payments into the early seventh century at least; once reliance on personal armies became the norm by the latter half of the century, however, every impression is that soldiers were not paid salaries.[540] Garrison troops in various cities and *castella* formed the only element of the standing army, which would normally suffice for the defense of the kingdom.[541] How these soldiers were rewarded is not known from extant sources, but it would be in keeping with earlier custom and with the

538 *Vita Aviti*, 2. Pérez Sánchez, *El ejército*, 69 and 77, believes this *donativum* was irregular; he notes that Clovis rewarded the support of nobility with cash. See also Avitus of Vienne, *Ep.* LXXXVII, on Alaric's disastrous debasement of his gold currency at that time. Haldon, "Late Rome," 363f, 368 discusses the military's high portion of costs in the early Byzantine Empire.
539 Procopius, *Bell. Goth.* 5.12.48 (ed. and trans, H. B. Dewing, *History of the Wars*, vol. 3 [Cambridge, MA: Harvard University Press, 1961], 131): "[...] he ordered that the rulers of [Gaul and Spain] should bring tribute to him. And though he received this every year, in order not to give the appearance of being greedy for money he sent it as an annual gift to the army of the Goths and the Visigoths." On Theodoric's donatives to Ostrogothic soldiers, not usually annual and sometimes under the name *munera*, see Goffart, *Barbarians and Romans*, 83-84; also Jones, *Later Roman Empire*, I, 256 and III, 49 n. 45. García Moreno makes a rather convincing case for a whole system of satisfying the expenses of the army – the greatest output of the state – through taxation: "Estudios," 113-14 and idem, "Cecas visigodas," 333-45. One should note Jones's suggestion, taken from Procopius, that Justinian converted the quinquennial donative into an annual payment of one solidus a year and combined it with the commutation for *annona*: *Later Roman Empire*, II, 670.
540 See the next section; the same opinion can be found in Margarita Vallejo Girvés, *Bizancio y la España tardoantigua (ss. V-VIII): Un capítulo de historia mediterránea* (Alcalá de Henares: Universidad de Alcalá de Henares, 1993), 243 and Damián Fernández, *Aristocrats and Statehood in Western Iberia, 300-600 C.E.* (Philadelphia, PA: University of Pennsylvania Press, 2017), 201. The shifting Visigothic military is treated extensively in Amancio Isla Frez, *Ejército, sociedad y política en la Península Ibérica entre los siglos VII y XI* (Madrid: Consejo Superior de Investigaciones Científicas, 2010); see 100f for the observation that no minting in Septimania can be connected to the rebellion of Duke Paul in 672.
541 On the army, see Pérez Sánchez, *El ejército*; Orlandis, *Historia de España*, 226-29; Thompson, *Goths in Spain*, 262-67; Isla Frez, *Ejército, sociedad*, esp. 9-22 and P. D. King, *Law and Society*, 72-76 (both basing their relevant commentary on seventh-century evidence); García Moreno, "Estudios," 65f. Just as right after the conquest of Suevic Gallaecia there were many Gothic bishops, doubtless because of the presence of many Gothic soldiers, so too once Málaga was taken over from the Byzantines the first two bishops appointed to the see were Goths: José Orlandis, *Historia social y économica de la España visigoda* (Madrid: Confederación Española de Cajas de Ahorros, 1975), 44. I discuss evidence of the military-monetary links in the following section.

contemporary imperial administrative system to pay them in coin.[542] It is difficult to imagine the troops not being thus placated at times, especially during long campaigns. Men drafted into service whenever a serious threat arose would probably have been similarly rewarded.

Félix Retamero has added to the evidence of taxation some considerations about the specific uses of coin. He concludes that the Visigothic monetary economy was overwhelmingly geared to the fiscal mechanism and played little role as a redistributive instrument through market activities. He contends furthermore that tremisses were owned by *potentes*, who were the ones paying taxes in cash; peasants merely brought their crops to landlords and therefore did not touch the coinage used in tax collection. "Thus the low figures of surviving pieces would accurately reflect the reduced number of fiscal subjects responsible for handing over taxes in coin to the state."[543] This very limited monetization is contrasted with the much greater number of extant coins from tenth-century al-Andalus, in which responsibility for tax payments was laid upon peasant communities.[544] Retamero's general argument about the purpose of currency and its relatively limited quantity is not without merit, but he goes too far in proclaiming that the fiscal system was ineffective and that peasants never handled coinage when the process did work. This is the point of '*De fisco Barcinonensi*' and of the ecclesiastical and royal enactments seeking to protect the '*populos*' (*potentes* are not found in any such fiscal contexts).[545] By the author's own admission some of the slates found in northern Spain include demands for crops expressed not only in *modii* and *sextarii* and the like, but also in *solidi*.[546] We may

542 Donatives were still granted to soldiers of the Eastern Roman Empire by Heraclius (610-41), and there were "a number of temporary mints [...] clearly connected with military activity": Haldon, "Military Service," 11-12.

543 Retamero, "As Coins Go Home," 291. A rather similar view is proposed by Crusafont i Sabater, *El sistema*, 89, relying on the opinion of Grierson that "la moneda debió estar lejos de las clases humildes."

544 Ibid., 291f, with references.

545 'Populos' are mentioned repeatedly in the documents cited above, e.g. in Ervig's remission in XIII Tol. (Vives, ed., *Concilios*, 435-37).

546 Retamero, "As Coins Go Home," 290. I cannot see why "*solidi* can hardly be considered a unit of account for cereals," on the objection that in this way "different sets of units were needed to reckon the same product." In a region where coinage seems to have been less abundant, it might be natural for cash and kind equivalences to be adopted in various circumstances so that either unit of value may be employed. Retamero has unfortunately misread '*De fisco*' by claiming that the bishops "were held responsible for handing in taxes to the *fiscus* (*omnes episcopi ad civitatem Barcinonense fiscus inferentes*), and they had also to ensure the collection of crops" (p. 288; see similarly F. Retamero, "La moneda del *regnum gothorum* (ca. 575-714). Una revisión del registro numismático," in *Between Taxation and Rent: Fiscal Problems from Late Antiquity*

question whether the monetary cycle was as closed as Retamero – and others applying a less restricted model – have suggested, even if they are correct about the fiscal purpose of the currency.

Was Currency Issued for the Commercial Convenience of the People?

The particulars of this problem are not the same for the Roman Empire as for early medieval Spain, since the latter had nothing like the overflowing amounts of bronze coinage of Rome and Byzantium, and little if any silver.[547] The high value of gold coins makes it less plausible that the royal court minted in order to provide the means for the public to make ordinary transactions. Tremisses were suitable for large purchases but not for smaller ones.[548] The question, then, is whether the Visigothic monarchs were motivated by strictly 'higher-end' commercial needs within the kingdom when producing coins.

Merchants, nobles, and *possessores* of even modest means must have found tremisses useful for some of their needs. The high value of gold coins would, of course, greatly facilitate the state's frequent payments, but one should recognize that activities of the state were by no means the controlling principle of their circulation once they were issued. Hendy's notion of a massive redistributive cycle of late Roman gold coinage through the repetition of tax collection and state expenditure should not make us envision a closed economic system as Retamero has. Hendy's emphasis on Roman and

to Early Middle Ages, ed. Pablo C. Díaz and Iñaki Martín Viso (Bari: Edipuglia, 2011), 189-220, at 206f with n. 62). There is nothing here to require anything more than their participation in public finances, presumably as taxpayers themselves, but above all as the ones given the job of securing fair rates: see above, n. 523, where bishops are contrasted on a moral level with tax collectors. I am also skeptical about whether cancellations of arrears can be taken as a sure sign of the feebleness of fiscal practice (291). At one level, they record the continuation of taxation; they also should be recognized as having emerged from troubled situations and may suggest a certain level of administrative vitality.

547 For the fifth century, see Grierson and Mays, *Late Roman Coins*.

548 On prices and monetary values in Visigothic Spain, see Barral i Altet, *La circulation*, 72-74, and J. Orlandis, "Sobre el nivel de vida en la Hispania visigoda," *Anuario de Estudios Medievales* 8 (1972-73), 17-33. Dietrich Claude, "Zur Funktion des Münzgeldes im hispanischen Westgotenreich," in *Münstersche Beiträge zur Antiken Handelsgeschichte* 8 (no. 2, 1989), 32-51, shows fairly convincingly that gold coins were in the possession of ordinary people, who used them not only for tax payments but for the purchase of food. That does not mean tremisses were used for small purchases. We can get an idea of monetary value from the premise in the law code that the cost of a child's sustenance for one year was one solidus: *LV* IV.4.3. Roman monetary policy of the fourth and fifth centuries surrounding a standard solidus of extremely high purity, overvalued with respect to lower denominations and at the same time widely available, intended the solidus to be the predominant coin in transactions of any consequential amount. Banaji, *Exploring the Economy*, 105, 116.

Byzantine government and the actual making of coinage naturally leads him to focus on a single monetary cycle, but it does not take into much account the varieties of coin exchange. Let us assume that the Visigothic government maintained on a very reduced scale the sorts of spending of coin in which the late Empire engaged, a seemingly obvious conclusion though without explicit extant documentation. Payments to supply and reward the army, members of the court, and others in the service of the king would alone put a substantial amount of currency into many hands, and we should include in the latter list not only soldiers and counts and the like, but also landlords, state slaves, artisans, scribes, etc. Kings' demand for major goods and luxury items which pertain to royal status, such as gold-laden votive crosses or buildings within the *urbs regia* or elsewhere, must have immediately enlarged the orbit of circulation to include, among others, merchants and building workers.[549] The presumably vast amount of currency which flowed out from the state treasuries did not all come back in the form of taxation. Did the court recognize this and mint partly to supply the monetized portion of the economy?

Few modern scholars have thought in such terms.[550] Why would the state care about how coins were used as long as they made their way in

549 See P. D. King, *Law and Society*, 62-63 for references to royal foundations, endowment of churches, and rewards to informers (some of these themes are taken up below in Chapter Seven); the author holds that rents and taxes from lands of the crown and those in the personal possession of the king provided most of the needed revenue. Pliego, "La acuñación monetaria," 133f and idem, *La moneda visigoda*, v. 1, 215-30 believes the main purpose of Visigothic gold coinage was to facilitate royal payments and relations with nobility through gifts, but does not envision it in the full fiscal apparatus sustained in this chapter; tax exemption and evasion by nobles proved too great an inhibition. Re-supply of gold came more by way of fines and confiscations. Nor does she see much in the way of a monetary economy. On the other hand, she writes of regular re-minting and many dies and therefore a greater circulation than the current corpus seems to indicate. I concur that a lowered stock of gold through hoarding led to diminished weight and purity of currency in the last decades of the kingdom (*La moneda visigoda*, v. 1, 229), but would underscore that the same sort of constrictive pressure and its result supports the theory I have laid out on military minting in the south. (As noted in earlier footnotes, Pliego, "El *tremis* de los últimos años," widens her perspective of how the precious metal was utilized.) Gold currency and the theoretical tributary monopoly as means of confirming bonds between central and local authorities is a crucial notion in works of Iñaki Martín Viso, most recently "Circuits of Power in a Fragmented Space: Gold Coinage in the Meseta del Duero (Sixth-Seventh Centuries)," in *Scale and Scale Change*, ed. Escalona and Reynolds, 215-52, esp. 221. Naismith, "Gold Coinage and Its Use," 290 points to revenue sources apart from taxation but still views the fiscal dynamic and not commercial purposes as key to the gold currency (as referenced in this chapter as well as in Chapter Seven).

550 The common view may be summed up in the remark of Peter Spufford, "Currency and Coinage," in *Cambridge Economic History of Europe*, vol. 2, 791: "It was a basically non-commercial coinage of gold that the barbarians inherited."

sufficient numbers back to the fisc?[551] The point at which the court *might* have cared about trade is when gold became scarce, particularly if gold from the kingdom were being lost through imbalance of trade. A western Mediterranean gold drain to the East has been a conventional theory for a long time.[552] Scarcities of the precious metal on the part of the eastern Empire's administration may have been a factor in the supposed drain.[553] The Visigothic state would then take greater interest in melting down foreign coinage and in earning a profit from commercial transactions or 'monetary mutations.'[554] Yet, only in a remote way can the collection of commercial taxes be interpreted as a motive for minting in order to provide the means for commerce.

Barral i Altet has posited the "essentially commercial character" of Visigothic tremisses. As if using a different prism, which does not ignore the role of money in the fiscal system but gives it secondary emphasis,[555] he discusses the many signs of active trade in the Visigothic period. Internal and external commerce is indeed well-documented,[556] and we can be sure

551 Implied in Retamero, "As Coins Go Home,"esp. 293-94, although the interest kings had in the return of coins was frustrated by the weakness of the monarchy, according to the author's point of view.

552 Numerous references can be found in Barral i Altet, *La circulation*, 71 nn. 358-59, and in Crusafont i Sabater, *El sistema*, 89. See also Harl, *Coinage in the Roman Economy*, 185-86 and 311.

553 See below at n. 610; P. Grierson, "Coinage and Money in the Byzantine Empire, 498-c. 1090," *Settimane di studio centro italiano di studi sull'alto medioevo* VIII (1961), 411-53, here n. 21 and 448. Metcalf, "Some Geographical Aspects," 311 poses a favorable balance of payments from the Mediterranean world into Hispania suggested by the heavy minting in the south, but for reasons discussed later in this chapter this idea should be considered feeble.

554 A strategy treated, though not strictly in terms of scarcity, in Retamero, "As Coins Go Home," 279-86 and 293-94 and the discussion on 310.

555 Apparent in his treatment of fiscal activities toward the end of his chapter on "*l'économie du royaume visigot*" (*La circulation*, 67-77) and in the remark that "la fiscalité est essentiellement basée sur la monnaie," rather than the other way around. See also X. Barral i Altet, "Una moneda d'Egica trobada a Orense. Notes sobre la circulacio de les monedes d'Egica (687-695-702)," *Cuadernos de Estudios Gallegos* 29 (no. 87, 1974-75), 30-34 and 2 pll.

556 A rich variety of evidence, although not based on recent archeological findings, may be found in the following: Barral i Altet, *La circulation*, 69-71; Orlandis, *Historia de España*, 196-99; P. D. King, *Law and Society*, 194-201; García Moreno, "Colonias de comerciantes orientales en la península ibérica, s. V-VII," *Habis* 3 (1972), 127-54; Valdeavellano, "La moneda y la economía de cambio,"; Orlandis, *Historia económica*; Jeremy Knight, *The End of Antiquity: Archaeology, Society and Religion, AD 235-700* (Stroud: Tempus, 1999), 154-58. See further on these matters in Chapter Seven below. Archeology attests to ongoing (sixth- and seventh-century) importation of liturgical items, personal adornments, ceramic wares, and other goods from around the Mediterranean, in some cases from various parts of northern Africa or Italy, in others possibly the Levant or Greece or even beyond. Much of the commerce took specific kinds of goods to focused destinations, but even though place of origination often cannot be nailed down, as a

that coinage was involved in much exchange, though by far not all.[557] But was trade a factor in the production of coinage? Barral i Altet implies that it was as he explains patterns of coin circulation – from single finds and the composition of hoards – in terms of commerce. In a few cases, he takes as military losses the coincidence of finds from periods in which battles are known to have taken place in the same general area. What is indicated by his evidence, however, are possible circumstances of coin usage and coin loss. Only in one case, that of the south in the first decades of the seventh century, does he tentatively attribute minting to a military purpose.[558]

Barral i Altet's observations were taken further, though in the same general direction, by D. M. Metcalf. This Oxford numismatist emphasized the rapid, long-distance circulation of a high percentage of regal tremisses away from the mints. Yet, there is no guarantee that trade accounts for this or for specific areas of loss; furthermore, it cannot be proved that the court took any notice. Metcalf makes a valiant effort to combine the evidence of coin loss with that of minting; however, he may have disregarded his own admonition that the two phenomena require different approaches because "once coins have been put into circulation e.g. during a military campaign, their function may quickly change, they may circulate into a different province or region, anything may happen."[559] His examination of production from the perspective of needs is more useful for our question. A map that he has made of relative mint-output shows that two groups of large mints dominate the second tier of production, after the exceptional place held by Emerita, Ispali, Toleto and Cordoba. The first is the handful of central-southern mints located close together. The second is comprised of a few mints along the northeastern coast, plus the mint at Cesaragusta up the Ebro River.[560] The concentration of minting in the south goes hand in hand with a northward movement of much of this currency; in Tarraconensis, an unusually large percentage of finds traveled from very distant mints, including those in the south.[561] Metcalf discounts as likely motives for

whole even the limited record speaks of significant peninsular exchange within a broad Maritime spectrum. For a recent summary see Paul Reynolds, "Material Culture and the Economy in the Age of Saint Isidore of Seville (6th and 7th Centuries)," *Antiquité Tardive* 23 (2015), 163-210.

557 See the remarks on barter in Barral i Altet, *La circulation*, 69 n. 347 (citing C. M. Cipolla, *Money, Prices and Civilization in the Mediterranean World, Fifth to Seventeenth Century* [Princeton, NJ: Princeton University Press, 1956], 4f.) and 72.

558 Barral i Altet, *La circulation*, 114-15.

559 Metcalf, "For What Purposes Were Suevic and Visigothic Tremisses Used?," 18.

560 See Metcalf, "Some Geographical Aspects," 309, fig. 1.

561 Ibid., 313-15.

the southern minting both administrative and military needs, instead attributing the overwhelming part of it to international and inter-regional trade.[562] I shall demonstrate in the next section that the evidence points to war as the dominant motive for this minting, but Metcalf's explorations of the topic are provocative and it is probably true that economic factors were not entirely absent from large mintings.

Two rather basic questions are related to the problem of why the Visigoths struck the gold coinage. Unfortunately, neither can be definitively answered, nor could the answers resolve the larger problem addressed in this chapter, yet they are, nevertheless, important. The first question is whether minting was carried out strictly as an initiative of the state, or whether 'private minting' was carried out. The system by which bullion was converted into coinage is not too clear for any kingdoms in the early Middle Ages, and even if it were clearer for one or another kingdom, it would not necessarily shed much light on the way this operated in Visigothic Spain. Among the abuses Theodoric the Ostrogoth confronted during his regency was that of mint-workers seeking private profit, which in the context of *Variae* V.39 appears to mean profits made by minting for individuals.[563] The late Roman Empire had to confront the same situation.[564] But, as in the Roman world, so too in early sixth-century Hispania the state reacted. The measure of success is not documented, but in the Visigothic kingdom from Leovigild onward the presumption is that royal control of monetary production was tight. This subject is addressed in more detail in the next chapter.

The other pertinent issue is the volume of coinage. Many remarked on the small corpus of surviving specimens even before the work of Miles, but especially in the light of his extensive research. How much taxation could there have been, or what scale of monetary economy, if there were only approximately four thousand regal coins surviving by the mid-twentieth century? The number is small, even compared to contemporary Merovingian coins, of which some ten thousand were already known then, and the corpus

562 See especially "For What Purposes Were Suevic and Visigothic Tremisses Used?," 20-21.
563 Hendy, "From Public to Private," 43, 55 (see also my treatment of *Variae* V.39 in Chapter One; the same interpretation here as an instance of private minting is made by Naismith, "Gold Coinage and Its Use," 288). The private right to mint and individuals bringing metal to the mint did occur regularly in the Carolingian world, but this was a new situation influenced by changing circumstances (Hendy, "From Public to Private, 37-40).
564 Ibid., 35-36. A simplified version of a key thesis of Hendy's runs as follows: the late Roman and early Byzantine government's spending of coin on foodstuffs provided taxpayers with currency with which to return the gold. If people did not possess gold coins and the minting of private metal was "prohibited or rendered prohibitively expensive," by implication there was not a truly monetary economy.

is miniscule compared to the many thousands of coins from various 150-year periods of the Roman Empire and Byzantium. It was noted in Chapter Three that in the 1980s the number of known Visigothic regal coins increased by as much as two times or more. Hendy may be correct to caution that a doubling of the corpus as it stood thirty years ago from a single hoard proves that volume was small. The interpretation could go the other way, however; not only did several thousand more specimens suddenly become known, but it is quite likely that substantial hoards will continue to be found (such as the two- or three-hundred coin hoard retrieved a few years ago).[565] If, in addition, it can be shown that the number of dies is larger than generally believed, doubts that Visigothic coinage was struck on a major scale will likely wane. The question cannot be resolved at present, but there is no reason to assume categorically that the volume of currency was small.[566]

B Other Reasons for Minting

The Military Factor

The patterns of minting in two regions merit separate attention since special circumstances appear to have affected output there. We begin with the apparent predominance of coin production by the southern mints in the kingdom during the years 612-36, when a much higher proportion of Visigothic coins were struck than during the rest of the regal period lasting from c. 573 to c. 713.[567] There must have been some reason why the majority of Visigothic coins between 612 and 636 came from the south. Apparently, the area had a special need for currency, which peaked in the second through fourth decades of the seventh century. A clear connection can be drawn between military engagements and minting, which suggests

565 Above, Chapter Three, section B.

566 As pointed out by Metcalf, "For What Purposes Were Suevic and Visigothic Tremisses Used?," 16-17. In one brief discussion of volume of coinage, Retamero makes no mention of any significant finds since Miles's day (Retamero, "As Coins Go Home," 287); a later, more extensive discussion incorporates newer data (Retamero, "La Moneda," 193-6). On the basis of the number of isolated finds, it has been observed that we have more indicators of circulation for Visigothic gold than we do for the imperial period in Hispania, and yet the latter is not thereby regarded as a period of monetary scarcity or decline: T. Marot, "La península ibérica," 149. Pliego, *La moneda visigoda*, v. 1, 226, 228f raises important considerations for both sides of the volume question without a final resolution.

567 See Appendix I, Figure I.9, a graph of the southern mints' percentage of the total corpus of known coins.

that coin production was sometimes greatly influenced by the needs of maintaining an army. This is a kind of fiscal requirement, but one of an extraordinary nature.

In about 554, eastern imperial troops entered the Visigothic kingdom on the request of a usurper, Athanagild, who was in the middle of a civil war. Once Athanagild had won the throne he found that his foreign collaborators did not want to leave. The call for help had been a convenient pretext for an invasion of barbarian Spain, which formed the last and certainly the least successful campaign in Justinian's reconquest. For nearly seventy-five years, Byzantine and Visigothic troops were engaged intermittently in war in the south and the southeast of Spain. A few sites that Visigothic kings recovered from imperial troops were recorded by name by the two main chroniclers of this period in Spain, John of Biclar, and Isidore of Seville.[568] From the former it is known that in 570 the regions around Málaga and Basti (east of Acci) were recovered by Leovigild; then, in 571, Asidona, near the southern tip of Spain, was re-taken.[569]

It has often been asserted that Cordoba fell to imperial troops, a conclusion based on an inscription found there and on John of Biclar's entry for the year 572, in which the author says Leovigild occupied the city, killed the enemy troops and many common people, and brought numerous towns and forts back to Visigothic control.[570] But the slaughtered enemy troops, '*caesis hostibus*,' do not refer in John of Biclar's language to the imperial army.[571] Still, the possibility of a northern extension of the Byzantine zone from the coast exists, since in 552 the army is known to have moved towards Ispali to assist Athanagild's forces.[572] Imperial troops must have been near

568 John of Biclar's *Chronicon* covers the period 568-590, while Isidore's *Historia Gothorum* (= *HG*) begins its coverage much earlier and ends, at least in one version, in 625/6.

569 John of Biclar, *Chronicon*, a. 570 & 571 (*MGH.AA*. XI, 212).

570 Ibid., a. 572 (*MGH.AA* XI, 213): "Leovegildus rex Cordubam civitatem diu Gothis rebellem nocte occupat et caesis hostibus propriam facit multasque urbes et castella interfecta rusticorum multitudine in Gothorum dominium revocat." There is no question that Cordobans had been rebellious against the Goths for a long time ('diu Gothis rebellem'); in fact, ever since 550, during Agila's reign and thus before the Byzantines came to Spain. They do not seem to have linked up with imperial troops in 572.

571 When John refers to imperial troops, he always uses the term 'milites' or 'Romani': Thompson, *The Goths in Spain*, 323 n. 1.

572 See the interpretation of events in ibid., 322-26, based on *HG* 46 (*MGH.AA* XI, 286), where Seville is the location of battle between Agila and Athanagild. In 566/7, Athanagild lost Seville, but Byzantine involvement in that episode is doubtful. Archeological work has shown that from 562 to 642 twenty per cent of the funerary inscriptions in the *conventus* of Cordoba were for people with Gothic names, a proportion higher than usual which has been attributed to the presence of mostly Gothic troops fighting in the south: Orlandis, *Historia del reino*, 191. Vizcaíno,

Ispali in 584 when the rebel prince Hermenegild, having made an alliance with them, counted on their imminent intervention there at the height of the civil war with his father Leovigild. Gregory of Tours, a contemporary and a moderately well-informed source regarding Spain, reported that "Hermenegild called upon the Greeks to support him, left his wife in his capital and went out to fight his father. As soon as Leovigild ordered his troops to advance Hermenegild found himself deserted by the Greeks," for he was unaware the King had bribed them with thirty thousand pieces of gold.[573]

The city of Málaga, either recaptured by imperial soldiers or never itself wrested from them by the Visigoths, is found under a Byzantine bishop in 603. But it was certainly in Visigothic control again by 619, when a bishop from there signed his name to the conciliar canons of II Seville.[574] King Witteric (603-09) won control of Saguntia, just north of Asidona, in 607. Because Saguntia is inland from the coast and located on the Roman road leading north from Asidona, it has reasonably been supposed that Asidona was once more in Byzantine control until at least that time. Byzantine control of the latter fort city would fit the testimony of Isidore, who wrote that Witteric, "though he often exerted himself in battle against the army of the Romans, accomplished nothing of much glory except that he captured through his generals some soldiers at Sagunt[ia]," whereas his successors did gain notable victories over the Romans.[575] Though Isidore's words in regard to these more successful kings are unspecific as to place, Sisebut's

La presencia bizantina, 138, 156f discards an imperial occupation of Cordoba but sees it highly influenced by Byzantium.

573 *Historiae Francorum*, V.38 (trans. Lewis Thorpe, *History of the Franks* [Toronto: Penguin, 1974], 302). John of Biclar's chronicle narrates the episode in this way: "King Leovigild entered Seville by force after his son Hermenegild had fled to imperial territory (*ad rem publicam*). Leovigild captured the cities and fortresses that his son had seized and not long after apprehended him in the city of Cordoba" (*MGH.AA*, XI, 217; trans. Wolf, *Conquerors and Chroniclers*, 74). Vallejo Girvés, *Bizancio y la España*, 210-11 stresses instead the absence of the imperial army from the actual fighting at Seville at this time. On the precariousness of the independent-minded lower Baetican territory for both Visigoths and Romans, see P. C. Díaz Martínez, "En tierra de nadie: Visigodos frente a bizantinos. Reflexiones sobre la frontera", in *Bizancio y la península ibérica. De la antigüedad tardía a la edad moderna*, ed. I. Pérez Martín and P. Bádenas de la Peña (Madrid: Consejo Superior de Investigaciones Científicas, 2004), 37-60.

574 Thompson, *The Goths in Spain*, 330, points out the strict ecclesiastical separation between the two sides.

575 *HG* 58 (*MGH.AA* XI, 291; trans. Wolf, *Conquerors and Chroniclers*, 105-6, quoted here with a corrected version of the name of the town, which Wolf mistakenly has taken to be Saguntum near Valencia). On Saguntia and Asidona see Vallejo Girvés, *Bizancio y la España*, 154-55. Asidona's bishop was absent from both III Toledo (589) and I Seville (590).

general (and the future king) Suinthila is said to have captured Roman 'fortresses,' a term that could well apply to Asidona.[576] Furthermore, the city was located on the road leading up to Ispali from Baesippo near the Strait of Gibraltar, no doubt controlled by the Byzantines in 584 when they approached the Baetican capital.

On the southeastern coast, Carthago Nova (= Cartagena) was in Byzantine hands from around 555 until its capture and total destruction by the Goths some time before 625/6, when Isidore had finished the first, longer version of his history. The reference to Cartagena's destruction by the Goths in *Etymologies* can no longer be used as a firm support for dating this event to c. 615, for the current view is that Isidore was at work on the book into the 630s.[577] Further up the coast, the Byzantines may have had possession of Dianium, which did not send a bishop or representative to III Toledo in 589 and which was not far south of the monastery of St. Martin raided by an army of Leovigild, perhaps as a consequence of its nearness to the frontier.[578]

It is unfortunate that Isidore, who provides the only history from early seventh-century Spain, often does not give precise information about the occupation and Visigothic counterattacks. Several times he records that many sites were recaptured without naming them or specifying where they were. In the case of Reccared (586-601), victory itself is not certain, for it is ambiguously stated that he "often pitted his strength against the excesses of the Romans [i.e. Byzantines] and the attacks of the Basques."[579] Gundemar

576 *HG* 62 (*MGH.AA*, XI, 292): "Iste sub rege Sisebuto ducis nanctus officium Romana castra perdomuit." John of Biclar called Asidona a "civitas fortissima" (ibid, 212).

577 Collins, *Early Medieval Spain*, 63 and esp. M. C. Díaz y Díaz, "Introducción general a las Etimologías," in *San Isidoro de Sevilla, Etimologías*, ed. J. Oroz-Reta and M. A. Marcos Casquero (Madrid: BAC, I, 1982), 3-257, here 172-74. The word *nunc* in the phrase at the end of Isidore's description of Carthage may point not only to the contemporary status of the famous city but to a recent event at the time of writing: "Nunc autem a Gothis subversa atque in desolationem redacta est" (Etym., XV, 1, 67). On the dating see Vizcaíno, *La presencia bizantina*, 233. Margarita Vallejo Girvés, *Hispania y Bizancio: Una relación desconocida* (Madrid: Akal, 2012), 143-51 stresses the possible dates of 551-555 for the initial incursion; see 169-72 for the conclusion that Carthage was the capital of Spania.

578 Vallejo Girvés, *Bizancio y la España*, 206-07; Greg. of Tours, *Lib. de Glor. Conf.*, XII-XIII. Vizcaíno, *La presencia bizantina*, 127f. See the discussion of the probable Byzantine control of Denia and, under Reccared, Játiva, and the related minting at Sagunto and Valencia, in García Moreno, "Cecas visigodas," 340. Also attributing this minting to campaigns against the Byzantines, although not elaborating its exact purpose, are Barral i Altet, *La circulation*, 64, and Mateu y Llopis, "Sobre el numerario visigodo de la Tarraconense. Las cecas de Sagunto y Valencia en el primer tercio del siglo VII," *Ampurias* 3 (1941), 85-95.

579 And further, "In these cases, he seemed not so much to be waging wars as to be exercising his people to keep them fit as in the sport of wrestling": *HG* 54 (*MGH.AA* XI, 290; trans. Wolf,

(609-612) besieged the army of the enemy on one expedition.[580] Isidore wrote that King Sisebut "In person [...] had the good fortune to triumph twice over the Romans and to subject certain of their cities to himself in battle.[581] He was so merciful in the wake of victory that he ransomed many of the enemy who had been reduced to slavery as booty by his army [...]."[582] Of Suinthila, the *Historia Gothorum* tells only in general terms that he brought about the end of the imperial occupation:

> Having risen to the position of general under King Sisebut, he captured Roman fortresses and overcame the Ruccones.[583] After he had ascended to the summit of royal dignity, he waged war and obtained the remaining cities which the Roman army held in Spain and, with amazing fortune, triumphed even more gloriously than had the other kings. He was the first to rule the entire Iberian peninsula north of the straits, which had not been achieved by any previous ruler. He increased his claim to fame in that battle by capturing two patricians, one by cunning, the other by force.[584]

In an earlier entry of the *Historia Gothorum*, Isidore explained that, "Up until this time there has been fighting against [the Romans]. But [they are] diminished by frequent battles[...]."[585]

In order to understand what relation minting may have had to this military activity, let us first examine the output of coinage in the areas where fighting took place.[586] The period of the climax of the war and shortly

Conquerors and Chroniclers, 104). In fact, the Byzantines probably gained territory during Reccared's reign: Thompson, *The Goths in Spain*, 331-32, and Vallejo Girvés, *Bizancio y la España*, 219-54.

580 *HG* 59 (*MGH.AA* XI, 291): "Wascones una expeditione vastavit, alia militem Romanum obsedit."

581 It is significant that he refers to several cities having been in Byzantine hands ("quasdam eorum urbes").

582 *HG* 61 (*MGH.AA* XI, 291; trans. Wolf, *Conquerors and Chroniclers*, 107).

583 A people somewhere in northwestern Spain.

584 *HG* 62 (*MGH.AA* XI, 292; trans. Wolf, *Conquerors and Chroniclers*, 107).

585 *HG* 47 (ibid., 286; trans. Wolf, *Conquerors and Chroniclers*, 101).

586 Mints of southern Spain are defined here as any mint south of Castelona: see the map in Appendix I, Figure I.4. Reckoning of output is precarious, since of necessity it hinges on the happenstance of discovery, which in turn involves hoards which are likely to have a strong bias of mints near to the place of recovery. Because of the very uncertain contents of the giant 1984 Fuentes de Andalucía discovery, it is removed from the equation here. The percentages mentioned are based on the table in Miles, *The Coinage of the Visigoths*, 70-75, along with the regal Visigothic coins included in Grierson and Blackburn, *Medieval European Coinage*.

afterwards has left by far the greatest bulk of surviving tremisses. The mints of southern Spain account for over thirty per cent of the corpus during most reigns. For the reign of Sisebut (612-621), the percentage exceeds forty-five per cent of the total, then for the next two reigns (Suinthila [621-631] and Sisenand [631-636]), it jumps to its highest level, roughly sixty per cent of the total. It might be objected that the reason for such remarkable figures is the exceptional hoard of La Capilla. Dated precisely to c. 632/3, it was buried near Ispali, and therefore naturally comprised mostly coins from southern mints.[587] No doubt this objection is partly valid, so that the minting of this period might be supposed to have been in reality less weighted to the area closest to Byzantine territory. Still, several arguments can be made against a complete mistrust of the data from this hoard. The first is that southern minting accounts for a relatively high percentage of the total during several other reigns as well; some hoards buried later than 632/3 reflect this fact.[588] Second, even northern hoards from this period and later display a predominance of southern mints.[589] Third, a map of La Capilla's mint distribution demonstrates that the hoard was formed from coins which had circulated from very distant mints and not simply from southern coins, suggesting the make-up of this treasure was governed by a random flow of coins, not by mere proximity to its place of burial. For example, by far the most specimens originated not in nearby Ispali or any other southern mint but rather in Emerita; coins from Toleto are fairly numerous; the number of Galician mints represented (as opposed to the level of their output) is exceptionally high, and several other mints contributed to the hoard.[590]

587 Barral i Altet, *La circulation*, 109-10, has a useful discussion of the date of burial; see ibid., 96 on the site. Essential now is Pliego, *La moneda visigoda*, v. 1, 234-41; ibid., 192f gives general adherence to the idea of southern minting in these years owing much to the war front against imperial forces.
588 As Appendix I, Figure I.9 demonstrates, long after La Capilla's burial date the average of southern minting is still over thirty per cent of the total. Pliego, "El *tremis* de los últimos años," 20 relates that in spite of the Abusejo hoard's burial very near Salamanca in the near northwestern area of Spain, while Toleto and then Emerita are the most represented individual mints, Baetica and Carthaginensis are the dominant provinces. Other hoards or multiple discoveries from what was central and lower Carthaginensis ('La Condenada' hoard and the El Tolmo de Minateda site) reveal a vast majority from Baetica: ibid., 21-3.
589 See Barral i Altet, *La circulation*, 116, 122, 130, 139.
590 Barral i Altet's maps of the hoard's mints of origin according to various periods illustrate my point. A geographical bias is naturally apparent for coins from the reign of Sisenand, since the hoard was very likely buried a year or two into his reign: there was not yet much time for his coins to have circulated from their mints of origin (ibid., 114, fig. 9). By contrast, a much wider range of circulation occurred further from the time of burial, i.e. for coins from 621-631 and c. 600-621. Thus, these latter maps are more representative of actual production. Essential on La

Fourth, while a hoard may easily bear a geographical bias, a large hoard which contains coins from a broad geographical range of mints could be without a bias. That is, the hoard's particularly high number of coins from mints near the find is not necessarily due to the proximity of the keeper of the treasure to those mints. It might result from a real, exceptional volume of minting for a time in that region, and the hoard's indication of minting volume there could even be low.[591] The argument is clearly borne out when the hoard of La Capilla is simply subtracted from the entire corpus, in so far as this can be done.[592] Without La Capilla's known coins in the equation, southern mints contribute eighty-eight per cent and fifty-seven per cent of all coins during the two reigns from 612 to 631, and more than thirty per cent during most other reigns.[593]

The coin output within different provinces can be examined in order to see how individual mints behaved. A graph of mints in Baetica demonstrates a shift in production from primary mints to a cluster of secondary mints exactly in the period coinciding with the final campaigns against the Byzantines (especially 621-631).[594] To judge from surviving coins from Sisebut's reign (612-621), Ispali had accounted for eighty-five per cent of Baetican output. Precisely during that time, the mints at Barbi and Acci (the latter in Carthaginensis) opened, and Cordoba's mint surged after an apparent drop-off for ten years, while the mint at Tucci records its first activity. During the next reign, Ispali's relative output sank as the smaller mints expanded their production – Ispali, Eliberri, Barbi, and Tucci all share roughly twenty per cent of the total. The beginning of a return to the normal

Capilla is Pliego, *La moneda visigoda*, v. 1, 226 and 234-41, the latter pages a study of the hoard with more pieces now identified.

591 The indication of regional volume of minting would be low if for some reason coins from mints outside the area of burial were over-represented in comparison with actual output in those places, which could occur through the treasure-keeper's long stay elsewhere or mixture of his coins with a locally-biased hoard from another area.

592 This is possible to do with reasonable confidence thanks to the excellent research on the composition of the hoard which appears in Barral i Altet, *La circulation* , 96-116. The state of the corpus used for calculation here is prior to the 1980s, when the huge Fuentes hoard's quiet discovery began to bring an untraced but quite obvious accretion to coins coming from the south.

593 While I cannot deny that the figures may be the result of our incomplete knowledge of the La Capilla hoard, I offer this calculation to show that the hoard does not *necessarily* distort our picture of actual production. Single finds, which can be presumed to be random, show a significant but much lower amount of coins from southern mints (c. 20-30 per cent): Metcalf, "Some Geographical Aspects," 315-16. As Metcalf sensibly remarks, "the truth probably lies somewhere in between the two sets of percentages."

594 See Appendix I, Figure I.10.

predominance of one or two mints occurred from 631-636, but Ispali picked up an absolute majority of the province's output again only after several secondary mints had ceased by 639. Based on the data from finds, Ispali and Cordoba were again the principal workshops in terms of the number of coins issued and in terms of consistency. Temporary circumstances gave way to the normal fiscal pattern.

A similar trend is apparent in the minting of Carthaginensis during the reigns of Sisebut, Suinthila, and Sisenand. From 601-621, the Mentesa mint went from having a very minor role to assuming a large percentage of production along with the mint at Toleto. From 621-631 it even surpassed Toleto's output, if the surviving corpus may be trusted, and in the next reign three minor mints in the south operated along with the one at Toleto, which normally took an 80-100 per cent share of minting in the province.[595]

Most of the mints from the Guadalquivir River Valley to the southern coast were opened along four rough geographical lines that correspond fairly closely in chronology to Visigothic reconquests nearby, as well as can be determined from the evidence.[596] The first line of mint openings was in the north of the region, where Italica and Tucci joined Ispali's and Cordoba's minting during the reign of Leovigild, between c. 575-586. From the style of the one surviving coin from Italica, a city just 7-8 km northwest of Ispali, its issue can be dated to between 582 and early 584. The legend on the coin's reverse points to a victory won there by Leovigild: CVM DEO ETALICA.[597] The one reference to Italica in the histories of this period is from John of Biclar, who wrote that in 583/4 "Leovigild restored the walls of the ancient city of Italica, which proved a great disadvantage for the people of Seville," where Hermenegild was still resisting his father.[598] If the issue was made shortly after the possible recapture of Italica – a rapidity in harmony with

595 For graphs of relative shares of minting in Carthaginensis and Lusitania see Andrew Kurt, "Visigothic Minting," 165-166. These graphs would now appear slightly different due to a number of new discoveries. Changes highlight even more the contrasting centralization of production at Emerita in the western province.

596 One may wish to refer to Appendix I, Figure I.7 [mint-ruler table] and Figure I.4 [map of mints].

597 Pliego, *La moneda visigoda*, v. 1, 81-83 and v. 2, 69-71, nos. 45-49. Miles, *The Coinage of the Visigoths*, 111, 192, pl. III, 1. "The inscription is probably to be read CVM DE[O] O[BTINVIT] ETALICA," on the basis of similar victory legends and recorded re-occupations of the sites from which these issues proceeded (p. 111). After Ispali was recaptured from Hermenegild, Leovigild had coins struck with the legends CVM D[E]O OPTINVIT SPALI and perhaps CVM DEO SPALI ADQVISITA. (pp. 110, 191-92)

598 John of Biclar, *Chronicon*, s.a. 584, 1 (*MHG.AA* XI, 216; trans. Wolf, *Conquerors and Chroniclers*, 73).

other Visigothic victory issues – then Leovigild ordered the striking of coins there while unable to mint in Ispali, by far his main workshop in the south.[599] What was the reason for the special minting at this time in Italica, one of only perhaps five workshops in the south under Leovigild? The king may have wanted to make a small issue of coins for purposes of propaganda, or he may have had a particular need for coinage there during the months of the siege of Ispali. The coincidence of the presence of a large royal army, the brief activity of a new mint while the principal one close by was in his son's control, and the victory legend, suggests the coinage was needed in order to support the army. Perhaps late in Leovigild's reign a workshop was possibly started at Tucci.[600] Although no specific evidence links this site to skirmishes with the Byzantines, minting at Tucci may have begun a southward progression of workshops that cut right toward the middle of the entire territory the Byzantines held from Asidona to Carthago Nova and very probably further up the southeastern coastline. The mint may not have been too far from the territory in southern or eastern Baetica which Hermenegild is thought to have ceded to the imperial forces in order to win their support of his rebellion.[601]

While the mint at Tucci – if it existed – seems to have ceased production by 586 and would not show activity until at least 612, as the current corpus indicates, in Reccared's reign (586-601) a mint was established a few kilometers east from there at Mentesa. Also under Reccared, a mint was set up at Eliberri. Together, they reveal a third line of expansion. A Spanish scholar has put forth the argument that both were frontier mints.[602] They would have been close to the front, which Reccared established against the imperial aggressions ('*romanas insolentias*') he frequently had to confront.[603]

599 At least eleven of Leovigild's coins from Ispali are known, compared to six from Cordoba, two from Roda, and one each from Italica and possibly Tucci. That the Roda in question is to be distinguished from Rodas on the NE coast of Iberia has been demonstrated by Balaguer, "El problema." She is absolutely correct that the style and the victory type place the coins from Roda in the same group of victory issues made in connection with the crushing of Hermenegild's rebellion. The article concludes with the suggestion that the mint site is "perhaps the Roda of Andalucía, near Ispali," a site I have tentatively proposed as modern Ronda la Vieja: see above, p. 88, and the map in Appendix I, Figure I.4.

600 Miles accepted the authenticity of the single Leovigild-Tucci coin, but its whereabouts were unknown to him and no photo of it is available. If it has a facing bust on both sides, it was issued between 584 and 586. Miles, *The Coinage of the Visigoths*, 45-47 and 192-93. Pliego, *La moneda visigoda*, v. 1, 121 (implied) does not accept the existence of this coin.

601 See Vallejo Girvés, *Bizancio y la España*, 214.

602 Ibid., 243.

603 *HG* 54 (*MGH.AA* XI, 290): "saepe etiam et lacertos contra Romanas insolentias et inruptiones Vasconum movit." I concur with Thompson, *The Goths in Spain*, 332 n. 1, that *insolentias* implies

It is not surprising, following the theory of military minting, that in the years 601-612 no new workshops were set up in the southern part of the kingdom, for in the three reigns of this period only two apparently modest victories were won.[604] On the other hand, literary evidence regarding heightened military activity under Sisebut correlates with the starting of workshops in Barbi, Acci, Iliocrici and, from recent discovery, Aorariola: a third line. The latter three appear to have operated in conjunction with campaigns against Byzantine holdouts on the southeastern coast[605] and eastward past Basti, perhaps in preparation for the later attack on Cartagena. Barbi, located on the road leading northwest from Málaga, was the point from which the latter was recaptured before 619. This was the reason why the workshop of Barbi, which was not a bishopric, far outproduced the one in Málaga (minting under the name Malaka), an important port city and a metropolitan see. Several Sisebut-Barbi coins with a victory legend that have recently come to light offer further proof of the drive toward the southern coast at this time. A more elaborate study of die styles than I have been able to carry out until now holds out the possibility of dating this issue more precisely.[606]

some kind of offensive by the Byzantines and balances the *inruptiones* of the Basques. See idem, 331-32, for other evidence indicating Byzantine successes in this reign.

604 See above, nn. 575 and 580, on the expeditions of Witteric and Gundemar, respectively.

605 Acci: see Vallejo Girvés, *Bizancio y la España*, 296. Iliocrici/Eliocrica and Aorariola: see Pliego, *La moneda visigoda*, v. 1, 115; also ibid., 100 in relation to a long-suspected *limes* possibly already under the name Aurariola, as in the time of Muslim conquest.

606 See Pliego, *La moneda visigoda*, v. 2, 172f, nos. 268 (1,2), 269(c) (1,2), 269(d) (1); the reverse legend of the last three reads '*PIVS BARBI VI*,' the letters VI expanding to *VICTOR* or *VICTORIA*. See also Peter Bartlett and Gonzalo Cores, "The Coinage of the Visigothic King Sisebut (612-21) from the Mint of Barbi," *Gaceta Numismática* 158-159 (Sep.-Dec. 2005), 13-21; and Sebastián Corzo Pérez and Susana Sempere Díaz, "La ceca visigoda de Barbi: aspectos historiográficos y arqueológicos," *Numisma* 45 (no. 236, 1995), 125-38, esp. 136, where the authors believe the purpose of the mint of Barbi was to assist the army.

A basic chronology of events may be proposed from literary sources. Vallejo Girvés sees in a law of Sisebut of 612 a provision for a military build-up precisely for this campaign: idem, *Bizancio y la España*, 291-92, where the law in question (*LV* XII.2.13) forced Jews to relinquish ownership of Christian slaves precisely in twelve towns across a wide area just north of Barbi and Acci, and including Barbi itself. According to Thompson, *The Goths in Spain*, 162 and 329, in c. 614-15 the imperial commander Caesarius initiated an exchange of letters for the purpose of seeking a peace, implying that a Visigothic advance had already taken place. Both Caesarius and the king refer to the terrible slaughter and the great capture of soldiers suffered by the two sides. Isidore's *Chronicle* gives 615 as the year in which Sisebut seized various cities of the Roman army ("quasdam eiusdem Romanae militiae urbes cepit": *Chron.*, 129). A secure final date for the struggle over Málaga is 619, when the bishop not only signed the acts of II Seville but also sought recovery of a few of his city's *parrochiae* taken over by the three surrounding dioceses "ante militarem hostilitatem" (Vives, ed., *Concilios*, 163). The chronologies offered by

The fourth line of mint openings represents the extension of Gothic authority all the way to the coast, where one might expect them to be since the workshops operated in the reigns of Suinthila and Sisenand, who took the throne a few years after hostilities on the peninsula were ended. The sites of new workshops were Asidona and Málaga, with minting also renewed at Iliocrici,[607] the last one a small city 60 km west of Cartagena with access to the sea by possibly two different roads. If they had a direct relationship to Visigothic troops, they enabled the king to guard the surrounding regions and the shore itself.

Mints of the south issued gold currency of notably low fineness and lower weights in the years 621 to 642.[608] Average weights for all the mints of the kingdom, accounting for less than ten per cent of known volume, began to fall after Reccared's reign (586-601), and were especially low from Sisenand through Chintila, falling to under 1.3g.[609] The lowered quality of eastern imperial gold coinage at this time is attributed to a shortage of gold in the eastern Mediterranean, and it may be that the same conditions explain the Visigothic debasements.[610] The state's supply of gold did not necessarily

the several unearthed hoards from the first decades of the seventh century can be compared with one another.

607 For the identification from a coin of Sisenand of this remote site, modern Lorca (province of Murcia), see Kurt and Bartlett, "Ceca visigoda nueva." Suinthila minted at Asidona; the recovery of one or more specimens of his reign from Iliocrici would demonstrate continuous if low-volume minting there.

608 See Appendix I, Figure I.11 and Marques et al., *Ensaios*, 137, Fig. 5 (all Baetican mints) and 141, Fig. 9 (Ispali alone).

609 See Appendix I, Figure I.14. As first observed by Barceló, "A Statistical Approach," dispersion of weights is also characteristic of the mints.

610 This reason for Visigothic debasements can be seen, for example, in Orlandis, *Historia del reino*, 282, and in García Moreno, "Cecas," 336, where the shortage of gold is said to be largely the effect of kings' gift-giving to the Church and to the nobility. See Banaji, *Exploring the Economy*, 12f on depletion of western gold currency; ibid., 111f observes there were less gold reserves in the late empire's coffers but more gold coins in circulation generally, a fact attributed to aggrandizing trade activity which put increasing amounts of money into private individuals' possession, counter to the theory of an exodus of gold beyond the empire as sometimes suggested. On Eastern imperial shortage see Haldon, "Military Service," 13ff and idem, *Byzantium*, 173-207; Harl, *Coinage in the Roman Economy*, 186-203; P. Yannopoulos, "Production monétaire à l'époque byzantine, avant l'an mil," in *Rythmes de la production monétaire, de l'antiquité à nos jours*, ed. G. Depeyrot et al. (Louvain-la-neuve: l'Université Catholique de Louvain, 1987), 359-72, here 370. On the gold shortage in the Merovingian kingdom beginning about 580 see Harl, 184 and esp. Hendy, "From Public to Private," 62-65. Regarding a suggestion that the quality of Merovingian gold currency was significantly improved after, perhaps as a result of, Sisenand's gift of 200,000 solidi to the Frankish king Dagobert for his help in defeating the sitting Visigothic ruler Suinthila, see Ian Wood, *The Merovingian Kingdoms, 450-751* (New York: Longman, 1994), 174.

decrease in Spain during this period; it is possible that it stayed about the same, but that a much greater production of tremisses for military needs required a reduction in quality. In either case, the lower standards appear to be a matter of policy (albeit one born of necessity), to judge by their occurrence especially at southern peripheral mints and even at the primary mints during periods of heavy warfare and decreasing supply of gold.[611] This conclusion differs from the common notion that the low standards were the result of the dishonesty of minters, which, in turn, proceeded from the difficulties of supervision of these secondary workshops. Lack of supervision is said to have resulted from a lack of control by the state, but the minting of low-standard coins by design would mean that the king had a firm command over monetary affairs. It would be strange if he did not, since for all kings the war was a matter of the greatest interest and kings were often at the front.[612]

We should consider whether it seems likely that the southern mints' high proportion of total production would be due to trade, as Metcalf believes. There was certainly a heavy Mediterranean trade in the south of the peninsula, and the rivers on which several mint cities were located undoubtedly were involved in trade.[613] Large riverine cities such as Ispali, Cordoba, and

611 See Appendix I, Figure I.11. Observe the decreasing amounts of gold coin output particularly under Sisebut, Suinthila, and Sisenand, including at Toleto and Emerita. I do not yet have an explanation for the fact that Tarraconensian mints have low standards during most reigns. It should be pointed out that *seigniorage*, minting fees exacted by a ruler, does not appear to be the reason for Visigothic debasement. If it were, it seems odd that it should have been imposed or increased primarily or even solely at military mints. I am unconvinced by the argument for the general supply of western gold from Byzantium in the post-Roman period, so that Visigothic acquisition via purchase and not recycling or use of gold from Hispania itself explains how most tremisses were made and why they were subject to fluctuations: Fernando López Sánchez, "The Mining, Minting, and Acquisition of Gold in the Roman and Post-Roman World," in *Ownership and Exploitation of Land and Natural Resources in the Roman World*, ed. P. Erdkamp et al. (Oxford: Oxford University Press, 2015), 315-36 esp. at 334. Even the evidence to suggest some portion of supply in this manner is sparse and indirect.

612 On the king's departure for war and the ceremonies of victory see McCormick, *Eternal Victory*, esp. 302-25; see Collins, *Early Medieval Spain*, 36 and idem, *Visigothic Spain*, 38-40 on the necessities of war-leadership for survival. Isidore, *HG* 61, specifically records that Sisebut fought in person against the Romans. It was not unusual, and was possibly customary, for the king to travel along with the royal treasure or at least a part of it: e.g. Isidore, *HG* 45 (Agila's loss of his entire treasure in his impious attack on Cordoba), and possibly ibid., 61 (Sisebut using his treasure for the redemption of captives); also Greg. of Tours, *HF* III, 10 (Amalaric attempting to take part of his treasure in a doomed escape). This is also suggested in Thompson, "The Suevic Kingdom in Galicia," in idem, *Romans and Barbarians*, 161-87, here 169.

613 For a brief summary and maps, see J. J. Sayas Abengochea and Luis A. García Moreno, *Romanismo y germanismo: El despertar de los pueblos hispánicos (siglos IV-X)*, vol. 2 of *Historia de España dirigida por Manuel Tuñón de Lara* (Barcelona: Labor, 1982), 388-90.

Emerita were more involved in trade than smaller ones, probably on a large enough scale to necessitate heavy minting of gold pieces, whether with the intention of facilitating commercial transactions or as a corollary for taxation purposes.[614] Yet, the record of surviving coins indicates a greater volume of minting in certain years in what were clearly less important cities.[615] It is improbable that the needs of trade would require mints in smaller cities to take on a sudden, temporary, and collectively a very large production of coins in the period 612-639. Nor does this minting fit well with administrative necessities. The pattern of minting in the south of the Visigothic kingdom at this time can convincingly be explained only by the military campaigns against the Byzantines, especially if we consider the timing of the opening of mints. Debasement at peripheral mints operating on an immense scale was driven by extraordinary needs that cannot be accounted for by commerce or administrative circumstances. Taken together, the data linking minting and Visigothic military campaigns form a strong case for the military hypothesis of coin production, however imprecise the geographical zones of imperial occupation remain.

There are four main ways to explain the connection of war and minting in southern Spain:

1. *The requirements of Visigothic troops*

Earlier in this chapter, we discussed the likelihood of expenses and rewards of the army being paid at least partly in currency. Cash grants were one way to for kings to secure loyalty,[616] which could never be taken for granted among the Visigoths. That the Byzantine government in Spain also made cash payments to its troops is implied by the military minting attributed to Justinian and his successors. "Anomalous features" present in Byzantine minting can be linked to military purposes, but the irregularities were

614 In addition to the comment of Barral i Altet, *La circulation*, 69 that "the coinage has an essentially commercial character" (see above at n. 555), which I do not share as a broad assessment, see the evidence gathered by P. D. King, *Law and Society*, 192f, who concludes that "the apparatus for a developed economic and commercial life based upon money transactions existed and needed regulation." While more recently it has been proved that Visigothic Spain was not monometallic, too few bronze pieces have been discovered so far to believe gold did not predominate in the still highly active trading scene well into the sixth century: see Chapter Two, section C.

615 The map of Suinthila's coins in the La Capilla hoard best demonstrates the surprising comparative outputs across Baetica and s. Carthaginensis: Barral i Altet, *La circulation*, 113.

616 P. D. King, *Law and Society*, 71. Recently, Pliego has lent support to the idea that army campaigns stilled elicited the transfer of coinage by the state even as the late trend toward privatized troops ensued: Pliego, "El *tremis* de los últimos años," 38.

quickly eliminated once hostile circumstances returned to normal.[617] We can see much the same process in southern parts of *Gothia* during the Byzantine war. The law codes make clear that all able-bodied men of age – Goth or Roman, freemen or freedmen, clergy and *servi fiscales* alike – were required not only to join a king's campaign but also to bring their slaves, well-equipped, when called in times of disturbance.[618] The Byzantine war presented frequent scenes of military engagement; it was the most formidable military challenge the Visigothic kingdom faced. If a type of *donativum* was still in use, it would have been given out frequently in the south during the nearly seventy-five-year occupation.

It also seems likely that the provisioning of the troops would be taken care of by payments in coin.[619] Payments for food would be directed to the local landowners who would sell their goods to provisions officers, who are, in fact, mentioned in the laws.[620] This is nothing more than the system of *coemptio* – obligatory sale of grain to organs of the state – employed in the late Roman period and still used at this time in the eastern Empire. It would not be surprising that the Visigoths should have kept this system in place among the majority Hispano-Roman population.[621] In the case either of rewards to troops or securing provisions, minting near the army's engagements offered greater convenience and new opportunities for royal propaganda in frontier zones. The extraordinarily high output from 621-636

617 Hendy, *Studies*, 405 (Justinian), 414-20 (Heraclius).

618 Esp. book IX of the *LV*, many of which laws are labeled *antiqua*, thus dateable to the time of Leovigild or earlier. See P. D. King, *Law and Society*, 71-77. Pérez Sánchez, *El ejército*, 116-17 discusses private armies involved in military operations on the part of the state.

619 By the sixth century, supplies for the Byzantine frontier forces were probably as a rule commuted to gold; by the reign of Maurice (582-602) annual cash allowances were granted to soldiers for uniforms and arms: Jones, *Later Roman Empire*, 670-74. See also Haldon, "The Army and the Economy," 140-41. At the time of his intervention in favor of the Visigoths in southern Gaul, shortly after Alaric II's defeat, Theodoric released local inhabitants from paying for the expenses of garrison troops. He wrote to his administrative Vicar of the Prefect there: "We will transmit to the Duces and Praepositi sufficient money to provide food to our Goths (*alimonia nostris Gothis*)" (Cass., *Variae* III.42; trans. Tomasini, *The Barbaric Tremissis*, 58).

620 *LV* IX.2.6; the *annonarius* is the same as the *erogator annone*, or the distributor of rations, who appears to have worked in this capacity or in providing the supplies for levy troops alongside the *comes civitatis:* P.D. King, *Law and Society*, 74 and n. 3. As King notes (at n. 4), "living off the land was sternly forbidden" by the law code (VIII.1.9), and the men in charge of provisions may have stored up supplies in case the army were mobilized. Here too, the Visigothic court may have acted in a way similar to the contemporary Byzantine state. Constantinople took steps to increase the provincial or local role in providing for troops, not only billeting but also compulsory purchases of foodstuffs in kind and other measures, a process nonetheless centrally controled: Haldon, "The Army and the Economy," esp. 145.

621 Cf. García Moreno, "Cecas visigodas," esp. 339.

at Ispali, Cordoba, Tucci, and Mentesa can be explained by the role of those cities on the second line of the Visigothic *limes*, a military frontier organization with many fortified locations along the front connected by roads to a few strong cities some distance behind.[622]

Chris Wickham's massive work on late ancient-early medieval structures and economy surveys the evidence of taxation maintained until late in the Visigothic period, perhaps to the end. He asks what purpose taxation still served at that point, since there was not a standing army. "Even specialist army service [...] was not associated with salaries, in other words with tax." In this environment taxes exacted increasingly in the fruit of the land, as sources seem to relate, would make much more sense, while cessions of land in exchange for tax liability maintained the wealth of the monarchy. The implication is that coinage was not much needed. Wickham's answer to the question is that tax proceeds must have provided for the court personnel and ceremonial.[623] However, from minting output it can be discerned that taxes paid in gold (in at least the sixth century) had not all been channeled to Toledo but must instead have been remitted to provincial centers and distributed provincially or locally. Needs at these levels are thereby evoked.[624] Specifics are not revealed in the surviving record, but even the highly centralized eastern Roman empire had regional distributions for sub-levels of government, garrisons, and the like. Wickham's own observation is that he fails to see a supposed crisis now that Rome's salaried army no longer existed and a public levy operated instead, except for the urgency of "an unfeedable army of hundreds of thousands" on call-up.[625] Here is an obvious case where either gold for food or food itself was needed. Rewards in tremisses may also have been made periodically. From the legal evidence on taxation as well as the minting habits, it appears that Visigothic Hispania

622 Visigothic use of the *limes* following Byzantine models of the time has been asserted by Sayas Abengochea and García Moreno, *Romanismo y germanismo*, 330, and Vallejo Girvés, *Bizancio y la España*, 243, 291f. Vizcaíno, *La presencia bizantina*, 88-92 (Byzantine) and 92-94 (Visigothic) sees a similar version of the *limes* adapted in Spain.

623 Wickham, *Framing*, 100. Earlier we noted a similar perspective in Pliego, *La moneda visigoda*, v. 1, 222-24.

624 On local variation in fiscal arrangements see Valverde Castro, "La ideología fiscal."

625 Wickham, *Framing*, 98. There is possibly significance in this regard in the inclusion of *dux* – denoting a military role – in the full titles of *comes thesaurorum et dux* first known from XIII Tol. (683) as well as of *comes patrimonii et dux* already present in the sixth century, emblematic of the army's association with fiscal workings. Isla Frez, "El *Officium Palatinum*," 837. Despite attempts within the Visigothic administrative evolution to keep military supervisors separate from tributary matters, support of the army was likely an area of pressure forcing an amplified role on military administrators: see Fernández, "Statehood, Taxation," 254.

of the final half-century or more may have foreshadowed a somewhat later Byzantine trend in transitioning from extraction-and-expenditure in gold coinage to a cycle based on land and its produce. Yet, gold currency was still being produced – and used. Evidently, it retained a significant role from the state's viewpoint as a convenient means of satisfying expenses.

2. *Recovery of taxation zones from Byzantine control*

This hypothesis is related to the first one. The newly recovered lands, which had presumably been paying taxes to the Byzantine administration, were probably now subject to taxation by the Visigothic administration and thereby provided some portion of the gold for local minting. It is perfectly in line with contemporary evidence to suppose that the Visigothic kings soon imposed taxes on the lands they had won back to the kingdom and, furthermore, turned this revenue into coin. One problem with the argument is simply that the minting at the new workshops did not last. What happened to the taxation? It is unlikely that it ceased after a few years (we have no record of Visigothic tax revolts, as we do for the Merovingians). On the other hand, the theory that coins were struck there for paying troops or providing for them fits with the transitoriness of the mints, since employment of garrisons probably did not last indefinitely, but rather only until the serious threat from remaining Byzantines or their sympathizers subsided.

Miquel Barceló, who sees Visigothic minting as purely fiscal, believes that taxation in the territories of what now comprises Andalucía was destined for the military expenses incurred there.[626] He attributes the differences in the quality of coins from the kingdom's mints to the relative strength of tax collection. Unequal gold content in the early seventh century "would be the result of unequal tax collecting: either lower fiscal liability of certain zones, lesser fiscal capacity or more resistance to pay, or even creakiness of the fiscal process itself." He therefore links gold supply directly to taxation.[627] Under different circumstances, there may be a parallel in the eastern Mediterranean from a slightly later period. Late seventh-century economic decline befell most of the remaining Byzantine lands due to the shrinking revenue base after the Muslim conquests, and while a 'functioning monetary economy' and Mediterranean commerce persisted never the less

626 Miquel Barceló, "A Statistical Approach to Multiple Mint Issues of Royal Coinage: The Case of the Visigoths in Hispania (585-711)," *PACT* 5 (1981), 138-54, in which a historical parallel is drawn to other fiscal coinage systems of former ages, including that of early Islamic Egypt.

627 Ibid., 153. Comparative scarcity is the consequence of "poor tax gathering which would result in the production of cheaper coin at the local mints choosing to produce relatively large issues instead of better but smaller ones" (152). Barceló rules out planned fraud by the moneyers.

a monetary recession set in, which among other matters affected the ability of the general populace to pay taxes in specie. The circumstance in common in near contemporary scenarios is that a decrease in the availability of gold affects taxation and thereby the re-minting of gold taken in by the state.[628]

3. *Re-minting of Byzantine gold*

We can now discern that the Byzantines used imperial gold coinage in the south of Spain, just as they did elsewhere throughout imperial territory. Imperial bronze coinage from the Visigothic era has been found in abundance on the peninsula, but only a handful of gold coins have been known until recent research brought awareness to some two dozen verifiable pieces.[629] Certain features of the known specimens led Philip Grierson to conclude long ago that a mint was established at Carthago Nova.[630] Why, then, are the discoveries still few? The reason may be that the Visigothic administration required any imperial gold coins to be re-minted. There is evidence for the same practice in Merovingian France.[631] Possibly, the main motive was to avoid differences in numismatic standards, but the desire to utilize coinage for propaganda should not be underestimated.[632] One real possibility not considered plausible until lately is that the Byzantines in Spain may well have re-minted Visigothic tremisses. A discernable imitation of lower Visigothic metallurgical values in the Byzantine pieces is a remarkable observation.[633]

4. *Taking of war booty*

This is an age-old practice of armies. King Leovigild himself was known to have taken or at least to have kept booty, and the collection of spoils by the Visigothic armies is attested to in numerous places.[634] But how was booty in

628 Banaji, *Exploring the Economy*, 19f, 85f deals with Byzantine and early Islamic territories.

629 Barral i Altet, *La circulation*, 64-66; see now Bartlett et al., "Byzantine Gold Coinage of *Spania*."

630 Ph. Grierson, "Una ceca bizantina en España," *Numario Hispánico* 4 (1955), 305-14.

631 Barral i Altet, *La circulation*, 65; Metcalf, "Some Geographical Aspects," 310ff, extends the discussion. Also Pliego, *La moneda visigoda*, v. 1, 193.

632 See Hillgarth, "Coins and Chronicles," and McCormick, *Eternal Victory*, 304, 317-19.

633 Bartlett et al., "Byzantine Gold Coinage of *Spania*," 371-74. Pliego, *La moneda visigoda*, v. 1, 225f notes the idea of Byzantine re-minting of Visigothic tremisses proposed in R. Doehaerd, *Le haut moyen âge occidental: Économies et sociétés* (Paris: Presses Universitaires de France, 1971), but instead suggests as more likely that merchants in Spania used Roman or Byzantine currency.

634 Leovigild's enlargement of the treasury (*aerarium*) through robbery from citizens and the collection of spoils from enemies is recorded by Isidore in *HG* 51 (*MGH.AA* XI, 288), where a distinction seems to be drawn between the treasury (*aerarium*) and state lands (the other meaning of *fiscus*): "fiscus quoque primus iste locupletavit primusque aerarium de rapinis civium

the form of gold turned into coin, if indeed this was a factor in the short-term minting with which we are concerned? Were soldiers gathering gold and having it minted on a private basis? Did they have to turn in any gold they found to royal officials, so that the coins minted in the workshops near their campaigns were in the first place state revenues?[635] If some spoils went at times to the king, not all did. We know that a certain class of a Gothic lord's retainers had by law to turn in any spoils to his patron, while another class did not;[636] in either case, the spoils remained in private hands. But we are left on shaky ground if we want to attribute all the minting in the south of the kingdom to booty alone. One reason is that it is doubtful whether booty – a new source of gold hypothetically turned into coin – would lead directly to an enormous rise in Ispali's minting during Sisebut's reign.[637] There is also no evident reason why booty would bring about a huge swell of minting at the provincial capital. Another problem is that the amount of gold booty recovered would have to have been enormous given the total of all secondary minting in the region, a fact one might expect to hear of in Isidore's history or somewhere else, but which receives no specific mention.

The best theory to account for the southernmost mints on which I have focused here is a combination of military minting and re-minting of Byzantine gold. These reasons for establishing the mints may have been combined with the desire to facilitate local taxation. Given the temporary existence of the mints, we must then conclude that the new tax zones came after a few years to depend on more distant, permanent mints. We have seen that there is indeed some evidence implying a rotation of taxation centers (*fisci*) within the provinces, or the existence of two or three at a time, with the result that tax revenues would be channeled to these cities

hostiumque manubiis auxit." The primary meaning of *manubiae* is money derived from the sale of booty. The only booty of Sisebut's army specifically referred to is slaves, i.e. captured Romans brought into servitude (*HG* 61). See also P. D. King, *Law and Society*, 75 on laws regarding war spoils which slaves collected for their masters.

635 John of Biclar makes an interesting report about a victory of Justin over the Persians: "The booty taken by the Romans was sold, along with a multitude of Persians, resulting in no small profit to the public finances" (*Chronicon*, a. 575, 1 [*MGH.AA.* XI, 212; trans. Wolf, *Conquerers and Chroniclers*, 68]).

636 War loot won by a *saio* belonged to the lord, whereas the booty of a *buccellarius* was his own property, the only stipulation being that if the latter were to change lords, as he was free to do, one half of the goods won had to be returned to his patron at the time of the campaign. See on this Thompson, *The Goths in Spain*, 264f and P. D. King, *Law and Society*, 187f. From Greg. of Tours, *HF* II.27, we know that the Frankish king Clovis evenly shared booty, including gold, with his soldiers.

637 Cf. the table in Appendix I, Figure I.7.

(and in the end presumably to their mints) during at least a brief period.[638] Yet, in the case of Baetica, the fact that the frontier mints were very close to each other, and that they either are never heard from again or revive with only a minor status, makes their existence look like a special case rather than part of ordinary fiscal practice.

In the previous chapter, we saw that there were numerous die cutters operating in the south in the war period.[639] Elsewhere, I have shown in detail the connection through a single engraver between several southern mints during the final decades of the Visigothic-Byzantine war. The engraver was at work in the 620s and 630s at Cordoba, Tucci, Mentesa, Castelona, Eliberri, Acci, and Iliocrici.[640] The traveling of die engravers – or their sending out dies to several cities – can be seen in other regions and other periods of Visigothic Spain, but in the south the circumstances of war brought about much more (possibly itinerant) mint activity, and furthermore blurred the distinctions of style which normally obtained between provinces.

One point may be added to the considerations above. Miles noted that among the inferior die engraving work in the regal period of coinage, the worst was at several secondary mints examined above. In commenting on the growing use or misuse of punches for parts of both letters and images of the coins, he observed that: "the technique is most clearly revealed in the coins of Suinthila and Sisenand, especially at such mints as Acci, Barbi, Eliberri, and Tucci [...] [where] the die engravers were so careless in constructing their letters that the several punches used frequently are improperly coordinated or stand free, or else elements of letters are missing because certain punches were omitted. [...] Probably the worst die execution from [the standpoint of R or P appearing only as I or I.] is that at Acci during Sisenand's rule."[641] My own extensive examination of the coins confirms Miles's observations. I would add that the quality of coins issued from Málaga and Mentesa are almost as poor as those from Acci.[642] Careless workmanship is what one would expect from minting workshops which had few expert engravers.

638 See above, n. 525. Hendy, "From Public to Private," 55-56 argues for a rotating or multiple fisc in Tarraconensis from the combined evidence of '*De fisco Barcinonensis*' and Reccared's temporarily heavy minting at Barcinona. To his observations should be added the fact that Tarracona was a capital city, and yet it was paying taxes along with other cities on the northeastern coastline to Barcelona.

639 Chapter Three, section C. See also Appendix II, Plates IV and V.

640 Kurt and Bartlett, "Nueva ceca visigoda."

641 Miles, *The Coinage of the Visigoths*, 153.

642 Cf. ibid, pl. XVII, 13-14 and pl. XVIII, 1-3, and J. Amorós and A. M. Berruezo, *Catálogo de las monedas visigodas del Gabinete Numismático de Cataluña* (Barcelona: Ayuntamiento, 1952), pl. X, 107-10.

Such a shortage of skilled labor may well have prevailed at the secondary mints which became important between 612 and 640 if, as I have argued, several new southern mints were established somewhat hastily to produce coins – perhaps under the pressure of deadlines – above all to maintain an army and to mint new receipts of gold from reconquered areas.

In short, literary evidence of warfare in southern Spain, the special organization of minting there during the period of engagements and just after, military inscriptions, inferiority of style, and the lowered quality of the tremisses in question, combine to indicate firmly the specific motivations for some minting in the Visigothic kingdom.[643] The specialized pattern is one that can be seen in various periods of antiquity.[644] One example from southeastern Asia Minor of this very period (615/616) links the provisioning of arms with a mint briefly established in the same place. In a related imperial parallel of these same years and in the immediate vicinity of the Visigoths, two Byzantine Spania tremisses of Heraclius with a low intrinsic value near those of Suinthila, from different dies and of cruder style than nine other Spania coins in Heraclius's name, can circumstantially be deemed to have come from a point late in the Byzantine occupation but before the conclusion in 624. Perhaps these were made under stress of an eroding military situation.[645] In Hispania, in so far as needs and the output of coins were extraordinary, military minting may serve to highlight normal minting operations that, considering mint distribution and regularity, appear much more conducive to ordinary public finance.

643 The data satisfies at least three of five possible indicators of military coinage summarized by Howgego, *Ancient History*, 37: "[...] military inscriptions on the coins, highly specific military typology, an unambiguously military context, a monetary phenomenon apparently explicable in no other way, and clear literary evidence that a particular coinage was struck for military purposes."

644 To name but a few, in addition to Byzantine military minting covered by Hendy, *Studies*, 405, 409-20, I quote Howgego, *Ancient History*, 36 (where appropriate references are provided): "[...] the building of the Athenian fleet in the 480s BC to fight the Persians coincided with 'probably [...] one of the most intensive periods of minting in the history of Greek coinage' [...] there was a significant increase in coinage in many regions of Alexander's empire when a substantial part of his army was paid off and sent home from c. 324 BC [...] Rome's massive coinage in 90 BC during the Social War was larger than that in any other year of the Republic."

645 Arms-mint: Hendy, *Studies*, 416 and idem, "From Antiquity to the Middle Ages: Economic and Monetary Aspects of the Transition," in *De la antigüedad al medievo, siglos IV-VIII* (III Congreso de Estudios Medievales) (Ávila: Fundación Sanchez-Albornoz, 1993), 325-60 at 343. Heraclius tremisses: Bartlett et al., "Byzantine Gold Coinage of *Spania*," 369. In the 590s, and perhaps earlier, payment of daily expenses of the city of Rome's military was made by the *sacellarius*, a role played at this time by Pope Gregory I: Hendy, *Studies*, 411; on the *sacellarius* see also Haldon, *Byzantium*, 190f.

Mints of Gallaecia and of Northern Tarraconensis

Like the south, Gallaecia is a special case. The terms of the problem are well put in the title of an article by Michael Metcalf: "Many Mint-Places, Few Coins: Visigothic Coinage in Gallaecia and Northern Lusitania."[646] Scholars have offered several possible reasons for the peculiarities of minting in the northwest: to provide for normal taxation in a mountainous region;[647] extraction of gold;[648] military needs;[649] post-war plunder and re-minting; reuse of Suevic administrative structure or as part of compacts with local settlements in the wake of conquest.[650] Metcalf has wisely cautioned against declaring a single explanation for all the northwestern mints, in light of their varying longevities and the diverse size of the towns or in some cases villages or simply place-names.

It is impossible to prove or disprove fully that exploitation of gold deposits, known for the late imperial period, and normal tax collection had much to do with the setting up of mints in the northwest, though both remain potential reasons.[651] Firmer ground in many cases is evidence which points

646 D. M. Metcalf, "Many Mint-Places, Few Coins: Visigothic Coinage in Gallaecia and Northern Lusitania," in *Homenagem a Mário Gomes Marques*, ed. Mário de Castro Hipólito (Sintra: Instituto de Sintra, 2000), 175-94.

647 Gil Farrés, "La moneda sueva y visigoda," 188ff., believed the reason for Gallaecia's many small mints – "mobile mints" incorrectly presumed to have used some dies at more than one place – was in order to facilitate payment of taxes on the spot (but see below, n. 659). Also Hendy, "From Public to Private," 58 (taxation directly related to extraction of gold).

648 Grierson, *Coins of Medieval Europe*, 22; Hendy, "From Public to Private," 58; Orlandis, *Historia de España: La España visigótica*, 201; P. D. King, *Law and Society*, 194. The theory is that *yacimientos*, alluvial gold deposits, gave the Visigoths much gold for a time but then dried up, producing shortage. See more below, n. 666.

649 Miquel Barceló, "La cuestión del 'Limes Hispanus': los datos numismáticos," *Acta Numismática* 5 (1975), 31-45; García Moreno, "Cecas visigodas," 342-43. Spaulding, "Mint-cities," esp. 180-238, 256-59, makes a fascinating argument that supposes the outbreak of two unrecorded civil wars in Gallaecia. Unfortunately, this latter conclusion is unreliable, founded as it is on drops in the number of extant specimens, which fail to account for relative lengths of reigns or the possibility – now established fact – of more finds coming to light.

650 Plunder and re-minting: Metcalf, "Many Mint-Places," attributes small Gallaecian mints to re-minting of Suevic tremisses. Orlandis, *Historia del reino*, 282 attributes the strange pattern in the NW to minting of the Suevic treasure and of alluvial gold; it is hard to see why the treasure should have gone out to a great number of obscure sites, and why the sites should have increased long after the acquisition of the treasure. Administrative arrangements: see below, n. 655.

651 The former has never been demonstrated, as notes Metcalf, "Many Mint-Places," (p. 13 of the ms. copy sent to me, the only complete version I have been able to access): "Not a scrap of evidence has been adduced that particular small mint-places lay beside auriferous rivers, or near gold-mines. Much less is there any dateable evidence of the winning of gold (except that it was known already to Isidore) which could be correlated with the reigns of particular kings.

directly in favor of the military motive and, by extension of the argument, a combination of loot, re-minting of Suevic coins, and possibly extraordinary taxation. In a 1970, dissertation which seems to have attracted little notice, Spaulding elaborated a thesis of military minting not only in the south but also in the northwest.[652] He associated the establishment of mints with victory legends and literary documentation of wars against the Sueves and other peoples in or near Gallaecia from 585 to about the first quarter of the seventh century. While he takes 'negative evidence' of gaps in the minting record too far, for example supposing Gundemar to have lost Gallaecia when in fact several finds from his mints there have since been made, the 'positive evidence' is compelling if brought up to date and elaborated.

Metcalf lays aside the explanation of the workshops as campaign mints set up to coin war booty and inflows of gold from a taxation similar to what we have envisioned in the south, instead seeing re-minting of Suevic currency as the primary reason for abundance of mints.[653] There are good reasons why booty is hardly suggested by the data as a principal incentive in striking Gallaecian coins.[654] It is also correct that victory legends do not have to indicate military minting, since they could be a statement of propaganda on coins minted for other reasons, or they might have been the result of "administrative arrangements for the supply of dies," some of which were possibly produced at a central point such as the capital city Bracara (modern Braga). But significant insight can be gained by carefully considering the location of the mints of Leovigild, Reccared, and later kings, keeping an eye on where and when the words *VICTOR* or *VICTORIA* appear

What we can say quite confidently is that these mysterious, tiny mint-places had only a trivial importance in the monetary affairs of the north-west: they contributed only a very small part of its coinage." See below, n. 666.

652 Spaulding, "Mint-cities," esp. 180-238, 256-59. F. Cebreiro Ares, "Dificultades que plantea el estudio de la historia monetaria sueva," in *Introducción a la Historia Monetaria de Galicia* (*s. II a. C. – XVII d. C.*), ed. F. Cebreiro Ares (A Coruña: Labirinto de Paixóns, 2012), 31-63 traces the main theories on LATINA MVNITA gold coins from Suevia, which appear to come from the last years of the kingdom. If so, (a) there were multiple mints in the NW already before the Visigothic annexation, and (b) evidentiary contexts have led to suggestions that these coins are related to a religious-political front against the Visigoths (see ibid., 48-54).

653 He comments on the argument laid out by Barceló, "La cuestión del 'Limes Hispanus'," who makes a passing reference to Spaulding.

654 Metcalf, "Many Mint-Places," (p. 2 of the ms.). In the first place, Metcalf doubts that a rather large number of small mints would be necessary or that this would be administratively appropriate, given that it required the preparation of so many separate dies. One fact that might be deemed to support Metcalf's notion of re-minting in Gallaecia, but which admits of other interpretations such as tax revenue, is the high standard of several coins from the northwest (see Appendix I, Figure I.11). Testing of more coins is necessary to know the real trend there.

on reverses. We can now do so with the help of the larger number of recently discovered tremisses.[655]

In 585, Leovigild rapidly conquered the Suevic kingdom, making it part of his own. At the same time, he captured the Suevic royal treasure. From the known coins, which came from the last year of his life, we can conjecture that his minting was carried out exclusively at three principal cities of Suevia. According to an early report, at Bracara Leovigild's tremisses included the epithet *VICTOR*. From Portocale were issued coins inscribed with *PORTOCALE VICTI*.[656] From Luco, a regional nucleus far to the north, we find a version of *IN LVC(O?)*. So far, re-minting of Suevic gold might be thought to hold as good a claim to the motive of minting as the military-minting hypothesis. When Reccared took power at Leovigild's death in 586, he did not merely continue the minting at these key Gallaecian sites. More than twenty mints operated at some time during his reign, and while the known Bracara coins do not employ the term *VICTOR*, the inscription *IN BRACARA* on one informs us of the continuation of the triumphant message there, and at least eight sites did include an announcement of victory.[657]

655 See the table in Appendix I, Figure I.7; the statistics in Metcalf's article need to be adjusted slightly. For the mint-map see Appendix I, Figure I.4. A recent update can be found in Pliego, "*Gallaecia*"; Leovigild's very few Gallaecian finds present problems, but I concur on her ultimate acceptance of their probable authenticity. Her treatment of Victory legends (96-101) shows the possibility that, despite little clarification from written sources, such inscriptions could point to some resistance to the Goths. She explains the region's dispersed coin-making up to the reforms of Chindasvinth as the result of concessions granted as agreements were reached with the disparate population centers. This is sensible if not comprehensive, and I believe is harmonious with my interpretation. There was no close correspondence with Suevic mint locations or episcopal sees if the current table of mints and rulers closely reflects actual production; the evocative suggestions of Martín Viso, "Circuits of Power" are without reference to Pliego, *La moneda visigoda*, v. 2 and idem, Pliego, "*Gallaecia*," which would render more complete information on the geography and timing of currency issuance in NW Iberia. Visigothic coopting of the Suevic administrative structure for fiscal purposes, as in Pablo C. Díaz Martínez, "Acuñación monetaria y organización administrativa en la *Gallaecia* tardoantigua," *Zephyrus* 57 (2004), 367-75 and Martín Viso, "Tremisses y potentes," is persuasive to a point but the timing of mint activity as currently known by remaining tremisses largely accords with military activity as suggested here (a somewhat different picture from what is cited on this point in Martín Viso). Díaz's article offers excellent bibliography and essentials of the various arguments on post-conquest Gallaecian minting and lays out clearly his linkage of Visigothic mints to many towns in the *Parrochiale Suevum*; cf. also Cf. Daniel Osland, "Tribute and Coinage in the Visigothic Kingdom: On the Role of the Bishop," *Anas* 24 (2011), 71-95.

656 The single coin of Bracara for this reign is not without some serious question of authenticity, although it is included in the catalog of Pliego, *La moneda visigoda*, v. 2, 76, no. 58. Portocale coins also present questions, though they seem on firmer ground.

657 LIVVICVVRE – INLVCIDDIVS (last letters signifying 'Pius'): this inscription from a list from the Hermitage collection in St. Petersburg as well as the other three coins (two from Portocale)

The others did not, according to the current state of the corpus. We may suspect that Reccared's specific use of the victory legend initiated under his father has significance.

During the fifteen years of Reccared's reign, tremisses were issued across the breadth of the province. Places known to have inscribed with *VICTOR* or *VICTORIA* were the western *civitas* of Tude (IN TVDE and VICTORIA IN TVDE, the latter confirming the meaning of the Bracara legend) and nearby Tornio on the Atlantic coast; the important northern city of Luco (IN LVCO VICTOR); and a cluster of small sites in the center formed by Pincia, Senabria, Calapa, and Bergancia.[658] Why did some mint sites employ *VICTOR*(*IA*), and why did the workshops at three principal cities up and down western Gallaecia proclaim "IN"? The answer may be that mints that took on the special inscriptions were on a war front, while those with normal legends, scattered far and wide, opened once the battles were over.[659] The legend *IN BRACARA*,

can be found in Pliego, *La moneda visigoda*, v. 2, 76, nos. 59 and 60.1, 2 respectively; ibid., 114-19 catalogs Reccared's Gallaecian coins; ibid., v. 1, 128-46 details the region's mint attributions and known specimens. For the table of mints see ibid., v. 2, 49f or now Pliego, "*Gallaecia*," 74f. Twenty mints of Reccared have now been attributed to Gallaecia, and future finds will perhaps reveal more. We might have reasonably expected the city of Leione to have a mint under the Gothic kings soon after annexation (at this time only coins of Suinthila are on record); Grierson and Blackburn, *Medieval European Coinage*, v. 1, 452, no. 293 and pl. 15 propose a little-commented Suevic-style tremissis with LEIOI A COTIS MVNITA on obverse and L-I on reverse as probably having been struck just after the Gothic takeover (see also Grierson, *Coins of Medieval Europe*, 14 for photo). I suspect finds of early Visigothic trientes from León will one day be uncovered.

658 Bergancia was possibly in the vicinity of Flavas (= Chaves) instead: Spaulding, "Mint-cities," 186. António Marques de Faria, "On Finds of Suevic and Visigothic Coins in the Iberian Peninsula and Their Interpretation," in Marques and Metcalf, *Problems of Medieval Coinage*, vol. 3, 71-88, places it between Pincia and Calapa, which would only strengthen the hypothesis about a line of military mints half-way into the province, from the lower Miño valley eastward (see ibid., p. 87, map 1). The preferable location of Bergancia in Pliego, *La moneda visigoda*, v. 1, 101 and 130 is only a slight adjustment. For the Calapa tremissis, I follow Miles, *The Coinage of the Visigoths*, 231, no. 104, which correctly transcribes CALABACIA V:CTOR (see reproduction of the original illustration in Vico et al., *Corpus Nummorum Visigothorum*, 282, no. 79D). The Tude tremisses of Reccared are described in Pliego, *La moneda visigoda*, v. 2, 118, nos. 150-52. Enrique Ariño Gil and Pablo C. Díaz, "La frontera suevo-visigoda. Ensayo de lectura de un territorio en disputa," in *Fortificaciones en la Tardoantigüedad: Élites y articulación del territorio (siglos V-VIII d. C.)*, ed. R. Catalán, P. Fuentes, and J. C. Sastre (Madrid: La Argástula, 2014), pp. 179-90 pose a number of fortifications along a North-South border area very close to the mints mentioned here.

659 Long ago, Gil Farrés speculated that the mints with insignificant production were not really mints as such, but rather places where the army passed through or where a royal expedition stopped and a small issue was struck: Gil Farrés, "Algunos aspectos," 32. Since completion of the manuscript for this book, I have come across an interpretation similar to my own of much of the known Visigothic monetary output as triumphal minting and continued issues to support

VICTORIA/IN TVDE and *IN LVCO VICTOR[IA]* are possibly references to the presence of Reccared himself at these sites. He may have been in these key cities in 585 in a wave of assault after an immediate post-conquest rebellion in Suevia, as one of the generals of Leovigild noted to have been entrusted with the offensive. A strategic path suggests itself. The presumption is that money in his name was issued only once he ascended to the throne in 586 on his father's death, which may have occurred shortly after this significant expedition still fresh in memory and worth broadcasting. Or, the minting could pertain to a moment following coronation. Neither John of Biclaro, nor Isidore mention continued fighting against Suevic hold-outs, but this cannot be ruled out.[660] If Reccared did not have to complete the operation, he must at least have had many garrisons in the occupied zone, and these would be obvious places to start. Orlandis observed that out of the eight converted Arian bishops at the Third Council of Toledo in 589 four were from Gallaecia, and he suggests that the installment of several Gothic bishops there is an indication of a significant concentration of Gothic soldiers.[661]

garrisons in the Iberian northwest and the south. For artful integration of numismatic and contemporary historical sources concerning the takeover of Suevia, see López Sánchez, "Moneda civil y moneda militar," 248-52; similarly, idem, "La moneda del reino visigodo de Toledo: ¿Por qué? ¿Para quién?," *Mainake* 31 (2009),175-86, esp. 179-83. The same author exposes the real possibility that Egica's son Wittiza, crowned in Tude over the Suevic territory in 694 (or perhaps later), was not put in place by his father to cap suppression of a Gallaecian revolt but instead came to power as a result of that regional rebellion.

660 Biclar, *Chron.*, a. 585, 2, 5, 6, informs us of the rebellion immediately after Leovigild devastated Gallaecia and deprived Audeca of his rule, and presumably had returned home: "Malaric immediately seized power in Galicia, as if wanting to be king. He was immediately defeated by King Leovigild's generals and was captured and presented in chains to Leovigild" (trans. Wolf, *Conquerors and Chroniclers*, 74-75). Sueves were not eliminated in 585, rather survivors were pushed back, as inferred by Isidore when he wrote many years after the conquest: "The Suevi, too, forced into inaccessible corners of Spain, have now experienced the danger of extermination at the hands of the Goths" (*HG* 68; trans. Wolf, *Conquerors and Chroniclers*, 109). The northern pockets of resistance in general took a long time to finally die. "Some of the most difficult areas of the peninsula, as far as authority based in Toledo was concerned, were the northern regions of Galicia, the Asturias and Cantabria": Collins, *Early Medieval Spain*, 110. Spaulding, "Mint-cities," 175-76 suggests on the basis of Greg. of Tours, *HF* VIII.35, that the Gallican ships which Leovigild attacked in 585 on their way to Gallaecia were a fleet sent by King Guntram. Literary accounts of the day narrate continued Frankish-Gothic hostilities in the Spanish northeast until Reccared's triumph via Duke Claudius in 589, but Thompson and others believe the reference can only be to trade ships: Thompson, *Goths in Spain*, 88.

661 Orlandis, *Historia del reino*, 190. An alternative to continued battles against Sueves is the possibility of Visigothic rebellion in the province against Reccared, who converted near the beginning of his reign (*HG* 62). While Spaulding weaves too grand a theory founded almost entirely on coins extant in 1952, a Galician uprising is not implausible. Leovigild installed a number of Arian bishops in Gallaecia in 585, four of which renounced Arianism and signed on

Reccared's triumphal numismatic labels may with some confidence be considered to have been early issues. Victory legends only appear in places and during reigns for which there are grounds for deducing military victories (we have seen Leovigild's in Emerita, in the south, and in lower Gallaecia, and Sisebut's in Barbi; see also the following paragraphs).

The victory legends, possibly ended already in Reccared's reign, do not appear among known pieces struck in Gallaecia in the following years under Liuva II (601-603) and Witteric (603-609). There are very few known issues from Liuva II's short term. Minting was carried out during Witteric's rule in several of the same places where Reccared had coined, and given the even spread of sites throughout the province in both reigns it appears that Witteric's network was similar to that of his predecessor. Discoveries made in the last few decades show that numerous mints also struck for Gundemar (although his short reign inevitably left fewer finds) and for Sisebut. It is not merely by the chance of finds that most of Sisebut's mints form a line running north-south down approximately the center of Gallaecia.[662] I take this to have been the frontier against the Ruccones, possibly linked with an opposite front to the east involving Saldania and Mave. Suinthila was able to mint in at least two sites located exactly in the zone between these sets of mints.[663] It is also not a mere coincidence that both Sisebut and Suinthila

to the Catholic faith at III Tol.; two were in places where Reccared minted with victory legends (Tude, Luco), while the other Arian bishops, including of Braga, did not. John of Biclar, and Reccared himself at III Tol., expressly lamented that Leovigild had won over many Sueves (see Thompson, *Goths in Spain*, 88, 90). The province did not return as a whole to Catholicism until III Tol. in 589. We should not be surprised if the atmosphere of tension should have brought about an uprising in the area. We know in fact of four separate rebellions in the kingdom during the new monarch's very first years on the throne (see ibid., 101-06). The suppression of the one in Emerita in 588 may be the reason for Reccared's many issues there inscribed with *VICTOR*: so Miles, *The Coinage of the Visigoths*, 119. Perhaps Gallaecia was the site of the rebellion of Argimund, the military commander of an unnamed province (*'dux provinciae'*: John of Bicl., *Chron.*, a. 590, 3), which could not have been Lusitania, where Duke Claudius held the office, nor probably Narbonensis where a probably more involved insurrection is narrated separately. Marques de Faria, "Finds,"80-81, briefly alludes to the possibility that Reccared's 'triumphal coinage' may be related to aristocratic rebellion in the northwest.

662 These mints included – in addition to Luco (VICTOR) and several western mints – Pesicos, Bergio, Georres, Pincia, Senabria (5 known tremisses), Calapa, Bergancia, Turico (?), Laetera (?), Vallearitia, and Semure (? = supposed location). Finds from previous kings demonstrate previous coining along this central line, but not to the same extent. Many of these mints and others in the center are also known to have continued activity under Suinthila.

663 I.e. Leione and Ventosa. Note that in relation to my conjectural frontier mints, these places fit neatly within an area that corresponds to what Isidore writes of the Ruccones, "who were protected by steep mountains on all sides" (*HG* 61). See the topographical-historical map in Collins, *Early Medieval Spain*, xvii. The Ruccones, who had also warred against the Sueves (see

revived the use of the '*VICTOR*' legend at Luco, since they were probably conjointly involved in the victory over the Asturians as they were against the Ruccones.[664] The establishment of a mint at Pesicos in the Asturian mountains must bear witness to the army's activity under Gundemar and Sisebut. By contrast to all the mint locations in the northwest, which can be associated with troop activity,[665] no currency has been shown to come from Vigo, the one coastal site that recent archeological research confirms as having been intensely involved even into the seventh century in trade from the eastern and southern Mediterranean shores as well as from western Gaul. In fact, none of the production sites along the whole Galician coast match Visigothic or for that matter Suevic mint locations, an indication that the trade economy was not a determinant of mint placement and perhaps not even a factor in currency production itself. Some trace gold mining in the area is being scientifically demonstrated of late, but pairing this with mint sites is problematic. It may be suspected that tin was the greater export good at Vigo, and trace gold deposits are to be associated with the mints by way of general supply – and perhaps taxation – but not in any full correspondence of sites.[666]

John of Biclar, *Chron.*, a. 572, 3) and may have presented a threat to the Visigothic order in years prior to Sisebut, are never heard from again.

664 King Sisebut won his Gallaecian victories through his generals, and in the next passage Isidore specifically mentions that Suinthila is the one who defeated the Ruccones: Isidore, *HG* 61, 62. Miles, *The Coinage of the Visigoths*, 137, connects the inscription at Lucu/o with the triumph over the Asturians, and possibly in Suinthila's reign over the Cantabrians.

665 Very little of which is taken into specific account in Martín Viso, "Circuits of Power." The argument made here from the ensemble of evidence matters, because otherwise it is probably correct to link the sporadic minting in Gallaecia with an inability to provide coin consistently for *adaeratio*, resulting in limited tax gathering (ibid., 237f, envisioning the entrusting of the mints to local elites). Yet, irregular minting applies to many other parts of the peninsula, where association can be drawn not to ineffective fiscal operations but rather incidents of campaign.

666 José Carlos Sánchez Pardo, "Power and Rural Landscapes in Early Medieval Galicia (400–900 AD): Towards a Re-incorporation of the Archaeology into the Historical Narrative," *Early Medieval Europe* 21.2 (2013), 140-68, at 150-52, 157, 160; idem, "Sobre las bases económicas de las aristocracias en la *Gallaecia* suevo-visigoda (ca. 530-650 d.c.). Comercio, minería y articulación fiscal," *Anuario de Estudios Medievales* 44.2 (2014), 983-1023. See also M. F. Guerra et al., "The Treasure of Guarrazar: Tracing the Gold Supplies in the Iberian Peninsula," *Archaeometry* 49.1 (2007), 53-74 at 60-63 and M. F. Guerra, "The Circulation of Monetary Gold in the Portuguese Area from the 5th Century to Nowadays," *Anejos de Archivos Español de Arqueología* 32 (2004), 423-31 at 425: analyses of some Suevic and Visigothic gold pieces suggest local gold sourcing from this corner of Iberia rather than the southern region from which other Visigothic gold coinage seems, based on Roman tradition, to have drawn (given the inconsistencies in the results, however, M. Metcalf's salient observation here is that the circulation, melting down and re-minting of coins is corroborated). Sánchez Pardo implies a matching of many Galician mints

Solid arguments have been made that certain mints bordering the regions of the Cantabrians and the Basques had a military purpose.[667] The brief minting under Leovigild at Lebea far on the upper Ebro accords with the campaign in which the king "seized part of Vasconia and founded the city which is called Victoriacum," probably modern Vitoria.[668] Reccared's issues at Cestavi as well as Tirasona and Calagorre on the eastern and southern edges of the same area may be related to the ongoing skirmishes. Isidore writes of his frequent attacks on the Basques.[669] Minting in the area north of Tirasona is known from the time of Gundemar, under whom the obscure mint of Volotania saw presumably limited activity (two coins with this name have been discovered), and this king is reported to have led a campaign against the Basques.[670] An apparently small issue from Sisebut at Labeclosa

with mining sites, and writes of a lively trade in tin and gold passing through Vigo. Although a map displaying locations of mints near some of the apparent gold mining sites is suggestive, it is equally impressive how many gold mining spots do not match mint placement, and vice versa (see "Sobre las bases económicas," 993). I believe the chronological and spatial patterns of currency-making, alongside a spate of suggestively positioned 'Victory mints,' tell a different story at least on the whole. His associating northwestern mints with pacts made with local and regional potentates is nevertheless intriguing, and alluvial mining in the region merits further investigation. For now, I can only offer the obvious question: If the Visigothic monarchy had such a source of gold at hand just as the need for coin production in the kingdom increased, why permit the selling of much of the gold and resort to considerable currency adulteration in Baetica and elsewhere?

667 Perhaps first put forward by F. Mateu y Llopis, "Sobre los límites de la conquista visigoda en Vasconia y Cantabria," in *Ampurias* 6 (1949), 222-225. M. Vigil and A. Barbero, *Sobre los orígenes sociales de la Reconquista* (Barcelona: Ariel, 1974), relied on this article but also previous works; their discussion of the minting and the northern *limes* was critically reviewed by Barceló, "La cuestión." The arguments of Spaulding, "Mint-cities," are apparently independent of these authors.

668 Mateu y Llopis, "Sobre los límites," and idem, "Sobre el numerario visigodo," 88 pointed to minting at Egessa in this regard, but the coins have been suspected as fakes (see Pliego, *La moneda visigoda*, v. 2, 496, nos. 840 and 841); Lebea (modern Herramélluri, La Rioja), however, fits the same locational supposition. The quotation is from John of Biclar, *Chronicon*, a. 581, 3 (*MGH.AA.* XI, 216; trans. Wolf, *Conquerers and Chroniclers*, 73). Vitoria is several dozen kilometers further north from both Lebea and the supposed mint site of Egessa. The cross-on-steps style of the two Egessa coins would make perfect sense if connected with a campaign in 581, though authenticity remains a problem (see above, n. 409); the Lebea coin is Facing Bust type, so would have come from between 584 and 586.

669 *HG* 54. Spaulding, "Mint-cities," 184, infers the presence of a large garrison at Tirasona to prevent incursions of Basques and Cantabrians. Pío Beltrán Villagrasa, "Nueva ceca goda en el Pirineo aragonés. Reducción de la ciudad de Cestavvi al pueblo oscense de Gistau," *Caesaraugusta* 5 (1954), 129-40, saw Cestavi as a military mint intended to assist against the Franks. Beltrán draws a fascinating argument from medieval and modern documentation to equate Cestavi with present-day Gistau, near Osc.

670 *HG* 59.

comes from the same remote area. Suinthila's striking at Calagorre, up the Ebro River beyond Tirasona and where minting is otherwise unknown apart from a single specimen from Reccared's rule, can be related directly to his expedition aimed at curbing Basque incursions into Tarraconensis.[671] Upon their surrender, the Basques "built the city of Ologicus for the Goths with their own taxes and labour, promising to be obedient to Suinthila's rule and dominion [...]."[672] An observation should not be missed: no coins of either Ologicus or Victoriacum have been found, while tremisses of Calagorre and Lebea, for example, have long been known. Might this not suggest that the very peripheral minting in question was carried out to pay and supply the army from points nearby, and that re-minting or providing money in the new cities was not a factor?[673]

In sum, military costs perhaps paid for by special taxation or forced tribute hold the soundest answer why the gold coinage of most peripheral sites in the north was struck. Re-minting was possibly an added part of the

671 Barceló, "La cuestión," 41; García Moreno, "Cecas visigodas," 339-40, where it is asserted that Calagorra (-e) and Osca were the natural points of access to the Basque country (ref. Julian of Tol., *Historia Wambae*, 10: after defeat of the *Vascones* Wamba's army goes on to Septimania 'per Calagurrem et Oscam civitates transitum faciens'). Pliego, *La moneda visigoda*, v. 1, 104 mentions the importance of the city including its location on the Roman road connecting to Caesaraugusta; the two Suintila-Calagorre trientes are catalogued in ibid., v. 2, 211, no. 337 (a and b).

672 "[...] stipendiis suis [...]": Isidore, *HG* 63 (*MGH.AA*, XI, 292; trans. Wolf, *Conquerers and Chroniclers*, 107-08). Ologicus is commonly believed to be modern Olite, not many km northeast of Calahorra: see García Moreno, "Cecas visigodas," 340 n. 28.

673 One is left to wonder in what the taxes of the Basques consisted. It may be best to regard this as either extraction in kind or a tribute rather than actual taxation. In either case, lack of monetary finds and sustained minting in the region makes the regular use of coined money doubtful. A less clear-cut case for military minting is Dertosa, from which several coins of Reccared now look to be confirmed: see Pliego, "Dertosa." Miles was led by the apparently short duration of the minting and a special legend with *DERTOSA IEECIT* (*fecit?*) to think in terms of some special event (Miles, *The Coinage of the Visigoths*, 83). At least two later scholars imply a relation to the large campaign of Duke Claudius against the Franks in Septimania in 589, which Isidore calls the greatest victory of the Goths: Spaulding, "Mint-cities," 184 and García Moreno, "Cecas visigodas," 340; *HG* 54. The Ebro valley was possibly the most highly militarized region in Spain in the latter third of the sixth century: see Collins, *Early Medieval Spain*, 40. For the view that Reccopolis was a military city, and its legends *RECCOPOLI*[*T*] *FECI*[*T*] under Leovigild and Reccared a testimony of this purpose, see Spaulding, "Mint-cities," 169-70, 178 (cf. the argument of López Sánchez, "Moneda civil y moneda militar," 248 that Reccopolis was a natural garrison town and access point for the eastern coast, the place from which Witteric's successful siege of Sagunto must have been launched). The geography of coin losses, admittedly difficult to interpret, is certainly compatible with military engagements. See Barceló, "La cuestión," 33-40; Marques de Faria, "Finds"; Barral i Altet, *La circulation*, 83, 85, 91, 152; and for an interpretation rather of *aemulatio imperii* and economic advantage, Castro, "*Reccopolis*."

puzzle in Gallaecia, as it may have been in the south, but spotty gathering of alluvial gold must be said to at least fit as the reason behind several locations. There is little in the record of surviving tremisses to suggest normal taxation had any role in the mints before about the mid-seventh century. Bracara is indeed the most productive mint in the Gallaecian region overall, but the table of finds indicates that before Suinthila's rule in the 620s other mints in Gallaecia produced roughly on par. After Reccesvinth came to the throne, which mints remain? Only Bracara, Tude, and Lucu – the largest towns of the region – and perhaps two or more others which may have been opened only during Egica-Wittiza's joint reign. The fiscal reforms of mid-century once again stand in contrast to the earlier monetary situation.

C The Addition of Bronze to the Corpus

Still rather little is known about the bronze or copper coins of the Visigothic era in Spain. The wide variety of weights opens the possibility that the coins had different values. From the limited corpus built up by a single scholar they do not appear to have been minted in great abundance, but this impression may be due to the inherent difficulties of finding, identifying and dating bronzes, as mentioned above.[674] Crusafont i Sabater has so far attributed bronze pieces primarily to the four major cities of the center-south of the kingdom – Toleto, Emerita, Ispali, and Cordoba – but they also may have come from a few smaller, yet significant cities in Lusitania and lower Gallaecia. The finds published to date have come almost solely from the region around Ispali.

Our scant knowledge of this low-denomination currency makes it difficult to determine why it was made. We cannot even be certain who produced it. The legend *CIVITA* which appears on pieces assigned to Emerita reinforces Crusafont i Sabater's hypothesis that bronzes formed a parallel coinage to the royal tremisses and were minted by certain large cities and perhaps others as well. Such a source gives little reason to think this minting was destined for the military, although some contemporary bronzes in the eastern Empire certainly served this purpose.[675] In this case, the simplest answer is probably the best one. Bronze or copper coins were made to provide small change. That is the prime function which they served throughout Roman and Byzantine

674 See Chapter Three, section C.
675 On Heraclius's bronze minting for military needs see Haldon, "Military Service, Military Lands," 12, and Hendy, *Studies*, 415-17.

history and in other ancient societies, and no doubt in Visigothic Spain (the kingdom of Toulouse had plenty of Roman coinage to rely on). Low-value coinage was extremely useful for constant small transactions, all the more so in large cities where commerce abounded and barter was harder to come by. In this light, in contrast to the not uncommon view that the Visigothic kingdom was engulfed in decadence which contributed to its end, bronze coinage might be an additional sign that some cities were thriving. If a few, or perhaps many, cities needed both gold and bronze currency for a variety of transactions, then trade was not in decadence.[676] That is also the impression one gets from the ample evidence of trade in Spain in spite of limited documentation from the period.

D Visigothic Minting in the Context of Contemporary Monetary Systems

Visigothic coins were made for a variety of reasons. As occasionally observed in the scholarship, the data available to us from the gold coins show a great variety in the production rates, the permanence, and the number of mints in each region, as well as in standards. All of the viewpoints commented on in this chapter add potential insight, but some of them suffer from exclusion of other motives. Retamero's model is too enclosed on itself, though his explorations of coinage's precise place in the taxation process is commendable and his considerations about displays of wealth by nobility and the church are significant. Metcalf is probably correct that trade and "the life of populous and wealthy cities" was a factor in Visigothic monetary policy, just as it seems to have been in some Merovingian minting.[677] Administrative, fiscal, and commercial activity were, after all, linked in many ways: by the desire of the court or regional administrators to ensure the smooth operation of

676 Crusafont i Sabater, *El sistema*, 106f and idem, "The Copper Coinage." I cannot agree with Spufford, "Coinage and Currency," 790, when he writes: "It is perhaps a measure of the collapse of urban society that only in Sicily did the necessary copper coinage survive [...] to provide for the enormous number of extraordinarily small payments [...] Elsewhere in the West the great cities of antiquity had dwindled away." Nor can I agree that the absence of silver should be read as an indication of the demise of commerce. The Roman / Byzantine Empire did not always make use of silver, either. In this interpretation, Spufford is perhaps relying on the conclusions of Pierre Le Gentilhomme, "Le monnayage et la circulation."

677 Commercial needs appear to have been a factor in some of the minting in Merovingian France, particularly that of Provence and of a few northern trading posts: Grierson, *Coins of Medieval Europe*, 25; Hendy, "From Public to Private," 68-70; P. Spufford, "Coinage and Currency," 2nd ed., 790-92.

trade and its associated taxes, by the process of *adaeratio*, by the payment of officials, by the supply of currency to taxpayers (at least in the fifth and sixth centuries), etc. But Metcalf is unconvincing when he writes, "the urban prosperity of Baetica dominated the kingdom's monetary affairs, and [if] coins were minted for reasons connected with military activity, that was quite a minor theme."[678] War was the great determinant of minting in the south and the far north, and possibly elsewhere. That mints concurrent with conflict evidently disappeared after a while is a sign of their special purpose. In the end, it is most fitting to call their possibly multi-layered purpose 'fiscal'. The evidence, though circumstantial and not explicit, weighs overwhelmingly in that direction. We should not doubt that currency then went on to have many uses, including as a means of trade and monarchical propaganda, but these have a rather tenuous claim upon the ultimate motive for striking coins.

The fiscal foundation of Visigothic gold currency helps to answer the directly related problem of why the Visigothic state employed so many mints, and why mints were placed where they were. The great multiplicity of mints presents a problem since there were other ways of handling taxation even if similarly based on coinage. One way to look at this question is to compare how states in the West and around the Mediterranean in these centuries addressed financial needs, to see if the huge variation in mint placement represented similar or different ends. In view of the general monetary continuity after the fall of the western empire, grounded on barbarian dependence on Rome in this one of many aspects where outsiders had no previous experience, it has been said that the break between Roman and medieval currency was not completed until silver was widely adopted in the late seventh and early eighth century and the weight of the *denarius* was reduced.[679] Yet, in the material production of coinage nothing so differentiated certain successor states from the Roman empire as the profusion of mints. Whereas Rome centralized the making of precious metal currency at very few mints providing for a vast territory, some new kingdoms issued coins from dozens or even hundreds of mints within a much smaller area.

678 Metcalf, "For What Purposes Were Suevic and Visigothic Tremisses Used?," 21. Of the two very general arguments about the network of mints as a whole in idem, "Some Geographical Aspects," 320, I agree wholly with the first, "that minting was carried on in so many places as to suggest that it was in response to or in relation to local needs." I believe the second is an erroneous conclusion based on a fairly accurate observation: "[...] most of the mints have long histories [...] The mints, in other words, were not set up temporarily to meet some special need, e.g. military needs, but fulfilled a persistent need."

679 See Blackburn, "Money and Coinage," v. 2, 538.

Numbers of mints varied widely among the kingdoms, and we must ask whether this was because the purposes of minting differed.

While the quite diverse coining operations might appear to indicate widely differing state involvement and purposes in making currency, in fact all precious metal coinages in the post-Roman West with the possible exception of the early Anglo-Saxon gold series were monopolized by the crown and were fiscal in nature.[680] Probing the rationale behind the numerous workshops of several kingdoms is linked to conjecture on the purpose behind specific mint locations. Particular need for currency in certain locales determined the situating of mints. The most obvious, if rather general, reason a mint might have operated at a given place was to supply coin where it was unavailable; others include re-minting of foreign coins, facilitation of taxation including in areas taken in war, and perhaps most importantly funding an army on campaign. Yet, the Roman system, employing central mints and transporting its products elsewhere, demonstrates that setting up a myriad of mints was only one way to satisfy the need for currency in areas distant from the court.

Scrutiny of the early medieval monetary scene indicates that for the incipient states the general need for coinage corresponded to administrative needs, in other words for fiscal revenues,[681] and in certain kingdoms officials determined that it would be more efficacious to mint at few sites, such as

680 Rory Naismith, "Mints, Moneyers and the Geography of Power in Early Medieval England and Its Neighbours," paper given at the conference Power and Place in Later Roman and Early Medieval Europe: Interdisciplinary Perspectives on Governance and Civil Organization held at University College London, November 2011 (forthcoming proceedings), available at https://www.academia.edu/24992893/Mints_Moneyers_and_the_Geography_of_Power_in_Early_Medieval_England_and_its_Neighbours, accessed 20 October 2016; see 7-10 on the largely commercial association of much of Anglo-Saxon coinage.

681 On fiscalism as the very reason why gold minting prevailed after the demise of Rome see Naismith, "Mints, Moneyers," 3 and idem, "Gold Coinage and Its Use." Pliego, *La moneda visigoda*, 97-153, 187-98 and idem, "La acuñación monetaria," 133f sustains only a minimal sense of the fiscal foundation of Visigothic gold minting, and she avers the monarchy had the will but not the mechanisms for robust taxation. The main reason for minting was along the same lines as in other contemporary barbarian societies, according to Pliego – for ransoms, tributes and gifts given for example in diplomacy at home or abroad, and payments and collections for fundamental services between the king and nobles, creating a web of mutual dependence. Warfare was a factor only in the early seventh century against the Byzantine occupation ("La acuñación monetaria," 129, without explanation of how the extraordinary outputs were accomplished). Most income to the king flowed not from widespread taxation but rather a cycle of tribute between crown and aristocracy, fines, and confiscations; the volume of coinage was based on concrete needs and available metal. My contention is that the evidence for fiscal engagement, regular as well as irregular minting, association with campaigns, patterns of coin quality, and volume itself all leads to a different conclusion.

was the case in the Ostrogothic, Burgundian, and African Vandal kingdoms (it was probably no mere coincidence the empire employed central mints in these very regions). In others the establishment of multiple sites, as we have seen among the Visigoths and much more so in Merovingian France, was deemed a better solution. The minting networks varied among the kingdoms according to the point(s) at which governments combined their fiscal and monetary operations, either near or far from the center, and it is this which explains all or close to all of the locations where coins were made. Thus, in the Ostrogothic kingdom, for example, the foundation of a tight Roman financial organism based heavily on taxation of land and trade was a rather obvious course for Theodoric and his successors to follow, and gold and silver coins were issued strictly from Rome and to a far lesser extent Ravenna. As in the Roman empire, the state made coinage available for revenue gathering and expenditure in a concentrated format. Although the Ostrogothic army rested primarily on the levy and only secondarily on standing or garrison units, still currency was required even if few details about payments can be discerned, and furthermore employment of currency in *coemptio* is recognizable.[682] As discussed in the first chapter, a letter from late in Theodoric's reign implies that mints in Italy as in Spain were meant for state functions instead of private needs.[683] Lombard state apparatus was rather consolidated; however, recent acceptance of the kingdom's continuation of taxation confines it solely to the first decades of rule;[684] Lombard minting was not completely centralized, but this has mostly to do with regional individuation by gradual territorial acquisition of Lombardy, then Tuscany, and eventually Benevento. Earlier the Burgundian kings from the 470s to 534 minted gold currency at a few sites including Lyon and probably Geneva and Valence, though evidence suggests that under each king only one mint may have been used. The kingdom seems to have maintained the land tax, city administrators, and expenditures at least on the part of

682 Naismith, "Gold Coinage and Its Use," 285 gathers the essential evidence. See Hendy, "From Public to Private," p. 43, with references for the Ostrogothic *donativum* and discussion of tax allotments as proposed by W. Goffart, *Barbarians and Romans, A.D. 418-584*, which would presumably not have affected the amount of coinage in production.

683 This letter written between 523 and 526 to Theodoric's joint governors in *Hispania* includes among its corrections of abuse: "Monetarios autem, quos specialiter in usum publicum constat inventos, in privatorum didicimus transisse compendium. Qua praesumptione sublata pro virium qualitate functionibus publicis applicentur." Cassiodorus, *Variae* V.39.8 (ed. Mommsen, MGH.AA 12:165).

684 See Wickham, *Framing*, 115-22. Predictably, Justinian's reconquest from the Ostrogoths was followed immediately by a concerted effort to reinstitute the fiscal system, a plan with only partial success. On minting, see Blackburn, "Money and Coinage," v. 2, 666f.

the army consisting of former Roman troops, the basis for a money system revolving around the necessities of government. Suevic minting was mostly centralized at León and probably Braga and a few mints in between, at least in the brief period of regal gold coinage before Leovigild's triumph in 585.

The Muslim conquerors who moved with great success into the eastern Mediterranean lands and from there eastward and westward, and who like the European barbarians had no previous coinage of their own, mimicked the Roman fiscal arrangements extremely successfully. In the early Islamic territories, taxation was even accelerated, with a mix of money and land taxes and the addition of a head tax for non-Muslims. Arab rulers established a regionalization of administration and to some extent minting; monetary taxes in the regions went predominantly toward the army and soon the navy, with the remainder for the government.[685] (When Islamic forces took Spain starting from the invasion in 711 the new fiscal structure was not as monetarily driven, given the post-tax Visigothic setting by the time of conquest.)[686] A parallel to the nascent Arab empire was contemporary Byzantium, which remained capital-centered. What occurred in the eastern empire, though subject to interpretation, may serve to enhance the overall point about the close connection between taxation and minting of precious metal.[687] Late

685 In the first decades, the Caliphate made use of Byzantine gold and Persian silver coinage, then issued close copies. A Muslim gold currency distinct from the Byzantine prototype did not emerge until the late 690s. Minting was sometimes placed near troop concentrations for several decades in lands which Muslim armies captured from the Byzantine and Sasanian empires: Hugh Kennedy, "Military Pay and the Economy of the Early Islamic State," *Historical Research* 75 (May 2002), pp. 155-69. See also idem, *The Armies of the Caliphs: Military and Society in the Early Islamic State* (New York: Routledge, 2001), 67-71, on huge amounts of currency presumed to exist mostly in support of the armies, and on mints possibly moving in the early Muslim world with the principal governors, much as we saw with the Byzantine comitatensian mint; copper minting was, on the other hand, quite scattered. In the western Islamic territories, the site of the main mint was probably Damascus. On the fiscal operations, see Wickham, *Framing*, 130-44. Within the regions the tax system was in fact more centralized than the Roman empire's, which had to work with more independent cities and a potent aristocracy, and was more aggressive; see esp. ibid., 767-69 on Egypt. Banaji, *Exploring the Economy*, calls attention to the economic continuity in the Umayyad period and the massive streams of money that flowed to the army wages, caliphs, and elites (e.g., 33f, 211-18). In his view, the monetization and monetary markets were more significant than allowed for in Wickham's model of a divide in economic integration between ancient and medieval systems.

686 Wickham, *Framing*, 100-02. Chapter Six of the present book looks at the transition.

687 The Byzantine involvement in the patchwork of Italian states around the turn of the eighth century, it is true, meant that by exception several mints operated in this western sector: see Blackburn, "Money and Coinage," v. 2, 542f. Wickham, *Framing*, 124-29 traces the debate on whether the eastern empire maintained monetary fiscalism past the seventh-century crisis and concludes that it did indeed, even if there was reduction and localization. Tremendous

seventh-century economic decline befell most of the remaining Byzantine lands due to the shrinking revenue base after the Muslim conquests, and despite the persistence of a 'functioning monetary economy' and Mediterranean commerce a monetary recession set in which, among other effects, decreased the ability of the general populace to pay taxes in specie.[688]

Much less tidy circumstances of coin production apply to Merovingia, where perhaps 2000 minters are named at several hundred sites across the span from c. 500 to 670, when minting in gold gave way to a silver series. No regular royal mint operated, but for that matter few of all minting sites were regular from what can be made of inscriptions. However, elemental central authority behind the coinage is strongly implied by the overall uniformity of metallic standards and harmonizing of many of the artistic types. A more traditional explanation of the moneyers is that they were itinerant goldsmiths working on behalf of lords, including the kings, who occasionally needed new currency. This generic postulation is less than convincing as a comprehensive explanation, and has ceded primacy to the inference that many places on the coins were tax collection points or places where rents in produce were turned into coin for the landowners.[689] Coins feature *monetarii* because minting was undertaken in the name of this low- or mid-level official in charge of local collection or conversion, probably as guarantor of monetary quality and a guarantee of revenue amounts. Other strong evidence supports the view that what appears to be a privatized minting landscape was at least largely a 'public' structure serving taxation in coin.[690] Merovingian minting fit the intense localism of the kingdom. Taxation revenue itself came to be

stress fell upon Anatolia in wake of Arab annexations. The eighth century and the rise of the theme organization of the army brings the empire into a new phase beyond the scope of this brief comparative sketch.

688 Banaji, *Exploring the Economy*, 19f, 85. The question might be asked if a parallel to the final half-century or more of Visigothic rule is apparent: Did the economic constriction in Iberia, affecting agricultural exchange and perhaps coinciding with gold drainage, cause erosion of the base for taxation and thus a shift away from state-sponsored monetary support of troops?

689 Tax basis: Stahl, *The Merovingian Coinage*; Hendy, "From Public to Private"; Durliat, *Les finances publiques*; Grierson later adopted the fiscal explanation for Frankish coinage: see CME, pp. 24-25. See more recently, with emphasis on *civitates* named on coins as a key part in the collection system, Jürgen Strothmann, "Königsherrschaft oder nachantike Staatlichkeit? Merowingische Monetarmünzen als Quelle für die politische Ordnung des Frankenreiches," *Millennium* 5 (2008): 353–81. In a similar light Naismith, "Gold Coinage and Its Use," 289-300 and 306 considers both commutation of crops and taxation to be the main motives for the minting; ibid., 291 refers to 2000 moneyers.

690 This is not to say taxation was only in coin or that it was anywhere near Roman levels. My fuller argument for fiscally-oriented Merovingian minting and how the different post-Roman systems coincide at core in a mainly fiscal purpose can be found in Andrew Kurt, "The Places and Purposes of Minting in the Earliest Medieval Kingdoms," in *Worlds of History and Economics:*

directed in highly localized fashion to privileged institutions or persons (and to some degree to the royal court), while early taxation blended into rents or what appear to be rents and the large landowners who did owe fiscal dues paid them in cash. The Visigothic kingdom's mode of coin-making lies between the two poles of the early Frankish state and the others discussed above, with several major administrative centers in Iberia each served by a permanent mint, contingencies or special circumstances such as war zones or royally-supported foundations provided for by short-term facilities, and currency needs within an exceptional situation in the northwest met by extremely dispersed but apparently very light minting which after a few decades came under a general consolidation.

The decentralizing of minting is equivalent to the regionalization and localization of minting. I have made the case that much minting can be explained by military needs, but much can also be explained by the downsized state in the post-Roman West. Simpler administrative forms and lower-scaled government operations including taxation corresponded to changes in the countryside. The Visigothic regime may have adapted both taxation and minting apparatus to the new rural realities. Fifth-century Iberia experienced a transformational process in the countryside whereby aristocrats increasingly abandoned their great residences, the *villae*, while at the same time a proliferation of peasant villages was underway, yet a good portion of the peasants may have found themselves under the domination of local lords, some of whom especially in the center-north and west now resided in fortified hilltop settlements (*castra* or *castella*), a form of habitation which also attracted peasant populations. Management of production was more scattered and occasionally in the hands of peasants.[691] The varied rural situations comprised of environmental setting, economic functions, socio-political relations, and personal status relate to coinage by way of arrangements of surplus extraction and the range of usage in the full life of each coin. Although not recoverable in any exact way, recognizing the full scope in which currency existed is indispensable when attempting to understand the coinage and the contemporary society.[692] Under the late

Essays in Honour of Andrew M. Watson, ed. Brian A. Catlos (Valencia: Universitat de Valencia, 2990), 33-54.

691 Fernández, *Aristocrats and Statehood*, 146, 188-90, 204, 211, 222. *Castra, oppida*, and localized arrangements of power-sharing are examined at length in Santiago Castellanos and Iñaki Martín Viso, "The Local Articulation of Central Power in the North of the Iberian Peninsula (500-1000)," *Early Medieval Europe* 13 (2005), 1-42.

692 See ibid. for extensive and stimulating discussion of the rural conditions as they are beginning to be better known, not only in the western peninsula but to some extent more widely.

Roman administration and in the Visigothic Kingdom of Toulouse, the local responsibility for taxation had rested with *curiales*, city councilors from among ranking landowners, who no longer had privileged legal status or exemption. Collection activity was the task of the *exactor*.[693] By the time the unification and progression of the kingdom in Iberia and Septimania began to be accomplished by Leovigild and his son Reccared, a probably amalgamated fiscal system operating through provincial and local rungs engaged the oversight of bishops and the direct work of locally appointed or elected officials in the cities who had charge over the countryside, as explained earlier. The officials may still have utilized the assistance of major landowners who served as conduits for peasant taxation (and presumably their own).[694] To acquire coin, the peasants needed large landowners and people of some means in the cities to purchase their crops in the market.

Some of the consolidated gathering of local farm production that took place under later Roman rule – centralization at the micro-level under large landowners – continued as barbarian groups occupied parts of the peninsula, but this was on a smaller scale commensurate with the reduced markets of the period. Such a trend coincided with a vast reduction of exchange, as inter-regional networks within the peninsula and across Mediterranean waterways slowed to become only a minor factor in the non-coastal areas

The picture I have drawn in this section demonstrates my agreement with the postulation of Naismith, "Mints, Moneyers," 7: "Numerous mints generally reflect localised structures of power and communication rather than a strong monetary economy." While I am highly sympathetic with the view of gold coinage in Martín Viso, "Circuits of Power," 247-52 as providing "channels of participation in Visigothic political networks that were very attractive to local aristocrats," clearly there is an assumption of elite-only usage of the currency guiding the outlook on the distribution of finds (in this case northern Lusitania, where *civitates* and *castra* form the majority of sites): see 238-47, esp. 246. The presumption may be correct, but is not a necessary conclusion for all of the coins considered.

693 *Curiales*' responsibility: as apparent from contemporary laws. See Thompson, *Goths in Spain*, 118-21, 129; and reflecting the somewhat modified role of *curiales* who in the Kingdom of Toledo owed specific tributes, Fernández, "Statehood, Taxation," 256 and idem, *Aristocrats and Statehood*, 169f, 202, 206, and 260 nn. 19 and 20 (tax collection as the duty of the *numerarius*, however, as stated on 202 seems to be true only of the general level – see above, nn. 522 and 523 on the ongoing work of the *exactor*).

694 Fernández, "Statehood, Taxation," 256-63 and idem, *Aristocrats and Statehood*, 204-07. See also the interpretation of enumerations in slates as tax records, linking landowners directly to satisfaction of tax dues, in Iñaki Martín Viso, "Tributación y escenarios locales en el centro de la península ibérica: Algunas hipótesis a partir del análisis de las pizarras 'visigodas'," *Antiquité Tardive* 14 (2006), 263-90 and idem, "Prácticas locales de la fiscalidad en el reino visigodo de Toledo," in *Lo que vino de Oriente: Horizontes, praxis y dimensión material de los sistemas de dominación fiscal en Al-Andalus (ss. VII-IX)*, ed. Xavier Ballestín and Ernesto Pastor (Oxford: Archaeopress, 2013), 72-85; so also Castellanos, "Tributa and *Historiae*," 204f.

during most of the final Visigothic century.[695] The preponderance of local exchanges matches the coin movements, roughly half of which circulated 200 km or less from their place of emission.

Intensified Visigothic rule begun under Leovigild obliged the involvement of non-bureaucratic actors – bishops, prominent local men, and large landowners – in the taxation process. Damián Fernández rejects the assumption that a shrunken state fiscal apparatus and the need to rely on figures outside official institutional channels corresponds to an enfeebled state, and instead convincingly demonstrates that by employing an adaptive strategy of extraction the Visigothic regime was able to succeed in a relatively vigorous revenue collection and maintain a durable state. His advancement of an existing argument for the collection of taxes by large landowners remains somewhat conjectural, but it makes sense especially in the Mediterranean context of late antiquity when many similar situations are known to have obtained. The interpretation draws on a few slates from the northern Meseta whose accounting notations may well record tribute figures alongside estate incomes and outflows. The direct legal evidence we have for Visigothic Spain, however, and indeed going back to the *Codex Theodosianus* of fifth-century Rome, is not of major landowners but instead of royal officials doing the collecting. It is possible that landowners might have been in charge of collection before the proceeds were handed over to the state's local tax officials. The key point here is that the state exactions continued to function, and the supra-local gathering of payments and processing of at least some of the gold through the mints and treasuries provided a suitable order in the kingdom. It is easily accepted that the procedures would enhance the stature of local figures who remain mostly silent in our sources. We are being continually instructed by recent scholarship of the important interplay between royal and aristocratic power in early medieval Iberia. The next chapter sets out to confirm monarchical control over the production of gold coin in terms of the many aspects of the Visigothic currency we have seen so far.

695 Fernández, *Aristocrats and Statehood*, 197, 211-22. As he observes, rural farmlands continued to use major road networks because the dictates of the Roman state in taxation and tributary demands established production patterns still in effect as the specific large-scale imperial coercion evaporated in the fourth century (95).

5. The Royal Control of Visigothic Minting

Abstract

Chapter Five demonstrates that, although specific record of minting is lacking, there can be little doubt of the ultimate royal authority behind minting, as can be ascertained from numerous numismatic and documentary elements in combination. Minting of gold was the king's affair, a prerogative based on its fiscal functionality. Gold coinage was the major medium employed to capture the wealth of the agricultural base as well as to assess and levy fines, and on the other end of the cycle to implement royal projects or otherwise make payments. Transfers in kind may still have formed a significant part of Visigothic society, but currency was without doubt a major component of state activity.

Keywords: royal; authority; control; wealth; centralization; fiduciary

> "Visigothic coinage is not a measure of commercial exchanges, in which of course it can intervene, but of political power that kings can gather."[696]

A Evidence of Royal Control

Because documentation on Visigothic minting is lacking, the fundamental question of the degree of royal authority over the striking of gold can best be fully addressed only here, at a later point of this book. One is forced to rely on the sum of the coin evidence discussed in detail above. Several aspects of the gold coinage from both the Kingdom of Toulouse and the Kingdom of Toledo have led to the common opinion that minting was tightly controlled

696 Barceló, "A Statistical Approach," 153-54.

Kurt, A., *Minting, State, and Economy in the Visigothic Kingdom: From Settlement in Aquitaine through the First Decade of the Muslim Conquest of Spain.*
Taylor & Francis Group, 2020
DOI 10.5117/9789462981645_CH05

by the Visigothic kings, in spite of the plethora of mints in the later period. For the fifth-century kingdom, these aspects are mainly the small number of mint sites and stable weights and fineness. For the regal period they include the placing of the king's name on all tremisses from early in Leovigild's reign, the rapid dissemination of generalized inscriptions, specific legends relating to royal victory, changes in type, the maintenance of theoretical standards, and royal laws concerning coined money. Our treatment of these aspects and of the primary reasons for the production of the gold coinage reinforce the notion that minting was a '*regalía*,' as it is sometimes called in Spanish scholarship. We now explore this matter further.

It is hard to tell how much power the sixth-century Visigothic kings before Leovigild had over monetary affairs. The letter of Theodoric the Ostrogoth indicates that it was not complete even late in his regency.[697] On the strength of the numismatic data, Leovigild was possibly the first king after 507 to establish effectively a royal monopoly of the monetary system. This is one possible conclusion about pre-regal 'VPW' currency based on the observation that the earliest regal coinage seems to have lacked central direction.[698] By the final two phases under Leovigild the coins exhibit signs of a firm control by their standardization and quality of workmanship and clearer propagandistic legends. Our examination of numismatic standards and style confirms that a process of deterioration was indeed occurring in the sixth century. The further the Visigothic kingdom was from the political and cultural ties with the Roman Empire in fifth-century Gaul, the less its currency reflected imperial standards of workmanship and the concentrated, well-regulated Roman monetary system. The first few decades of pre-regal coinage in Spain exhibit high standards and low dispersion, probably in part because the number of workshops was still low. But by about the middle of the sixth century minting became more erratic. It took a series of changes by Leovigild to bring greater stability to the tremissis. When Athanagild died in 567, he was the first Visigothic king of the sixth century to die a natural death; how different was the course of Leovigild's kingship, culminating after his long reign in the establishment of a dynasty.

How much Leovigild adjusted the network of mints is not known, since we have no explicit information on where the pre-regal mints-sites were. It is quite evident, however, that he made significant modifications to the coins themselves. Besides having his name inscribed on the currency, he also soon had the name of the mint site included on reverse. At least twice

697 Cassiodorus, *Variae* V.39: see above, Chapter One at n. 136.
698 Tomasini, *The Barbaric Tremissis*, 66.

he altered the standard of the tremissis, and perhaps on account of these changes created new types. The 'regalization' of coinage which occurred in Frankish Gaul and in the Suevic kingdom in the 570s/580s may not have been strictly concurrent. The early date for Leovigild's first regal coinage, put forward in the second chapter, suggests that the work of the Visigothic king inspired the regular regal gold coinage in the neighboring barbarian kingdoms (though the Suevic series would not last for long).

A movement toward regularization is already apparent in the series of '*curru*' and '*Rex Inclitus*' coins. As the existence of the '*Rex Inclitus*' coin of Toleto can now be confirmed, it provides further evidence that Toleto was leading the innovation in coinage.[699] A higher degree of regularization of the currency is apparent between 584 and 586, when the enormous variety of spellings of the king's or the emperor's name becomes everywhere LEOVIGILDVS REX. At this time, an original type is created which displays what is clearly an image of the king, a change that coincides with a return to the full imperial weight standard for tremisses. On the basis of the uniformity of the changes, we may conclude that it was not individual mint officials but rather Leovigild who controlled all significant aspects of the currency. Of course, the king must have received information and advice from one or other members of his court, particularly the *comes thesaurorum* or his equivalent at that time.

One very basic example of the control exercised by Leovigild over the production of coinage should not be overlooked. Grierson correctly summarizes a mystery concerning the facing busts type when he writes, "It has been conjectured that the second bust was intended to represent Reccared, who like his half-brother had been consors regni since 573." Yet, he goes on to assert that "it is more likely that the mints received a simple order to place the king's facing bust on the coins and, in default of further instruction, thought it safest to employ it on both sides."[700] In fact, the universal application of the double bust does not seem likely to have happened by coincidence, considering the enormous regional variation in minting even after Leovigild's initial reforms. Whether the second bust was supposed to represent the dynastic line (as I believe)[701] or not, it was a small but radical innovation in coinage by a king who had long taken a direct interest in the generation of specie in his kingdom.

Thus, the complete control of the making of gold coinage throughout the kingdom at this time is beyond doubt, and it is impossible not to see

699 See above, Chapter Two, section A.

700 Grierson and Blackburn, *Medieval European Coinage*, v. 1, 50.

701 Miles, *The Coinage of the Visigoths*, 45f, reviews this question.

the authority of Leovigild behind it.[702] He was as jealous of control over the production of money as he was in other fields,[703] as the changes in types, the adjustments in weight and fineness levels, and the use of propaganda indicate. Uniformity of type then continued after Leovigild for seventy years. Nevertheless, as discussed in Chapter Three, regional variety of styles of the facing bust type developed, more or less according to a provincial scheme. The theoretical standards which Leovigild and his son Reccared imposed on the tremissis – in spite of the latter's increased minting and opening of new mint sites – remained until late in the Visigothic era.[704] But the gradual decrease of real weights and fineness thereafter show that this father-son duo formed a tough act to follow. Already in the reign of Liuva II (601-603), Reccared's short-lived son, both elements of the tremisses were in decline.[705]

Royally framed monetization can be seen as part of ethnic differentiation.[706] Leovigild's drastic move commanding that coins bear his name as well as his image meant something in the mixed ethnic atmosphere in which identity in the kingdom was still being sorted out. This is easy enough to see in line with numerous other steps by Leovigild and in the historical context of sixth-century Visigothic rule as discussed in Chapter Two. Regal coinage was, like his attempt to create a religious unity between Gothic Arians and Hispano-Roman Catholics by a compromise formula of faith at an Arian synod in 580, also a resolution of contested intercultural contact. But it was decidedly a move toward distinction and parity at the same time. A Roman instrument – gold coins – now bore a Visigothic stamp. Their emanation throughout the kingdom not only proclaimed but effected self-sufficiency. In the final stage of reconceptualizing the Visigothic currency, it could no longer be confused with those of imperial issue; it also underwent a measurable modification of weight and a distinct imagery, demonstrating the king was completely sovereign here, too.

Coins were crucial to the successful exercise of power in the Visigothic kingdom, in a way different and probably greater than in the Merovingian

702 The "initial reduction in fineness, carried out by Leovigild, must have been the result of definite directions on his part, as were the changes in weight and type which he made. But it is less clear how far the later changes were ordered by the central government or were due to irregularities in the working of the mints, as the variations in the weights of the coins between mint and mint undoubtedly were." Grierson, "Visigothic Minting," 86-87. Pliego, *La moneda visigoda*, v. 1, 190f et passim depicts the regal gold series as clearly under monarchical direction.

703 See Chapter Two above; also García Moreno, "Estudios," and idem, *El fin del reino visigodo*, 140-42.

704 See above, Chapter Three, section D.

705 See Appendix I, Figures I.12 and I.13.

706 The notion is raised by Kulikowski, "Ethnicity, Rulership," 248-51.

Figure 14: Coinage within the kingdom's political-economic system

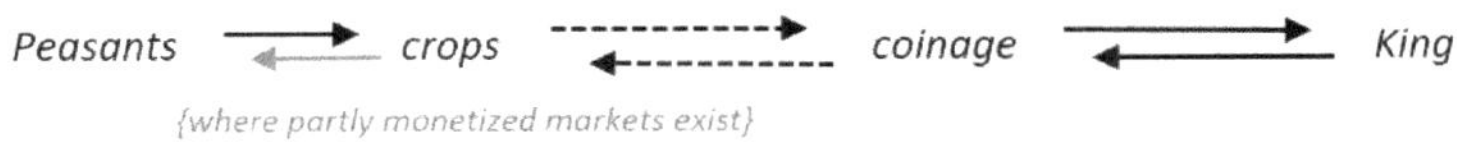

and Anglo-Saxon kingdoms (where wealth was more based on land and controled trade entrepôts, and in England currency was not even manufactured through the fifth and sixth centuries). Currency and its use in a regular taxation of agricultural production was the mechanism for converting harvested grain into easily transferable wealth, and so a hinge on which a most basic element of social domination revolved. Retamero has demonstrated the relationship in a graphic form essentially as follows.

It was not a direct relationship between king as producer and controler of coinage and peasant as generator of crops, since *potentes* in the form of rural lords, bishops and bureaucrats involved in taxation and minting stood between the two ends of the circuit. In Retamero's elaboration, peasants did not actually themselves employ coinage in rendering taxes, and likewise did not take in large-value currency. As he admits, this part is quite obscure to us, and so we should consider it equally possible that the free small-time landholders and even tenant farmers used tremisses in their tax obligations. Retamero's argued, if debatable, small volume of gold minting fittingly corresponds to his conception that the commoners were uninvolved with gold coin. Though royally directed, gold currency enhanced the power of the limited elite circle directly engaged with money, not simply in the mediated role and the political give and take entailed in the taxation process but also in the acquisition and valuation of wealth in convertible form.[707] There must be a good deal of truth in this, even if the possibility remains that some coin did trickle back to freeholding peasants and perchance renting tenants to thereby enable them to make tax payments – or indeed purchases or payments of fines and the like, as elaborated in Chapter Seven. What

707 I base the graph and much of the discussion on Retamero, "As Coins Go Home," 286-92. The author notes, "As the lines indicate, crops – the product of the peasant – do not necessarily require coins to ensure their existence. However, coins must be made exchangeable for crops to become money. Otherwise, they could never transcend their original condition as a product." (286, an excerpt from Miquel Barceló and Félix Retamero, "From Crops to Coin: Which Way Back?," *Gaceta Numismática* 122 (1996), 53-60, at 55.) See also the important treatment of the landlords' roles and specific incorporation of bishops' oversight in tax collection in Fernández, "Statehood, Taxation"; contemporary legal references to common landholders in his discussion (esp. 250f and 256f) and elsewhere leads me to suppose *pace* Retamero that peasants also utilized tremisses sometimes, if not completely regularly. See more on this in Chapter Seven below.

should not be forgotten, nevertheless, is that the entire process depended on the power of the monarch; gold coinage stands as its emblem, tangible proof of the reach of central authority which remained capable of capturing wealth in the kingdom.[708]

Periodic fluctuations in the quality of the Visigothic regal tremisses have often been associated with the relative political strength of the kings. Leovigild possessed the throne so commandingly that he could lower and raise standards as he pleased. The tremisses of his manifestly vigorous son Reccared have high and stable standards at all mints even as minting becomes more widespread. In the following years, a trend of debasement and lowered weight begins possibly before the gold shortage is felt, under several kings whose weakness is underlined by their violent deaths at the hands of Gothic nobles.[709] The manufacture of tremisses suffers further under Chintila (r. 636-39), who appears from the acts of ecclesiastical councils to have worried about rebellion and to have sought out protection from the church;[710] and it reaches a low point under Tulga (r. 639-42), who was doomed by the ruthless Chindasvinth. At the moment of the latter's rebellion, the variability of fineness and weight had reached unprecedented levels,[711] and it would be hard to refute that this is a sign of the loss of royal control of monetary production. Improvements were made in stages by Chindasvinth and his son Reccesvinth, both of whom enjoyed long lives and wielded much power over secular and ecclesiastical affairs. As described in the section on standards, a rapid deterioration in the coinage began just a few years after Reccesvinth; the worst slide came in the troubled reign of Egica[712] and during his joint rule with Wittiza. The latter was able to make a brief reversal of lost standards at some point in his individual rule. In conformity with the theory of political strength and monetary power, he was able to defeat several insurrections and possibly the Arabs or Byzantines at sea.

708 Castellanos, "Tributa and *Historiae*," 202; similarly Martín Viso, "Circuits of Power," 221, who later also discusses the instrumentality of gold coinage in the interplay of authority at various levels (see above, n. 692).

709 *HG* 58 to 64, covering the years 601 to c. 625. Sisebut and Suinthila may have formed exceptions by their military victories, but at least the latter and possibly the former were overcome by internal enemies (see *HG* 61 for the implication that Sisebut was poisoned). Pliego, *La moneda visigoda*, v. 1, 199-213 provides a wealth of metal analysis data from Leovigild to Roderic suggestive of the shifting fortunes of the monarchy, though the tie-in with political events is not explicit.

710 See Thompson, *The Goths in Spain*, 180-88.

711 See Appendix I, Figure I.16.

712 Thompson, *The Goths in Spain*, 243-44 discusses his persecutions and the rebellion of Suniefred, from whom a coin from Toleto itself survives.

B The Significance of Centralized Monetary Authority

Along the same lines, the low weights and fineness which were prevalent at the many secondary mints have sometimes been seen as the result of the lack of firm central control of these workshops. Dishonesty or sloppiness thus set in.[713] However, the evidence we have examined with regard to minting within the kingdom, as well as the evidence of contemporaneous foreign coinages, suggests that the inferior observed standards are most directly related to the supply of gold. One must remember that the production of tremisses increased in the early decades of the seventh century and occurred at a number of new sites. At the same time, polities in the entire Mediterranean world experienced a shortage of gold.[714] One scenario for the low weights and fineness would be that of a higher production dependent on a stable amount of gold in Spain. In that case, manipulations would have been deliberately effected by the state, possibly in order to draw a profit (if its creditors did not recognize or could do nothing about the lower gold content). Another possibility is that higher production occurred at a period of shortage of the precious metal in Spain, so the state ordered provisional reductions in quality in order to issue the desired amount of coins. The most likely scenario combines elements of both. In a period in which gold was scarce, a higher production at temporary mints depended on new but inadequate amounts of gold from taxation, some re-minting, and possibly plunder. Here, manipulations could also be deliberate, but supply of gold depends on inflows in very specific areas and includes private gold brought to the mints in unpredictable amounts. Hence the greater variability in weights and fineness at the peripheral sites.[715]

If the military hypothesis set out in Chapter Four is correct, the kings were indeed in control of minting associated with campaigns, in other words the peripheral mints.[716] Such mint sites existed primarily for the

713 Grierson, "Visigothic Metrology," 82: The decline in average weight from Suinthila's through Tulga's reign "is to be attributed to the weakness of the crown, allowing the exploitation of the mints by local officials, not to manipulation of the central mints in the royal interest." Here and in Grierson and Blackburn, *Medieval European Coinage*, v. 1, the author contrasts this with the major mints, which would have been more easily supervised by the king and his court.

714 See above, nn. 505 and 610. Hendy, "From Public to Private," 68ff reviews the extreme debasement of Merovingian tremisses c. 620-45. Orlandis, *Historia económica*, 580-81, ascribes the huge increase in the price of "composition" and the price of the law code in Visigothic Spain to the devaluation of coined money.

715 We saw that major mints also had diminished weights and fineness in the period of shortage, but not quite at the level of the secondary mints. See Chapter Three, section D.

716 Grierson pictures the main mints of the Visigothic monetary system as firmly under the control of the throne, but writes that "it is difficult to believe that the many petty mints were in

army acting on behalf of the king, who, at times, personally led his troops. The amount minted presumably depended on need; apparently the need for coin exceeded the precious metal supply. The lower weights and fineness of military pay was perhaps a trend going back to Alaric II's debasement on the eve of his great battle against Clovis. Attempts to save gold while making extraordinary expenditures is not out of the question, but kings' minters were necessarily influenced by the reduced availability of gold. This added factor holds true especially in the case of the southern mints at the height of the Byzantine war. Admittedly, it appears to be much less true of Gallaecian mints in a period beginning slightly earlier, judging from our small sample of tested coins from the region, some of which have elevated weights combined with average fineness or better, particularly during Reccared's reign.[717] This high quality makes sense if we consider that Reccared had at his disposal the Suevic treasure and melted-down Suevic gold coinage, which has been estimated on the order of a million pieces.[718] Even if it were not this fresh source of gold that prompted the opening of numerous mints, its utilization at a few or all mints there would have allowed the striking of higher-quality coins.

Oscillations in the metallic content in Visigothic Spain raise the question of whether administrators were in fact attempting to profit from a fiduciary gold currency, and more fundamentally how sensitive they were to currency value.[719] Roman government had been determined to maintain a stable solidus because of reliance by the fourth century on revenues and

any sense 'government' creations [...]" (Grierson and Blackburn, *Medieval European Coinage*, v. 1, 53). On the contrary, for several reasons it is difficult to imagine that they were not: the types and legends undergo changes at the same time; regional styles are closely obeyed on the whole (the 'Toleto engraver,' if indeed representing a special circumstance in the west, adapted to the regional style); their placement has to have some rationale, and this is inescapably connected to warfare or conquest.

717 See Appendix I, Figure I.11.

718 J. M. Peixoto Cabral and D. M. Metcalf, *A moeda sueva / Suevic Coinage* (Porto: Sociedade Portuguesa de Numismática, 1997).

719 T. Marot, "La península ibérica," 149, echoing Marques et al., *Ensaios*, 251, considers the gold currency of the kingdom fiduciary, meaning that it had a high level of surplus value (a nominal value greater than commodity value), pointing to the fluctuations in intrinsic quality which proved difficult to detect and therefore not an impediment to acceptance. Despite fluctuations, coins seem to have been accepted on the basis of the authority behind their declared royal designation. ("Coins were apparently accepted based on their regal appearance and associations, not simply on their (variable) intrinsic quality." Naismith, "Gold Coinage and Its Use," 302, ref. Retamero, "La moneda.") Such acceptance would provide the rationale for manipulations. It should not be assumed, however, that fluctuations had no effect on acceptance, and as argued in the first chapter weighing might have been utilized for payment adjustment.

satisfaction of administrative costs in gold. Commutation as the norm in the following century required further mass-production of gold. This was kept up in the eastern empire, with a solidus (Greek: *nómisma*) of very high purity. Valentinian III's Novel 16 from 445, which moved to stave off buyers' rejection of older coins, is interpreted as arising from wear that brought about lighter coins. Much sixth- and seventh-century Byzantine gold coinage shows obvious wear, which can be taken as a sign of heavy circulation. Wear is also a depreciation and opened up the market's need to adjust for transactions involving coins under full weight. Heavy rates of discount on such coins were drawn up.[720] Such sophisticated commercial or state responses are not evident for the Visigothic kingdom. Tremisses there also typically show wear, and some clipping probably occurred as suggested by the law made against such practice, but a more degrading effect on value was low weight and fineness at the point of minting. We remain in the dark about what adjustments may have been made as coin flowed into the public's hands. There is good reason to believe transactions of significant worth would involve weighing and assaying.[721] The crown endeavored to maximize its spending capability under stress, and some perhaps believed enforced value leveling of uneven currency pieces could do the trick. However, under the same basic template as the empire, though on much smaller scale, the Visigothic monarchy's neglect of the stability rule meant it suffered the consequences of fiscal 'cheating' through punctuated bursts in minting and simultaneous coin adulteration. Only extraordinary efforts could temporarily arrest the slide, but the unavoidable trend was gold of greatly compromised value. It may not seem to have mattered much if tremisses were actually accepted equally despite varying levels of gold content, as might be understood by the dispersed values consistently found within hoards as well as by the contemporary references to gold coins without stipulation about value. Yet, if the gold coinage came under a truly fiduciary policy, why not make all the gold currency of low quality? Intrinsic value of the tremisses must have mattered, since coin reforms were instituted by a few attentive and forceful Visigothic rulers, and a few seminal mints generated coins with more elevated gold levels. Rather than a profit principle per se, we should perceive reactions at a central or regional level stemming from pressing conditions.

After several decades of declining standards, due largely to extensive military minting, Chindasvinth and Reccesvinth shored up the gold

720 Wear and adjustments: Banaji, *Exploring the Economy*, 101-03; Nov. 16: ibid., 121.

721 See nn. 87, 209, as well as 466 above.

currency.[722] Chindasvinth was able to address the poor quality no doubt because the severity of his rule was felt at the mints, large and small, as it was felt in other aspects of government. A remarkable warrior-king even in his old age, he is reported to have killed hundreds of nobles and must have expropriated their properties.[723] Such massive confiscation could support a reform of coinage while a great number of mints remained active or were opened for the first time. But the only way to sustain a good currency in the face of an enduring gold shortage was to reduce minting. Reccesvinth closed many peripheral mints, reducing the total number of workshops from around two dozen to perhaps eleven seemingly with the aim of creating a more controllable network of coin production. It is probably correct to see a relationship between the concentration of minting in major cities and the military reorganization carried out by Chindasvinth and Reccesvinth.[724] It may also be true that Chindasvinth and Reccesvinth imitated Heraclius's reduction and improvement of Byzantine minting a few years earlier, reforms which were also related to changes in military organization and pay.[725]

722 Barceló, "A Statistical Approach," 153 characterized Visigothic gold currency as largely fiduciary. The value of a tremissis was independent of purity, so that high or low gold content did not matter. The inclusion of both "bad" and "good" coins in several hoards is called upon as proof. One should not fail to recognize, however, that low-weight and/or impure coins could circulate equally but not be accepted equally – it was probably this kind of rejection which prompted *LV* VII.6.5, "that no one will refuse a solidus of full weight." Some numismatists believe that when low-standard coins were detected in ancient societies they were sometimes made up for with additional payment, often satisfied with base metal currency. (I have heard this suggested with respect to a large variety of ancient and Islamic coinage systems by Dr. Michael Bates of the American Numismatic Society. See also Spaulding, "Mint-cities," 82, and Haldon, *Byzantium in the Seventh Century*, 190 n. 66, where the *zugostatēs* – or Latin *zygostatēs* – is thought to have been responsible for controling the purity and weight of coinage in Byzantium in the seventh century.) If money was fiduciary, it was only up to a certain point, otherwise what would be the point of the reforms of the seventh century?

723 See Collins, *Early Medieval Spain*, 113-16.

724 García Moreno, "Estudios," 152-53. Thompson, The Goths in Spain, 217, remarked that "the reasons which led to the great reforms of Chindasuinth and Reccesuinth are one of the darkest mysteries of Visigothic Spain." Pablo C. Díaz, "Confiscations," views royal confiscation as having become a necessity for running the royal administration by that time.

725 See Haldon, "Administrative Continuities," esp. 4 n. 4; idem, "Military Service, Military Lands"; and idem, *Byzantium in the Seventh Century*, esp. 190-92. See Crusafont i Sabater, *El sistema*, 63 for the supposition that changes were also made in the minting of bronze currency under Chindasvinth and Reccesvinth. Since the same author entertains the opinion that Visigothic bronzes were first struck in these years, one wonders if they formed any part of military salaries for a time. They did for Heraclius (610-641), but then died out almost completely at some point during the reign of Constans II (641-668), when means other than coin were used to maintain the imperial troops: see Hendy, *Studies*, 417-20, and Haldon, "Military Service, Military Lands," 13 n. 28 and 17 n. 45. Visigothic consolidation of mints was loosened in the last quarter of the century or so, and it is precisely the time when inconsistency of weights and fineness again cropped up: Appendix I, Figures 7, 14, 16.

The fact that large improvements occurred under the kings who wielded the strongest authority is an indication that minting was in the hands of the throne. As Mark Blackburn averred, with good reason, "The maintenance of an efficient coinage requires strong political and economic control, but also a degree of administrative sophistication."[726] Leovigild, Chindasvinth, Reccesvinth, and Ervig were also the important legislating kings.[727] During the one hundred year period in which they reigned, the Visigothic kingdom witnessed the growth of a centralized government, whose laws attempted to regulate minutiae.[728] It was precisely the law-making kings whose coinage had the highest standards. Legislation sometimes specifically touched on financial and monetary matters. We have just seen that Leovigild promulgated a law which made the acceptance of gold coins of full weight obligatory.[729] He made laws protecting public funds and re-building the fiscal administration, perhaps to make it resemble the Byzantine structure.[730] He also seems to have acquired much new gold for the treasury through both confiscation and the conquest of the Suevic kingdom, which would enable him to maintain a standard of eighteen karats (seventy-five per cent) with a weight in keeping with Roman standards. In Reccesvinth's legislation the king takes a special role in deciding punishment of those who debase, pare, file, or counterfeit '*solidi*,' by which we must understand tremisses.[731] Barceló showed that the provincial centralization of minting imposed by Chindasvinth and Reccesvinth was very efficient in maintaining the regularity of the gold currency for many years. There was, therefore, not a steady deterioration of Visigothic tremisses that "accompanied as a permanent shadow the ruin of Visigothic power in Hispania, as some hurried authors like to point out." What was this normalization based on? Barceló asserts that it was secured by a "harder fiscal pressure and smoother tax collection. That is what really measures Visigothic coinage: the taxing capacity of the kings."[732] Reccesvinth's consolidation of power over the Gothic nobility incorporated a consolidation of mints.[733]

726 Blackburn, in Forward of Pliego, *La moneda visigoda*, v. 1, 11.

727 Ervig's improvement was confined to the weight, but though small it was important in that it reversed a downward trend: see Appendix I, Figure I.14.

728 Collins, *Early Medieval Spain*, 141.

729 See n. 722.

730 See above at n. 520, and Pérez Sánchez, *El ejército*, 113-17.

731 *LV* VII.6.2; see P. D. King, *Law and Society*, 78.

732 Barceló, "A Statistical Approach," 148, 153. I am therefore puzzled as to why Barceló, as co-author with Retamero, should decry the successful accomplishment of taxation in general: "Crops," 58; also Retamero, "As Coins Go Home," 289, 291.

733 Barceló, "A Statistical Approach," 153.

Alterations in coin design by the reforming kings of the mid-seventh century also point to a reorganization of the monetary system, and it is tempting to see direct royal involvement here as with Leovigild's type changes. Chindasvinth returned to the use of the abbreviation DN (*Dominus Noster*) in inscriptions on the tremisses, a practice copied from Byzantine coinage during the reigns of Leovigild through Liuva II (c. 570 – 603), but in neither period did this herald any change in types. The most noticeable change on the tremisses is that Reccesvinth returned to the obverse-reverse combination of profile bust and cross-on-steps types of Leovigild's second-phase coinage. The continued use of the combined profile bust and cross-on-steps types by all the successors of Reccesvinth suggests that this design had some special significance in the monetary reforms.[734]

At this point of our extensive inquiry, it may be asked anew how similar the Visigothic mint system ultimately was to that of the Roman Empire. In the first chapter, we saw that in monetary affairs the differentiation from the Empire began while the kingdom was still in Gaul. The Visigothic monetary system became gradually more unlike the imperial system, as occurred in other early medieval kingdoms. Examples of the disjuncture are the lowered standards that probably provoked Majorian's law of 458, the opening of permanent mints in places where no Roman mint had existed, such as Toulouse and Narbonne and possibly elsewhere, and the exclusive and increasingly stylized use of a new reverse type for the tremisses, the 'VPW.' In Spain, the trend continued with the opening of more mints and the striking at standards which varied from those of the Eastern imperial gold coinage. Above all, under Leovigild the tremissis became non-imitative and

734 On the types combination, see Pliego, *La moneda visigoda*, v. 1, 166f. Changes began under Chindasvinth when the main Lusitanian/Emeritan sub-types (Miles's 8c on obverse and 7 on reverse) were taken up at several Gallaecian mints then in operation. These types, employed in all eleven reigns from Reccared to Chindasvinth, were replaced in Reccesvinth's sole reign by new styles of Leovigild's profile bust (1i and 1j), certain varieties of which had been re-introduced in the joint rule of Chindasvinth and Reccesvinth. Under Chindasvinth the sub-types formerly used exclusively at Cordoba began to appear at Eliberri as well. Then under Reccesvinth completely different designs were created for Cordoba's mint.
Two and a half centuries ago, Velázquez pointed out Chindasvinth's use of the monogram in a reverse legend at Beatia, just northeast of Cordoba and Tucci (Velázquez, *Congeturas sobre las medallas de los reyes godos, y suevos de España*, 81). It stands for VI, as it does in the king's name on the other side. It was already in Sisebut's time and perhaps before that an abbreviation of VICTOR or VICTORIA (above n. 606), which Velázquez associates here with the civil war that brought Chindasvinth into power. Such an inscription may signal a return to the triumphal theme of early Leovigildan money, yet another indication that the king's reforms were bent on revisiting past greatness.

strictly royal in character, and through the reverse inscription connected the king's authority with every city or place where the coin was issued.

In Gothic Spain, the widely varying coinage from nearly one hundred mints is ample evidence against the centralized amassing of gold and minting in Toleto, a system unlike the centuries-earlier "siphoning off to Rome of vast quantities of precious metals from around the Mediterranean."[735] We have referred on numerous occasions to the concentration of imperial minting at very few sites. In the first century, one city, Lugdunum, produced almost all the gold currency for the Roman Empire and had a dominant role in the production of silver and base metal coinage. As Cristopher Howgego observed, "that such a degree of centralization was maintained is a dramatic testimony to the scale of transfers of bullion and coin possible within the Roman economy."[736] The same holds true in the late western Empire and in the early Byzantine world, where minting was concentrated at the comitatensian mints and occasionally one or two others. The same level of concentration and superior real standards was clearly not maintained in the Visigothic kingdom.[737] We have suggested that the difference was largely due to the change in administrative scale after the disintegration of the Empire in the West. But the reason why mints were set up and grew in number was not so much to supply the economy but as an instrument of the fiscal and military machinery. Impinging on its operations was the limited supply of gold. In these last two aspects, despite the difference in the number of mints, Visigothic minting closely resembled the Roman and Byzantine system.[738] Tight control of such dispersed coin production, however, was only attained by exceptional Visigothic kings.

The very fact that a non-minting related legend or mark from a locale did not occasionally take over an issue reinforces the point that gold minting remained a strictly royal prerogative through the chain of command. In the Visigothic social-military system, after all, considerable power was entrenched among landowning elites. Usurpation attempts could radically

735 Howgego, *Ancient History from Coins*, 56.

736 Ibid., 101.

737 See the references in Naismith, "Mints, Moneyers," 3 n. 7.

738 Debasement of Roman coinage was sometimes accompanied by increased output. "One is left with the impression that by far the most significant causes of monetary reform at Rome were a shortage of state funds in relation to expenditure, and a more conservative desire to return to older and better standards," although there are other possibilities as well (Howgego, *Ancient History from Coins*, 121). Debasements also appear to have been linked to military pay: see Duncan-Jones, *Money and Government*, 238-39. On comparison with the Roman/Byzantine system: cf. the section on the territorial organization of minting in Pliego, *La moneda visigoda*, v. 1, 97-153.

affect not merely central power arrangements but also local and regional ones, most severely by sometimes large-scale killing of an enemy's supporters but also by confiscations.[739] But through the shifting dynamics of local networks that reached strength in some cases to the point of rebellion, apart from two very confined monetary promulgations of uprising, mints across the kingdom maintained inscriptions of monarchical character. That local forces at play did not effect a single display of a beloved saint, an especially powerful magnate, a site or point of pride on the gold currency speaks of the firm grasp over gold minting directed from the capital.

Finally, how does the Visigothic monetary system compare with the contemporary Merovingian system in general? There were many similarities to Gaul: a multitude of sites (in the case of Francia over 800); regional and local variations of types; fluctuations in real standards and consistently better quality in certain places; and possibly a direct relation between minting and tax collection which may account for the striking of coins at obscure, apparently unimportant places. Tomasini maintained that sixth-century Merovingian coinage, because of the greater local role in minting, has "a greater variation in technique and bust types [...]. The individual differences in Visigothic mints are displayed within a narrower range of controlled possibilities."[740] In other words, Visigothic tremisses are much more conservative, staying within a specific type and traditional styles. When new types were created near the beginning and towards the end of the sixth century they were adopted in all parts of the kingdom. By contrast, Frankish coinage of the pre-regal and regal eras was extremely complex.[741]

What seems to be most similar about the gold currencies of the Merovingian Franks and the Visigoths is the fiscal purpose for which they were minted, under the strong influence of the Roman and Byzantine Empire. It is the imperial monetary system which gave to both kingdoms the tremissis and the practice of regular taxation. How minting and taxation then evolved in Gaul and Hispania, however, was rather different as far as we can tell. As described in the fourth chapter, much of the tax system under the Visigoths stayed in place for many decades at least. The core of the minting network, centered on the most important cities, served the administration of taxation

739 See Collins, *Early Medieval Spain*, 112-14 on the power dynamics and pressures regarding monarchy and nobility.

740 Tomasini, *The Barbaric Tremissis*, 87.

741 See the remarks of Grierson, *Coins of Medieval Europe*, 16 and 24. Alessia Rovelli, "From the Fall of Rome to Charlemagne (c. 400-800)," in *Money and Coinage*, ed. Naismith, 63-92 furnishes a very useful survey of various barbarian currencies in the West and their Roman roots, albeit precious little regarding Iberia.

and expenditures. Many other less permanent mints primarily supported the army on expeditions. Merovingian mints served the first purpose, at least up to about the first quarter of the seventh century, but apparently not the second. By c. 630, the system of public revenue was shifting toward private rents while kings depended more on landed resources. At the same time, some minting came into private hands.[742] The whole process may have influenced the transformation to a silver coinage by about 670. At all stages, fiscal administrators evidently were convinced that a vast network of mints best responded to the situation and to the need for currency for fiscal and at times commercial ends.

The many hundreds of moneyers whose names appear on the majority of Merovingian coins from the early sixth century were probably the guarantors of quality; in Visigothic Spain the kings were.[743] Royal supervision was maintained in Spain in spite of appearances. The standards of weight and quality, notwithstanding variations of real weight and quality among the many hundreds of minters over time, are thought to be the same everywhere at any given time, an achievement which could only result from central, royal oversight.[744] The significant difference between the two systems is neatly summarized by Grierson. Some may wish to debate whether he overplays the small role of the state in minting, but it is true that the Merovingian kings "made no attempt to treat [minting] as a royal monopoly, as the Visigoths, following the Roman tradition, succeeded in doing."[745]

742 Ildar H. Garipzanov, "The Coinage of Tours in the Merovingian Period and the Pirenne Thesis," *Revue Belge de Numismatique et de sigillographie* 147 (2001) pp. 79-118. Garipzanov bases his view of the fiscal function of the gold coinage up to this time largely on Hendy, "From Public to Private," and on his own investigation of two mints at Tours; for Merovingian finance he relies mostly on Goffart, *Barbarians and Romans*, and idem "Old and New in Merovingian Taxation," in *Rome's Fall and After* (London: Hambledon, 1989), 213-231. See also the important conclusions about the underlying royal control of the coinage and the connection with taxation in Stahl, *Merovingian Coinage*, esp. 131-37. Stahl argues that the inclusion of the names of mint and moneyer on each coin assisted in accounting and quality control (p. 134); here only the function of the mint name can apply to Visigothic tremisses (see above, p. 105).

743 In addition to the literature cited in the previous note, see Grierson, *Coins of Medieval Europe*, 16-18 and 24-26; Grierson and Blackburn, *Medieval European Coinage*, v. 1, 91-115 and ff.; and Stahl, *Merovingian Coinage*. Pliego, *La moneda visigoda*, v. 1, esp. 190f and 215-30 affirms control within Iberia of the Visigothic monarchy.

744 Barral i Altet, *La circulation*, 119.

745 Ibid., 16. On the small role of the state see especially Grierson and Blackburn, *Medieval European Coinage*, v. 1, 97.

6. Coinage in Spain in the Aftermath of the Islamic Conquest

Abstract
Chapter Six considers the end of the Visigothic kingdom, which came in 711 with the Muslim invasion from northwest Africa, and how the new Islamic state and its minting compared with that of the previous regime. In ten years, Islamic coinage in Iberia moved from wholly Latin inscriptions to bilingual to wholly Arabic legends. It is believed that multiple minting sites were rapidly consolidated into one single gold mint at the new capital, Cordoba. The strictly gold minting of the late Visigothic era gave way to minting in gold dinars (solidi) and copious issues of bronze coins. Temporarily, Islamic coins in Iberia had reduced gold purity levels, but these were soon raised to the high Islamic and Byzantine standards.

Keywords: Islamic; Muslim; invasion; transitional; dinar; Roderic

Visigothic rule and its structures would be brought to a dramatic end after more than two hundred years in Iberia. That story has relevance for the theme of this book since altered circumstances offer perspective by way of contrast but also of transition. As the series of victorious Islamic campaigns sprang from the Arab lands, we may begin our brief look at this stage in the direction of the Near East.

In a small palatial complex from the early or mid-eighth century at Qasr 'Amra in eastern Jordan, an intriguing fresco depicts six kings. Nearby is inscribed the word '*Nike*', victory. Included among the rulers of lands where Islam successfully marched in this display of domination is the short-lived Visigothic king of distant Spain, Roderic. He had been defeated in the summer of 711 by the forces of the Berber commander of the Maghrib, Ṭāriq ibn Ziyad. The story is slightly complicated by the contestation of the monarchy at just this time, and the numismatic evidence stands in the center of the events at the

Kurt, A., *Minting, State, and Economy in the Visigothic Kingdom: From Settlement in Aquitaine through the First Decade of the Muslim Conquest of Spain.*
Taylor & Francis Group, 2020
DOI 10.5117/9789462981645_CH06

end of one regime and the beginning of a quite different one, most especially because literary evidence is not available until several decades, or in the case of Arab texts over two centuries, later.[746] The rather sudden takeover puts us in position to see two administrations and two cultures in comparison. Among the significant questions which arise are how the new authority would run affairs, and within the focus of this study, how coinage in particular would develop. Would there be a direct inheritance in this respect from the previous state? The answer would be dictated largely by the immediate background of the conquest, namely, the combination of a series of adaptations already having occurred in the path of Islamic expansion and the Visigothic currency form.

Coins tell the tale in a number of ways. We have already seen in this book the heavy decline in later seventh-century gold minting, in terms of raw numbers of production centers and their output as well as in the weight and fineness, factors that point to a decline in the strength of the throne itself. Islamic coins after the invasion of 711 naturally mark a point of departure by their very appearance, but even before this point extant Visigothic tremisses provide testimony of a dual claim to the throne on the part of Roderic and Agila, or Achila (II) as he is known from the coinage. This is important because written evidence is incomplete on this matter, mentioning one or the other rulers but rarely both. As has been observed, mint placement and coin finds infer divided zones of influence in the peninsula, with Achila II holding sway in the northeast and Roderic apparently operating in the central and southern parts, a fact that would not otherwise be known. At the same time, the currency supports the limited literary record that after the Muslim incursion was initiated the monarchy, and with it minting, persevered for a few years.[747] This occurred after Roderic was defeated and killed at the battle of

746 Roger Collins, *The Arab Conquest of Spain, 710-797* (Oxford: Blackwell, 1989) and Hugh Kennedy, *Muslim Spain and Portugal: a Political History of al-Andalus* (Harlow, UK: Longman, 1996) cover the events and the source problems of the conquest. Alejandro García Sanjuan, *La conquista islámica de la península ibérica y la tergiversación del pasado. Del catastrofismo al negacionismo* (Madrid: Marcial Pons Historia, 2013) demonstrates at length how the early Muslim coinage out of Spain is crucial in the historical and ideological battle over the very truth of the Muslim invasion and continuing presence.

747 Two key sources for the events of those years, the *Chronicle of 754* and the *Laterculus regum visigothorum*, have some discrepancies between them and some manuscript variations. For good discussion of the evidentiary background and the place of coinage in filling out the story, see Ruth Pliego, "La moneda en el ocaso del reino godo de Hispania," *Zona arqueológica*, No. 15, 2011 (Dedicated issue title: *711: Arqueología e historia entre dos mundos*), v. 2, 321-38 at 333-37. Tremissis finds at Ruscino near Perpignan, solely from Narbona, and El Bovalar, solely of Spanish mints, seem to testify to Achila II's leaving behind a territory he once held in the far northeast: idem, "El *tremis* de los últimos años," 26. Ibid., 37 echoes a recent suggestion that the pair of extant coins of the usurper Sunifred from Toleto, long taken as issued earlier by a few decades or

Guadalete near the southern tip of Iberia, while Achila continued 'for three years' after Wittiza (d. 710), as a key source indicates. His stated successor, one Ardo (or Artabado), has not left any currency, but the taking of Zaragoza in 714 by Mūsā ibn Nuṣayr and the initial conquest of Narbonne the following year by his son seems to have spelled the beginning of the end for any claim to Visigothic rulership. All the northeast was under Muslim domination by 717.

The substitution of authority brought with it the replacement of the minting system. The gold issued immediately following the invasion was of a 'pseudo-Byzantine' character, based on a North African Islamic form which was in turn modeled on seventh-century Byzantine gold coins.[748] These dinars, as well as their divisions of halves (*nisf*) and thirds (*thulth*), were based on solidi but were slightly lower in weight, with a standard of 4.25 g.[749] They do not proclaim any ruler but instead a religious message and a date. Their purely Latin inscriptions conveyed on the obverse abbreviated monotheistic formulas already found on the only recently established Islamic currency distinct from Byzantine coinage utilized by Muslims. For example, various versions of INNDINNNDSSLSNNDSA stood for 'IN Nomine DominI NoN Nisi DeuS SoLuS NoN DeuS Alius' (see Figure 15 below). In the center of the reverse was a numeral for the indiction date, the fifteen-year cycle of rulership used by the Byzantine empire. On the outer rim, the letters SPN denoted the province – Spania – while the rest of the legend indicated the Hijri year. Five years later, bilingual inscriptions in Latin and Arabic began to appear on the dinars minted under governor al-Hurr (r. 716-718);

more, reflects a three-way struggle at this time in which Sunifred was able to claim the throne in the royal city – the reason why no trientes from there are known from either of the other rivals (Roderic's only known coins were struck at Egitania): ref. Luis A. García Moreno, *España 702-719: La conquista musulmana* (Seville: Universidad de Sevilla, 2013), 155-75.

748 'Pseudo-Byzantine' is the apt term of Blackburn, "Money and Coinage," v. 2, 540. "The first North African issues, like the first Syrian [Islamic] coins, do not perpetuate the coins being struck at Carthage when the Arabs took the city about 698, but rather are an adaptation of Byzantine coins of seventy years before. They have inscriptions in Latin that translate those of the reformed Arabic coinage of Damascus and the East [...]": Michael L. Bates, "History, Geography, and Numismatics in the First Century of Islamic Coinage," *Revue suisse de Numismatique* 65 (1986), 231-62 and pl. 32, at 234. The Byzantine model and the disjuncture with Gothic minting is discussed in idem, "The Coinage of Spain Under the Umayyad Caliphs of the East, 711-750," in *III Jarique de numismática hispano-árabe* (Madrid: Museo Arqueológico Nacional, 1992), 171-89.

749 Byzantine minting at this time included the solidus, its half, and its third. Essential bibliography on the post-conquest transitional coinage begins with A. M. Balaguer, *Las emisiones transicionales árabe-musulmanas de Hispania* (Barcelona: Asociación numismática española, 1976). Idem, "Las emisiones transicionales árabe-musulmanas de Al-Andalus: Nueva síntesis," in *I Jarique de estudios numismáticos hispano-árabes* (Zaragoza: Institución Fernando el Católico, 1988), 11-28 offers largely a summary of that work and several articles in subsequent years.

the Arabic on the reverse cited Quranic affirmation of Muhammad as the Messenger of God (see Figure 16 below). Together with some of the numerous lead seals of administrative purpose from the first years of the conquest, these survive as the first dated instance of Arabic text and display the first use of the term 'al-Andalus', perhaps referring to the land of the Vandals, for this westernmost Muslim territory.[750] The name is the closest indication all the coins of Islamic Spain offer for the place of minting. It is generally assumed the coins emanated from Cordoba, the city chosen for the capital after a very brief period when Seville served in that capacity. The amirs may have minted in other cities under the single regional label, as there is thought to be enough variety of dies to make that a possibility, but the prevailing conclusion is that the new regime established a highly centralized minting.[751] In this sense, too, Muslim Spain followed the Byzantine pattern rather than adopt Visigothic practice. A peculiarity of the coins is that all have a star on the obverse, presumed to be taken from the story of Hesperis as a regional signifier. If so, the Greek influence is again apparent. The star can be seen as a tiny marker of the intermingling of the eastern and western Mediterranean on cultural, political, and economic levels.[752]

750 'Al-Andalus' possibly appeared on seals slightly before coins. Tawfiq Ibrahim, "Los precintos de la conquista y el dominio Omeya de Hispania," *Manquso* 4 (2016), 7-38; idem, "Nuevos documentos sobre la conquista Omeya de Hispania: Los precintos de plomo," *Zona arqueológica*, No. 15, 2011 (Dedicated issue title: *711: Arqueología e historia entre dos mundos*), v. 1, 145-61; and more recently the extensive draft of idem, "https://rah-es.academia.edu/TawfiqIbrahimتوفيقابراهيم (accessed online on 22 September 2018) and Ph. Sénac and Tawfiq Ibrahim, *Los precintos de la conquista omeya y la formación de al-Andalus (711-756)* (Granada: Universidad de Granada, 2017), esp. 27-30. For the suggestion that al-Andalus has a meaning based on the lots granted to Visigoths see Heinz Halm, "Al-Andalus and Ghotica Sors", in *The Formation of al-Andalus*, v. 1: *History and Society*, ed. M. Marín (London: Routledge, 1998), 39-50. Tracing the main suggestions for the etymology and their problems is A. García Sanjuán, "al-Andalus, etymology and name," in *Encyclopaedia of Islam, Three*, ed. Kate Fleet et al., http://dx.doi.org/10.1163/1573-3912_ei3_COM_24223 (accessed online on 08 October 2018).

751 Ruth Pliego Vázquez, "El dinar epigráfico latino acuñado en al-Andalus. Una reinterpretación a la luz de nuevos hallazgos," *Numisma* 245 (2001), 139-54 is appropriately cautious concerning the hypothetical mobile mints moving along with the army in the first years of the conquest in southern Spain, since sustained minting at *Ishbiliya* as at *Qurtuba* is strongly implied by the local nature of finds. The idea of traveling mints recommended by Balaguer, *Las emisiones transicionales* has found echoes in later scholarship, e.g., Bates, "The Coinage of Spain," 276f; A. Canto García, "Las monedas de la conquista," *Zona arqueológica*, No. 15, 2011 (Dedicated issue title: *711: Arqueología e historia entre dos mundos*), v. 1, 135-143; F. Regueras Grande and I. Rodríguez Casanova, "Triente de Sisebuto y dinar de indicción en dos *villae* romanas leonesas," 27 (2017), 11-24, at 23; and E. Manzano Moreno, *Conquistadores, emires y califas. Los omeyas y la formación de al-Andalus* (Barcelona: Crítica, 2006), 59.

752 The same star found on dinars of Homs with Abd al-Malik's standing caliph motif may refer to the northern (Syrian) star Sirius and thus symbolize in Spain the enduring caliphal call to

Figure 15: Transitional dinar in Latin letters of 94H = 712-713 (ANS, currently catalogued as HSA 57.1255)

Obv.: Margin from 12:00 – DINIMDMNIISISCSSDSNS (*garbled approximation of IN NOMINE DOMINI NON DEUS NISI DEUS SOLUS NON DEUS NON SOCIUS DEO*). Rev.: Center – IN̄dC̄XI (Indiction XI). Margin from 6:00 – HIISPANNANISNINIRFSDIS (? / *garbled approximation of a version of FERITUS SOLIDUS HIC IN SPANIA ANNUS XCIIII*).

Figure 16: Bilingual dinar of 98H = 716-717 (ANS 1994.55.1)

Obv.: Center – Muhammad ra/sul Allah; Margin – ḍuriba hādhā al-dinar bi'l-Andalus sana thaman wa-tisʿin. Rev.: FERITOSSOLINSPANANXVCI

Figure 17: Thulth (1/3 dinar) in Arabic of 102H = 720-721 (ANS 1917.215.3437)

Obv.: Center – La ilaha i/la Allah / wahdah; Margin – Muhamad rasul Allah arsala bi'l-huda wadeen al-haqq. Rev.: Center – Bismallah / al-rahman / al-raheem; Margin – ḍuriba hādhā al-thulth bi'l-Andalus sana thanateen wa-miat.

After a decade, the coinage of al-Andalus was transformed as a new series of Arabic-only dinars, dirhams, and feluses were made employing the epigraphic model of the monetary reform initiated by 'Abd al-Malik Ibn Marwān in 696. The dinars from 720 to 729 (AH 102-110), in Spain as in North Africa starting two years before, now bore on reverse the Islamic invocation placed only on divisions of the dinar in Syria: *bism Allah al-rahman al-rahim* ('in the name of God the merciful, the compassionate'; see Figure 17 above).[753] From the small number of Muslim Spanish gold pieces recovered from these early years, their volume can be said to have been quite limited. Silver and copper-based currency became much more abundant, especially as the Umayyad province became essentially independent following the toppling of the dynasty in Damascus in 750. Dirhams were probably first struck in 721/722 (AH 103) and were a consistent feature until the late ninth century, though they were restored a quarter-century later in the era of the Caliphate. Minting of the undated coppers of low value, the *fulus*, commenced sometime after the invasion.[754]

The reason Muslim authorities minted coin in Spain was the same essential reason for producing currency as elsewhere in the Islamic territories,

jihad: see Regueras and Rodríguez , 21f.

753 Balaguer, "Las emisiones transicionales," 12; Bates, "History, Geography and Numismatics," 259.

754 See the brief treatment on silver and copper in Blackburn, "Money and Coinage," v. 2, 550f.

for the ease of taxation and governmental transactions such as payment of troops, or in a related vein to facilitate the distribution of war spoils.[755] A similar question to that of the case of the original Gothic settlement applies to the Berber troops relied upon in the conquest of the peninsula: were they settled on land as a reward? At very least, settlement took several years, and it is understood that in the meantime the new gold coinage – or perhaps some of the old currency from Ifriqiya (northern Africa) or the Visigothic kingdom – was used to pay military salaries. Payment required a fiscal system, and the very progression of the coinage "suggests a development of financial administration."[756] The coinage is one of several main evidentiary supports for the very rapid establishment of a fiscal system.[757] If the system can be seen as borrowed, it was not from the Visigoths, but rather from the Byzantines in the preceding decades, and had become well developed. The fiscal-monetary apparatus was imported into Spain rather than taken over. The 'Visigothic' remnants, the Christians of the kingdom now under subjection, had a part in the new scheme. They were the majority and paid taxes, or perhaps a tribute that looked a lot like a tax. The famous Pact of Theodemir from the southeast in 713 demonstrates a monetary element (gold coins) payable each year in addition to a variety of produce.[758]

755 As suggested by Kennedy, *Muslim Spain and Portugal*, 21, echoing a common perspective of the specialized scholarship. Cf. Manzano Moreno, *Conquistadores, emires y califas*, Chap. 2: "El pago de los conquistadores. Las monedas de la conquista," 55-86, who observes that the much greater amount of copper than gold coinage as well as the comparative unimportance of the region gives reason to conclude gold was not the regular form of salary of the ordinary soldier but did likely have a part in commanders' salaries and army maintenance (64-70). On the other hand, P. Chalmeta, A. Canto, and T. Ibrahim consider gold (and later silver) as the normal channel for salary and for booty distribution, while copper or bronze currency was for other payments: Pedro Chalmeta, "Los primeros 46 años de economía andalusí (1)," *Alhadra* 1 (2015), 41-88 at 50f. Letters of the year 710 from the Arab governor of Egypt expressing to a high official the urgent need of coin and kind for soldiers' salaries and supply affords a glimpse into the operations one could expect to be in operation in Iberia (65). Tawfiq Ibrahim's work on the lead seals of al-Andalus demonstrates the presence, even in the tumultuous first years, of a system built on pacts and payments capable of satisfying troops: see Ibrahim, "Nuevos documentos," and Sénac and Ibrahim, *Los precintos*. He believes the very limited NW African coinage – a small amount of copper – at the point of Mūsā b. Nusair's departure for the peninsula was for administrative costs of the army, not salaries: Ibrahim, "Los precintos," 9.

756 Kennedy, *Muslim Spain and Portugal*, 21. See also Wickham, *Framing*, 101. Berbers and Arabs of the conquest were possibly paid initially, but they were also given parcels of land within decades. The same occurred with the Syrian forces brought into Spain in the 740s.

757 Sénac and Ibrahim, *Los precintos*, 40-46, where the Mozarabic Chronicle, seals, coins, and the high quality of coin production are brought together to underline this point.

758 Discussed in Chapter Seven below, in the context of the monetization question.

While the northern parts of Europe including the Merovingian and Anglo-Saxon kingdoms no longer minted gold coinage at this point, the Lombard, Byzantine and, until 711, Visigothic lands did. Apart from this common Mediterranean monetary resemblance, some harmony between the Muslim coinage and that of its predecessor is reflected in the occasional continued circulation of Visigothic tremisses for several decades after the conquest, and sometimes circulation together of coins from the two eras.[759] In spite of the differences in the gold currency, a certain adaptation was made to the monetary situation Muslim authorities came across. As was noted above in the discussion on metrology (see nn. 500-502), a number of Visigothic tremisses minted in the seventh century were struck at weights of 1.5 g or even higher, exceptional even for contemporary imperial mints, perhaps an attempt to hide or make up for inferior metallic quality.[760] Minting of debased coinage at or above the legal weight standard was copied and even exaggerated by Muslim minters in Spain in the initial years of the conquest, a sharp contrast to the inchoate Muslim practice of minting gold coins in the Near East, where regular weights and high fineness were the norm.[761] Within a short time, the minters in al-Andalus brought dinars and thulths (one third dinars) back to nearly twenty-four-karat quality.[762] By 745, al-Andalus stopped production of gold currency and issued only the silver *dirham* and copper *fals*. Gold coinage would not be issued again until 'Abd al-Rahman III's disavowal of 'Abbasid authority in 929. While the Islamic invaders of Spain did not copy the monetary system they encountered there, divergence in this part of administration between the two regimes

759 I.e. in limited cases, leaving Visigothic tremisses sometimes found with one or a few Islamic copper coins. Manuel Castro Priego, "Absent Coinage: Archaeological Contexts and Tremisses on the Central Iberian Peninsula in the 7th and 8th Centuries AD," *Medieval Archaeology* 60.1 (2016), 27-56. A. Canto García, "El Pacto de Tudmîr: Aspectos económicos," *eHumanista/IVITRA Journal of Iberian Studies* 5 (2014), 370-91, at 378f on circulation of Visigothic and Roman coins in areas under treaty with the new Muslim government, ref. S. Gutiérrez Lloret, "El Tolmo de Minateda en torno al 711," *Zona arqueológica*, No. 15, 2011 (Dedicated issue title: *711: Arqueología e historia entre dos mundos*), v. 1, 359-372.

760 Grierson and Blackburn, *Medieval European Coinage*, v. 1, 54.

761 Ibid. See also Balaguer, *Las emisiones transicionales*, 101; idem, "Las emisiones transicionales," 25; and Pliego, "El dinar epigráfico latino," 150f. The great variability in Latin transitional gold coinage for 93-95 AH (711-713/14) could derive mostly from the taking of whatever booty, Visigothic coins, jewelry, etc. was found by the rapacious soldiers, as sources describe them – cf. Chalmeta, "Los primeros 46 años," 42-45. The fineness, weight, and craftsmanship of the gold is vastly improved from 98 AH (716-717) onwards, indubitably the result of normalized collection of tribute: Canto, "El Pacto de Tudmîr," 382, 387, cf. 379 on the Gothic population's inevitable melting down of precious metal goods to meet treaty requirements.

762 Appendix I, Figure I.17.

should not be overemphasized. One system of gold minting was replaced by another primarily minting in gold as well, with copper and silver gaining prominence only after several years.[763] Adjustments in gold content in addition to some co-circulation of coinages in the post-invasion period reveals a stage of negotiated currency management that was still possible because Visigothic coinage, though independent and developed along its own lines, originated like Islamic coinage from a Roman foundation.

763 García Sanjuan, *La conquista islámica* stresses the rupture the new coinage represented. Some of his points in this regard are quite valid; however, he rejects Visigothic minting of copper coins (154), which he bases on the opinion of Eduardo Manzano Moreno, specifically in *Conquistadores, emires, y califas*, 68f. Even the observation of the non-use of indictional dates on Visigothic coins (163) should be qualified by mentioning that Hispano-Roman writers of that era often did use that dating system. Furthermore, in countering the ridiculous assertion of Ignacio Olagüe, *Les Arabes n'ont jamais envahi l'Espagne* (1970), that the transitional bilingual dinars are in fact Visigothic solidi, it is nevertheless incorrect to state that the Goths in Spain never minted solidi (250f), rather they did not do so after several years into Leovigild's reign.

7. Visigothic Currency in the Early Medieval Economy

Abstract
Chapter Seven addresses the use of coinage in the kingdom, considering the level of monetization in Visigothic society and the Mediterranean contexts of currency's functioning. An argument for a largely monetized economy draws from both written references to gold coins and archeological studies. Copper-based currency is seen to have played the larger role in society across large areas especially in southern Iberia, where monetary circumstances and contacts with Mediterranean regions display greater commonality than has been widely supposed. Economic interactivity is linked to early medieval Spain's shifting regionalism.

Keywords: economy; monetization; circulation; bronze; Mediterranean; currency

A The Other Side of the Coin

This book has addressed why coinage was struck, bronze and silver briefly in Chapter Two and gold more extensively in Chapter Four. In this final chapter, we flip to the other side of the coin, so to speak, to focus on how coinage was used. From the start, it is important to recognize usage is not the same as the state's purpose in minting, especially from the point of view taken in the earlier chapters. Under consideration here is the role of coinage in the economy, after and apart from minting. Bringing together a range of evidence will help to address the broader – and rather challenging – issue of the degree of monetization, signified by currency availability and utility, but by a strict definition "the share of transactions that are handled via

Kurt, A., *Minting, State, and Economy in the Visigothic Kingdom: From Settlement in Aquitaine through the First Decade of the Muslim Conquest of Spain.*
Taylor & Francis Group, 2020
DOI 10.5117/9789462981645_CH07

the market and which involve the use of money."[764] By no means can the full scope of the Visigothic economy be surveyed in this section, and the backdrop of causative factors in economic behavior will rest on references to specific studies. One major point of reference in the last dozen years may serve for the general setting in which the place of early medieval currency must be underscored. Chris Wickham's *Framing the Early Middle Ages: Europe and the Mediterranean, 400-800* established an excellent framework for considering the grand scale, in which economy and state are examined in interrelation and are viewed in one realm astride another for depth of comparison as well as an understanding of a whole process through several centuries. However, coinage is not incorporated. In the literature on this transformative age, it is often left to specialized scholarship. The intention here is to widen the narrow bridge between interest in socio-economic developments and the activity of currency.

Parts of Wickham's interpretation of the late antique state and economy have inevitably been criticized from different angles. While appreciating his view of the structure in which the states of the Mediterranean functioned, Jairus Banaji departs from Wickham on two main points: his overemphasis on the part of the economy represented by the fiscal machinery, and the view of taxation still mostly in kind as the Roman West was disintegrating. Banaji's general concern is primarily with the economy itself, however, and he is careful to recognize as Metcalf and Millar have enunciated that minting and the movement of money through exchange are separate questions.[765] Along a similar line as Wickham in regard to the overall economic configurations of late antiquity, Michael Hendy's works affirmed that Byzantine coinage, just as western Roman coinage, had the one main purpose of enabling the imperial fiscal administration, whereas the function of "public utility (the provision of a convenient medium of exchange for the private sector of the economy) ranked as very secondary."[766] Distribution of gold and very

764 Philipp Robinson Rössner, "Money, Banking, Economy," in *Handbook of Medieval Culture: Fundamental Aspects and Conditions of the European Middle Ages*, V. 2, ed. Albrecht Classen (Berlin/Boston, MA: De Gruyter, 2015). Ebook Collection (Ebscohost), Ebscohost (Accessed August 28, 2017), 326-46 at 332.

765 Banaji, *Exploring the Economy*, esp. 10-12.

766 Hendy, *Studies*, 4. So also much of the work of John Haldon cited in this book; see Banaji, *Exploring the Economy*, 111f, who sees the currency operating far beyond fiscal mechanisms. Hendy wrote from the so-called substantivist perspective then popular in the UK, describing distributionism and reciprocalism far more than the economic dynamics of scarcity and utility, which is the lens of formalism. Cf. the balance of state/private forces in F. Carlà, *L'oro nella tarda antichità: aspetti economici e sociali* (Torino: Zamorani, 2009), esp. 479-97; J. Iluk, *Aspects économiques et politiques de la circulation de l'or au Bas-Empire* (Wetteren: Moneta, 2007).

occasionally silver was strictly determined by expenditures of the state, of which those of the military ranked in first place.[767] This had a direct effect on placement of regional imperial mints, which corresponded to military locations and frequently did not happen to coincide with economic factors such as high agricultural yield areas or heavily urbanized zones. Copper and copper-alloy coinage distribution through a wider and more voluminous minting was also governed by fiscal purposes of the state, but the expenditure scale was different and, unlike gold, the base-metals were not intended for return in revenue cycles.[768] Hence base-metal currency pivoted into more widespread use apart from the state.

The same dynamics were at work in successor states of the West, at least initially. Rory Naismith has reestablished this conclusion from the perspective of a basic question with wide implications for early medieval economies. Amid the changes to the currency in the post-Roman West, among which was the overall dwindling of currency levels and a wide variation in denominations produced, why was gold coinage a steady feature? The answer is because of the essential role it had come to play in the taxation system in the later Roman period, and which continued in most barbarian kingdoms. Although the fiscal capabilities eventually waned with new socio-economic circumstances in France and Italy, for example, and were

Retamero, "La moneda," 192f rightly perceives that the debate on the volume and use of gold currency has usually viewed it apart from the political order that brought it into being. Placing money in its central role is essential for understanding both the currency and the political regime. He considers neither the purely fiscal, nor the purely commercial explanations convincing because both uses of currency are intertwined. Circulation is, in fact, the total sequence of where coinage appears. This chapter as well as Chapter Four seek a holistic approach which incorporates these astute reminders.

767 See Hendy, *Studies*, 164-68 on the huge bureaucratic and military costs associated with northern Africa and the West in Justinian I's reign. For estimates of over one third of total expenses in sixth-century Byzantium dedicated to the military, and more in the following two turbulent centuries, see Haldon, "Late Rome," 363f. Wickham, *Framing*, 73 estimates a third of the Roman expenditure went toward the army, with another third for the administration and another for the cities of Rome and Constantinople. The debate over the problem of the late Roman flow of gold coin on which the massive fiscal machinery depended looks at the depth of commercialization that could buy and transport products interregionally. Otherwise how could taxation overwhelmingly in gold provide the more essential need of food? Wickham sees in *coemptio* the only way the state could ensure availability of actual food, together with taxes necessarily based in kind in a certain portion of the empire (ibid., 74-76).

768 In a sharp disjunction of denominations Pliego, *La moneda visigoda*, v. 1, 230 applies Karl Polanyi's notion of the different conceptions and uses of coinage within the same system to Gothic Spain. I would differ from this application in so far as gold is thought to have little to do with exchange and exercised functions of gift-giving and accumulating treasure for nobles far more than taxation, ultimately.

completely absent in England and survived without gold coin in Vandal Africa, in Visigothic Spain continuation of fiscal operations upheld the longevity of the tremissis to the fall of the kingdom in 711.[769] Ramifications of the taxation-expenditure objectives of the imperial currency system described by Hendy and Wickham find parallels in the Visigothic kingdom. One is that shortage of gold currency is seen to correspond to the state's lack of concern to supply it.[770] So, also the circumstances of a massive as well as tightly systematic and inflexible fiscal administration lent quite easily, as the power of magnates grew, to the state's increasing difficulty in collecting the requisite revenues. Budgetary deficit, compounded by periodic spending surfeits, occasioned debasement of precious-metal currency.[771] And because political disintegration, economic structure, and minting systems went hand in hand, while the magnitude in the Visigothic kingdom was far lesser

769 I fully concur with his response to this same question posed in Naismith, "Gold Coinage and Its Use" and directly answered on 273f and 288. Naismith presents the Merovingian case wherein an empowered aristocracy and simultaneously weakened monarchy – and with it tax collection – helped shape a coinage system eventually geared more toward the monetary needs of elites than of the kingdom, and not by mere coincidence non-royal on the whole. Coin production devolved to a huge number of mostly localized mints and shifted in the later seventh century from gold to silver. Interdependence of fiscality and currency is expressed succinctly, "Decline in taxation therefore meant decline of the coinage" (Ibid., 274). The Vandal kingdom had no gold but three silver denominations, many with regal inscriptions and stamped only with the name of Carthage, indicating centralized control. A tax regime existed, but the situation was different without either a standing army or a past as Roman troops: Wickham, *Framing*, 88-92. Copper-alloy coinage could still serve for the *donativa* to troops: A. Merrills and R. Miles, *The Vandals* (Chichester: Wiley-Blackwell, 2010), 168. The diminished fiscal scheme was unable to support gold minting, as pointed out long ago by Hendy, "From Public to Private," 48. Yet, gold's convenience is demonstrated by the use of foreign gold: see below at n. 820 and Carlà, "The End of Roman Gold Coinage," 64.

770 Hendy, *Studies*, 4. The same idea, though combined with lower availability of bullion, is present in the fiscal framework presented by Naismith, "Gold Coinage and Its Use," (bullion shortage: 295, 299) and Crusafont, *El sistema*, 88-101. On the diminution of late Rome's state gold reserves due to their increased transfer to private individuals to supply the needs of a surge in commerce see Banaji, *Exploring the Economy*, 111f. Taxation-expenditure in the Visigothic realm is discussed judiciously albeit with a largely negative assessment in Pliego, *La moneda visigoda*, v. 1, 215-30 and Martín Viso, "Prácticas locales de la fiscalidad."

771 Hendy, *Studies*, 4 on Byzantine debasements. See above nn. 610f and 738. Crusafont et al., "Silver Visigothic Coinage," 245 attributes the debasing activity strictly to a perennial shortage of gold; what I argue here is essentially the same root problem but seen within the overarching circumstances. See Naismith, "Gold Coinage and Its Use," 299 on debased Western coinage in general due to scarcity of bullion. Debasement also occurred in the Byzantine Spanish province, as traced in Bartlett et al., "Byzantine Gold Coinage of *Spania*." The data compels the conclusion that this debasement was patterned after Visigothic debasement, in such a way that Spania's authorities were getting away with the lowest gold level possible given their local circumstances.

forms of administration there would also naturally affect monetization. One further note relates to the correlations here. It has been observed that there was a price increase between Leovigild and Ervig. At the same time, the salaries in the early Byzantine empire were higher than in Spain. The cause of both is plausibly seen in the relative abundance of gold in the East as opposed to the Visigothic kingdom. In the latter, gold itself must have retained a high value especially in the face of scarcity, but the markets picked up on the devaluations of gold coinage.[772]

B Use and Circulation of Currency in the Kingdom

Gold coinage was thus utilized on the part of the government in early medieval Iberia chiefly in payment of expenses and on the part of the kingdom's inhabitants in payment of tax assessments. This is not to say that all people paid in such a way, and not all currency out among the public at any given moment went into the fiscal stream, as stands to reason but is also indicated by common incorporation of older coins in hoards, for example. There is no getting around the lack of information to determine the specific sorts of distribution by the state, but the sharp distinction from the Roman Empire in minting localities denotes local as opposed to centralized distribution, though Byzantium did administer some regional and sub-regional distribution of gold.

As a separate stage from the fiscally-oriented operation of solidi and tremisses, the extent of monetization cannot be fully known, though some idea of it can be pieced together. This inquiry brings us beyond what can be gleaned with respect to the volume of minting, instances of currency use, and the circulation of the coinage, since we also must consider the kingdom's permeability.[773] As seen in Chapter Four, there are interesting

772 Crusafont, *El sistema*, 85; although not in given in comparison with the West, high prices and wages in the East coterminous with the Visigothic kingdom are evident in C. Morrisson and J.-C. Cheynet, "Prices and Wages in the Byzantine World," in *The History of the Byzantine Economy*, v. 2, ed. Angeliki E. Laiou (Washington, DC: Dumbarton Oaks, 2002), 815-78, esp. 860, 864f. Salaries and prices in the Visigothic kingdom are taken from J. Orlandis, "Sobre el nivel de la vida en Hispania visigoda," *Anuario de Estudios Medievales* 8 (1972-1973), 17-33, where the average cost of food for an adult per year in Euric's day is estimated at three tremisses (= one solidus), and a good annual salary at three solidi. This is adjusted from valuation of a child's upkeep in the law code at one tremiss per annum.

773 The term of Crusafont to denote 'the kings' acceptance of any gold coinage comparable to their own, such as the Merovingian or Suevian tremissis, which were not re-struck': Crusafont et al., "Silver Visigothic Coinage," 245; see also idem, *El sistema*, 96-101.

possibilities for increasing our knowledge of the volume of gold coinage, both solidi and tremisses, of Visigothic Iberia. The main takeaway for now is that the volume was not miniscule by any means; in fact, at least some series were apparently much more sizeable than could be supposed based on the number of currently known specimens, without examination of single versus repeated die samples.[774] Even the partial information with regard to numbers of dies, however, could never eliminate the conundrum of how many coins emerged from each die, a matter of educated guesswork. Emphasis on volume is limited in another way. Even *if* volume were known, population is not, and the problem of coin usage – essentially monetary economic activity – would remain.[775] Reliance is necessarily on contemporary literary references to currency and on the conglomeration of mostly indirect indicators that together resemble what might be expected in a relatively monetized or non-monetized economy.

At the level of the king and his court, were the many costs of power, such as maintaining the palace and other royal buildings, supporting a large household and retainers, building, administering, and defending cities such as Reccopolis, and meting out funds for artisans, regalia, stables, munificence, and the assuredly huge costs of war. This put a great deal of money into people's hands. That the king had vast sums from which he could dole out can scarcely be doubted. Leovigild paid 30,000 solidi to the Byzantine governor of Spania to induce him to withdraw support from Hermenegild. To become king, count Sisenand paid Dagobert 200,000

774 See above, 95 n. 262, 191 esp. n. 566, and 190f. Retamero, "La moneda," 194f points out that limited die duplication, which might be taken to signal high volume based on the use of many different dies, does not actually necessitate a great deal of minting from each die, and so volume of coinage could actually be low despite a large number of dies as known from the coins. He also equates what he deems as the generally minimal coin wear with a less heavy usage than the commercial perspective of Michael Metcalf would suggest; however, the independent observation of Peter Bartlett, myself, and others is that noticeable die wear appears on many coins. See the astute commentary on volume estimates by Pliego, *La moneda visigoda*, v. 1, 195-98; even without any certainty regarding use of dies or even their approximate number, as she points out, her die study of Sisebut-Ispali alone makes possible an emission of – by conservative estimate – many hundreds of thousands of tremisses in just one locale. Metcalf decried the perception of a low volume in the Visigothic as well as the Merovingian and post-600 Anglo-Saxon lands, in all of which he evoked heavy utilization of coined money. Visigothic: Metcalf, "Some Geographical Aspects"; Idem, "For What Purposes"; Idem, "Many Mint-Places." Merovingian: Idem, "Monetary Circulation in Merovingian Gaul, 561-674. A propos des Cahiers Ernest Babelon," *Revue numismatique*, 6e série, Tome 162 (2006), 337-393. Anglo-Saxon: Idem, "How Large Was the Anglo-Saxon Currency?," *English Historical Review* 18 (1965), 475-82.

775 Hendy, *Studies*, 8.

solidi in 631 to support his rebellion.[776] Costs of administration, while not like Rome's or Constantinople's, were a constant. The royal treasure was of such importance that it had its own 'Count of the Treasury', an official within the ranks of the 'Palatine Office', the highest organ of the central administration. The treasure's stature was great enough that in 507 the Franks attempted to seize it when they defeated the Visigoths at Vouillé, but when the Ostrogoths intervened it was instead taken to Ravenna where it stayed until Theodoric's death in 526, after which it was returned to the Visigoths in exchange for Provence. It drew the amazement of the Muslim invaders of Spain in the early eighth century, and even if our skepticism is aroused by reports of its inclusion of the gold-embroidered Table of Solomon, its contents impressed sufficiently to be highlighted in Islamic histories.[777]

The testimony of sustained minting itself and coin finds indicate demand on some level and imply usage engaging social ranks below the king. Yet, merely the presence of money in movement is too vague to demonstrate monetization as such. How gold currency was involved in society in the fifth century, when the manner of barbarian settlement is itself uncertain, is not a point on which there is much light in the case of the Visigothic kingdom. Research demonstrating the mostly local circulation of coins in the Toulouse era, with few found outside the Visigothic zone in Gaul, would be the result of short-distance interactions as opposed to long-distance trade, for example.[778] Monetary activity relatable to Visigothic authority is more discernable after the kingdom concentrated in Spain. Elites had their own costs, and evidence of their having and spending coinage is redolent of monetization among the upper echelon. Dower was set at ten percent of a husband's patrimony; for the high nobility, the *primates palatii* or *seniores gothorum*, the declared amount was 1000 solidi, to which could be added ten male and ten female slaves and twenty horses. This was based on a supposed possession of 10,000 solidi. The same law stipulates a 100 solidi donation if the patrimony were 1000, a hint at what was considered an average fortune.[779] Some light is

776 Leovigild: Greg. of Tours, *HF* V.38. Sisenand: Fredegar, *Chronicle*, IV.73.

777 On the sums and treasure see J. Orlandis, *La vida en España en tiempo de los godos* (Madrid: Rialp, 1991), 55f, 57, 93.

778 See Naismith, "Gold Coinage and Its Use," 284 and 286, where it is noted that the payments to Goths referred to in Euric's law are not specified as to whether in kind or currency. Circulation in Gaul: Depeyrot, "Les émissions wisigothiques" (see above, 37 n. 65), countering Barral's arguments for the coinage's association with major trade routes.

779 Orlandis, *La vida en España*, 60f, ref. *LV* III.1.v of Chindasvinth, affirmed by Ervig but setting the maximum gift at 1000 solidi. Orlandis suggests that recovered hoards appear to confirm such resources, an observation reaffirmed since he wrote.

shed on major commercial transactions by a rare account of a sum of 758 solidi for shipping costs in a tax payment of wheat from Spain to Rome in the 520s.[780] The several churches built in the southeast before the turn of the seventh century by Gudiliuva, a *vir inlustris*, are examples of activities that very likely required coinage, as did the church building and repair work as well as support of religious festivals by Bishop Justinian of Valencia in the 540s.[781] Similar instances that may have no name attached to them occurred in Mérida, Cordoba, Valencia, Seville, and a host of other cities.

In Crusafont's conception gold moved in a rather closed circuit of magnates and state within a fiscal orientation, and with Grierson he believes the ordinary people would not have much dealing with solidi or tremisses.[782] The activity of traders from across the sea, controled for purposes of taxation as in similar commerce in the Mediterranean and the North Sea in antiquity and in the post-Roman age, has been seen in terms of gold currency usage among a limited group.[783] Yet, both higher and lower social strata appear in association with coin use in a variety of sources. On the eve of the kingdom's removal into Spain, when Alaric II ordered tax collection specifically in order to pay soldiers a donative, coin was put into the hands of Goths and non-Goths alike.[784] At the point of conquest, Theodemir's pact with the Muslim authorities in the southeast required each Christian under him to pay annually an assorted tribute in kind as well as a *dinar*, essentially the

780 Cassiodorus, *Variae* 5.35 (a. 523/526).

781 See Kulikowski, *Late Roman Spain*, 289f.

782 Crusafont, *El sistema*, 89-91. We saw in Chapter Four that this is the model adopted by Retamero and Pliego as well. Metcalf on the other hand saw the Visigothic currency as largely commercially oriented, and took the evidence of short-, medium-, and long-distance circulation within the peninsula as emblematic of currency use. See above, p. 191. According to Pliego, the limited fiscalism (see above, n. 681) operated within what she characterizes as an essentially gift or prestige economy, which nevertheless coincided with coin payments to troops and rather regular access to currency on the part of merchants: Pliego, "El *tremis* de los últimos años," 37-41.

783 Retamero, "As Coins Go Home," 279-85; see esp. 280 on the tax points, *teloneum* and *cataplus*, and the remark on 285 that control (taxing) of domestic trade within the peninsula is less well known but probable. In a similar light, on controled commerce at long-distance trading spots or warehouses cum tax collection points, see Hendy, "From Public to Private," 69 and idem, "From Antiquity," 335-37 (and 339 for what becomes in al-Andalus the *alcaicería*); the similar *apotheke* of the eastern empire from perhaps the time of Anastasius may well have derived from the western trade/tax warehouses (344). Pliego, "El *tremis* de los últimos años," 39 briefly rehearses the direct trade for the luxury trade (taxation) and the indirect evidence (art and craftwork with eastern motifs).

784 Orlandis, *La vida en España*, 141; the *Life of St. Avitus of Périgord* narrates the saint being pressed into battle as a young man.

Islamic solidus. How else would these *dhimmi* satisfy the separate monetary requirement unless currency were at their disposal?

Several laws in the *Liber Iudiciorum* with traditions extending back into laws from the Gallic period demonstrate a preoccupation about coinage that pertains to all classes.[785] Severe punishments for fraud or adulteration of gold pieces on the one hand, and demanding acceptance of full value of a coin though of proper weight on the other, suggest a need for the Crown to act against repeated practices. We saw earlier that *LV* VII.6.ii supposes fraudulent behavior by free man or slave alike, and the law immediately preceding it permitted the torture of slaves to gain such information about either a lord or a lady. The law demanding 'that no one will refuse a solidus of full weight' (*LV* VII.6.v)[786] may seem ironic in light of the many official emissions below the normal standards, but if it were in a passable weight range, and potentially subject to payment adjustment after weighing, it could not legally be refused. The regulation infers that rejection of coins occurred, as could be comprehended even by the street level economics of the time. Implied behind the laws is transmission of coinage. Frequent mention of fines stipulated in monetary units is another indication of commonplace monetary conventions and even possession. From a fine of one solidus for destruction of another's patch of grapevine or a few solidi in the case of a tree – five for ruining an olive tree – to 300 for killing another's skilled slave, the laws repeatedly express pecuniary penalty. While reverse commutation to payment in kind may sometimes have occurred, it is never mentioned and valuation in currency indicates at very least familiarity with currency.[787]

785 See Javier de Santiago Fernández, "Legislación y moneda en la Hispania visigoda", *Mélanges de la Casa de Velázquez*, 41.2 (2011), 55-74.

786 Zeumer, ed., MGH.LL I.I, p. 311. "Solidum aureum integri ponderis, cuiuscumque monete sit, si adulterinus non fuerit, nullus ausus sit recusare nec pro eius aliquid moneta requirere preter hoc, quod minus forte pensaverit. [...]" The frequent debasement of official coinage necessitates the reading of 'si adulterinus non fuerit' as reference to unofficial alterations: Santiago, "Legislación y moneda," 57. See the analysis in Pliego, "La falsificación." Could this law refer to non-Visigothic coinage of equal quality and standard, or perhaps older Visigothic coinage? It has been pointed out to me by Andrei Gandila that Byzantine legislation, for instance, stipulated that old gold coinage was still legal tender and should not be avoided.

787 Many fines from the *Leges Visigothorum* are recorded in Naismith, "Gold Coinage and Its Use," 282 and Orlandis, *La vida en España*, 53f; see also Pliego, "La falsificación." As observed by Santiago, "Legislación y moneda," 58-62, fines may have been always valued though not always paid in cash form. Nevertheless, his own reasoning (61) that payments to the state would be greatly facilitated by currency transfer should be borne in mind. Fines are so common in the Visigothic law code that is has been remarked exaggeratedly that their testimony alone confirms monetization. For the whopping fine of 360 solidi in an early period for taking up the legal office of *defensor* before being confirmed by the city council, see *C. Th.*, i.29.6.

This is likewise the case with the slates from this era in Iberia that contain money values. Most often the references to payments in these writing tablets are expressed in kind, making it all the more possible that the few mentions of coinage amounts (solidi or tremisses) are simply units of account. But certain expressions such as '*suscepto solido uno*' or a '*securitas*' of ten solidi for several pigs leave little doubt currency itself changed hands.[788] Or a law on loans specifies lending of money (*pecuniam*) among other, non-monetary loans, and furthermore expresses the maximum of 1/8 interest in monetary units.[789] The evidence suggests coinage was part of urban and rural life. The mixed assortment of payment types may not constitute monetization by strict definition, though broad monetary habits are inferred in the written record.

The Church, too, had interactions involving hard currency, which only occasionally is cited explicitly. On feast days, some of the people would make monetary offerings.[790] Reports from the exceptionally prosperous city of Mérida must have had large or small echoes elsewhere. The tremendous building and charity works of bishop Masona (ca. 570-606) would have necessitated utilization of actual currency, and while we hear in his story of large amounts of goods donated and doled out at times, coinage is also on display. Masona not only directed half of the bishop's entire patrimonial revenues into the hands of the doctors of his *xenodochium*, a quasi-hospital 'to serve travelers and the sick', to be given to those suffering illness, he also set up a fund of 2000 solidi to help anyone in monetary crisis.[791] One episode in particular puts us in view of the everyday currency reality like perhaps no other instance. When Masona was in exile imposed by Leovigild and had given away everything of his own as well as of his servants, a poor widow with many difficulties came petitioning alms. The bishop and servants searched

788 Santiago, "Legislación y moneda," 60.

789 *LV* V.5.8: '*tres siliquas de unius solidi* [...] *et de solidis octo nonum solidum*'; see Santiago, "Legislación y moneda," 59.

790 Council of Mérida, canon 16, Vives, ed., *Concilios*, 335. Such gifts were to be equally distributed among the clergy once or twice a year: First Council of Braga, canon 21 (ibid., p. 76). John S. Huffstot, "Reverse Designs on the Sixth-century Iberian Coppers: An Alternative to the Municipal-Monogram Theory," *Gaceta Numismática* 160 (2006), 5-17, at 14f, makes the claim for bishops' authority behind bronze mintings, with the possible motive of receiving coins in return from the people by dint of tithing and alms. Such an intriguing idea supposes a large amount of specifically church expenses and tithing in coin for which documentation is lacking.

791 *Vitas Sanctorum Patrum Emeritensium*, in *Lives of the Visigothic Fathers*, ed. and trans. A. T. Fear (Liverpool: Liverpool University Press, 1997), *xenodochium* at 5.3.4 (ed. Fear, 74), the fund at 5.3.9 (ed. Fear, 75f). Towards the end of his life Masona is said to have manumitted a number of slaves who had served him well, providing them with a bit of both money and land – which would put money in the hands of freedmen still in semi-servile status on church lands if a later trend was already being followed: *VSPE* 13.4 (ed. Fear, 101).

for something left to give, until the head servant spoke up, "I have a single solidus, but if I give you this we will have nothing at all with which to buy food for ourselves and our mule." The holy bishop ordered the solidus to be given. We have here already a verification of the kinds of common use of gold coins, a commonplace that quite naturally found its way into hagiography meant for public reading in liturgy as an example easily understood by the congregation. But the rest of the story is also instructive. The servant after some moments "ran after the woman and begged her as he had nothing with which to buy food for himself to give back at least a tremiss of the sum [...] She gave him one tremiss without any sadness and took the other two off with her, glad at heart." The unfolding lesson includes repetition of the exact interchange as well as mention of a much larger amount of solidi and goods that Masona declares would have been the reward had the servant been fully generous.[792] Even if solidi were no longer minted in Spain by the last third of the sixth century, this traditional unit of account should not therefore be assumed to have applied solely or even predominantly to in-kind conversion. Laws and slates move between references to solidi and tremisses.

To return to the imperial model that had such influence on the earliest medieval kingdoms, emphasis has been placed on the state-driven economy and initial flow of gold only from the fiscal machinery.[793] A widespread phenomenon of the later Roman centuries obtained also in Visigothic Spain, whereby magnates served a role as middlemen in converting taxes gathered in a mix of currency and kind into gold alone.[794] Whether small

792 *VSPE* 5.7, in *Lives*, ed. and trans. Fear, 87f. No sooner did the head servant get his tremiss than a huge cargo of foodstuffs from well-wishers showed up – 200 loaded asses. Masona scolded his servant by remarking, "You gave two tremisses and, behold, you have obtained two thousand solidi and two hundred asses [...] had you not taken that third tremiss you would have received three hundred loaded asses."

793 See esp. Hendy, "From Antiquity," 329, 335f, 355f, 359. We have seen how the same engine is described in other works by Hendy such as *Studies* and "From Public to Private," as well as in Wickham, *Framing* (72 n. 43: tending more toward seeing the movement of goods across the empire caused by fiscal mechanisms than by private commercial enterprise), and how García Moreno and Crusafont relate this to Hispania.

794 Most recently Fernández, "Statehood, Taxation" and idem, *Aristocrats and Statehood*. Retamero, "La moneda," esp. 208-10, and Naismith, "Gold Coinage and Its Use," 303-05 also discuss mediation of magnates and cite some of the growing literature, among which should be highlighted Martín Viso, "Tremisses y potentes," Castellanos, "The Political Nature of Taxation". See also Barceló and Retamero, "From Crops to Coin"; Wickham, *Framing*, 93-100. The ultimate handing over of gold to the state does not answer whether or not it was melted down and reminted each time. The long circulating life (ave. roughly 40-50 years) leads to the conclusion that most tremisses in the tributary cycle were not renewed; Retamero sees re-striking as a phenomenon mostly of Leovigild's day.

landholders or peasants tied to local lords played their part in the taxation by using tremisses is a more difficult question. In the transformation of crops into coinage, *De fisco barcinonensi* calculates in monetary terms the tax assessment as well as the rather large percentage allocated for the collection and monetization process, which leaves the strong possibility that peasant and currency sometimes, at minimum, had a direct link too easily dismissed.[795] In other western territories, the currency system was forced to change radically over time to adapt to structural shifts. This was the main point of Hendy's article titled 'From Public to Private,' which between the state-oriented minting for public purposes of the Roman government to the private orientation of (by then silver) minting of the Carolingian realm, an altered reason for and concomitant usage of coin applied, since major aristocratic estate-holding and the collection of rents as opposed to taxes was the new norm. In Spain, the process may quietly have begun to occur in terms of reduced minting, but a regally organized minting network at some 'public' level still was in place. It had a heavily urban orientation.[796] By the same token, reduced minting translated into reduced gold currency availability and transaction, whether for taxation or commerce. Meanwhile urban topography saw major transformations during the Visigothic tenure. Yet, it is hard to imagine urban development, however much affected by demographic decline and turning from classical lines to largely ecclesiastical focus, did not involve money. The rough maintenance of Roman urban structures well into the mid-sixth century, or the continuing sea-borne trade in which coastal cities engaged,[797] plus the comparative detachment of urban inhabitants from rural resources, could only have entailed the utility of coins. The stories of Bishop Masona and Bishop Paul in Mérida provide examples. Find patterns show circulation revolving around urban locations and fortified aristocratic centers.[798] The substantial role of bronze

795 As in Retamero, "As Coins Go Home," and in Barceló and Retamero, "From Crops to Coin," 57, which nevertheless lays out the key monetary elements of the document superbly. A wide spectrum of money use such as I am arguing for in early medieval Spain is in evidence in France and Italy, albeit the preponderance was among the upper echelon of society: see Naismith, "Gold Coinage and Its Use," esp. 285-89 and 305f. Gold currency inflow via taxation requires an underlying productive economy engaging a complex of short- and long-range exchanges: Morrisson, "Regio dives," 194.

796 Pliego, "El *tremis* de los últimos años," 20.

797 Kulikowski, *Late Roman Spain* (esp. 256f, 287-309) and Wickham, *Framing*, esp. 656-65 and 748-55 provide solid treatment of the changes. On trade see n. 806 below.

798 Bishops: Retamero, "As Coins Go Home," 271-74. Find patterns: Castro, "Absent Coinage," 30-32, however it may be overstated to claim that circulation is limited to these areas. The example of Bovalar and a few others discussed below qualifies this statement. The fortified sites,

in these milieux, whether apart from or in conjunction with tremisses, will be explored below.

Evidence of coinage in situ in a rural archeological site called El Bovalar (Lleida) is illuminating.[799] Visigothic tremisses were found not in one single hoard, but instead in several locations on the site, thereby revealing the dispersal of currency among presumably ordinary residences in a remote village. The precise manner of Bovalar's integration suggested by its distribution of tremisses at several habitations is a mystery, more so because the findings from it do not include objects that would indicate sixth-century trade. The archeological work on the village gives some clues as to how currency must have been used. The raison d'etre of holding coinage is ultimately to facilitate convenient exchange of some sort. Possessions of Bovalar's inhabitants included livestock, farming tools, and, of course, houses and barns. The use of tremisses for purchasing of goods, especially more costly items such as these, would have been entirely fitting. Until used, currency is a convenient store of wealth. Taxes were most easily paid in coin, provided that coinage was available, which the dig at El Bovalar suggests was the case in this insignificant settlement. Another reason for having coins on hand was the payment of fines discussed above. If a wandering animal of a farmer in Bovalar or any other rural settlement in the kingdom damaged a neighbor's property, or a severe altercation arose, and a farmer was found guilty before a judge, he would have to be prepared to pay or face ruinous punishment. Fines were always expressed in gold coinage, with no commutation mentioned. The default arrangement assumes availability of coinage for the average person. How typical was El Bovalar? Without similar archeological digs centered on sites separate from cities and significant

whose utility is understood as maintaining control of extra-urban territory, stand somewhere between city and countryside.

799 See Kulikowski, *Late Roman Spain*, 301 and references. See the brief report in Pliego, *La moneda visigoda*, 254. Idem, "El *tremis* de los últimos años," 23-25 reports the suggestion that El Bovalar may have been a monastic site, but this is only a hypothesis; in any case the nature of the finds (separate belt sacks hung on walls in separate dwellings in a settlement ruined by fire shortly after 711) implies no intentional burial and instead provides a meaningful hint of the monetary use of gold pieces in the particular setting – a small rural settlement – and chaotic political circumstances. Retamero, "La moneda," 209 asks whether the tremisses from this site or the one found in La Vega near Madrid, for example, were accumulated and used by farmers. It is precisely this possibility about which I elaborate here. If urban orientations have proven to be by far most predominant in finds, this has much to do with the lesser attention to rural archeology. Some recent rural finds of tremisses have been recorded: see Fernando Regueras Grande and Isabel Rodríguez Casanova, "Triente de Sisebuto y dinar de indicción en dos *villae* romanas leonesas," *Brigecio* 27 (2017), 11-24, at 13-16.

churches it is not known, but we have no reason to think El Bovalar was anything but ordinary, and there must have been countless villages like it where tremisses were not rare.[800]

Monetization, furthermore, is related to circulation, a necessity for availability and a symptom of coin usage. In Hispania, as elsewhere, movements of the two most coined metals, gold and bronze, largely occurred separately.[801] The production of gold was for the kingdom, principally for the state's acquisition of revenue and satisfaction of expenditures as this book has argued; from Leovigild's time, it may have circulated almost entirely within the borders, as far as find data indicates. So, it makes perfect sense that the focus when it comes to use should be fixed primarily within the Visigothic realm.[802] The archeological context of finds changed somewhat after the dawn of the regal series in the 570s, with less tomb finds or stringing together. Félix Retamero identifies the fiscal authority – demanding tributes and paying salaries, for example – as the growing force preventing the use of coin as mere token.[803] But prior to that time a small portion of gold from the

800 The specific contexts of El Bovalar and Puig Rom finds beckon us to consider uses apart from fiscal orientation or by upper classes alone: Carolina Doménech Belda, "Numismática y Arqueología Medieval: La moneda de excavación y sus aportaciones," in *XIII Congreso Nacional de Numismática*, v. 2 (Cádiz, 22-24 octubre de 2007), ed. Alicia Arévalo González (Madrid-Cádiz, 2009), 731-60. Pliego, "El *tremis* de los últimos años," 40, despite an overall viewpoint of limited circulation of gold pieces among non-elites, admits rural inhabitants would be quite likely to utilize gold currency for their periodic large transactions. She also considers that gold found at the site was possibly used to pay a small garrison for protection. It is worth remarking here that the imbedded notions of so-called proto-feudalization and the concomitant economic constriction as serfdom supposedly commenced already in the Visigothic period are further challenged by this site. See Kulikowski, *Late Roman Spain*, 301 & n. 55. Wickham, *Framing*, 99 is convinced a full feudal process had taken place by the last Visigothic decades, however I believe this to be an overstatement.

801 T. Marot, "La península ibérica en los siglos V-VI: consideraciones sobre provisión, circulación y usos monetarios," *Pyrenae* nos. 31-32 (2000-2001), 133-60 discusses the dual metallic movement patterns. Separate movement and production of low denomination coinage is also described in Pliego, "The Circulation of Copper Coins."

802 Metcalf, "Some Geographical Aspects," 313-15 and idem, "Many Mint-Places," 190 saw the rather even and rapid distribution of tremisses as indicators of a 'national coinage', although from a different causative perspective.

803 See Retamero, "La moneda," 197f and 207 for the two parts of this consideration. Yet, there are findings in tombs in the final period of the Visigothic kingdom: Pliego, "El *tremis* de los últimos años," 43. One major instance of continuing use of tremisses apparently as a marker of death or religious honorific would be an elusive seventh-century hoard, sometimes called 'La Capilla II' because it was found on the other side of the La Capilla hoard site, in which coins in great number were spread out below the entryway of the chapel. Burials of loved ones with monetary offerings, whether contemporary or centuries old, gold or bronze, have come to light in a number of areas: see Castro, "Absent Coinage."

kingdom spread well beyond Spain, and conversely foreign coinages made their way westward to the peninsula.[804] This opens the question of the sort of interactivity in which Visigothic gold was involved. The answer appears, in a number of ways, connected to trade, as discussed in Chapter Four. Not only the circulation patterns based on finds, but also minting itself both of gold and of bronze, are dominated by the southern half of the peninsula. Locations of Suevic and Visigothic gold mints in the sixth century have been attributed, perhaps with an exaggerated causal link but not without a strong association, to 'the wealth and Mediterranean contacts of Baetica'. Already from the fifth century a shift in international commerce from the northeast (Ebro R. region) to the south was under way.[805] Although known locations of gold coin deposits are rarely linked to the evidence of pottery production and distribution, a continued vitality of trans-Mediterranean and intra-peninsular trade traceable into the first half of the sixth century had to involve gold at times. But a vast reduction in imperial commerce with the West in the latter half of the century, together with simultaneous shifts elaborated below, had a role in the diminished use of gold internationally.[806]

804 Pliego, "El *tremis* de los últimos años," 40: Visigothic tremisses were probably not accepted by foreign merchants, and they were probably usually melted down (we do not see large numbers from contemporary Gaul or Byzantium, for instance, where occasionally great amounts were directed as sources indicate).

805 Fernando López Sánchez, "Coinage, Iconography and the Changing Political Geography of Fifth-century Hispania," in *Hispania in Late Antiquity: Current Perspectives*, ed. and trans. Kim Bowes and Michael Kulikowski (Leiden: Brill, 2005), 487-518, esp. 517f; also Pliego, "The Circulation of Copper Coins," 148-54. On the trade orientation of gold in the analyses of Metcalf and Barral see above, pp. 188-90. On the greater movement of Merovingian gold coin before c. 575 and more local circulation afterward see Naismith, "Gold Coinage and Its Use," 294f.

806 On diminishing imperial commerce with the West see Carlà, "The End of Roman Gold Coinage," 89. Paul Reynolds, "Hispania in the Late Roman Mediterranean: Ceramics and Trade," in *Hispania in Late Antiquity*, ed. Bowes and Kulikowski, 369-485 considers the continuation of many trade circuits within Iberia and with other regions (esp. Tunisia, southern Gaul and the East) even through the fifth century, but apart from some continuing strands of note in the sixth century a constriction becomes apparent. In NE Spain, Tarragona's commercial prosperity lingered. Eastern commercial engagement with Britain was the driver of some trading in NW Iberia. Though fifth- and sixth-century imported wares had some rural dimensions, for the most part commerce was highly concentrated in cities along the eastern coast. More recently, the picture of Iberia's commercial contacts with distant points of the sea region has been enlarged geographically and in certain sites chronologically: see Reynolds, "Material Culture." For a fuller understanding of long-distance commerce enmeshed with the monetary economy, these and other studies by the same author focused on ceramics should be complemented and compared with the scholarship cited on this page and in the following section. Vizcaíno, *La presencia bizantina*, 310, 317f brings together studies which convey a flourishing Spanish coastal trade through the sixth century, then into the seventh certainly deterioration but with modifications rather than collapse. In fact, based on the smaller scales of commercial production in Hispania

The circulation pattern that applied to bronze was different than that of gold. As mentioned in the section on the minting of bronze coins in Chapter Two, bronzes traveled among different states in great numbers throughout much of late antiquity, in some regions far more so than gold. In fact, one of the most enlightening features of archeological research in recent decades on the late Roman and Visigothic eras has been its building up of insights on the circulation of foreign base-metal coinage in Spain. On a larger scale, a picture is developing of a vibrant product and money exchange in many parts and cycles in the Mediterranean, in which Spain played but one, no means minimal, part. To achieve a better understanding of Visigothic bronze currency after it emerges from the mints, we must therefore appreciate it on both a domestic level and in the broader context of the post-Roman world. Today, it is possible to glimpse Spain within the larger dynamics of high- and low-denomination circulation. There was more commercial and monetary interaction than is commonly known.

C Bronze Currency in Spain and its Mediterranean Context

In the early centuries after Roman authority in the West transferred to barbarian monarchies and each part developed its own administrative forms, we find not only echoes of the old fiscal and minting systems but at the same time cross-regional interaction.[807] The Vandal kingdom of North Africa did not itself strike gold, yet the usage of gold is attested by the ample circulation of gold from Italy and Constantinople. It is thought that trade and raid were the sources of gold intake.[808] Need for gold in the Ostrogothic and Merovingian kingdoms (and the Burgundian kingdom while it lasted) persisted for a time, until, as we have seen, altered fiscal circumstances brought different currency arrangements.

Taking the whole study of Mediterranean-wide circulation into consideration is a requirement for a balanced understanding of the early medieval

in so far as currently ascertained, the coastal cities appear to have relied heavily on imports from the Mediterranean. Both written and material evidence demonstrates ample exchange in both directions between Iberia and N. Africa, under the Vandals as well as – in this indirect way – the eastern Romans (298-306, 310). Within Byzantine Spain there is abundant evidence of exchange with other littoral urban points.

807 On the interregional circulation of gold coinage see the references to works by Metcalf in n. 774 above and by Cécile Morrisson in nn. 820 and 824 below; see also Carlà, "The End of Roman Gold Coinage."

808 See Naismith, "Gold Coinage and Its Use," 286 and references in n. 78.

economy, however much a trend toward more local economic levels and even self-sufficiency of estates and hamlets was a reality. At a point when pre-modern Mediterranean studies has fruitfully taken on the perspective of numerous micro-economies within the broader connecting maritime space, and of transregional interaction cutting across frontiers, the study of money circulation and use in the post-Roman western regions has been given less attention.[809] Coin-making and currency flows in the peninsula have been at the periphery of scholarship on early medieval Iberia, though the tide is slowly turning.

There is now abundant evidence of the continued Mediterranean-wide circulation of fourth-century bronze money as production of this metal declined in the following century. The decreased availability had a heavier impact on the West where minting had been more curbed than in the East, and especially in Spain where no imperial mints had been active since the first century.[810] Archeological evidence has continued to demonstrate monetary adaptations in the peninsula in the form of re-use, imitation bronzes on the eastern Iberian seaboard and even in the interior, an influx of foreign emissions (late Roman, Vandal, and Byzantine) of the fifth and sixth centuries into Spain, partitions of external currency, and local production in Spain itself primarily in the south.[811] The bronzes of various classes were of very small value but indispensable for the daily,

809 For antiquity, see Peregrine Horden and Nicholas Purcell, *The Corrupting Sea: A Study of Mediterranean History* (Oxford and Malden, MA: Blackwell, 2000), to which can be added a growing number of works on the later medieval period. See the recent discussion of the pre-modern Mediterreanean frame and its evolution in Brian A. Catlos and Sharon Kinoshita, eds., *Can We Talk Mediterreanean?: Conversations on an Emerging Field in Medieval and Early Modern Studies* (Cham, Switzerland: Palgrave Macmillan, 2017). Unfortunately, Horden and Purcell describe numismatic sources as "ambiguous" and of "occasional use" only (160). The Mediterranean's numerous micro-regions conjoined in the sea's "ready connectivity," as described by Richard Hodges, review of Horden and Purcell, *Corrupting Sea* in *The International History Review* 23.2 (2001), 377-79 at 378. Michael McCormick, *The Origins of the European Economy* (Cambridge: Cambridge University Press, 2001) served to stimulate a fresh analysis of the data on medium- and long-distance activity of the early Middle Ages, though primarily in the Carolingian era and with less attention to Iberia than other parts, and also emphasizing exchanges by elites.

810 Marot, "La península ibérica," 134 et passim.

811 Even blank tokens occasionally circulated with other monies. Imitation bronzes, referred to sometimes as coins of necessity, endured into the sixth century in a number of key cities such as Barcino, Tarraco, Iluro and the Balearic Islands. Marot, "La península ibérica," 135ff. Weight reduction of these imitation bronzes occurred frequently, just as was true of the imperial money on which they were based. Fragmentation of coins produced what today we call smaller change: see ibid., 137f. Most of the Byzantine coinage was from Carthage, though some came from the workshop at Constantinople (139) and after the mid-sixth century at Carthago Spartaria (146).

mundane level of transaction and indicators of a monetary economy. They functioned likewise as a "complement to other economic activities."[812] Numerous discoveries of weights (*exagia*) in Spain and the Balearic Islands are further testimony of commercial and monetary activity.[813] In fact, archeological research is demonstrating across a wide span of time and a wide array of deposit sites the habitual use of coins. This is corroborated by urban as well as semi-urban and rural finds and, for example, the continued use of older AE2 coins in fifth- and sixth-century northern Africa as well as the re-use and often countermarking of large pieces (sestercii, equivalent of 42 numii) in the Vandal kingdom and in Byzantium in the first half of the seventh century and perhaps earlier.[814] Such was the need for the lowest-level currency in the sixth century, it has long been noted that, apart from higher value coins in circulation, the territories of the old Roman world had "a separate *nummus* economy operating," and those involved in regular money exchange were loath to give up their *nummi*.[815]

Iberia under the Visigothic domain by no means stood in isolation from the economic activity of the Mediterranean world. The eastern coast enjoyed direct trading with Carthage in the late Vandal through early Byzantine period, especially in passage between Alicante-Carthage, and what is deemed derivative commerce of fine wares and amphorae of the eastern Mediterranean extended by sea into Portugal and western Britain. Visigothic copper-alloy emissions in the south of Spain is only one indication of a need for this economic medium and signals a greater economic sophistication than might otherwise be understood.[816] Foreign currency, by far mostly bronze rather than gold, came to Spain's littoral not by imperial policy, but through normal, private commercial life that had linked distant shores of

812 Mora "Old and New Coins," 140.

813 A point not always appreciated, and in fact even denied in the past. On the weights see Mora, "Old and New Coins," 139f; Marot, "La península ibérica," 150.

814 Marot, "La península ibérica," 149-52.

815 Pliego, "The Circulation of Copper Coins," 146; see the references to recent works by S. Moorhead and several others before him.

816 Hillgarth, *The Visigoths in History and Legend*, 12 n. 30. Spain's integration within the Mediterranean in late antiquity is emphasized from different directions throughout much of Bowes and Kulikowski, eds., *Hispania*. A contemporary example of the economic significance of copper-based currency across the sea can be seen in Florin Curta, "Byzantium in Dark-Age Greece (the numismatic evidence in its Balkan context)," *Byzantine and Modern Greek Studies* 29 (2005), pp. 113-146, at 113: "Instead of signalising decline, low-denomination coins, especially from Athens, may point to local markets of low-value commodities, such as food, as well as to the permanent presence of the fleet."

the middle sea for hundreds of years.[817] Sixth-century bronzes from abroad still circulated decades later.[818] There does not seem to have been any effort to abolish the small denomination currency coming from below the royal administration. The state ignored this base currency manufacture, perhaps acknowledging its usefulness.[819] North African influence on Spain's bronze coinage, though hard to pinpoint, appears to have been more direct than that of Byzantium. The trading network of the Vandal North Africa is what most singularly contributed to the long-distance diffusion of bronzes reaching all the way to and around Spain into the Atlantic coast of Iberia. While the crucial role central northern Africa played in the commercial-monetary network would be taken over by the Byzantine authority after the conquest of the 530s, the eastern empire apparently did not originally provide the impetus.[820] Visigothic minting of gold, silver, and copper-based coinage in the sixth century permits the conjecture that, in a combined sense at least, the Spanish kingdom was attempting to keep a currency parallel with other regimes of the central Mediterranean to facilitate economic integration.[821]

Coinciding with Vandal North Africa's increased commercial interaction, the source of most of its coinage starting in the mid-fifth century swung from Rome and Italy to eastern imperial mints. Yet, although eastern bronze units took up a larger share, their volume had dropped, which led to the

817 "Beyond political frontiers again, [bronze] flowed by land and sea routes [...]," an observation which applies to late Roman, locally produced Hispanic, and Byzantine coins; Mora, "Old and New Coins," 149. See also Marot, "La península ibérica," 138f; there is an insufficient number of gold finds to tell if foreign gold circulated widely in Spain, while in Gaul it was re-minted. The Vandal bronzes still circulating in Spain as well as the Peloponnese in the decades after the Byzantine conquest of North Africa are attributed to trade primarily because of their association with ceramics. See Cécile Morrisson, "Regio dives in Omnibus bonis ornata. The African Economy from the Vandals to the Arab Conquest in the Light of Coin Evidence," in *North Africa under Byzantium and Early Islam*, ed S. T. Stevens and J. P. Conant (Washington, DC: Dumbarton Oaks Publications, 2016), 173-198 at 196.

818 Castro, "Los hallazgos numismáticos," 135.

819 Marot, "La península ibérica," 137. Pliego, "The Circulation of Copper Coins," 142-44.

820 Cécile Morrisson, "Tra Vandali e Bizantini: la prosperità dell'Africa (V-VII secolo) attraverso le fonti e la documentazione monetale," *Incontri de filología classica* 10 (2010-2011), 145-69; idem, "L'atelier de Carthage et la diffusion de la monnaie frappée dans l'Afrique vandale et byzantine (439-695)," *Antiquité Tardive* 11 (2003), 65-84. Cf. Pliego, "The Circulation of Copper Coins," 143, 146, 154. Vizcaíno, *La presencia bizantina*, 699f: Byzantine currency mostly from Carthage, and only secondarily from Constantinople.

821 See Hendy, *Studies*, 399 for a snapshot of the multiform minting in the Byzantine prefectures of Italy and Africa, founded on Ostrogothic and Vandal practice (and in turn built on Roman precedence). In the immediate term, these Byzantine mints can be said to have catered to the West in their tri-fold denominations, apparent from the table of unit-mint-products under Justinian in ibid., 401.

appearance of anonymous bronzes later in the century.[822] Other 'makeshift' bronze pieces likewise signify a shortage. The emerging smaller denominations foreshadowed the Anastasian reform. The Vandal region ended up with more bronze denominations than the empire, implying the minting authorities made a specific effort to supply the needs of small exchange, presumably those required in local trade above all.[823] Byzantine North Africa followed the monetary model instigated under the Vandals[824] and served as the vehicle for continued dispersion of the previous currency. Archeological work reveals most of the Vandal bronze coinage that came into Iberia arrived primarily in the first half of the sixth century.[825] The association of Vandal bronze coin finds with ceramics in Spain points to trade relations.[826] Under imperial control, a more flourishing ceramics exchange across the sea developed, albeit the westward flow was now to less integrated markets.[827] The Byzantine administration of North Africa undertook plentiful silver minting, while the bronze values were brought lower than in the eastern Mediterranean mints – but were still larger than Spanish bronzes.[828] This and occasional increases in output of solidi belie the traditional outlook of a full downward economic trend in central northern Africa after 550.[829]

Regional differentiation with regard to minting of bronze currency was already cited in Chapter Two. Coin use was bound to be affected by this, but also by the variety in topography.[830] Bronze coins even of very small size and value clearly circulated widely in the late ancient Mediterranean basin. The explanation for this is their capacity to be easily used across many parts and systems. This proved especially useful in commercial locales associated most often with coasts or riverine access

822 Morrisson, "Tra Vandali e Bizantini," 177f.

823 Ibid., 178f.

824 Ibid., 181ff. In a reversal for how minting in the post-Roman period is normally conceived, it is clear that the Byzantine monetary authorities copied barbarian practice in Italy, central North Africa, and to some extent southeastern Spain after the takeover of these territories in the sixth century, by producing small bronzes even as these emissions were being phased out in the eastern half of the empire. Huffstot, "Reverse Designs," 13f; cf. C. Morrisson and J. P. Sodini, "The Sixth-century Economy," in *The Economic History of Byzantium: From the Seventh through the Fifteenth Century*, ed. E. Laiou (Washington DC: Dumbarton Oaks Publications, 2003), 171-220 at 212, 215.

825 Morrisson, "Tra Vandali e Bizantini," 180.

826 Ibid., 196.

827 Ibid., 192.

828 Ibid., 182.

829 Ibid., 192.

830 Hendy, *Studies*, 13.

where *nummi* tended to originate as well as to be deposited.[831] It may be obvious enough that cities on the eastern Iberian coast might be linked to Mediterranean trading networks, and indeed the archeological evidence including foreign and domestic bronzes circulating astride bears this out. But it is significant that a wealth of evidence connects Seville, distant from the coast but also linked by the river Guadalquivir (ancient Baetis), to transregional exchange.[832] And in this setting, the city has yielded what is at this time the greatest number of local bronze coins, adding to the substantial availability of tremisses turned out at the local royal mint alone. Economic connectivity including well in the interior is in evidence for cities such as Toletum and Reccopolis and Eio-El Tolmo de Minateda (Albacete province), for instance. In the last mentioned, a recovered bronze coin has been most convincingly attributed to Byzantine Carthago Spartaria (modern Cartagena).[833] On the sea itself, while Menorca was never within the kingdom's possession, a mélange of Visigothic, Byzantine, Vandal, and older Roman coins found there is one key sign of the wide commercial importance of the Balearic Islands well before and after the fall of imperial authority in Rome.[834]

In the early sixth century, the Byzantine supply of bronze currency increased, and mints producing them grew from two to six. Most were in the east, but one of these mints was Carthage, in the middle of the African coast, a city from which earthenware and amphorae and other goods made

831 Pliego, "The Circulation of Copper Coins," 147, citing S. Moorhead, "The Coinage of the Later Roman Empire, 364-498," in *The Oxford Handbook of Greek and Roman Coinage*, ed. W. E. Metcalf (Oxford: Oxford University Press, 2014), 601-32, at 621.

832 See Pliego, "The Circulation of Copper Coins," 149. Ceramics from northern Africa, Italy, and the eastern Mediterranean, in addition to citations of customs collection, commercial officials (*telonarii*), and other literary documentation, indicates the city's wide commercial links; so also does coinage from the east. Evidence of similar extended trading links applies likewise to nearby Aljarafe, the setting of numerous finds and judiciously highlighted by Pliego (ibid., 151).

833 Pliego, "The Circulation of Copper Coins," 143f; Crusafont, *El sistema*, 21-22. Treatment of the ceramics including from North Africa may be found in Sonia Gutiérrez Lloret and Julia Sarabia Bautista, "The Episcopal Complex of Eio-El Tolmo de Minateda (Hellín, Albacete, Spain). Architecture and Spatial Organization, 7th to 8th Centuries AD," *Hortus Artium Medievalium* 19 (2013), pp. 267-300. See also Lauro Olmo Enciso and Manuel Castro Priego, "La época visigoda a través de la arqueología," in *711: Arqueología e historia entre dos mundos* [Exhibition catalog: Museo Arqueológico Regional, Alcalá de Henares, Madrid, 16 December 2011 to 1 April 2012] (Museo Arqueológico Regional de la Comunidad de Madrid, 2011), 48-77. M. Castro Priego, "Circulación monetaria de los siglos VII-VIII en la Península Ibérica: Un modelo en crisis," *Zona arqueológica*, No. 15, 2011 (Dedicated issue title: 711: Arqueología e historia entre dos mundos), v. 2, 225-44, (Museo Arqueológico Regional de la Comunidad de Madrid, 2011).

834 Pliego, "The Circulation of Copper Coins," 153.

their way along the eastern and southern coast of Iberia.[835] Included in Crusafont's study were a couple of specimens of unique type, bearing a cross on obverse and a delta on the reverse, which he attributed to Cartagena under Byzantine control. Today, some two dozen published examples of this same type are known, with a significant number still to be published. Mostly of local circulation, they have, nevertheless, been uncovered in Menorca, Albacete (at Tolmo de Minateda), and possibly Clermont-Ferrand.[836]

An increasing number of *nummi* and occasionally larger bronze coins of Carthage, from early in the Justinian era to after the turn of the century (Phocas, r. 602-610), have been identified in Málaga and Benalúa (Alicante) from either new discoveries or reexamination of previously known coins. Imitations are also coming to light, as is the very large portion of fourth-century currency circulating amongst Byzantine issues in a number of towns between today's Gibraltar and Cartagena, and separately, late Roman pieces.[837] Circulation of local 'Visigothic' together with Byzantine small bronzes down the Guadalquivir from Seville can be gleaned from discovered specimens in a handful of towns outside the city recently, with more finds currently under investigation.[838] Seville itself has revealed less Byzantine and more older low-value coinage than Málaga, for instance, which is to be expected not only considering the latter's geographical accessibility to seaborne trade but also its possession by Byzantine authorities for decades. Málaga may have been the source of the bronze attributed to the Byzantines in Spain.[839] Visigothic bronzes have been identified in Cartagena. Outside that city there is not much in the way of Byzantine bronzes, which is somewhat curious given the significance of its port and the Byzantine zone of occupation.[840] One might also find surprising

835 See Marot, "La península ibérica."

836 Pliego, "The Circulation of Copper Coins," 134. Eio (El Tolmo de Minateda) was probably a new episcopal see founded to fill a need in the area due to the Byzantine occupation: cf. Pliego, "El *tremis* de los últimos años," 22.

837 Mora, "Old and New Coins," 145f; in several cases over ¾ of the finds. See also idem, "The Circulation of Bronze Currency in Málaga During the Sixth Century AD: New Findings," *Numismatic Chronicle* 169 (2009), 424-30. Vizcaíno, *La presencia bizantina*, 690-94, 705-07 furnishes a solid working inventory of Byzantine coins in Hispania, though the list is necessarily provisional as discussed in this chapter on coinage, 687-725.

838 Mora, "Old and New Coins," 148.

839 The finds: Mora, "Old and New Coins," 148. On Malaca's possible mint for the base-metal currency see Bartlett et al., "Byzantine Gold Coinage of *Spania*, 377." Cartagena as the lone minting site for Byzantine gold is nearly certain. Vizcaíno, *La presencia bizantina*, 714-16 rehearses the debate on this mint but is himself highly skeptical, I believe unnecessarily so.

840 Pliego, "The Circulation of Copper Coins," 133, refs. in n. 30; cf. Mora, "Old and New Coins," 143 who appears not to accept these. Murcia, 40 miles inland, has yielded twenty-three coins to date.

the lack of discoveries of bronze coinage from beyond c. 450 in numerous southern cities of importance such as Cordoba, Eliberri, Asidona, and others.[841] Further work may serve to provide some clarity, but for now questions remain.

Intake of foreign currency spiked in the latter half of the sixth century, coinciding with the strongest period of Byzantine occupation, but so too 'Visigothic bronzes' may have begun at that time,[842] both signs of a large need for small currency. Valencia's particular archeological yield from the latter half of the sixth century, not only of small currency but of ceramics, demonstrates that proximity to the Byzantine zone in wartime did not result in isolation from the important lower-Iberian and northern African corridor, but rather that it was quite engaged in this commercial activity,[843] as seen in the case of Seville. Cities further north up the coastline display similar relations. The flow of bronzes from the eastern Empire slowed after Justinian's rule and all but ceased shortly after the turn of the seventh century. The near end of the Byzantine hold on the southeast may be inferred as the reason.[844]

Further gain comes from the advancing knowledge of bronze coinages in early medieval Spain as regional patterns of circulation are becoming clearer.[845] Foreign coin finds of any denomination and archeological contexts are much more scarce in the center and north of Iberia. Nevertheless, numerous finds across this large area from over a half-century straddling Justinian's reconquest demonstrate a prevalence of Byzantine large bronzes (folles) or gold. Together with the several weights for commercial and monetary use discovered in the same large expanse, there is sufficient evidence to posit trading routes reaching far beyond the coast.[846] If this is so and

841 Mora, "Old and New Coins," 144; he offers archeological reasons why this may be due to modern circumstances and the situation could change.

842 Marot, "La península ibérica," 139; see Pliego, "The Circulation of Copper Coins." See Doménech, "Numismática y arqueología," 738-40 on 'Visigothic' coppers as local production within the kingdom, more or less in sync metrologically with Byzantine issues and often found alongside these as well as older Vandal money.

843 Marot, "La península ibérica," 142.

844 Ibid., 143f. Cf. Vizcaíno, *La presencia bizantina*, 696f, and 718-22 (discussing the circulation).

845 Mora, "Old and New Coins," 140; Pliego, "The Circulation of Copper Coins," stresses the usually local circulation of Visigothic low-value coins but also touches on the flow of Byzantine copper-alloys into Seville, for example. A. Martín Esquivel, "La moneda en los siglos IV-VIII d.C.: tipos, función y usos monetarios," in *Fortificaciones, poblados y pizarras: La Raya en los inicios del Medievo* (Salamanca: Ayuntamiento de Ciudad Rodrigo, 2018), 263-75 emphasizes the continuing use of copper currency but also references Visigothic tremisses discovered in various sorts of presumed socio-economic contexts.

846 Marot, "La península ibérica," 152. Another datum from the archeology of the center-north is the absence of Vandalic currency.

small bronzes do not turn up with frequency, a somewhat different level of monetary exchange may have predominated in the interior. Bartolomé Mora's observation of the absence of Visigothic bronzes in the southern tip and southwestern coast of the peninsula addresses a similar departure from the situation on the eastern coast.[847]

Several lessons can be drawn from the amassed discoveries of foreign bronzes, re-used older imperials, and Spanish-made *nummi*. Monetary need and exercise of an extensive monetary economy is undeniable. By the same token, the old notion of commercial isolation of Visigothic and Byzantine territories must be put to rest. Although wartime circumstances and a lack of documentation might seem to support the case for a rupture, there exists too much evidence of the movement of Byzantine coinage, weights, and ceramics through the sixth century – not to mention Vandalic currency in coastal urban sites in the early decades – for this model to be sustained.[848] Barcinona, Tarraco, Valencia, and cities southward along the coast to Gibraltar, shared much the same sort of Mediterranean trading activity. Great similarities with other Mediterranean zones as far as Carthage, Antioch or other Levantine cities can be seen in the distribution and apparent use of coined money.[849]

Specific archeological contexts are only known for some of the coinage, an inhibiting factor in drawing firm conclusions as to chronology or burial or usage. But more of this specific information continues to emerge. Perhaps the richest find area, La Punta de l'Illa Cullera (Valencia), affords a rare combination of material data which permits specialists to think in terms of a link between vessels, market, and bronze currency, and furthermore connects the local religious sights with this activity. In fact, the association of consumption and purchase by religious centers by way of currency, trade vessels or ware, and sometimes a port or exchange area is becoming possible elsewhere as well.[850] Episcopal contexts of finds of mid-seventh century tremisses from the central-western area have been elaborated.[851]

At a fundamental level, the small bronze currency, easily neglected for its unremarkable physical characteristics and worth, takes its position in the debate over whether the economy of the imperial economy of late ancient Rome and Byzantium was in essence a product of the state functions or whether it was more fully derived from private commercial initiative. Cécile

847 Mora, "Old and New Coins," 144f.

848 Marot, "La península ibérica," 153.

849 Ibid.

850 Mora, "Old and New Coins," 142.

851 See Castro, "Absent Coinage," 30, 32.

Morrisson addresses this especially by way of the monetary evidence, which demonstrates a dual level with respect to gold and bronze. Vandal authorities filled the needed stock of bronzes with local mintings.[852] Byzantine, Italian, and Spanish mints did much the same at diverse levels of government, apparently directing production largely for quotidian exchange. Gold had a distinct rationale in terms of its minting and different patterns of circulation in accord with its different purpose and value. The case has been made repeatedly that Vandal Africa was a monetized province,[853] while this argument has long been made concerning the contemporary Byzantine Empire.[854] There is growing data on finds of gold and bronze in Spain to suggest Visigothic Spain was monetized in some measure. It bears observing that Iberia was in fact largely re-monetized under the Visigothic regime shortly after its centering in Spain shortly after 507, since the influx of Roman gold and to some degree copper-alloy coinage had stalled after the early fifth century.

Contrary to antiquated notions of an almost complete collapse of the integrated and active economy sustained by Rome, it is correct to assert "the continuing openness of Mediterranean society in the sixth century."[855] Coastal exchange in which currency had a considerable role flourished. Discoveries of Merovingian and Byzantine gold coins and other foreign manufactures at Reccopolis testify to the reach well beyond the coast of goods coming from afar. Findings at Seville and Eio do likewise, but in association with copper alloys. New finds of Byzantine bronze pieces in Portugal, including on the Atlantic coast, are expanding the known reach of circulation from the Justinian era, while in addition fine ware and amphorae discoveries add to the sense of a still active Mediterranean-Atlantic trade.[856] Traffic in goods and currency is much reduced the further one looks into the seventh century. A revival underscoring specific aspects of a general post-Roman continuity would take place with the westward advance of the Islamic conquests.

852 Morrisson, "Tra Vandali e Bizantini," 149.

853 Morrisson, "Tra Vandali e Bizantini," with numerous references including to the author's own works over decades; on 174 the specific label is employed.

854 Banaji, *Exploring the Economy*, esp. 52-66, 84-88, extending the view to the very late Roman empire as a whole, counter to the Weberian model of the era's decline and contraction.

855 Collins, *Visigothic Spain*, 50f. Marot, "La península ibérica" confirms this view, as do Reynolds, "Hispania"; Pliego, "The Circulation of Copper Coins"; and Morrisson and Sodini, "The Sixth-century Economy," among others. In fact, the state of archeology today has expanded the view of inter-Mediterranean commerce which, though altered from previous centuries, still incorporated the Peninsula: Reynolds, "Material Culture."

856 Reccopolis: see Castro, "Los hallazgos numismáticos." Recent finds: Mora, "Old and New Coins," 140.

Conclusion

It is hoped that the reader of these chapters will appreciate that it is imperative to connect the historiography of the Visigothic kingdom's lengthy rule with its coinage. Failing to do so will leave a very incomplete picture. This book began with consideration of the problem of the perspective of continuity or discontinuity of the Visigothic monetary system set in the framework of the very late ancient Mediterranean world. Treatment of the many facets involved in the currency point to an abundance of both traits. Minting as well as use of currency, of different denominations as has been explained in detail, underwent a process of frequent change. No less than the Roman empire from which it took inspiration, the Visigothic kingdom cannot be seen as static across its three-hundred-year existence. Study of the vicissitudes of the currency afford a deeper understanding of structures and life in the kingdom.

As seen in taxation, agricultural practices, law, administration, and other matters there was more continuity than fracture, but adaptations occurred that eventually bear less resemblance to the Roman foundation.[857] In the regal gold currency, the early adaptation is evident in the royal image and inscription, reduced real fineness and weight standards, the plethora of mints and their regional-local association with tax payments and in numerous instances with apparent military expenditures. Later adaptation is visible in the high level of adulteration of the tremisses and the further stylistic distinctions of the coins. Yet, in the mid-seventh century reforms, and even in the imagery employed in the final decades of Visigothic Iberia, the imperial model was of key importance.

The establishment of a state derived much from Roman foundations, but government and culture took on their own character, and these combined

857 As a single example in recent literature of the force of tradition versus innovation, Fernández, *Aristocrats and Statehood*, 227 rehearses the essential continuity exemplified throughout his book, but on 204 the same author writes of "a minimum level of continuity between the post-Roman and the Visigothic periods in terms of tax collection administration."

Kurt, A., *Minting, State, and Economy in the Visigothic Kingdom: From Settlement in Aquitaine through the First Decade of the Muslim Conquest of Spain.*
Taylor & Francis Group, 2020
DOI 10.5117/9789462981645_CONCL

forces[858] were at work in shaping the Visigothic solidus and tremissis and the system that produced them. The first chapter of this book reviewed the earliest Visigothic coinage in Roman Gaul. From the perspective of the later chapters one can see a basic continuity in the development of the minting system as the Visigoths began to center their kingdom on the Iberian peninsula. The currency continued to be based essentially on gold even when the striking of solidi ceased and bronze or copper coinage appeared in mostly southern locales. The permanence of the tremissis and the use of a single numismatic type at any one time until the mid-seventh century[859] offer a little light on the make-up of pre-regal coinage, which still defies complete identification and a precise knowledge of chronology and geography. In gaining a better picture of the nature, the purpose, and the extent of royal control of the regal coinage it is hoped that new pieces can be fitted into the puzzle of pre-regal coinage.

Chapter Two looked carefully at the transition from a coinage struck under Visigothic royal authority for well over a century but veiled under imperial guise to the 'unmasking' that occurred under Leovigild. The chronology of that major evolution in Visigothic minting is significant not only for specific numismatic problems but also for the very nature of Leovigild's character, his rule, and a better understanding of the rebellion of his son Hermenegild. In this context, the increased manipulation of values and standards of the tremissis unfolded in parallel with an appreciation of the propagandizing use of minting. An apparent increase in gold mints and a strong association of minting with military operations suggest the beginning of a trend that was to last during the remainder of the Byzantine presence in Spain and beyond. A short-lived silver and much more abundant if sporadic bronze currency also came under examination. It is inconclusive at this point whether the bronze production began during or, as seems more likely, before Leovigild's reign, but apart from the few named specimens of the period known as of now, the vast majority were non-regal and should be considered city- or Church-sponsored emissions. The intention of the local leaders was to provide a low-value currency otherwise lacking except for the inflow of copper alloys from elsewhere in the Mediterranean region.

Scientific testing of coins and a closer examination of style groups, discussed in the first two chapters, allows us to see more clearly a trend

858 See Hillgarth, *The Visigoths*, 16.

859 With the exception of a few of Leovigild's transitional issues, which in any case were moving toward unification of type.

in diminished coin values occurring in the decades immediately preceding the regal series, just as would be manifest in the early seventh century. It is to be expected that minting would be affected by the political and military turmoil in Spain from 548-568, evident in monarchical assassination, a successful revolt in Córdoba that cost Agila the royal treasure and many men, civil war and the resultant entrée of imperial troops that quickly became occupation and demanded a new and prolonged state of war. Effects on currency-making were poorer coins with respect to their weight and fineness but also in terms of consistency, an indication of feeble regulation of the work of some minters. That could entail forgery (contemporary forgeries have been detected). Leovigild's early gold coinage was purposely adulterated in some places. Ultimately, after numerous stages he was able to create a uniform gold currency for his unified kingdom, coinciding with the establishment of centralized control, regained in some places and created anew in others.

Chapter Three looked closely at the arrangement of regal minting and its modifications over time. We saw that not all mints operated in the same way, and this variation forces us to consider what the full nature of the monetary system really was. The reasons behind the large number of regal mint sites have been a central question concerning Visigothic monetary history. Chapter Four has attempted to clarify the answer. It is in this light that the close examination of the placement and characteristics of the mints themselves bears most fruit. We have proposed that García Moreno was correct to attribute the primary mints to fiscal operations in Visigothic Spain. Taxation in the kingdom is an established fact despite its apparent waning over time, even if it is known only in rough outline and it has received little attention until the last twenty-five or so years. Literary evidence, particularly a tax document from Barcelona and information confirming the wealth and importance of Toleto, Emerita, and a few other cities, suggest a fitting match between leading metropolises and greater coin output. Comparatively high standards at the mints of these cities, above all at Toleto, can now more confidently be claimed as a corroboration of the central position of these mints. As the regular destination-points of tax money, the leading cities were able to sustain a primary role in minting.

Dispersed minting over a large network of sites, however, is how the Visigothic regime chose to create coined money. The vast majority of mints were secondary, if one keeps in view the whole course of the minting network throughout the regal period. The military motive that some have ascribed to much of the peripheral minting can now be reaffirmed for many of the secondary sites,[860] though we have suggested that other factors may have entered into the decision to carry out temporary minting. In addition to financing the frequent engagements of troops, taxation and re-minting probably figured in the south as important elements in the decision about where to produce coinage, in what quantity, and for how long. The low numbers of finds in the north offer less evidence of additional possible factors there beyond the needs of the soldiers. Propaganda, a royal message of reinforcement to local populations, was joined to the production of species.

It is the special circumstances of war, the evidence of which correlates so neatly with temporary and debased minting, which explain the curious choice of minting places which has exercised the minds of historians and numismatists for many generations. Some sites were bishoprics while others were not;[861] some were close to other workshops operating more or less contemporaneously while others were not; some were in cities where one would expect them to have been while others appear in quite obscure locations. Trade, administration, and extracting gold provide no clear solution to the irregular pattern. The occurrence of 'victory legends' at certain moments does not prove a military motivation for striking tremisses, but in perhaps every instance it does show the concurrence of minting and the work of the Gothic army. The combined evidence can leave little doubt of this specialized purpose behind the peripheral workshops. There can also be little question of the ultimate royal authority behind minting, as emphasized in Chapter Five as the obvious conclusion from a host of data, though again no specific record of minting on any level is extant. A quite different arrangement of minting obtained under the Islamic state established from 711, but as explained in Chapter Six the same essential state purposes as seen widely

860 The claim was already articulated in García Moreno, "Cecas visigodas," and Barceló, "La cuestión del 'Limes Hispanus'." Also Spaulding, "Mint-cities," however with excesses which can no longer be accepted; the quite general conclusions of Crusafont i Sabater, *El sistema* and idem, "Monete suebe e visigote" run along the same lines.

861 For example, neither Barbi, nor Reccopolis were bishoprics, but both had mints; Pax Julia and Ossonoba were bishoprics yet the present corpus gives no evidence that they produced coins. An inference about the many secondary sites in Grierson and Blackburn, *Medieval European Coinage*, v. 1, 53, is intriguing, if not very satisfying: "The surprisingly large number [of mints] in obscure or even unidentified places is a consequence of subsequent political changes in the Peninsula, for many ancient towns and villages disappeared in the aftermath of the Arab occupation or during the resettlement that followed the Reconquista from the eleventh century onwards." Apart from the weak premise for supposing the significance of towns in the northern mountains, the brevity of most of the minting has to be taken into account. Significantly, Grierson lent almost no attention to the military hypothesis in his works.

in the late antique world were still operative. The transition period saw some characteristics influenced by the Visigothic scene.

Mediterranean contexts have been seen in a number of ways in this study, from the very framework of Roman administration and minting from which post-imperial states developed their own characteristics to the economic interactivity examined in the final chapter. By the same token, a heightened sense of early medieval Spain's regionalism has been one main feature of scholarship in the last forty years. Close study of its coined money adds new hues to this picture. Alongside the refined level of argument for different tax arrangements,[862] it should also be clear from the present work that there were different monetary arrangements, for gold as well as for locally-produced bronze, whether official or unofficial. The exact correspondence of the many elements involved in the currency system is not so clear. Military interventions and perhaps post-campaign arrangements, trade patterns, the needs of royal cities, in addition to aristocratic and demographic variables, all brought specific factors into the making of currency, but above all this at least as far is gold is concerned was an underlying unity. Minting of gold was the king's affair, a prerogative based on its fiscal functionality. But the life of a coin beyond that would entail more or less interchange. How and to what extent money was utilized is only hinted at by discovery patterns. From the ensemble of evidence including written reference to solidi and tremisses and occasional archeological details we can make out a partial monetization of society. Bronze currency played a much larger role in society across large areas especially in the south of the kingdom, where monetary circumstances and contacts with Mediterranean regions display greater commonality than has been widely supposed. Visigothic Spain's supposed seclusion is no longer viable.

Considerable progress in Visigothic coin study especially since the turn of the century has opened new paths of investigation. Much can still be done to test the theory of military minting. Better knowledge of where peripheral mints were located will provide a firmer background from which to judge whether mint sites correspond closely with the areas where skirmishes are thought to have taken place. Of course, as the locations of battles or the territories of peoples fighting the Goths is made more precise, geographical relationships should be easier to confirm or deny. Further examining known sites in the context of major Roman roads would be useful in order to see if there is a regular correspondence between mints and roads. It is likely that the archeological record, formerly often handled by separate regional

862 See Valverde Castro, "La ideología fiscal."

bodies in Spain, could be profitably investigated for information which may relate to military minting. Finds of bronzes in context may yet broaden the picture of that parallel currency and its use. As more analyses of the purity of the tremisses are undertaken we will know more about the activity of individual mints and whole regions, such as Gallaecia. Various analytical results included in this study expose the instability of observed standards in certain areas under the pressure of what looks by all accounts to be urgent spikes in the desire to produce gold coin within a setting of limited raw material. Chronologies within some reigns can be explored further with the help of hoards as well as fineness studies. With painstaking work, it is, in theory, possible to assign coins as early or late in a particular reign, and a certain type or style before another. This could be extremely useful knowledge if it can be related to the years given in the histories to specific campaigns. Chronologies would also be helpful in tracing transitions, for example, in the wake of reforms.[863] The study of engraving styles is tedious and not ensured of establishing conclusions which will meet with acceptance. It is our hope that the research in this area described in the third chapter shows the rich possibilities of demonstrating the close connection between many mints.

These are some of the areas ripe for future research. Others include fifth- and sixth-century coin attributions, the search for more parallels in other barbarian states, which could prove to have been the inspiration for particular issues or changes in weight and fineness, evidence on the Hermenegild-Leovigild interchange, or metallurgical testing which might shed more light on regional sources of gold. As more low-denomination coinage from various production centers are found in Iberia, and more archeological evidence is brought to light on commerce, a greater sense of the economic connections and monetary vitality treated in Chapter Seven may become apparent. Bronze coinage chronology, mint attribution, issuing authority, archeological contexts, and circulation will, it may be hoped, become clearer in the decades to come. New finds from locations quite distinct from the current find pattern would signal an enlarged local minting of base-metal currency and could augment the present picture of early medieval Spain's participation in the widespread exercise of a multi-tiered monetary economy. Not least of all, more gold mints, more reigns for different mints, and more hoards and single finds will no doubt reveal themselves over time, and this will only enhance the picture that

863 Also, if coins were issued mainly for fiscal purposes, one might expect much re-minting of earlier coins toward the beginning of a new reign and less later in the reign.

is being developed in this and other scholarly works. With more material to work with, volume questions and metallurgical problems can be amply explored. In combination with stylistic considerations, metal analysis also holds the potential to refine our knowledge of the order of issues and thereby reveal a relative chronology that might be placed in association with documented political events.

The many figures in the two appendices furnish specifics and visualizations of matters discussed throughout the text. In conjunction with the main body of this work they will provide much food for thought. The updated map of mint sites and the table of mint activity, as currently known, in the first Appendix (Figures I.4 and I.7) are essential points of reference. I have little doubt that my specific arguments for die engraving attributions in Appendix II will generate some disagreement. But if there is consensus by specialists on the core matter, that certain 'hands' were responsible for a good range of gold currency including across several cities and several kings' reigns, then a significant advance will have been made in an important area of the material history of the Visigothic kingdom. As I have suggested, the strong association of single die engravers at several sites especially in southern Iberia during the height of the Byzantine war appears unsurprising given the perspective laid out in this work.

New coins entering the market continue to be added to the record, though they must always be approached with a healthy skepticism. Some of these will represent previously unknown sites, others will be from kings not previously known to have minted in a certain place. New discoveries increase the ability of scholars to carry out die studies. If we cannot know very accurately how many coins were produced in the Visigothic realm, we can at least gain a rough idea of the number of dies employed in certain periods at specific mints.[864] In this way, we have a better idea of the output of one workshop compared to another. This one area alone could make a difference in the way the Visigothic monetary system is viewed. Whether the amount of minting was enormous or very small is a question that has not yet been answered satisfactorily, but that is fundamental to our understanding of this coinage. It proffers one of many potential rewards for future investigations.

864 Some of this work has already been undertaken. See e.g. for example Gonzalo Cores et al., "Visigothic Mint Practice," 195-218 and 3 plates.

Appendix I

Figure I.1: Weight and fineness measurements of Visigothic pre-regal tremisses at the ANS

(Except where indicated otherwise under 'Notes', tests were conducted by Lauris Olson – see introduction to Fig. I.11. The author's own tests [AK] were conducted in January 2016 and David Yoon's [DY] in March 2017, both using Decalin with a density of 1.9638.)

Tomasini#	Tomasini Grp	Weight(g)	SpecGrav	Gold(%)	SG Method	Coin Number	Notes
1	A1	1.52				HSA 16708	
2	A1	1.51				ANS	
3	A1	1.49				HSA 16705	
7	A1	1.55				HSA 16682	
9	A1	1.48				HSA 16693	
10	A1	1.5				HSA 16696	
11	A1	1.47				HSA 16716	
12	A1	1.5				HSA 16695	
14	A1	1.5				HSA 16710	
16	A1	1.51				HSA 16706	
19	A1	1.48				HSA 16681	
21	A1a	1.47	18.9	97.4	Water	HSA 16746	Tom: 1.48g
25	A1a	1.47	19.1	98.9	Water	HSA 16687	Tom: 1.51g
27	A1b	1.5	19.1	98.4	Water	HSA 16718	Tom: 1.55g
29	A1c	1.46	18.8	96.6	Water	HSA 16719	
33	A1e	1.43	18.8	96.7	Water	HSA 16679	Tom: 1.48g
42	A2	1.46				ANS	ex-Reinhart
43	A2	1.5				HSA 16684	
46	A2a	1.5				HSA 16689	
52	A2a	1.49				HSA 16680	
55	A2a	1.48				HSA 16690	
58	A2b	1.49				HSA 16691	
59	A2b	1.52				HSA 16713	
64	A2c	1.47				HSA 16688	
65	A3	1.45				HSA 16683	
70	A3	1.47				HSA 16773	
71	A3	1.45				HSA 16737	
75	A3	1.43				HSA 16714	
77	A3	1.38				HSA 522	
85	A3b	1.44				ANS	ex-Reinhart
95	A4	1.45	19	98.1	Water	HSA 16747	
96	A4	1.46	18.8	96.4	Water	HSA 16685	Tom: 1.49g
99	A4a	1.46	19	98	Water	HSA 16717	Tom: 1.48g

100	A4a	1.46	19.1	98.9	Water	HSA 16692	Tom: 1.50g
103	A5	1.48	18.6	95.1	Water	HSA 16699	Tom: 1.47g
104	A5	1.45	19	97.9	Water	HSA 16704	Tom: 1.47g
105	A5	1.43	18.3	93.6	Water	HSA 16703	Tom: 1.42g
106	A5	1.45	18.9	97.3	Water	HSA 16702	Tom: 1.36g
107	A5	1.48	18.7	96	Water	HSA 16701	
108	A5	1.49	18.8	96.8	Water	HSA 16698	Tom: 1.57g
110	A5	1.46	18.8	97	Water	HSA 16707	Tom: 1.45g
111	A5	1.47	18.9	97.4	Water	HSA 16697	Tom: 1.46g
115	A5a	1.46	18.9	97.4	Water	HSA 16738	Tom: 1.48g
117	A6	1.41	17.8	89.6	Water	HSA 16709	Tom: 1.43g
123	A6	1.36	19	97.7	Water	HSA 16700	Tom: 1.38g
125	A6a	1.47	19	98	Water	HSA 16715	Tom: 1.49g
126	A6b	1.45	18.1	91.6	Water	HSA 16740	Tom: 1.47g
127	A6c	1.45	18.9	97.3	Water	HSA 16767	Tom: 1.47g
132	JI1	1.37				ANS	ex-Reinhart
134	JI1	1.21	18.3	93.1	Water	HSA 16723	Tom: 1.24g
136	JI1	1.42	18.6	95.3	Water	HSA 16722	Tom: 1.43g
153	JI1	1.43	18.1	92.2	Water	ANS	Tom: 1.44g
158	JI1	1.4	18.1	92	Water	HSA 519	Duplicate HSA no. to T. 495. Tom: 1.43g
164	JI1	1.5				HSA 517	
191	JI2	1.48				HSA 16739	
193	JI2	1.44				HSA 16742	
194	JI2	1.48				HSA 16721	
195	JI2	1.44				HSA 16748	
202	JI2	1.44				HSA 16720	
205	JI2a	1.46				HSA 16724	
207	JI3	1.45	18.8	97	Water	HSA 16758	Tom: 1.46g
212	JI3	1.5	19	97.8	Water	HSA 16725	Tom: 1.54g
222	JI4	1.5				HSA 16694	
224	JI4	1.44				HSA 16732	
232	1-Jan	1.45				HSA 16775	
238	1-Jan	1.47				HSA 16727	
242	1-Jan	1.39				HSA 16757	
247	2-Jan	1.42				HSA 503	
249	2-Jan	1.43	17	83.3	Decalin [AK]	HSA 16768	Olson’s wt: 1.46
254	2-Jan	1.44				HSA 514	
256	2-Jan	1.43	18.2	92.6	Decalin [DY]	HSA 515	Olson’s wt: 1.46

257	2-Jan	1.47				HSA 8117	
258	2-Jan	1.47				HSA 511	
262	2-Jan	1.44				HSA 16744	
280	JAN2a	1.44				HSA 16750	
285	JAN2a	1.46				HSA 512	
288	JAN2b	1.45				HSA 16772	
289	JAN2b	1.25				HSA 16769	
303	3-Jan	1.45				HSA 16726	
304	3-Jan	1.43				HSA 16730	
306	3-Jan	1.44				HSA 516	
308	3-Jan	1.43				HSA 16728	
309	3-Jan	1.08				ANS	ex-Reinhart
313	JAN3a	1.29				HSA 16735	
314	JAN3a	1.43				ANS	ex-Reinhart
316	4-Jan	1.43				HSA 16736	
329	4-Jan	1.36				HSA 16785	
344	5-Jan	1.35	17.5	87.7	Decalin [DY]	HSA 16786	Olson’s wt.: 1.38
345	5-Jan	1.43				HSA 502	
349	5-Jan	0.95				HSA 510	
350	5-Jan	1.25				HSA 505	
351	5-Jan	1.01				HSA 506	
357	5-Jan	1.46				HSA 10619	
358	5-Jan	1.42				HSA 16733	
362	6-Jan	1.42				HSA 16780	
363	6-Jan	1.43				HSA 504	
365	7-Jan	1.37				HSA 16761	
366	7-Jan	1.39				HSA 498	
367	7-Jan	1.38				HSA 10618	
368	8-Jan	1.42				HSA 507	
369	8-Jan	1.4				HSA 16741	
380	8-Jan	1.45				HSA 15979	
392	9-Jan	1.43				HSA 518	
395	10-Jan	1.52				HSA 16778	
396	11-Jan	1.46				HSA 16712	
399	11-Jan	1.36				HSA 16755	
---	11-Jan	1.44	18.4	94.2	Decalin [DY]	ANS 1956.25.58	
407	JAN11c	1.46				ANS	ex-Reinhart
408	JII1	1.37	18.2	92.6	Freon 113	HSA 16729	
453	JII3	1.09	18.3	93.3	Freon 113	ANS	ex-Reinhart

479	JII4	1.4	18.2	92.6	Freon 113	HSA 499	
486	JII4	1.31	15.7	72.1	Freon 113	HSA 15590	Tom: 1.34g. Miles 7(e)1, 1.34g
495	JII4a	1.13	16.7	81.1	Freon 113	HSA 519	Tom: 1.15g. duplicate
498	JII4a	1.25	15	65.1	Freon 113	ANS	Tom: 1.24g. ex-Reinhart
502	JII5	1.49	18.1	91.8	Freon 113	HSA 16665	Tom: 1.51g
516	JII5	1.18	16.9	82.7	Freon 113	HSA 500	Tom: 1.19g
549	C1	1.38	18.4	94	Freon 113	HSA 8116	Tom: 1.41g
551	C1	1.44	18.3	93.2	Decalin [AK]	HSA 508	Olson's wt.: 1.46
552	C1	1.42	18.6	95.3	Freon 113	HSA 15975	Tom: 1.41g
553	C1	1.45	18.2	92.6	Freon 113	HSA 15980	Tom: 1.48g
554	C1	1.46	18.1	91.8	Freon 113	HSA 16731	Tom: 1.48g
560	C2	1.47	18.4	94	Freon 113	HSA 15976	
561	C2	1.44	18.4	94	Freon 113	HSA 15977	Tom: 1.45g
562	C2	1.44	18	91.2	Freon 113	HSA 15978	Tom: 1.45g
565	C2	1.37	18.4	94	Freon 113	HSA 7891	
569	C3	1.27	17.9	90.5	Freon 113	HSA 15981	Tom: 1.29g
574	C3	1.28	17.6	88.3	Freon 113	HSA 497	Tom: 1.29g
575	C3	1.28	18.4	94	Freon 113	HSA 16756	Tom: 1.30g
577	C3	1.27	18.4	94	Freon 113	ANS	
578	C3	1.35	17	83.5	Freon 113	HSA 501	Tom: 1.34g
593	C4	1.32	15.1	66.2	Freon 113	HSA 16734	Tom: 1.34g
594	C4	1.27	15.2	67.2	Freon 113	HSA 16771	
602	C5	1.46	18.6	95.3	Freon 113	HSA 513	
615	IR	1.37				HSA 7892	broken, repaired. Miles 8(d)1
619	IR	1.29	15.5	70.1	Freon 113	HSA 16002	Tom, Miles: 1.31g. Miles 8(h)1
620	IR	1.31	15.6	71.1	Freon 113	HSA 16003	Tom, Miles: 1.32g. Miles 8(i)1
621	IR	1.31	15.8	73	Freon 113	HSA 16781	Tom: 1.32g. Miles 8(j)1, 1.30g
631	H1	1.43	18.8	96.7	Freon 113	HSA 16013	Tom: 1.42g. Miles 46(a)1
640	A?	1.35				HSA 16686	
653	JI/JII	1.41				HSA 521	
654	JI/JII	1.44				HSA 16789	
655	JI/JII	1.45				HSA 16788	
656	JI/JII	1.27				ANS	ex-Reinhart
659	JI/JII	1.45				HSA 16760	

Figure I.2: Comparison of intrinsic values between tremisses of Byzantine Spania, Constantinople and the Visigothic Kingdom

(Adapted from P. Bartlett et al, "The Byzantine Gold Coinage of *Spania*," p. 358, Fig. 3)

From Catalogue (cf. Bartlett et al.)	**Summary of measurements of Byzantine coins of *Spania***				
Emperor	**Dates**	**No. of Coins**	**Au %**	**Weight, g**	**Intrinsic Value, g**
Justinian	552-565	3 of 5 for SG	89.8	1.48	1.33
Justin II	565-578	4 of 4 for SG	87*	***1.33***	***1.15****
Maurice	582-602	5 of 5 for SG	***83.1***	***1.41***	***1.17***
Phocas	602-610	3 of 5 for SG	***72.1***	***1.42***	***1.02***
Heraclius	610-626	8 of 11 for SG	***72.3***	***1.41***	***1.02***
From Appendix I in Bartlett et al.	**Summary of measurements of Byzantine coins from Constantinople**				
Emperor	**Dates**	**Sample**	**Au %**	**Weight, g**	**Intrinsic Value, g**
Justinian	552-565	8	96.7	1.48	1.43
Maurice	582-602	10	97.2	1.44	1.40
Phocas	602-610	9	94.7	1.46	1.38
Heraclius	610-626	8	97.0	1.44	1.40
From Appendix II in Bartlett et al.	**Summary of measurements of Visigothic coins**				
Ruler	**Dates**	**Sample**	**Au %**	**Weight, g**	**Intrinsic Value, g**
Justinian	552-565	19[⌖]	92.6	1.38*	1.28
Justin II-Leovigild	565-573	32[X]	88.8	1.41	1.21
C-3 Leovigild?	c. 573-576	15[X]	91.5	1.30	1.19
Leovigild IR	c. 576-580	10	***77.0***	1.31	***1.01***
Leovigild COS	> 578-584	18	***73.3***	1.26	***0.93***
Leovigild FB	584-586	26	***74.0***	1.46	***1.08***
Reccared I	586-601	104	***72.7***	1.48	***1.08***
Liuva II	601-603	13	***71.6***	1.47	***1.06***
Witteric	603-609	31	***70.8***	1.46	***1.03***
Gundemar	609-612	20	***69.2***	1.44	***1.00***
Sisebut	612-621	105	***66.4***	1.44	***0.96***
Reccared II	621	12	***64.8***	1.44	***0.93***
Suinthila (< 625)	621-624	68	***62.4***	1.42	***0.89***

Observations on the data:

Starting under Justin II clear reductions in weight and fineness are evident, as is diminished instrinsic value. (See italic font.)

Constantinople-issued tremisses have values superior to both other groups.

*Possibly two weight standards in use: c. 1.25g and 1.42g (cf. ibid., 360).

Lower intrinsic value than coins from Spania already during Justinian's rule. A drop in fineness as well as intrinsic value was initiated by the time of Leovigild's *Inclitus Rex* coins, apparently already in some J II series.[X] The lowered weight in his tremisses is raised for the Facing Bust issues. Improved intrinsic value then begins a slow, continuous decline.

* Minimal modification based on improved testing results of one coin now rendering a marginally lower Au% and intrinsic value, as reported in Bartlett et al., "Weight, Fineness and Debasement."

[⌖] Modified from the published source by the addition of three tremisses at the American Numismatic Society tested for weight and SG by Andrew Kurt and David Yoon. The new averages remain close to the original sample of 16 specimens from the Ashmolean Museum and Grierson and Blackburn, *Medieval European Coinage*, v. 1: Au % 93.4, weight 1.38 g, intrinsic value 1.28 g.

[X] The detailed research in Bartlett et al., "Weight, Fineness and Debasement" offers up-to-date results and recommends reclassification of some coins. As such a major drop in weight as well as fineness – and consequently intrinsic value averages as low as .70 g Au – can be said to have begun in J II groups such as J II 2, 3, 5b, 6, and 7, in which it is unsurprising to find at the same time much greater variation in values even in coins from the very same dies. Such data is taken to reflect "poor control over the minting process." The fact that certain categories or subcategories have much better intrinsic value (including fineness percentages in the low 90s) may result from an improvement in metrological standard late in the series, just before the opening stages of Leovigild's regal currency, or perhaps alongside these issues. See the table of JII/Leovigild issues and especially Figure 2 in ibid.

Figure I.3: Graph comparison of intrinsic values – tremisses of Byzantine Spania, Constantinople and the Visigothic Kingdom

(from P. Bartlett et al, "The Byzantine Gold Coinage of *Spania,*" p. 371, Fig. 7)

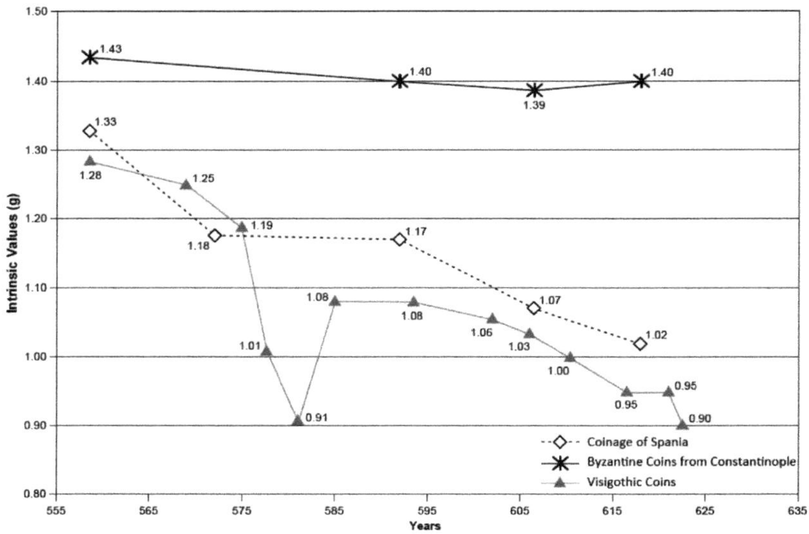

Figure I.4: Map of gold mints in Visigothic Spain (c. 575 – c. 714)

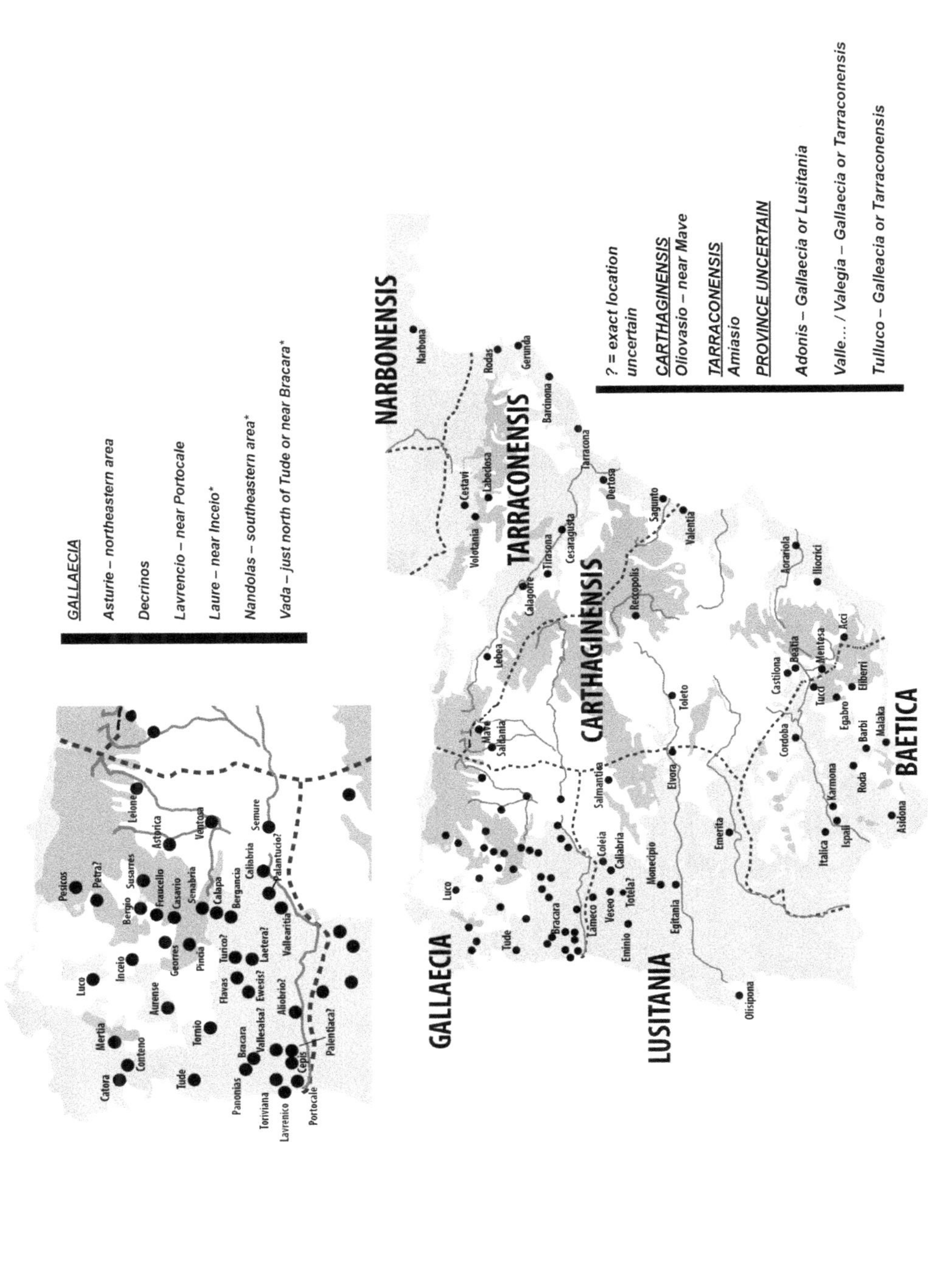

* Cf. Pliego, "La moneda visidogda: Anexo I," SPAL 21 (2012), 212f.

Figure I.5: Schema of bust types of Visigothic regal tremisses

(from M. Crusafont i Sabater, *El sistema monetario visigodo: cobre y oro* [Barcelona, 1994], 79)

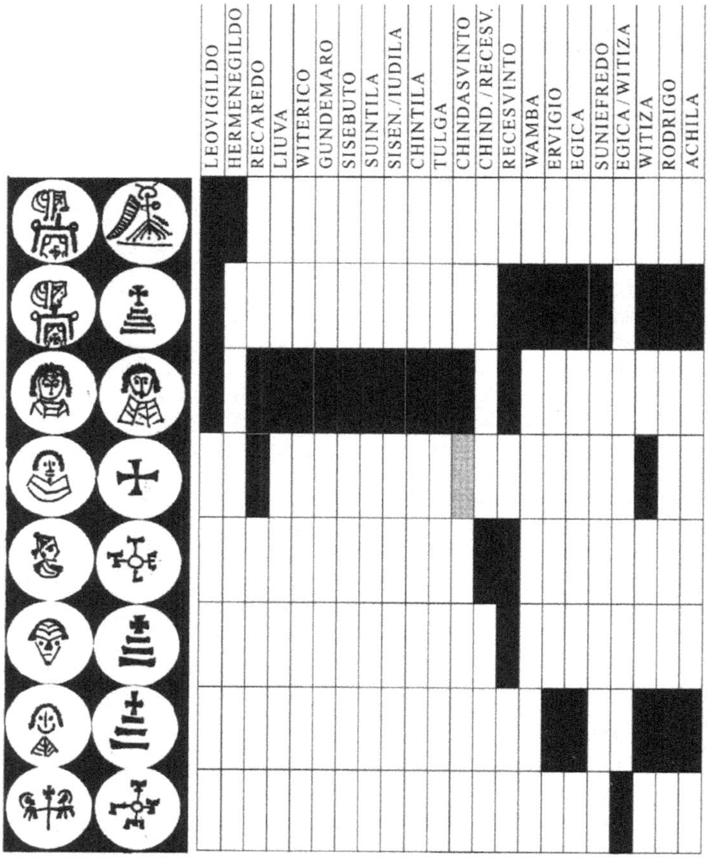

Figure I.6: Visigothic copper-alloy coins compared to tremisses

(from Crusafont, *El sistema monetario*, 35)

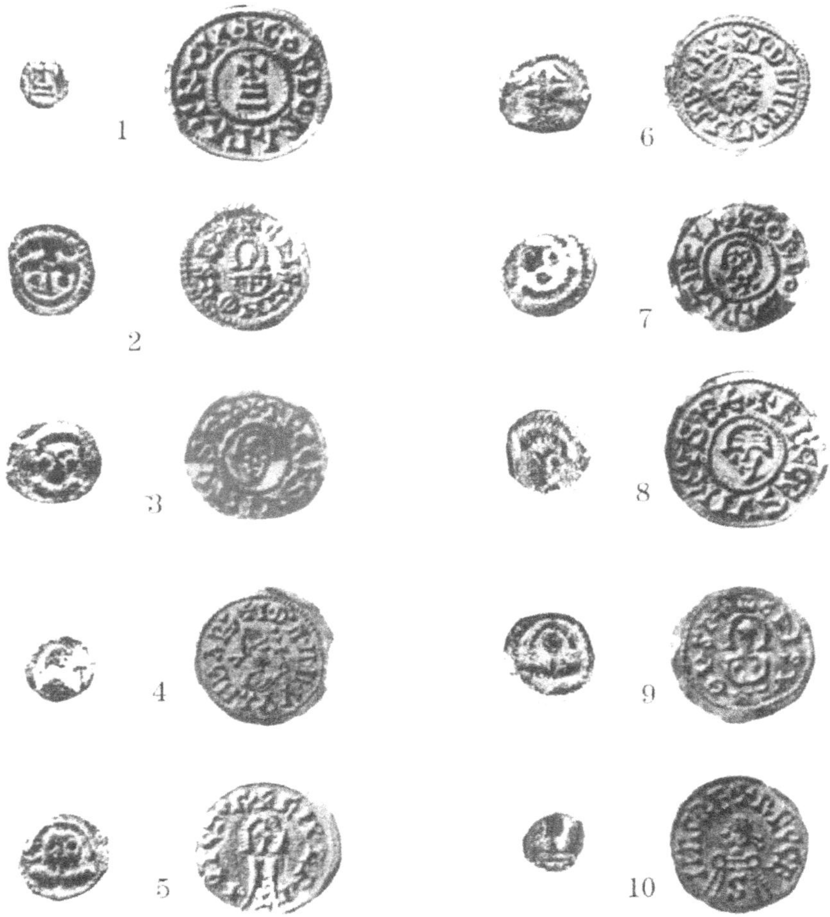
1
2
3
4
5
6
7
8
9
10

Figure I.7: Table of known regal mints

MINT Based on Ruth Pliego, *La moneda visigoda*, v. 2 (Seville: University of Seville, 2009), 47-50 and idem, "La moneda visigoda: Anexo I," *SPAL* 21 (2012), 209-33.	LEOVIGILD (573-586)	*HERMENEGILD (c. 579-584)*	RECCARED (586-601)	LIUVA II (601-603)	WITTERIC (603-610)	GUNDEMAR (610-612)	SISEBUT (612-621)	RECCARED II (621)	SUINTHILA (621-631)	SISENAND (631-636)	*IUDILA (632-633)*	CHINTILA (636-639)	TULGA (639-642)	CHINDASVINTH (642-653)	CHIND. - RECCES. (649-653)	RECCESVINTH (653-672)	WAMBA (672-680)	ERVIG (680-687)	EGICA (687-700)	*SUNIFRED (c. 692-693)*	EGICA - WITTIZA (700-702)	WITTIZA (702-710)	RODERIC (710-711)	ACHILA II (710/11-713)	*TOTALS: MINTS & PROVINCES*
No Mint Name	86	8		1																					***95***
Narbonensis (1)																									***150***
Narbona	4		11		5		3		1	2			1	21		4		25	26		25	12		10	
Tarraconensis (14)																									**697**
Amiasio (?)	1																								1
Barcinona	3		22	2	2	1	2												3		6	2			43
Calagorre			1						2																3
Cesaragusta	12		39	3	16	8	22		32	4		1	7	1			1	7	17		28	23		2	223
Cestavi			4																						4
Dertosa			1																						1
Gerunda					3		2			4		2				2		1	24		35	19		1	93
Labeclosa							1																		1
Lebea	1																								1
Rodas	4		3		1														4			1			13
Sagunto						2	4														1				7
Tarracona	1		30	5	13	15	46		50	12			4	2		29	8	8	18		18	6		2	267
Tirasona	2		20	1	3	2	1		5			1	3												38
Volotania						2																			2
Carthaginensis (12)																									**1500**
Acci							23	2	58	21		3						1	3			1			112
Aorariola							1																		1
Beatia													3	2											5
Castelona										26		6													32
Iliocrici							1			1															2
Mave							1			1		1		1											4
Mentesa			4		8	9	37		139	27		4		1					6		6	10			251
Oliovasio					1																				1
Reccopolis	7		7				1		4													2			21
Saldania	2		1		1		1		3					1											9
Toleto	66		114	13	41	25	101	14	113	47		20	10	37	10	109	64	76	91	2	63	30			1046
Valentia									6			3						1	3		3				16

MINT

Based on Ruth Pliego, *La moneda visigoda* , v. 2 (Seville: University of Seville, 2009), 47-50 and idem, "La moneda visigoda: Anexo I," *SPAL* 21 (2012), 209-33.

MINT	LEOVIGILD (573-586)	*HERMENEGILD (c. 579-584)*	RECCARED (586-601)	LIUVA II (601-603)	WITTERIC (603-610)	GUNDEMAR (610-612)	SISEBUT (612-621)	RECCARED II (621)	SUINTHILA (621-631)	SISENAND (631-636)	*IUDILA (632-633)*	CHINTILA (636-639)	TULGA (639-642)	CHINDASVINTH (642-653)	CHIND. - RECCES. (649-653)	RECCESVINTH (653-672)	WAMBA (672-680)	ERVIG (680-687)	EGICA (687-700)	*SUNIFRED (c. 692-693)*	EGICA - WITTIZA (700-702)	WITTIZA (702-710)	RODERIC (710-711)	ACHILA II (710/11-713)	*TOTALS: MINTS & PROVINCES*
Baetica (11)																									**2772**
Asidona									13	12											5				30
Barbi							29	2	186	35		3	5	3											263
Cordoba	5		29	1	2	1	24		132	81		12	39	28		54	27	21	6		49	42			553
Egabro												2									3				5
Eliberri			21	5	21	12	86	5	193	44	2	5	2	3				4	13		14				431
Ispali	11		91	27	76	40	311	2	173	83		15	9	38	7	90	60	58	47		85	20			1243
Italica	2																								2
Karmona																		2							2
Malaka										4															4
Roda	2																								2
Tucci							6		174	32		3	2	1				4			10	5			237
Lusitania (13)																									**2071**
Caliabria					1							1													2
Coleia			3				1		3																7
Egitania			2			3	15		9	11		1	2	1		6		4	4		14	5	13		90
*Elissa (Olisipona?)	1																								1
Elvora	35		58	10	32	13	39		19			1						2	3		39	5			256
Emerita	31		165	39	84	35	219	15	352	158	1	39	11	86	4	75	75	69	47		87	33			1625
Eminio			11	1	2	2	14		3			4													37
Lameco					1		3		1	2				1											8
Monecipio			5				1																		6
Olisipona (see *)			1																						1
Salamantica			4		1				6									2	2		16				31
Totela			1				1																		2
Veseo							2		1						1	1									5

MINT Based on Ruth Pliego, *La moneda visigoda*, v. 2 (Seville: University of Seville, 2009), 47-50 and idem, "La moneda visigoda: Anexo I," *SPAL* 21 (2012), 209-33.	LEOVIGILD (573-586)	*HERMENEGILD (c. 579-584)*	RECCARED (586-601)	LIUVA II (601-603)	WITTERIC (603-610)	GUNDEMAR (610-612)	SISEBUT (612-621)	RECCARED II (621)	SUINTHILA (621-631)	SISENAND (631-636)	*IUDILA (632-633)*	CHINTILA (636-639)	TULGA (639-642)	CHINDASVINTH (642-653)	CHIND. - RECCES. (649-653)	RECCESVINTH (653-672)	WAMBA (672-680)	ERVIG (680-687)	EGICA (687-700)	*SUNIFRED (c. 692-693)*	EGICA - WITTIZA (700-702)	WITTIZA (702-710)	RODERIC (710-711)	ACHILA II (710/11-713)	*TOTALS: MINTS & PROVINCES*
Gallaecia (45)																									**302**
Adonis			1																						1
Aliobrio									3																3
Arofre[1]			1																						1
Astorica									1																1
Asturie			1											8											9
Aurense							2		2					1											5
Bergancia			1		2	1	3																		7
Bergio							3																		3
Bracara	1		3		1		11		17	2		2		22		4			1		2	2			68
Calapa			2			1	3		3					2											11
Casavio									1																1
Catora					2																				2
Cepis			2				2		2																6
Conteno			2																						2
Decrinos							1																		1
Ewesis							1																		1
Flavas			1		1																				2
Fraucello					2				4					1											7
Georres			1	1	3	2	3		5																15
Inceio							1																		1
Laetera					1		3		1				1												6
Laure							3																		3
Lavrencio					1				1																2

[1] A Reccared tremissis of Arofre was auctioned recently: see CNG (https://www.cngcoins.com/Coin.aspx?CoinID=325293, accessed March 19, 2009); Ex Numismatica Genevensis SA VII (27 November 2012), lot 1245, sale price 42,000 Swiss francs. Its close resemblance to a coin of Reccared from Senabria (Pliego 2009, v. 2, 147.1) strongly suggests an authentic Gallaecian issue.

MINT Based on Ruth Pliego, *La moneda visigoda* , v. 2 (Seville: University of Sevillie, 2009), 47-50 and idem, "La moneda visigoda: Anexo I," *SPAL* 21 (2012), 209-33.	LEOVIGILD (573-586)	*HERMENEGILD (c. 579-584)*	RECCARED (586-601)	LIUVA II (601-603)	WITTERIC (603-610)	GUNDEMAR (610-612)	SISEBUT (612-621)	RECCARED II (621)	SUINTHILA (621-631)	SISENAND (631-636)	*IUDILA (632-633)*	CHINTILA (636-639)	TULGA (639-642)	CHINDASVINTH (642-653)	CHIND. - RECCES. (649-653)	RECCESVINTH (653-672)	WAMBA (672-680)	ERVIG (680-687)	EGICA (687-700)	*SUNIFRED (c. 692-693)*	EGICA - WITTIZA (700-702)	WITTIZA (702-710)	RODERIC (710-711)	ACHILA II (710/11-713)	*TOTALS: MINTS & PROVINCES*
Leione									3																3
Luco	1		3				1		5			1	3	7							2	1			24
Mertia			1																						1
Nandolas				2	2	3	3		2																12
Palentiaca									1																1
Palantucio			1		1																				2
Panonias					2		2																		4
Pesicos						1	1																		2
Petra			1						1			1		1											4
Pincia			2				1		1																4
Portocale	2		4	1			2		2																11
Semure							2																		2
Senabria			1		3	1	5		1																11
Susarres			1		2																				3
Toriviana									2	2		1		2											7
Tornio			1																						1
Tude			3		5	4	12		11					2		1	1		3						42
Turico							1		2																3
Vada									1																1
Vallearitia					1	1	1																		3
Vallesalsa			1																						1
Ventosa									2																2
Province Unknown (2)																									2
Tulluco							1																		1
Valle.../Vallegia?			1																						1
TOTALS (98 mints)	280	8	683	112	343	184	1066	40	1752	611	3	130	102	273	22	375	236	285	321	2	511	219	13	15	7589

Figure I.8: Number of known mints from each reign

N.b.: The locations of one mint of Reccared and one of Sisbeut are unknown.

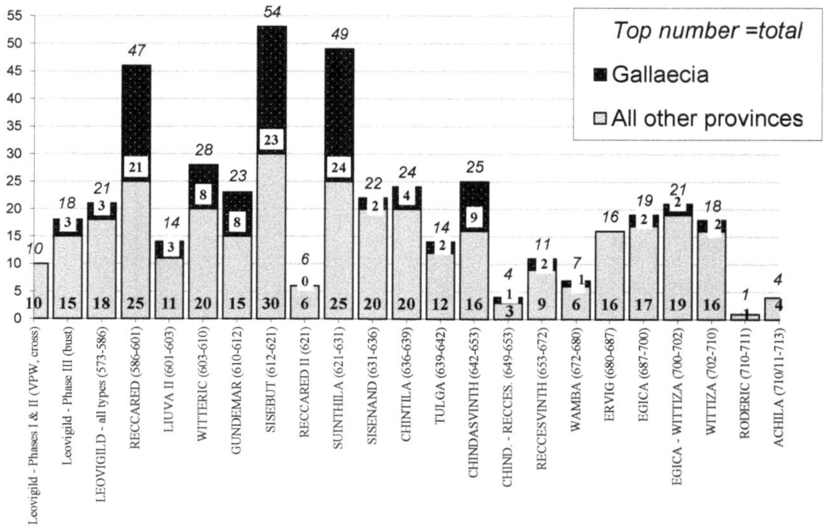

Figure I.9: Southern mints' percentage of total corpus

(based on Miles, *The Coinage of the Visigoths*, 70 74 and Grierson and Blackburn, *Medieval European Coinage*, v. 1 , 442 51 , pls. 12 14)

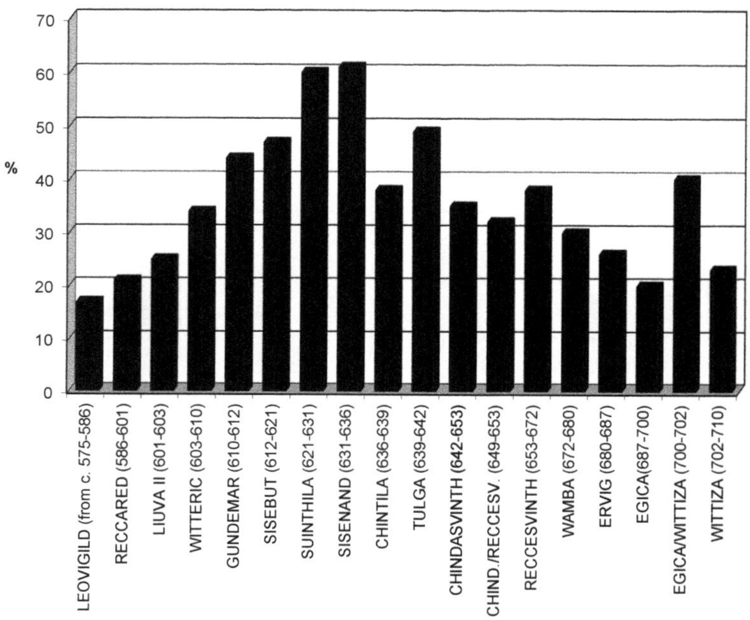

Figure I.10: Individual mints' percentage of total in southern-central Visigothic Spain

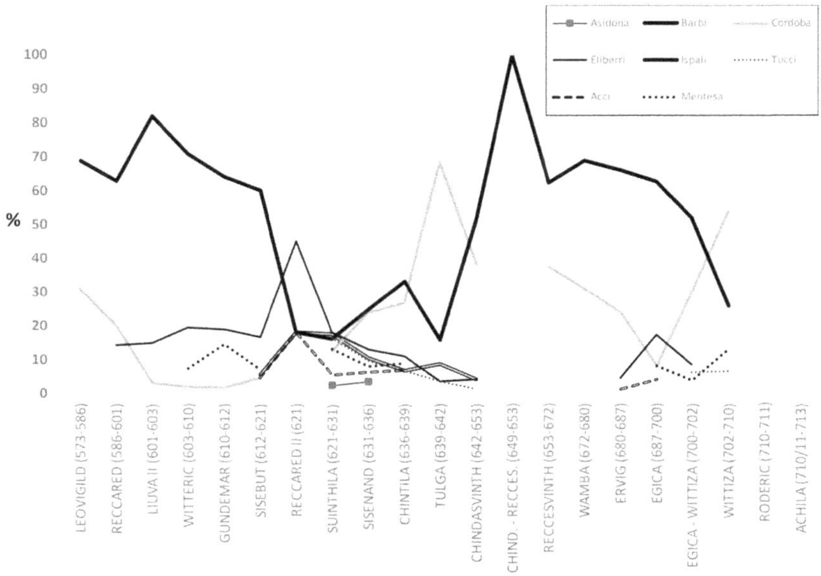

Figure I.11: Weight and fineness measurements by Lauris Olson of 377 Visigothic regal tremisses

The information in the table which follows was compiled in 1987 by Lauris Olson, then a doctoral student at the University of Pennsylvania. The subsequent table in this appendix (Figure I.12) uses data from this table and other sources, including results from Olson's own research on pre-regal coinage, to indicate the averages of fineness of gold coins from early medieval Spain, c. 507 to 721.

In 1987 Olson, a student in the graduate summer seminar at the American Numismatic Society (New York, NY), carefully measured the weight and fineness of 299 tremisses in the ANS collection. The weight measurements are undoubtedly to be preferred to those in Miles's catalog, since Olson used better equipment and weighed each coin three times. His results, a portion of which he kindly made available to me, are extremely consistent for each coin measured. While they differ from Miles's weights in perhaps most cases, they almost always fall within the same or an adjacent weight class in the frequency tables of this appendix.

In addition to the tremisses which Olson himself tested, the present table includes the published figures of weight and fineness of seventy-eight additional specimens: seventy-three which appear in Ph. Grierson and Mark Blackburn, *Medieval European Coinage, v. I: The Early Middle Ages (5th-10th Centuries)* (Cambridge), 1986, 442-51, and five from W. A. Oddy and M. J. Hughes, "The Specific Gravity Method for the Analysis of Gold Coins," in E. T. Hall and D. M. Metcalf, eds., *Methods of Chemical and Metallurgical Investigation of Ancient Coinage* (London, 1972), 82. The three samples combined in the table all used the specific gravity method.

Olson was the first person to have carried out an analysis of fineness on the Visigothic tremisses at the ANS, the preeminent collection of such coins. His specific gravity determinations were made on the Sartorius 1602 MP digital balance located in the second-floor coin room at the ANS. Before testing, each coin was soaked in acetone for ten minutes; remaining encrustations visible under low magnification were removed with an acetone-soaked soft bristle brush. The procedure used followed the instructions of Dr. Michael Bates of the ANS and ultimately derive from Earle Caley, *Analysis of Ancient Metals. International Series of Monographs on Analytical Chemistry, 19* (New York) and Oddy and Hughes. Olson weighed the coins three times each in trifluorotrichloroethane (Freon 113, or "Dissolve"), recalibrating the scale between each batch, checking the temperature of the liquid with each measurement, and making determinations on the same day except in the case of a widely divergent outcome. Interpretation of the specific gravity values is based on Caley, on Oddy and Hughes, and on W. A. Oddy and S. M. Blackshaw, "The Accuracy of the Specific Gravity Method for the Analysis of Gold Alloys," *Archaeometry* XVI (1974), 81-90.

Coins here are identified by their catalog numbers in George C. Miles, *The Coinage of the Visigoths of Spain: Leovigild to Achila II* (New York, 1952) [= HSA and ANS] and idem, "The Ferreira Collection of Visigothic Coins," *American Numismatic Society Museum Notes* XII (1966), 129-37 [= F], and by their numbers in Grierson and Blackburn [= MEC] and in Oddy and Hughes [= O]. 'HSA' refers to the Hispanic Society of America, whose Visigothic coin collection was on indefinite loan to the ANS. 'O' refers to Oxford University, the Ashmolean Museum. Olson published the table for a time on the internet, and only minor adjustments have been made here. I accessed the full table in digital archive on 3 January 2018 at http://web.archive.org/web/20020704101742/http://pobox.upenn.edu/~olson/visicoins/allsg.prn.

Miles No.	*Ruler*	*Date*	*Mint*	*Province*	***Weight (g)***	***Gold (%)***	*Specific Gravity*	*Location*	
7(e)1	Leovigild	581	None	None	1.31	72.1	15.7	HSA	15990
8(h)1	Leovigild	581	None	None	1.29	70.1	15.5	HSA	16002
8(i)1	Leovigild	581	None	None	1.31	71.1	15.6	HSA	16003
8(j)1	Leovigild	581	None	None	1.31	73	15.8	HSA	16781
1(b)...	Leovigild	581	None	None	1.3	86	17.37	MEC	209
Cross-on-steps									
31(a)1	Leovigild	584	Ispali	Baetica	1.24	75.8	16.1	HSA	16004
31(b)1	Leovigild	584	Ispali	Baetica	1.29	78.5	16.4	HSA	15988
34.1	Leovigild	584	Italica	Baetica	1.21	75.8	16.1	HSA	16751
23(a)1	Leovigild	584	Reccopolis	Carthaginensis	1.23	76.7	16.2	HSA	16006
28(a)1	Leovigild	584	Toleto	Carthaginensis	1.3	71.1	15.6	HSA	15993
28(a)2	Leovigild	584	Toleto	Carthaginensis	1.29	71.1	15.6	HSA	15994
28(a)3	Leovigild	584	Toleto	Carthaginensis	1.24	73.9	15.9	HSA	16000
36(a)1	Leovigild	584	Elvora	Carthaginensis	1.1	67.2	15.2	HSA	15982
36(a)2	Leovigild	584	Elvora	Carthaginensis	1.36	70.1	15.5	HSA	15987
36(b)1	Leovigild	584	Elvora	Carthaginensis	1.19	74.8	16	HSA	15986
36(a)3	Leovigild	584	Elvora	Carthaginensis	1.28	71	15.58	MEC	210
38(b)1	Leovigild	584	Emerita	Lusitania	1.26	69.2	15.4	HSA	16498
38(c)1	Leovigild	584	Emerita	Lusitania	1.29	74.8	16	ANS	56.25.12
38(c)2	Leovigild	584	Emerita	Lusitania	1.17	72.1	15.7	HSA	F 4
22.1	Leovigild	584	Tirasona	Tarraconensis	1.22	70.1	15.5	HSA	16670
Facing Bust									
33(a)1	Leovigild	586	Ispali	Baetica	1.49	80.3	16.6	HSA	8114
33(e)1	Leovigild	586	Ispali	Baetica	1.54	76.7	16.2	HSA	16668
26.1	Leovigild	586	Saldania	Carthaginensis	1.36	76.7	16.2	HSA	16001
29(a)1	Leovigild	586	Toleto	Carthaginensis	1.45	73.9	15.9	HSA	15992
29(a)2	Leovigild	586	Toleto	Carthaginensis	1.49	73.9	15.9	HSA	15996
29(a)4	Leovigild	586	Toleto	Carthaginensis	1.48	72.1	15.7	HSA	15998
29(b)1	Leovigild	586	Toleto	Carthaginensis	1.53	73	15.8	HSA	15991
29(c)1	Leovigild	586	Toleto	Carthaginensis	1.49	71.1	15.6	HSA	15995
29(a)13	Leovigild	586	Toleto	Carthaginensis	1.52	77	16.2	MEC	212
37(a)1	Leovigild	586	Elvora	Carthaginensis	1.49	72.1	15.7	HSA	15984
37(a)2	Leovigild	586	Elvora	Carthaginensis	1.51	69.2	15.4	HSA	16008
37(a)3	Leovigild	586	Elvora	Carthaginensis	1.51	70.1	15.5	HSA	16010
37(b)1	Leovigild	586	Elvora	Carthaginensis	1.46	71.1	15.6	HSA	15983
37(b)2	Leovigild	586	Elvora	Carthaginensis	1.53	69.2	15.4	HSA	16009
38(a)...	Leovigild	586	Elvora	Carthaginensis	1.52	70	15.47	MEC	211
39.2	Leovigild	586	Emerita	Lusitania	1.33	73	15.8	HSA	F 5
9.1	Leovigild	586	Narbona	Narbonensis	1.44	70.1	15.5	HSA	16005
11(a)1	Leovigild	586	Narbona	Narbonensis	1.48	77.6	16.3	HSA	15989
17.1	Leovigild	586	Cesaragusta	Tarraconensis	0.94	81.9	16.8	HSA	16669

Miles No.	*Ruler*	*Date*	*Mint*	*Province*	***Weight (g)***	***Gold (%)***	*Specific Gravity*	*Location*	
19(a)1	Leovigild	586	Rodas	Tarraconensis	1.45	68.2	15.3	HSA	16007
82(c)1	Reccared I	593	Cordoba	Baetica	1.5	75.8	16.1	HSA	16020
82(m)1	Reccared I	593	Cordoba	Baetica	1.41	68.2	15.3	HSA	16019
82(k)var.	Reccared I	593	Cordoba	Baetica	1.5	74	15.96	MEC	215
83(a)1	Reccared I	593	Eliberri	Baetica	1.42	63	14.8	HSA	16065
83(c)1	Reccared I	593	Eliberri	Baetica	1.39	62	14.7	HSA	16023
83(d)2	Reccared I	593	Eliberri	Baetica	1.41	63	14.8	HSA	F 10
83(a)...	Reccared I	593	Eliberri	Baetica	1.47	67	15.19	MEC	216
85(a)6	Reccared I	593	Ispali	Baetica	1.46	71.1	15.6	HSA	F 11
85(c)1	Reccared I	593	Ispali	Baetica	1.48	72.1	15.7	HSA	16037
86(a)1	Reccared I	593	Ispali	Baetica	1.51	74.8	16	HSA	16041
86(a)2	Reccared I	593	Ispali	Baetica	1.49	72.1	15.7	HSA	16509
86(b)1	Reccared I	593	Ispali	Baetica	1.49	71.1	15.6	HSA	16038
86(b)2	Reccared I	593	Ispali	Baetica	1.52	73.9	15.9	HSA	16036
86(d)1	Reccared I	593	Ispali	Baetica	1.5	72.1	15.7	HSA	16039
85(e)1	Reccared I	593	Ispali	Baetica	1.46	72	15.67	MEC	222
86(e)4	Reccared I	593	Ispali	Baetica	1.55	75	16.06	MEC	221
80.1	Reccared I	593	Saldania	Carthaginensis	1.55	73.9	15.9	HSA	16045
81(a)1	Reccared I	593	Toleto	Carthaginensis	1.48	73.9	15.9	HSA	16055
81(b)1	Reccared I	593	Toleto	Carthaginensis	1.42	72.1	15.7	HSA	16052
81(c)1	Reccared I	593	Toleto	Carthaginensis	1.49	73.9	15.9	HSA	16049
81(c)2	Reccared I	593	Toleto	Carthaginensis	1.56	73.9	15.9	HSA	16051
81(c)3	Reccared I	593	Toleto	Carthaginensis	1.48	70.1	15.5	HSA	16053
81(c)4	Reccared I	593	Toleto	Carthaginensis	1.52	73	15.8	HSA	16054
81(c)5	Reccared I	593	Toleto	Carthaginensis	1.43	73.9	15.9	HSA	16057
81(c)6	Reccared I	593	Toleto	Carthaginensis	1.45	70.1	15.5	HSA	16058
81(c)7	Reccared I	593	Toleto	Carthaginensis	1.48	71.1	15.6	HSA	16059
81(c)8	Reccared I	593	Toleto	Carthaginensis	1.54	73	15.8	HSA	16060
81(c)9	Reccared I	593	Toleto	Carthaginensis	1.51	71.1	15.6	HSA	16063
81(c)10	Reccared I	593	Toleto	Carthaginensis	1.43	75.8	16.1	HSA	8102
81(c)37	Reccared I	593	Toleto	Carthaginensis	1.51	73	15.8	HSA	F 17
81(c)27	Reccared I	593	Toleto	Carthaginensis	1.53	74	15.94	MEC	223
...	Reccared I	593	Calapa	Gallaecia	1.5	71	15.63	MEC	213
101.1	Reccared I	593	Susarros	Gallaecia	1.57	73.9	15.9	HSA	16061
115.1	Reccared I	593	Vallegia	Gallaecia	1.48	74.8	16	HSA	16064
90(a)1	Reccared I	593	Elvora	Carthaginensis	1.49	72.1	15.7	HSA	16021
90(a)2	Reccared I	593	Elvora	Carthaginensis	1.45	69.2	15.4	HSA	16022
90(b)1	Reccared I	593	Elvora	Carthaginensis	1.56	72.1	15.7	HSA	16024
90(b)2	Reccared I	593	Elvora	Carthaginensis	1.49	69.2	15.4	HSA	16071
90(c)1	Reccared I	593	Elvora	Carthaginensis	1.47	76.7	16.2	HSA	16025
90(b)6	Reccared I	593	Elvora	Carthaginensis	1.51	74	15.89	MEC	217
91.1	Reccared I	593	Elvora	Carthaginensis	1.45	59	14.45	MEC	218
93(a)1	Reccared I	593	Emerita	Lusitania	1.44	76.7	16.2	HSA	16027
93(a)2	Reccared I	593	Emerita	Lusitania	1.42	73	15.8	HSA	16028

Miles No.	*Ruler*	*Date*	*Mint*	*Province*	***Weight (g)***	***Gold (%)***	*Specific Gravity*	*Location*	
93(a)35	Reccared I	593	Emerita	Lusitania	1.5	71.1	15.6	HSA	F 13
93(a)36	Reccared I	593	Emerita	Lusitania	1.49	73	15.8	HSA	F 14
93(a)37	Reccared I	593	Emerita	Lusitania	1.46	72.1	15.7	HSA	F 16
93(d)1	Reccared I	593	Emerita	Lusitania	1.51	73	15.8	HSA	16029
93(e)1	Reccared I	593	Emerita	Lusitania	1.51	78.5	16.4	HSA	F 15
93(f)1	Reccared I	593	Emerita	Lusitania	1.51	73.9	15.9	HSA	16030
93(f)2	Reccared I	593	Emerita	Lusitania	1.52	73.9	15.9	HSA	16042
93(f)3	Reccared I	593	Emerita	Lusitania	1.51	81.9	16.8	HSA	16032
93(f)4	Reccared I	593	Emerita	Lusitania	1.51	72.1	15.7	HSA	16034
93(f)14	Reccared I	593	Emerita	Lusitania	1.52	75.8	16.1	ANS	69.222.78
93(f)18	Reccared I	593	Emerita	Lusitania	1.52	76.7	16.2	HSA	F 12
94(a)1	Reccared I	593	Emerita	Lusitania	1.46	79.4	16.5	HSA	16033
94(b)1	Reccared I	593	Emerita	Lusitania	1.44	73.9	15.9	HSA	16026
94(d)1	Reccared I	593	Emerita	Lusitania	1.48	73	15.8	HSA	16035
94(f)1	Reccared I	593	Emerita	Lusitania	1.49	71.1	15.6	HSA	16031
93(a)14	Reccared I	593	Emerita	Lusitania	1.46	76	16.14	MEC	220
94(d)2	Reccared I	593	Emerita	Lusitania	1.49	75	16.03	MEC	219
96(d)1	Reccared I	593	Eminio	Lusitania	1.48	70	15.44	MEC	214
48(b)1	Reccared I	593	Narbona	Narbonensis	1.51	72.1	15.7	HSA	16043
49(a)1	Reccared I	593	Narbona	Narbonensis	1.43	73.9	15.9	HSA	16044
51(a)1	Reccared I	593	Barcinona	Tarraconensis	1.51	72.1	15.7	HSA	10620
51(d)1	Reccared I	593	Barcinona	Tarraconensis	1.47	71.1	15.6	HSA	16067
52(d)1	Reccared I	593	Barcinona	Tarraconensis	1.47	68.2	15.3	HSA	16582
55(a)1	Reccared I	593	Cesaragusta	Tarraconensis	1.5	73.9	15.9	HSA	16015
55(c)1	Reccared I	593	Cesaragusta	Tarraconensis	1.48	75.8	16.1	HSA	16016
55(e)1	Reccared I	593	Cesaragusta	Tarraconensis	1.46	70.1	15.5	HSA	16018
55(i)2	Reccared I	593	Cesaragusta	Tarraconensis	1.47	73	15.8	HSA	NOT F 1
56.1	Reccared I	593	Cesaragusta	Tarraconensis	1.46	70.1	15.5	HSA	16069
57(b)1	Reccared I	593	Cesaragusta	Tarraconensis	1.45	78.5	16.4	HSA	16017
65(a)1	Reccared I	593	Tarracona	Tarraconensis	1.4	70.1	15.5	HSA	16050
66.1	Reccared I	593	Tarracona	Tarraconensis	1.46	69.2	15.4	HSA	16046
68(c)1	Reccared I	593	Tarracona	Tarraconensis	1.47	69.2	15.4	HSA	16047
69(c)1	Reccared I	593	Tarracona	Tarraconensis	1.5	69.2	15.4	HSA	F 8
70(b)1	Reccared I	593	Tarracona	Tarraconensis	1.51	74.8	16	HSA	16056
70(c)1	Reccared I	593	Tarracona	Tarraconensis	1.49	78.5	16.4	HSA	16048
74(d)1	Reccared I	593	Tirasona	Tarraconensis	1.45	67.2	15.2	HSA	16072
120(b)1	Liuva II	602	Ispali	Baetica	1.51	74.8	16	HSA	16076
120(b)6	Liuva II	602	Ispali	Baetica	1.49	69.2	15.4	HSA	F 18
120(b)3	Liuva II	602	Ispali	Baetica	1.48	76	16.17	MEC	225
119.1	Liuva II	602	Toleto	Carthaginensis	1.46	71.1	15.6	HSA	16075
122(a)1	Liuva II	602	Emerita	Lusitania	1.49	69.2	15.4	HSA	16077
122(a)3	Liuva II	602	Emerita	Lusitania	1.43	74	15.86	MEC	224
118(a)1	Liuva II	602	Tarracona	Tarraconensis	1.47	67.2	15.2	HSA	16074
139(a)...	Witteric	606	Eliberri	Baetica	1.44	66	15.1	MEC	226

Miles No.	*Ruler*	*Date*	*Mint*	*Province*	***Weight (g)***	***Gold (%)***	*Specific Gravity*	*Location*	
140(b)1	Witteric	606	Ispali	Baetica	1.44	71.1	15.6	HSA	16082
140(b)2	Witteric	606	Ispali	Baetica	1.32	67.2	15.2	HSA	16086
140(c)...	Witteric	606	Ispali	Baetica	1.5	71	15.58	MEC	228
137(a)1	Witteric	606	Toleto	Carthaginensis	1.49	71.1	15.6	HSA	16087
137(a)2	Witteric	606	Toleto	Carthaginensis	1.52	70.1	15.5	HSA	16088
137(a)10	Witteric	606	Toleto	Carthaginensis	1.46	73	15.8	HSA	F 23
137(a)11	Witteric	606	Toleto	Carthaginensis	1.52	72.1	15.7	HSA	F 24
137(a)5	Witteric	606	Toleto	Carthaginensis	1.5	75	15.71	MEC	229
147.1	Witteric	606	Bergancia	Gallaecia	1.48	76.7	16.2	HSA	16094
152(a)1	Witteric	606	Georres	Gallaecia	1.41	77.6	16.3	HSA	16091
142(a)1	Witteric	606	Elvora	Carthaginensis	1.51	69.2	15.4	HSA	16081
142(a)2	Witteric	606	Elvora	Carthaginensis	1.48	70.1	15.5	HSA	16095
143(b)1	Witteric	606	Emerita	Lusitania	1.45	68.2	15.3	HSA	16083
143(b)2	Witteric	606	Emerita	Lusitania	1.45	71.1	15.6	HSA	16084
143(e)1	Witteric	606	Emerita	Lusitania	1.43	73	15.8	HSA	16085
143(k)1	Witteric	606	Emerita	Lusitania	1.46	71.1	15.6	HSA	F 21
143(g)1	Witteric	606	Emerita	Lusitania	1.51	72	15.71	MEC	227
129(a)1	Witteric	606	Cesaragusta	Tarraconensis	1.47	69.2	15.4	HSA	16092
129(d)1	Witteric	606	Cesaragusta	Tarraconensis	1.45	68.2	15.3	HSA	16090
129(f)bis	Witteric	606	Cesaragusta	Tarraconensis	1.5	70.1	15.5	HSA	F 20
134.1	Witteric	606	Tirasona	Tarraconensis	1.4	70.1	15.5	HSA	16093
168(b)2	Gundemar	610	Eliberri	Baetica	1.45	67	15.14	MEC	230
166(a)1	Gundemar	610	Mentesa	Carthaginensis	1.42	64.1	14.9	HSA	16096
167.1	Gundemar	610	Toleto	Carthaginensis	1.4	65.1	15	HSA	16089
162(b)1	Gundemar	610	Cesaragusta	Tarraconensis	1.46	69.2	15.4	HSA	16098
164(a)1	Gundemar	610	Tarracona	Tarraconensis	1.46	66.2	15.1	HSA	16759
185.1	Sisebut	616	Cordoba	Baetica	1.52	76.7	16.2	HSA	16105
186(a)1	Sisebut	616	Eliberri	Baetica	1.47	66.2	15.1	HSA	16106
186(f)1	Sisebut	616	Eliberri	Baetica	1.33	63	14.8	HSA	F 27
187(a)1	Sisebut	616	Ispali	Baetica	1.46	70.1	15.5	HSA	16121
187(a)2	Sisebut	616	Ispali	Baetica	1.49	67.2	15.2	HSA	16244
187(a)3	Sisebut	616	Ispali	Baetica	1.48	68.2	15.3	HSA	16376
187(a)4	Sisebut	616	Ispali	Baetica	1.47	69.2	15.4	HSA	16418
187(c)1	Sisebut	616	Ispali	Baetica	1.45	68.2	15.3	HSA	16120
187(c)2	Sisebut	616	Ispali	Baetica	1.49	70.1	15.5	HSA	16124
187(c)3	Sisebut	616	Ispali	Baetica	1.54	69.2	15.4	HSA	16426
187(c)4	Sisebut	616	Ispali	Baetica	1.48	71	15.54	MEC	232
180.1	Sisebut	616	Acci	Carthaginensis	1.4	59.9	14.5	HSA	16103
182.1	Sisebut	616	Mentesa	Carthaginensis	1.03	62	14.7	HSA	16127
183(a)1	Sisebut	616	Toleto	Carthaginensis	1.52	61	14.6	HSA	16116
183(a)2	Sisebut	616	Toleto	Carthaginensis	1.49	62	14.7	HSA	16132
183(a)3	Sisebut	616	Toleto	Carthaginensis	1.44	64.1	14.9	HSA	16133
183(a)4	Sisebut	616	Toleto	Carthaginensis	1.44	63	14.8	HSA	16135
183(a)16	Sisebut	616	Toleto	Carthaginensis	1.51	66.2	15.1	HSA	F 31

Miles No.	*Ruler*	*Date*	*Mint*	*Province*	***Weight (g)***	***Gold (%)***	*Specific Gravity*	*Location*	
183(a)17	Sisebut	616	Toleto	Carthaginensis	1.46	68.2	15.3	HSA	NOT F 2
183(a)...	Sisebut	616	Toleto	Carthaginensis	1.39	67	15.18	O 1	74
183(a)...	Sisebut	616	Toleto	Carthaginensis	1.42	65	14.95	MEC	234
203.1	Sisebut	616	Laetera	Gallaecia	1.38	72.1	15.7	HSA	16112
205.1	Sisebut	616	Lucu	Gallaecia	1.54	72.1	15.7	HSA	16113
207.1	Sisebut	616	Pincia	Gallaecia	1.24	66.2	15.1	HSA	16114
210(a)1	Sisebut	616	Tude	Gallaecia	1.5	64.1	14.9	HSA	16117
192(a)1	Sisebut	616	Emerita	Lusitania	1.45	68.2	15.3	HSA	8109
192(a)2	Sisebut	616	Emerita	Lusitania	1.51	68.2	15.3	HSA	16119
192(b)1	Sisebut	616	Emerita	Lusitania	1.43	68.2	15.3	HSA	16108
192(b)2	Sisebut	616	Emerita	Lusitania	1.48	72.1	15.7	HSA	16454
192(b)5	Sisebut	616	Emerita	Lusitania	1.45	69	15.4	MEC	231
195(b)1	Sisebut	616	Eminio	Lusitania	1.48	73.9	15.9	HSA	16109
174(a)1	Sisebut	616	Cesaragusta	Tarraconensis	1.41	64.1	14.9	HSA	16100
174(a)2	Sisebut	616	Cesaragusta	Tarraconensis	1.36	64.1	14.9	HSA	16101
174(a)3	Sisebut	616	Cesaragusta	Tarraconensis	1.42	66.2	15.1	HSA	16102
175.1	Sisebut	616	Cesaragusta	Tarraconensis	1.39	64.1	14.9	HSA	16104
177(a)1	Sisebut	616	Tarracona	Tarraconensis	1.49	65.1	15	HSA	16128
177(b)2	Sisebut	616	Tarracona	Tarraconensis	1.43	70.1	15.5	HSA	F 29
177(c)1	Sisebut	616	Tarracona	Tarraconensis	1.4	66.2	15.1	HSA	16115
177(c)2	Sisebut	616	Tarracona	Tarraconensis	1.44	66.2	15.1	HSA	F 30
178(a)1	Sisebut	616	Tarracona	Tarraconensis	1.47	64.1	14.9	HSA	16129
178(d)2	Sisebut	616	Tarracona	Tarraconensis	1.33	59.9	14.5	HSA	F 28
178(b)...	Sisebut	616	Tarracona	Tarraconensis	1.43	62	14.65	MEC	233
224(c)...	Suinthila	626	Barbi	Baetica	1.44	63	14.81	MEC	235
226(c)var.	Suinthila	626	Cordoba	Baetica	1.28	51	13.72	MEC	236
227(b)...	Suinthila	626	Eliberri	Baetica	1.36	59	14.43	MEC	237
228(c)...	Suinthila	626	Ispali	Baetica	1.47	68	15.26	MEC	240
229(i)2	Suinthila	626	Tucci	Baetica	1.19	58	14.3	MEC	243
223(a)...	Suinthila	626	Toleto	Carthaginensis	1.42	58	14.3	MEC	242
235(a)4	Suinthila	626	Emerita	Lusitania	1.47	61	14.6	HSA	16175
235(a)8	Suinthila	626	Emerita	Lusitania	1.42	61	14.6	HSA	16178
235(a)9	Suinthila	626	Emerita	Lusitania	1.51	59.9	14.5	HSA	16179
235(a)10	Suinthila	626	Emerita	Lusitania	1.52	58.8	14.4	HSA	16180
235(a)11	Suinthila	626	Emerita	Lusitania	1.35	61	14.6	HSA	16182
235(a)12	Suinthila	626	Emerita	Lusitania	1.43	64.1	14.9	HSA	16184
235(a)13	Suinthila	626	Emerita	Lusitania	1.42	62	14.7	HSA	16186
235(a)17	Suinthila	626	Emerita	Lusitania	1.49	63	14.8	HSA	16190
235(a)18	Suinthila	626	Emerita	Lusitania	1.43	64.1	14.9	HSA	16192
235(a)19	Suinthila	626	Emerita	Lusitania	1.5	61	14.6	HSA	16453
235(a)20	Suinthila	626	Emerita	Lusitania	1.52	59.9	14.5	HSA	16193
235(a)21	Suinthila	626	Emerita	Lusitania	1.43	62	14.7	HSA	16208
235(a)22	Suinthila	626	Emerita	Lusitania	1.51	64.1	14.9	HSA	16196
235(a)23	Suinthila	626	Emerita	Lusitania	1.48	62	14.7	HSA	16197

Miles No.	*Ruler*	*Date*	*Mint*	*Province*	***Weight (g)***	***Gold (%)***	*Specific Gravity*	*Location*	
235(a)31	Suinthila	626	Emerita	Lusitania	1.47	61.7	14.67	O 1	75
235(a)35	Suinthila	626	Emerita	Lusitania	1.43	64	14.89	MEC	238
235(i)2	Suinthila	626	Emerita	Lusitania	1.4	66	15.06	MEC	239
212var.	Suinthila	626	Calagorre	Tarraconensis	1.47	59.9	14.5	ANS	59.129.1
213(a)1	Suinthila	626	Cesaragusta	Tarraconensis	1.33	54.1	14	HSA	16150
213(e)1	Suinthila	626	Cesaragusta	Tarraconensis	1.38	50.4	13.7	HSA	16149
214(b)1	Suinthila	626	Tarracona	Tarraconensis	1.34	56.5	14.2	HSA	16278
214(c)1	Suinthila	626	Tarracona	Tarraconensis	1.47	56.5	14.2	HSA	16277
215(d)1	Suinthila	626	Tarracona	Tarraconensis	1.43	58.8	14.4	HSA	16280
215(e)1	Suinthila	626	Tarracona	Tarraconensis	1.39	57.7	14.3	HSA	16279
215(f)1	Suinthila	626	Tarracona	Tarraconensis	1.3	52.9	13.9	HSA	16265
215(h)1	Suinthila	626	Tarracona	Tarraconensis	1.35	58	14.29	MEC	241
279.1	Iudila	632	Emerita	Lusitania	1.45	58.8	14.4	HSA	16299
267(d)3	Sisenand	633	Cordoba	Baetica	1.25	54	13.99	MEC	244
267(j)...	Sisenand	633	Cordoba	Baetica	1.46	55	14.04	MEC	245
262(a)1	Sisenand	633	Mentesa	Carthaginensis	1.12	49	13.63	MEC	246
273(g)...	Sisenand	633	Emerita	Lusitania	1.5	52	13.8	MEC	247
286(c)1	Chintila	637	Cordoba	Baetica	1.48	49.1	13.6	HSA	F 43
286(c)2	Chintila	637	Cordoba	Baetica	1.42	49.1	13.6	HSA	NOT F 6
290.1	Chintila	637	Eliberri	Baetica	1.23	49.1	13.6	HSA	16457
290var.	Chintila	637	Eliberri	Baetica	1.12	45	13.3	MEC	248
291(a)1	Chintila	637	Ispali	Baetica	1.48	50.4	13.7	HSA	16458
291(b)...	Chintila	637	Ispali	Baetica	1.41	54	13.95	MEC	250
292(c)1	Chintila	637	Tucci	Baetica	1.21	44.6	13.27	O 1	76
283(a)1	Chintila	637	Acci	Carthaginensis	1.23	47.7	13.5	HSA	16455
285(d)1	Chintila	637	Toleto	Carthaginensis	1.47	68.2	15.3	HSA	16459
285(d)2	Chintila	637	Toleto	Carthaginensis	1.52	73.9	15.9	HSA	16470
285(d)5	Chintila	637	Toleto	Carthaginensis	1.49	72	15.67	MEC	251
293(b)2	Chintila	637	Emerita	Lusitania	1.41	54	13.96	MEC	249
280.1	Chintila	637	Cesaragusta	Tarraconensis	1.39	35.8	12.6	HSA	16461
306(a)1	Tulga	640	Cordoba	Baetica	1.25	50.4	13.7	HSA	16465
306(b)1	Tulga	640	Cordoba	Baetica	1.15	46.4	13.4	HSA	16462
306(b)2	Tulga	640	Cordoba	Baetica	1.33	45.1	13.3	HSA	16464
306(d)1	Tulga	640	Cordoba	Baetica	1	45.1	13.3	HSA	16463
304(b)1	Tulga	640	Toleto	Carthaginensis	1.47	69.2	15.4	HSA	16468
301var.	Tulga	640	Cesaragusta	Tarraconensis	1.4	50	13.68	MEC	252
320.1	Chindasuinth	645	Cordoba	Baetica	1.41	58.8	14.4	ANS	58.184.1
322(e)1	Chindasuinth	645	Cordoba	Baetica	1.55	55.3	14.1	ANS	56.25.15
319...	Chindasuinth	645	Cordoba	Baetica	1.01	50	13.69	MEC	253
324var.	Chindasuinth	645	Ispali	Baetica	1.44	46	13.38	MEC	255
318(a)1	Chindasuinth	645	Toleto	Carthaginensis	1.54	67.2	15.2	HSA	16478
318(a)2	Chindasuinth	645	Toleto	Carthaginensis	1.53	63	14.8	HSA	16479
318(a)3	Chindasuinth	645	Toleto	Carthaginensis	1.52	56.5	14.2	HSA	16480
318(a)4	Chindasuinth	645	Toleto	Carthaginensis	1.41	56.5	14.2	HSA	8110

Miles No.	*Ruler*	*Date*	*Mint*	*Province*	***Weight (g)***	***Gold (%)***	*Specific Gravity*	*Location*	
318(a)5	Chindasuinth	645	Toleto	Carthaginensis	1.47	70.1	15.5	HSA	16481
318(a)7	Chindasuinth	645	Toleto	Carthaginensis	1.5	63	14.8	HSA	16483
318(c)...	Chindasuinth	645	Toleto	Carthaginensis	1.48	63	14.84	MEC	256
330(a)1	Chindasuinth	645	Emerita	Lusitania	1.53	46.4	13.4	HSA	16475
330(d)1	Chindasuinth	645	Emerita	Lusitania	1.42	51.7	13.8	HSA	16473
330(f)1	Chindasuinth	645	Emerita	Lusitania	1.54	70.1	15.5	HSA	16474
330(a)7	Chindasuinth	645	Emerita	Lusitania	1.27	55	14.06	MEC	254
348(a)1	Chind.-Recces	651	Ispali	Baetica	1.45	61	14.6	HSA	16536
350(a)var.	Chind.-Recces	651	Emerita	Lusitania	1.49	67	15.19	MEC	257
361.1	Reccesuinth	653	Cordoba	Baetica	1.54	54.1	14	HSA	16490
366.1	Reccesuinth	653	Ispali	Baetica	1.45	71	15.6	MEC	258
362(a)1	Reccesuinth	662	Cordoba	Baetica	1.47	75.8	16.1	HSA	16484
362(b)1	Reccesuinth	662	Cordoba	Baetica	1.52	70.1	15.5	HSA	16489
364(b)1	Reccesuinth	662	Cordoba	Baetica	1.46	64.1	14.9	HSA	16487
364(f)1	Reccesuinth	662	Cordoba	Baetica	1.5	69.2	15.4	HSA	16486
364(g)1	Reccesuinth	662	Cordoba	Baetica	1.51	71.1	15.6	HSA	16491
364(i)1	Reccesuinth	662	Cordoba	Baetica	1.48	65.1	15	HSA	16520
365.1	Reccesuinth	662	Cordoba	Baetica	1.41	65.1	15	HSA	16485
364(f)3	Reccesuinth	662	Cordoba	Baetica	1.4	68	15.31	MEC	260
367(a)1	Reccesuinth	662	Ispali	Baetica	1.49	64.1	14.9	HSA	16507
368(d)4	Reccesuinth	662	Ispali	Baetica	1.51	61	14.6	HSA	F 46
369(a)1	Reccesuinth	662	Ispali	Baetica	1.52	64.1	14.9	HSA	16040
369(a)2	Reccesuinth	662	Ispali	Baetica	1.44	67.2	15.2	HSA	16503
369(a)3	Reccesuinth	662	Ispali	Baetica	1.44	63	14.8	HSA	16505
369(f)1	Reccesuinth	662	Ispali	Baetica	1.54	65.1	15	HSA	16501
369(f)2	Reccesuinth	662	Ispali	Baetica	1.5	63	14.8	HSA	16508
369(a)...	Reccesuinth	662	Ispali	Baetica	1.5	66	15.06	MEC	262
360(a)1	Reccesuinth	662	Toleto	Carthaginensis	1.48	69.2	15.4	HSA	16523
360(a)2	Reccesuinth	662	Toleto	Carthaginensis	1.39	65.1	15	HSA	16534
360(a)3	Reccesuinth	662	Toleto	Carthaginensis	1.45	66.2	15.1	HSA	16524
360(a)4	Reccesuinth	662	Toleto	Carthaginensis	1.52	67.2	15.2	HSA	16525
360(a)5	Reccesuinth	662	Toleto	Carthaginensis	1.39	64.1	14.9	HSA	16527
360(a)6	Reccesuinth	662	Toleto	Carthaginensis	1.43	66.2	15.1	HSA	16528
360(a)7	Reccesuinth	662	Toleto	Carthaginensis	1.37	68.2	15.3	HSA	16529
360(c)4	Reccesuinth	662	Toleto	Carthaginensis	1.46	66	15.1	MEC	263
378(a)1	Reccesuinth	662	Bracara	Gallaecia	1.5	82.7	16.9	O 1	77
374(a)1	Reccesuinth	662	Emerita	Lusitania	1.47	69.2	15.4	HSA	8119
374(a)2	Reccesuinth	662	Emerita	Lusitania	1.49	66.2	15.1	HSA	16492
375(a)1	Reccesuinth	662	Emerita	Lusitania	1.52	69.2	15.4	HSA	16496
375(a)7	Reccesuinth	662	Emerita	Lusitania	1.38	68.2	15.3	HSA	F 44
376(a)1	Reccesuinth	662	Emerita	Lusitania	1.54	67.2	15.2	HSA	16493
376(a)2	Reccesuinth	662	Emerita	Lusitania	1.5	66.2	15.1	HSA	16494
376(a)3	Reccesuinth	662	Emerita	Lusitania	1.5	66.2	15.1	HSA	16495
376(a)4	Reccesuinth	662	Emerita	Lusitania	1.45	67.2	15.2	HSA	16499

Miles No.	*Ruler*	*Date*	*Mint*	*Province*	***Weight (g)***	***Gold (%)***	*Specific Gravity*	*Location*	
376(a)5	Reccesuinth	662	Emerita	Lusitania	1.5	68.2	15.3	HSA	16497
376(a)6	Reccesuinth	662	Emerita	Lusitania	1.5	65.1	15	HSA	16500
376(a)7	Reccesuinth	662	Emerita	Lusitania	1.48	68.2	15.3	ANS	1937.56.6
374(e)var.	Reccesuinth	662	Emerita	Lusitania	1.5	73	15.83	MEC	261
353(a)1	Reccesuinth	662	Narbona	Narbonensis	1.39	70.1	15.5	HSA	16511
356(a)1	Reccesuinth	662	Tarracona	Tarraconensis	1.36	64.1	14.9	HSA	16512
356(c)1	Reccesuinth	662	Tarracona	Tarraconensis	1.5	71.1	15.6	HSA	16513
356(c)2	Reccesuinth	662	Tarracona	Tarraconensis	1.55	71.1	15.6	HSA	16519
357(a)1	Reccesuinth	662	Tarracona	Tarraconensis	1.46	61	14.6	HSA	16515
357(d)1	Reccesuinth	662	Tarracona	Tarraconensis	1.41	59.9	14.5	HSA	16514
386(b)11	Wamba	676	Toleto	Carthaginensis	1.59	57	14.27	MEC	266
394(a)7	Wamba	676	Emerita	Lusitania	1.47	59	14.42	O 1	78
394(a)8	Wamba	676	Emerita	Lusitania	1.5	58	14.29	MEC	264
394(b)1	Wamba	676	Emerita	Lusitania	1.38	63	14.76	MEC	265
409(b)2	Ervig	683	Ispali	Baetica	1.47	57	14.22	MEC	268
410(a)4	Ervig	683	Ispali	Baetica	1.46	53	13.87	MEC	269
412(a)var.	Ervig	683	Tucci	Baetica	1.49	55	14.06	MEC	271
399(a)14	Ervig	683	Toleto	Carthaginensis	1.43	57	14.36	MEC	270
415(a)23	Ervig	683	Emerita	Lusitania	1.46	59	14.41	MEC	267
436(f)1	Egica	691	Toleto	Carthaginensis	1.26	42.5	13.1	HSA	16616
436(i)2	Egica	691	Toleto	Carthaginensis	1.49	42	13.08	MEC	276
437(b)var.	Egica	691	Toleto	Carthaginensis	1.48	58	14.31	MEC	277
448(a)1	Egica	691	Emerita	Lusitania	1.37	53	13.93	MEC	273
449(a)...	Egica	691	Emerita	Lusitania	1.43	53	13.94	MEC	274
424(c)...	Egica	691	Gerunda	Tarraconensis	1.23	40	12.91	MEC	272
426(c)...	Egica	691	Tarracona	Tarraconensis	1.17	47	13.44	MEC	275
471(d)1	Egica-Wittiza	698	Cordoba	Baetica	1.47	43.8	13.2	HSA	16625
473(a)1	Egica-Wittiza	698	Cordoba	Baetica	1.38	28.5	12.1	HSA	16629
480(d)1	Egica-Wittiza	698	Ispali	Baetica	1.43	38.5	12.8	HSA	16641
480(e)1	Egica-Wittiza	698	Ispali	Baetica	1.4	37.2	12.7	HSA	16631
480(m)1	Egica-Wittiza	698	Ispali	Baetica	1.32	28.5	12.1	HSA	16642
480(n)1	Egica-Wittiza	698	Ispali	Baetica	1.35	30	12.2	HSA	16623
480(o)1	Egica-Wittiza	698	Ispali	Baetica	1.33	34.4	12.5	HSA	16632
480(p)1	Egica-Wittiza	698	Ispali	Baetica	1.38	31.5	12.3	HSA	16627
480(r)1	Egica-Wittiza	698	Ispali	Baetica	1.26	26.9	12	HSA	8137
481(c)1	Egica-Wittiza	698	Ispali	Baetica	1.26	39.8	12.9	HSA	16620
483(a)1	Egica-Wittiza	698	Tucci	Baetica	1.08	34.4	12.5	HSA	16630
483(b)1	Egica-Wittiza	698	Tucci	Baetica	1.22	38.5	12.8	HSA	16589
467(b)1	Egica-Wittiza	698	Mentesa	Carthaginensis	1.13	25.4	11.9	HSA	16654
467(c)1	Egica-Wittiza	698	Mentesa	Carthaginensis	1.32	47.7	13.5	ANS	56.25.19
467(f)1	Egica-Wittiza	698	Mentesa	Carthaginensis	1.35	43.8	13.2	HSA	F 69
468(a)1	Egica-Wittiza	698	Toleto	Carthaginensis	1.43	38.5	12.8	HSA	16588
468(a)2	Egica-Wittiza	698	Toleto	Carthaginensis	1.25	34.4	12.5	HSA	16622
468(l)1	Egica-Wittiza	698	Toleto	Carthaginensis	1.58	35.8	12.6	HSA	F 73

Miles No.	*Ruler*	*Date*	*Mint*	*Province*	***Weight (g)***	***Gold (%)***	*Specific Gravity*	*Location*	
468(m)1	Egica-Wittiza	698	Toleto	Carthaginensis	1.51	49.1	13.6	HSA	F 72
468(j)var.	Egica-Wittiza	698	Toleto	Carthaginensis	1.5	49	13.62	MEC	282
468(j)var.	Egica-Wittiza	698	Toleto	Carthaginensis	1.4	48	13.53	MEC	283
485(a)1	Egica-Wittiza	698	Elvora	Carthaginensis	1.49	41.2	13	HSA	16587
485(c)1	Egica-Wittiza	698	Elvora	Carthaginensis	1.38	38.5	12.8	ANS	56.25.20
485(c)1	Egica-Wittiza	698	Elvora	Carthaginensis	1.09	37	12.72	MEC	278
486(a)1	Egica-Wittiza	698	Emerita	Lusitania	1.34	35.8	12.6	HSA	16619
486(h)1	Egica-Wittiza	698	Emerita	Lusitania	1.2	31	12.26	MEC	280
486(k)1	Egica-Wittiza	698	Emerita	Lusitania	1.37	37	12.67	MEC	279
455(a)1	Egica-Wittiza	698	Narbona	Narbonensis	1.41	45.1	13.3	HSA	16647
455(b)1	Egica-Wittiza	698	Narbona	Narbonensis	1.41	41.2	13	HSA	16590
455(e)1	Egica-Wittiza	698	Narbona	Narbonensis	1.45	38.5	12.8	HSA	16626
456(b)1	Egica-Wittiza	698	Narbona	Narbonensis	1.16	42.5	13.1	HSA	F 70
460(a)1	Egica-Wittiza	698	Cesaragusta	Tarraconensis	1.52	47.7	13.5	HSA	16644
460(e)1	Egica-Wittiza	698	Cesaragusta	Tarraconensis	1.32	25.4	11.9	HSA	16643
461...	Egica-Wittiza	698	Gerunda	Tarraconensis	1.03	10.2	11	ANS	62.30.2
462(a)1	Egica-Wittiza	698	Gerunda	Tarraconensis	0.98	30	12.2	HSA	16648
503(a)1	Wittiza	706	Cordoba	Baetica	1.36	54.1	14	HSA	16652
507(a)1	Wittiza	706	Ispali	Baetica	1.02	23.9	11.8	HSA	16661
499(a)1	Wittiza	706	Toleto	Carthaginensis	1.57	65.1	15	HSA	16658
499(c)1	Wittiza	706	Toleto	Carthaginensis	1.34	69.2	15.4	ANS	56.25.21
500(b)1	Wittiza	706	Toleto	Carthaginensis	1.51	69.2	15.4	HSA	16653
500(c)2	Wittiza	706	Toleto	Carthaginensis	1.51	70.1	15.5	HSA	F 75
500(d)1	Wittiza	706	Toleto	Carthaginensis	1.46	65.1	15	HSA	F 76
491(c)1	Wittiza	706	Narbona	Narbonensis	1.27	34.4	12.5	HSA	16649
493(a)1	Wittiza	706	Cesaragusta	Tarraconensis	1.27	66.2	15.1	HSA	16651
494(c)1	Wittiza	706	Gerunda	Tarraconensis	1.12	30	12.2	HSA	16662
512(b)4	Roderic	710	Egitania	Lusitania	1.48	52.9	13.9	HSA	F 77
f105(b)6	Roderic	710	Toleto	Carthaginensis	1.35	61	14.6	HSA	0

Figure I.12: Averages of fineness and other measurements of gold coins at the ANS

(tests conducted by Lauris Olson; see Figure I.11)

Ruler	Number of coins	Year	Mean AU (SG)	Max AU (SG)	Min AU (SG)	SD AU (SG)	SD + AU (SG)	SD - AU (SG)	Coeffic. of Variation (%)
PseudoAnastasius	17	504	**18.616**	19.1	16.5	0.775	19.391	17.842	
PseudoJustin I	11	523	**18.591**	19	18.1	0.323	18.914	18.268	
PseudoJustinian	10	546	**17.991**	18.71	15.89	0.86	18.851	17.131	
PseudoJustin II	13	571	**17.669**	18.67	15	1.001	18.67	16.668	
CURRU legend	20	576	**17.9**	18.6	15.1	1.012	18.912	16.888	
Leovigild--VPW	5	581	**15.994**	17.37	15.5	0.777	16.771	15.217	4.9
Hermenegild (forgery)	1	582	**18.8**						
Leovigild--COS	15	584	**15.785**	16.4	15.2	0.341	16.126	15.445	2.2
Leovigild-2FB	20	586	**15.844**	16.8	15.3	0.417	16.261	15.426	2.6
Reccared I	79	593	**15.746**	16.8	14.45	0.389	16.134	15.357	2.5
Liuva II	7	602	**15.661**	16.17	15.2	0.357	16.019	15.304	2.3
Witteric	22	606	**15.586**	16.3	15.1	0.282	15.868	15.304	1.8
Gundemar	5	610	**15.108**	15.4	14.9	0.188	15.296	14.92	1.2
Sisebut	42	616	**15.162**	16.2	14.5	0.38	15.542	14.783	2.5
Suinthila	32	626	**14.51**	15.26	13.7	0.365	14.875	14.146	2.5
Iudila	1	632	**14.4**						
Sisenand	4	633	**13.865**	14.04	13.63	0.188	14.053	13.677	1.4
Chintila	13	637	**13.996**	15.9	12.6	0.996	14.992	13.001	7.1
Tulga	6	640	**13.797**	15.4	13.3	0.806	14.602	12.991	5.8
Chindasvinth	15	645	**14.391**	15.5	13.38	0.695	15.086	13.696	4.8
Chindasvinth-Reccesvinth	2	651	**14.895**	15.19	14.6	0.417	15.312	14.478	2.8
Reccesvinth A	2	653	**14.8**	15.6	14	1.131	15.931	13.669	7.6
Reccesvinth B	43	662	**15.209**	16.9	14.5	0.415	15.624	14.795	2.7
Wamba	4	676	**14.435**	14.76	14.27	0.227	14.662	14.208	1.6
Ervig	5	683	**14.184**	14.41	13.87	0.222	14.406	13.962	1.6
Egica	7	691	**13.53**	14.31	12.91	0.535	14.065	12.995	4
Egica-Wittiza	35	698	**12.691**	13.62	11	0.576	13.268	12.115	4.5
Wittiza	10	706	**14.19**	15.5	11.8	1.466	15.656	12.724	10.3
Roderic (one forgery)	2	710	**14.25**	14.6	13.9	0.495	14.745	13.755	3.5
Arabic-94 A.H.	9	713	**12.892**			1.791	14.914	11.332	
Arabic-96 A.H.	2	715	**16.95**			0.348	17.304	16.609	
Arabic-102 A.H.	5	721	**18.893**			0.225	19.12	18.671	
Total (royal only)	377		**14.927**	18.8	11	1.092	16.019	13.835	7.3
Total (all)	464								

Figure I.13: Frequencies of weights of Visigothic regal tremisses

(based on Marques et al., *Ensaios*, 108-13 and Lauris Olson – see Fig. I.11)

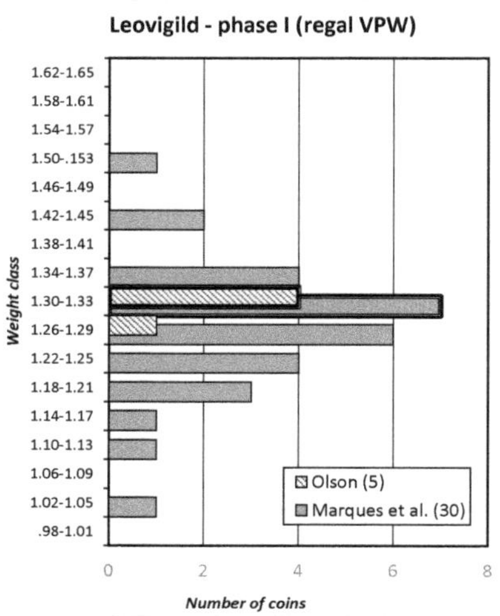

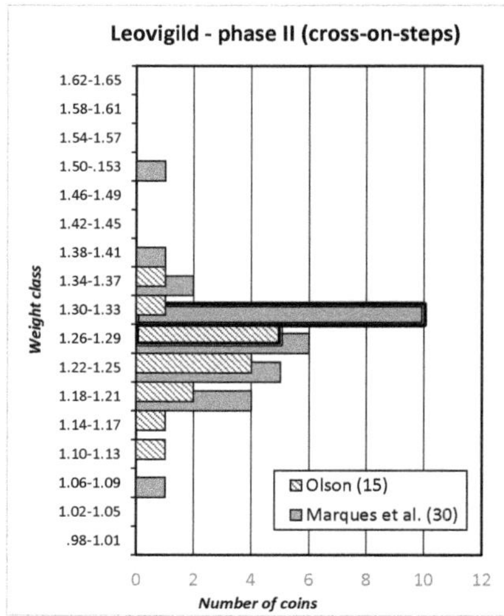

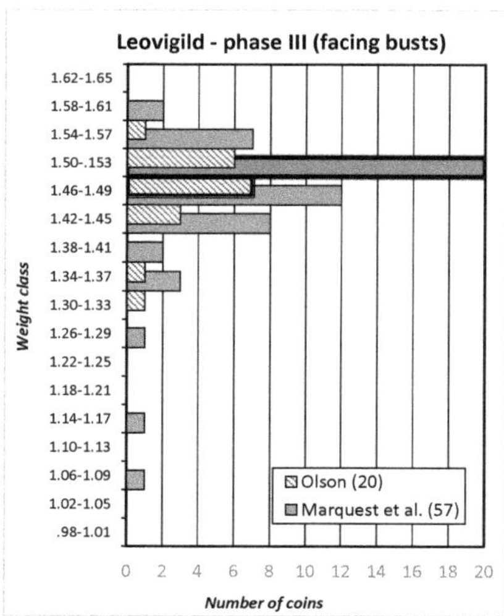

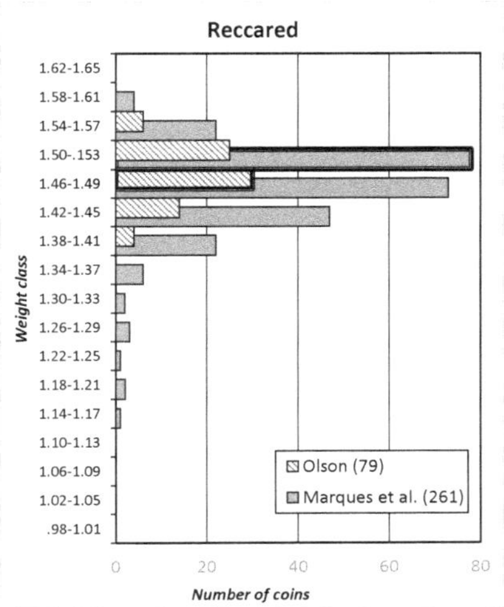
Reccared
Weight class
1.62-1.65
1.58-1.61
1.54-1.57
1.50-.153
1.46-1.49
1.42-1.45
1.38-1.41
1.34-1.37
1.30-1.33
1.26-1.29
1.22-1.25
1.18-1.21
1.14-1.17
1.10-1.13
1.06-1.09
1.02-1.05
.98-1.01
0 20 40 60 80
Number of coins
Olson (79)
Marques et al. (261)

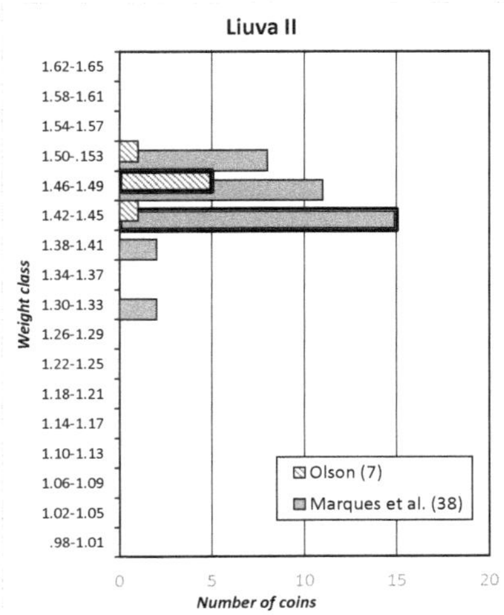
Liuva II
Weight class
1.62-1.65
1.58-1.61
1.54-1.57
1.50-.153
1.46-1.49
1.42-1.45
1.38-1.41
1.34-1.37
1.30-1.33
1.26-1.29
1.22-1.25
1.18-1.21
1.14-1.17
1.10-1.13
1.06-1.09
1.02-1.05
.98-1.01
0 5 10 15 20
Number of coins
Olson (7)
Marques et al. (38)

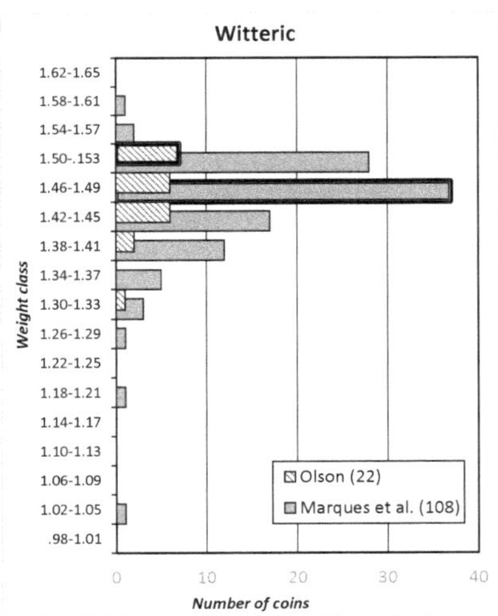
Witteric
Weight class
1.62-1.65
1.58-1.61
1.54-1.57
1.50-.153
1.46-1.49
1.42-1.45
1.38-1.41
1.34-1.37
1.30-1.33
1.26-1.29
1.22-1.25
1.18-1.21
1.14-1.17
1.10-1.13
1.06-1.09
1.02-1.05
.98-1.01
0 10 20 30 40
Number of coins
Olson (22)
Marques et al. (108)

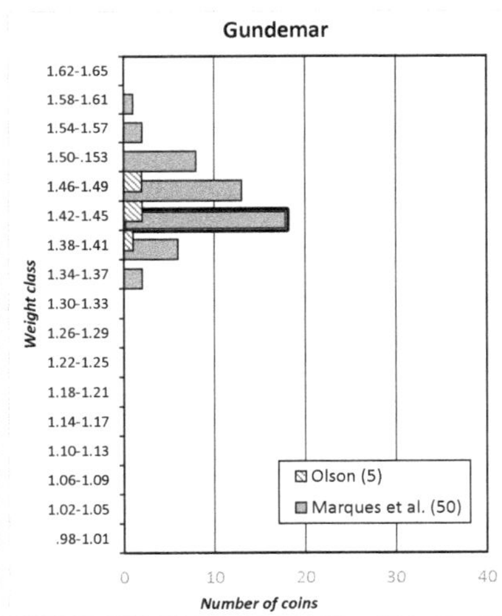
Gundemar
Weight class
1.62-1.65
1.58-1.61
1.54-1.57
1.50-.153
1.46-1.49
1.42-1.45
1.38-1.41
1.34-1.37
1.30-1.33
1.26-1.29
1.22-1.25
1.18-1.21
1.14-1.17
1.10-1.13
1.06-1.09
1.02-1.05
.98-1.01
0 10 20 30 40
Number of coins
Olson (5)
Marques et al. (50)

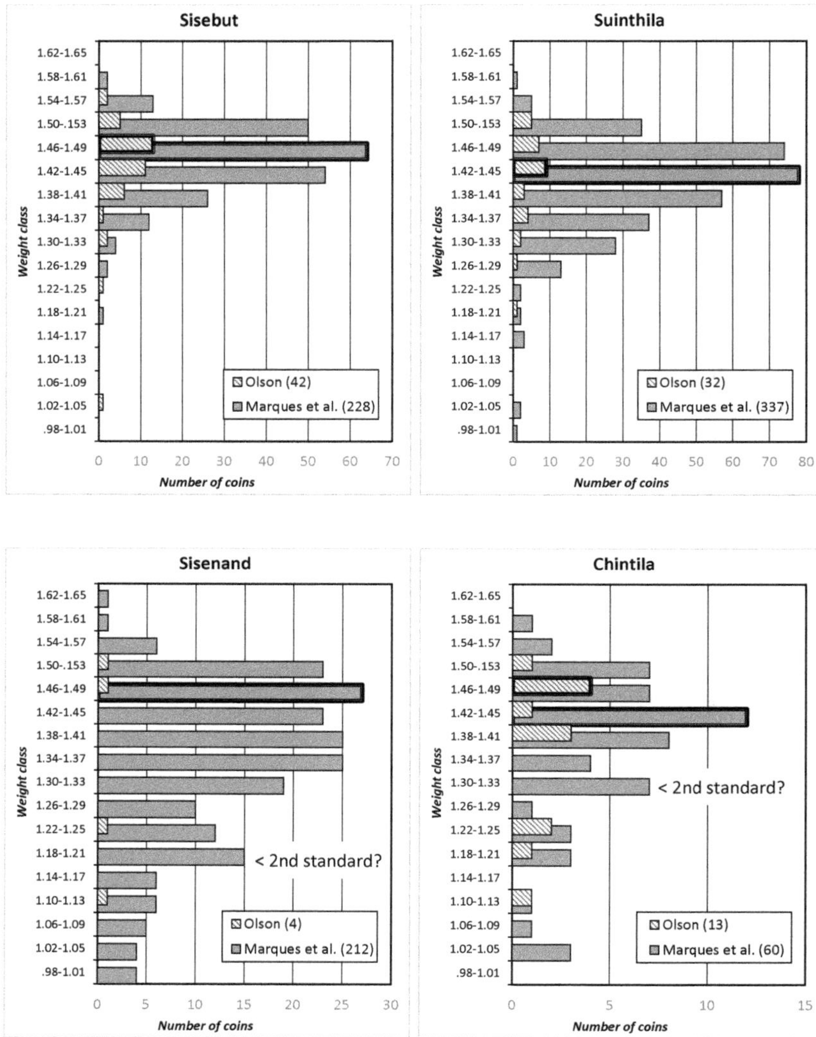
Sisebut
Olson (42)
Marques et al. (228)
Suinthila
Olson (32)
Marques et al. (337)
Sisenand
< 2nd standard?
Olson (4)
Marques et al. (212)
Chintila
< 2nd standard?
Olson (13)
Marques et al. (60)
Weight class
Number of coins
1.62-1.65
1.58-1.61
1.54-1.57
1.50-.153
1.46-1.49
1.42-1.45
1.38-1.41
1.34-1.37
1.30-1.33
1.26-1.29
1.22-1.25
1.18-1.21
1.14-1.17
1.10-1.13
1.06-1.09
1.02-1.05
.98-1.01

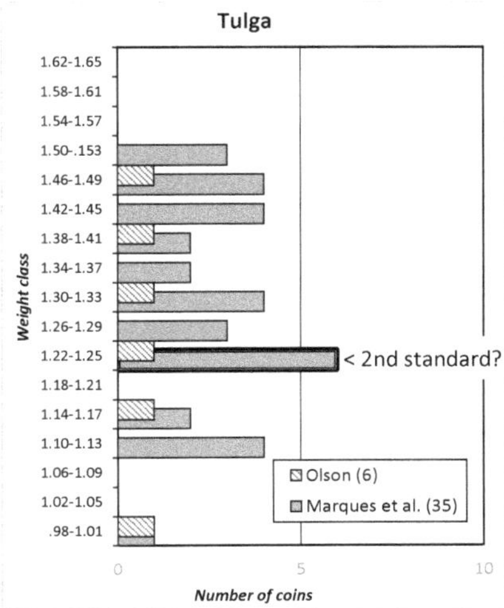
Tulga
Weight class
1.62-1.65
1.58-1.61
1.54-1.57
1.50-.153
1.46-1.49
1.42-1.45
1.38-1.41
1.34-1.37
1.30-1.33
1.26-1.29
1.22-1.25
1.18-1.21
1.14-1.17
1.10-1.13
1.06-1.09
1.02-1.05
.98-1.01
< 2nd standard?
Olson (6)
Marques et al. (35)
0
5
10
Number of coins

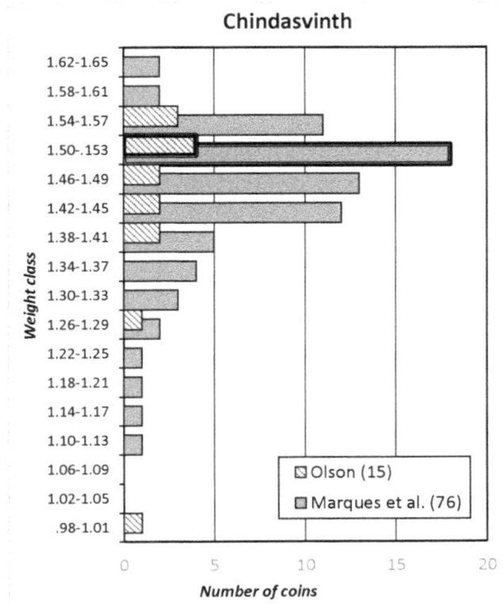
Chindasvinth
Weight class
1.62-1.65
1.58-1.61
1.54-1.57
1.50-.153
1.46-1.49
1.42-1.45
1.38-1.41
1.34-1.37
1.30-1.33
1.26-1.29
1.22-1.25
1.18-1.21
1.14-1.17
1.10-1.13
1.06-1.09
1.02-1.05
.98-1.01
Olson (15)
Marques et al. (76)
0
5
10
15
20
Number of coins

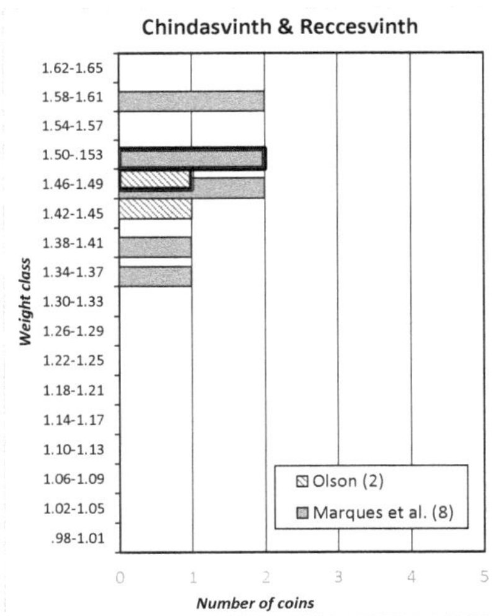
Chindasvinth & Reccesvinth
Weight class
1.62-1.65
1.58-1.61
1.54-1.57
1.50-.153
1.46-1.49
1.42-1.45
1.38-1.41
1.34-1.37
1.30-1.33
1.26-1.29
1.22-1.25
1.18-1.21
1.14-1.17
1.10-1.13
1.06-1.09
1.02-1.05
.98-1.01
Olson (2)
Marques et al. (8)
0
1
2
3
4
5
Number of coins

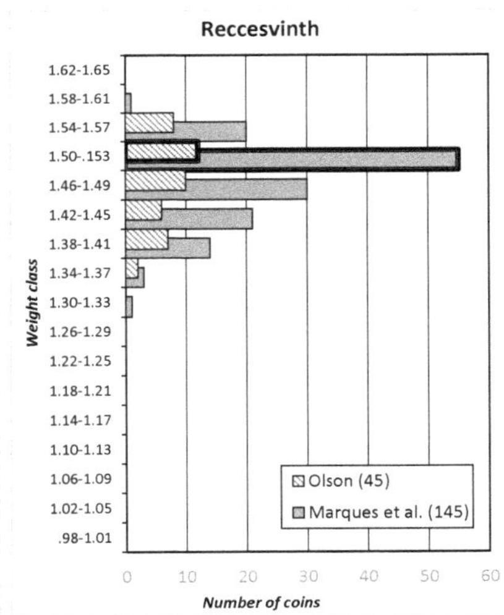
Reccesvinth
Weight class
1.62-1.65
1.58-1.61
1.54-1.57
1.50-.153
1.46-1.49
1.42-1.45
1.38-1.41
1.34-1.37
1.30-1.33
1.26-1.29
1.22-1.25
1.18-1.21
1.14-1.17
1.10-1.13
1.06-1.09
1.02-1.05
.98-1.01
Olson (45)
Marques et al. (145)
0
10
20
30
40
50
60
Number of coins

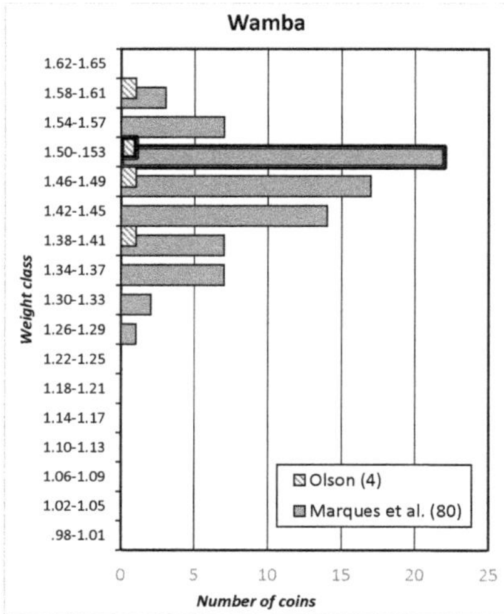
Wamba
Weight class
1.62-1.65
1.58-1.61
1.54-1.57
1.50-.153
1.46-1.49
1.42-1.45
1.38-1.41
1.34-1.37
1.30-1.33
1.26-1.29
1.22-1.25
1.18-1.21
1.14-1.17
1.10-1.13
1.06-1.09
1.02-1.05
.98-1.01
0 5 10 15 20 25
Number of coins
Olson (4)
Marques et al. (80)

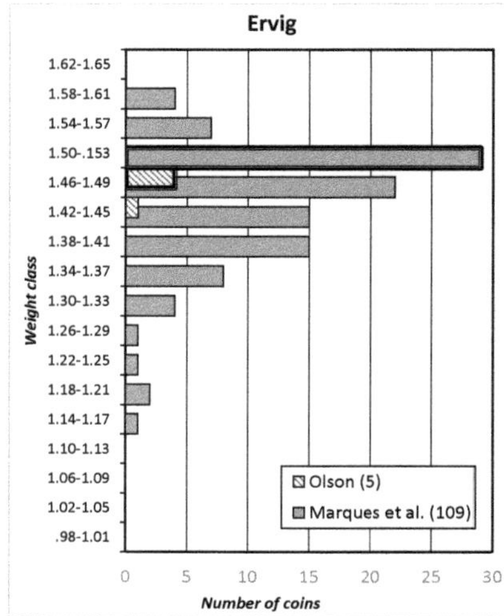
Ervig
Weight class
1.62-1.65
1.58-1.61
1.54-1.57
1.50-.153
1.46-1.49
1.42-1.45
1.38-1.41
1.34-1.37
1.30-1.33
1.26-1.29
1.22-1.25
1.18-1.21
1.14-1.17
1.10-1.13
1.06-1.09
1.02-1.05
.98-1.01
0 5 10 15 20 25 30
Number of coins
Olson (5)
Marques et al. (109)

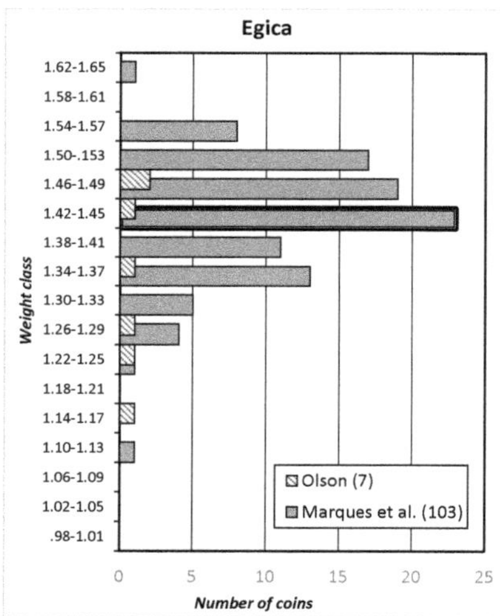
Egica
Weight class
1.62-1.65
1.58-1.61
1.54-1.57
1.50-.153
1.46-1.49
1.42-1.45
1.38-1.41
1.34-1.37
1.30-1.33
1.26-1.29
1.22-1.25
1.18-1.21
1.14-1.17
1.10-1.13
1.06-1.09
1.02-1.05
.98-1.01
0 5 10 15 20 25
Number of coins
Olson (7)
Marques et al. (103)

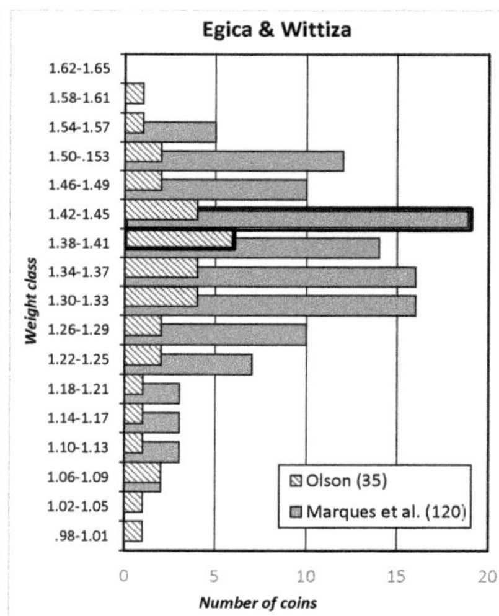
Egica & Wittiza
Weight class
1.62-1.65
1.58-1.61
1.54-1.57
1.50-.153
1.46-1.49
1.42-1.45
1.38-1.41
1.34-1.37
1.30-1.33
1.26-1.29
1.22-1.25
1.18-1.21
1.14-1.17
1.10-1.13
1.06-1.09
1.02-1.05
.98-1.01
0 5 10 15 20
Number of coins
Olson (35)
Marques et al. (120)

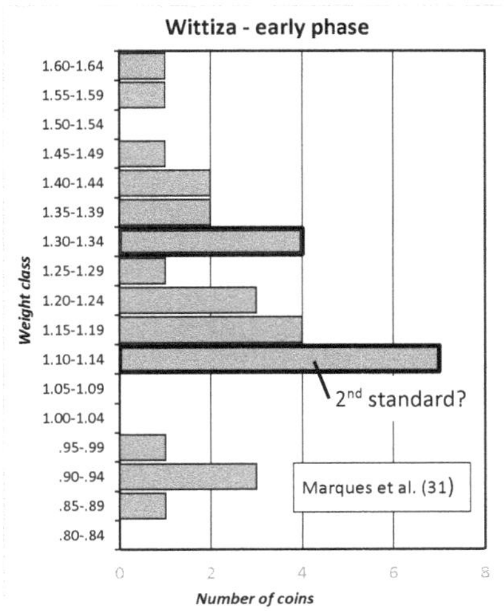
Wittiza - early phase
Weight class
1.60-1.64
1.55-1.59
1.50-1.54
1.45-1.49
1.40-1.44
1.35-1.39
1.30-1.34
1.25-1.29
1.20-1.24
1.15-1.19
1.10-1.14
1.05-1.09
1.00-1.04
.95-.99
.90-.94
.85-.89
.80-.84
2nd standard?
Marques et al. (31)
0 2 4 6 8
Number of coins

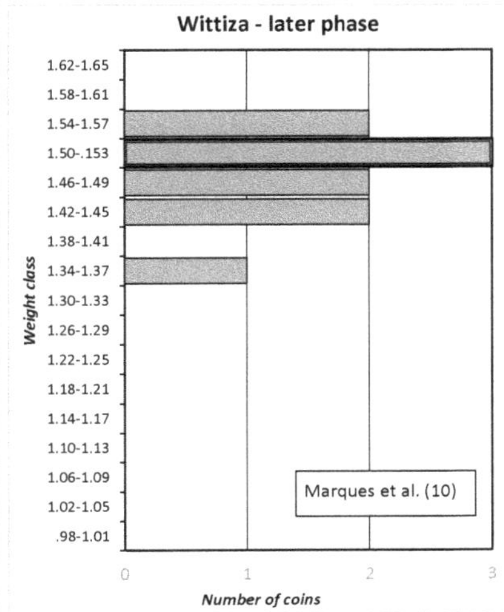
Wittiza - later phase
Weight class
1.62-1.65
1.58-1.61
1.54-1.57
1.50-.153
1.46-1.49
1.42-1.45
1.38-1.41
1.34-1.37
1.30-1.33
1.26-1.29
1.22-1.25
1.18-1.21
1.14-1.17
1.10-1.13
1.06-1.09
1.02-1.05
.98-1.01
Marques et al. (10)
0 1 2 3
Number of coins

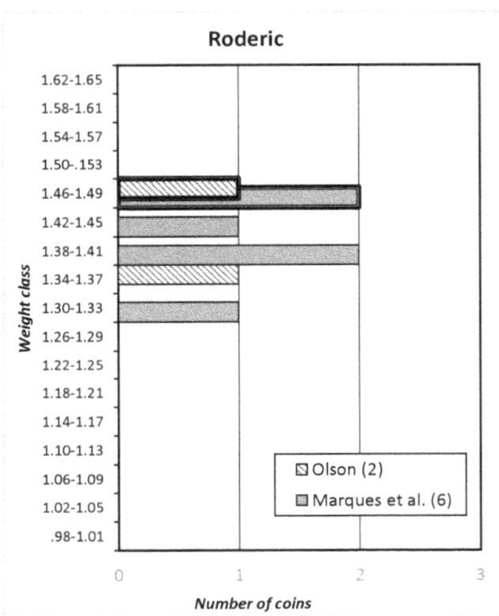
Roderic
Weight class
1.62-1.65
1.58-1.61
1.54-1.57
1.50-.153
1.46-1.49
1.42-1.45
1.38-1.41
1.34-1.37
1.30-1.33
1.26-1.29
1.22-1.25
1.18-1.21
1.14-1.17
1.10-1.13
1.06-1.09
1.02-1.05
.98-1.01
Olson (2)
Marques et al. (6)
0 1 2 3
Number of coins

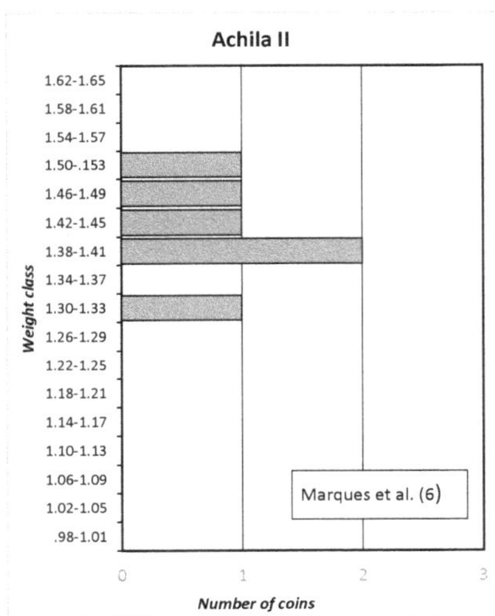
Achila II
Weight class
1.62-1.65
1.58-1.61
1.54-1.57
1.50-.153
1.46-1.49
1.42-1.45
1.38-1.41
1.34-1.37
1.30-1.33
1.26-1.29
1.22-1.25
1.18-1.21
1.14-1.17
1.10-1.13
1.06-1.09
1.02-1.05
.98-1.01
Marques et al. (6)
0 1 2 3
Number of coins

Figure I.14: Average weights of tremisses at mints of diverse volumes of output

(derived from Marques et al., *Ensaios*, 104, Quadro VI)

REIGN / PHASE	AVE. WEIGHT / Standard Deviation at largest mint	>10%	3-10%	<3%
Leovigild				
Phase II	1.307 ±0.030	1.276 ±0.104	1.263 ±0.040	---
Phase III	↑ 1.506 ±0.048	↑ 1.501 ±0.040	↑ 1.437 ±0.125	1.420 ±0.060
Reccared	1.475 ±0.053	1.483 ±0.051	1.464 ±0.075	1.431 ±0.099
Liuva II	1.475 ±0.034	1.474 ±0.034	1.443 ±0.056	---
Witteric	1.475 ±0.038	1.469 ±0.060	1.435 ±0.039	1.426 ±0.110
Gundemar	1.491 ±0.032	1.475 ±0.046	1.435 ±0.038	---
Sisebut	1.483 ±0.034	1.480 ±0.038	1.446 ±0.064	1.428 ±0.075
Suinthila	1.461 ±0.042	↓ 1.418 ±0.084	↓ 1.412 ±0.080	↓ 1.356 ±0.084
Sisenand	1.442 ±0.089	1.414 ±0.108	↓ 1.286 ±0.148	↓ 1.292 ±0.095
Chintila	1.435 ±0.065	1.437 ±0.064	↓ 1.279 ±0.148	---
Tulga	↓ 1.181 ±0.149	↓ 1.270 ±0.179	↑ 1.341 ±0.110	---
Chindasvinth	↑ 1.496 ±0.051	↑ 1.476 ±0.080	↑ 1.422 ±0.111	1.389 ±0.144
Chind.& Recces.	↑ 1.537 ±0.118	↑ 1.507 ±0.077	---	---
Reccesvinth	↓ 1.483 ±0.057	1.492 ±0.058	↑? 1.460 ±0.068	↑? 1.478 ±0.065
Wamba	↓ 1.422 ±0.073	↓ 1.458 ±0.074	1.471 ±0.052	---
Ervig	1.445 ±0.072	1.452 ±0.082	↓ 1.446 ±0.090	1.457 ±0.050
Egica	1.455 ±0.107	1.439 ±0.098	1.434 ±0.072	1.459 ±0.054
Egica & Wittiza	↓ 1.376 ±0.080	↓ 1.389 ±0.099	↓ 1.328 ±0.208	↓ 1.284 ±0.208
Wittiza				
Phase I	↓ 1.311 ±0.127	↓ 1.215 ±0.175	↓ 1.175 ±0.094	---
Phase II	↑ 1.483 ±0.074	↑ 1.483 ±0.074	---	---
Phase III	1.477 ±0.120	1.445 ±0.117	---	---
Roderic	↓ 1.396 ±0.057	↓ 1.407 ±0.057	---	---
Achila II	1.418 ±0.079	1.423 ±0.072	---	---

1st column – Average weight and standard deviation of tremisses struck at the most productive mint in the reign or phase (according to the number of extant coins)

>10% -- as above, but for mints which account for more than 10% of the total corpus

3-10% -- as above, but for mints which account for 3-10% of the total corpus

<3% -- as above, but for mints which account for less than 3% of the total corpus

Note: ↑ denotes a significant increase in the average weight compared to the previous reign or phase, ↓ denotes a significant decrease. Sudden or gradual downward trends generally correspond to a rise in standard deviation, whereas improved weights have generally lower standard deviations.

Figure I.15: Percentage of fineness in Visigothic tremisses of three major samples

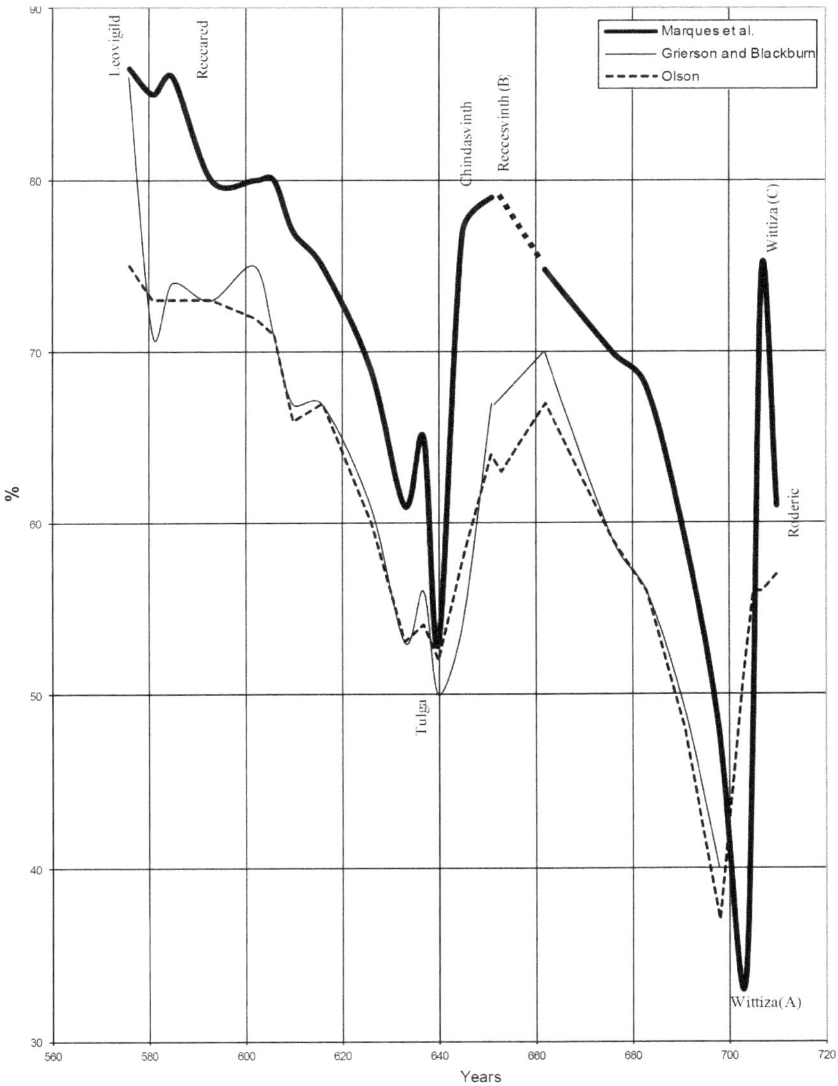

Figure I.16: Average fineness of 238 tremisses tested using X-ray fluorescent spectrometry method

(derived from Marques et al., *Ensaios*, 131, Quadro VI)

REIGN / PHASE	Number of Coins	Percentage of Fineness*	Fineness Expressed in karats*
Leovigild			
Phase I	2	86.5 ± 0.2	20.7 ± 0.1
Phase II	2	84.6 ± 4.1	20.3 ± 1.0
Phase III	1	85.7	20.6
Reccared	27	80.4 ± 2.6	19.3 ± 0.6
Liuva II	6	79.7 ± 2.9	19.1 ± 0.7
Witteric	19	79.6 ± 2.9	19.1 ± 0.7
Gundemar	9	77.3 ± 2.0	18.6 ± 0.5
Sisebut	32	74.5 ± 3.3	17.9 ± 0.8
Reccared II	1	74	17.8
Suinthila	34	69.1 ± 5.0	16.6 ± 1.2
Sisenand	14	↓60.8 ± 5.3	14.6 ± 1.3
Chintila	8	64.9 ± 5.1	15.6 ± 1.2
Tulga	3	↓53.4 ± 10.2	12.8 ± 2.4
Chindasvinth			
Phase I	9	59.7 ± 4.3	14.3 ± 1.0
Phase II	1	↑77.1	18.5
Chind.& Recces.	1	79.2	19.0
Reccesvinth	16	75.0 ± 4.2	18.0 ± 1.0
Wamba	6	70.4 ± 3.6	16.4 ± 0.9
Ervig	8	67.91± 4.7	16.3 ± 1.1
Egica	14	↓58.5 ± 5.0	14.0 ± 1.2
Egica & Wittiza	18	↓48.0 ± 7.5	11.5 ± 1.8
Wittiza			
Phase I	2	32.5 ± 2.1	7.8 ± 0.5
Phase II	2	47.5 ± 1.1	11.5 ± 0.3
Phase III	2	↑74.5 ± 1.8	17.9 ± 0.4
Roderic	1	60.6	14.5

**Average value ± standard deviation*

↑ and ↓ indicate the most notable increases and decreases in finenesss

Figure I.17: Fineness of Visigothic pseudo-imperial tremisses, Visigothic regal tremisses, and early Muslim dinars in Spain

(based on a graph by Lauris Olson of 464 coins tested at the ANS in 1987 see data in Fig. I.12)

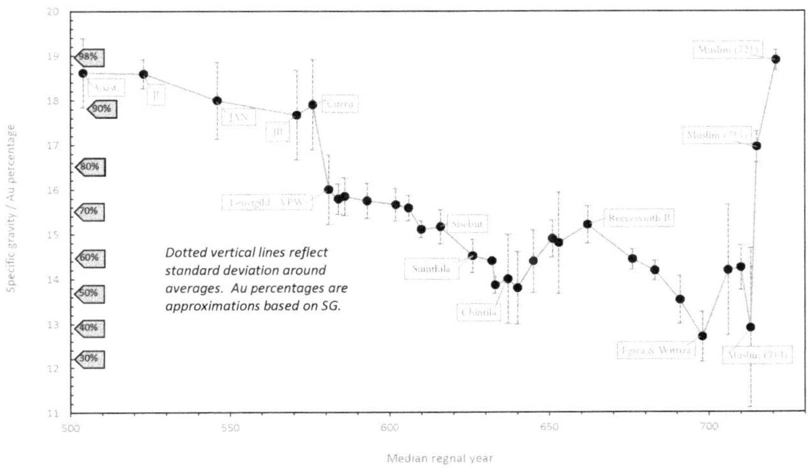

Appendix II

The identification of die engravers at multiple mints

An explanation should be given of the sources and of the method of analysis for the attributions of die engravers in Chapter Three, and in the photos and commentary as well as the full table that follow. I have conducted my die study over a number of years, with intermittent visits to the American Numismatic Society (ANS) in New York City. Apart from my visits, I initially relied on the photo plates in Miles's catalog and a few key sources below, to which are attached the abbreviations used in the following pages. (Plate numbers from books are given in Roman numerals, followed by Arabic numerals corresponding to the numbers of the coins on the plates.) In recent years, any detailed work on Visigothic coins in general has been greatly aided by two superb tools. Ruth Pliego's catalog (volume 2 of *La moneda visidogda*) provides a nearly comprehensive corpus from the time of publication in 2009 as well as a huge number of good photographs. In addition, the online digitized image bank of the ANS, called MANTIS, furnishes color images of the vast majority of the gold coins of the kingdom housed at this singular repository. At the end of this introduction to this second appendix, a concordance of old Hispanic Society of America (HSA) numbers of the ANS Visigothic regal collection and the new acquisition numbers is provided.[865]

Abbreviations

ANS American Numismatic Society coins studied firsthand or from photos from the collection.

Aureo Auction catalogs of Aureo, S. A., under the title of *Subasta Numismática*.

865 Most of the Visigothic coins, among many others at the ANS, were on indefinite loan from the HSA (Hispanic Society of America) for decades. After the ANS moved to a different part of New York City over ten years ago, the ANS lost guardianship of the coins, which then became inaccessible to all. In recent years, a generous donor purchased half of some 38,000 coins sold by the HSA, including all the Visigothic pieces, for permanent possession by the ANS. ANS enumeration of this coinage is composed of year of acquisition, followed by group number within that year, then object number within that group (e.g., 2015.48.81). The 2013 Visigothic acquisitions were of die duplicates of the HSA. In 2014, the imitative and pseudo-imperial gold coins were received. In 2015, lower-value Visigothic regal pieces were acquired, then, in 2016, those of high value.

Bartlett	Peter Bartlett, private collection, Costa Rica; photos shared by owner.
BM	British Museum, coins as referenced in Pliego 2009.
Bruxelles	Photos from the *Cabinet des medailles* of the Bibliotheque royale Albert Ier.
Chaves	Rafael Chaves and María José Chaves, *Acuñaciones previsigodas y visigodas en Hispania, desde Honorio a Achila II* (Madrid, 1984).
Ensaios	Mário Gomes Marques, J. M. Peixoto Cabral, and J. Rodriguez Marinho, *Ensaios sobre história monetária da monarquia visigoda* (Porto, 1995). After p. 188, the book provides twelve plates of photos of regal coins in Portuguese collections, both private and public.
GNC	J. Amorós and Antonia Mata Berruezo, *Catálogo de las monedas visigodas del Gabinete Numismático de Cataluña* (Barcelona, 1952).
Heiss	Aloïss Heiss, *Description générale des monnaies de rois wisigoths d'Espagne* (Paris, 1872).
HSA	Hispanic Society of America
IVDJ	Instituto de Valencia de Don Juan, coins as referenced in Pliego 2009.
JV	Auction catalogues of Jesus Vico, S. A.
Leu Photos	Photos of four hundred Visigothic tremisses obtained by Bank Leu (now Leu Numismatik) in the 1980s, the originals of which were given to the ANS and the author was able to review at length.
M.	George C. Miles, *The Coinage of the Visigoths of Spain: Leovigild to Achila II* (New York, NY, 1952). It contains thirty-eight plates of black-and-white photos of coins from the American Numismatic Society's collection. For each specimen there is a corresponding catalog number.
Madrid	Felipe Mateu y Llopis, *Catálogo de las monedas previsigodas y visigodas del Gabinete Numismático del Museo Arqueológico Nacional* (Madrid, 1936).
MAN	Museo Arqueológico Nacional, Madrid.
MEC	Philip Grierson and Michael Blackburn, *Medieval European Coinage* (vol. I: *The Early Middle Ages [5th-10th centuries]*) (London, 1986).
NAC	*Numismatic Ars Classica* (London-Zurich-Milan), coins as referenced in Pliego 2009.
Pliego 2009	Ruth Pliego Vázquez, *La moneda visigoda*, vol. 2 (Seville, 2009). Includes photos from many private collections cited in the table by name and item number followed by Pliego's catalog number.
SB 42	Swiss Bank Corporation, *Gold- und Silbermünzen: Auktion 42* (*Basel, 21-23 January 1997*). The Visigothic tremisses, mostly from one or more hoards of the 1980s, are numbers 2548 to 2709.
Yndias	*Colección del Caballero de las Yndias*, Aureo y Calicó (21/22 – 10 – 2009), coins as referenced in Pliego 2009.

This study incorporates a limited but not small number of samples of regal tremisses between Leovigild and Chintila as a starting point for discussion. The decision to attribute a coin to a particular engraving style has been done in each case only after careful observation of busts, letters, and crosses. Whenever there has been some doubt I have indicated so. Most of the Visigothic coins at the ANS dating from the late sixth century to the first third or so of the seventh century were examined under stereoscope. This helped to confirm most of my opinions where minute aspects of die engraving are concerned. Yet, even to the naked eye, many similarities between coins are so great that they are immediately evident. Coins of the same city usually present no difficulty in attribution to a single engraver, but similar specimens from other cities were brought together to form a core group. From here a few coins were chosen as models with which to test other coins, beginning with those from areas nearby.

To further test my attributions, I have compared coins from different groups; usually, my original judgment on an individual die cutter's work was confirmed after rounds of comparison. Occasionally, a coin on the margin of a group has had to be reassigned or left as a query. One must account for the fact that an engraver's work will not always be perfectly uniform over a long period of time and in many locations. Small differences in the style of busts or letters of various coins do not disqualify an attribution to the same engraver, since variations in these features often occur even on the same coin. Sometimes, a coin will be similar to one or several other coins in the group, but will have some noticeable differences vis-à-vis other coins definitely in the same group. This is probably the result of one die cutter changing his manner of engraving over time or for some unknown reason, such as the use of different instruments. For example, if an engraver ceases to have at his disposal a punch with a very large wedge and, furthermore, spells the legend in different ways, there will inevitably be coins with similarities and differences simultaneously. An analogy can be made to variations in signatures by the same person, who perhaps uses a different pen or employs multiple styles for some letters. Varied signatures can often be linked to one person if studied carefully. Periodically, I have observed that two different engravers may have worked on the bust and the inscription within the same die, but this scenario seems quite rare.

In the photos and tables that follow, abbreviations are used in order to conserve space.

> = the reasons for an attribution to a particular engraver

* = very similar; the resemblance suggests the work of a single engraver

** = extremely similar; the resemblance strongly indicates the work of a single engraver

obv. = obverse
rev. = reverse
+ = the cross at 12:00 on facing-busts tremisses
pl. = plate
incl. = including
esp. = especially

The photo plates and accompanying commentary demonstrate several key engraver styles, as determined by the author, by way of comparison and contrast. From here, the many selections and notes within the table for each attribution invite further investigation. Three main engraving styles employed across multiple sites in the south of the Visigothic kingdom, which I attribute to three different hands, share enough similar aspects that an explanation of the distinctions between them may be helpful.

'Carthaginensis / Baetica' (C/B) – The cross comprises four very wide wedges, at least some of which are connected by thin lines; sometimes it is formed like a capital I with two separated wedges to left and right. In the bust, the hair generally hangs down lower than on 'Ispali' coins. Loops forming the eyebrows come together, frequently flowing into the line forming the nose (a feature that appears most consistently on the 'Toleto' engraver's coins). Up until Sisebut's reign, the cuirass is open at the bottom, with no horizontal line drawn across; once it is added it tends to be slanted in one direction. Letters have long stems and are therefore taller than those of the other two engravers. The wedges are wider and usually not at much of an angle. Several letters are distinctive. The wedge of R is often at an odd angle. The wedge of L is more detached than that of 'Ispali'. T has connecting lines between the wedges. E is frequently formed with quite detached wedges off the stem. The loop of P is almost always attached to the stem.

'Ispali' (Isp.) – Generally shorter hair, ending in a single dot. Usually, the loops forming the eyebrows do not quite meet, and do not form a single line with the nose. Letters have shorter stems – though from Sisebut onwards they become longer – and many letters are formed primarily by small wedges (e.g. A and V, made by three wedges connected by short lines; the bases of the wedges are always at an angle to the outer rim instead of being on the same circular frame as the rim as in 'C / B' coins). The loop of P is always detached, often considerably, a characteristic exaggerated in the letter R (in which the diagonal line is generally a small detached wedge). R is formed differently than by the other hands, with the diagonal stem reaching half-way up the vertical stem and the wedge detached but otherwise normal.

‘Southern’ (So.) – Crosses are formed by detached wedges. Execution of the busts and letters are similar to ‘Isp.’, notably with respect to letters A and V. The S of this hand resembles that of Ispali except that it is habitually large on the upper half and quite small on the bottom. The R differs in that it has a shorter right stem often unconnected to the vertical stem, above which is a half-crescent likewise unattached. T is constructed of wedges that are sometimes connected by a thin line. Coins of this engraver do not have the same thin, neat epigraphy as ‘Isp.’ coins, instead employing a somewhat awkward composition of large wedges.

Plate I descriptions

The coins on the plate opposite this page demonstrate the progression toward the quintessential regal type produced late in the reign of Leovigild. They also show distinctions and likenesses in engraving style that facilitate the identification of certain hands responsible for tremisses from different cities, although categorization is not yet applied to these early issues.

(a) through (e) are reproduced from Marques et al., *Ensaios*, p. 24, Fig. 4. These five regal tremisses of Leovigild illustrate transition from Justinian-Leovigild issue through facing busts. (a), (b), and (c) were made shortly after the beginning of Leovigild's sole rule, the first two in c. 573-c. 575 and c. 575-c. 579 respectively, and (c) in c. 577-c. 580. The inscriptions start from the bottom left: (a) IIIVSTIINIVA – CLIVVIGILDIREGISV; (b) VCLIVVIGILDIREGI – VCLIVVGILDIRECIS; (c) XIVVIC✠IXDVS – REXINCXIVI / ONO. The first two coins are possibly from the same hand > all aspects of both busts*, and most letter forms*, esp. L, D, R, E* (rounded), S, positions within I-L-D-I sequence*.

(d) and (e) were made in c. 582-584 and c. 584-586 respectively. The inscriptions are: DNLIV-VICILDVSREX – EMERITAVICTORIA; and ✠DNLEOVIGILDVSRE – ✠PIVSEMERITAVICTOR. While there are some similar letter forms (D, N, E, M, perhaps R), there is enough differentiation in forms (e.g., S, T, A), spelling (Livv- vs. Leov-) and inclusion of a cross (none in (d)) to question whether they are products of the same engraver.

(f), ANS 57.540, reads, from the top, ✠DNLEOVIGILDVSRE – ✠PIVSEMERITAVICTOR. It shares the same essential type and the same legend as (e) and is clearly from the same hand > bust** (incl. downward leaning top of cuirass), esp. face and hair; all letter forms and angles**. These and many other Visigothic tremisses demonstrate that one hand could employ varying types, sub-types, and symbol forms, e.g. whether a crown or helmet is added or of what size.

Tremisses (a) through (f) suggest the progression of a Victory legend, from VC to VI to VICTORIA to VICTOR.

(g) is from Heiss, *Description générale des monnaies des rois wisigoths*, pl. I.26. Heiss's drawings do not reflect exact epigraphic and type features but do approximate type, letters, and spaces. This illustration suggests the same hand at work as on the die for (c), and therefore a Toleto origin for at least some INCLITVS REX coins: specific execution of the obv. profile bust; the spelling (XIVVIC✠IXDVSI, with L's formed by X); the heavy tilt of obv. S; the rev. Victory form, and R-E combination.

Plate I

Plate II descriptions

(A) LIVVICILDVSREX – RECCOPOLIT / CONOB	(ANS 2016.29.7 = HSA 16006; Pliego 2009, 36a.1)
(B) DNLIVVICILDVS – TOLETOREX / CONOB	(ANS 2015.48.6 = HSA 15993; Pliego 2009, 42c.1)
(C) ✠LVVIG• |LDV∽R – RODACVMDEA• / ONO	(SB 42, #2551; Pliego 2009, 50b.1)
(D) ✠LEOVICILDVSRE – ✠CVMDOPTINITSPL	(ANS 2016.29.12; Pliego 2009, 46b.1)
(E) ✠LEOVIGILDVSREX – ✠TOLETOIVSTV∽	(ANS 2016.29.9 = HSA 15991; Pliego 2009, 43d.1)
(F) ✠LEOVIGILDVSREX – ✠TOSELVORAIVS	(ANS 2016.29.16 = HSA 15984; Pliego 2009, 53b.1)
(G) ✠RECCAREDVSREX – ✠TOLETOPIV∽	(ANS 2015.48.36 = HSA 16058; Pliego 2009, 98b.7)
(H) ✠RECCAREDVSREX – ✠PIVSISPALI	(ANS 2015.48.48 = HSA 16509; Pliego 2009, 106a.2)

(A) and (B) are from the 'Toleto hand'[1] > Bust*, including the hair** and hairpiece that comes straight down, and the circular brooches formed above the cuirass (all of which, by comparison with other profile bust – cross on steps tremisses, bear close resemblance); the cross on rev., with ends formed by neat wedges; all letter forms, esp. key letters such as L (left-leaning stem on both coins), R (3 separate but neat parts), E (wedges almost on an even plane), V (with a minimal bottom wedge), X (diagonal cross). Contrast these coins with (C), struck at Roda probably a couple of years later. The style of bust and letters is quite different. (D) is a later, facing-busts tremiss from Ispali; similarities to Toleto coins of letter forms, esp. L and E, and of the face and hair, which ends in double dots, may indicate that the 'Toleto engraver' was responsible for its dies, or that the gold coins of Toledo served as direct models.

Also from the 'Toleto hand' but from the facing busts period, (E) and (F) employ the same bust type** (short hair ending in multiple dots, face with several dots on forehead, eyebrows and nose line joined, cuirass) and epigraphic style, right down to shapes, positions, and leftward lean. A distinctive L, G, R, and S (larger than neighboring letters on obv., sideways at end of rev.) are shared. D-V-S/T-V-S and T-O-L/T-O-S sequences form a rounded angle at bottom, with the middle letter upraised – so also the D-V-S of (D). The style undergoes small modifications under Reccared (G), but there is little doubt this coin's dies are from the same hand > Eyebrows and nose still formed as if a single feature, to which the mouth and eyes are closely joined, traits that this hand will continue over the course of many reigns). As in (E), (F), and (B), R has attached stem halfway down plus a barely attached loop; D-V-S sequence has a rounded bottom; S is generally larger and final S on (E) and (F) rev. is sideways; T is very wide. Similar also to (B), O is very small; the D loop is not completely attached.

(E) and (G) provide examples, as do many other coins, that the same engraver could over several years have some variation in letter formation, for example in size.

(G) and (H), together with numerous tremisses from Toleto and Ispali in the next several decades, are sufficiently close to suggest a cross-influence between the two hands. Were it not for small but consistent variations in bust and epigraphic features between the two mints, the same hand might be thought to have worked in both places. One subtle distinction in Ispali coins is the outward angle of the bottom wedges of A and top wedges of V, so that they are not on a circular frame as in Toleto coins; others are the larger serif size on Ispali's coins and normally the slight separation between eyebrows and nose.

1 For an explanation and context of the engraver attributions determined from the style study represented in this appendix see pp. 149-55 of this book.

Plate II

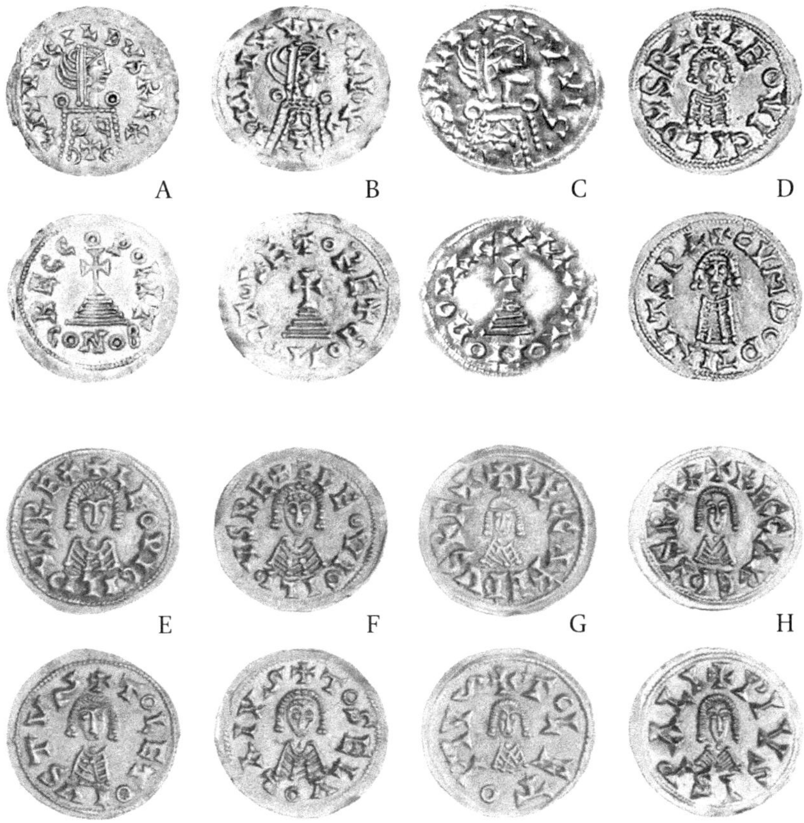

Plate III descriptions

All of the tremisses on the plate, with the exception of the last coin on bottom right, are reproduced from Marques et al., *Ensaios*, pl. II on p. 190. The last coin is from Swiss Bank Corp., Auction 42, Basel: 23 January 1997, #2572.

(31) ✠RECCARIDVSREX – ✠IMINIOPIVS	(private coll., António Miranda 69; Pliego 2009, 119.4)
(32) ✠RECCARIDVSRE – ✠PORTOCALEPIVS	(private coll., António Miranda 70; Pliego 2009, 146c.2)
(33) ✠DNLIVVAREX – ✠TOLETOPIV∽	(private coll., António Miranda 71; Pliego 2009, 160b.1)
(38) ✠DNLEVVARE^{X} – ✠PORTOCALEPI•S	(Museu Numismático Português 3834; Pliego 2009, 169.1)
(36) ✠DNLIVVAREX – ✠EMERITAPIV∽	(private coll., António Miranda 72; Pliego 2009, 165a.5)
(37) ✠DNLIVVAREX – ✠EMERETAPIV∽	(Museu Numismático Português 3833; Pliego 2009, 165b.2)
(39) ✠VVITTERICVSRE – ✠CE:AR:C•O:TAIV✷	(Museu Numismático Português 3835; Pliego 2009, 174c.3)
(s.n.) ✠VVITTERICVSRE – ✠✷PIV:TARR:CO:	(SB 42, #2572; Pliego 2009, 179a.1)

The first four coins are likely from the 'Toleto hand' or school. (31) and (32) of Reccared's reign are from Gallaecian mints, Eminio and Portocale. (33) and (38) are from Toleto and Portocale during the following reign (Liuva II, 601-603). The likeness of busts and crosses of (32) and (38) are immediately evident; most of the epigraphy is nearly the same, including a leftward lean (also true of crosses), although small differences in style may have entered over time. The busts of all four coins are remarkably alike, with arched eyebrows coming down into the long nose, a rounded but slightly triangular face (more fully angled in 31), and similar hair length – even multiple dots are similarly used at the end of braids in (33) and (38). Compare the letter forms of (31) and (32) > esp. R-I-D-V-S-R-E (obv.) and P-I-V-S (rev.); and of (32) and (33) > esp. R, A (flat top), E (almost perfectly rectangular). The crosses on all the coins are quite similar. N.B.: a minute local variation in the bust at Toleto is the dot in the neck. The bust of the Eminio coin is in the style of Emerita below.

(36) and (37) emanated from different dies but very clearly the same hand, possibly the same one as the previous coins ('Tol.'). If one compares these with (33) from Toleto several similar traits are visible. (33) shows sharper similarity with (f) in Plate I above (a Leovigild-Emerita issue) > crosses** (obv. – not centered, rev. – tall stems); many letters** such as L (backward leaning, bottom wedge hanging down at times), E, O (small, upraised), A (bottom wedged angled), R-E; leftward orientation of the cuirass; uneven hair. (36) and (37) exhibit some of these characteristics and the sideways S on rev., but there the letters are more slender. D and M forms are similar to the coins mentioned here, although M in the Eminio tremiss (31) is at variance. If not all products of one engraver, at least some cross-influence is strongly suggested.

(39) and SB 42, #2572 are coins of Witteric by the 'Cesaragusta engraver' from mints in Cesaragusta and Tarracona. Resemblances between the coins are apparent in all aspects: rim, cross,** bust* (esp. the cross which makes up the eyebrows and nose), letters** (esp. obv. V-V, E-R-I; R-E, this final E having a longer middle stem; rev. A-R with A's leftward lean and angle on right), abbreviations and mint mark (✷).

Plate III

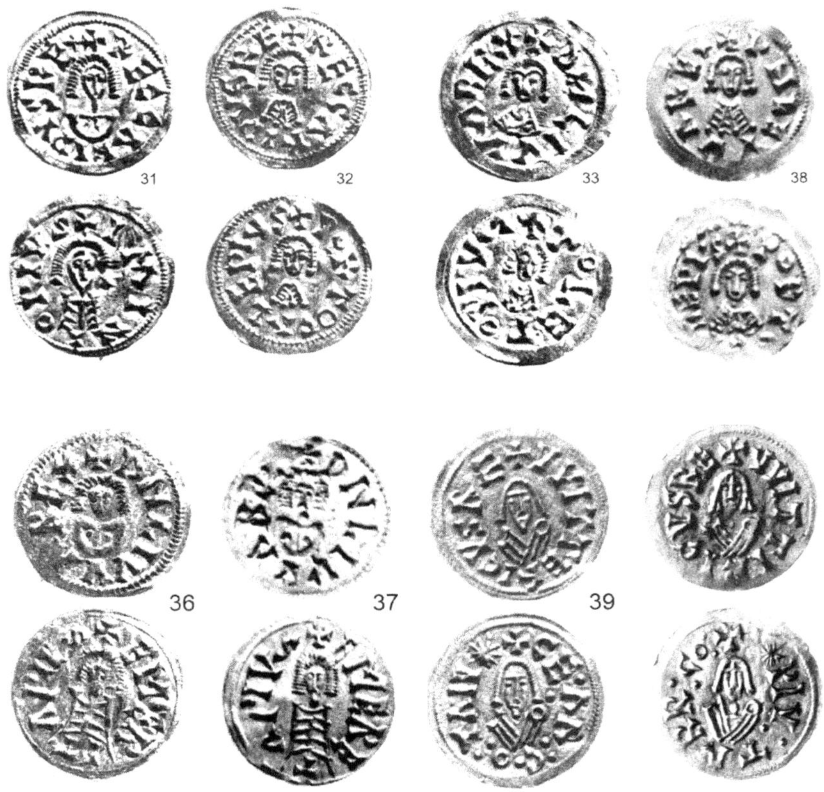

Plate IV descriptions

(A) ✠SISEBVTVSRE – ✠IVSTVSACCI:	(private coll., Bartlett 54; Pliego 2009, 257c.5)
(B) ✠SISEBVTVSRE – ✠VICTORBARBI	(private coll., Bartlett 67B; not in Pliego 2009)
(C) ✠SISEBVTVSRE – ✠PIVSELIBERI	(ANS 2015.48.109 = HSA 16106; Pliego 272b.1)
(D) ✠SISEBVTVSRI – ✠PIVSELIBERR.·.	(ANS 2015.48.110 = HSA 57.566; Pliego 272o.1)
(E) ✠SVINTHILARE – ✠ISPALIPIVS	(ANS 2015.48.208 = HSA 16222; Pliego 2009, 381a.2)
(F) ✠SVINTHIL.·.RE: – ✠IVSTVSTV:CI	(ANS 2015.48.227 = HSA 16292; Pliego 2009, 384h.1)
(G) ✠SVINTILARI: – ✠IVSTVSACC·	(ANS 2015.48.138 = HSA 16236; Pliego 2009, 348a.1)
(H) ✠SVINTILARE – ✠IVSTVSTVCI	(ANS 2015.48.230 = HSA 16230; Pliego 2009, 387a.1)

(A) and (B) are from dies made by the 'B/C' hand[2] > **Face (incl. eyebrows), hair* (often hanging lower on one side at these mints, and alternating between triangular or dot ends), bust*; cross** (often only top and bottom wedges are connected). (B) **Obv. Inscription, including similar left lean and positions; S (larger than other letters), esp. E (wedges do not touch stem), T (lines drawn between wedges), R (a slanted 'A' with a small crescent-shaped wedge to upper right). **Rev. V, T, A (slanted left, straight wedge top), R (slanted left, as in Acci obv.), B (see Acci obv.). In (A) the same two dots at end of rev. legend were utilized at least in one issue in Barbi, following "VI" (see Pliego 2009 269d.1 = Bartlett 67).

(C) and (D), both made at Eliberri, come from the same 'B/C' hand. Most of the same features as the previous two coins are apparent in these examples.

The dies of (E) and (F) were engraved by the 'Ispali hand' > +** (wedges of all four crosses connected by lines scratched in by hand); bust**, esp. mouth and hair; epigraphy (the neat scratching in between wedges, different from most other mints; spelling – regularly THI rather than TI of 'So.' hand), notably S, A/V (wide angles meeting at the tip of the lower wedge rather than at the middle or bottom), N, T, R (diagonal line formed by a small, separated wedge; on top a small, detached loop). Many of the Ispali coins of this engraver have a dot on the forehead or within the inscription, probably a privy mark. The use of dots as a substitute for C – or as a privy mark – is common at Tucci.

In comparison with (F), tremisses (G) and (H), from what I designate as from 'So.' or the Southern hand, demonstrate a great likeness between Tucci and Acci coins by what must have been two separate engravers during these decades. > bust*; the same or similar letter shapes and characteristics are evident, esp., A/V and often S (with variants). But since the mints of 'So.' including Acci almost invariably have a top-heavy S and a different R (normally *not* a fully extended, connected diagonal line; half-crescent above is also detached), and a drawn-in T, they have been classified as a separate engraving origin. In general, 'Isp.' tremisses appear neater and have thinner letters. A careful look at the photos within the appropriate sections of Pliego, *La moneda visigoda*, v. 2 will confirm the slightly distinct styles.

2 See p. 151 above.

Plate IV

'B/C' engraving style

A B C D

'Isp.' engraving style

E F

'So.' engraving style

G H

Plate V descriptions

All of the tremisses on the plate are from Aureo, Subasta Numismática, 16-17 December 1997 (Barcelona, 1997). The auction arrangement of photos conveniently provides examples for different engraver designations to supplement those treated above and in the table.

1324 and 1325 once again display close similarities between the engravers of Toleto and Ispali, but the letters on the latter show heavier use of wedges. Furthermore, there are differences such as in the A (angled bottom wedges) and S (wider, and here as common at Ispali with a long, straight line at top). The Liuva II-Ispali specimen 1328 exhibits the same features as 1325 of Reccared-Ispali.

Close similarities are likewise evident between Toleto and Emerita issues, as can be seen in 1324 and 1327. Note the face*, R-E-C* and several other letter sequences, including D-V-S. But as the 1327 rev. employs much wider wedges and serifs (esp. E, A/V), a smaller S, and a more neatly round frame, these can be considered products of distinct hands. It is possible the 1327 rev. and obv. are from different engravers. Between the three specimens here from Emerita (1327/Reccared, 1329/ Liuva II, 1333/Witteric) the likenesses are evident enough, however the 1327 rev. is more highly serifed, the M is straighter, and the entire look is neater and more exact in the circular frame; it also has a variant spelling, Emerita. Otherwise the Emerita letter features (e.g., R, slanted or sideways S) resemble those of the Toleto coin, and it may be suspected that the same 'Tol.' is behind coins of both mints.

1336 of Gundemar-Emerita can also suggested as possibly by 'Tol.' > G (see Leovigild coins of 'Tol.'), E, R, S.

1332 of Elvora is a coin of the 'Tol.' Engraver > bust**; letter forms* or **, esp. R, E, A/V, S (thin, slanted).

The separate hand 'Isp.' is clear enough in 1325 and 1328 from the same distinctive characteristics as discussed in the previous plate, esp. the tall letters and S (straight top), A/V (angled wedges), and P (detached loop).

The last two coins, 1337 and 1338 from Sisebut issues from Acci and Mentesa respectively, come from dies of the 'B/C' engraver > Bust** incl. face; heavy left lean of letters; S (large and fairly thin; wide serifs), E (detached, small triangular wedges; left lean), S-R-E sequence on obv. The 'B/C' hand is likewise behind the Sisebut-Acci coin illustrated in Pliego 2009, p. 167, no. 258.1, an example of one engraver exhibiting variations within the same style (here the spelling of the mint as HACCI). The next two photos on the same page in Pliego 2009, nos. 259.1 and 260.1, of Aorariola and Iliocrici, give every indication that these coins share the same origin.

Plate V

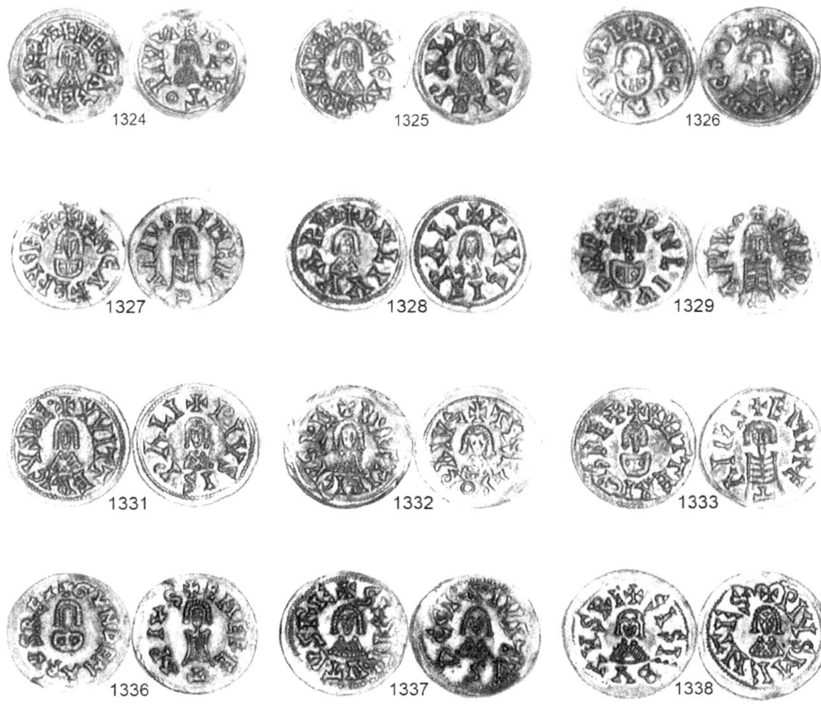

Tables of Regal Visigothic Tremisses Attributed to Separate Engravers

Explanatory Notes

The following tables list specific coins that form the author's basis for attributions to several distinct engravers during the regal period. Given the time required to conduct such a study of coin styles, the list is necessarily incomplete. But for each engraver it includes a good number of coins from more than one city and typically from several reigns. It is therefore a starting point from which one can test the theory of itinerant engravers elaborated in Chapter Three. Coins from a wide range of sources have been examined. For the sake of comparison, most of the references are to coins within the tables.

The majority of the coins of each style, i.e. of each engraver attribution, have been compared against a standard, labeled here as prototypes. For some coins, I have noted even closer similarities with another coin in the attribution group. Both the bust and epigraphy have been considered. Specific styles of epigraphy are discernable from the shape of letters, from their formation by wedge and/or engraved lines, and often from the position of letters and their spacing relative to one another. It must be observed that the letters within the same engraving style sometimes vary in size, and this is true even when the coins are from the same city in the same reign.

Unless otherwise noted, notations are primarily based on a comparison of obverses (obv.) with obverses and reverses (rev.) with reverses. Abbreviations used in the tables are those at the beginning of Appendix II on pp. 329-30 and 331-32.

'SOUTHERN ENGRAVER'

King	Mint	Coin	Reasons for attribution of obverse	Additional comments about style of reverse
Suinthila	Acci	M. 218(a) / HSA 16236 (pl. XI.4); in App. II, pl. IV.	**Prototype.** In App. II, pl. IV.	
"	Acci	M.218(b)/HSA 16136 (pl. XI.5)		
"	Acci	M. 218(e) / HSA 16237	All aspects **, esp. letters S, T, R.	All aspects **, esp. T, S, A,C.
"	Acci	M. 218(f) / HSA 8095 (pl. XI.6)		
"	Acci	SB 42, no. 2618		
"	Acci	GNC, pl. VI.67	Probably by the 'Southern engraver'.	
"	Cordoba	SB 42, no. 2630		
"	Cordoba	GNC, pl. VI.72 (ref. Pliego 2009, 370a.1ph.)		
"	Eliberri	M. 227(a) / HSA 8097 (pl. XIII.10)		
"	Eliberri	M. 227(b) / HSA 16239 (pl. XIII.2)	**Prototype.** See HSA 16290 (Suinthila-Tucci).	
"	Eliberri	M. 227(d) / HSA 16169 (pl. XIII.3)		
"	Eliberri	M. 227(g) / HSA 16167 (pl. XIII.6)		
"	Eliberri	M. 227(h) / HSA 16168 (pl. XIII.7)		
"	Eliberri	M. 227(i) / HSA 16166 (pl. XIII.8)		
"	Eliberri	M.227(1)/ HSA 16172 (pl. XIII.II)		
"	Eliberri	M.227(0)/ HSA 16170 (pl. XIII.13)		
"	Eliberri	M. 227(p) / HSA 16162		
"	Eliberri	M. 227(p) / HSA 16163 (pl. XIII.14)		
"	Eliberri	M. 227(q) / HSA 16241 (pl. XIV.I)		
"	Eliberri	MEC, no. 237		
"	Eliberri	SB 42, nos. 2632 & 2633		
"	Eliberri	Madrid 1936, p. 321, nos. 173 & 174		
"	Eliberri	GNC, pl. VII.76--79		

King	Mint	Coin	Reasons for attribution of obverse	Additional comments about style of reverse
"	Mentesa	M. 219(b) I HSA 16213	(Mentesa coins listed here) > Bust**; letters**, esp. A/V (angled wedges), T, L, R. E, P-I-V-S.	
"	Mentesa	M. 2 I 9(b) / HSA 16215		
"	Mentesa	M. 219(b) / HSA 16266 (pl. XI.8)		
"	Mentesa	M. 219(c) / HSA 16255 (pl. XI.9)		
"	Mentesa	M. 219(d) / HSA 16212 (pl. XI.10)		
"	Mentesa	M. 219(f) / HSA 16267 (pl. XI.11)		
"	Mentesa	GNC, pl. VIII.85		
"	Tucci	M. 229(a) / HSA 16230 (pl. XIV.12); this coin with photo is Pliego 2009, 387a.1. In App. II, pl. IV.	All Pliego 2009 387 and 388 series shown in photos are of this 'So.' hand. Spelling is somewhat erratic; king's name usually without H.	
"	Tucci	M. 229(j) / HSA 16290 (pl. XV.4)	**Prototype.** Note the formation of cross and letters almost solely by the use of triangle wedges, the left lean of letters, the top-heavy initial S, the dot or triangle horizontal stem of L, the distinctive R, the use of small punches for all parts of the face, the forked cuirass.	
"	Tucci	M. 229(k) / HSA 16429 (pl. XV.5)		
"	Tucci	M. 229(0) / HSA 16233 (pl. XV.7)		
"	Tucci	M. 229(p) / HSA 8096 (pl. XV.8)	**Prototype.**	
"	Tucci	M. 229(q) / HSA 16430 (pl. XV.9)		
"	Tucci	M. 230(a) / HSA 16295 (pl. XV.10)		
"	Tucci	Madrid 1936, p. 321, no. 167		
Iudila	Eliberri	GNC, pl. VIII.90		

King	Mint	Coin	Reasons for attribution of obverse	Additional comments about style of reverse
Sisenand	Acci	GNC, pl. VIII.92 & pl. IX.93	As with all the coins listed on this page, these Sisenand tremisses are distinct from 'Isp.' coins > cf. top-heavy S, lack of neat execution, minimal D, less neat R (more a separated right wedge, with no connector drawn to main stem; detached loop).	
"	Castelona	M. 258(f) / HSA 16305 (pl. XVII.9)	Cf. HSA 16400 (Sisenand-Tucci) > All aspects **, esp. bust, letters S and R.	
"	Castelona	GNC, pl. IX.96 (probably 97 also)		
"	Eliberri	M. 268(c) / HSA 16318 (pl. XIX.13)	Probably 'Southern engraver'> Bust**;+ **; letters , esp. S, R, E (wide wedges for stem, tiny wedges to the right).	
"	Eliberri	GNC, pl. IX.102, 103		
"	Iliocrica	SB 42, no. 2658	Cf. esp. HSA 16400 (Sisenand-Tucci) > All aspects**, esp. S-I-S, S-R.	
"	Mentesa	M. 262(b) / HSA 16378 (pl. XVIII.2)		
"	Mentesa	MEC, no. 246		
"	Tucci	M. 271(i) / HSA 16400 (pl. XXI.11)	**Prototype.**	
Chintila	Acci	M. 283(b) (pl. XXII.13)	Obverse probably by this engraver> Bust*;+ **; letters**, though backwards here.	All aspects **, esp. bust, letter S.
"	Eliberri	M. 290 / HSA 16457 (pl. XXII.16)	Probably the 'Southern engraver' > All aspects * or **, though less neat here.	
"	Eliberri	MEC, no.248		

'ISPALI ENGRAVER'

King	Mint	Coin	Reasons for attribution of obverse	Additional comments about style of reverse
Reccared	Ispali	M. 86(a) / HSA 16509 (pl. V.18); in App. II, pl. II	Busts** have the typical long, thin face of this engraver. Drawn-in letters use wide and neat wedges. E (with arched back) and S are thin.	
"	Ispali	M. 86(b) / HSA 16038 (pl. V.19)	Busts**; all letters**; S (ends below circular frame).	
"	Ispali	Ensaios, pl. 1.10		
"	Ispali	Bruxelles, no. 4		
"	Ispali	Aureo, 16-17 Dec. 1997; in App. II, pl. V, 1325		
Liuva II	Ispali	Aureo, 16-17 Dec. 1997; in App. II, pl. V, 1328		
Witteric	Ispali	Aureo, 16-17 Dec. 1997; in App. II, pl. V, 1331		
Sisebut	Ispali	(Cores, private coll., Madrid) = Pliego 2009, 274f.1	This and the following specimen share all the typical characteristics of this hand, incl. the S-R sequence with S slightly larger and hanging low.	Note the heavy use of dots, presumably mint marks or distinctive accounting marks.
"	Ispali	(FAJO, private coll., Seville) = Pliego 2009, 274g.3		
"	Tucci	(Cores, private coll., Madrid) = Pliego 2009, 279.4	Cf. Pliego 2009, 275b.1 (Sisebut-Ispali) > +**; letters**, esp. S-R sequence. Wider eyebrows connected to nose suggest bust was by B/C hand.	
Reccared II	Acci	(Cores, private coll., Madrid) = Pliego 2009, 330a.1	Cf. Pliego 2009, 334.1, 2 below (Sisebut-Ispali)**	
"	Acci	(Bartlett 88, private coll., Costa Rica) = Pliego 2009, 330b.1		
"	Ispali	(Cores, private coll., Madrid) = Pliego 2009, 334.1		
"	Ispali	(Bartlett 91, private coll., Costa Rica) = Pliego 2009, 334.2		

King	Mint	Coin	Reasons for attribution of obverse	Additional comments about style of reverse
Suinthila	Acci	(FAJO, private coll., Seville) = Pliego 2009, 347a.1; see also 347b.1, 347c.1-3, 347d.1, 347f.1	The vast majority of Suinthila-Acci coins are of 'So.', but these demonstrate characteristics of 'Isp.' described below and under 'So.' above.	
"	Asidona	(Cores, private coll., Madrid) = Pliego 2009, 365a.2	Cf. Pliego 2009, 381a.56 (Suinthila-Ispali) > all aspects * or **, incl. wide eyebrows.	
"	Asidona	(FAJO, private coll., Seville) = Pliego 2009, 365a.10		
"	Asidona	(Ex Bartlett 123, private coll., Costa Rica) = Pliego 2009, 365b.1		
"	Ispali	M. 228(a) / ANS 57.569		
"	Ispali	M. 228(a) / HSA 16218 (pl. XIV.3)	**Prototype**.	
"	Ispali	M. 228(a) / HSA 16227	Cf. HSA 16218 (Suinthila-Ispali) >Bust*; +*; letters (esp. R, T, not formed only by wedges as with the 'Southern engraver') and spacing.	
"	Ispali	M. 228(a) / HSA 16249	See HSA 16227	
"	Ispali	M. 228(a) / HSA 16222 (pl. XIV.4); in App. II, pl. IV.	See HSA 16227	
"	Ispali	M. 228(a) / HSA 16283	See HSA 16227	
"	Ispali	M. 228(a) / HSA 16223	See HSA 16227	
"	Ispali	M. 228(a) / HSA 16224	See HSA 16227	
"	Ispali	M. 228(a) / HSA 16245	**Prototype.**	
"	Ispali	M. 228(a) / HSA 16225 (pl. XIV.5)	Cf. HSA 16218 (Suinthila-Ispali) > Bust; cross; all letters *.	
"	Ispali	M. 228(a) / HSA 16226	Cf. HSA 16225 (Suinthila-Ispali) > Bust; cross; all letters *.	
"	Ispali	M. 228(a) / HSA 16228		
"	Ispali	M. 228(b) / HSA 16217 (pl. XIV.6)		
"	Ispali	M. 228(d) / HSA 16219 (pl. XIV.7)		
"	Ispali	M. 228(c) / HSA ANS 56.25.14		
"	Ispali	M. 228(f) / HSA 16262		
"	Ispali	M. 228(f) / HSA 16231 (pl. XIV.8)		
"	Ispali	M. 228(f) / HSA 16229		

King	Mint	Coin	Reasons for attribution of obverse	Additional comments about style of reverse
"	Ispali	M. 228(g) / HSA 16261 (pl. XIV.9)	'Ispali engraver'?> Cross is not the same (not touching in center) and bust is of a different type; letters *, but not spacing and position.	
"	Ispali	M. 228(h) / HSA 16254 (pl. XIV.10)	N.B.: closer to HSA 16262 than to 16245, but apparently in between both. Spelling is SVINTIHLA.	
"	Ispali	M. 228(h) / HSA 16220	Same style and the same curious spelling indicate it is by the same hand as HSA 16254.	
"	Ispali	M. 228(h) / HSA 16221		
"	Ispali	M. 228(j) / HSA 16264 (pl. XIV.11)		
"	Ispali	Ensaios, pl. VI.114	Cf. esp. HSA 16228 * (Suinthila-Ispali).	
"	Ispali	Ensaios, pl. VI.115	Cf. esp. HSA 16224 * (Suinthila-Ispali) > The HSA coin's die has been re-worked; under stereoscope one can see an exact match beneath the present very slight differences; same diagonal line in letter N.	Cf. HSA 16224 rev.**
"	Ispali	Ensaios, pl. VI.116	Cf. esp. HSA 16222 * (Suinthila-Ispali) > See esp. details of cuirass; face ** to HSA 16263.	
"	Ispali	MEC, no. 240	Cf. esp. HSA 16221 ** (Suinthila-Ispali).	
"	Ispali	SB 42, no. 2640	Cf. esp. HSA 16222 " (Suinthila-Ispali) > See esp. indentation of first I and slightly crooked center line of second I.	
"	Ispali	SB 42, no. 2641	Cf. esp. HSA 16217 * and HSA 16245 ** (both Suinthila-Ispali).	
"	Ispali	SB 42, no. 2642	Cf. esp. HSA 162 I 8 * (Suinthila-Ispali).	
"	Ispali	SB 42, no. 2643	Cf. esp. HSA 16245 and 16219 ** (Suinthila-Ispali).	
"	Ispali	Leu photos, nos. 355-360	Cf. esp. HSA 16225 * (Suinthila-Ispali).	
"	Ispali	Leu photos, no. 361	Cf. esp. HSA 16224 ** (Suinthila-Ispali) only + and position of T are slightly different.	
"	Ispali	Leu photos, no. 362	Cf. esp. HSA 16219 * (Suinthila-Ispali).	

King	Mint	Coin	Reasons for attribution of obverse	Additional comments about style of reverse
"	Ispali	GNC, pl. VII.82	Cf. ANS 56.25.14 * (Suinthila-Ispali) > Incl. the horizontal line in 'H' (= N); note L•.	
"	Ispali	Madrid 1936, p. 217, pl. XXI	Cf. esp. HSA 16219 * (Suinthila-Ispali).	
"	Ispali	JV III/13/97, no. 190	Cf. esp. HSA I 6219 * (Suinthila-Ispali).	
"	Ispali	JV VI/05/97, no. 242		
"	Ispali	JV V/16/96, no. 234	Cf. esp. HSA 16231 * (Suinthila-Ispali).	
"	Ispali	JV II/29/96, no. 156	Cf. esp. HSA 16222.* (Suinthila-Ispali).	
"	Ispali	JV III/04/92, no. 211	Cf. esp. HSA 16225 * (Suinthila-Ispali) > See esp. blotch on right corner of cuirass; letter S.	
"	Tucci	M. 229(c) / HSA 16256	Cf. esp. HSA 8100 (Suinthila-Mentesa) > All aspects **, incl. letter height (3.6mm) and band width (17.5mm) and large flan size; same letter forms, esp. peculiar L followed by ∴. Cf. HSA 16155 (Suinthila-Cordoba) **> Bust * (on all 3 coins the hair ends even with the chin, formed in a wedge shape - Ispali coins have a dot instead; cuirass: form *, bottom has connected dots); see letter forms and position of S-V, N-T-H-I, R-E; L with dots omits final A of Suinthila; + formed by wedges connected by thin lines in the center.	Cf. esp. HSA 8100 rev.> Bust**;+ *; size, spacing and form of letters, esp. T. Cf. HSA 16155 rev. > See esp. size, spacing and form of P-1-V-S.
"	Tucci	M.229(c) /HSA 16257 (pl. XIV.13)	All aspects *.	All aspects *.
"	Tucci	M. 229(d) / HSA 16292 (pl. XIV.14); in App. II, pl. IV.	All aspects *.	All aspects *.
"	Tucci	M. 229(e) / HSA 16293 (pl. XV.I)	General appearance *, though there are several slight differences.	All aspects *, esp. +.
"	Tucci	M. 229(h) / HSA 16275 (pl. XV.2)		
"	Tucci	M. 229(h) / HSA 16276		

King	Mint	Coin	Reasons for attribution of obverse	Additional comments about style of reverse
"	Tucci	M. 229(m) / HSA 16270 (pl. XV.6); in App II, pl. IV	Cf. esp. HSA 16256 ** (Suinthila-Tucci) > Bust**; +*; all letters*, esp. S-V, N-T, L·.	Bust, +, letter forms *.
"	Mentesa	M. 219(a) / HSA 8100 (pl. XI.7)	Cf. HSA 16256 (Suinthila-Tucci)	Cf. HSA 16256
"	Mentesa	M.219(a) / HSA 16216	Bust**; +*; letters*, esp. S, V, T, H, R.	Bust, +, letters* esp. P-I-V-S, A.
"	Cordoba	M. 226(a) / HSA 16155 (XII.IO)		
"	Cordoba	M. 226(a) / HSA 16157 (XII.12)	Bust**; +*; letters*, esp. S, V, T, H, R.	
"	Cordoba	M. 226(a) / HSA 16154	Cf. HSA 16245 (Suinthila-Ispali) >Bust**; + *; most letters*, esp. S, V.	Bust, +, letters* esp. P-I-V- S, A.
Sisenand	Asidona	M. 265(a) / HSA 16407 = Pliego 2009, 451a.5		
"	Asidona	Bode Museum, Berlin = Pliego 2009, 451b.2	Cf. esp. Pliego 2009, 459m.1 and 460b.3 (Sisenand-Ispali) > Bust **; letters, esp. awkward S-R sequence with S larger	P-I-V-S very similar to these two Ispali coins and the others in the series.
"	Ispali	M. 269(g) / HSA 16428	Cf. esp. HSA 16245 (Suinthila-Ispali) > Bust*; +**; esp. letters S, N, V, R-E. Also cf. HSA 16222 (in App II, pl. IV).	Bust*; +*; all letter forms **
"	Ispali	M. 269(m) / HSA 16351 (XX.11)	Same notes as HSA 16428.	
"	Ispali	M. 269(m) / HSA 16360	Same notes as HSA 16428; same dies as 16351.	Bust*; +*; P-I-V-S.
"	Ispali	M. 269(n) / HSA 16374 (XX.12)	Same notes as HSA 16428.	Bust*; +*; P-I-V-S.
"	Ispali	M. 269(n) / HSA 16389	Same notes as HSA 16428.	Bust*; +*; P-I-V-S.
"	Ispali	M. 269(q) / ANS 57.576		
"	Ispali	M. 269(q)/ HSA 16359 (XX.14)		
"	Ispali	M. 269(q) / HSA 16361		
"	Ispali	M. 269(s) / HSA 16399 (XXI.1)	Cf. esp. HSA 16245 (Suinthila-Ispali) > Bust*; + **; esp. letters S, E, A, R-E.	Bust*; + *; all letter forms **

'BAETICA / CARTHAGINENSIS ENGRAVER'

King	Mint	Coin	Reasons for attribution of obverse	Additional comments about style of reverse
Witteric	Eliberri	M. 139(a)I (pl. VII.11) = BM 1849, 0620.11, or 18A	Bust**; +**; letters ** (very tall, thin; typical leftward lean of 'B/C'), R (fully formed and as prototypes). Cf. coins of Mentesa (this coin = Pliego 2009, 198a.1 close to Witteric-Mentesa tremisses in ibid., esp. 183e.1).	
"	Eliberri	Pliego 2009, 183d.1	Same as above.	
"	Mentesa	Yndias 1263 = Pliego 2009, 183e.1	Same as above.	
Sisebut	Acci	(Bartlett 54, private coll., Costa Rica) = Pliego 2009, 257c.5	Same as above.	
"	Barbi	(Bartlett 67, private coll., Costa Rica) = Pliego 2009, 269d.1	Same as above.	
"	Eliberri	M. 186(a)I / HSA 16106 (pl. IX.8); in App. II, pl. IV	**Prototype.** Note distinctive R of this hand, a slanted, complete A with a small wedge on top right. Busts of this hand possibly copied bust style of 'So.'	
"	Eliberri	M. 186(f)I / ANS 57.566; in App. II, pl. IV	**Prototype.** Bust**; thin, tall letters** with mostly backward lean; S (small, top-heavy), wide wedges, B (thin, defined loop), R (sloppier, right stem begins lower than 'So.' coins).	
"	Eliberri	M. I 86(b)3 / ANS 57.565	Same as above.	
"	Eliberri	Leu photos, no. 129	Cf. HSA 16140 (Suinthila-Barbi) > Bust*; +*; decorative rim**; letters I, E, B, T **.	
"	Eliberri	Leu photos, no. 131		
"	Mentesa	M. 18l(a) / see Heiss, no. 8 (pl. IX.4)	Cf. HSA 16106 (Sisebut-Eliberri) > Bust*; +**; letter forms and position, esp. S-I-S, B-V, S-R; E's horizontal wedges go well beyond vertical stem, unlike Ispali coins on same pl.	Cf. HSA 16106 > Cuirass *; +**; most letter forms, esp. P (see also 16106 obv. T).

King	Mint	Coin	Reasons for attribution of obverse	Additional comments about style of reverse
"	Barbi	Ensaios, pl. IV.72	Bust**; +* (see HSA 16106 rev.); all letter forms**.	All aspects**, esp. P-I-V-S, R.
"	Barbi	SB 42, no. 2584		
"	Acci	SB 42, no. 2583		
Suinthila	Barbi	M. 224(a) / HSA 16143 (pl. XII.4)	**Prototype.** Note the use of wide, thin wedges for the letters, while the stems rely less on wedges and more on engraved lines than those of other engravers. Cf. HSA 16106 (Sisebut-Eliberri) >Bust*;+** (cf. 16106 rev.); letter forms, esp. R, E, A/V, B (wedges unattached to stem); same severe left lean of letters.	Cf. HSA 16106 > All aspects **, esp. letters B, R, I (very short).
"	Barbi	M. 224(c) / HSA 16145		
"	Barbi	M. 224(c) / HSA 16138		
"	Barbi	M. 224(c) / HSA 16140	Cf. HSA 16143 (Suinthila-Barbi) > All aspects**	
"	Barbi	M. 224(c) / HSA 16238	Cf. HSA 16140 (Suinthila-Barbi) > All aspects**, esp. S, N, T, A.	Cf. HSA 16140 > All aspects**, esp. P-I-V-S.
"	Barbi	M. 224(c) / HSA 16141 (pl. XII.5)	Cf. Ensaios, pl. IV.72 (Sisebut-Barbi) > Bust*; + **; letters, esp. R.	Cf. Ensaios, pl. IV.72 > Bust, + *; all letters*, esp. V-S-B **
"	Barbi	M. 224(c) / HSA 16144		
"	Barbi	M. 224(c) / ANS 57.567		
"	Barbi	M. 224(d) / HSA 16137 (pl. XII.6)		
"	Barbi	M. 224(d) / HSA 16146		
"	Barbi	M. 224(d) / HSA 16139		
"	Barbi	M. 224(d) / HSA 16147		
"	Barbi	M. 224(e) / HSA 16148 (pl. XII.7)		
"	Barbi	M. 224(f) / HSA 16142		
"	Barbi	M. 224(f) / HSA 16248		
"	Barbi	M. 224(f) / HSA 8093 (pl. XII.8)		
"	Barbi	M. 224(h) / HSA 16240 (pl. XII.9)		
"	Barbi	Ensaios, pl. VI.106 -108	107 is a die duplicate of HSA 16137; 108 obv. die is linked to HSA 16145.	

King	Mint	Coin	Reasons for attribution of obverse	Additional comments about style of reverse
"	Barbi	MEC, no. 235		
"	Barbi	Madrid 1936, p. 168, pl. XVII		
"	Barbi	GNC, pl. VI.68-69		
"	Barbi	SB 42, nos. 2620-2624	2623 is a die duplicate of HSA 16137 and Leu photos 333-351 (Suinthila-Barbi); 2624 is a die duplicate of HSA 16148.	
"	Barbi	Chaves 1984, p.94, no. 182		
"	Barbi	Leu photos, nos. 328-352 (328-329 & 333-351 are die duplicates)	Cf. 328 and HSA 16238 (** with exception of letters A and E, this last possibly re-worked.). 328-35l are die duplicates of HSA 16137 (Suinthila-Barbi).	
"	Barbi	Aureo VI/94, no. 347	Obv. die link to HSA 16139.	
"	Barbi	Aureo XII/94, no. 244	Obv. die link to Ensaios, pl. VI.106.	
"	Barbi	Aureo XII/94, no. 245	Obv. die link to HSA 16139.	
"	Barbi	Aureo I/95, no. 494	Obv. die link to Ensaios, pl. VI.106.	
"	Barbi	Aureo VI/95, nos. 184-186	Obv. die link to HSA 16240.	
"	Barbi	Aureo IX/95, no. 475	Obv. die link to HSA 16139.	
"	Barbi	Aureo XII/95, no. 213	Obv. die link to HSA 16139.	
"	Barbi	Aureo IV/96, no. 120	Obv. die link to HSA 16139.	
"	Barbi	Aureo V/96, nos. 72-73	Obv. die link to HSA 16137.	
"	Barbi	Aureo VII/96, no. 183	Obv. die link to Ensaios, pl. VI.106.	
"	Barbi	Aureo XII/96, no. 121	Obv. die link to Ensaios, pl. VI.106.	
"	Barbi	Aureo III/05/97, no. 154		
"	Barbi	Aureo IV/15/97, no. 109	Obv. die link to Ensaios, pl. VI. I 06.	
"	Barbi	Aureo VI/97, no. 239	Obv. die link to MEC, no. 235 (Suin.-Barbi)	

'TOLETO ENGRAVER'

King	Mint	Coin	Reasons for attribution of obverse	Additional comments about style of reverse
Leovigild	Elvora	M.37(a)/ HSA 16010	**Prototype**	
"	Elvora	M. 37(a) / HSA 15984 (pl. III.5); in App. II, pl. II		
"	Elvora	M. 37(a) / HSA 16008 (pl. III.6)		
"	Elvora	M. 37(b) / HSA 16009		
"	Ispali	M. 33(a) / HSA 8114 (pl. II.18)	Cf. HSA 15996 & HSA 15995 (Leovigild- Toleto) > Bust**; +*; letters, esp. L-E-O, D-V-S (S taller than other letters).	
"	Reccopolis	M. 23(a) / HSA 16006 (cross-on-steps) (pl. II.9); in App. II, pl. II	Cf. HSA 15993 > All aspects**, esp. letters L, S, R (but not B).	
"	Toleto	M. 28(a) / HSA 15993; in App. II, pl. II		
"	Toleto	M. 29(a) / ANS 69.1164		
"	Toleto	M. 29(a) / HSA 15992		
"	Toleto	M. 29(a) / HSA 15998		
"	Toleto	M. 29(a) / HSA 15996 (pl. II.12)	All aspects **, but letters slightly larger here.	
"	Toleto	M. 29(b)/ HSA 15991 (pl. II.13); in App. II, pl. II		
"	Toleto	M. 29(c) / HSA 15995 (pl. II.14)	All aspects **.	
Reccared	***Central Carthaginensis***			
	Elvora	M. 90(a) / HSA 16022	All aspects **, but letters slightly larger here.	
"	Elvora	M. 90(c) / HSA 16025 (pl. VI.4)	Cf. HSA 16035 (Reccared-Emerita) > Bust (face)*; legend**.	Cf. HSA 16035 > Letters A, I-V-S, R, E (tall)**.
"	Elvora	Ensaios, pl. I.15	Cf. Ensaios, pl. I.9 (Reccared-Toleto) & 1.20 (Reccared-Emerita) > Bust*; legend**.	Cf. Ensaios, pl. I.9 & I.20 > Bust (cuirass) *; letters T, E, L.
"	Elvora	SB 42, no. 2555	Cf. Bruxelles, no. 5 (Reccared-Toleto) > Bust *;+*;letters, esp. R, D.	Cf. Bruxelles, no. 5 > Letters E, L, T (but top line of 2nd T of Bruxelles coin is more hand-engraved than formed by wedges).
"	Toleto	M. 81(c) / HSA 16060	**Prototype**	
"	Toleto	M. 81(a) / HSA 16055 (pl. V.6)	Closest of these examples to Tude triens below (HSA 16062)*.	
"	Toleto	M. 81(b) / HSA 16052 (pl. V.7)	Close to Tude triens below (HSA 16062)*.	

King	Mint	Coin	Reasons for attribution of obverse	Additional comments about style of reverse
"	Toleto	M. 8l(c) / HSA 16049 (pl. V.8)	Close to Tude triens below (HSA 16062)*.	
"	Toleto	M. 8l(c) / HSA 16063 (pl. V.9)		
"	Toleto	Ensaios, pl. 1.9		
"	Toleto	SB 42, no. 2561		
"	Toleto	Bruxelles, no. 5		
"	***Gallaecia***			
	Sussarres/ Susarros	M. 101 / HSA 16061 (pl. VI.16)	Cf. Ensaios, pl. 1.9 (Reccared-Toleto) * > Bust, letters. Cf. M. 103(a) (Reccared-Bergancia) ** > See busts, + (both coins omit reverse +), letter S.	Cf. Ensaios, pl. I.9 > Bust**
"	Bergancia	M. 103(a) / see Heiss, no. 4 (pl. VI.18)	Several letters * > R (note two different forms), D (also formed in two ways), A (3 wedges), S (thin and larger than other letters; set apart and sometimes horizontal).	
"	Mertia	(Alba, private coll., France) = Pliego 2009, 141.1	All aspects **, incl. face, although cuirass diverges in type on both sides.	Letters on rev. are larger here.
	Palantucio	(private coll.) = Pliego 2009, 142.1	All aspects **, except face and cuirass seem adapted.	
"	Portocale	(Costa, private coll., Portugal) = Pliego 2009, 146a.1; also 146b.1, 146c.1,2	All aspects **	
"	Portocale	Ensaios, pl. II.32; in App. II, pl. III.	Cf. Ensaios, pl. II.33 (Liuva II-Toleto) > Letters *, esp. A, R, E, P. Cf. Ensaios, pl. II.31 (Eminio) > +*; letters *, esp. D-V-S (S on this coin is larger).	Cf. Ensaios, pl. II.33 > Letters O and L are both small but positioned high, P-1-V-S *. Cf. Ensaios, pl. II.31 > letters*; P-1-V-S **.
"	Tude	M. 113 / HSA 16062 (pl. VI.19) = Pliego 2009, 151	Several letters * > R (note two different forms), D (also found in two ways), A (3 wedges), S (thin and larger than other letters; set apart and sometimes horizontal). Cf. Toleto trientes above.	
"	***Lusitania***			
	Contosolia	M. 88 (pl. VI.I)	Cf. HSA 16025 (Reccared-Elvora) > Bust*; + **; all aspects of epigraphy**.	Cf. HSA 16025 > Letters T, S (large).
"	Egitania	Madrid 1936, p. 358 (= Heiss, no. 10)	Cf. Ensaios, pl. II.28 (Reccared-Emerita) > Bust**; +**; all aspects of epigraphy *.	Cf. Ensaios, pl. II.28 > All aspects of epigraphy *.

King	Mint	Coin	Reasons for attribution of obverse	Additional comments about style of reverse
"	Emerita	M. 93(a) / HSA 16027 (pl. VI.7) M. 93(b) (pl. VI.8) M. 94(d) / HSA 16035 (pl. VI.13)	Some letters * > R (in two different forms, one of them the style found on most Toleto coins), D (loop very small or detached on Emerita Coins), A, S.	
"	Emerita	Ensaios, pl. II.28	Cf. SB 42, no. 2561 & M. pl. V.6, 7 (all Reccared-Toleto) > All aspects *.	
"	Eminio	Ensaios, pl. II.30	Many letters * > R, E, A, D, P, D-V-S	Slanted S as in 'Tol.'
"	Eminio	Ensaios, pl. II.31 = Pliego 2009, 119.4; in App. II, pl. III	See above.	
"	***<u>Baetica – s. Carthaginensis</u>***			
	Eliberri	M. 83(a) / HSA 16065 (pl. V.13)	Cf. M. pl. V.9 (Reccared-Toleto) > Bust**; +**; obv. letters and slant**; R, E, A, S-R-E. Cf. M. pl. V.6 (Reccared-Toleto) > All aspects *, though cuirass style is slightly different. Cf. HSA 16509 (Reccared-Ispali) > All aspects**	
"	Eliberri	M. 83(c) / HSA 16023 (pl. V.14)	Cf. HSA 16038 (Reccared-Ispali) > All aspects**	
"	Mentesa	Madrid 1936,p.313	Cf. SB 42, no. 2561 (Reccared-Toleto) > All aspects **.	
"	Mentesa	IVDJ 3554 = Pliego 2009, 95b.1	Cf. Pliego 2009, 98a.9 and 98b.58 (Reccared-Toleto) > All aspects **.	
Liuva II	Elvora	Madrid 1936, p. 304, pl. XXIX		
"	Elvora	NAC 25, 671 = Pliego 2009, 164a.8	Cf. MAN 105.298 (Liuva II-Toleto) > All aspects **.	
"	Emerita	Ensaios, pl. II.36; in App. II, pl. III		
"	Emerita	Ensaios, pl. II.37; in App. II, pl. III		
"	Portocale	Ensaios, pl. II.38; in App. II, pl. III	Cf. Ensaios, pl. II.32 (Reccared-Portocale) > + *; bust **; most letter forms *.	
"	Toleto	M. 119 / HSA 16075 (pl. VII.2)	Cf. HSA 16060 (Reccared-Toleto) > All aspects **. Cf. HSA 16022 (Reccared-Elvora) > All aspects *.	Cf. HSA 16060 > All aspects**. Cf. HSA 16022 > All aspects**, esp. letters T, E.
"	Toleto	Ensaios, pl. II.33; in App. II, pl. III.		
Witteric	Bergancia	M. 147 / HSA 16094 (pl. VIII. I)	Probably 'Toleto engraver'; cf. HSA 16088 (Witteric-Toleto) & HSA 16081 (Witteric- Elvora) >Bust*;+**; epigraphy*, esp. R.	

King	Mint	Coin	Reasons for attribution of obverse	Additional comments about style of reverse
"	Bracara	Heiss, pl. IV.3	Probably 'Toleto engraver'; cf. Heiss, pl. IV.19 (Witteric-Toleto) & HSA 16088 (same)> Face and hair *; + *; letters *.	
"	Bracara	HSA 57.559 = ANS 2016.29.45	Same as above.	
"	Elvora	M. 142(a) / HSA 16081 (pl. VII.13)	Cf. HSA 16088 (Witteric-Toleto) > All aspects **	Cf. HSA 16088 > All aspects **,esp. face, letters T, E, I-V, R (see 16088 obverse).
"	Emerita	M. 143(e) / HSA 16085 (pl. VII.15)	Possibly 'Toleto engraver'; cf. HSA 16088 (Witteric-Toleto) > Face (eyebrows formed together with nose, ending in a triangular wedge); letters T, C-V-S. Cf. M. I 39(a)1 (Witteric-Eliberri) > Face (but not the rest of the bust);+*; letters, esp. C-V- S-R-E **.	Cf. HSA 16088 > + *; letters I-V-S (S on its side). Cf. M. 139(a)I > Face;+*; letters P-I-V.
"	Eminio	M. 144 / Stuttgart, no. 1344 (pl. VII.16)	Cf. HSA 16081 (Witteric-Elvora) > Head; +; epigraphy. For similarities to Toleto coins see Pliego 2009, 186a.2 (note obv. face**) and 186e.1.	Reverse is more like HSA 16085 (Emerita).
"	Mentesa	M. 135(a) = Ensaios, pl. III.41 = Pliego 2009, 183a.1	Probably 'Toleto engraver'; cf. HSA 16088 (Witteric-Toleto) > Bust; epigraphy* (except R). Appears definitely to be by the same engraver as M. 139(a)I (Witteric-Eliberri) > Bust; epigraphy**. Cf. this coin (= Pliego 2009, 183a.1) plus another of this mint (ibid., 183d.1) and Witteric-Iminio (ibid., 195a.1). Cf. also IVDJ 3554 above (Reccared-Mentesa).	
"	Toledo	M. 137(a) / HSA 16088 (pl. VII.10)	**Later prototype**	Cf. HSA 16075 (Witteric- Toleto) > All aspects**.
Gundemar	Elvora	Ensaios, pl. IV.61	Cf. Ensaios, pl. III. 59 (Gundemar-Toleto) > Bust**; +*; letters*, esp. S and backward lean of M-A-R.	
"	Mentesa	(Cores, private coll.) = Pliego 2009, 222d.1	Epigraphy by 'Tol.' engraver, but not face and bust? Cf. IVDJ 3554 above (= Pliego 2009, 95b.1) > letter forms and spacing * or **. **Face and bust seem to be by 'Isp.' hand: cf. many examples in Pliego 2009, pp. 154-55.**	
"	Toleto	Ensaios, pl. III.59		

King	Mint	Coin	Reasons for attribution of obverse	Additional comments about style of reverse
"	Toleto	M. 167 / HSA 16089 (pl. VIII.9)	Cf. HSA 16081 (Witteric-Elvora) > Bust*; + **; letters V, R, E **.	Cf. HSA 16088 (Witteric- Toleto) > All aspects**, esp. epigraphy. Cf. HSA 16081 (Witteric-Elvora) > All aspects **; see T, E, L, S.
Sisebut	Bracara	Leu photos, no. 320	Possibly 'Toleto engraver' (almost certainly the same engraver as the coin of Nandolas); cf. Leu photos, no. 113 (Sisebut-Toleto). Another Bracara triens (= Pliego 2009, 299.1) is possibly also a 'Tol.' coin: cf. ibid., 267f.13 > face *; bust; B, R, P-I-V.	
"	Egitania	Leu photos, no. 229	Probably 'Toleto engraver'; appearance is closer to Emerita and Bracara than Toleto. Cf. Leu photos, no. 285 (Sisebut- Emerita) > All aspects **. Cf. Leu photos, no. 320 (Sisebut-Bracara) > + *; epigraphy *.	Cf. Leu photos, no. 285 > Reverse of no. 229 appears to have been made hastily, thus the comparison shows less similarity.
"	Egitania	BNF 39 (= Pliego 2009, 281d.1)	Probably 'Toleto engraver' > face *, but not bust; letter forms * or **. Cf. Pliego 2009, 267a.42 and 267a.5 (Sisebut-Toleto), face *, but not bust. Ibid. 267e.1 (Sisebut-Toleto) is very similar to ibid., 281b.1 (Sisebut-Egitania).	
"	Elvora	M. 19l(a) / HSA 16107 (pl. IX.17)	Cf. HSA 16081 (Witteric-Elvora) > Bust*; +**; all letters **. Cf. HSA 16089 (Gundemar-Toleto) > Bust**; +**; letter size and most forms**, esp. R, E.	Same as obverse.
"	Elvora	M. 191(a) / HSA 16372 (pl. X.I)		
"	Elvora	Leu 41, no. 30	Cf. Leu 41, no. 38 (Suinthila-Toleto) > All aspects**; see letters R-E-X, reverse S (on its side).	
"	Elvora	Ensaios, pl. V.82-85	Cf. Ensaios, pl. V.70, 71 (Sisebut-Toleto) > Bust**; letters*, esp. S-I-S (see positions), B, R **; all include the full word REX. Compare pl. V.83 to pl. V.90 (Sisebut-Emerita) > +**; epigraphy*.	Ensaios, pl V.71 & 85 both have a faint circle around the field.

King	Mint	Coin	Reasons for attribution of obverse	Additional comments about style of reverse
"	Elvora	SB 42, no. 2594	Cf. SB 42, no. 2615 (Sisebut-Toleto) > Bust*; +**; letters*, esp. R, B.	Cf. SB 42, no. 2615 > letters *, esp. T, E, L (small stem, large wedge).
"	Elvora	Leu photos, no. 232	See Leu photos, no. 321 (Sisebut-Nandolas).	
"	Emerita	Ensaios, pl. V.90-96	Possibly by 'Tol.' hand. Cf. Ensaios, pl. V.71 (Sisebut-Toleto)- compare both sides > All letters *, except X; S- I-S similar (angle and form in V.90-93 of Emerita **).	
"	Emerita	SB 42, no. 2595	Possibly by 'Tol.' hand. See above.	
"	Emerita	SB 42, no. 2596	Possibly by 'Tol.' hand. Cf. SB 42, no. 2615 (Toleto) > +**; epigraphy**.	Cf. SB 42, no. 2615 > epigraphy**, esp. E, T, P-I- V-S.
"	Eminio	Ensaios, pl. V.97	Possibly by 'Tol.' hand; at least probably same hand as at Emerita. Cf. Ensaios, pl. V.96 (Sisebut-Emerita) > Face?; +**; most letters**, esp. S-I-S-E-B, T (but V, R not very similar).	For a very similar cuirass on the reverse of an Emerita coin see Ensaios, pl. V.95.
"	Eminio	SB 42, no. 2602	Possibly by 'Tol.' hand; at least probably same hand as at Emerita. Cf. SB 42, no. 2614 & 2615 (both Sisebut- Toleto) > Face; +*; letters similar, with very slight differences.	Cf. SB 42, no. 2614 & 2615 > see esp. P-1-V-S ** (esp. the distinctive S).
"	Mentesa	Ensaios, pl. V.69	Possibly 'Toleto engraver'; cf. Ensaios, pl. IV.70 (Sisebut-Toleto) > +*; epigraphy * (except R, and Mentesa letters are larger). Cf. Ensaios, pl. V.85 (Sisebut-Elvora) > + *; letters similar, esp. A, V, T, E, X.	
"	Nandolas	Leu photos, no. 321	Probably 'Toleto engraver'; cf. Leu photos, no. 113 (Sisebut-Toleto) > Bust*; +**; epigraphy *. Cf. Leu photos, no. 232 (Sisebut-Elvora) > Bust*; +*; epigraphy**. Cf. Pliego 314.1 (Sisebut-Nandolas) and ibid., 267a.43 (Sisebut-Toleto) > obv. face*; bust; letter forms; rev. similar letter forms, esp. L, A/V (but S on Toleto coins are usually sideways).	Cf. Leu photos, no. 113 > same as obverse. Cf. Leu photos, no. 232 > same as obverse, but epigraphy *.
"	Toleto	Ensaios, pl. V.70, 71	See Ensaios, pl. V.82-85 (Sisebut-Elvora).	See Ensaios, pl. V.82-85.

King	Mint	Coin	Reasons for attribution of obverse	Additional comments about style of reverse
"	Toleto	SB 42, no. 2614		
"	Toleto	SB 42, no. 2615	See SB 42, no. 2594 (Sisebut-Elvora).	
"	Toleto	Leu photos, no. 113	See Leu photos, no. 321 (Sisebut-Nandolas).	
"	Veseo	Ensaios, pl. V.98	Probably *not* from 'Tol.' hand, but same engraver as at Emerita and Eminio. Cf. Ensaios, pl. V.96 (Sisebut-Emerita) > Bust**; +*; epigraphy*, esp. E-B, S-R-E. Cf. Ensaios, pl. V.97 (Sisebut-Eminio) > Bust?; +**; epigraphy*, esp. E and S (irregular, sometimes backwards).	Cf. Ensaios, pl. V.96 > see esp. E, P-1-V-S (S **).
Suinthila	Elvora	Ensaios, pl. VI.119	Cf. Ensaios, pl. VI.104, 105 (Suinthila-Toleto) > All aspects *; cf. the S after the +, E, L, R **, and the thin horizontal line of H (unlike coins of Emerita at that time).	
"	Elvora	SB 42, no. 2635	Cf. SB 42, no. 2649 (Suinthila-Toleto) > All aspects *; position and form of +-S-V **. N.B.: both coins have a distinctive faint circle in the field.	
"	Toleto	M. 223(a) / HSA 16271 (pl. XI.13)	Bust**; +*; letters T, L, E (curved stem), final S (slanted), R **. Obverse linked to HSA 16288.	Same as obverse.
"	Toleto	M. 223(a) / HSA 16286		
"	Toleto	M. 223(a) / HSA 16288		
"	Toleto	M. 223(a)12 / ANS 69.222.79	Obverse linked to HSA 16288.	
"	Toleto	M. 223(a) / HSA 16282		
"	Toleto	M. 223(a) / HSA 16283		
"	Toleto	M. 223(a) / HSA 16274		
"	Toleto	M. 223(a) / HSA 16281		
"	Toleto	M. 223(a) / HSA 16273 (pl. XI.14)		
"	Toleto	M. 223(b) / HSA 16285 (pl. XII.2)		
"	Toleto	M. 223(c) / HSA 16284 (pl. XII.3)		
"	Toleto	Ensaios, pl. VI.104, 105	104 obverse linked to HSA 16273.	
"	Toleto	MEC, no. 242	Obverse linked to HSA 16281.	
"	Toleto	Madrid, p. 130		
"	Toleto	Chavez, p. 93, no. 180		
"	Toleto	SB 42, no. 2649		
"	Toleto	Leu 41, no. 38		

King	Mint	Coin	Reasons for attribution of obverse	Additional comments about style of reverse
"	Toleto	Aureo, VII/01/97, no. 124	Obverse linked to Chaves, no. 180.	
Sisenand	Toleto	Ensaios, pl. VII.137, 138	Cf. HSA 16271 (Suinthila-Toleto) > All aspects **.	
"	Toleto	SB 42, no. 2661	'Toleto engraver'? > Most aspects*. The style of Toleto coins seems to undergo change in this reign, perhaps due to a new engraver; cf. SB 42, no. 2662 > bust and several letters, esp. R, T, 0, are different. Cf. also no. 2669 (Chintila-Toleto) > the fabric differs substantially from no. 2661, and is closer to no. 2662. So also M. 285(d) / HSA 16470 / pl. XXII.14 (Chintila-Toleto), M. 304(a, b) / HSA 16469, 16468 / pl. XXIII.11, 12 (Tulga-Toleto), and Chindasvinth-Toleto coins in Miles> these differ from 'Toleto engraver' in the bust, incl. cuirass; in their thicker decorative rim; in letters N, S, 0, and possibly P.	
Chintila	Toleto	M. 285(d) / HSA 16470 (pl. XXII.14)	Cf. HSA 16445 & HSA 16448 (Sisenand-Toleto) > Bust*; +*; see A and most letters on reverse.	

'BARCINONA ENGRAVER'

King	Mint	Coin	Reasons for attribution of obverse	Additional comments about style of reverse
Reccared	Barcinona	M. 5l(a) / HSA 10620 (pl. IV.3)	**Prototype.**	
"	Barcinona	M. 5l(d) / HSA 16067 (pl. IV.4)		
"	Barcinona	M. 5 l(g) (pl. IV.5)	All aspects *; same wide E, narrow C, backwards S.	
"	Barcinona	M. 5l(d) / HSA 16582 (pl. IV.6)	Probably by the same engraver > Cf. pl. IV.5: Bust and most letters **; S not backwards.	
"	Rodas	M. 63(a) (pl. IV.13)	All aspects**, esp. left lean of letters; see distinctive A (left stem at 90°, right stem at ca. 45°, wide thin wedge on top), R, backwards S.	
"	Tarracona	M. 72. l / see Heiss, no. 35 (pl. IV.20)	All aspects ** except cuirass and cross in center of reverse. The nose and eyes are formed in the same way.	
Witteric	Barcinona	M. 128(a) / HSA 16080 (pl. VII.5)	All aspects * or **.	See esp. letters B, A, R.

'NARBONA ENGRAVER'

King	Mint	Coin	Reasons for attribution of obverse	Additional comments about style of reverse
Leovigild	Narbona	M. 11(a) / HSA 15989 (pl. II.2)	Bust* (face & hair**); most letters *, esp. L, E, D, R, S (thin, slightly larger than surrounding letters, slanting to right).	Same as obv.; see esp. P-I- V- S.
"	Narbona	M. 12 (pl. II.3)	**Prototype.**	
"	Rodas	M. 19(a) / HSA 16007 (pl. II.7)		
"	Rodas	GNC, pl. III.27		
Reccared	Narbona	M. 48(b) / HSA 16043 (pl. IV.l)		
"	Narbona	M. 49(a) / HSA 16044 (pl. IV.2)		

'CESARAGUSTA ENGRAVER'

King	Mint	Coin	Reasons for attribution of obverse	Additional comments about style of reverse
Leovigild	Cesarau-gusta	M. 16(e) (= pl. II.4)	All aspects *; cf. SB 2553 ** (Reccared-Cesaraugusta).	
Reccared	Cesarau-gusta	M. 55(a) / HSA 16015 (= pl. IV.7) M. 55(c) / HSA 16016 (= pl. IV.8) M. 55(e) / HSA 16018 (= pl. IV.9) M. 55(h) / see Heiss, no. 6 (pl. IV.10) M. 56 / HSA 16069 (= pl. IV.11) M. 57(b) / HSA 16017 (= pl. IV.12)	**HSA 16015 is prototype.** Note in this hand the peculiar engraving of the face, with a 'T' in the center: letters are mostly engraved by hand, with small wedge punches at the ends; R's diagonal stem goes all the way to the vertical stem; D's loop is often not closed, is often backwards; S is thin and tall. Pl. nos. 8-12: All aspects**, incl. abbreviation (:) and thin decorative rim.	
"	Cesarau-gusta	M. 55(i) / ANS 57.542	**Prototype**	
"	Cesarau-gusta	SB 42, no. 2553	All aspects *.	
"	Tarracona	M. 65(a) / HSA 16050 (= pl. IV.14) M. 66 / HSA 16046 (= pl. IV.15) M. 67(a) (pl. IV.16) M. 68(c) / HSA 16047 (pl. IV.17) M. 70(6) / HSA 16056 (pl. IV.18) M. 70(c) / HSA 16048 (pl. IV.19)	**HSA 16015 is prototype.** HSA 16046: Bust** (esp. face); +* (lines are engraved between wedges, but the wedge ends are very wide); all letters **, incl. size and spacing*; several dots in legend.	Overall style is very similar to that of obverse.
"	Tirasona	M. 74(d) / HSA 16072 (= pl. V. I)	Bust**; +**; all letters**, esp. T (slanted stem), R, D, S.	Bust**; all letters**, esp. T, R.
"	Tarracona	M. 118(a)/ 16074 (=pl. VII.I)	Bust * (extremely similar to HSA 16046 [Reccared-Tarracona], as are letters D, A, R); +*; letter forms*, esp. R, E, A.	All aspects **, incl. style of +, dots in legend, and esp. letter T.
"	Cesarau-gusta	SB 42, no. 2563	All aspects and control marks *.	
Witteric	Cesarau-gusta	SB 42, no. 2568	Bust **; letters *, L **.	

King	Mint	Coin	Reasons for attribution of obverse	Additional comments about style of reverse
"	Cesarau-gusta	SB 42, no. 2572	Bust and decorative rim**; all other aspects similar.	
"	Cesarau-gusta	SB 42, no. 2573	Uncertain: most aspects similar; E and R *.	
"	Cesarau-gusta	M. 129(d) / HSA 16090 (pl. VII.7)	Bust**; +**; A, R, S, E (with uneven stems) **; decorative rim (very close to edge)**.	
"	Cesarau-gusta	M. 129(f)bis / ANS 57.555	Same as previous coin; even more similar to prototype.	
"	Cesarau-gusta	Ensaios, pl. II.39 (= Pliego 2009, 174c.3); in App. II, pl. III		
"	Tarraco	SB 42, #2572 (= Pliego 2009, 179a.1); in App. II, pl. III		
"	Tirasona	M. 134 / HSA 16093 (pl. VII.9)	All aspects**, except this coin is slightly larger, as are the letters of its legend. Cf. also ANS 57.555 ** (Witteric-Cesaraugusta).	
Gundemar	Cesarau-gusta	M.162(b) / HSA 16098 (= pl. VIII.5)	**Later prototype.** Cf. ANS 57.542 reverse (Reccared-Cesaraugusta) > Bust**; +**; letters E, R, A, V, O, C/G **.	All aspects **, esp. letters and inclusion of dots in legend.
"	Sagunto	GNC pl. V.57	Cf. other Gundemar coins here > most aspects*, esp. letters (and: in place of S). Most similar to HSA 16759 (Gundemar-Tarracona) > module, light decorative rim.	
"	Tarracona	M. 164(a) / HSA 16759 (= pl. VIII.6)	All aspects *. Cf. HSA 16098 (Gundemar-Cesaraugusta) > all aspects** (except M), but size of coin and letters is smaller.	
"	Tirasona	M. 165(a) / see Heiss, no. 4 (= pl. VIII.7)	All aspects*. Cf. HSA 16098 (Gundemar- Cesaraugusta) > all aspects**.	
Sisebut	Cesarau-gusta	M.174(a)/HSA 16102 (=pl. VIII.12)	All aspects *. Cf. HSA 16098 (Gundemar- Cesaraugusta) > esp. Bust, +, S, E, R **.	Cf. HSA 16098 > All aspects **, esp. letters (incl. size and spacing).

King	Mint	Coin	Reasons for attribution of obverse	Additional comments about style of reverse
"	Cesarau-gusta	M. 174(a) / HSA 16100		
"	Tarracona "	M. 177(a) / HSA 16128 (= pl. VIII.14)	All aspects *. Cf. HSA 16100 (Sisebut- Cesaraugusta) > Bust**; +**; letters*, esp. E-X **.	All aspects *. Cf. HSA 16100 > All aspects**.
"	Tarracona	M. I 77(e)2 / ANS 57.560	Same as above	Same as above
Suinthila	Calagorre	M. 212 / ANS 59.129.I	Cf. esp. 16149 > Bust**; +*; All letters*, but larger on this coin.	Bust**; + *; see letters C, E, A, 0, I, V (all**) and same dots in legend.
"	Cesarau-gusta	M. 213(e)/ 16149 (= pl. X.15)	All aspects *. Cf. HSA 16098 (Gundemar- Cesaraugusta) and 16100 (Sisebut- Cesarau-gusta) > Bust**; shape of +*; letters S, R-E (-X on 16100), T, N **.	Cf. esp. HSA 16098 and 16100 > Bust *, all letters * (except larger on this coin).
"	Tarracona	M. 215(f) / HSA 16265 (= pl.XI.I)	All aspects*. Cf. HSA 16759 (Gundemar- Tarracona) >Bust**; +**; letters** (esp. R-E), but larger here and the die has deteriorated.	Same as obv.
"	Tarracona	SB 42, no. 2648	All aspects *. Cf. SB 42, no. 2654 (Suinthila- Valentia) > Bust, esp. face *; + **; letters *.	
"	Valentia	SB 42, no. 2654	Bust, +, letters. See previous coin. However, Valentia coins have reversed S's.	
Sisenand	Tarracona	M. 256(d) / HSA 16441 (= pl. XVII.2)	Cf. esp. 16265 (Suinthila- Tarracona) > Style of bust*, but small differences begin to appear; +**; most letters similar, but S, N, R differ slightly.	Cf. 16265 > Bust**; +**; letters *, with possible exception of R.

Concordance of new ANS accession numbers for ex-HSA regal Visigothic tremisses

HSA number	Ruler	Mint	Miles type	Pliego type	New ANS number
1001.1.15990	Leovigild	no mint	Miles.7e	Pliego2009.9d	2015.48.1
1001.1.7892	Leovigild	no mint	Miles.8d	Pliego2009.11d	2015.48.2
1001.1.16003	Leovigild	no mint	Miles.8i	Pliego2009.13a	2015.48.3
1001.1.16002	Leovigild	no mint	Miles.8h	Pliego2009.13c	2015.48.4
1001.1.16781	Leovigild	no mint	Miles.8j	Pliego2009.13e	2015.48.5
1001.1.16005	Leovigild	Narbona	Miles.9	Pliego2009.19	2016.29.1
1001.1.15989	Leovigild	Narbona	Miles.11a	Pliego2009.22	2016.29.2
1001.1.16669	Leovigild	Cesaragusta	Miles.17	Pliego2009.29	2016.29.3
1001.1.16007	Leovigild	Rodas	Miles.19a	Pliego2009.32b	2016.29.4
1001.57.538	Leovigild	Tarracona	Miles.21	Pliego2009.33	2016.29.5
1001.1.16670	Leovigild	Tirasona	Miles.22	Pliego2009.34	2016.29.6
1001.1.16006	Leovigild	Recopoli	Miles.23a	Pliego2009.36a	2016.29.7
1001.1.16001	Leovigild	Saldania	Miles.26	Pliego2009.39	2016.29.8
1001.1.15993	Leovigild	Toleto	Miles.28a	Pliego2009.42c	2015.48.6
1001.1.15994	Leovigild	Toleto	Miles.28a	Pliego2009.42c	2015.48.7
1001.1.16000	Leovigild	Toleto	Miles.28a	Pliego2009.42c	2015.48.8
1001.1.15992	Leovigild	Toleto	Miles.29a	Pliego2009.43c	2015.48.9
1001.1.15995	Leovigild	Toleto	Miles.29c	Pliego2009.43c	2015.48.10
1001.1.15996	Leovigild	Toleto	Miles.29a	Pliego2009.43c	2015.48.11
1001.1.15997	Leovigild	Toleto	Miles.29a	Pliego2009.43c	2015.48.12
1001.1.15998	Leovigild	Toleto	Miles.29a	Pliego2009.43c	2015.48.13
1001.1.15991	Leovigild	Toleto	Miles.29b	Pliego2009.43d	2016.29.9
1001.1.16004	Leovigild	Ispali	Miles.31a	Pliego2009.45a	2016.29.10
1001.1.15988	Leovigild	Ispali	Miles.31b	Pliego2009.45b	2016.29.11
1001.1.8114	Leovigild	Ispali	Miles.33a	Pliego2009.46b	2016.29.12
1001.1.16668	Leovigild	Ispali	Miles.33e	Pliego2009.48b	2016.29.13
1001.1.16751	Leovigild	Italica	Miles.34	Pliego2009.49	2016.29.14
1001.1.15982	Leovigild	Elvora	Miles.36a	Pliego2009.52b	2015.48.14
1001.1.15987	Leovigild	Elvora	Miles.36a	Pliego2009.52b	2015.48.15
1001.1.15986	Leovigild	Elvora	Miles.36b	Pliego2009.52e	2016.29.15
1001.1.16008	Leovigild	Elvora	Miles.37a	Pliego2009.53a	2015.48.16
1001.1.16010	Leovigild	Elvora	Miles.37a	Pliego2009.53a	2015.48.17
1001.1.15984	Leovigild	Elvora	Miles.37a	Pliego2009.53b	2016.29.16
1001.1.15983	Leovigild	Elvora	Miles.37b	Pliego2009.53d	2016.29.17
1001.1.16009	Leovigild	Elvora	Miles.37b	Pliego2009.53d	2016.29.18
1001.57.539	Leovigild	Emerita	Miles.38c	Pliego2009.54d	2015.48.18
1001.1.16498	Leovigild	Emerita	Miles.38b	Pliego2009.54e	2015.48.19
1001.57.540	Leovigild	Emerita	Miles.39	Pliego2009.56b	2015.48.20
1001.1.16043	Reccared I	Narbona	Miles.48b	Pliego2009.63b	2015.48.21
1001.1.16044	Reccared I	Narbona	Miles.49a	Pliego2009.64a	2015.48.22
1001.1.10620	Reccared I	Barcinona	Miles.51a	Pliego2009.67a	2016.29.19
1001.1.16067	Reccared I	Barcinona	Miles.51d	Pliego2009.67d	2016.29.20
1001.1.16582	Reccared I	Barcinona	Miles.52d	Pliego2009.68e	2016.29.21

HSA number	Ruler	Mint	Miles type	Pliego type	New ANS number
1001.1.16015	Reccared I	Cesaragusta	Miles.55a	Pliego2009.70a	2016.29.22
1001.1.16016	Reccared I	Cesaragusta	Miles.55c	Pliego2009.70d	2016.29.23
1001.1.16018	Reccared I	Cesaragusta	Miles.55e	Pliego2009.71b	2015.48.23
1001.57.542	Reccared I	Cesaragusta	Miles.55i	Pliego2009.71c	2015.48.24
1001.1.16069	Reccared I	Cesaragusta	Miles.56	Pliego2009.72c	2015.48.25
1001.1.16017	Reccared I	Cestavi	Miles.57b	Pliego2009.76b	2016.29.24
1001.1.16050	Reccared I	Tarracona	Miles.65a	Pliego2009.80a	2016.29.25
1001.1.16046	Reccared I	Tarracona	Miles.66	Pliego2009.81b	2015.48.26
1001.1.16047	Reccared I	Tarracona	Miles.68c	Pliego2009.83d	2015.48.27
1001.57.543	Reccared I	Tarracona	Miles.69c	Pliego2009.85	2016.29.26
1001.1.16056	Reccared I	Tarracona	Miles.70b	Pliego2009.86b	2016.29.27
1001.1.16048	Reccared I	Tarracona	Miles.70c	Pliego2009.86c	2016.29.28
1001.1.16072	Reccared I	Tirasona	Miles.74d	Pliego2009.91f	2016.29.29
1001.1.16045	Reccared I	Saldania	Miles.80	Pliego2009.97	2016.29.30
1001.1.16052	Reccared I	Toleto	Miles.81b	Pliego2009.98a	2015.48.28
1001.1.16055	Reccared I	Toleto	Miles.81a	Pliego2009.98a	2015.48.29
1001.1.8102	Reccared I	Toleto	Miles.81c	Pliego2009.98b	2015.48.30
1001.1.16049	Reccared I	Toleto	Miles.81c	Pliego2009.98b	2015.48.31
1001.1.16051	Reccared I	Toleto	Miles.81c	Pliego2009.98b	2015.48.32
1001.1.16053	Reccared I	Toleto	Miles.81c	Pliego2009.98b	2015.48.33
1001.1.16054	Reccared I	Toleto	Miles.81c	Pliego2009.98b	2015.48.34
1001.1.16057	Reccared I	Toleto	Miles.81c	Pliego2009.98b	2015.48.35
1001.1.16058	Reccared I	Toleto	Miles.81c	Pliego2009.98b	2015.48.36
1001.1.16059	Reccared I	Toleto	Miles.81c	Pliego2009.98b	2015.48.37
1001.1.16060	Reccared I	Toleto	Miles.81c	Pliego2009.98b	2015.48.38
1001.1.16063	Reccared I	Toleto	Miles.81c	Pliego2009.98b	2015.48.39
1001.57.544	Reccared I	Toleto	Miles.81c	Pliego2009.98b	2015.48.40
1001.1.16020	Reccared I	Cordoba	Miles.82c	Pliego2009.100c	2015.48.41
1001.1.16019	Reccared I	Cordoba	Miles.82m	Pliego2009.100j	2015.48.42
1001.1.16065	Reccared I	Eliberri	Miles.83a	Pliego2009.101a	2016.29.31
1001.57.545	Reccared I	Eliberri	Miles.83d	Pliego2009.101e	2015.48.43
1001.1.16023	Reccared I	Eliberri	Miles.83d	Pliego2009.101f	2015.48.44
1001.57.546	Reccared I	Ispali	Miles.85a	Pliego2009.105b	2015.48.45
1001.1.16037	Reccared I	Ispali	Miles.85c	Pliego2009.105h	2015.48.46
1001.1.16041	Reccared I	Ispali	Miles.86a	Pliego2009.106a	2015.48.47
1001.1.16509	Reccared I	Ispali	Miles.86a	Pliego2009.106a	2015.48.48
1001.1.16036	Reccared I	Ispali	Miles.86b	Pliego2009.106b	2015.48.49
1001.1.16038	Reccared I	Ispali	Miles.86b	Pliego2009.106b	2015.48.50
1001.1.16039	Reccared I	Ispali	Miles.86d	Pliego2009.106d	2015.48.51
1001.1.16021	Reccared I	Elvora	Miles.90a	Pliego2009.112a	2015.48.52
1001.1.16022	Reccared I	Elvora	Miles.90a	Pliego2009.112a	2015.48.53
1001.1.16024	Reccared I	Elvora	Miles.90b	Pliego2009.112b	2015.48.54
1001.1.16071	Reccared I	Elvora	Miles.90b	Pliego2009.112b	2015.48.55
1001.1.16025	Reccared I	Elvora	Miles.90c	Pliego2009.112c	2015.48.56
1001.1.16027	Reccared I	Emerita	Miles.93a	Pliego2009.114a	2015.48.57

HSA number	Ruler	Mint	Miles type	Pliego type	New ANS number
1001.1.16028	Reccared I	Emerita	Miles.93a	Pliego2009.114a	2015.48.58
1001.57.547	Reccared I	Emerita	Miles.93a	Pliego2009.114a	2015.48.59
1001.57.548	Reccared I	Emerita	Miles.93a	Pliego2009.114a	2015.48.60
1001.57.549	Reccared I	Emerita	Miles.93a	Pliego2009.114a	2015.48.61
1001.57.550	Reccared I	Emerita	Miles.93e	Pliego2009.114b	2015.48.62
1001.1.16029	Reccared I	Emerita	Miles.93d	Pliego2009.114d	2015.48.63
1001.1.16030	Reccared I	Emerita	Miles.93f	Pliego2009.114g	2015.48.64
1001.1.16032	Reccared I	Emerita	Miles.93f	Pliego2009.114g	2015.48.65
1001.1.16034	Reccared I	Emerita	Miles.93f	Pliego2009.114g	2015.48.66
1001.1.16042	Reccared I	Emerita	Miles.93f	Pliego2009.114g	2013.40.65
1001.57.551	Reccared I	Emerita	Miles.93f	Pliego2009.114g	2015.48.67
1001.1.16033	Reccared I	Emerita	Miles.94a	Pliego2009.115a	2015.48.68
1001.1.16026	Reccared I	Emerita	Miles.94b	Pliego2009.116e	2015.48.69
1001.1.16035	Reccared I	Emerita	Miles.94d	Pliego2009.116g	2015.48.70
1001.1.16031	Reccared I	Emerita	Miles.94f	Pliego2009.117a	2015.48.71
1001.57.552	Reccared I	Salmantica	Miles.99c	Pliego2009.127	2016.29.32
1001.1.16014	Reccared I	Asturie	Miles.102	Pliego2009.129	2016.29.33
1001.57.553	Reccared I	Cepis	Miles.105a	Pliego2009.135a	2016.29.34
1001.1.16061	Reccared I	Susarres	Miles.101	Pliego2009.148	2016.29.35
1001.1.16062	Reccared I	Tude	Miles.113	Pliego2009.151	2016.29.36
1001.1.16064	Reccared I	Vallegia (?)	Miles.115	Pliego2009.154	2016.29.37
1001.1.16074	Liuva II	Tarracona	Miles.118a	Pliego2009.158b	2016.29.38
1001.1.16075	Liuva II	Toleto	Miles.119	Pliego2009.160c	2015.48.72
1001.1.16076	Liuva II	Ispali	Miles.120b	Pliego2009.163b	2015.48.73
1001.57.554	Liuva II	Ispali	Miles.120b	Pliego2009.163b	2015.48.74
1001.1.16077	Liuva II	Emerita	Miles.122a	Pliego2009.165a	2015.48.75
1001.1.16080	Witteric	Barcinona	Miles.128a	Pliego2009.173a	2016.29.39
1001.1.16092	Witteric	Cesaragusta	Miles.129a	Pliego2009.174a	2016.29.40
1001.1.16090	Witteric	Cesaragusta	Miles.129d	Pliego2009.175a	2016.29.41
1001.57.555	Witteric	Cesaragusta	Miles.129f	Pliego2009.175d	2016.29.42
1001.1.16093	Witteric	Tirasona	Miles.134	Pliego2009.181a	2016.29.43
1001.1.16087	Witteric	Toleto	Miles.137a	Pliego2009.186b	2015.48.76
1001.1.16088	Witteric	Toleto	Miles.137a	Pliego2009.186b	2015.48.77
1001.57.556	Witteric	Toleto	Miles.137a	Pliego2009.186b	2015.48.78
1001.57.557	Witteric	Toleto	Miles.137a	Pliego2009.186b	2015.48.79
1001.1.16082	Witteric	Ispali	Miles.140b	Pliego2009.190a	2015.48.80
1001.1.16086	Witteric	Ispali	Miles.140b	Pliego2009.190a	2015.48.81
1001.57.558	Witteric	Ispali	Miles.140b	Pliego2009.190a	2015.48.82
1001.1.16081	Witteric	Elvora	Miles.142a	Pliego2009.192c	2015.48.83
1001.1.16095	Witteric	Elvora	Miles.142a	Pliego2009.192c	2015.48.84
1001.1.16085	Witteric	Emerita	Miles.143e	Pliego2009.193d	2015.48.85
1001.57.29966	Witteric	Emerita	Miles.143k	Pliego2009.193f	2015.48.86
1001.1.16083	Witteric	Emerita	Miles.143b	Pliego2009.194c	2015.48.87
1001.1.16084	Witteric	Emerita	Miles.143b	Pliego2009.194c	2015.48.88
1001.1.16094	Witteric	Bergancia	Miles.147	Pliego2009.198	2016.29.44

HSA number	Ruler	Mint	Miles type	Pliego type	New ANS number
1001.57.559	Witteric	Bracara	Miles.148	Pliego2009.199	2016.29.45
1001.1.16091	Witteric	Georres	Miles.152a	Pliego2009.203a	2016.29.46
1001.1.16098	Gundemar	Cesaragusta	Miles.162b	Pliego2009.217d	2016.29.47
1001.1.16759	Gundemar	Tarracona	Miles.164a	Pliego2009.219a	2015.48.89
1001.1.16096	Gundemar	Mentesa	Miles.166a	Pliego2009.222a	2016.29.48
1001.1.16089	Gundemar	Toleto	Miles.167	Pliego2009.224a	2015.48.90
1001.1.16100	Sisebut	Cesaragusta	Miles.174a	Pliego2009.247a	2015.48.91
1001.1.16101	Sisebut	Cesaragusta	Miles.174a	Pliego2009.247a	2015.48.92
1001.1.16102	Sisebut	Cesaragusta	Miles.174a	Pliego2009.247a	2015.48.93
1001.1.16104	Sisebut	Cesaragusta	Miles.175	Pliego2009.249a	2015.48.94
1001.57.560	Sisebut	Tarracona	Miles.177b	Pliego2009.254a	2015.48.95
1001.1.16128	Sisebut	Tarracona	Miles.177a	Pliego2009.254b	2016.29.49
1001.1.16115	Sisebut	Tarracona	Miles.177c	Pliego2009.254e	2015.48.96
1001.57.561	Sisebut	Tarracona	Miles.177c	Pliego2009.254e	2013.40.1
1001.57.562	Sisebut	Tarracona	Miles.178d	Pliego2009.255a	2015.48.97
1001.1.16129	Sisebut	Tarracona	Miles.177a	Pliego2009.255d	2015.48.98
1001.1.16103	Sisebut	Acci	Miles.180	Pliego2009.257f	2015.48.99
1001.1.16127	Sisebut	Mentesa	Miles.182	Pliego2009.262a	2015.48.100
1001.1.16116	Sisebut	Toleto	Miles.183a	Pliego2009.267a	2015.48.101
1001.1.16132	Sisebut	Toleto	Miles.183a	Pliego2009.267a	2015.48.102
1001.1.16133	Sisebut	Toleto	Miles.183a	Pliego2009.267a	2015.48.103
1001.1.16135	Sisebut	Toleto	Miles.183a	Pliego2009.267a	2015.48.104
1001.57.563	Sisebut	Toleto	Miles.183a	Pliego2009.267a	2015.48.105
1001.57.564	Sisebut	Toleto	Miles.183a	Pliego2009.267a	2015.48.106
1001.1.16105	Sisebut	Cordoba	Miles.185	Pliego2009.271c	2015.48.107
1001.57.565	Sisebut	Eliberri	Miles.186b	Pliego2009.272a	2015.48.108
1001.1.16106	Sisebut	Eliberri	Miles.186a	Pliego2009.272b	2015.48.109
1001.57.566	Sisebut	Eliberri	Miles.186f	Pliego2009.272o	2015.48.110
1001.1.16121	Sisebut	Ispali	Miles.187a	Pliego2009.274a	2015.48.111
1001.1.16244	Sisebut	Ispali	Miles.187a	Pliego2009.274a	2015.48.112
1001.1.16376	Sisebut	Ispali	Miles.187a	Pliego2009.274a	2015.48.113
1001.1.16418	Sisebut	Ispali	Miles.187a	Pliego2009.274a	2015.48.114
1001.1.16120	Sisebut	Ispali	Miles.187c	Pliego2009.274d	2015.48.115
1001.1.16124	Sisebut	Ispali	Miles.187c	Pliego2009.274d	2015.48.116
1001.1.16426	Sisebut	Ispali	Miles.187c	Pliego2009.274d	2015.48.117
1001.1.16416	Sisebut	Ispali	Miles.187d	Pliego2009.274n	2015.48.118
1001.1.16125	Sisebut	Ispali	Miles.187e	Pliego2009.275a	2015.48.119
1001.1.16110	Sisebut	Ispali	Miles.187f	Pliego2009.275d	2015.48.120
1001.1.16111	Sisebut	Ispali	Miles.187f	Pliego2009.275d	2013.40.3
1001.1.16122	Sisebut	Ispali	Miles.187f	Pliego2009.275d	2013.40.2
1001.1.16123	Sisebut	Ispali	Miles.187f	Pliego2009.275d	2015.48.121
1001.1.16126	Sisebut	Ispali	Miles.187f	Pliego2009.275d	2013.40.4
1001.1.16427	Sisebut	Ispali	Miles.187f	Pliego2009.275d	2013.40.5
1001.1.8094	Sisebut	Ispali	Miles.187g	Pliego2009.277g	2015.48.122
1001.1.16437	Sisebut	Ispali	Miles.187g	Pliego2009.277g	2015.48.123

HSA number	Ruler	Mint	Miles type	Pliego type	New ANS number
1001.1.16107	Sisebut	Elvora	Miles.191a	Pliego2009.283a	2015.48.124
1001.1.16118	Sisebut	Elvora	Miles.191a	Pliego2009.283a	2015.48.125
1001.1.16372	Sisebut	Elvora	Miles.191b	Pliego2009.283e	2015.48.126
1001.1.8109	Sisebut	Emerita	Miles.192a	Pliego2009.285a	2015.48.127
1001.1.16119	Sisebut	Emerita	Miles.192a	Pliego2009.285a	2015.48.128
1001.1.16108	Sisebut	Emerita	Miles.192b	Pliego2009.285c	2015.48.129
1001.1.16454	Sisebut	Emerita	Miles.192b	Pliego2009.285c	2015.48.130
1001.1.16109	Sisebut	Eminio	Miles.195b	Pliego2009.289a	2016.29.50
1001.1.16112	Sisebut	Laetera	Miles.203	Pliego2009.310a	2016.29.51
1001.1.16113	Sisebut	Luco	Miles.205	Pliego2009.313	2016.29.52
1001.1.16114	Sisebut	Pincia	Miles.207	Pliego2009.319	2016.29.53
1001.1.16117	Sisebut	Tude	Miles.210a	Pliego2009.325b	2016.29.54
1001.1.16150	Suinthila	Cesaragusta	Miles.213a	Pliego2009.338a	2015.48.131
1001.1.16149	Suinthila	Cesaragusta	Miles.213e	Pliego2009.338f	2015.48.132
1001.1.16277	Suinthila	Tarracona	Miles.214c	Pliego2009.340b	2015.48.133
1001.1.16278	Suinthila	Tarracona	Miles.214b	Pliego2009.340c	2015.48.134
1001.1.16280	Suinthila	Tarracona	Miles.215d	Pliego2009.341b	2015.48.135
1001.1.16265	Suinthila	Tarracona	Miles.215f	Pliego2009.341c	2015.48.136
1001.1.16279	Suinthila	Tarracona	Miles.215e	Pliego2009.341f	2015.48.137
1001.1.16236	Suinthila	Acci	Miles.218a	Pliego2009.348a	2015.48.138
1001.1.16136	Suinthila	Acci	Miles.218e	Pliego2009.348b	2016.29.55
1001.1.8095	Suinthila	Acci	Miles.218f	Pliego2009.348g	2015.48.139
1001.1.16237	Suinthila	Acci	Miles.218e	Pliego2009.348h	2015.48.140
1001.1.16268	Suinthila	Mentesa	Miles.220a	Pliego2009.350a	2015.48.141
1001.1.8100	Suinthila	Mentesa	Miles.219a	Pliego2009.352c	2015.48.142
1001.1.16216	Suinthila	Mentesa	Miles.219a	Pliego2009.352c	2015.48.143
1001.1.16267	Suinthila	Mentesa	Miles.219f	Pliego2009.354c	2015.48.144
1001.1.16247	Suinthila	Mentesa	Miles.219e	Pliego2009.354e	2015.48.145
1001.1.16212	Suinthila	Mentesa	Miles.219d	Pliego2009.356b	2015.48.146
1001.1.16213	Suinthila	Mentesa	Miles.219b	Pliego2009.356d	2015.48.147
1001.1.16215	Suinthila	Mentesa	Miles.219b	Pliego2009.356d	2015.48.148
1001.1.16266	Suinthila	Mentesa	Miles.219b	Pliego2009.356d	2015.48.149
1001.1.16255	Suinthila	Mentesa	Miles.219c	Pliego2009.356e	2015.48.150
1001.1.16274	Suinthila	Toleto	Miles.223a	Pliego2009.361a	2015.48.151
1001.1.16281	Suinthila	Toleto	Miles.223a	Pliego2009.361a	2015.48.152
1001.1.16282	Suinthila	Toleto	Miles.223a	Pliego2009.361a	2015.48.153
1001.1.16283	Suinthila	Toleto	Miles.223a	Pliego2009.361a	2015.48.154
1001.1.16286	Suinthila	Toleto	Miles.223a	Pliego2009.361a	2015.48.155
1001.1.16287	Suinthila	Toleto	Miles.223a	Pliego2009.361a	2015.48.156
1001.1.16288	Suinthila	Toleto	Miles.223a	Pliego2009.361a	2015.48.157
1001.1.16285	Suinthila	Toleto	Miles.223b	Pliego2009.361c	2015.48.158
1001.1.16271	Suinthila	Toleto	Miles.223a	Pliego2009.361d	2015.48.159
1001.1.16273	Suinthila	Toleto	Miles.223a	Pliego2009.361d	2015.48.160
1001.1.16284	Suinthila	Toleto	Miles.223c	Pliego2009.361e	2015.48.161
1001.1.16143	Suinthila	Barbi	Miles.224a	Pliego2009.366a	2015.48.162

HSA number	Ruler	Mint	Miles type	Pliego type	New ANS number
1001.1.16138	Suinthila	Barbi	Miles.224c	Pliego2009.366d	2015.48.163
1001.1.16140	Suinthila	Barbi	Miles.224c	Pliego2009.366d	2015.48.164
1001.1.16141	Suinthila	Barbi	Miles.224c	Pliego2009.366d	2015.48.165
1001.1.16144	Suinthila	Barbi	Miles.224c	Pliego2009.366d	2015.48.166
1001.1.16145	Suinthila	Barbi	Miles.224c	Pliego2009.366d	2015.48.167
1001.1.16238	Suinthila	Barbi	Miles.224c	Pliego2009.366d	2015.48.168
1001.57.567	Suinthila	Barbi	Miles.224c	Pliego2009.366d	2015.48.169
1001.1.16137	Suinthila	Barbi	Miles.224d	Pliego2009.366f	2015.48.170
1001.1.16139	Suinthila	Barbi	Miles.224d	Pliego2009.366f	2015.48.171
1001.1.16146	Suinthila	Barbi	Miles.224d	Pliego2009.366f	2015.48.172
1001.1.16147	Suinthila	Barbi	Miles.224d	Pliego2009.366f	2015.48.173
1001.1.16148	Suinthila	Barbi	Miles.224e	Pliego2009.366h	2015.48.174
1001.1.8093	Suinthila	Barbi	Miles.224f	Pliego2009.366i	2015.48.175
1001.1.16142	Suinthila	Barbi	Miles.224f	Pliego2009.366i	2015.48.176
1001.1.16248	Suinthila	Barbi	Miles.224f	Pliego2009.366i	2015.48.177
1001.1.16240	Suinthila	Barbi	Miles.224h	Pliego2009.366k	2015.48.178
1001.1.16153	Suinthila	Cordoba	Miles.226a	Pliego2009.367a	2015.48.179
1001.1.16154	Suinthila	Cordoba	Miles.226a	Pliego2009.367a	2015.48.180
1001.1.16155	Suinthila	Cordoba	Miles.226a	Pliego2009.367a	2015.48.181
1001.1.16157	Suinthila	Cordoba	Miles.226a	Pliego2009.367a	2015.48.182
1001.1.16158	Suinthila	Cordoba	Miles.226a	Pliego2009.367a	2013.40.6
1001.1.16159	Suinthila	Cordoba	Miles.226a	Pliego2009.367a	2015.48.183
1001.1.16151	Suinthila	Cordoba	Miles.226c	Pliego2009.367b	2015.48.184
1001.1.16152	Suinthila	Cordoba	Miles.226c	Pliego2009.367b	2015.48.185
1001.1.8101	Suinthila	Cordoba	Miles.226b	Pliego2009.367d	2015.48.186
1001.1.16156	Suinthila	Cordoba	Miles.226d	Pliego2009.367e	2015.48.187
1001.1.16160	Suinthila	Cordoba	Miles.226d	Pliego2009.367e	2015.48.188
1001.1.16161	Suinthila	Cordoba	Miles.226a	Pliego2009.367h	2015.48.189
1001.1.8099	Suinthila	Eliberri	Miles.227f	Pliego2009.375b	2015.48.190
1001.1.16243	Suinthila	Eliberri	Miles.227f	Pliego2009.375b	2015.48.191
1001.1.16242	Suinthila	Eliberri	Miles.227e	Pliego2009.375i	2016.29.56
1001.1.16169	Suinthila	Eliberri	Miles.227d	Pliego2009.376b	2015.48.192
1001.1.16168	Suinthila	Eliberri	Miles.227h	Pliego2009.376d	2015.48.193
1001.1.16239	Suinthila	Eliberri	Miles.227b	Pliego2009.376g	2015.48.194
1001.1.16170	Suinthila	Eliberri	Miles.227o	Pliego2009.376h	2015.48.195
1001.57.568	Suinthila	Eliberri	Miles.227o	Pliego2009.376h	2015.48.196
1001.1.16166	Suinthila	Eliberri	Miles.227i	Pliego2009.376i	2015.48.197
1001.1.16171	Suinthila	Eliberri	Miles.227j	Pliego2009.376o	2015.48.198
1001.1.16167	Suinthila	Eliberri	Miles.227g	Pliego2009.376p	2016.29.57
1001.1.16172	Suinthila	Eliberri	Miles.227l	Pliego2009.377a	2013.40.8
1001.1.16259	Suinthila	Eliberri	Miles.227l	Pliego2009.377a	2015.48.199
1001.1.16251	Suinthila	Eliberri	Miles.227m	Pliego2009.377b	2015.48.200
1001.1.8097	Suinthila	Eliberri	Miles.227k	Pliego2009.378a	2015.48.201
1001.1.16162	Suinthila	Eliberri	Miles.227p	Pliego2009.379c	2015.48.202
1001.1.16163	Suinthila	Eliberri	Miles.227p	Pliego2009.379c	2015.48.203

HSA number	Ruler	Mint	Miles type	Pliego type	New ANS number
1001.1.16164	Suinthila	Eliberri	Miles.227p	Pliego2009.379c	2015.48.204
1001.1.16165	Suinthila	Eliberri	Miles.227p	Pliego2009.379c	2013.40.9
1001.1.16206	Suinthila	Eliberri	Miles.227p	Pliego2009.379c	2013.40.7
1001.1.16252	Suinthila	Eliberri	Miles.227r	Pliego2009.379d	2015.48.205
1001.1.16241	Suinthila	Eliberri	Miles.227q	Pliego2009.379e	2015.48.206
1001.1.16253	Suinthila	Eliberri	Miles.227q	Pliego2009.379e	2015.48.207
1001.1.16218	Suinthila	Ispali	Miles.228a	Pliego2009.381a	2013.40.11
1001.1.16222	Suinthila	Ispali	Miles.228a	Pliego2009.381a	2015.48.208
1001.1.16223	Suinthila	Ispali	Miles.228a	Pliego2009.381a	2015.48.209
1001.1.16224	Suinthila	Ispali	Miles.228a	Pliego2009.381a	2015.48.210
1001.1.16225	Suinthila	Ispali	Miles.228a	Pliego2009.381a	2015.48.211
1001.1.16226	Suinthila	Ispali	Miles.228a	Pliego2009.381a	2015.48.212
1001.1.16227	Suinthila	Ispali	Miles.228a	Pliego2009.381a	2013.40.10
1001.1.16228	Suinthila	Ispali	Miles.228a	Pliego2009.381a	2015.48.213
1001.1.16245	Suinthila	Ispali	Miles.228a	Pliego2009.381a	2015.48.214
1001.1.16249	Suinthila	Ispali	Miles.228a	Pliego2009.381a	2015.48.215
1001.1.16263	Suinthila	Ispali	Miles.228a	Pliego2009.381a	2015.48.216
1001.57.569	Suinthila	Ispali	Miles.228a	Pliego2009.381a	2013.40.12
1001.1.16217	Suinthila	Ispali	Miles.228b	Pliego2009.381c	2015.48.217
1001.1.16220	Suinthila	Ispali	Miles.228h	Pliego2009.381g	2013.40.14
1001.1.16221	Suinthila	Ispali	Miles.228h	Pliego2009.381g	2015.48.218
1001.1.16254	Suinthila	Ispali	Miles.228h	Pliego2009.381g	2015.48.219
1001.1.16219	Suinthila	Ispali	Miles.228d	Pliego2009.381l	2015.48.220
1001.1.16229	Suinthila	Ispali	Miles.228f	Pliego2009.382a	2013.40.13
1001.1.16231	Suinthila	Ispali	Miles.228f	Pliego2009.382a	2015.48.221
1001.1.16262	Suinthila	Ispali	Miles.228f	Pliego2009.382a	2015.48.222
1001.1.16264	Suinthila	Ispali	Miles.228j	Pliego2009.382e	2015.48.223
1001.1.16256	Suinthila	Tucci	Miles.229c	Pliego2009.384a	2015.48.224
1001.1.16257	Suinthila	Tucci	Miles.229c	Pliego2009.384a	2015.48.225
1001.1.16293	Suinthila	Tucci	Miles.229e	Pliego2009.384f	2015.48.226
1001.1.16292	Suinthila	Tucci	Miles.229d	Pliego2009.384h	2015.48.227
1001.1.16275	Suinthila	Tucci	Miles.229h	Pliego2009.385c	2013.40.15
1001.1.16276	Suinthila	Tucci	Miles.229h	Pliego2009.385c	2015.48.228
1001.1.16270	Suinthila	Tucci	Miles.229m	Pliego2009.386e	2015.48.229
1001.1.16230	Suinthila	Tucci	Miles.229a	Pliego2009.387a	2015.48.230
1001.1.16290	Suinthila	Tucci	Miles.229j	Pliego2009.387d	2015.48.231
1001.1.16429	Suinthila	Tucci	Miles.229k	Pliego2009.387e	2016.29.58
1001.1.16430	Suinthila	Tucci	Miles.229q	Pliego2009.387j	2016.29.59
1001.1.8096	Suinthila	Tucci	Miles.229p	Pliego2009.387n	2015.48.232
1001.1.16296	Suinthila	Tucci	Miles.229p	Pliego2009.387n	2013.40.16
1001.1.16233	Suinthila	Tucci	Miles.229o	Pliego2009.387q	2015.48.233
1001.1.16232	Suinthila	Tucci	Miles.229i	Pliego2009.387r	2016.29.60
1001.1.16291	Suinthila	Tucci	Miles.230c	Pliego2009.388a	2015.48.234
1001.1.16258	Suinthila	Tucci	Miles.230b	Pliego2009.388b	2015.48.235
1001.1.16294	Suinthila	Tucci	Miles.230a	Pliego2009.388b	2013.40.17

HSA number	Ruler	Mint	Miles type	Pliego type	New ANS number
1001.1.16295	Suinthila	Tucci	Miles.230a	Pliego2009.388b	2015.48.236
1001.1.16204	Suinthila	Egitania	Miles.233	Pliego2009.391c	2013.40.18
1001.1.16210	Suinthila	Egitania	Miles.233	Pliego2009.391c	2015.48.237
1001.1.16173	Suinthila	Emerita	Miles.235a	Pliego2009.393a	2015.48.238
1001.1.16175	Suinthila	Emerita	Miles.235a	Pliego2009.393a	2015.48.239
1001.1.16176	Suinthila	Emerita	Miles.235a	Pliego2009.393a	2015.48.240
1001.1.16177	Suinthila	Emerita	Miles.235a	Pliego2009.393a	2015.48.241
1001.1.16178	Suinthila	Emerita	Miles.235a	Pliego2009.393a	2015.48.242
1001.1.16179	Suinthila	Emerita	Miles.235a	Pliego2009.393a	2015.48.243
1001.1.16180	Suinthila	Emerita	Miles.235a	Pliego2009.393a	2015.48.244
1001.1.16182	Suinthila	Emerita	Miles.235a	Pliego2009.393a	2015.48.245
1001.1.16184	Suinthila	Emerita	Miles.235a	Pliego2009.393a	2015.48.246
1001.1.16185	Suinthila	Emerita	Miles.235a	Pliego2009.393a	2013.40.19
1001.1.16186	Suinthila	Emerita	Miles.235a	Pliego2009.393a	2015.48.247
1001.1.16187	Suinthila	Emerita	Miles.235a	Pliego2009.393a	2015.48.248
1001.1.16188	Suinthila	Emerita	Miles.235a	Pliego2009.393a	2015.48.249
1001.1.16190	Suinthila	Emerita	Miles.235a	Pliego2009.393a	2015.48.250
1001.1.16192	Suinthila	Emerita	Miles.235a	Pliego2009.393a	2013.40.20
1001.1.16193	Suinthila	Emerita	Miles.235a	Pliego2009.393a	2015.48.251
1001.1.16196	Suinthila	Emerita	Miles.235a	Pliego2009.393a	2015.48.252
1001.1.16197	Suinthila	Emerita	Miles.235a	Pliego2009.393a	2015.48.253
1001.1.16199	Suinthila	Emerita	Miles.235a	Pliego2009.393a	2015.48.254
1001.1.16205	Suinthila	Emerita	Miles.235a	Pliego2009.393a	2015.48.255
1001.1.16208	Suinthila	Emerita	Miles.235a	Pliego2009.393a	2015.48.256
1001.1.16211	Suinthila	Emerita	Miles.235a	Pliego2009.393a	2015.48.257
1001.1.16453	Suinthila	Emerita	Miles.235a	Pliego2009.393a	2015.48.258
1001.57.570	Suinthila	Emerita	Miles.235a	Pliego2009.393a	2015.48.259
1001.57.571	Suinthila	Emerita	Miles.235a	Pliego2009.393a	2015.48.260
1001.57.572	Suinthila	Emerita	Miles.235a	Pliego2009.393a	2013.40.21
1001.1.16209	Suinthila	Emerita	Miles.235a	Pliego2009.393b	2015.48.261
1001.1.16181	Suinthila	Emerita	Miles.235b	Pliego2009.393c	2015.48.262
1001.1.16203	Suinthila	Emerita	Miles.235c	Pliego2009.393d	2015.48.263
1001.1.16207	Suinthila	Emerita	Miles.235d	Pliego2009.393f	2015.48.264
1001.1.16183	Suinthila	Emerita	Miles.235i	Pliego2009.393j	2015.48.265
1001.1.16195	Suinthila	Emerita	Miles.235e	Pliego2009.394b	2015.48.266
1001.1.16174	Suinthila	Emerita	Miles.235f	Pliego2009.394d	2013.40.22
1001.1.16191	Suinthila	Emerita	Miles.235f	Pliego2009.394d	2015.48.267
1001.1.16194	Suinthila	Emerita	Miles.235f	Pliego2009.394d	2013.40.23
1001.1.16269	Suinthila	Salmantica	Miles.237a	Pliego2009.400a	2016.29.61
1001.1.16235	Suinthila	Bracara	Miles.240c	Pliego2009.409e	2015.48.268
1001.1.16260	Suinthila	Nandolas	Miles.247	Pliego2009.421	2016.29.62
1001.1.16441	Sisenand	Tarracona	Miles.256d	Pliego2009.437d	2016.29.63
1001.1.16300	Sisenand	Acci	Miles.257b	Pliego2009.438a	2016.29.64
1001.1.16234	Sisenand	Acci	Miles.257a	Pliego2009.438b	2016.29.65
1001.1.16434	Sisenand	Acci	Miles.257d	Pliego2009.438d	2016.29.66

HSA number	Ruler	Mint	Miles type	Pliego type	New ANS number
1001.1.16364	Sisenand	Acci	Miles.257c	Pliego2009.438e	2016.29.67
1001.1.16425	Sisenand	Castilona	Miles.259a	Pliego2009.439a	2016.29.68
1001.1.16424	Sisenand	Castilona	Miles.259b	Pliego2009.439c	2016.29.69
1001.1.16340	Sisenand	Castilona	Miles.259e	Pliego2009.439e	2016.29.70
1001.1.16338	Sisenand	Castilona	Miles.258a	Pliego2009.441a	2016.29.71
1001.1.16305	Sisenand	Castilona	Miles.258f	Pliego2009.441d	2016.29.72
1001.1.16395	Sisenand	Castilona	Miles.258e	Pliego2009.441f	2016.29.73
1001.1.16246	Sisenand	Castilona	Miles.258g	Pliego2009.441g	2016.29.74
1001.1.16214	Sisenand	Mentesa	Miles.261a	Pliego2009.445c	2016.29.75
1001.1.16404	Sisenand	Mentesa	Miles.261b	Pliego2009.445d	2016.29.76
1001.1.16439	Sisenand	Mentesa	Miles.261c	Pliego2009.445e	2016.29.77
1001.57.573	Sisenand	Mentesa	Miles.262e	Pliego2009.447a	2016.29.78
1001.1.16396	Sisenand	Mentesa	Miles.262c	Pliego2009.447b	2016.29.79
1001.1.16406	Sisenand	Mentesa	Miles.262d	Pliego2009.447c	2015.48.269
1001.1.16378	Sisenand	Mentesa	Miles.262b	Pliego2009.447d	2016.29.80
1001.1.16446	Sisenand	Toleto	Miles.264d	Pliego2009.449b	2015.48.270
1001.1.16447	Sisenand	Toleto	Miles.264d	Pliego2009.449b	2015.48.271
1001.1.16443	Sisenand	Toleto	Miles.264e	Pliego2009.449c	2015.48.272
1001.1.16444	Sisenand	Toleto	Miles.264e	Pliego2009.449c	2015.48.273
1001.1.16450	Sisenand	Toleto	Miles.264e	Pliego2009.449c	2015.48.274
1001.1.16445	Sisenand	Toleto	Miles.264b	Pliego2009.449e	2015.48.275
1001.1.16448	Sisenand	Toleto	Miles.264c	Pliego2009.449f	2015.48.276
1001.1.16442	Sisenand	Toleto	Miles.264a	Pliego2009.450b	2015.48.277
1001.1.16301	Sisenand	Asidona	Miles.265a	Pliego2009.451a	2016.29.81
1001.1.16407	Sisenand	Asidona	Miles.265a	Pliego2009.451a	2016.29.82
1001.1.16408	Sisenand	Asidona	Miles.265a	Pliego2009.451a	2013.40.24
1001.1.16415	Sisenand	Asidona	Miles.265a	Pliego2009.451a	2016.29.83
1001.1.16421	Sisenand	Asidona	Miles.265a	Pliego2009.451a	2016.29.84
1001.1.16250	Sisenand	Barbi	Miles.266d	Pliego2009.453a	2015.48.278
1001.1.16304	Sisenand	Barbi	Miles.266d	Pliego2009.453a	2013.40.25
1001.1.16367	Sisenand	Barbi	Miles.266d	Pliego2009.453a	2015.48.279
1001.1.16380	Sisenand	Barbi	Miles.266a	Pliego2009.453a	2015.48.280
1001.1.16385	Sisenand	Barbi	Miles.266d	Pliego2009.453a	2015.48.281
1001.1.16417	Sisenand	Barbi	Miles.266a	Pliego2009.453a	2015.48.282
1001.1.16422	Sisenand	Barbi	Miles.266d	Pliego2009.453a	2015.48.283
1001.1.16423	Sisenand	Barbi	Miles.266a	Pliego2009.453a	2015.48.284
1001.1.16303	Sisenand	Barbi	Miles.266b	Pliego2009.453b	2016.29.85
1001.1.16302	Sisenand	Barbi	Miles.266e	Pliego2009.453d	2016.29.86
1001.1.16409	Sisenand	Barbi	Miles.266c	Pliego2009.453f	2016.29.87
1001.1.16369	Sisenand	Barbi	Miles.266g	Pliego2009.453h	2013.40.27
1001.1.16379	Sisenand	Barbi	Miles.266g	Pliego2009.453h	2013.40.26
1001.1.16433	Sisenand	Barbi	Miles.266g	Pliego2009.453h	2015.48.285
1001.1.16435	Sisenand	Barbi	Miles.266g	Pliego2009.453h	2015.48.286
1001.1.16311	Sisenand	Cordoba	Miles.267d	Pliego2009.454c	2016.29.88
1001.1.16316	Sisenand	Cordoba	Miles.267e	Pliego2009.454d	2016.29.89

HSA number	Ruler	Mint	Miles type	Pliego type	New ANS number
1001.1.16306	Sisenand	Cordoba	Miles.267b	Pliego2009.454f	2016.29.90
1001.1.16381	Sisenand	Cordoba	Miles.267d	Pliego2009.454g	2016.29.91
1001.1.16312	Sisenand	Cordoba	Miles.267j	Pliego2009.455d	2016.29.92
1001.1.16310	Sisenand	Cordoba	Miles.267k	Pliego2009.455e	2016.29.93
1001.1.16307	Sisenand	Cordoba	Miles.267h	Pliego2009.455i	2013.40.28
1001.1.16314	Sisenand	Cordoba	Miles.267h	Pliego2009.455i	2015.48.287
1001.1.16432	Sisenand	Cordoba	Miles.267h	Pliego2009.455i	2015.48.288
1001.1.16308	Sisenand	Cordoba	Miles.267i	Pliego2009.455j	2016.29.94
1001.1.16313	Sisenand	Cordoba	Miles.267o	Pliego2009.455m	2016.29.95
1001.1.16315	Sisenand	Cordoba	Miles.267n	Pliego2009.455n	2016.29.96
1001.1.16377	Sisenand	Cordoba	Miles.267n	Pliego2009.455n	2016.29.97
1001.1.16309	Sisenand	Cordoba	Miles.267f	Pliego2009.456c	2016.29.98
1001.1.16394	Sisenand	Eliberri	Miles.268d	Pliego2009.457a	2016.29.99
1001.1.16318	Sisenand	Eliberri	Miles.268c	Pliego2009.458d	2013.40.34
1001.1.16319	Sisenand	Eliberri	Miles.268c	Pliego2009.458d	2013.40.32
1001.1.16320	Sisenand	Eliberri	Miles.268c	Pliego2009.458d	2015.48.289
1001.1.16355	Sisenand	Eliberri	Miles.268c	Pliego2009.458d	2013.40.31
1001.1.16410	Sisenand	Eliberri	Miles.268c	Pliego2009.458d	2015.48.290
1001.1.16419	Sisenand	Eliberri	Miles.268c	Pliego2009.458d	2015.48.291
1001.1.16431	Sisenand	Eliberri	Miles.268c	Pliego2009.458d	2013.40.30
1001.1.16363	Sisenand	Eliberri	Miles.268c	Pliego2009.458e	2016.29.100
1001.1.16401	Sisenand	Eliberri	Miles.268c	Pliego2009.458e	2013.40.33
1001.1.16317	Sisenand	Eliberri	Miles.268b	Pliego2009.458f	2016.29.101
1001.1.16321	Sisenand	Eliberri	Miles.268b	Pliego2009.458f	2013.40.29
1001.1.16393	Sisenand	Eliberri	Miles.268f	Pliego2009.458h	2016.29.102
1001.1.8098	Sisenand	Eliberri	Miles.268e	Pliego2009.458i	2016.29.103
1001.1.16391	Sisenand	Ispali	Miles.269c	Pliego2009.459c	2015.48.292
1001.1.16397	Sisenand	Ispali	Miles.269c	Pliego2009.459c	2015.48.293
1001.57.574	Sisenand	Ispali	Miles.269c	Pliego2009.459c	2015.48.294
1001.1.16420	Sisenand	Ispali	Miles.269e	Pliego2009.459d	2015.48.295
1001.1.16350	Sisenand	Ispali	Miles.269f	Pliego2009.459e	2013.40.38
1001.1.16354	Sisenand	Ispali	Miles.269f	Pliego2009.459e	2013.40.36
1001.1.16362	Sisenand	Ispali	Miles.269f	Pliego2009.459e	2015.48.296
1001.1.16365	Sisenand	Ispali	Miles.269f	Pliego2009.459e	2013.40.35
1001.1.16383	Sisenand	Ispali	Miles.269f	Pliego2009.459e	2015.48.297
1001.1.16436	Sisenand	Ispali	Miles.269f	Pliego2009.459e	2013.40.37
1001.1.16358	Sisenand	Ispali	Miles.269g	Pliego2009.459f	2013.40.39
1001.1.16388	Sisenand	Ispali	Miles.269g	Pliego2009.459f	2015.48.298
1001.1.16428	Sisenand	Ispali	Miles.269g	Pliego2009.459f	2015.48.299
1001.1.16366	Sisenand	Ispali	Miles.269j	Pliego2009.459g	2013.40.40
1001.1.16382	Sisenand	Ispali	Miles.269j	Pliego2009.459g	2015.48.300
1001.1.16371	Sisenand	Ispali	Miles.269k	Pliego2009.459h	2015.48.301
1001.1.16351	Sisenand	Ispali	Miles.269m	Pliego2009.460b	2015.48.302
1001.1.16360	Sisenand	Ispali	Miles.269m	Pliego2009.460b	2013.40.41
1001.1.16374	Sisenand	Ispali	Miles.269n	Pliego2009.460c	2015.48.303

HSA number	Ruler	Mint	Miles type	Pliego type	New ANS number
1001.1.16389	Sisenand	Ispali	Miles.269n	Pliego2009.460c	2013.40.42
1001.1.16357	Sisenand	Ispali	Miles.269o	Pliego2009.460e	2013.40.43
1001.57.575	Sisenand	Ispali	Miles.269d	Pliego2009.460e	2015.48.304
1001.1.16399	Sisenand	Ispali	Miles.269s	Pliego2009.460g	2016.29.104
1001.1.16356	Sisenand	Ispali	Miles.269q	Pliego2009.460h	2015.48.305
1001.1.16359	Sisenand	Ispali	Miles.269q	Pliego2009.460h	2015.48.306
1001.1.16361	Sisenand	Ispali	Miles.269q	Pliego2009.460h	2013.40.44
1001.1.16370	Sisenand	Ispali	Miles.269q	Pliego2009.460h	2013.40.45
1001.1.16449	Sisenand	Ispali	Miles.269q	Pliego2009.460h	2015.48.307
1001.57.576	Sisenand	Ispali	Miles.269q	Pliego2009.460h	2015.48.308
1001.1.16375	Sisenand	Ispali	Miles.269r	Pliego2009.460i	2015.48.309
1001.1.16412	Sisenand	Ispali	Miles.269t	Pliego2009.460k	2016.29.105
1001.1.16387	Sisenand	Malaka	Miles.270b	Pliego2009.461c	2016.29.106
1001.1.16368	Sisenand	Tucci	Miles.271j	Pliego2009.462a	2016.29.107
1001.1.16384	Sisenand	Tucci	Miles.271a	Pliego2009.462a	2016.29.108
1001.1.16440	Sisenand	Tucci	Miles.271a	Pliego2009.462a	2013.40.46
1001.1.16438	Sisenand	Tucci	Miles.271k	Pliego2009.462b	2016.29.109
1001.1.16403	Sisenand	Tucci	Miles.271b	Pliego2009.462c	2016.29.110
1001.1.16373	Sisenand	Tucci	Miles.271c	Pliego2009.462d	2015.48.310
1001.1.16386	Sisenand	Tucci	Miles.271c	Pliego2009.462d	2013.40.47
1001.1.16390	Sisenand	Tucci	Miles.271c	Pliego2009.462d	2015.48.311
1001.1.16392	Sisenand	Tucci	Miles.271c	Pliego2009.462d	2015.48.312
1001.1.16411	Sisenand	Tucci	Miles.271c	Pliego2009.462d	2015.48.313
1001.1.16398	Sisenand	Tucci	Miles.271d	Pliego2009.462e	2016.29.111
1001.1.16414	Sisenand	Tucci	Miles.271g	Pliego2009.462g	2016.29.112
1001.1.16413	Sisenand	Tucci	Miles.271h	Pliego2009.462h	2016.29.113
1001.1.16402	Sisenand	Tucci	Miles.271e	Pliego2009.462i	2016.29.114
1001.1.16405	Sisenand	Tucci	Miles.271f	Pliego2009.462j	2016.29.115
1001.1.16400	Sisenand	Tucci	Miles.271i	Pliego2009.465	2016.29.116
1001.1.16341	Sisenand	Egitania	Miles.272b	Pliego2009.466b	2016.29.117
1001.57.577	Sisenand	Egitania	Miles.272f	Pliego2009.466e	2016.29.118
1001.1.8121	Sisenand	Emerita	Miles.273a	Pliego2009.467a	2015.48.314
1001.1.16198	Sisenand	Emerita	Miles.273a	Pliego2009.467a	2015.48.315
1001.1.16200	Sisenand	Emerita	Miles.273a	Pliego2009.467a	2015.48.316
1001.1.16201	Sisenand	Emerita	Miles.273a	Pliego2009.467a	2015.48.317
1001.1.16322	Sisenand	Emerita	Miles.273a	Pliego2009.467a	2013.40.50
1001.1.16324	Sisenand	Emerita	Miles.273a	Pliego2009.467a	2013.40.51
1001.1.16325	Sisenand	Emerita	Miles.273a	Pliego2009.467a	2013.40.55
1001.1.16326	Sisenand	Emerita	Miles.273a	Pliego2009.467a	2013.40.53
1001.1.16327	Sisenand	Emerita	Miles.273a	Pliego2009.467a	2013.40.48
1001.1.16332	Sisenand	Emerita	Miles.273a	Pliego2009.467a	2013.40.52
1001.1.16334	Sisenand	Emerita	Miles.273a	Pliego2009.467a	2015.48.318
1001.1.16336	Sisenand	Emerita	Miles.273a	Pliego2009.467a	2013.40.49
1001.1.16339	Sisenand	Emerita	Miles.273a	Pliego2009.467a	2013.40.54
1001.1.16346	Sisenand	Emerita	Miles.273a	Pliego2009.467a	2015.48.319

HSA number	Ruler	Mint	Miles type	Pliego type	New ANS number
1001.1.16347	Sisenand	Emerita	Miles.273a	Pliego2009.467a	2015.48.320
1001.1.16352	Sisenand	Emerita	Miles.273a	Pliego2009.467a	2015.48.321
1001.1.16451	Sisenand	Emerita	Miles.273f	Pliego2009.467c	2015.48.322
1001.1.8123	Sisenand	Emerita	Miles.273b	Pliego2009.467e	2015.48.323
1001.1.16202	Sisenand	Emerita	Miles.273b	Pliego2009.467e	2013.40.56
1001.1.16297	Sisenand	Emerita	Miles.273b	Pliego2009.467e	2015.48.324
1001.1.16323	Sisenand	Emerita	Miles.273b	Pliego2009.467e	2015.48.325
1001.1.16329	Sisenand	Emerita	Miles.273b	Pliego2009.467e	2013.40.57
1001.1.16330	Sisenand	Emerita	Miles.273b	Pliego2009.467e	2013.40.58
1001.1.16337	Sisenand	Emerita	Miles.273b	Pliego2009.467e	2015.48.326
1001.1.16344	Sisenand	Emerita	Miles.273b	Pliego2009.467e	2015.48.327
1001.1.16345	Sisenand	Emerita	Miles.273b	Pliego2009.467e	2013.40.59
1001.1.16333	Sisenand	Emerita	Miles.273d	Pliego2009.467f	2013.40.62
1001.1.16335	Sisenand	Emerita	Miles.273d	Pliego2009.467f	2015.48.328
1001.1.16342	Sisenand	Emerita	Miles.273d	Pliego2009.467f	2013.40.61
1001.1.16348	Sisenand	Emerita	Miles.273d	Pliego2009.467f	2015.48.329
1001.1.16349	Sisenand	Emerita	Miles.273d	Pliego2009.467f	2013.40.64
1001.1.16452	Sisenand	Emerita	Miles.273d	Pliego2009.467f	2013.40.63
1001.1.16298	Sisenand	Emerita	Miles.273c	Pliego2009.467h	2013.40.60
1001.1.16328	Sisenand	Emerita	Miles.273c	Pliego2009.467h	2015.48.330
1001.1.16331	Sisenand	Emerita	Miles.273c	Pliego2009.467h	2015.48.331
1001.1.16353	Sisenand	Emerita	Miles.273c	Pliego2009.467h	2015.48.332
1001.1.16343	Sisenand	Emerita	Miles.273g	Pliego2009.467i	2015.48.333
1001.57.578	Sisenand	Emerita	Miles.273g	Pliego2009.467i	2015.48.334
1001.1.16299	Iudila	Emerita	Miles.279	Pliego2009.472	2016.29.119
1001.1.16461	Chintila	Cesaragusta	Miles.280	Pliego2009.473	2016.29.120
1001.1.16455	Chintila	Acci	Miles.283a	Pliego2009.476b	2016.29.121
1001.57.579	Chintila	Toleto	Miles.285a	Pliego2009.482a	2015.48.335
1001.1.16459	Chintila	Toleto	Miles.285d	Pliego2009.482b	2015.48.336
1001.1.16470	Chintila	Toleto	Miles.285d	Pliego2009.482b	2015.48.337
1001.57.580	Chintila	Cordoba	Miles.286c	Pliego2009.487d	2016.29.122
1001.57.581	Chintila	Cordoba	Miles.286c	Pliego2009.487e	2016.29.123
1001.1.16457	Chintila	Eliberri	Miles.290	Pliego2009.491a	2016.29.124
1001.1.16458	Chintila	Ispali	Miles.291a	Pliego2009.492a	2016.29.125
1001.1.16469	Tulga	Toleto	Miles.304a	Pliego2009.512a	2016.29.126
1001.1.16468	Tulga	Toleto	Miles.304b	Pliego2009.512b	2015.48.338
1001.1.16465	Tulga	Cordoba	Miles.306a	Pliego2009.515a	2016.29.127
1001.1.16462	Tulga	Cordoba	Miles.306b	Pliego2009.515b	2015.48.339
1001.1.16464	Tulga	Cordoba	Miles.306b	Pliego2009.515b	2015.48.340
1001.1.16463	Tulga	Cordoba	Miles.306d	Pliego2009.515e	2016.29.128
1001.1.16477	Chindasuinth	Narbona	Miles.314a	Pliego2009.526c	2015.48.341
1001.1.8110	Chindasuinth	Toleto	Miles.318a	Pliego2009.533a	2015.48.342
1001.1.16478	Chindasuinth	Toleto	Miles.318a	Pliego2009.533a	2015.48.343
1001.1.16479	Chindasuinth	Toleto	Miles.318a	Pliego2009.533a	2015.48.344
1001.1.16480	Chindasuinth	Toleto	Miles.318a	Pliego2009.533a	2015.48.345

HSA number	Ruler	Mint	Miles type	Pliego type	New ANS number
1001.1.16481	Chindasuinth	Toleto	Miles.318a	Pliego2009.533a	2015.48.346
1001.1.16482	Chindasuinth	Toleto	Miles.318a	Pliego2009.533a	2015.48.347
1001.1.16483	Chindasuinth	Toleto	Miles.318a	Pliego2009.533a	2015.48.348
1001.1.16472	Chindasuinth	Cordoba	Miles.319	Pliego2009.537b	2016.29.129
1001.1.16476	Chindasuinth	Cordoba	Miles.322d	Pliego2009.541f	2016.29.130
1001.1.16475	Chindasuinth	Emerita	Miles.330a	Pliego2009.550a	2015.48.349
1001.1.16473	Chindasuinth	Emerita	Miles.330d	Pliego2009.550e	2015.48.350
1001.1.16474	Chindasuinth	Emerita	Miles.330f	Pliego2009.550g	2016.29.131
1001.1.16510	Chind.-Recces.	Ispali	Miles.349	Pliego2009.567	2016.29.132
1001.1.16536	Chind.-Recces.	Ispali	Miles.348a	Pliego2009.568a	2016.29.133
1001.1.16511	Reccesuinth	Narbona	Miles.353a	Pliego2009.572	2016.29.134
1001.1.16512	Reccesuinth	Tarracona	Miles.356a	Pliego2009.575a	2015.48.351
1001.1.16513	Reccesuinth	Tarracona	Miles.356c	Pliego2009.575b	2015.48.352
1001.1.16519	Reccesuinth	Tarracona	Miles.356c	Pliego2009.575b	2015.48.353
1001.1.16515	Reccesuinth	Tarracona	Miles.357a	Pliego2009.576b	2016.29.135
1001.57.582	Reccesuinth	Tarracona	Miles.357e	Pliego2009.576f	2015.48.354
1001.1.16514	Reccesuinth	Tarracona	Miles.357d	Pliego2009.576g	2016.29.136
1001.1.16518	Reccesuinth	Toleto	Miles.360f	Pliego2009.579a	2015.48.355
1001.1.16530	Reccesuinth	Toleto	Miles.360f	Pliego2009.579a	2015.48.356
1001.57.587	Reccesuinth	Toleto	Miles.360f	Pliego2009.579a	2015.48.357
1001.1.16524	Reccesuinth	Toleto	Miles.360a	Pliego2009.580a	2015.48.358
1001.1.16525	Reccesuinth	Toleto	Miles.360a	Pliego2009.580a	2015.48.359
1001.1.16527	Reccesuinth	Toleto	Miles.360a	Pliego2009.580a	2015.48.360
1001.1.16528	Reccesuinth	Toleto	Miles.360a	Pliego2009.580a	2015.48.361
1001.1.16529	Reccesuinth	Toleto	Miles.360a	Pliego2009.580a	2015.48.362
1001.1.16532	Reccesuinth	Toleto	Miles.360a	Pliego2009.580a	2015.48.363
1001.1.16533	Reccesuinth	Toleto	Miles.360a	Pliego2009.580a	2015.48.364
1001.57.583	Reccesuinth	Toleto	Miles.360a	Pliego2009.580a	2015.48.365
1001.57.584	Reccesuinth	Toleto	Miles.360a	Pliego2009.580a	2015.48.366
1001.57.585	Reccesuinth	Toleto	Miles.360a	Pliego2009.580a	2015.48.367
1001.1.16517	Reccesuinth	Toleto	Miles.360g	Pliego2009.580b	2015.48.368
1001.1.16523	Reccesuinth	Toleto	Miles.360a	Pliego2009.580c	2015.48.369
1001.1.16534	Reccesuinth	Toleto	Miles.360a	Pliego2009.580c	2015.48.370
1001.1.16526	Reccesuinth	Toleto	Miles.360c	Pliego2009.580d	2015.48.371
1001.1.16535	Reccesuinth	Toleto	Miles.360c	Pliego2009.580d	2015.48.372
1001.1.16521	Reccesuinth	Toleto	Miles.360d	Pliego2009.580e	2015.48.373
1001.1.16522	Reccesuinth	Toleto	Miles.360d	Pliego2009.580e	2015.48.374
1001.1.16516	Reccesuinth	Toleto	Miles.360b	Pliego2009.580f	2015.48.375
1001.1.16531	Reccesuinth	Toleto	Miles.360b	Pliego2009.580f	2015.48.376
1001.57.586	Reccesuinth	Toleto	Miles.360b	Pliego2009.580f	2015.48.377
1001.1.16490	Reccesuinth	Cordoba	Miles.361	Pliego2009.583b	2015.48.378
1001.1.16484	Reccesuinth	Cordoba	Miles.363a	Pliego2009.584	2015.48.379
1001.1.16489	Reccesuinth	Cordoba	Miles.363b	Pliego2009.584	2015.48.380
1001.1.16485	Reccesuinth	Cordoba	Miles.365	Pliego2009.586	2016.29.137
1001.1.16487	Reccesuinth	Cordoba	Miles.364b	Pliego2009.587c	2015.48.381

HSA number	Ruler	Mint	Miles type	Pliego type	New ANS number
1001.1.16491	Reccesuinth	Cordoba	Miles.364g	Pliego2009.587e	2016.29.138
1001.1.16486	Reccesuinth	Cordoba	Miles.364f	Pliego2009.587h	2015.48.382
1001.1.16520	Reccesuinth	Cordoba	Miles.364i	Pliego2009.587k	2016.29.139
1001.1.16040	Reccesuinth	Ispali	Miles.369a	Pliego2009.591b	2015.48.383
1001.1.16503	Reccesuinth	Ispali	Miles.369a	Pliego2009.591b	2015.48.384
1001.1.16505	Reccesuinth	Ispali	Miles.369a	Pliego2009.591b	2015.48.385
1001.1.16501	Reccesuinth	Ispali	Miles.369f	Pliego2009.591i	2015.48.386
1001.1.16504	Reccesuinth	Ispali	Miles.369f	Pliego2009.591i	2015.48.387
1001.1.16506	Reccesuinth	Ispali	Miles.369f	Pliego2009.591i	2015.48.388
1001.1.16508	Reccesuinth	Ispali	Miles.369f	Pliego2009.591i	2015.48.389
1001.1.16502	Reccesuinth	Ispali	Miles.369g	Pliego2009.591j	2015.48.390
1001.57.588	Reccesuinth	Ispali	Miles.368d	Pliego2009.592b	2015.48.391
1001.1.16507	Reccesuinth	Ispali	Miles.367a	Pliego2009.594a	2015.48.392
1001.1.16493	Reccesuinth	Emerita	Miles.376a	Pliego2009.600a	2015.48.393
1001.1.16495	Reccesuinth	Emerita	Miles.376a	Pliego2009.600a	2015.48.394
1001.1.16497	Reccesuinth	Emerita	Miles.376a	Pliego2009.600a	2015.48.395
1001.1.16500	Reccesuinth	Emerita	Miles.376a	Pliego2009.600a	2015.48.396
1001.1.16494	Reccesuinth	Emerita	Miles.376a	Pliego2009.600b	2015.48.397
1001.1.16499	Reccesuinth	Emerita	Miles.376a	Pliego2009.600b	2015.48.398
1001.1.8119	Reccesuinth	Emerita	Miles.374a	Pliego2009.602	2015.48.399
1001.1.16492	Reccesuinth	Emerita	Miles.374a	Pliego2009.602	2015.48.400
1001.1.16496	Reccesuinth	Emerita	Miles.375a	Pliego2009.604	2015.48.401
1001.57.589	Reccesuinth	Emerita	Miles.375a	Pliego2009.604	2015.48.402
1001.1.16552	Wamba	Toleto	Miles.384	Pliego2009.617a	2015.48.403
1001.1.16556	Wamba	Toleto	Miles.384	Pliego2009.617a	2015.48.404
1001.1.16557	Wamba	Toleto	Miles.384	Pliego2009.617a	2015.48.405
1001.1.16660	Wamba	Toleto	Miles.386a	Pliego2009.618a	2015.48.406
1001.1.16553	Wamba	Toleto	Miles.386b	Pliego2009.618e	2015.48.407
1001.1.16554	Wamba	Toleto	Miles.386b	Pliego2009.618e	2015.48.408
1001.1.16555	Wamba	Toleto	Miles.386b	Pliego2009.618e	2015.48.409
1001.57.590	Wamba	Toleto	Miles.386b	Pliego2009.618e	2015.48.410
1001.57.591	Wamba	Toleto	Miles.386b	Pliego2009.618e	2015.48.411
1001.1.16537	Wamba	Cordoba	Miles.390a	Pliego2009.620a	2015.48.412
1001.1.16545	Wamba	Ispali	Miles.392a	Pliego2009.624a	2015.48.413
1001.1.16549	Wamba	Ispali	Miles.392a	Pliego2009.624a	2015.48.414
1001.57.592	Wamba	Ispali	Miles.392a	Pliego2009.624a	2015.48.415
1001.1.16546	Wamba	Ispali	Miles.392b	Pliego2009.624b	2015.48.416
1001.1.16548	Wamba	Ispali	Miles.392c	Pliego2009.624c	2015.48.417
1001.1.16547	Wamba	Ispali	Miles.392e	Pliego2009.624e	2015.48.418
1001.1.16551	Wamba	Ispali	Miles.392e	Pliego2009.624e	2015.48.419
1001.1.16550	Wamba	Ispali	Miles.392h	Pliego2009.624g	2016.29.140
1001.1.8113	Wamba	Ispali	Miles.392g	Pliego2009.624h	2016.29.141
1001.1.16540	Wamba	Emerita	Miles.393f	Pliego2009.626b	2016.29.142
1001.1.16543	Wamba	Emerita	Miles.393a	Pliego2009.627a	2015.48.420
1001.1.16538	Wamba	Emerita	Miles.393c	Pliego2009.627c	2015.48.421

HSA number	Ruler	Mint	Miles type	Pliego type	New ANS number
1001.1.16539	Wamba	Emerita	Miles.393j	Pliego2009.627e	2015.48.422
1001.57.594	Wamba	Emerita	Miles.394b	Pliego2009.628a	2015.48.423
1001.1.16541	Wamba	Emerita	Miles.394a	Pliego2009.628b	2015.48.424
1001.1.16542	Wamba	Emerita	Miles.394a	Pliego2009.628b	2015.48.425
1001.1.16544	Wamba	Emerita	Miles.394a	Pliego2009.628b	2015.48.426
1001.1.16655	Wamba	Emerita	Miles.394a	Pliego2009.628b	2015.48.427
1001.1.16659	Wamba	Emerita	Miles.394a	Pliego2009.628b	2015.48.428
1001.57.593	Wamba	Emerita	Miles.394a	Pliego2009.628b	2015.48.429
1001.1.16571	Ervig	Narbona	Miles.396a	Pliego2009.631b	2015.48.430
1001.1.16572	Ervig	Narbona	Miles.396a	Pliego2009.631b	2015.48.431
1001.1.16558	Ervig	Cesaragusta	Miles.397c	Pliego2009.633f	2016.29.143
1001.1.7894	Ervig	Toleto	Miles.399a	Pliego2009.637a	2015.48.432
1001.1.16574	Ervig	Toleto	Miles.399a	Pliego2009.637a	2015.48.433
1001.1.16577	Ervig	Toleto	Miles.399a	Pliego2009.637a	2015.48.434
1001.57.595	Ervig	Toleto	Miles.399a	Pliego2009.637a	2015.48.435
1001.57.596	Ervig	Toleto	Miles.399d	Pliego2009.637f	2016.29.144
1001.1.16615	Ervig	Toleto	Miles.399b	Pliego2009.637h	2015.48.436
1001.57.597	Ervig	Toleto	Miles.399h	Pliego2009.637h	2015.48.437
1001.1.16573	Ervig	Toleto	Miles.399f	Pliego2009.637k	2015.48.438
1001.1.16576	Ervig	Toleto	Miles.399f	Pliego2009.637k	2015.48.439
1001.1.16559	Ervig	Cordoba	Miles.400b	Pliego2009.643c	2016.29.145
1001.1.16567	Ervig	Ispali	Miles.407	Pliego2009.647	2015.48.441
1001.1.16568	Ervig	Ispali	Miles.407	Pliego2009.647	2015.48.440
1001.1.16569	Ervig	Ispali	Miles.409a	Pliego2009.649b	2016.29.146
1001.1.16575	Ervig	Ispali	Miles.409c	Pliego2009.649e	2016.29.147
1001.57.598	Ervig	Ispali	Miles.410g	Pliego2009.649f	2015.48.443
1001.57.599	Ervig	Ispali	Miles.410d	Pliego2009.649f	2015.48.442
1001.1.16578	Ervig	Tucci	Miles.412b	Pliego2009.653b	2016.29.148
1001.1.16566	Ervig	Egitania	Miles.413a	Pliego2009.654a	2016.29.149
1001.1.16560	Ervig	Emerita	Miles.415a	Pliego2009.658a	2015.48.444
1001.1.16561	Ervig	Emerita	Miles.415a	Pliego2009.658a	2015.48.445
1001.1.16562	Ervig	Emerita	Miles.415a	Pliego2009.658a	2015.48.446
1001.1.16563	Ervig	Emerita	Miles.415a	Pliego2009.658a	2015.48.447
1001.1.16564	Ervig	Emerita	Miles.415a	Pliego2009.658a	2015.48.448
1001.1.16565	Ervig	Emerita	Miles.415a	Pliego2009.658a	2015.48.449
1001.57.600	Ervig	Emerita	Miles.415c	Pliego2009.658a	2015.48.450
1001.57.603	Ervig	Emerita	Miles.415e	Pliego2009.658a	2015.48.451
1001.57.602	Ervig	Emerita	Miles.415d	Pliego2009.658d	2015.48.452
1001.57.601	Ervig	Emerita	Miles.415c	Pliego2009.658h	2015.48.453
1001.1.16601	Egica	Narbona	Miles.419b	Pliego2009.662c	2015.48.454
1001.1.16602	Egica	Narbona	Miles.419b	Pliego2009.662c	2015.48.455
1001.1.16617	Egica	Narbona	Miles.419c	Pliego2009.662d	2016.29.150
1001.1.16581	Egica	Barcinona	Miles.420a	Pliego2009.664b	2016.29.151
1001.1.16583	Egica	Cesaragusta	Miles.421a	Pliego2009.665a	2015.48.456
1001.1.16636	Egica	Cesaragusta	Miles.421a	Pliego2009.665a	2015.48.457

HSA number	Ruler	Mint	Miles type	Pliego type	New ANS number
1001.1.16584	Egica	Cesaragusta	Miles.421c	Pliego2009.665e	2016.29.152
1001.1.16603	Egica	Tarracona	Miles.426b	Pliego2009.671d	2016.29.153
1001.57.604	Egica	Tarracona	Miles.427b	Pliego2009.672c	2016.29.154
1001.1.16607	Egica	Tarracona	Miles.428	Pliego2009.673	2016.29.155
1001.1.16605	Egica	Acci	Miles.430a	Pliego2009.674b	2016.29.156
1001.1.16595	Egica	Mentesa	Miles.431a	Pliego2009.675a	2016.29.157
1001.1.16634	Egica	Toleto	Miles.438	Pliego2009.677	2016.29.158
1001.1.16639	Egica	Toleto	Miles.433a	Pliego2009.678d	2015.48.458
1001.1.16614	Egica	Toleto	Miles.434	Pliego2009.679	2016.29.159
1001.1.16633	Egica	Toleto	Miles.435	Pliego2009.680	2015.48.459
1001.1.16608	Egica	Toleto	Miles.436a	Pliego2009.681a	2015.48.460
1001.1.16613	Egica	Toleto	Miles.436a	Pliego2009.681a	2015.48.461
1001.1.16610	Egica	Toleto	Miles.436g	Pliego2009.681e	2015.48.462
1001.1.16616	Egica	Toleto	Miles.436f	Pliego2009.681f	2015.48.463
1001.1.16612	Egica	Toleto	Miles.437b	Pliego2009.683b	2016.29.160
1001.57.605	Egica	Toleto	Miles.437c	Pliego2009.683e	2016.29.161
1001.1.16012	Egica	Toleto	Miles.437d	Pliego2009.684a	2015.48.464
1001.57.606	Egica	Toleto	Miles.437e	Pliego2009.684a	2015.48.465
1001.1.16011	Egica	Toleto	Miles.437h	Pliego2009.684b	2016.29.162
1001.57.607	Egica	Toleto	Miles.437l	Pliego2009.684d	2016.29.163
1001.1.16611	Egica	Toleto	Miles.437f	Pliego2009.685a	2016.29.164
1001.1.16609	Egica	Toleto	Miles.437l	Pliego2009.685c	2015.48.466
1001.1.16618	Egica	Toleto	Miles.437g	Pliego2009.685d	2016.29.165
1001.1.16628	Egica	Toleto	Miles.437k	Pliego2009.685i	2016.29.166
1001.1.16272	Egica	Valentia	Miles.429a	Pliego2009.686b	2016.29.167
1001.1.16586	Egica	Cordoba	Miles.440b	Pliego2009.688b	2016.29.168
1001.1.16585	Egica	Cordoba	Miles.440a	Pliego2009.688c	2016.29.169
1001.1.16592	Egica	Cordoba	Miles.439a	Pliego2009.689	2016.29.170
1001.1.16606	Egica	Ispali	Miles.442a	Pliego2009.696a	2015.48.467
1001.1.16599	Egica	Ispali	Miles.442b	Pliego2009.696c	2015.48.468
1001.1.15999+16594	Egica	Ispali	Miles.442c	Pliego2009.696e	2015.48.469
1001.1.16635	Egica	Ispali	Miles.444a	Pliego2009.698b	2015.48.470
1001.1.16597	Egica	Emerita	Miles.449a	Pliego2009.703a	2015.48.471
1001.57.608	Egica	Emerita	Miles.449b	Pliego2009.704c	2015.48.472
1001.1.16593	Egica	Emerita	Miles.447	Pliego2009.705	2015.48.473
1001.1.16647	Egica & Wittiza	Narbona	Miles.455a	Pliego2009.713b	2016.29.171
1001.1.16590	Egica & Wittiza	Narbona	Miles.455b	Pliego2009.713d	2016.29.172
1001.1.16626	Egica & Wittiza	Narbona	Miles.455e	Pliego2009.713f	2016.29.173
1001.57.609	Egica & Wittiza	Narbona	Miles.456b	Pliego2009.714a	2016.29.174
1001.1.16644	Egica & Wittiza	Cesaragusta	Miles.460a	Pliego2009.718f	2016.29.175
1001.1.16643	Egica & Wittiza	Cesaragusta	Miles.460e	Pliego2009.718j	2015.48.474
1001.1.16648	Egica & Wittiza	Gerunda	Miles.462a	Pliego2009.720o	2015.48.475
1001.57.610	Egica & Wittiza	Mentesa	Miles.467f	Pliego2009.726e	2016.29.176
1001.57.612	Egica & Wittiza	Toleto	Miles.468m	Pliego2009.727ii	2015.48.476
1001.57.611	Egica & Wittiza	Toleto	Miles.468l	Pliego2009.727l	2015.48.477

HSA number	Ruler	Mint	Miles type	Pliego type	New ANS number
1001.1.16588	Egica & Wittiza	Toleto	Miles.468a	Pliego2009.727n	2015.48.478
1001.1.16622	Egica & Wittiza	Toleto	Miles.468a	Pliego2009.727n	2015.48.479
1001.1.16629	Egica & Wittiza	Cordoba	Miles.473a	Pliego2009.731k	2015.48.480
1001.1.16625	Egica & Wittiza	Cordoba	Miles.471d	Pliego2009.732b	2015.48.481
1001.1.16632	Egica & Wittiza	Ispali	Miles.480o	Pliego2009.742aa	2015.48.485
1001.1.16620	Egica & Wittiza	Ispali	Miles.481c	Pliego2009.742c	2015.48.482
1001.1.16627	Egica & Wittiza	Ispali	Miles.480p	Pliego2009.742dd	2015.48.486
1001.1.16641	Egica & Wittiza	Ispali	Miles.480d	Pliego2009.742kk	2015.48.487
1001.1.16631	Egica & Wittiza	Ispali	Miles.480e	Pliego2009.742ll	2015.48.488
1001.1.16642	Egica & Wittiza	Ispali	Miles.480m	Pliego2009.742r	2015.48.483
1001.1.16623	Egica & Wittiza	Ispali	Miles.480n	Pliego2009.742v	2015.48.484
1001.1.16589	Egica & Wittiza	Tucci	Miles.483b	Pliego2009.743d	2016.29.177
1001.1.16630	Egica & Wittiza	Tucci	Miles.483a	Pliego2009.745	2016.29.178
1001.1.16587	Egica & Wittiza	Elvora	Miles.485a	Pliego2009.750j	2016.29.179
1001.1.16624	Egica & Wittiza	Emerita	Miles.486m	Pliego2009.753aa	2015.48.494
1001.57.613	Egica & Wittiza	Emerita	Miles.486b	Pliego2009.753c	2015.48.489
1001.1.16637	Egica & Wittiza	Emerita	Miles.486n	Pliego2009.753cc	2015.48.495
1001.1.16619	Egica & Wittiza	Emerita	Miles.486a	Pliego2009.753d	2015.48.490
1001.1.16621	Egica & Wittiza	Emerita	Miles.486c	Pliego2009.753e	2015.48.491
1001.57.614	Egica & Wittiza	Emerita	Miles.486f	Pliego2009.753k	2015.48.492
1001.1.16638	Egica & Wittiza	Emerita	Miles.486g	Pliego2009.753o	2015.48.493
1001.1.16654	Egica & Wittiza	Salmantica	Miles.467b	Pliego2009.755c	2016.29.180
1001.1.16650	Egica & Wittiza	Salmantica	Miles.487b	Pliego2009.756f	2016.29.181
1001.1.16649	Wittiza	Narbona	Miles.491c	Pliego2009.760f	2016.29.182
1001.1.16651	Wittiza	Cesaragusta	Miles.493a	Pliego2009.763a	2016.29.183
1001.1.16662	Wittiza	Gerunda	Miles.494c	Pliego2009.764c	2016.29.184
1001.1.16658	Wittiza	Toleto	Miles.499a	Pliego2009.774a	2015.48.496
1001.1.16653	Wittiza	Toleto	Miles.500b	Pliego2009.774c	2015.48.497
1001.57.615	Wittiza	Toleto	Miles.500c	Pliego2009.774d	2015.48.498
1001.57.616	Wittiza	Toleto	Miles.500d	Pliego2009.774e	2015.48.499
1001.1.16652	Wittiza	Cordoba	Miles.503a	Pliego2009.776a	2016.29.185
1001.1.16661	Wittiza	Ispali	Miles.507a	Pliego2009.781a	2016.29.186
1001.57.617	Roderic	Egitania	Miles.512b	Pliego2009.794c	2016.29.187
Counterfeit:					
1001.1.16289	*Suinthila*	*Toleto*	*Miles.525.48a*	*Pliego2009.811a*	*2015.48.500*
1001.1.16261	*Suinthila*	*Ispali*	*Miles.228g*	*Pliego2009.812*	*2015.48.501*
Fantasy:					
1001.1.8136	*Theudis*	*Ispali*	*Miles.525.4*	*Pliego2009.824*	*2015.48.502*
Forgery:					
1001.57.619	*Leovigild*	*Cordoba*	*Miles.525.11c*	*Pliego2009.838a*	*2015.48.503*
1001.1.8084	*Leovigild*	*Cordoba*	*Miles.525.11b*	*Pliego2009.838b*	*2015.48.504*
1001.1.8083	*Leovigild*	*Cordoba*	*Miles.525.11b*	*Pliego2009.838b*	*2015.48.505*
1001.57.618	*Leovigild*	*Cordoba*	*Miles.525.11b*	*Pliego2009.838b*	*2015.48.506*
1001.1.8086	*Leovigild*	*Cordoba*	*Miles.525.11b*	*Pliego2009.838b*	*2015.48.507*
1001.1.8085	*Leovigild*	*Cordoba*	*Miles.525.11b*	*Pliego2009.838b*	*2015.48.508*

HSA number	Ruler	Mint	Miles type	Pliego type	New ANS number
1001.1.15985	*Leovigild*	*Elvora*	*Miles.525.13*	*Pliego2009.844a*	*2015.48.509*
1001.1.8126	*Leovigild*	*Emerita*	*Miles.525.14*	*Pliego2009.849b*	*2015.48.510*
1001.1.8129	*Leovigild & Reccared*	*Toleto*	*Miles.525.16*	*Pliego2009.879*	*2015.48.511*
1001.1.8118	*Hermenegild*		*Miles.525.17a*	*Pliego2009.882a*	*2015.48.512*
1001.1.16013	*Hermenegild*		*Miles.46a*	*Pliego2009.886*	*2015.48.513*
1001.57.541	*Reccared I*	*Barcinona*	*Miles.50c*	*Pliego2009.889*	*2015.48.514*
1001.1.16073	*Reccared I*	*Cestavi*	*Miles.525.19b*	*Pliego2009.900*	*2015.48.515*
1001.1.8103	*Reccared I*	*Mentesa*	*Miles.525.22*	*Pliego2009.922*	*2015.48.517*
1001.1.8104	*Reccared I*	*Mentesa*	*Miles.525.22*	*Pliego2009.922*	*2015.48.518*
1001.1.16068	*Reccared I*	*Mentesa*	*Miles.525.22e*	*Pliego2009.922*	*2015.48.516*
1001.1.16070	*Reccared I*	*Oliovasio*	*Miles.525.30*	*Pliego2009.924*	*2015.48.519*
1001.1.10617	*Liuva II*	*Elvora*	*Miles.525.33*	*Pliego2009.937a*	*2015.48.520*
1001.1.10616	*Liuva II*	*Ispali*	*Miles.525.32b*	*Pliego2009.946*	*2015.48.521*
1001.1.16079	*Liuva II*	*Ispali*	*Miles.525.32b*	*Pliego2009.946*	*2015.48.522*
1001.1.8125	*Liuva II*	*Ispali*	*Miles.525.32b*	*Pliego2009.946a*	*2015.48.523*
1001.1.16078	*Liuva II*	*Ispali*	*Miles.525.32a*	*Pliego2009.946a*	*2015.48.524*
1001.57.620	*Gundemar*	*Ispali*	*Miles.525.37*	*Pliego2009.982*	*2015.48.525*
1001.1.16097	*Gundemar*	*Ispali*	*Miles.525.37*	*Pliego2009.982*	*2015.48.526*
1001.1.16099	*Gundemar*	*Ispali*	*Miles.525.37*	*Pliego2009.982*	*2015.48.527*
1001.1.8124	*Sisebut*	*Portocale*	*Miles.525.46a*	*Pliego2009.1023a*	*2015.48.528*
1001.1.16134	*Sisebut*	*Portocale*	*Miles.525.46a*	*Pliego2009.1023a*	*2015.48.529*
1001.1.16131	*Sisebut*	*Tarracona*	*Miles.525.39*	*Pliego2009.1027*	*2015.48.530*
1001.1.16130	*Sisebut*	*Tarracona*	*Miles.525.39*	*Pliego2009.1027*	*2015.48.531*
1001.57.621	*Sisenand*	*Cordoba*	*Miles.525.52b*	*Pliego2009.1072*	*2015.48.532*
1001.1.8120	*Sisenand*	*Egitania*	*Miles.525.54*	*Pliego2009.1075*	*2015.48.533*
1001.1.8122	*Sisenand*	*Egitania*	*Miles.525.54*	*Pliego2009.1075*	*2015.48.534*
1001.1.16456	*Chintila*	*Emerita*	*Miles.525.60a*	*Pliego2009.1103*	*2015.48.535*
1001.1.16460	*Chintila*	*Valentia*	*Miles.525.58*	*Pliego2009.1115*	*2015.48.536*
1001.1.16466	*Tulga*	*Emerita*	*Miles.525.62b*	*Pliego2009.1125a*	*2015.48.537*
1001.1.16467	*Tulga*	*Emerita*	*Miles.525.62a*	*Pliego2009.1125b*	*2015.48.538*
1001.1.8105	*Tulga*	*Toleto*	*Miles.525.61*	*Pliego2009.1129a*	*2015.48.539*
1001.57.622	*Tulga*	*Toleto*	*Miles.525.61*	*Pliego2009.1129b*	*2015.48.540*
1001.1.16471	*Chindasuinth*	*Ispali*	*Miles.525.65*	*Pliego2009.1139*	*2015.48.541*
1001.1.8115	*Chind.-Recces.*	*Toriviana*	*Miles.525.67*	*Pliego2009.1153*	*2015.48.542*
1001.1.8106	*Chind.-Recces.*	*Ispali*	*Miles.525.70c*	*Pliego2009.1156*	*2015.48.543*
1001.1.8108	*Chind.-Recces.*	*Ispali*	*Miles.525.70c*	*Pliego2009.1156*	*2015.48.544*
1001.1.16066	*Chind.-Recces.*	*Ispali*	*Miles.525.70c*	*Pliego2009.1157*	*2015.48.545*
1001.1.8107	*Chind.-Recces.*	*Ispali*	*Miles.525.70d*	*Pliego2009.1159*	*2015.48.546*
1001.1.16666	*Chind.-Recces.*	*Toleto*	*Miles.525.69*	*Pliego2009.1161*	*2015.48.547*
1001.1.16488	*Reccesuinth*	*Cordoba*	*Miles.525.73c*	*Pliego2009.1165*	*2015.48.548*
1001.1.8128	*Reccesuinth*	*Cordoba*	*Miles.525.73c*	*Pliego2009.1165*	*2015.48.549*
1001.1.8134	*Wamba*	*Emerita*	*Miles.525.81d*	*Pliego2009.1198a*	*2015.48.550*
1001.1.16656	*Wamba*	*Emerita*	*Miles.525.81d*	*Pliego2009.1198a*	*2015.48.551*
1001.1.8111	*Wamba*	*Emerita*	*Miles.525.81c*	*Pliego2009.1201*	*2015.48.552*

HSA number	Ruler	Mint	Miles type	Pliego type	New ANS number
1001.1.16667	*Wamba*	*Ispali*	*Miles.525.79d*	*Pliego2009.1207*	*2015.48.553*
1001.1.8135	*Wamba*	*Toleto*	*Miles.525.77e*	*Pliego2009.1222*	*2015.48.554*
1001.1.8133	*Ervig*	*Cordoba*	*Miles.525.84*	*Pliego2009.1227*	*2015.48.555*
1001.1.16570	*Ervig*	*Ispali*	*Miles.525.85b*	*Pliego2009.1238*	*2015.48.556*
1001.1.8091	*Ervig*	*Salmantica*	*Miles.525.87*	*Pliego2009.1241*	*2015.48.557*
1001.1.10615	*Ervig*	*Salmantica*	*Miles.525.87*	*Pliego2009.1241*	*2015.48.558*
1001.1.8092	*Ervig*	*Salmantica*	*Miles.525.87*	*Pliego2009.1241*	*2015.48.559*
1001.1.16580	*Ervig*	*Salmantica*	*Miles.525.87*	*Pliego2009.1241*	*2015.48.560*
1001.1.16579	*Ervig*	*Salmantica*	*Miles.525.87*	*Pliego2009.1241*	*2015.48.561*
1001.57.623	*Egica*	*Cordoba*	*Miles.525.91b*	*Pliego2009.1252*	*2015.48.562*
1001.1.16591	*Egica*	*Cordoba*	*Miles.525.91b*	*Pliego2009.1252*	*2015.48.563*
1001.1.8089	*Egica*	*Ispali*	*Miles.525.92*	*Pliego2009.1259*	*2015.48.564*
1001.1.8090	*Egica*	*Ispali*	*Miles.525.92*	*Pliego2009.1259*	*2015.48.565*
1001.1.8088	*Egica*	*Ispali*	*Miles.525.92*	*Pliego2009.1259*	*2015.48.566*
1001.1.16600	*Egica*	*Ispali*	*Miles.525.92*	*Pliego2009.1259*	*2015.48.567*
1001.1.16604	*Egica*	*Ispali*	*Miles.525.92*	*Pliego2009.1259*	*2015.48.568*
1001.1.16598	*Egica*	*Ispali*	*Miles.525.92*	*Pliego2009.1259*	*2015.48.569*
1001.1.8087	*Egica*	*Ispali*	*Miles.525.92*	*Pliego2009.1259*	*2015.48.570*
1001.1.8132	*Egica*	*Narbona*	*Miles.525.88d*	*Pliego2009.1263*	*2015.48.571*
1001.1.16645	*Egica*	*Salmantica*	*Miles.525.94b*	*Pliego2009.1266b*	*2015.48.572*
1001.1.10614	*Egica*	*Salmantica*	*Miles.525.94b*	*Pliego2009.1266b*	*2015.48.573*
1001.1.16596	*Egica*	*Salmantica*	*Miles.525.94b*	*Pliego2009.1266b*	*2015.48.574*
1001.1.16640	*Egica*	*Tarracona*	*Miles.525.89a*	*Pliego2009.1269*	*2015.48.575*
1001.1.16646	*Egica-Wittiza*	*Cordoba*	*Miles.525.96*	*Pliego2009.1280*	*2015.48.576*
1001.1.8130	*Egica-Wittiza*	*Cordoba*	*Miles.525.96*	*Pliego2009.1280*	*2015.48.577*
1001.1.8137	*Egica-Wittiza*	*Ispali*	*Miles.480r*	*Pliego2009.1291*	*2015.48.578*
1001.1.16657	*Wittiza*	*Toleto*	*Miles.525.101c*	*Pliego2009.1314*	*2015.48.579*
1001.1.8127	*Wittiza*	*Toleto*	*Miles.525.101c*	*Pliego2009.1314*	*2015.48.580*
1001.1.8131	*Roderic*	*Egitania*	*Miles.525.106e*	*Pliego2009.1318c*	*2015.48.581*
1001.1.16663	*Roderic*	*Egitania*	*Miles.525.106e*	*Pliego2009.1318c*	*2015.48.582*
1001.1.8112	*Roderic*	*Toleto*	*Miles.525.105b*	*Pliego2009.1326*	*2015.48.583*
1001.1.16664	*Roderic*	*Toleto*	*Miles.525.105b*	*Pliego2009.1326*	*2015.48.584*

Bibliography

Primary Sources

Bank Leu A.G. *Auktion 41: Mittelalter/Neuzeit. Zürich, 14 October, 1986.*

Cassiodorus. *Variae*. Ed. Theodor Mommsen. Monumenta Germaniae Historica. Auctores Antiquissimi 12. Berlin: Weidmann, 1894.

Concilia Hispaniae. Ed. José Vives, *Concilios visigóticos e Hispano-romanos*. Barcelona: Consejo Superior de Investigaciones Científicas, 1963.

Consularia Caesaraugustana. Ed. C. Cardelle de Hartmann. Corpus Christianorum, Series Latina 173A. Turnhout: Brepols, 2001.

Continuatio isidoriana hispana. Crónica mozárabe de 754. Ed. and trans. J. Eduardo López Pereira. León: Centro de Estudios e Investigación San Isidoro – Caja España de Inversiones – Archivo Histórico Diocesano, 2009.

Ennodius. *Vita Epiphanii*. Ed. F. Vogel. In Monumenta Germaniae Historica. Auctores Antiquissimi 7: 84-109. Berlin: Weidmann, 1885.

Gregory of Tours. *Historiae Francorum*. Trans. Lewis Thorpe, *History of the Franks*. Toronto: Penguin, 1974.

Gregory of Tours. *Historiarum libri X*. Ed. B. Krusch and W. Levison. Monumenta Germaniae Historica. Scriptores rerum Mervingicarum 1.1. Hannover: Hahn, 1951.

Hydatius. *Chronicle*. In *The Chronicle of Hydatius and the Consularia Constantinopolitana: Two Contemporary Accounts of the Final Years of the Roman Empire*, ed. and trans. R. W. Burgess, 9-124. Oxford: Oxford University Press, 1993.

Ildephonse of Toledo. *De viris illustribus*. Ed. C. Codoñer, *El 'De viris illustribus de Ildefonso de Toledo. Estudio y edición crítica*. Salamanca: Universidad de Salamanca 1972.

Inscripciones cristianas de la España romana y visigoda. Ed. J. Vives. 2nd ed. Barcelona: Consejo Superior de Investigaciones Científicas, 1969.

Isidore of Seville. *Historia Gothorum, Wandalorum, Sueborum*. Ed. C. Rodríguez Alonso. Fuentes y estudios de historia leonesa 13: 167-321. León: Centro de Estudios e Investigación San Isidoro – Caja de Ahorros y Monte de Piedad de León, 1975.

John of Biclar. *Chronicon*. Ed. C. Cardelle de Hartmann. Corpus Christianorum, Series Latina 173A: 57-83. Turnhout: Brepols, 2001.

Jordanes. *Getica*. Ed. Theodor Mommsen. Monumenta Germaniae Historica. Auctores Antiquissimi 5.1. Berlin: Weidmann, 1882.

Leges Burgundionum. Ed. L. R. de Salis. Monumenta Germaniae Historica. Leges 1.2 (Hannover: Hahn, 1892.

Leges Visigothorum. Ed. K. Zeumer. Monumenta Germaniae Historica. Leges 1.1. Hannover: Hahn, 1902.

Mantis: a Numismatic Technologies Integration Service (American Numismatic Society, New York, NY). "Visigothic." http://numismatics.org/search/.

Procopius, *Bellum Gothicum*. In *Opera omnia*. 3 vols. Vol. 2, ed. J. Haury. Leipzig: Teubner, 1905.

Procopius, *Bellum Gothicum*. Ed. and trans, H. B. Dewing, *History of the Wars*. 6 vols. Vol. 3, Books V and VI. Cambridge, MA: Harvard University Press, 1961.

Sidonius Apollinaris. *Carmina*. Ed. Christian Luetjohann. In Monumenta Germaniae Historica. Auctores Antiquissimi 8: 173-264. Berlin: Weidmann, 1887.

Swiss Bank Corporation. *Auction 42, Basel. January 23, 1997*.

Theodosius. *Theodosiani libri 16 cum Constitutionibus Sirmodianis et Leges novellae ad Theodosianum pertinentes*. Ed. Theodor Mommsen, Paul M. Meyer, and Paul W. A. Krüger. Berlin: Weidmann, 1962.

Vitas Sanctorum Patrum Emeritensium. Ed. A. Maya Sánchez. Corpus Christianorum, Series Latina 116. Turnhout: Brepols, 1992.

Vitas Sanctorum Patrum Emeritensium, Ed. and trans. A. T. Fear. *Lives of the Visigothic Fathers*. Liverpool: Liverpool University Press, 1997.

Secondary Sources

Amorós, Josep, and Antonia Mata Berruezo. *Catálogo de las monedas visigodas del Gabinete Numismático de Cataluña*. Barcelona: Ayuntamiento, 1952.

Arce, Javier. "La transformación de Hispania en época tardorromana: Paisaje urbano, paisaje rural." In *De la antigüedad al medievo: ss. IV-VIII* (III Congreso de Estudios Medievales), 227-49. León: Fundación Sánchez-Albornoz, 1993.

Ariño Gil, Enrique and Pablo C. Díaz. "La frontera suevo-visigoda. Ensayo de lectura de un territorio en disputa." In *Fortificaciones en la Tardoantigüedad: Élites y articulación del territorio (siglos V-VIII d. C.)*, ed. R. Catalán, P. Fuentes, and J. C. Sastre, 179-90. Madrid: La Argástula, 2014.

Arslan, E. "Ancora sulla questione della cosiddetta 'moneta in rame nell'italia longobarda'. Una replica e problem di método." *Rivista Italiana di Numismatica* 108 (2007): 11-28.

Balaguer, Anna M. "El problema de la localización de la Roda visigoda." *Acta Numismática* 13 (1983): 109-18.

——. "Las emisiones transicionales árabe-musulmanas de Al-Andalus: Nueva síntesis." In *I Jarique de estudios numismáticos hispano-árabes*, 11-28. Zaragoza: Institución Fernando el Católico, 1988.

——. *Las emisiones transicionales árabe-musulmanas de Hispania.* Barcelona: Asociación numismática española, 1976.

Banaji, Jairus. *Exploring the Economy of Late Antiquity: Selected Essays.* Cambridge: Cambridge University Press, 2016.

Barceló, Miquel. "La cuestión del 'Limes Hispanus': los datos numismáticos." *Acta Numismática* 5 (1975), 31-45.

——. "A Statistical Approach to Multiple Mint Issues of Royal Coinage: The Case of the Visigoths in Hispania (585-711)." *PACT* 5 (1981): 138-54.

Barceló, Miquel and Fèlix Retamero. "From Crops to Coin: Which Way Back?" *Gaceta Numismática* 122 (1996): 53-60.

Barral i Altet, Xavier. *La circulation des monnaies suèves et visigotiques. Contribution á l'histoire économique du royaume visigot.* Munich: Artemis Verlag, 1976.

Barral i Altet, Xavier. "Una moneda d'Egica trobada a Orense. Notes sobre la circulacio de les monedes d'Egica (687-695-702)." *Cuadernos de Estudios Gallegos* 29 (no. 87, 1974-75): 30-34 and 2 pll.

Bartlett, Peter. "Reccopolis, ceca inédita de Suinthila (621-631)." *Gaceta Numismática,* no. 135 (1999): 19-20.

Bartlett, Peter, Andrew Oddy, and Cécile Morrisson. "The Byzantine Gold Coinage of *Spania* (Justinian I to Heraclius)." *Revue Numismatique* 167 (2011): 351-401.

Bartlett, Peter, and Gonzalo Cores. "The Coinage of the Visigothic King Sisebut (612-21) from the Mint of Barbi." *Gaceta Numismática* 158-159 (Sep.-Dec. 2005): 13-21.

Bartlett, Peter, Gonzalo Cores Uría and María Cruz Cores Gomendio. "The Use of Dots as Control Marks in the Coin Legends at the Visigothic Mint of Ispali During the Reign of Sisebut (612-21)." In *XIII Congreso Internacional de Numismática,* 1127-33. Madrid: Ministerio de Cultura, 2003.

Bartlett, Peter, Ruth Pliego, and David Yoon. "Weight, Fineness, and Debasement in Visigothic Tremisses from Theudis to Leovigild: New Evidence from the Hoards of Seville and Reccopolis." *American Journal of Numismatics* 29 (2017): 149-211.

Bates, Michael L. "The Coinage of Spain Under the Umayyad Caliphs of the East, 711-750." In *III Jarique de numismática hispano-árabe,* 171-89. Madrid: Museo Arqueológico Nacional, 1992.

——. "History, Geography, and Numismatics in the First Century of Islamic Coinage." *Revue suisse de Numismatique* 65 (1986): 231-62.

Bautier, Robert-Henri. *The Economic Development of Medieval Europe.* London: Harcourt Brace Jovanovich, 1971.

Beltrán Villagrasa, Pío. "Monedas de Leovigild en el tesorillo de Zorita de los Canes (año 1945)." In *Numario Hispánico* II, 3 (1953): 19-52.

——. "Nueva ceca goda en el Pirineo aragonés. Reducción de la ciudad de Cestavvi al pueblo oscense de Gistau." *Caesaraugusta* 5 (1954): 129-40.

Blackburn, Mark. "Money and Coinage." In *The New Cambridge Medieval History*, 7 vols; vol. 2: c. 500-700, ed. Paul Fouracre, 660-74. Cambridge: Cambridge University Press, 2005.

Blackburn, Mark. "Money and Coinage." In *The New Cambridge Medieval History*, 7 vols.; vol. 2: c. 700-900, ed. Rosamond McKitterick, 538-60. Cambridge: Cambridge University Press, 1995.

Bost, Jean-Pierre, et al. "Hallazgos de aurei y solidi en la Península Ibérica: introducción a su circulación en época imperial," *Numisma* 33, (1983): 137-76.

Bowes, Kim and Michael Kulikowski, eds. *Hispania in Late Antiquity: Current Perspectives.* Leiden: Brill, 2005.

Brenot, Cl., J.-N. Barrandon, J.-P. Callu, J. Poirier, R. Halleux, and C. Morrisson. *L'or monnayé*, vol. 1: *purifications et altérations de Rome à Byzance* (Cahiers Ernest-Babelon 2). Paris: Centre National de la Recherche Scientifique, 1985.

Bruun, Patrick. "The Charm of Quantitative Studies in Numismatic Research." In *Die Münze: Bild – Botschaft – Bedeutung: Festschrift für Maria R.-Alföldi*, 65-83. Frankfurt am Main: Peter Lang, 1991.

Burgess, R. W. "From Gallia Romana to Gallia Gothica: The View from Spain." In *Fifth-century Gaul*, ed. John Drinkwater and Hugh Elton, 19-27. New York: Cambridge University Press, 1992.

——. "The Gallic Chronicle of 511: A New Critical Edition with a Brief Introduction." In *Society and Culture*, ed. Ralph Mathisen and Danuta Shanzer, 85-100. Aldershot: Ashgate, 2001.

Bursche, Aleksander. "Gold barbarian imitations of Roman coins: the Ulów type." In *Honoratissimum assensus genus est armis laudare. Studia dedykowane Profesorowi Piotrowi Kaczanowskiemu z okazji siedemdziesiątej rocznicy urodzin*, ed. R. Madyda-Legutko and J. Rodzińska-Nowak, 317-327. Kraków: Towarzysto Wydawnicze – Historia Lagiellonica, 2014.

Bursche, Aleksander, and Kirill Myzgin. "Gold coins, Alexandria Troas and Goths." In *Studies in Ancient Coinage in Honour of Andrew Burnett*, ed. R. Bland & D. Calomino, 232-58. London: Spink, 2015.

Cabré Aguiló, Juan. *Crónica del II Congreso Arqueológico del Sudeste Español.* Albacete: Imprenta Provincial, 1947.

——. *El tesorillo visigodo de trientes de las excavaciones del plan nacional de 1944-45 en Zorita de los Canes (Guadalajara).* Madrid: Ministerio de Educación Nacional, 1946.

Callu, J.-P. "The Distribution and the Role of the Bronze Coinage from A.D. 348 to 392," 95-124.

——. "Silver Hoards and Emissions from 324 to 392." In Imperial revenue, expenditure and monetary policy in the fourth century A.D., ed. C. E. King, pp. 213-54. Oxford: B.A.R., 1980.

Cameron, Averil. *The Later Roman Empire, A.D. 284-430.* London: Fontana, 1993.
——. *The Mediterranean World in Late Antiquity, AD 395-600.* London: Routledge, 1993.
Canto García, Alberto. "El Pacto de Tudmîr: aspectos económicos." *eHumanista/IVITRA Journal of Iberian Studies* 5 (2014), 370-91.
——. "Las monedas de la conquista." *Zona arqueológica* 15, no. 1, dedicated issue *711: Arqueología e historia entre dos mundos* (2011): 135-143.
Carlà, Filippo. "The End of Roman Gold Coinage and the Disintegration of a Monetary Area," *Annali dell'Istituto Italiano di Numismatica* 56 (2010): 45-114.
——. *L'oro nella tarda antichità: aspetti economici e sociali.* Torino: Zamorani, 2009.
Casariego, Anton, and Gonzalo Cores. "Nota sobre las monedas de Recaredo II." *Numisma* 35-36, nos. 192-203 (1985-86): 39-46.
Cascio, E. Lo. "State and Coinage in the Late Republic and Early Empire." *Journal of Roman Studies* 71 (1981): 76-86.
Castellanos, Santiago. "The Political Nature of Taxation in Visigothic Spain." *Early Medieval Europe* 12, (2003): 201–28.
——. "Tributa and *Historiae*: Scale and Power at a Turning Point in Post-Roman Spain." In *Scale and Scale Change in the Early Middle Ages: Exploring Landscape, Local Society, and the World Beyond*, ed. Julio Escalona and Andrew Reynolds, 187-214. Turnhout: Brepols, 2016.
Castellanos, Santiago and Iñaki Martín Viso. "The Local Articulation of Central Power in the North of the Iberian Peninsula (500-1000)." *Early Medieval Europe* 13, no. 1 (2005), 1-42.
Castro Hipólito, Mário., ed. *Homenagem a Mário Gomes Marques.* Sintra: Instituto de Sintra, 2000.
Castro Priego, Manuel. "Absent Coinage: Archaeological Contexts and Tremisses on the Central Iberian Peninsula in the 7th and 8th Centuries AD." *Medieval Archaeology* 60, no. 1 (2016): 27-56.
——. "Circulación monetaria de los siglos VII-VIII en la Península Ibérica: un modelo en crisis." *Zona arqueológica* 15, no. 2, dedicated issue *711: Arqueología e historia entre dos mundos* (2011): 225-44.
——. "Los hallazgos numismáticos de Recópolis: aspectos singulares de su integración en la secuencia histórica del yacimiento." *Zona arqueológica,* no. 9 (2008): 131-141.
——. "*Reccopolis* y los contextos numismáticos de época visigoda en el Centro de la Península Ibérica." *Revue Numismatique* 6, no.171 (2014): 463-95.
Catlos, Brian A. and Sharon Kinoshita. eds. *Can We Talk Mediterreanean?: Conversations on an Emerging Field in Medieval and Early Modern Studies.* Cham, Switzerland: Palgrave Macmillan, 2017.

Cebreiro Ares, Francisco. "Dificultades que plantea el estudio de la historia monetaria sueva." In *Introducción a la Historia Monetaria de Galicia (s. II a. C. – XVII d. C.)*, ed. F. Cebreiro Ares, 31-63. A Coruña: Labirinto de Paixóns, 2012.

Chalmeta, Pedro. "Los primeros 46 años de economía andalusí (1)." *Alhadra* 1 (2015), 41-88.

Claude, Dietrich. *Adel, Kirche und Königtum im Westgotenreich.* Sigmaringen: Jan Thorbecke Verlag, 1971.

——. "Zur Funktion des Münzgeldes im hispanischen Westgotenreich," in *Münstersche Beiträge zur Antiken Handelsgeschichte* 8 (no. 2, 1989), 32-51.

Collins, Roger. *The Arab Conquest of Spain, 710-797.* Oxford: Blackwell, 1989.

——. *Early Medieval Spain: Unity in Diversity, 400-1000.* 2nd ed. London: Macmillan, 1995.

——. "Mérida and Toledo, 550-585." In *Visigothic Spain: New Approaches*, ed. Edward James, 189-219. Oxford: Oxford University Press, 1980.

——. *Spain: An Oxford Archaeological Guide.* Oxford: Oxford University Press, 1998.

——. *Visigothic Spain, 409-711.* Malden: Blackwell, 2004.

Cores, Gonzalo, J. M. Peixoto Cabral, L. C. Alves, and P. Bartlett. "Visigothic Mint Practices, March 621: What Can the Coins of Reccared II Tell Us?" In *Homenagem a Mário Gomes Marques*, ed. M. Castro Hipólito, 195-223. Sintra: Instituto de Sintra, 2000.

Cores Gomendio, María Cruz, Jesús Vico Monteoliva, and Gonzalo Cores Uría. *Corpus Nummorum Visigothorum: ca. 575-714, Leovigildus-Achila.* Madrid: the authors, 2006.

Corzo Pérez, Sebastián and Susana Sempere Díaz. "La ceca visigoda de Barbi: aspectos historiográficos y arqueológicos." *Numisma* 45 (no. 236, 1995): 125-38.

Crawford, Michael H. "Money and Exchange in the Roman World." *Journal of Roman Studies* 60 (1970): 40-48.

Crusafont i Sabater, Miquel. "The Copper Coinage of the Visigoths of Spain." In *Problems of Medieval Coinage in the Iberian Area.* 3 vols. Vol. 3, ed. Mário Gomes Marques and D. M. Metcalf, 35-88. Santarém: Instituto Politécnico de Santarém, 1988.

——. "The Copper Coinage of the Visigoths of Spain: New Evidence." *Spinks Numismatic Circular* 98, no. 9 (Nov. 1990): 303-04.

——. *El sistema monetario visigodo: cobre y oro.* Barcelona: Asociación Numismática Española, 1994.

——. "Monete suebe e visigote." In *I Goti*, ed. V. Bierbrauer, O. Von Hessen, and E. A. Arslan, 348-51. Milan: Electa Lombardia, 1994.

——. "¿Un numerario visigodo de cobre?." *Gaceta Numismática*, nos. 74-75 (1984): 131-41.

Crusafont i Sabater, Miquel, Jaume Benages, and Jaume Noguera. "Silver Visigothic Coinage." *Numismatic Chronicle* 176 (2016): 241-60.

Curta, Florin. "Byzantium in Dark-Age Greece (the Numismatic Evidence in its Balkan Context)." *Byzantine and Modern Greek Studies* 29 (2005): 113-146.

Delmaire, Roland. *Largesses sacrées et* res privata: *L'*aerarium *impérial et son administration du IVe au VIe siècle.* Rome: Ecole Française de Rome, 1989.

Depeyrot, Georges. *Le Bas-Empire Romain: Économie et numismatique*. Paris: Errance, 1987.

——. "Les émissions wisigothiques de Toulouse (Ve siècle)." *Acta numismática* 16 (1986): 79-104.

——. "Les *solidi* gaulois de Valentinien III." *Revue suisse de numismatique* 65 (1986): 111-32.

Dhénin, M., and C. Landes. "Le tresor 'de Roujan' (VIe siecle)." *Etudes Héraultaises* 26-27 (1995-96): 11-14.

Díaz y Díaz, Manuel C. *Index Scriptorum Latinorum Medii Aevi Hispanorum*. 2 vols. Salamanca: Universidad de Salamanca, 1958.

——. "Introducción general a las Etimologías." In *San Isidoro de Sevilla, Etimologías*, ed. J. Oroz-Reta and M. A. Marcos Casquero, 3-257. Madrid: BAC, I, 1982.

Díaz Martínez, Pablo C. "Acuñación monetaria y organización administrativa en la *Gallaecia* tardoantigua." *Zephyrus* 57 (2004): 367-75.

——. "Confiscations in the Visigothic Reign of Toledo: A Political Instrument." In *Expropiations et confiscations dans les royaumes barbares. Une approche régionale*, ed. P. Porena and Y. Rivière, 93-112. Rome: École Française de Rome, 2012.

——. "En tierra de nadie: Visigodos frente a bizantinos. Reflexiones sobre la frontera." In *Bizancio y la península ibérica. De la antigüedad tardía a la edad moderna*, ed. I. Pérez Martín and P. Bádenas de la Peña, 37-60. Madrid: Consejo Superior de Investigaciones Científicas, 2004.

Díaz Martínez, Pablo C. and M. R. Valverde. "The Theoretical Strength and Practical Weakness of the Visigothic Monarchy of Toledo." In *Rituals of Power From Late Antiquity to the Early Middle Ages*, ed. Frans Theuws and Janet L. Nelson, 59-93. Leiden: Brill, 2000.

Doehaerd, Renée. *Le haut moyen âge occidental: Économies et sociétés.* Paris: Presses Universitaires de France, 1971.

Doménech Belda, Carolina. "Numismática y Arqueología Medieval: La moneda de excavación y sus aportaciones." In *XIII Congreso Nacional de Numismática* (Cádiz, 22-24 octubre de 2007), 2 vols.; vol. 2, ed. Alicia Arévalo González, 731-60. Madrid-Cádiz: Museo Casa de la Moneda; Universidad de Cádiz, 2009.

Domingo, Agustín. "Sobre la autenticidad de los trientes visigodos." *Acta Numismática* 20 (1990): 79-82.

Drinkwater, John, and Hugh Elton, eds. *Fifth-century Gaul: A Crisis of Identity?* Cambridge: Cambridge University Press, 1992.

Duncan-Jones, Richard. *Money and Government in the Roman Empire*. Cambridge: Cambridge University Press, 1994.

Durliat, Jean. *Les finances publiques de Diocletien aux Carolingiens (284-889)*. Sigmaringen: Thorbecke, 1990.

Elton, Hugh. "Roman Gold and Barbarian Kings." In *Medieval Europe, 1992* (Conference on Medieval Archaeology in Europe, 21-24 September 1992, University of York), 8 vols.; vol. 5: *Exchange and Trade*, 25-30. York: University of York, 1992.

Fernández Guerra, Aureliano. *Historia de España desde la invasión de los pueblos germánicos hasta la ruina de la monarquía visigoda*. Madrid: El progreso editorial, 1854.

Fernández, Damián. *Aristocrats and Statehood in Western Iberia, 300-600 C.E.*, 201. Philadelphia: University of Pennsylvania Press, 2017.

——. "Statehood, Taxation, and State Infrastructural Power in Visigothic Iberia." In *Ancient States and Infrastructural Power Europe, Asia, and America*, ed. Clifford Ando and Seth Richardson, 243-71. Philadelphia: University of Pennsylvania Press, 2017.

Fernández-Flores, Álvaro, Ruth Pliego Vázquez, and Gabriel Carvajal Mateos. "Nuevos hallazgos de bronces visigodos en la provincia de Sevilla: una aproximación metrológica y de composición metálica." *Journal of Archaeological Numismatics* 3 (2013): 275-304.

Finley, Moses. *The Ancient Economy*. Berkeley, CA: University of California Press, 1973.

Florez, Henrique. *Medallas de las colonias, municipios y pueblos antiguos de España hasta hoy no publicadas, con las de los reyes Godas*. 3 vols. Vol. 3. Madrid: D. Antonio de Sancha, 1773.

Fossella, Jason. "'Waiting Only For a Pretext': a New Chronology for the Sixth-century Byzantine Invasion of Spain." *Estudio Bizantinos* 1 (2013): 30-38.

Fulford, Michael. "Coin Circulation and Mint Activity in the Late Roman Empire: Some Economic Implications." *Archaeological Journal* 135 (1978): 67-114.

García Moreno, Luis A. "Algunos aspectos fiscales de la Península Ibérica durante el siglo VI." *Hispania Antiqua* 1 (1971): 233-56.

——. "Cecas visigodas y sistema económico." In *II^a reunió d'arqueologia paleocristiana hispànica*, 333-45. Barcelona: Institut d'Arqueologia i Prehistòria, 1982.

——. "Colonias de comerciantes orientales en la península ibérica, s. V-VII," *Habis* 3 (1972), 127-54.

——. *España 702-719: La conquista musulmana*. Seville: Universidad de Sevilla, 2013.

——. "Estudios sobre la organización administrativa del reino visigodo de Toledo." *Anuario de Historia del Derecho Español* 44 (1974): 5-155.

——. *Historia de España visigoda*. Madrid: Cátedra, 1989.

——. *Leovigildo. Unidad y diversidad de un reinado.* Madrid: Real Academia de la Historia, 2008.

García Moreno, Luis A. and Sebastián Rascón Marqués, eds. *Complutum y las ciudades hispanas en la antigüedad tardía* (Actas del encuentro hispania en la antigüedad tardía, Alcalá de Henares, 16 de octubre de 1996). Alcalá: Universidad de Alcalá, 1999.

García Sanjuan, Alejandro. "al-Andalus, etymology and name." In *Encyclopaedia of Islam, Three*, ed. Kate Fleet et al. http://dx.doi.org/10.1163/1573-3912_ei3_COM_24223, accessed online on 08 October 2018.

——. *La conquista islámica de la península ibérica y la tergiversación del pasado. Del catastrofismo al negacionismo.* Madrid: Marcial Pons Historia, 2013.

Garipzanov, Ildar H. "The Coinage of Tours in the Merovingian Period and the Pirenne Thesis." *Revue Belge de Numismatique et de sigillographie* 147 (2001): 79-118.

——. "Monograms as Graphic Signs of Authority on Early Medieval Coins (from the Mid-Fifth to Seventh Centuries)." In *Graphic Signs of Identity, Faith, and Power in Late Antiquity and the Early Middle Ages*, ed. Ildor Garipzanov, Caroline Goodson, and Henry Maguire, 325-350. Turnhout: Brepols, 2017.

Geary, Patrick. *The Myth of Nations.* Princeton, NJ: Princeton University Press, 2002.

Gil Farrés, Octavio. "Algunos aspectos de la numismática visigoda: consideraciones acerca del 'tipo tercero' de Leovigildo." *Numisma* 5, no. 1 (1955): 25-61.

——. "La moneda sueva y visigoda." In *Historia de España*, 37 vols.; vol. 3, ed. Ramón Menéndez Pidal. Madrid: Espasa Calpe, 1963, pp. 177–191.

Gillett, Andrew. "The Accession of Euric." *Francia* 26, no. 1 (1999): 1-40.

——, ed. *On Barbarian Identity: Critical Approaches to Ethnicity in the Early Middle Ages.* Turnhout: Brepols, 2002.

Goffart, Walter. *Barbarians and Romans, A.D. 418-584: The Techniques of Accommodation.* Princeton, NJ: Princeton University Press, 1980.

——. "Old and New in Merovingian Taxation." *Past & Present* 96, no. 1 (1982): 3-21. Repr. in W. Goffart, *Rome's Fall and After*, 213-231. London: Hambledon, 1989.

——. *Rome's Fall and After.* London: Hambledon, 1989.

Greene, Kevin. *The Archaeology of the Roman Economy.* London: B. T. Batsford, 1986.

Grierson, Phillip. *Byzantine Coins.* Berkeley: University of California Press, 1982.

——. "Coinage and Money in the Byzantine Empire, 498-c. 1090," *Settimane di studio centro italiano di studi sull'alto medioevo* VIII (1961), 411-53.

——. *Coins of Medieval Europe.* London: Seaby, 1991.

——. "Note on Stamping of Coins and Other Objects." In *A History of Technology*, 2 vols.; vol. 2, ed. C. Singer et al., 485-92. Oxford: Oxford University Press, 1956.

——. "Numismatics." In *Medieval Studies: An Introduction*, 2nd ed., ed. James M. Powell, 114-61. Syracuse: Syracuse University Press, 1992.

——. "Una ceca bizantina en España." *Numario Hispánico* 4 (1955), 305-14.

——. "Visigothic Metrology." *Numismatic Chronicle* 6th ser., 13 (1953): 74-87.

Grierson, Phillip, and Mark Blackburn. *Medieval European Coinage*. 14 vols. Vol. 1: *The Early Middle Ages (5th-10th Centuries)*. Cambridge: Cambridge University Press, 1986.

Grierson, Phillip, and Melinda Mays. *Catalogue of Late Roman Coins in the Dumbarton Oaks Collection and in the Whittemore Collection: From Arcadius and Honorius to the Accession of Anastasius.* Washington, DC: Dumbarton Oaks, 1992.

Guerra, María Filomena. "The Circulation of Monetary Gold in the Portuguese Area from the 5th Century to Nowadays." *Anejos de Archivos Español de Arqueología* 32 (2004): 423-31.

Guerra, María Filomena, Thomas Calligaro, and Alicia Perea. "The Treasure of Guarrazar: Tracing the Gold Supplies in the Iberian Peninsula." *Archaeometry* 49, no. 1 (2007): 53-74.

Gurt Esparraguera, Josep M. and Cristina Godoy Fernández. "*Barcino*, de sede imperial a *urbs regia* en época visigoda." In *Sedes regiae (ann. 400-800)*, ed. Gisela Ripoll López and Josep M. Gurt, 425-66. Barcelona: Reial Acadèmia de Bone Lletres, 2000.

Gutiérrez Lloret, Sonia. "El Tolmo de Minateda en torno al 711." *Zona arqueológica*, No. 15, vol. 1 (2011) (Dedicated issue title: *711: Arqueología e historia entre dos mundos*): 359-372.

Gutiérrez Lloret, Sonia and Julia Sarabia Bautista. "The Episcopal Complex of Eio-El Tolmo de Minateda (Hellín, Albacete, Spain). Architecture and Spatial Organization, 7th to 8th Centuries AD." *Hortus Artium Medievalium* 19 (2013): 267-300.

Haldon, John F. "Administrative Continuities and Structural Transformations in East Roman Military Organisation c. 580-640." In *State, Army and Society in Byzantium*, ed. John Haldon, 1-20. Brookfield, VT: Variorum, 1995.

——. "The Army and the Economy: the Allocation and Redistribution of Surplus Wealth in the Byzantine State." *Mediterranean Historical Review* 72 (1992): 133-53.

——. *Byzantium in the Seventh Century.* Cambridge: Cambridge University Press, 1990.

——. "Late Rome, Byzantium, and Early Medieval Western Europe." In *Fiscal Regimes and the Political Economy of Premodern States*, ed. Andrew Monson and Walter Scheidel, 345-89. Cambridge: Cambridge University Press, 2015.

——. "Military Service, Military Lands, and the Status of Soldiers: Current Problems and Interpretations," *Dumbarton Oaks Papers* 47 (1993): 1-67.

Halm, Heinz. "Al-Andalus and Ghotica Sors." In *The Formation of al-Andalus*, 2 vols.; vol. 1: *History and Society*, ed. M. Marín, 39-50. London: Routledge, 1998.

Halsall, Guy. *Barbarian Migrations and the Roman West, 376-568.* Cambridge: Cambridge University Press, 2007.

Harl, Kenneth. *Coinage in the Roman Economy, 300 B.C. to A.D. 700*. Baltimore, MD: Johns Hopkins University Press, 1996.

Heath, Sebastian, and David Yoon. "A Sixth-century Tremissis from Psalmodi (Gard, France)." *American Journal of Numismatics*, Second series 13 (2001): 63-80.

Heather, Peter. "The Emergence of the Visigothic Kingdom." In *Fifth-century Gaul*, ed. John Drinkwater and Hugh Elton, 84-94. New York: Cambridge University Press, 1992.

———. *Empires and Barbarians: The Fall of Rome and the Birth of Empire*. New York: Oxford University Press, 2010.

———. *The Goths*. Oxford: Wiley-Blackwell, 1996.

———. *Goths and Romans, 332-489*. Oxford: Oxford University Press, 1991.

———. "Migration." *Networks and Neighbours* 3, no. 1 (2015): 1-21.

Heather, Peter, and John Matthews. *The Goths in the Fourth Century*. Liverpool: Liverpool University Press, 1991.

Heiss, Aloïss. *Description générale des monnaies antiques de l'Espagne*. Paris: Imprimirie Nationale, 1870.

———. *Description générale des monnaies des rois wisigoths d'Espagne*. Paris: Imprimerie Nationale, 1872.

Hendy, Michael F. "From Antiquity to the Middle Ages: Economic and Monetary Aspects of the Transition." In *De la antigüedad al medievo, siglos IV-VIII* (III Congreso de Estudios Medievales), 325-60. León: Fundación Sanchez-Albornoz, 1993.

———. "From Public to Private: The Western Barbarian Coinages as a Mirror of the Disintegration of Late Roman State Structures." *Viator* 19 (1988): 29-78.

———. *Studies in the Byzantine Monetary Economy, c. 300-1450*. Cambridge: Cambridge University Press, 1985.

Hillgarth, J. N. "Coins and Chronicles: Propaganda in Sixth-Century Spain and the Byzantine Background." *Historia* 15 (1966): 483-508.

———. "Historiography in Visigothic Spain." In *La storiografia altomedievale*, Settimane di studio del centro italiano di studi sull'alto medioevo 17, 261-313. Spoleto: Presso la sede del centro, 1970.

———. "La conversión de los Visigodos: notas críticas." *Analecta Sacra Tarraconensia* 34 (1961): 21-64.

———. *The Visigoths in History and Legend*. Toronto: Pontifical Institute of Mediaeval Studies, 2009.

Hodges, Richard. Review of *The Corrupting Sea: A Study of Mediterranean History*, by Peregrine Horden and Nicholas Purcell. *The International History Review* 23, no. 2 (2001): 377-79.

Horden, Peregrine and Nicholas Purcell. *The Corrupting Sea: A Study of Mediterranean History*. Oxford and Malden, MA: Blackwell, 2000.

Howgego, Christopher. *Ancient History from Coins*. London: Routledge, 1995.
———. "Why Did Ancient States Strike Coins?" *Numismatic Chronicle* 150 (1990): 1-25.
Huffstot, John S. "Reverse Designs on the Sixth-century Iberian Coppers: An Alternative to the Municipal-Monogram Theory." *Gaceta Numismática* 160 (2006): 5-17.
Ibrahim, Tawfiq. "Los precintos de la conquista y el dominio Omeya de Hispania." *Manquso* 4 (2016): 7-38.
———. "Nuevos documentos sobre la conquista Omeya de Hispania: Los precintos de plomo." *Zona arqueológica*, No. 15, vol. 1 (2011) (Dedicated issue title: *711: Arqueología e historia entre dos mundos*): 145-61.
Iluk, J. *Aspects économiques et politiques de la circulation de l'or au Bas-Empire*. Wetteren: Moneta, 2007.
Innes, Matthew. "Economies and Societies in Early Medieval Western Europe." In *A Companion to the Medieval World*, ed. Carol Lansing and Edward D. English, 9-35. Malden: Wiley-Blackwell, 2013.
Isla Frez, Amancio. *Ejército, sociedad y política en la Península Ibérica entre los siglos VII y XI*. Madrid: Consejo Superior de Investigaciones Científicas, 2010.
———. "El *Officium Palatinum* visigodo. Entorno regio y poder aristocrático." *Hispania* LXII/3, no. 212 (2002): 823-47.
James, Edward. "Who are the barbarians?" In *Europe's Barbarians, AD 200-600*, ed. E. James, 1-20. London: Routledge, 2009.
Jones, A.H.M. *The Later Roman Empire, 284-602: A Social, Economic, and Administrative Survey*. 3 vols. Oxford: Blackwell, 1964.
Kennedy, Hugh. *The Armies of the Caliphs: Military and Society in the Early Islamic State*. New York: Routledge, 2001.
———. "Military Pay and the Economy of the Early Islamic State." *Historical Research* 75 (May 2002): 155-69.
———. *Muslim Spain and Portugal: a Political History of al-Andalus*. Harlow, Eng.: Longman, 1996.
Kent, John P. C. "Gold Coinage in the Later Roman Empire." In *Essays in Roman Coinage Presented to Harold Mattingly*, ed. R. A. G. Carson and C. H. V. Sutherland, 190-204. London: Oxford University Press, 1956.
———. *The Roman Imperial Coinage*. 10 vols. Vol. 10. London: Spink, 1994.
———. "Un monnayage irrégulier du début du Ve siècle de notre ère." *Bulletin du Cercle d'etudes numismatiques* (1974): 23-32.
King, C. E. "Roman, Local, and Barbarian Coinages." In *Fifth-Century Gaul*, ed. John Drinkwater and Hugh Elton, 184-95. Cambridge: Cambridge University Press, 1992.
King, C. E. "The *Sacrae Largitiones*: Revenues, Expenditure and the Production of Coin." In *Imperial Revenue, Expenditure and Monetary Policy in the Fourth Century*

A.D., ed. C. E. King, 141-73. Oxford: British Archeological Reports International Series, 1980.

King, P.D. *Law and Society in the Visigothic Kingdom.* Cambridge: Cambridge University Press, 1972.

Knight, Jeremy. *The End of Antiquity: Archaeology, Society and Religion, AD 235-700.* Stroud: Tempus, 1999.

Kulikowski, Michael. "Ethnicity, Rulership, and Early Medieval Frontiers." In *Borders, Barriers, and Ethnogenesis: Frontiers in Late Antiquity and the Middle Ages*, ed. Florin Curta, 247-54. Turnhout: Brepols, 2005.

——. *Late Roman Spain and its Cities.* Baltimore, MD: Johns Hopkins University Press, 2004.

——. Review of *Visigothic Spain*, by Roger Collins. *English Historical Review* 123 (2008): 160-61.

——. "The Visigothic Settlement in Aquitania: The Imperial Perspective." In *Society and Culture in Late Antique Gaul: Revisiting the Sources*, ed. Ralph W. Mathisen and Danuta Shanzer, 26-38. Aldershot: Ashgate, 2001.

Kurt, Andrew. "Lay Piety in Visigothic Iberia: Liturgical and Paraliturgical Forms." *Journal of Medieval Iberian Studies* 8, no. 1 (2016): 1-37.

——. "The Places and Purposes of Minting in the Earliest Medieval Kingdoms." In *Worlds of History and Economics: Essays in Honour of Andrew M. Watson*, ed. Brian A. Catlos, 33-54. Valencia: Universitat de Valencia, 2009.

——. "Visigothic Minting and the Expulsion of the Byzantines from Spain in the Early Seventh Century." *The Picus* (1996): 133-66.

Kurt, Andrew and Peter Bartlett. "Nueva ceca visigoda: Lorca (Iliocri[ca]) y sus nexos con las cecas del sur." *Numisma* 48, no. 241 (1998): 27-39.

Lafaurie, Jean. "Familia monetaria." *Bulletin de la Société française de numismatique* (July 1972): 267-71.

——. "Flan de monnaie mérovingienne trouvé a Bordeaux." *Bulletin de la Societé française de numismatique* (May 1970): 528-30.

——. "Les monnaies frappées à Lyon au VIe siècle." In *Mélanges de Travaux offerts à maître Jean Tricou*, 139-295. Lyon: Audin, 1972.

——. "Les trouvailles de monnaies des Visigots en Gaule." In *Actes du 94e congrès national des societés savantes, Pau 1969 (section d'archéologie)*, 111-128. Paris: Bibliothèque Nationale, 1971.

——. Review of *The Barbaric Tremissis in Spain and Southern France, Anastasius to Leovigild*, by Wallace J. Tomasini. *Revue numismatique*, ser. 6, 8 (1966): 336-38.

——. "Triens mérovingiens avec représentations d'un monétaire." *Bulletin de la Societé française de numismatique* 19 (1964): 342-43.

Le Gentilhomme, Pierre. "Le monnayage et la circulation monétaire dans les royaumes barbares en Occident (Ve-VIIIe siècle)." *Revue numismatique* 7 (1943): 46-112.

——. "Le monnayage et la circulation monétaire dans les royaumes barbares en Occident (Ve-VIIIe siècle)." *Revue numismatique* 8 (1944): 13-59.

Lechuga Galindo, M. "Una aproximación a la circulación monetaria de época tardía en Cartagena: los hallazgos del teatro romano." In *V Reunió d'Arqueologia Cristiana Hispànica: Cartagena, 16-19 d'abril de 1998* (Monografíes de la secció histórico-arqueologica 7), ed. J. M. Gurt and N. Tena, 333-49. Barcelona: Institut d'Estudis Catalans, 2000.

Liebeschuetz, J.H.W.G. "Alaric's Goths: Nation or Army?" In *Fifth-century Gaul: a Crisis of Identity?*, ed. John Drinkwater and Hugh Elton, 75-83. Cambridge: Cambridge University Press, 1992.

——. "Cities, Taxes and the Accommodation of the Barbarians: The Theories of Durliat and Goffart." In *Kingdoms of the Empire: The Integration of Barbarians in Late Antiquity*, ed. Walter Pohl, 135-51. Leiden: Brill, 1997.

Livermore, Harold V. "The Coinage of the Suevic Period." *Nummus*, 2nd ser., 12-13 (1989-90): 39-49.

Lo Cascio, Elio. "The Function of the Gold Coinage in the Monetary Economy of the Roman Empire." In *The Monetary Systems of the Greeks and Romans*, ed. W. V. Harris, 160-73. Oxford: Oxford University Press, 2008.

——. "State and Coinage in the Late Republic and Early Empire." *Journal of Roman Studies* 71 (1981): 76-86.

López Sánchez, Fernando. "Coinage, Iconography and the Changing Political Geography of Fifth-century Hispania." In *Hispania in Late Antiquity: Current Perspectives*, ed. and trans. by Kim Bowes and Michael Kulikowski, 487-518. Leiden: Brill, 2005.

——. "La moneda del reino visigodo de Toledo: ¿Por qué? ¿Para quién?" *Mainake* 31 (2009):175-86.

——. "The Mining, Minting, and Acquisition of Gold in the Roman and Post-Roman World." In *Ownership and Exploitation of Land and Natural Resources in the Roman World*, ed. P. Erdkamp et al., 315-36. Oxford: Oxford University Press, 2015.

——. "Moneda civil y moneda militar en Hispania (350-711)." In *Militares y civiles en la antigua Roma*, ed. Juan José Palao Vicente, 227-52. Salamanca: Universidad de Salamanca, 2010.

Manzano Moreno, Eduardo. *Conquistadores, emires y califas. Los omeyas y la formación de al-Andalus.* Barcelona: Crítica, 2006.

Marot, Teresa. "La ciudad de Barcino durante los siglos V I VI: Nuevas aportaciones sobre el circulante." *Anejos de Archivo Español de Arqueología* 20 (1999): 415-22.

——. "La península ibérica en los siglos V-VI: consideraciones sobre provisión, circulación y usos monetarios." *Pyrenae*, nos. 31-32 (2000-2001): 133-60.

Marques, Mário Gomes, J. M. Peixoto Cabral, and J. Rodrigues Marinho. *Ensaios sobre história monetária da monarquia visigoda.* Porto: Sociedade Portuguesa de Numismática, 1995.

Marques de Faria, António. "On Finds of Suevic and Visigothic Coins in the Iberian Peninsula and Their Interpretation." In *Problems of Medieval Coinage*, 3 vols.; vol. 3, ed. M. Gomes Marques and D. M. Metcalf, 71-88. Santarém: Instituto Politécnico de Santarém, 1988.

Martín Esquivel, Alberto. "La moneda en los siglos IV-VIII d.C.: tipos, función y usos monetarios." In *Fortificaciones, poblados y pizarras: la Raya en los inicios del Medievo*, 263-75. Salamanca: Ayuntamiento de Ciudad Rodrigo, 2018.

Martín Viso, Iñaki. "Circuits of Power in a Fragmented Space: Gold Coinage in the Meseta del Duero (Sixth-Seventh Centuries)." In *Scale and Scale Change in the Early Middle Ages: Exploring Landscape, Local Society, and the World Beyond*, ed. Julio Escalona and Andrew Reynolds, 215-52. Turnhout: Brepols, 2016.

——. "Prácticas locales de la fiscalidad en el reino visigodo de Toledo." In *Lo que vino de Oriente: Horizontes, praxis y dimensión material de los sistemas de dominación fiscal en Al-Andalus (ss. VII-IX)*, ed. Xavier Ballestín and Ernesto Pastor, 72-85. Oxford: Archaeopress, 2013.

——. "Tremisses y potentes en el nordeste de Lusitania (siglos VI–VII)." *Mélanges de la Casa de Velázquez* 38 (2008): 175–200.

——. "Tributación y escenarios locales en el centro de la península ibérica: Algunas hipótesis a partir del análisis de las pizarras 'visigodas'." *Antiquité Tardive* 14 (2006): 263-90.

Martínez Jiménez, Javier. "Crisis or crises? The End of Roman Towns in Iberia, Between the late Roman and the Early Umayyad Periods." In *Tough Times: The Archaeology of Crisis and Recovery. Proceedings of the GAO annual conferences 2010 and 2011*, BAR IS 2478, ed. E. Van der Wilt and J. Martínez Jiménez, 77-90. Oxford: Archaeopress, 2013.

Martínez Jiménez, Javier, Isaac Sastre de Diego, and Carlos Tejerizo García. *The Iberian Peninsula between 300 and 850: an Archaeological Perspective*. Amsterdam: Amsterdam University Press, 2018.

Mateos Cruz, Pedro, Antonio Pizzo, and Ruth Pliego Vázquez. "Un tesoro de tremises visigodos hallado en el llamado 'Foro Provincial' de *Augusta Emerita*." *Archivo Español de Arqueología* 78 (2005): 251-70.

Mateu y Llopis, Felipe. *Catálogo de las monedas previsigodas y visigodas del Gabinete Numismático del Museo Arqueológico Nacional*. Madrid: Imp. Gongora, 1936.

——. "El arte monetario visigodo. Las monedas como monumentos (un ensayo de interpretación)." *Archivo Español de Arqueología* 18 (1945): 34-58.

——. "Sobre el numerario visigodo de la Tarraconense. Las cecas de Sagunto y Valencia en el primer tercio del siglo VII." *Ampurias* 3 (1941): 85-95.

Mathisen, Ralph. Review of *Roman Imperial Coinage*, by J.P.C. Kent. *American Journal of Numismatics*, second ser., 7-8 (1995-96): 299-305.

Mathisen, Ralph W., and Danuta Shanzer, eds. *Society and Culture in Late Antique Gaul: Revisiting the Sources.* Aldershot: Ashgate, 2001.

Mathisen, Ralph W., and Hagith S. Sivan. "Forging a New Identity: The Kingdom of Toulouse and the Frontiers of Visigothic Aquitania (418-507)." In *The Visigoths,* ed. Alberto Ferreiro, 1-62. Leiden: Brill, 1999.

McCormick, Michael. *Eternal Victory: Triumphal Rulership in Late Antiquity, Byzantium and the Early Medieval West.* Cambridge: Cambridge University Press, 1986.

———. *The Origins of the European Economy.* Cambridge: Cambridge University Press, 2001.

Merrills, A. and R. Miles. *The Vandals.* Chichester: Wiley-Blackwell, 2010.

Metcalf, D. M. "For What Purposes Were Suevic and Visigothic Tremisses Used?." In *Problems of Medieval Coinage in the Iberian Area,* 3 vols.; vol. 3, ed. M. Gomes Marques and D. M. Metcalf, 15-34. Santarém: Instituto Politécnico de Santarém, 1988.

———. "How Large Was the Anglo-Saxon Currency?" *English Historical Review* 18 (1965): 475-82.

———. "The Joint Reign Gold of Justin I and Justinian I," in Hahn and Metcalf, eds., *Studies in Early Byzantine Gold Coinage,* 19-27

———. "Many Mint-Places, Few Coins: Visigothic Coinage in Gallaecia and Northern Lusitania." In *Homenagem a Mário Gomes Marques,* ed. Mário de Castro Hipólito, 175-94. Sintra: Instituto de Sintra, 2000.

———. "Monetary Circulation in Merovingian Gaul, 561-674. A propos des Cahiers Ernest Babelon." *Revue numismatique,* 6e série, vol. 162 (2006): 337-393.

———. "Some Geographical Aspects of Early Medieval Monetary Circulation in the Iberian Peninsula." In *Problems of Medieval Coinage in the Iberian Area,* 3 vols.; vol. 1, ed. Mário Gomes Marques and M. Crusafont i Sabater, 307-24. Ávila: Sociedad Numismatic Avilesina, 1986.

Metcalf, D. M. and F. Schweizer. "Milliprobe Analyses of Some Visigothic, Suevi, and Other Gold Coins of the Early Middle Ages." *Archaeometry* 12 (1970): 173-88.

Metcalf, D. M., J. M. P. Cabral, and L. C. Alves. "Sixth-Century Visigothic Metrology, Some Evidence from Portugal." *American Journal of Numismatics* 3-4, (1991-92): 65-90.

Miles, George C. *The Coinage of the Umayyads of Spain.* New York: American Numismatic Society, 1950.

———. *The Coinage of the Visigoths of Spain: Leovigild to Achila II.* New York: American Numismatic Society, 1952.

———. "The Ferreira Collection of Visigothic Coins." *Museum Notes* 12 (1966), 129-37.

———. "Notes on the Visigothic Coins in the Gabinete Numismático de Cataluña." *Numisma* 5, no. 16 (1955): 57-62.

Millar, F. "The World of the Golden Ass." *Journal of Roman Studies* 71 (1981): 63-75.

Moorhead, Sam. "Ever Decreasing Circles. The Nummus Economy at Butrint (Albania) and Beyond." In *Numismatic History and Economy in Epirus During Antiquity. Proceedings of the 1st International Conference (University of Ioannina, October 3rd-7th 2007)*, ed. K. Liampi, et al., 601-16. Athens: Society of Numismatics and Economic History, 2013.

Moorhead, Sam. "The Coinage of the Later Roman Empire, 364-498." In *The Oxford Handbook of Greek and Roman Coinage*, ed. W. E. Metcalf, 601-32. Oxford: Oxford University Press, 2014.

Mora Serrano, Bartolomé. "The Circulation of Bronze Currency in Málaga During the Sixth Century AD: New Findings." *Numismatic Chronicle* 169 (2009): 424-30.

——. "Old and New Coins in Southern Hispania in the 6th Century AD." In *Produktion und Recyceln von Münzen in der Spätantike. RGZM – TAGUNGEN 29*, ed. J. Chameroy and P.-M. Guihard, 139-53. Mainz: Schnell & Steiner, 2016.

Moreno, Eduardo Manzano. *Conquistadores, emires, y califas. Los omeyas y la formación de al-Andalus.* Barcelona: Crítica, 2006.

Morrisson, Cécile. "L'atelier de Carthage et la diffusion de la monnaie frappée dans l'Afrique vandale et byzantine (439-695)," *Antiquité Tardive* 11 (2003), 65-84.

Morrisson, Cécile. "Regio dives in Omnibus bonis ornata. The African Economy from the Vandals to the Arab Conquest in the Light of Coin Evidence." In *North Africa under Byzantium and Early Islam*, ed. S. T. Stevens and J. P. Conant, 173-198. Washington, D.C.: Dumbarton Oaks Publications, 2016.

Morrisson, Cécile. "Tra Vandali e Bizantini: la prosperità dell'Africa (V-VII secolo) attraverso le fonti e la documentazione monetale," *Incontri de filología classica* 10 (2010-2011), 145-69.

Morrisson, C. and J.-C. Cheynet. "Prices and Wages in the Byzantine World." In *The History of the Byzantine Economy*, 2 vols.; vol. 2, ed. Angeliki E. Laiou, 815-78. Washington, DC: Dumbarton Oaks, 2002.

Morrisson, C. and J. P. Sodini. "The Sixth-century Economy." In *The Economic History of Byzantium: From the Seventh through the Fifteenth Century*, ed. E. Laiou, 171-220. Washington D.C.: Dumbarton Oaks Publications, 2003.

Naismith, Rory. "Gold Coinage and Its Use in the Post-Roman West." *Speculum* 89 (2014): 273-306.

——. "Introduction." In *Money and Coinage in the Middle Ages*, ed. Rory Naismith, 1-18. Leiden: Brill, 2018.

——, ed. *Money and Coinage in the Middle Ages*. Leiden: Brill, 2018.

——. "Mints, Moneyers and the Geography of Power in Early Medieval England and its Neighbours." Paper given at the conference Power and Place in Later Roman and Early Medieval Europe: Interdisciplinary Perspectives on Governance and Civil Organization held at University College, London, November 2011. Forthcoming.

Nixon, C.E.V. "Relations Between Visigoths and Romans in Fifth-century Gaul." In *Fifth-century Gaul: A Crisis of Identity?*, ed. John Drinkwater and Hugh Elton, 64-74. New York: Cambridge University Press, 1992.

Oddy, W.A. "The Debasement of the Provincial Byzantine Gold Coinage from the Seventh to Ninth Centuries." In *Studies in Early Byzantine Gold Coinage*, ed. W. Hahn and W.E. Metcalf, 135-42. New York: American Numismatic Society, 1988.

Oddy, W. A. and M. J. Hughes. "The Specific Gravity Method for the Analysis of Gold Coins." In *Methods of Chemical and Metallurgical Investigation of Ancient Coinage*, ed. Edward T. Hall and David M. Metcalf, 75-87. London: Royal Numismatic Society, 1972.

Olmo Enciso, Lauro and Manuel Castro Priego. "La época visigoda a través de la arqueología." In *711: Arqueología e historia entre dos mundos* (Exhibition catalog: Museo Arqueológico Regional, Alcalá de Henares, Madrid, 16 December 2011 to 1 April 2012), 48-77. Museo Arqueológico Regional de la Comunidad de Madrid, 2011.

Olson, Lauris. "Gold contents of royal Visigothic tremisses at the American Numismatic Society." http://web.archive.org/web/20020704101742/http:/pobox.upenn.edu/~olson/visicoins/allsg.prn; accessed in digital archive 3 January 2018.

——. "Visigothic Coin Hoard Structure." Paper presented at the 24th International Congress on Medieval Studies, Kalamazoo, Michigan, 4-7 May 1989; accessed in digital archive 3 January 2018.

Orlandis, José. *Hispania y Zaragoza en la antigüedad tardía. Estudios varios.* Zaragoza: Caja de Ahorros – Monte de Piedad de Zaragoza, Aragón y Rioja, 1984.

——. *Historia de España: La España visigótica.* Madrid: Gredos, 1977.

——. *Historia del reino visigodo español.* Madrid: Rialp, 1988.

——. *Historia social y éconómica de la España visigoda.* Madrid: Confederación Española de Cajas de Ahorros, 1975.

——. *La vida en España en tiempo de los godos.* Madrid: Rialp, 1991.

——. "Sobre el nivel de la vida en Hispania visigoda." *Anuario de Estudios Medievales* 8 (1972-1973), 17-33.

Osland, Daniel. "Tribute and Coinage in the Visigothic Kingdom: On the Role of the Bishop. Moneda y tributo en el reino visigodo: sobre las funciones del obispo." *Anas* 24 (2011), 71-95.

Panvini Rosati, F. "La tecnica monetaria altomedievale." *Settimane di studio del Centro Italiano de studi sull'alto medioevo* 18 (1971), vol. 2: 713-44.

Peixoto Cabral, J. M. and D. M. Metcalf. *A moeda sueva / Suevic Coinage.* Porto: Sociedade Portuguesa de Numismática, 1997.

Pérez Sánchez, Dionisio. *El ejército en la sociedad visigoda.* Salamanca: Universidad de Salamanca, 1989.

Pliego Vázquez, Ruth. "The Circulation of Copper Coins in the Iberian Peninsula During the Visigothic Period: New Approaches." *Journal of Archaeological Numismatics* 5-6 (2015-2016): 125-60.

——. "Counterfeit Visigothic Gold." *Bulletin on Counterfeits* 20, no. 1 (1995): 8-10.

——. "Dertosa, ceca visigoda bajo el reinado de Recaredo I (586-601)." *Acta Numismàtica* 45 (2015): 81-90.

——. "El dinar epigráfico latino acuñado en al-Andalus. Una reinterpretación a la luz de nuevos hallazgos." *Numisma* 245 (2001): 139-54.

——. "El origen de la representación de Cristo en la moneda del rey visigodo Ervigio." *Numismatica e antichità classiche: quaderni ticinesi* 42 (2013): 251-62.

——. "El *tremis* de los últimos años del Reino Visigodo (702-714)." In *Monnaies du haut Moyen Âge: histoire et archéologie (péninsule Ibérique – Maghreb, VIIe-XIe siècle)*, ed. Philippe Sénac and Sébastien Gasc, 17-58. Toulouse: Presses universitaires du Midi – Collection Méridiennes, 2015.

——. "*Gallaecia* en tiempos del reino visigodo de Toledo: sus emisiones monetarias." In *Introducción a la Historia Monetaria de Galicia*, ed. F. Cebreiro Ares, 65-104. A Coruña: Labirinto de Paixóns, 2012.

——. "A hoard of Late Roman and Visigothic Gold." *Numismatic Chronicle* 176 (2016): 377-91.

——. "Kings' Names on Visigothic Bronze Coins: A New Minimus from Ispali in the Name of Leovigild." *American Journal of Numismatics* 30 (2018): 245-58.

——. "La acuñación monetaria en el Reino Visigodo de Toledo: El funcionamiento de las cecas." In *Els tallers monetaris: organització y producció, XII Curs d'Historia monetaria d'Hispania*, 117-41. Barcelona: Museu Nacional d'Art de Catalunya, 2008.

——. "La falsificación y manipulación de la moneda visigoda," In *Falsificació i manipulació de la moneda, XVI Curs d'Història monetaria d'Hispania*, 81-102. Barcelona: Museu Nacional d'Art de Catalunya, 2010.

——. "La moneda en el ocaso del reino godo de Hispania." *Zona arqueológica*, No. 15, vol. 2 (2011) (Dedicated issue title: *711: Arqueología e historia entre dos mundos*): 321-38.

——. "La moneda visigoda: Anexo I." *SPAL* 21 (2012): 209-31.

——. *La moneda visigoda*. 2 vols. Seville: Universidad de Sevilla, 2009.

Pounds, N. J. G. *An Economic History of Medieval Europe*, 2nd ed. London: Longman, 1994.

Regueras Grande, Fernando and Isabel Rodríguez Casanova. "Triente de Sisebuto y dinar de indicción en dos *villae* romanas leonesas." *Brigecio* 27 (2017): 11-24.

Reinhart, Wilhelm. "Die Münzen des tolosanischen Reiches der Westgoten." *Deutsches Jahrbuch für Numismatik* 1 (1938): 107-35.

——. "Die Münzen des westgotischen Reiches von Toledo." *Deutsches Jahrbuch für Numismatik* 3-4 (1940-41): 69-101.

——. "Los anillos hispano-visigodos." *Archivo español de arqueología* 20, no. 68 (1947): 167-78.

——. "Nuevas aportaciones a la numismatica visigoda." *Archivo español de arqueología* 18 (1945): 212-35.

Retamero, Félix. "As Coins Go Home: Towns, Merchants, Bishops and Kings in Visigothic Hispania." In *The Visigoths from the Migration Period to the Seventh Century: an Ethnographic Perspective*, ed. Peter Heather, 271-320. San Marino: Center for Interdisciplinary Research on Social Stress, 1999.

——. "Coinage, Minting of." In *Medieval Science, Technology, and Medicine: An Encyclopedia*, ed. Thomas F. Glick, Steven Livesey, and Faith Wallis, 130-31. New York: Routledge, 2005.

——. "La moneda del *regnum gothorum* (ca. 575-714). Una revisión del registro numismático." In *Between Taxation and Rent: Fiscal Problems from Late Antiquity to Early Middle Ages*, ed. Pablo C. Díaz and Iñaki Martín Viso, 189-220. Bari: Edipuglia, 2011.

Reynolds, Paul. "Hispania in the Late Roman Mediterranean: Ceramics and Trade." In *Hispania in Late Antiquity*, ed. and trans. Kim Bowes and Michael Kulikowski, 369-485. Leiden: Brill, 2005.

——. "Material Culture and the Economy in the Age of Saint Isidore of Seville (6th and 7th Centuries)." *Antiquité Tardive* 23 (2015): 163-210.

Ripoll López, Gisela. "*Sedes regiae* en la Hispania de la antigüedad tardía." In *Sedes regiae (ann. 400-800)*, ed. Gisela Ripoll López and Josep M. Gurt, 371-401. Barcelona: Reial Acadèmia de Bone Lletres, 2000.

Robinson Rössner, Philipp. "Money, Banking, Economy." In *Handbook of Medieval Culture: Fundamental Aspects and Conditions of the European Middle Ages*, 2 vols.; vol. 2, ed. Albrecht Classen. Berlin/Boston, MA: De Gruyter, 2015, pp. 1137–1166.

Romanowski, Andrzej. "An Extraordinary Barbarian Imitation of the 2nd-Century Roman Denarius from Central Poland (Osiny, Baranów Commune, Grodzisk Mazowiecki District)." *Notae Numismaticae/Zapiski Numizmatyczne* 10 (2015): 115-30.

Rovelli, Alessia. "From the Fall of Rome to Charlemagne (c. 400-800)." In *Money and Coinage in the Middle Ages*, ed. Rory Naismith, 63-92. Leiden: Brill, 2018.

Sánchez Pardo, José Carlos. "Power and Rural Landscapes in Early Medieval Galicia (400–900 AD): Towards a Re-incorporation of the Archaeology into the Historical Narrative." *Early Medieval Europe* 21, no. 2 (2013): 140-68.

——. "Sobre las bases económicas de las aristocracias en la *Gallaecia* suevo-visigoda (ca. 530-650 d.c.). Comercio, minería y articulación fiscal." *Anuario de Estudios Medievales* 44, no. 2 (2014), 983-1023.

Santiago Fernández, Javier de. "Legislación y moneda en la Hispania visigoda." *Mélanges de la Casa de Velázquez* 41, no. 2 (2011): 55-74.

Sayas Abengochea, J. J. and Luis A. García Moreno. *Romanismo y germanismo: el despertar de los pueblos hispánicos (siglos IV-X)*. Historia de España dirigida por Manuel Tuñón de Lara. 2 vols. Vol. 2, 388-90. Barcelona: Labor, 1982.

Schwarcz, Andreas. "The Visigothic Settlement in Aquitania: Chronology and Archaeology." In *Society and Culture*, ed. Ralph Mathisen and Danuta Shanzer, 15-25. Aldershot: Ashgate, 2001.

Sénac, Philip and Tawfiq Ibrahim. *Los precintos de la conquista omeya y la formación de al-Andalus (711-756)*. Granada: Universidad de Granada, 2017.

Spaulding, James. "The Mint-cities of Visigothic Spain: Leovigild to Achila II." PhD, Duke University, 1970.

Spufford, Peter. "Coinage and Currency." In *Cambridge Economic History of Europe from the Decline of the Roman Empire*, ed. M.M. Postan, 8 vols.; vol. 3, 576-602. Cambridge: Cambridge University Press, 1963.

——. "Coinage and Currency." In *Cambridge Economic History of Europe from the Decline of the Roman Empire*, 2nd ed., ed. M.M. Postan and H.J. Habakkuk, 8 vols.; vol. 2, 788-863. Cambridge: Cambridge University Press, 1987.

——. *Money and Its Use in Medieval Europe*. Cambridge: Cambridge University Press, 1988.

Stahl, Alan M. *The Merovingian Coinage of the Region of Metz.* Louvain-la-Neuve: Institut Superieur d'Archeologie et d'Histoire de l'Art, 1982.

Strothmann, Jürgen. "Königsherrschaft oder nachantike Staatlichkeit? Merowingische Monetarmünzen als Quelle für die politische Ordnung des Frankenreiches." *Millennium* 5 (2008): 353–81.

Suchodolski, Stanislaw. "Est-ce que les Burgondes ont été forcés d'accepter l'or au poids?" *Numismatica e antichità classica* 20 (1991): 247-51.

——. "Les débuts du monnayage dans les royaumes barbares." In *Mélanges de numismatique, d'archéologie et d'histoire offerts à Jean Lafaurie*, 249-56. Paris: Société Française de Numismatique, 1980.

Thompson, Edward A. *The Goths In Spain*. Oxford: Oxford University Press, 1969.

——. *Romans and Barbarians: The Decline of the Western Empire*. Madison, WI: University of Wisconsin Press, 1982.

Tomasini, Wallace J. *The Barbaric Tremissis in Spain and Southern France: Anastasius to Leovigild*. New York: American Numismatic Society, 1964.

Treadgold, Warren. *Byzantium and Its Army, 284-1081.* Stanford, CA: Stanford University Press, 1995.

Valdeavellano, L. G. de. "La moneda y la economía de cambio en la península ibérica desde el siglo VI hasta mediados del siglo XI." In *Moneta e scambi nell' alto medioevo*, 203-30. Spoleto: Presso la sede del Centro, 1961.

Vallejo Girvés, Margarita. *Bizancio y la España tardoantigua (ss. V-VIII): un capítulo de historia mediterránea*. Alcalá de Henares: Universidad de Alcalá de Henares, 1993.

——. *Hispania y Bizancio: Una relación desconocida*. Madrid: Akal, 2012.

Valverde Castro, María del Rosario. "La ideología fiscal en el reino visigodo de Toledo." In *Between Taxation and Rent: Fiscal Problems from Late Antiquity to Early Middle Ages / Entre el impuesto y la renta: problemas de la fiscalidad tardoantigua y altomedieval*, ed. Pablo C. Díaz and Iñaki Martín Viso, 163-88. Bari: Edipuglia, 2011.

——. "Monarquía y tributación en la Hispania visigoda: el marco teórico." *Historia Antigua* 31 (2007): 235-51.

Velázquez, Isabel, and Gisela Ripoll. "*Toletum*, la construcción de una *urbs regia*." In *Sedes regiae (ann. 400-800)*, ed. Gisela Ripoll López and Josep M. Gurt, 521-78. Barcelona: Reial Acadèmia de Bone Lletres, 2000.

Velázquez, Luis J. *Congeturas sobre las medallas de los reyes godos y suevos de España*. Málaga: Oficina de Francisco Martinez de Aguilar, 1759.

Vigil, M. and Barbero, A. "Algunos aspectos de la feudalización del reino visigodo en relación a su organización financiera y militar." *Monéda y Credito*, no. 112 (1970): 71-91.

——. *Sobre los orígenes sociales de la Reconquista*. Barcelona: Ariel, 1974.

Vizcaíno Sánchez, Jaime. *La presencia bizantina en Hispania, siglos VI-VII: la documentación arqueológica*. Murcia: Universidad de Murcia, 2009.

Von Reden, Sitta. *Money in Classical Antiquity*. Cambridge: Cambridge University Press, 2010.

Walker, Alan. "The Identification of the Coinage of Reccared II: New Evidence from the Visigothic Mints of Emerita and Eliberri." *Numismatics – Witness to History*, 73-86. Wetteren: IAPN Publications, no. 8, 1986.

Walker, John. *A Catalogue of Muhammadan Coins in the British Museum*. 2 vols. Vol.2: *Arab-Byzantine and Post-Reform Umaiyad Coins*. London: British Museum, 1956.

Watson, Andrew M. "Back to Gold – and Silver." *The Economic History Review*, second series 20, no. 1 (1967): 1-34.

Wickham, Chris. *Framing the Early Middle Ages: Europe and the Mediterranean, 400-800*. Oxford: Oxford University Press, 2005.

Wolf, Kenneth Baxter. *Conquerors and Chroniclers of Early Medieval Spain*. Liverpool: Liverpool University Press, 1990.

Wolfram, Herwig. *The History of the Goths*. Trans. Thomas J. Dunlop. Berkeley: University of California Press, 1988.

Wood, Ian. *The Merovingian Kingdoms, 450-751*. New York: Longman, 1994.

Yannopoulos, P. "Production monétaire à l'époque byzantine, avant l'an mil." In *Rythmes de la production monétaire, de l'antiquité à nos jours*, ed. G. Depeyrot, T. Hackens, Gh. Moucharte, 359-72. Louvain-la-neuve: l'Université Catholique de Louvain, 1987.

Yoon, David. "Art, Craft, Innovation, and Efficiency: Early Medieval Minting Technology." *American Numismatic Society Magazine* 14, no. 2 (2015): 18-27.

About the Author

Andrew Kurt (Ph.D., University of Toronto) is Associate Professor of History at Clayton State University in Morrow, Georgia.

Index

adaeratio 132 n.383, 180, 217 n.665, 222
American Numismatic Society (ANS), collection of 16 n.9, 73 n.196, 98 n.272, 107 n.297, 145 n.424, 147 n.430, 159, 167, 291, 295, 306, 307, 317, 327, 329, 330, 331, 344, 368–86
Anastasius 38, 41–42, 49, 51–54, 61, 66, 68, 70–73, 75 n.203, 76, 79, 117 n.339, 124 n.352, 177 n.515, 264 n.783
Anglo-Saxons 67 n.183, 223, 235, 254, 262 n.774
Aquitania 19, 28f
archeology 13, 27 n.26, 108, 110, 113 n.321, 115, 116 n.331, 119f, 142, 176, 188 n.556, 192 n.572, 217, 257, 269, 270, 272, 273f, 276f, 279–80, 281 n.855, 287–88
Arles 29, 31, 33 n.46, 41 n.78, 42, 45, 47, 51, 52 nn.115 and 118, 53 n.121, 110
army 22, 28 n.27, 29–33, 46, 47f, 53 n.119, , 83, 88, 107, 133 n.386, 144, 148 n 435, 152, 177, 179 n.521, 181 n.525, 182 n.529, 184f, 187, 192–95, 196 n.587, 199, 200 n.606, 201, 203–08, 210, 214 n.659, 215, 217, 218 n.669, 219, 223–25, 226 n.688, 238, 240 n.725, 245, 247, 250 n.751, 253, 254, 258 n.766, 259 n.767, 260 n.769, 264, 270 n.800, 285, 286
assaying 78, 239
Asturians 215 n.660, 217
Attalus 39 n.73, 40, 44 n.90
Avitus of Périgord 264 n.784
Avitus, bp. of Vienne, letter of 43, 44 n.88, 184 n.538

Baetica 27, 31, 58f, 132 n.384, 137, 141, 146f, 150–52, 166, 171, 193 n.573, 194, 196 n.588, 197, 199, 201 n.608, 203 n.615, 209, 218 n.666, 222, 271, 301, 308–16, 332, 353–55, 358
Banaji, Jairus 15 n.5, 225 n.685, 258, 281 n.854
Barceló, Miquel 165f, 206, 241
Barcelona 16 n.9, 27, 32 nn.41 and 43, 47–48, 60–61, 62 n.156, 77 n.208, 89, 93 n.254, 117–18, 132 n.383, 153, 180, 209 n.638, 285; *see also* mints, Visigothic
Barral i Altet, Xavier 16, 38, 64, 65 n.171, 66 n.174, 68, 104 n.288, 126 n.362, 188f, 196 n.590, 263 n.778
Bartlett, Peter 9, 262 n.774, 97 n.269, 262 n.774, 330
Basques 194, 200 n.603, 218–19
bishops, Visigothic 46 n.97, 83, 113, 115, 132, 133 n.387, 140 n.411, 179f, 183 n.537, 184 n.541, 185f n.546, 193, 194, 200, 215f, 228–29, 235, 264, 266–68, 278 n.836, 280, 286
bronze coinage *see* copper coinage
Burgundians 29–30, 34, 36f, 43f, 47, 52, 53f, 62 n.161, 114 n.325, 119, 224, 272
Byzantine Empire 36 n.61, 48, 82, 83f, 98, 107, 175 n.510, 184 n.538, 185, 186, 190 n.564, 204f, 225f, 236, 240f, 244, 249, 258, 259 n.767, 261, 264 n.783, 265 n.786, 274, 275, 280f

Cantabrians 215 n.660, 217 n.664, 218
Carthage
  Carthago Spartaria or Carthago Nova (mod. Cartagena, SE Spain) 55 n.127, 194, 199, 207, 273 n.811, 277
  in North Africa 249 n.748, 260 n.769, 273 n.811, 274, 275 n.820, 277f, 280
Carthaginensis 58, 137f, 140–41, 146f, 150, 151f, 155–56, 166, 171, 196 n.588, 197f, 203 n.615, 300f, 308–16, 332, 353–56, 358
Cherniakhiv culture 27 n.26
Chronicle of Caesaraugusta (*Consularia Caesaraugustana*) 32, 46
circulation of coinage 16, 23, 39, 48 n.104, 49, 64f, 68, 79, 82, 85, 109–12, 114–17, 120, 126 n.362, 146, 160, 174, 177 nn.513 and 517, 186f, 189, 191 n.566, 196, 201 n.610, 217 n.666, 228 n.692, 229, 239, 240 n.722, 254f, 258f, 261–81
cities 18, 22–23, 31, 33–34, 45f, 84, 88, 89 n.243, 103 n.287, 105, 110–16, 128–30, 133 n.387, 138, 145f, 148, 150, 152, 161, 175–76, 183f, 193 n.573, 195, 200, 202f, 205, 208f, 211, 213, 214f, 219–22, 225 n.685, 228, 240, 244, 250, 259, 262, 264, 266, 268f, 269 n.799, 271 n.806, 273 n.811, 274, 277–80, 285, 286f, 289, 331
Codex Theodosianus 229
coemption 179 n.521, 204, 224, 259 n.767
coinage
  Byzantine 23, 48 n.105, 50, 51f, 54, 55 n.127, 58, 70, 77 n.206, 78f, 81, 84, 85 n.226, 87, 93, 103 n.283, 106f, 109, 112, 118 n.340, 119f, 124, 129, 149 n.436, 161, 172 n.505, 185 n.542, 186, 190 n.564, 191, 201, 202 n.611, 203, 206–08, 210, 220, 221 n.676, 225, 239–40, 242, 249, 253–54, 258, 260, 271 n.804, 273–81, 283; *see also solidus*, Byzantine
  Islamic 240 n.722, 247–55; *see also dinar, dirham, fulus, nisf*
  Roman 15, 20, 22, 27, 34, 36 n.61, 38, 40, 45, 51, 53, 66, 108, 117, 160, 162, 175–78, 186f, 191, 221 n.676, 224, 243, 277, 280; *see also solidus*, Roman
  Visigothic
    attribution 38–40, 41 n.77, 42f, 60–63, 66f, 90 n.247, 111f, 114 n.324, 214 n.657
    copper (bronze) *see* copper coinage
    corpus of 17f, 21, 56 n.132, 60 n.150, 61f, 64 n.170, 65, 109, 120, 135–37, 140–45, 158, 187 n.549, 190f, 196–99, 214, 215 n.661, 220, 286 n.861, 300–04, 324, 329
    debasement 22, 43f, 64, 75, 79, 104, 120, 126–28, 169–72, 184 n.538, 201–03, 218 n.666, 236–39, 241, 243 n.738, 254, 260f, 265, 283, 285f, 295

discoveries of 18f, 21f, 49, 64, 66, 87 n.582, 88 n.241, 96, 109–12, 114, 117–21, 135–39, 191, 195 n.586, 196 n.588, 197 n.592, 198 n.595, 200, 207, 213, 216, 218, 278f, 288f
engraving 21, 51, 55, 57, 63f, 75, 87f, 89 n.241, 90, 94f, 96 n.571, 98, 108, 124–30, 139 n.409, 149–57, 175, 209, 238 n.716, 288f, 329–67
fiduciary character 238–40
fineness 18, 21, 42, 68–79, 98f, 109 n.306, 167–72, 186 n.548, 187 n.549, 202, 206, 236–40, 244f, 254f, 265 n.786, 291–95, 306–17, 326f
intrinsic value (weight and fineness combined) 77f, 99, 103, 109 n.306, 210, 238 n.719, 239, 295f
monograms on 36 n.59, 50 n.107, 53 n.121, 102 n.282, 111f, 115, 116 n.331, 128 n.365, 242 n.734
monometallism as erroneous view 18, 21, 108 n.302, 109, 203 n.614
pre-regal period gold 25–79, 81–100, 291–94, 327
regal period gold 81–121, 123–71, 173–229, 231–45, 257–89, 295–327, 335–86
silver 18–21, 35, 39, 108f, 117–19, 259, 275, 284
solidus 20, 36–45, 49–54, 56 n.131, 60, 66, 69 n.188, 73, 78 n.211, 79 n.212, 81, 85, 103 n. 283, 118, 125 n.355, 127, 160f, 163, 174, 183 n.537, 185, 186 n.548, 201 n.610, 240 n.722, 241, 255 n.763, 261–67, 276, 284, 287
standards 21, 39 n.75, 43, 56, 68–79, 87, 91, 98–100, 103, 105, 124, 128, 129 n.370, 130, 156–71, 175f, 202, 207, 212, 221, 226, 232–34, 236f, 239, 240 n.722, 241–45, 265, 283–85, 288, 295, 320f, 323
tremissis 15–18, 20f, 23, 37, 40 nn.75 and 76, 49–54, 56, 58–64, 65 n.174, 68–76, 78f, 81, 84f, 87–112, 114f, 117f, 124–26, 129f, 135–37, 139–43, 145, 147 n.431, 148 n.434, 149 n.436, 150, 152f, 153 n.451, 156–71, 174f, 178, 180, 181 n.525, 182f, 185f, 188f, 196, 202, 205, 207, 210, 211 n.650, 213f, 214 n.657, 216 n.662, 219f, 232–37, 239–42, 244, 245 n.742, 248, 254, 260–62, 264, 266–71, 277, 279 n.845, 280, 283f, 285, 287f, 291–386
weight 16, 18f, 21f, 42–44, 68–78, 87, 91, 95, 98f, 103, 116–19, 124, 129f, 156–72, 187 n.549, 196, 201, 220, 222, 232–34, 236–41, 245, 248f, 254, 265, 273 n.811, 283, 285, 288, 291–95, 306–16, 318–24
Collins, Roger 47, 83 n.215
comes metallorum 55
comes patrimonii, -iorum 132f, 134 n.387, 178 n.520, 180, 181 n.525, 205 n.625
comes sacrarum largitionum 131, 177, 178 n.520
comes thesaurorum 55, 131f, 157, 178 n.520, 183 n.533, 205 n.625, 233, 263
Consularia Caesaraugustana *see* Chronicle of Caesaraugusta
control marks 129–30, 139 n.409, 156, 183, 365
copper coinage 15–16, 19, 21–23, 102 n.282, 108–17, 119–21, 126, 177 n.516, 220f, 225 n.685, 240 n.722, 243, 252–55, 259, 260 n.769, 270–81, 284, 288, 299; *see also fulus*
bronze as term used interchangeably 19, 109 n.306
Córdoba 60, 62 n.156, 73, 90, 96 n.267, 102, 105, 107 n.297, 110 n.311, 111, 114, 116 n. 331, 140f, 143, 146, 150–53, 157, 189, 192f, 197–99, 202, 205, 209, 220, 242 n.734, 250, 264, 279, 285; *see also* mints, Visigothic
Corpus Nummorum Visigothorum (CNV) 17
Council of the Seven Provinces 28 n.28, 33
court, royal 33, 36, 89, 104, 132 n.384, 156, 182, 183, 186–89, 204 n.620, 205, 221, 227, 233, 237 n.713, 262–64
Crawford, Michael 176
Crusafont i Sabater, Miquel 14 n.5, 16, 109–21, 185 n.543, 220, 261, 264, 278
cuirass 38 n.71, 42, 50f, 55 n.127, 147–49, 152 n.444, 156, 332, 334, 336, 338, 346, 350–51, 353, 356–58, 361, 363–64
currency *see* coinage

De fisco Barcinonensi 118, 132 n.383, 133 n.387, 180, 183 n.533, 209 n.638, 268
die(s) 17f, 20f, 28 n.26, 37, 50, 57, 59, 63f, 66, 75f, 88–90, 94f, 113 n.322, 124–30, 139 n.409, 140, 146 n.429, 148 n.434, 149–57, 178 n.518, 187 n.549, 191, 200, 209–12, 250, 262, 289, 295, 329–34, 336, 338, 340, 342, 350, 352, 354f, 367
dinar 251f, 254, 327
dirham 252, 254, 264
donativum 184f, 204, 260 n.769, 264

economy 13f, 15f, 19f, 23, 27 n.26, 35 n.53, 49f, 61, 64, 103 n.283, 119f, 172 n.505, 174–78, 185–90, 203–06, 217, 225–28, 235, 241, 243, 257–81, 287f
Eio (El Tolmo de Minateda) 196 n.588, 277f, 281
ethnicity 234
exagia (measurement weights) 43 n.87, 274

Fernández, Damián 229, 283 n.857
fines 265, 269
fiscal
coinage 22, 121, 130, 174–86, 188, 192, 198, 206, 209, 217 n.665, 219, 222f, 224, 225 n.687, 226 nn.689 and 690, 238f, 241, 243–45, 253, 258–62, 264, 267, 270, 285, 287f
system 22, 28, 53, 103, 121, 130, 132–34, 174–88, 192, 205f, 209, 213 n.655, 217

n.665, 219–29, 238f, 241, 243–45, 253, 258–63, 264, 267, 270, 272, 283, 285, 287f
see also taxation
fiscus, -i (fisc) 118, 131–33, 180, 183 n.533, 185, 187f, 207 n.634, 208f, 268; *see also* *patrimonium*, treasure
forgery: 76, 138 n.409, 285, 317, 384
Franks *see* Merovingians
fulus 242, 254

Gallaecia 27, 31, 55, 137–43, 146, 147 n.430, 148 n.434, 152–54, 156, 161 n.467, 165 nn.483 and 487, 175, 184 n.541, 211–20, 238, 242 n.734, 288, 302–04, 309, 311f, 314, 338, 357
Gallia *see* Gaul
García Moreno, Luis A. 14 n.5, 15, 178, 285
García Sanjuan, Alejandro 255 n.763
Gaul 12, 18f, 20, 22, 27–47, 51–54, 61, 63, 85 n.225, 120 n.348, 125 n.355, 157 n.456, 173, 184 n.539, 204 n.619, 217, 232f, 242, 244, 263, 271, 275 n.817; *see also* Aquitania
gold
bullion, melted, or shaped 124–28, 131, 156, 160, 180, 183 n.537, 187, 204 n.619, 206–13, 218, 229, 238, 243, 260 n.770, 263, 267
supply of 23, 76, 120, 142, 144, 161 n.467, 172 n.505, 187f, 201f, 206–13, 217, 220, 226 n.688, 236–38, 240, 243, 260f, 267 n.794, 272, 275 n.817, 281, 286, 288
see also coinage, Visigothic: fineness, solidus, tremissis; purity of gold coins
goldsmiths 128, 226
Gregory of Tours 47 nn.102 and 103, 87 n.235, 88 n.237, 183 n.537, 193, 194 n.578, 202 n.612, 208 n.636, 215 n.660, 263 n.776
Grierson, Philip 38, 40 n.75, 69 n.189, 86 n.229, 128, 167, 207

Heiss, Aloïss 49 n.106, 138, 145, 155, 334
Hendy, Michael 177f, 180, 182, 186f, 190f, 209 n.638, 258, 260, 268, 275 n.821
Heraclius 185 n.542, 204 n.617, 210, 220 n.675, 240, 295
Hermenegild 48, 83, 85–104, 114f, 161 n.472, 193, 198f, 262, 284, 288, 300–03, 317, 385
Hispania 11f, 20, 22, 25, 27, 30–33, 48 n.105, 55, 57, 131, 161 n.467, 179, 188 n.552, 190, 191 n.566, 202 n.611, 205, 210, 224 n.683, 241, 244, 267 n.793, 270, 271 n.806, 278 n.837
hoards 16f, 21, 53 n.120, 54, 58, 64–68, 77f, 82 n.213, 96f, 108–10, 117, 126 n.362, 136f, 141–44, 181 n.525, 182, 187 n.549, 189, 191, 195 n.586, 196f, 201 n.606, 239f, 261, 263, 269, 270 n.803, 288, 330
Abusejo 196 n.588
Fuentes de Andalucía 136, 141, n.414, 143 n.420, 195 n.586, 197 n.592
La Capilla 136, 141 n.414, 143 n.420, 196f, 203 n.615, 270 n.803
La Capilla II 136, 270 n.803
Les Tres Cales 117
Mérida 87 n.235, 96f
Seville I (Calle Cuna) 66–68, 77–79
Zorita de los Canes 50 n.111, 54, 65f, 68, 75 n.201, 77 n.208, 95 n.263, 96, 98 n.272
Honorius 28 n.28, 30 n.31, 38–40, 66f
Howgego, Christopher 176 n.513, 210 nn.643 and 644, 243
Hydatius, chronicle of 26 n.23, 46 n.95

imitation coinage *see* coinage, Visigothic, pre-regal
inscriptions 14 n.5, 35, 36 n.61, 38, 40 n.74, 44f, 49, 55 nn.125 and 127, 56, 58f, 62f, 65 n.172, 66, 68, 70, 72, 73 n.195, 75, 79, 81, 85, 86 n.231, 87–91, 93–96, 98f, 100–07, 110, 112f, 118, 124 n.355, 125f, 128, 130 n.373, 131, 139 n.409, 145, 149, 152, 155 n.452, 156, 174f, 192, 198–200, 204, 210–20, 226, 232, 238, 242–44, 249f, 260 n.769, 283, 286, 331, 334, 340, 345–67 *passim*
CONOB (also CONO, ONO) 55 n.127, 89 n.242, 93 n.254, 94, 101, 128, 334, 336
cum Deo (*optinuit, intravit*) 88f, 91, 94, 102, 198
curru 62, 66 n.174, 68, 76 n.205, 77, 85, 92, 94–98, 100f, 103f, 118, 233, 317, 327
Islamic 249–52
iustus 91, 106 n.295, 139 n.409, 340
jumbled 58, 59 n.144, 70, 72f, 75, 85, 86 n.231, 92, 94f, 97, 100f, 104, 118, 251
pius 91, 93f, 106 n.295, 130 n.373, 200 n.606, 334, 336, 338, 340
regi a Deo vita 91, 92 n.252, 94, 95 n.263, 102
rex inclitus 68, 76 n.205, 87, 89, 91f, 94f, 96 n.267, 97–99, 101, 233, 295, 334
victor/victoria, victory issues not listed above 87 n.235, 88, 91, 96 n.266, 97 n.268, 100–04, 152, 175, 199f, 211–18, 232, 242 n.734, 286, 334, 340
war-related inscriptions in Gallaecia 152, 211–20
Islam *see* Muslim invasion of Spain in 711; *dinar*; *dirham*; *fulus*; *thulth*
Islamic territories, administration of 206 n.262, 207, 225, 252f
Iudila (usurper) 301, 313, 317, 346, 379

John of Biclar, chronicle of 32 n.42, 82f, 88, 99, 192f, 198, 208 n.635, 215f
Justin I 42, 49, 58, 61, 65 n.172, 66, 70f, 76, 79, 317
Justin II 49, 55 n.127, 58, 60 n.150, 62, 65 n.172, 70f, 72–75, 76f, 87, 91, 93, 95, 98 n.271, 99, 124 n.352, 295, 317
Justinian 42, 48f, 58, 61, 63, 65 n.172, 66, 68, 70–72, 75 n.202, 76–78, 94 n.260, 95, 112 n.319, 115, 117f, 178 n.518, 184 n.539, 192, 203, 204 n.617, 224 n.684, 259 n.767, 275 n.821, 278f, 281, 295, 317, 334

Kent, J.P.C. 38–41, 67 n.181
Kings, Visigothic
Athaulf (r. 410–415) 39
Wallia (r. 415–419) 27
Theodorid (Theodoric I) (r. 419–451) 29
Thorismund (r. 451–453) 30, 39
Theodoric II (r. 453–466) 31, 33
Euric (r. 466/477–484) 31–35, 39, 43 n.87, 44, 179 n.522, 261 n.722, 263 n.778
Alaric II (r. 484–507) 29, 32, 39, 41 n.78, 43f, 46, 48, 52, 178, 179 n.522, 183f, 204 n.619, 238, 264
Gesalic (r. 507/508–511) 46f
Amalaric (r. 526–531) 47f, 53, 62 n.161, 74, 202 n.612
Theudis (r. 531–548) 47f
Theudisclus (r. 548–549) 48
Agila (r. 549–554) 48, 61 n.153, 90, 192 nn.570 and 572, 202 n.612, 285
Athanagild (r. 554–567) 48, 61 n.153, 73, 192, 232
Liuva I (r. 568–571/573) 48, 82, 83 n.215, 86, 95 n.263
Leovigild (r. 568–586) 17, 20f, 46, 48, 54, 56 n.132, 58f, 62, 68, 74, 77f, 81–107, 114–16, 118f, 124, 130f, 139, 143, 146 n.427, 149, 151–57, 159, 160 n.466, 161–63, 168–70, 178 n.520, 183 n.537, 190, 192–94, 198f, 204 n.618, 207, 212f, 215f, 218f, 225, 228f, 232–36, 241f, 255 n.763, 261–63, 266, 267 n.794, 270, 284f, 288, 295, 298, 300–05, 308f, 317f, 324–27, 334–39, 342f, 356, 364f, 368, 384f
Reccared (r. 586–601) 62, 83, 105, 107 n.297, 115, 116 n.331, 129 n.372, 130 n.373, 133 n.387, 136 n.397, 139, 143, 148 n.435, 151–54, 162, 164, 169–71, 179 n.523, 180 n.525, 181 n.528, 183 n.537, 194f, 199, 201, 209 n.638, 212–16, 218f, 228, 233f, 236, 238, 242 n.734, 295, 298, 300–05, 309f, 317f, 319, 324–27, 336–39, 342f, 348, 352, 356–59, 364–66, 368–70, 385
Liuva II (r. 601–603) 143, 148 n.433, 152 n.445, 162, 216, 234, 242, 295, 298, 300–05, 310, 317, 319, 324, 326f, 338, 342, 348, 357f, 370, 385
Witteric (r. 603–610) 142f, 148 n.433, 151, 153f, 193, 200 n.604, 216, 219 n.673, 295, 298, 300–05, 310f, 319, 324–27, 338f, 342f, 348, 353, 358–60, 364–66, 370f
Gundemar (r. 610–12) 154, 194f, 200 n.604, 212, 216–18, 295, 300–05, 311, 317, 319, 324, 326, 342f, 359f, 366f, 371, 385
Sisebut (r. 612–621) 107 n.297, 136, 139, 150, 151 n.442, 183 n.537, 193–98, 200, 202, 208, 216–18, 236 n.709, 242 n.734, 262 n.774, 295, 298, 300–05, 311f, 317, 320, 324–27, 332, 342f, 348, 353f, 360–62, 366f, 371f, 385
Reccared II (r. 621) 137, 139f, 162 n.474
Suinthila (r. 621–631) 130 n.373, 136, 139, 147 n.431, 150f, 153f, 162, 166, 194–96, 198, 201, 202 n.611, 203 n.615, 209f, 214 n.657, 216f, 219f, 236 n.709, 237 n.713, 295, 298, 300–05, 312f, 317, 320, 324–27, 345, 349–55, 360, 362f, 367, 372–75, 384
Sisenand (r. 631–636) 153f, 161 n.467, 163–66, 183 n.537, 196, 198, 201, 202 n.611, 209, 262f, 300–05, 313, 317, 320, 324–27, 347, 352, 363, 367, 375–79, 385
Chintila (r. 636–639) 141, 147 n.431, 153, 162, 166, 201, 236, 300–05, 313, 317, 320, 324–27, 331, 347, 363, 379, 385
Tulga (r. 639–642) 162f, 165f, 236, 237 n.713, 300–05, 313, 317, 321, 324–27, 363, 379, 385
Chindasvinth (r. 642–53) 105f, 112, 116, 142, 143 n.421, 149, 151, 154, 163f, 169f, 171, 181, 183, 213 n.655, 236, 239–42, 263 n.779, 300–05, 313f, 317, 321, 324–27, 363
Reccesvinth (r. 649–72) 105f, 107 n.297, 112, 116, 127 n.363, 142f, 145, 154, 157, 163–66, 169f, 181, 183, 220, 236, 239–42, 300–05, 314f, 317, 321, 324–27
Wamba (r. 672–680) 106, 116, 164, 219, 300–05, 315, 317, 322, 324–27, 381f, 385f
Ervig (r. 680–687) 127 n.363, 164, 181, 182 n.528, 185 n.545, 241, 261, 263 n.779, 300–05, 315, 317, 322, 324–27, 382, 386
Egica (r. 687–702) 106, 142, 156, 157 n.456, 160 n.464, 163–65, 171, 181 n.527, 182 n.528, 215 n.659, 220, 236, 300–05, 315–17, 322, 324–27, 382–84, 386
Wittiza (r. 702–710) 106, 139 n.410, 142, 157 n.456, 160 n.464, 163–65, 170f, 215 n.659, 220, 236, 249, 300–05, 315–17, 322f, 324–27, 383f, 386
Roderic (r. 710–711/712) 140, 164, 236 n.707, 247–49, 300–05, 316f, 324–27, 384, 386
Achila II (r. c. 710/711–713/714) 164, 248, 300–05, 323–27
Ardo (Artabado) (r. c. 713–c. 717) 249

Lafaurie, Jean 38 n.68, 43 n.84, 44 n.87, 54, 63, 66
landowners 133f, 179 n.523, 185, 187, 204, 208 n.636, 226–29, 235, 243, 267f; *see also potentes*
La Punta de l'Illa Cullera 280
laws 33f, 42–44, 57, 84, 118, 126–28, 131, 133f, 148, 160 n.466, 178, 179 n.523, 181, 186 n.548, 200 n.606, 204, 208, 228 n.693, 232, 237 n.714, 239, 241f, 261 n.772, 263, 265–67, 283
Le Gentilhomme, Pierre 38, 120

limes 200 n.605, 205, 218 n.667
Lo Cascio, Elio 176
Lombards 117, 119, 224, 254
Lusitania 27, 90, 137f, 141, 143, 146, 148, 152f, 155f, 166, 171, 198, 211, 216, 220, 228 n.692, 242 n.734, 301, 308–16, 357
Lyon 51–53, 224

Majorian 31 n.37, 33 n.47, 39 n.73, 41–43, 46, 242
Málaga (ancient Malaka, Malaca) 96 n.267, 110, 111 n.315, 114, 184 n.541, 192f, 200f, 209, 278, 301, 378
Marques, Mário Gomes et al. 16f, 39 n.74, 58, 70 n.193, 75 n.202, 159f, 162 n.472, 167 n.492, 168–70, 238 n.719, 318–26, 330, 334, 338
Masona, bishop 266–67
Mateu y Llopis, Felipe 138, 145f, 153–55, 157
Mediterranean Sea 11–13, 23, 29 n.30, 31 n.41, 50f, 67 n.182, 79, 107, 112f, 120, 147, 161, 183, 188f, 201–02, 206, 217, 222, 225f, 228f, 237, 243, 250, 254, 258, 264, 271–81, 283f, 287
Mérida (Emerita Augusta) 30 n.36, 31, 32 n.41, 48, 58, 60f, 62 n.156, 66, 87f, 89–91, 96f, 101f, 107 n.297, 111, 112 n.317, 113, 130 n.373, 136 n.397, 140f, 143, 146, 148, 152, 159 n.459, 160f, 165 n.488, 171, 175, 182f, 189, 196, 198 n.595, 202 n.611, 203, 216, 220, 242, 264, 266, 268, 285, 301, 308–16, 334, 338, 342, 356–62, 368f, 372, 375, 378–85; *see also* mints, Visigothic
Merovingians 29, 32, 34, 35 n.56, 36f, 44, 47–49, 52–55, 61 n.152, 63, 64 n.168, 65 n.171, 67 n.182, 83, 85 n.226, 89 n.241, 103, 106, 112, 113 n.322, 114 n.325, 119f, 121 n.351, 125, 128 nn.364 and 365, 129 n.370, 130, 144, 171f, 184, 190, 201 n.610, 206f, 208 n.636, 215 n.660, 218 n.669, 219 n.673, 221, 224, 226f, 233f, 237 n.714, 244f, 254, 260 n.769, 261 n.773, 262 n.774, 263, 271 n.805, 272, 281
metallurgy 76 n.204, 77f, 157–67, 207, 288f, 306
Metcalf, D.M. (Michael) 56 n.133, 90 n.247, 98 n.273, 167, 188 n.553, 189–91, 202, 211–13, 217 n.666, 221f, 258, 262 n.774, 264 n.782
metrology 27 n.26, 66 n.175, 76 n.204, 77–79, 112, 116 n.332, 157–67, 169, 254, 279 n.842, 295
Milan 51, 52 n.118, 66, 68
Miles, George C. 15–17, 19, 21, 92, 95, 105–07, 126, 135, 136 n.395, 137f, 145–49, 151, 153, 155, 157, 159, 164, 167, 190, 198 n.597, 199 n.600, 209, 306f, 329f
minting
  late Roman 12, 21, 23, 36f, 42, 45, 51, 53, 55, 67f, 123–26, 128, 131, 144, 171, 175, 177f, 183, 186, 190, 203, 222, 224–25, 240, 242–44, 250, 259, 261, 273, 275f, 281
  military minting 22, 56 n.132, 61 n.151, 74–76, 96, 103–05, 138, 152, 174f, 177, 183–85, 187 n.549, 189f, 191–206, 208–20, 219 n.673, 220, 222, 225, 227, 237–40, 243, 253, 259, 283–88; *see also* inscriptions, *cum Deo (optinuit, intravit)*; *curru*; *regi a Deo vita*; *victor/victoria*, victory issues
  minting network 17–21, 27, 34, 45, 55–64, 67f, 74–76, 78f, 104f, 108–21, 128–32, 137–57, 164f, 180–86, 190, 197–229, 231–45, 249–55, 260f, 283–89, 297 (map)
    Visigothic and contemporary systems compared 34f, 49 n.107, 61 n.151, 67f, 119–21, 124–26, 130f, 144f, 171f, 183, 190f, 221–29, 233–35, 242–45, 249–55, 259f
  minting process 35, 59, 69f, 76, 85 n.226, 99, 123–31, 149–57, 162 n.472, 163, 188, 190, 201f, 206 n.627, 207–10, 214 n.659, 217, 225 n.685, 232, 236, 289, 329–43
  personnel 18, 21, 50f, 57–59, 63f, 75f, 87–90, 94f, 96 n.267, 98, 105, 108, 124–34, 139 n.409, 148 n.434, 149–57, 175, 209f, 232, 289, 329–43
  punches, use of 59 n.144, 124–26, 128, 209, 331, 346
  purpose 22, 102–04, 114–15, 120f, 143f, 173–229, 238 n.716, 244f, 252–55, 257–61, 281, 284–87
  re-minting 79 n.212, 187 n.549, 188, 207f, 211 n.650, 212 n.654, 238, 254 n.761, 267 n.794, 271 n.804, 286
  volume of minting 95, 117, 120, 135–40, 142f, 158f, 174, 189, 195–203, 223 n.681, 237, 261–71, 289, 324
mints, Visigothic *see* individual mints by province listed below
  identification of 16f, 45, 135, 137f, 201 n.607, 214 n.657
  main mints 45, 60f, 75, 114, 140f, 164–66, 171, 182 n.530, 189, 198,237 nn.713 and 716
  peripheral mints 22, 56 n.132, 75, 128, 144, 156, 159, 162, 164–66, 175, 202f, 208, 211, 212 n.654, 219, 237, 240, 285–87
  regal-period mints by province (in order as in Figure I.7 on pp. 300–04)
    Narbonensis
    Narbona 89 n.243, 93 n.254, 140, 146, 153f, 155, 248 n.747, 300, 308, 310, 315f, 364, 368, 379f, 382–84, 386
    Tarraconensis
    Amiasio (?) 137, 300
    Barcinona 89, 101, 129 n.372, 140, 146, 153, 180, 209 n.638, 300, 310, 364, 368, 370, 382, 385
    Calagorre 218f, 300, 313, 367
    Cesaragusta 89, 91, 101, 105, 140, 154, 189, 300, 308, 310–12, 316, 338, 365–67, 369–72, 379, 382–84
    Cestavi 137–39, 218, 300, 369, 385
    Dertosa 219 n.673, 300
    Gerunda 140, 143, 153f, 300, 315f, 383f

Labeclosa 137, 218, 300
Lebea 137, 138 n.404, 218f, 300
Rodas 88f, 107 n.297, 137, 153, 155, 199 n.599, 300, 309, 364, 368
Sagunto 147 n.431, 154, 194 n.578, 219 n.673, 300, 366
Tarracona 140, 143, 147, 153–55, 180f n.525, 209 n.638, 300, 310–13, 315, 338, 364–72, 375, 380, 383, 385f
Tirasona 89, 101, 140, 147, 154, 218f, 300, 308, 310f, 365f, 368–70
Volotania 137, 218, 300
Carthaginensis
Acci 138, 140, 150f, 192, 197, 200, 209, 300, 311, 313, 340–43, 245, 247–49, 253f, 371f, 375f, 379, 383
Aorariola 137f, 150, 200, 300, 342f
Beatia 242 n.734, 300
Castelona 150, 195 n.586, 209, 300, 347
Iliocrici 137f, 150, 200f, 209, 300, 342f, 347
Mave 137, 216, 300
Mentesa 140, 150–52, 198f, 205, 209, 300, 311, 313, 315, 342f, 346f, 351–53, 358f, 361, 371f, 376, 383, 385
Oliovasio 137, 300, 385
Reccopolis 89f, 96, 101, 139, 152, 219, 262, 277, 281, 286 n.861, 300, 308, 356
Saldania 216, 300, 308f, 368f
Toleto 61 n.152, 89, 90, 96 n.571, 98, 101, 107 n.297, 138, 140, 143, 147 n.431, 148 nn.433 and 434, 151–53, 156–61, 164 n.480, 165, 171, 175, 182f, 189, 196, 198, 202 n.611, 220, 233, 236 n.712, 238 n.716, 243, 248 n.747, 285, 300, 308–16, 332, 334–39, 342f, 356–63, 368–72, 376, 379–86
Valentia 137f, 147, 155, 300, 367, 383, 385
Baetica
Asidona 150, 201, 301, 349, 352, 376 (*see related* 192–94, 199)
Barbi 41, 151, 197, 200, 209, 216, 286 n.861, 301, 312, 340f, 353–55, 372f, 376
Cordoba 90, 96 n.571, 102, 105, 107 n.297, 111 n.315, 114 n.324, 140f, 143, 146, 150–53, 157, 189, 197–99, 202, 205, 209, 220, 242 n.734, 301, 309, 311–16, 345, 351f, 369, 371, 373, 376f, 379–86
Egabro 300
Eliberri 141, 150–52, 197, 199, 209, 242 n.734, 279, 301, 309–13, 340f, 345–47, 353f, 358f, 369, 371, 373f, 377, 379
Ispali 61 n.152, 89 n.241, 102, 105, 111f, 130 n.237, 140f, 143, 150–52, 159 n.459, 160, 161 n.467, 165 n.488, 171, 175, 182f, 189, 196–99, 201 n.608, 202, 205, 208, 262 n.774, 301, 308–16, 332f, 336f, 340–43, 348–53, 356, 358, 368–71, 374, 377–86 (*see related* 192–94)
Italica 88, 102, 105, 198f, 300, 308, 368
Karmona 301
Malaka 200, 301, 378
Roda 88f, 102, 105, 199 n.599, 301, 309, 336f, 364
Tucci 141, 150, 197–99, 205, 209, 301, 312f, 315, 340f, 345–48, 351f, 374f, 378, 382, 384
Lusitania
Caliabria 301
Coleia 30
Egitania 111, 114 n.324, 141, 249 n.747, 301, 316, 357, 360, 375, 378, 382, 384–86
Elissa (= Olisipona?) 137f, 301
Elvora 89f, 101, 130 n.373, 138, 141, 143, 152, 166 n.489, 301, 308f, 311, 316, 336f, 342f, 356–62, 368–70, 372, 384f
Emerita 61, 87–91, 96f, 101f, 107 n.297, 130 n.373, 140f, 143, 146, 148, 152, 159 n.459, 160f, 165 n.488, 171, 175, 182f, 189, 196, 198 n.595, 202 n.611, 203, 216, 220, 242 n.734, 285, 301, 308–16, 334f, 338f, 342f, 356–62, 368–70, 372, 375, 378–85
Eminio 141, 301, 312, 338f, 357–59, 361f, 372
Lameco 301
Monecipio 301
Olisipona (= Elissa?) *see* Elissa
Salamantica 301
Totela 301
Veseo 301, 362
Gallaecia
Adonis 137f, 302
Aliobrio 302
Arofre: 35, 143 n.419, 302
Astorica 302
Asturie 302, 370
Aurense 139, 302
Bergancia 139, 214, 216 n.662, 302, 311, 357f, 370
Bergio 216, 302
Bracara 107 n.298, 111, 141, 148, 212–14, 220, 302, 314, 359f, 371, 375
Calapa 214, 216 n.662, 302, 309
Casavio 302
Catora 302
Cepis 302, 370
Conteno 137, 302
Decrinos 137, 302
Ewesis 137, 302
Flavas 214 n.658, 302
Fraucello 302
Georres 139, 141, 216 n.662, 302, 311, 371
Inceio 138 n.404, 302
Laetera 216 n.662, 302, 312, 372
Laure 302
Lavrencio 302

Leione 214 n.657, 216 n.663, 303
Luco 141, 213f, 216f, 220, 303, 312, 372
Mertia 137, 303, 357
Nandolas 148, 303, 360–62, 375
Palentiaca 137, 303
Palantucio 303, 357
Panonias 303
Pesicos 216 n.662, 217, 303
Petra 303
Pincia 214, 216 n.662, 303, 312, 372
Portocale 152 n.445, 213, 303, 338f, 357f, 385
Semure 216 n.662, 303
Senabria 141, 214, 216 n.662, 302f
Susarres 138, 303, 309, 357, 370
Toriviana 303, 385
Tornio 214, 303
Tude 141, 214–16, 220, 303, 312, 356f, 370, 372
Turico 137, 216 n.662, 303
Vada 303
Vallearitia 216 n.662, 303
Vallesalsa 138, 303
Ventosa 216 n.663, 303
Province Unknown
Tulluco 138, 303
Valle.../Vallegia? 138, 303, 309, 370
monarchy
aristocracy in relation to 34, 46, 48, 82–84, 163, 184 n.538, 187 n.549, 201 n.610, 223, 227–29, 235f, 240f, 243f, 259 n.768, 260 n.769
confiscations by kings 84, 133 n.386, 163, 165 n.485, 187 n.549, 223 n.681, 240f, 244
royal control of Visigothic minting 21–23, 55, 57–59, 69, 73f, 76, 78f, 84, 86, 88–91, 94–105, 114, 131, 156f, 169, 190, 202, 226, 229, 231–37, 240f, 243, 245, 260 n.769, 284–86
see also individual kings
monetarius *see* moneyer
monetary history 12f, 16 n.11, 180, 285
monetization 23, 176, 178, 185, 187, 225 n.685, 234–36, 257f, 261–71, 281, 287
money *see* coinage
moneyer 37, 42, 45, 57, 63f, 125, 128, 130f, 157 n.456, 160 n.466, 183, 206 n.627, 226, 245
Mora, Bartolomé 280
Morrisson, Cécile 280f
Muslim invasion of Spain in 711 12f, 225, 247–50, 263f

Narbonensis 42, 83, 137, 140, 153, 161 n.467, 216 n.661, 300, 308, 310, 315, 316f
Narbonne 27, 29, 31, 33 n.46, 44f, 47f, 52, 56, 60–62, 73, 89 n.243, 93 n.254, 118, 140, 146, 153f, 155, 242, 248 n.747, 249, 300, 308, 310, 315f
nisf 249
numismatics 13–16, 19, 40, 49, 53, 55f, 57, 85 n.226, 86, 146f, 174, 176, 215 n.659, 232, 247, 273 n.809
nummus *see* copper coinage

Olson, Lauris
weight and fineness measurements 76 n.205, 159, 165 n.487, 167–71, 291–94, 306–23, 327
Ostrogoths 20, 27 n.24, 32 n.43, 34, 35 n.56, 36 n.61, 46f, 48, 50 n.110, 51, 53 n.121, 54, 55 n.127, 58, 74, 102 n.281, 114 n.325, 116 n.333, 117, 119, 130, 133 n.386, 179, 181 n.525, 184 n.539, 190, 224, 232, 263, 272, 275 n.821

Paludamentum 84
patrimonium (royal or imperial patrimony) 132, 133f, 163 n.477, 181 n.525, 266
Pliego, Ruth 17, 19, 64 n.170, 65 n.171, 86 n.229, 87 n.582, 91, 106f, 111, 114 n.325, 115 n.329, 116f, 135, 136 n.394, 148, 151, 157, 160 n.467, 182 n.529, 187 n.549, 196 n.588, 203 n.616, 213 n.655, 223 n.681, 259 n.768, 262 n.774, 264 n.782, 270 n.800, 300–03, 329f
Polanyi, Karl 259 n.768
Portugal 60, 90, 111, 135 n.392, 138, 167, 274, 281
potentes 185, 235
Prosper, chronicle of 26 n.23
provinces
as related to type and style 105, 107, 145–49, 150f, 153–57, 171, 182 n.530, 209, 234
as basis of territorial and minting organization 22, 28 n.28, 64, 105, 131 n.382, 132, 134 n.387, 137, 142, 145–49, 152, 160 n.467, 166, 171, 180f, 183, 196 n.588, 197, 205, 208, 228, 241, 304
see also individual provinces
pseudo-imperial coinage *see* coinage, Visigothic, pre-regal
purity of gold coins
Byzantine 93 n.254, 201, 239, 295
Visigothic *see* coinage, Visigothic, fineness

Ravenna 38, 40–42, 47 n.100, 51, 224, 263
rebellion 32 n.43, 46, 48, 58f, 75, 82f, 83 n.216, 86–88, 90f, 95, 96 n.571, 98, 104 n.288, 114–15, 161f n.472, 184 n.540, 192 n.570, 193, 199, 215f, 236, 244, 263, 284f
Reccopolis 68, 84 n.222, 89f, 96, 101, 139, 152, 219 n.673, 262, 277, 281, 286 n.861, 300, 308, 356
regal series (of Visigothic tremisses) *see* coinage, Visigothic
Reinhart, Wilhelm 37f, 40 n.76, 45, 49, 53, 60–62, 64, 66, 69, 146
Retamero, Félix 185f, 221, 235, 259 n.766, 262 n.774, 267 n.794, 270

Roman Empire 11–13, 15, 20–22, 25–38, 40–42, 45f, 49–52, 53 n.121, 67f, 70, 84, 108, 113, 120, 132f, 147 n.431, 160 n.466, 176, 177, 179, 183, 186, 190, 201 n.610, 204, 222, 225, 229 n.695, 232, 243f, 259 n.767, 267, 271, 280f, 283; *see also* Byzantine empire; minting, late Roman
Ruccones 195, 216f
rural population 184f, 227–29, 235, 266, 268–70, 271 n.806, 274

Septimania *see* Narbonensis
Severus 31, 38 n.71, 39, 41
Seville (Ispali) 48, 60, 61 nn.152 and 153, 62 n.156, 66–68, 73 n.197, 77f, 88, 89 n.241, 94, 96, 102, 105, 109 n.306, 110f, 114f, 130 n.373, 140f, 143, 150–52, 159 n.459, 160f, 165 n.488, 171, 175, 182f, 189, 200 n.606, 201 n.608, 202, 205, 208, 220, 250, 262 n.774, 264, 277–79, 281, 301, 308–11, 312–15, 332f, 336, 340, 342, 348–53, 356, 358, 368–71, 374, 377–79, 381–86; *see also* mints, Visigothic
siliquae 39 n.73, 98, 117f, 132 n.383, 159–63, 180, 266 n.789
Suniefred (usurper) 712
slates 185, 228 n.694, 229, 266f
Spania (Byzantine enclave in Hispania) 48, 59 n.143, 74f, 77f, 82f, 103 n.283, 104 n.288, 110, 119f, 151, 166, 183 n.537, 184, 192–97, 199f, 203f, 205 n.622, 206f, 209f, 223, 238, 260 n.771, 262, 272 n.806, 278–80, 284f, 289, 295–96
solidus
Byzantine 50, 160, 178 n.518, 184, 239, 249, 251
Roman 15, 35, 36 n.61, 38, 66–68, 117 n.337, 126 n.360, 129, 160 n.466, 161, 238
see also coinage, Visigothic
Stahl, Alan 61 n.152, 45 n.742
style, numismatic 16, 18, 20f, 36f, 38 n.66, 40 nn.75 and 76, 41 n.77, 50, 52–56, 58f, 61–64, 75–78, 87, 89 n.241, 90, 93–96, 99 n.274, 105–07, 112, 128f, 130 n.373, 136, 145, 147–57, 182, 198–200, 209f, 218 n.668, 232, 234, 238 n.716, 242 n.734, 244, 284, 288, 331
stylistic analysis 329–67
Sueves 27, 30f, 34, 35 n.56, 36f, 42, 46, 49, 55, 67 nn.181 and 182, 82f, 103, 120, 140 n.412, 143, 149 n.437, 156, 211f, 215, 216 n.661 and 663, 217, 225, 233, 238, 241, 261 n.773, 271

Tarraconensis 30–32, 33 n.48, 77 n.208, 137f, 140, 147, 154f, 166, 171, 180 n.525, 181 n.525, 189, 209 n.638, 211–21, 300, 308, 310–13, 315f
Taxation 22, 28, 33, 42, 53, 103, 118, 121, 130, 132–34, 142, 144, 174–88, 190, 192, 203, 205–09, 211f, 213 n.655, 217, 219–29, 235, 237–39, 241, 243–45, 253, 258–63, 264, 267–70, 272, 283, 285–88; *see also* fiscal, system
Theodemir, pact of 253, 264
Theodoric the Ostrogoth 20, 32 n.43, 36 n.61, 47, 48 n.104, 51–53, 55 n.127, 57f, 74, 79, 102 n.281, 131, 133 n.386, 179, 181 n.525, 184, 190, 204 n.618, 224, 232, 263
Theodosius II 38 n.70, 39 n.73, 40
thulth 171, 249, 252, 254
Toledo 48, 60f, 62 n.156, 84, 88 n.240, 89–91, 96 n.571, 98, 101, 107 n.297, 111, 112 n.317, 114, 116, 131 n.381, 133 n.387, 138, 140, 143, 147, 148 nn.433 and 434, 151–53, 156–61, 164 n.480, 173 n.523, 175, 180, 181 n.525, 182f, 189, 193 n.575, 194, 196, 198, 202 n.611, 205, 215, 220, 233, 236 n.712, 238 n.716, 243, 248 n.747, 285, 300, 308–16, 332, 334, 336, 338, 342, 356–63, 368–72, 376, 379–86; *see also* mints, Visigothic
Tomasini, Wallace J. 17, 49, 50 n.111, 51–64, 66f, 69f, 73f, 76f, 94, 95 n.263, 99 n.274, 100f, 105, 244, 291
Toulouse, Kingdom of 29, 32 n.41, 39, 48, 178, 221, 228, 231
trade 34, 49, 53 n.119, 109, 112–15, 120f, 144, 151, 176, 179, 182 n.530, 186–91, 201 n.610, 202f, 206, 215 n.660, 217, 218 n.666, 221f, 223f, 226, 235, 239, 245, 257, 259 nn.766 and 767, 260 n.770, 262 n.774, 263f, 267 n.793, 268f, 270 n.800, 271–81, 286, 288
treasure 48 n.104, 61, 96 n.570, 131, 134 n.388, 136, 183, 196f, 202 n.612, 211 n.650, 213, 238, 263, 285
thesaurus, thesauri 55, 131f, 134, 157, 178 n.520, 180 n.525, 183 n.533, 205 n.625, 233
tremissis 15–18, 20f, 23, 35f, 38 n.70, 39 n.73, 40 nn.75 and 76, 41f, 44, 48 n.105, 49–56, 58–60, 61 n.152, 62–64, 65 n.174, 66–76, 78f, 81, 84f, 87, 88–100, 102 n.282, 103–07, 110, 111 n.315, 112, 113 n.322, 114f, 117f, 124–26, 129f, 135–37, 139–45, 147 n.431, 149f, 152f, 154 n.451, 156–72, 147f, 178, 181 n.525, 182f, 185f, 188f, 196, 202, 205, 207, 210, 211 n.650, 213f, 216 n.662, 219f, 232–42, 244, 245 n.742, 248, 254, 260–64, 266–77, 279 n.845, 280, 283f, 286–88, 291–96, 298f, 306–86; *see also* coinage, Visigothic, regal period
triens *see tremissis*
types, numismatic 16, 21, 35, 37, 39 n.73, 40–42, 50f, 56, 62, 65 n.171, 66, 67 n.181, 81, 84, 86f, 92 n.253, 93, 95, 105–08, 110–12, 115–18, 124, 128 n.366, 131, 143, 145–57, 164, 165 n.483, 232–34, 238 n.716, 242, 244, 278, 284, 288, 298, 304, 334, 336, 368–86
confronting busts 106, 146
cross-on-steps (COS) 87–92, 96, 101f, 106, 168 n.495, 169, 242, 318, 324
facing busts 56, 62, 90, 92f, 96 n.571, 99, 101–03, 105–07, 115, 146f, 149, 151, 153, 155–57, 159, 162f, 168f, 199 n.600, 218 n.668, 233f, 295, 304, 308–24, 332, 334, 336

profile 146 n.427, 242
Victory with palm and wreath (VPW) 20, 35 n.54, 42, 50–55, 65 n.174, 66, 68, 87, 89, 91f, 94, 96, 100–02, 124 n.352, 145, 168f, 199 n.599, 232, 242, 304, 317f, 327

usurper 48, 55, 183 n.537, 192, 234f, 248 n.747

Valentinian III 39 n.73, 40–42, 44 n.87, 239
Vandals 27, 31 n.37, 34, 35 n.56, 46, 102 n.282, 108, 112 n.318, 114 n.325, 116 n.333, 119, 224, 250, 260, 272–77, 279 n.842, 279 n.846, 280f
Victoriacum 84 n.222, 218f
Victory goddess *see* types, numismatic
Visigoths
Gothic identity 26 n.22, 27 n.24 (name), 104, 234
settlement in Aquitania II 19f, 25f, 28, 29 n.29, 33, 38
settlement in Hispania 32, 46–48
volume of minting *see* minting, volume of

war 21f, 31, 34, 44, 46f, 48, 53, 61, 74f, 78f, 83, 87f, 90, 97f, 104, 107, 151f, 161 n.467, 166, 183, 189f, 192–95, 202–04, 207–20, 222f, 227, 238, 242 n.734, 248f, 253, 262, 279f, 285f, 287, 289
Wickham, Chris 205, 225, 258–60
Wielbark culture 27 n.26

Zeno 39, 41, 52 n.118

For Product Safety Concerns and Information please contact our EU
representative GPSR@taylorandfrancis.com
Taylor & Francis Verlag GmbH, Kaufingerstraße 24, 80331 München, Germany

www.ingramcontent.com/pod-product-compliance
Ingram Content Group UK Ltd.
Pitfield, Milton Keynes, MK11 3LW, UK
UKHW020024200926
475702UK00014B/2038

* 9 7 8 1 0 4 1 1 8 2 9 2 4 *